Shaw's Directory of Courts in the United Kingdom

2007/08

edited by **SARAH BRUTY** and **KELLY YOUNG**

SHAW & SONS LTD.
SHAWAY HOUSE,
21 BOURNE PARK,
BOURNE ROAD,
CRAYFORD,
KENT DA1 4BZ.

Tel: 01322 621100
Fax: 01322 550553
DX: 400700 CRAYFORD
E-mail: sales@shaws.co.uk
Web site: www.shaws.co.uk

ISBN: 978 0 7219 1634 7

ISSN: 0264-312X

A CIP catalogue record
for this book
is available from
The British Library

© SHAW & SONS LTD 2007
Typeset by Letterpart Limited, Reigate, Surrey
Printed in Great Britain by Bell and Bain Ltd., Glasgow

CONTENTS

Part I (CREAM)
The High Court and Crown Courts
Appellate Courts
Supreme Court of Judicature
Administrative Regions
Crown Court Offices, Court Managers and Court Houses
Numerical Index of Crown Court Codes

Part II (BLUE)
County Courts
County Court Offices, District Judges, Court Managers and Court Houses

Part III (WHITE)
Courts of Summary Jurisdiction (arranged under Commission Areas)
Her Majesty's Courts Service Areas and Area Directors
Names and Addresses of Clerks of Magistrates' Courts in England, Wales and Northern Ireland, with Normal Times and Places of Sittings of Courts
Sheriffs Courts and District Courts in Scotland, with Numerical Index of Court Codes for Sheriff and District Courts
Gazetteer of Places in the Greater London Area
Numerical Index of Court Codes of Courts in England and Wales
Alphabetical Index of Courts of Summary Jurisdiction.

Part IV (BLUE)
List of Coroners
Postal addresses, Telephone numbers and Fax numbers of Coroners and Coroners Officers

Part V (WHITE)
List of Probate Registrars
Postal addresses, Telephone numbers and Fax numbers of Probate Registrars

Appendix I (CREAM)
Crown Prosecution Service
Postal addresses, Telephone numbers and Fax numbers of Crown Prosecution Service Headquarters, Area, Branch and Sub-Branch Offices and references to the Crown Courts and Magistrates' Courts served.

Appendix II (CREAM)
Crown Office and Procurator Fiscal Service (Scotland)
Postal Addresses, Telephone numbers and Fax numbers of Service Headquarters and Branch Offices with references to the Sheriff Courts and District Courts served.

Appendix III (CREAM)
Penal Establishments
Postal Addresses, Telephone Numbers and Fax Numbers of Headquarters Establishments, High Security Establishments Local Prisons and Remand Centres, Training Prisons, Young Offender Institutions, Juvenile Institutions, Immigration and Removal Centres and Special Hospitals.

EDITORS' NOTES ON THIS RESTRUCTURED EDITION

Since its introduction in 2005, the unified system of courts administration, Her Majesty's Courts Service, has been subject to extensive review and, in April 2007, the structure of the administrative Areas and Regions was radically reformed. 46 Areas have been transformed into just 25, a move which has involved significant amounts of redefinition of Area/Region boundaries. This major new edition of the Directory reflects the restructured system, without significantly altering the traditional layout of the book. However, whilst updating the information to reflect the streamlining of HMCS, the opportunity has also been taken to introduce new features. As such, the Directory is now divided into five parts, with three appendices, as follows:

Part I introduces the Appellate Courts and the Supreme Courts, in England and Wales, Scotland and Northern Ireland. This is followed by details of the seven new regions in respect of Her Majesty's Court Service: the Midlands, the North East, the North West, the South East, London, HMCS Wales and the South West. The regional listings contain up-to-date contact information for the Regional Director and the Directors responsible for the Areas under the umbrella of the region. Circuit Judges for each particular region are listed. For the first time, all Crown, County and Magistrates' Courts under each Region's administration have been indexed within the Regional listing, for ease of location of courts within the dedicated Parts. Details of the Crown Courts, including the Circuit Judges and the Court Houses, complete Part I.

Part II contains details of County Courts, arranged in alphabetical order throughout, with reference to the appropriate Region and Area to which the court now belongs following the restructuring. Each entry is annotated to indicate any jurisdiction held by the court. District Registries are indicated against the relevant County Court office.

Part III sets out particulars of the Magistrates' Courts in England and Wales, including details of normal times and places of sittings. These are arranged alphabetically by Local Justice Area within the relevant Commission Areas, which themselves are arranged alphabetically within England and Wales. In addition to providing details of the Local Justice Areas, the Commission Area listings also provide full contact details for the appropriate Area Director. Courts of Summary Jurisdiction in Northern Ireland and Scotland continue to be shown separately, the latter being arranged under Sheriffdoms.

Court Code numbers are not listed in numerical order, so a separate Numerical Index is included so that any Court which has been referred to solely by its Court Code number can be readily traced.

A comprehensive alphabetical index can also be found at the end of Part III.

Part IV contains a List of Coroners and addresses of Coroners' Officers set out under their respective Coroners' Districts.

Part V contains, for the first time, extensive listings of Probate Courts in England and Wales; including names, addresses and contact numbers for all registrars, as well as normal opening times.

Appendix I contains details of the Crown Prosecution Service, setting out the Area and branch offices of the Service, together with references to the Crown Courts and Magistrates' Courts which each covers. This section has seen many changes this year, particularly in London.

Appendix II contains similar information in respect of the Crown Office and Procurator Fiscal Service (Scotland).

Appendix III sets out the postal addresses and telephone and fax numbers of Penal Establishments in England and Wales, Northern Ireland and Scotland, grouped into their various categories.

As ever, changes in the listings in this book (including staff members, addresses, telephone, fax and DX numbers, together with the times and places of sittings of courts), are published as notified to us up to the 15th August 2007, so the book is correct at the time of press.

Finally, we would like to express our sincere appreciation to all the people who have assisted us in collating the information that appears in this edition. Particular thanks must go to our contacts at Her Majesty's Courts Service who have provided valuable guidance during the compilation of this new edition. With their help, every effort has been made to ensure complete accuracy. We would ask to be advised of any amendments, and of any changes that may occur in the future, so that they can be incorporated into the next edition.

Sarah Bruty
Kelly Young

Shaw & Sons Limited

Suppliers of

FORMS ON DISK

Forms on Disk enables you to fill in your forms on screen and then print them out. The forms are customised for your organisation and all the updates to the forms and software are FREE of charge. There is never any need to re-order hard copy forms and waste old stock. Groups we have available include Legal forms and Local Government forms (including the new Housing Act 2004).

BOOKS

Shaw & Sons publish over sixty books covering a wide range of subjects for professionals, from definitive loose-leaf works to simple quick-reference guides. These texts are predominantly for legal and local government professionals but also include topics for businesses and environmental agencies.

At the forefront of *Shaw's* books list are its annual directories. These include:

> *Shaw's Local Government Directory* – provides extensive details of all local authorities
>
> *NAPO Probation Directory* – the "bible" of the probation service
>
> *Varsity Directory of Investigators and Process Servers*
>
> *Police and Constabulary Almanac* – published under the imprint of R. Hazell & Co, the official register of police forces and allied organisations in the UK.

Recently published titles of interest to the legal profession include:

> *Street Use and the Law* – a succinct, quick-reference guide to legal issues arising from the use of our streets
>
> *Alcohol and Entertainment Licensing: A Practical Guide* – a handy textbook explaining the new regime under the extensive Licensing Act 2003
>
> *Successful Use of Expert Witnesses* – a practical guide aimed at lawyers who seek advice from experts on the technical aspects of a case or instruct expert witnesses
>
> *The Conveyancers' Yearbook* – an invaluable annual which provide the busy property practitioner with an up-to-date and accessible ready reference guide to the most important changes in the law and practice of conveyancing.

For full details of the above and Shaw's other products and services, visit: www.shaws.co.uk

Shaw & Sons Limited, Shaway House, 21 Bourne Park,
Bourne Road, Crayford, Kent DA1 4BZ
Tel: 01322 621100; Fax: 01322 550553;
E-mail: sales@shaws.co.uk

PART I

THE HIGH COURT AND CROWN COURTS

	Page
Appellate Courts	2
Supreme Court of Judicature:–	
England and Wales	3
Northern Ireland	7
Scotland	8
Crown Courts:–	
Midlands Region	11
North East Region	16
North West Region	20
South East Region	24
London Region	29
HMCS Wales	34
South West Region	37
Crown Court Offices:–	
England and Wales	42
Northern Ireland	61
Numerical Index to Crown Court Codes	63

APPELLATE COURTS

THE JUDICIAL COMMITTEE OF THE PRIVY COUNCIL
Downing Street, London SW1A 2AJ
Tel: 020 7276 0483/85/87
Fax: 020 7276 0460
E-mail: judicial.committee@jcpc.x.gsi.gov.uk

Registrar to the Privy Council: M. E. MacDonald

Group Manager: Mrs J. Lindsay

THE HOUSE OF LORDS,
Westminster, London SW1A 0PW
Tel: 020 7219 3000
Fax: 020 7219 6156

The Lord High Chancellor and Secretary of State for Constitutional Affairs: The Rt. Hon. Jack Straw, M.P.

Permanent Secretary to the Lord Chancellor: Mr. Alex Allan Tel: 020 7210 8380

Lords of Appeal in Ordinary:
- The Rt. Hon. Lord Bingham of Cornhill
- The Rt. Hon. Lord Hoffmann
- The Rt. Hon. Lord Hope of Craighead
- The Rt. Hon. Lord Saville of Newdigate
- The Rt. Hon. Lord Scott of Foscote
- The Rt. Hon. Lord Rodger of Earlsferry
- The Rt. Hon. Lord Walker of Gestingthorpe
- The Rt. Hon. Baroness Hale of Richmond
- The Rt. Hon. Lord Carswell
- The Rt. Hon. Lord Brown of Eaton-Under-Heywood
- The Rt. Hon. Lord Mance
- The Rt. Hon. Lord Neuberger of Abbotsbury

Office Manager: Mrs. Helen McMurdo. Tel: 020 7219 3202

SUPREME COURT OF JUDICATURE

ENGLAND AND WALES

COURT OF APPEAL
Royal Courts of Justice, Strand, London WC2A 2LL
Tel: 020 7947 6000
Fax: 020 7947 6900
DX 44450 STRAND WC2

The Lord High Chancellor (The Rt. Hon. Jack Straw, M.P.)

Ex officio Judges:
The Lord Chief Justice of England and Wales (The Rt. Hon. the Lord Phillips of Worth Matravers)
The Master of the Rolls (The Rt. Hon. Sir Anthony Peter Clarke)
The President of the Queen's Bench Division (The Rt. Hon. Sir Igor Judge)
The President of the Family Division (The Rt. Hon. Sir Mark Howard Potter)
The Chancellor (The Rt. Hon. Sir Robert Andrew Morritt, CVO)

The Master of the Rolls: The Rt. Hon. Sir Anthony Clarke
   Secretary: Ms. Jackie Sears. Tel: 020 7947 6002
   Clerk: Ms. Dawn Rollason. Tel: 020 7947 6371

Lords Justices of Appeal:
The Rt. Hon. Sir Robin Ernest Auld
The Rt. Hon. Sir Malcolm Thomas Pill
The Rt. Hon. Sir Alan Hylton Ward
The Rt. Hon. Sir Mathew Alexander Thorpe
The Rt. Hon. Sir George Mark Waller
The Rt. Hon. Sir John Frank Mummery
The Rt. Hon. Sir John Murray Chadwick, ED
The Rt. Hon. Sir Richard Joseph Buxton
The Rt. Hon. Sir Anthony Tristram Kenneth May
The Rt. Hon. Sir Simon Lane Tuckey
The Rt. Hon. Sir John Grant McKenzie Laws
The Rt. Hon. Sir Stephen John Sedley
The Rt. Hon. Sir David Nicholas Ramsay Latham
The Rt. Hon. Sir Bernard Anthony Rix
The Rt. Hon. Dame Mary Howarth Arden, DBE
The Rt. Hon. Sir David Wolfe Keene
The Rt. Hon. Sir John Anthony Dyson
The Rt. Hon. Sir Andrew Centlivres Longmore
The Rt. Hon. Sir Robert John Anderson Carnwath, CVO
The Rt. Hon. Sir Thomas Scott Gillespie Baker
The Rt. Hon. Dame Janet Hilary Smith, DBE
The Rt. Hon. Sir Roger John Laugharne Thomas
The Rt. Hon. Sir Robert Raphael Hayim (Robin) Jacob
The Rt. Hon. Sir Nicholas Peter Rathbone Wall
The Rt. Hon. Sir Maurice Ralph Kay
The Rt. Hon. Sir Anthony Hooper
The Rt. Hon. Sir William Marcus Gage
The Rt. Hon. Sir Timothy Andrew Wigram Lloyd
The Rt. Hon. Sir Martin James Moore-Bick
The Rt. Hon. Sir Nicholas Allan Ray Wilson
The Rt. Hon. Sir Alan George Moses
The Rt. Hon. Dame Heather Carol Hallett, DBE
The Rt. Hon. Sir Anthony Philip Gilson Hughes
The Rt. Hon. Sir Stephen Price Richards
The Rt. Hon. Sir Brian Henry Leveson
The Rt. Hon. Sir Lawrence Anthony Collins
The Rt. Hon. Sir Roger Grenfell Toulson

Civil Appeals Office: Office Manager: Tel: 020 7947 6409
                                    Fax: 020 7947 6810

Criminal Appeal Office: Registry Enquiries: Tel: 020 7947 6014
                                        Fax: 020 7947 6900

HIGH COURT OF JUSTICE, CHANCERY DIVISION
Royal Courts of Justice, Strand, London WC2A 2LL
Tel: 020 7947 6000
Fax: 020 7947 7345
DX 44450 STRAND WC2

President: The Lord High Chancellor (The Rt. Hon. Jack Straw, M.P.)

The Chancellor of the High Court: The Rt. Hon. Sir Robert Andrew Morritt, CVO
   Clerk: Mrs. Sheila Glasgow. Tel: 020 7947 6412

SUPREME COURTS

Judges:
The Hon. Sir John Edmund Frederic Lindsay
The Hon. Sir Edward Christopher Evans-Lombe
The Hon. Sir William Anthony Blackburne
The Hon. Sir Gavin Anthony Lightman
The Hon. Sir Colin Percy Farquharson Rimer
The Hon. Sir Nicholas Richard Pumfrey
The Hon. Sir David Anthony Stewart Richards
The Hon. Sir David James Tyson Kitchin
The Hon. Sir Nicholas John Patten
The Hon. Sir Terrence Michael Elkan Barnet Etherton
The Hon. Sir Peter Winston Smith
The Hon. Sir Kim Martin Jordan Lewison
The Rt. Hon. Sir George Anthony Mann
The Rt. Hon. Sir Nicholas Roger Warren
The Hon. Sir Michael Townley Featherstone Briggs
The Hon. Sir Launcelot Dinadin James Henderson

Judges Chambers: Clerk of the Lists. Tel: 020 7947 6010
Bankruptcy Department: Chief Clerk. Tel: 020 7947 6870
Companies Court: Chief Clerk. Tel: 020 7947 6243

HIGH COURT OF JUSTICE, QUEEN'S BENCH DIVISION
Royal Courts of Justice, Strand, London WC2A 2LL
Tel: 020 7947 6000   DX 44450 STRAND WC2

The Lord Chief Justice of England: The Rt. Hon. The Lord Phillips of Worth Matravers
   Secretary: Miss. M. Souris. Tel: 020 7947 6776
   Clerk: Ms. Helen Tyler. Tel: 020 7947 6001

Judges:
The Hon. Sir Stuart Neil McKinnon
The Hon. Sir Peter John Cresswell
The Hon. Sir Christopher John Holland
The Hon. Sir Anthony David Colman
The Hon. Sir John Thayne Forbes
The Hon. Sir Thomas Richard Atkin Morison
The Hon. Sir Andrew David Collins
The Hon. Sir Alexander Neil Logie Butterfield
The Hon. Sir George Michael Newman
The Hon. Sir Gordon Julian Hugh Langley
The Hon. Sir Robert Franklyn Nelson
The Hon. Sir David Eady
The Hon. Sir Jeremy Mirth Sullivan
The Hon. Sir David Herbert Penry-Davey
The Hon. Sir David William Steel
The Hon. Sir Charles Anthony St. John Gray
The Hon. Sir Nicolas Dusan Bratza (Judge of the European Court of Human Rights)
The Hon. Sir Michael John Burton
The Hon. Sir Rupert Matthew Jackson
The Hon. Sir Patrick Elias
The Hon. Sir Richard John Pearson Aikens
The Hon. Sir Stephen Robert Silber
The Hon. Sir John Bernard Goldring
The Hon. Sir Peter Francis Crane
The Hon. Dame Ann Judith Rafferty, DBE
The Hon. Sir Geoffrey Douglas Grigson
The Hon. Sir Richard John Hedley Gibbs
The Hon. Sir Richard Henry Quixano Henriques
The Hon. Sir Stephen Miles Tomlinson
The Hon. Sir Andrew Charles Smith
The Hon. Sir Stanley Jeffrey Burnton
The Hon. Sir Christopher John Pitchford
The Hon. Sir Duncan Brian Walter Ouseley
The Hon. Sir Richard George Bramwell McCombe
The Hon. Sir Raymond Evan Jack
The Hon. Sir Robert Michael Owen
The Hon. Sir Colin Crichton Mackay
The Hon. Sir John Edward Mitting
The Hon. Sir David Roderick Evans
The Hon. Sir Brian Richard Keith
The Hon. Sir Jeremy Lionel Cooke
The Hon. Sir Richard Alan Field
The Hon. Sir Christopher John Pitchers
The Hon. Sir Colman Maurice Treacy
The Hon. Sir Peregrine Charles Hugo Simon
The Hon. Sir Roger John Royce
The Hon. Dame Laura Mary Cox, DBE
The Hon. Sir Adrian Bruce Fulford
The Hon. Sir Jack Beatson
The Hon. Sir Michael George Tugendhat
The Hon. Sir David Clive Clarke
The Hon. Dame Elizabeth Gloster, DBE
The Hon. Sir David Michael Bean
The Hon. Sir Alan Fraser Wilkie
The Hon. Dame Linda Penelope Dobbs, DBE
The Hon. Sir Henry Egar Garfield Hodge, OBE
The Hon. Sir Paul James Walker
The Hon. Sir David Calvert-Smith
The Hon. Sir Christopher Simon Courtenay Stephenson Clarke
The Hon. Sir Charles Peter Lawford Openshaw
The Hon. Dame Caroline Jane Swift
The Hon. Sir Brian Frederick James Langstaff
The Hon. Sir David Lloyd-Jones
The Hon. Sir Vivian Arthur Ramsay
The Hon. Sir Nicholas Edward Underhill
The Hon. Sir Stephen John Irwin
The Hon. Sir Nigel Anthony Lambert Davis
The Hon. Sir Peter Henry Gross
The Hon. Sir Nigel John Martin Teare
The Hon. Sir John Griffith Williams
The Hon. Sir Wyn Lewis Williams
The Hon. Sir Timothy Roger Alan King
The Hon. Sir Saunders
The Hon. Sir Morgan
The Hon. Sir Flaux

Chief Clerk to Q.B. Judges in Chambers: Tel: 020 7947 6511
Clerk of the Lists Office: Tel: 020 7947 6021
Commercial Listing: Tel: 020 7947 6826

SUPREME COURTS

TECHNOLOGY & CONSTRUCTION COURT
St Dunstans House, 133-137 Fetter Lane, London EC4A 1HD
Tel: 020 7947 6022
Fax: 020 7947 7428

T.C.C. Judges

Mr Justice Jackson (Presiding Judge)
His Honour Judge Peter Bowsher
" " " Richard Havery
" " " Humphrey Lloyd

His Honour Judge Anthony Thornton
" " " David Wilcox
" " " John Toulmin
" " " Richard Seymour

Court Manager: Ms L. Fletcher. Tel: 020 7947 7429

HIGH COURT OF JUSTICE, FAMILY DIVISION

First Avenue House, 42-49 High Holborn, London WC1V 6NP
Tel: 020 7947 6000
Fax: 020 7947 6709

President: The Rt. Hon. Sir Mark Howard Potter
   Secretary: Mrs. S. Leung. Tel: 020 7947 6084
   Clerk: Miss Ayo Onatade. Tel: 020 7947 6576

Judges:

The Hon. Sir Jan Peter Singer
The Hon. Sir Andrew Tristram Hammett Kirkwood
The Hon. Sir Hugh Peter Derwyn Bennett
The Hon. Sir Edward James Holman
The Hon. Dame Mary Claire Hogg, DBE
The Hon. Sir Christopher John Sumner
The Hon. Sir Arthur William Hessin Charles
The Hon. Sir David Roderick Lessiter Bodey
The Hon. Dame Jill Margaret Black, DBE
The Hon. Sir James Lawrence Munby

The Hon. Sir Paul James Duke Coleridge
The Hon. Sir Mark Hedley
The Hon. Dame Anna Evelyn Hamilton Pauffley, DBE
The Hon. Sir Roderic Lionel James Wood
The Hon. Dame Florence Jacquelene Baron, DBE
The Hon. Sir Ernest Nigel Ryder
The Hon. Sir Andrew Ewart McFarlane
The Hon. Dame Julia Wendy Macur, DBE
The Hon. Sir Andrew John Gregory Moylan

Clerk of the Rules: Miss R. Few. Tel: 020 7947 6591

Principal Registry of the Family Division (P.R.F.D.)

Family & Probate Service Group Manager: R. Knight. Tel: 020 7947 6989

District Judges:

Mr District Judge Philip Waller (Senior District Judge)
Mrs. District Judge Moorhouse
Mr District Judge Segal
Mr District Judge Maple
Miss District Judge Bradley
Mr District Judge White
Mr District Judge Bassett-Cross
Mr District Judge Berry
Ms District Judge Bowman

Mr District Judge Million
Mr District Judge Waller
Miss District Judge Cushing
Mr District Judge Harper
Mr District Judge Brasse
Miss District Judge Redgrave
Ms District Judge Black
Mr District Judge Green
Miss District Judge Roberts
Mr District Judge Robinson

SUPREME COURTS

CENTRAL OFFICE OF THE SUPREME COURT
Royal Courts of Justice, Strand, London WC2A 2LL
Tel: 020 7947 6000 (Central Switchboard)
DX 44450 STRAND

Senior Master of the Supreme Court (Q.B.D.) and Queen's Remembrancer: R. L. Turner
Masters of the Supreme Court (Q.B.D.)
P. Miller
I. H. Foster
G. H. Rose
P. G. A. Eyre
H. J. Leslie
J. G. G. Ungley
B. Yoxall
S. Whitaker
B. J. F. Fontaine

Clerk to Interim Applications Judge: B. Young. Tel: 020 7947 6508

CHANCERY CHAMBERS
Chief Master of the Supreme Court: J. I. Winegarten
Masters of the Supreme Court
J. A. Moncaster
Teveson
N. W. Bragge
T. J. Bowles
N. Price

Court Manager: G. Robinson. Tel: 020 7947 6075

ADMINISTRATIVE COURT
Royal Courts of Justice, Strand, London WC2A 2LL
Tel: 020 7947 6000
Fax: 020 7947 6802
DX 44450 STRAND WC2

Master of the Crown Office, and Queen's Coroner and Attorney: R. A. Venne
Head of Administrative Court: Mrs. L. G. Knapman
Group Manager: Ms H. Smith. Tel: 020 7947 6190
Administrative Court Office Associates: Tel: 020 7947 6106

SUPREME COURT COSTS OFFICE
Clifford's Inn, Fetter Lane, London EC4A 1DQ
Tel: 020 7947 6163
Fax Nos. 020 7947 6344 and 020 7947 6247
DX 44454 STRAND

Senior Cost Judge: P. T. Hurst
Court Manager: Geoff Waterhouse. Tel: 020 7947 7312

ADMIRALTY REGISTRY AND MARSHAL'S OFFICE
Royal Courts of Justice, Strand, London WC2A 2LL
Tel: 020 7947 6112

Admiralty Registrar and Queen's Bench Master: P. Miller
Admiralty Marshall and Court Manager: K. Houghton. Tel: 020 7947 6111

COURT OF PROTECTION
Archway Towers, 2 Junction Road, London N19 5SZ
Tel: 0845 330 2900

OFFICIAL SOLICITOR'S DEPARTMENT
Chichester Rents, 81 Chancery Lane, London WC2A 1DD
Tel: 020 7911 7127/7142

OFFICIAL RECEIVER'S OFFICE
21 Bloomsbury Street, London WC1B 3SS
Tel: 020 7823 3090
Fax: 020 7636 4709

CROWN PROSECUTION SERVICE: See Appendix 1 *post*

SUPREME COURTS

NORTHERN IRELAND

THE ROYAL COURTS OF JUSTICE
Chichester Street, Belfast BT1 3JF
Tel: 028 9023 5111
Fax: 028 9031 3508

Lord Chief Justice of Northern Ireland: The Rt. Hon. Sir Brian Kerr

Judges:
- The Rt. Hon. Lord Justice Campbell
- The Hon. Lord Justice Higgins
- The Hon. Lord Justice Girvan
- The Hon. Mr. Justice Coghlin
- The Hon. Mr. Justice Gillen
- The Hon. Mr. Justice McLaughlin
- The Hon. Mr. Justice Weatherup
- The Hon. Mr. Justice Weir
- The Hon. Mr. Justice Morgan
- The Hon. Mr. Justice Deeny
- The Hon. Mr. Justice Hart
- The Hon. Mr. Justice Stephens
- The Hon. Mr. Justice Treacy

NORTHERN IRELAND COURT SERVICE
Windsor House, Bedford Street, Belfast BT2 7LT
Tel: 02890 328594
Fax: 02890 439110

Director of the Court Service: David A Lavery

The Northern Ireland Court Service is comprised of 5 divisions and the work of these is described below. The Northern Ireland Court Service also has administrative responsibility for tribunals in Northern Ireland, together with responsibility for 2 non-departmental public bodies, namely the Northern Ireland Legal Services Commission and the Northern Ireland Judicial Appointments Commission.

Operations Division
Head of Division: Jacqui Durkin
Providing administrative support for criminal, civil and family court business, across all court tiers at the 21 courthouses in Northern Ireland; the Enforcement of Judgments Office; The Fixed Penalty Office; The Coroners Service for Northern Ireland; The provision of human resource services, information services and judicial support services; NDPB Sponsorship of the NI Judicial Appointments Commission; Business modernisation and development through the use of ICT and business redesign, operational policy, customer service continuous improvement and facilitating inspectorate activity.

Policy and Legislation Division
Head of Division: Laurene McAlpine
Advising the Lord Chancellor on the policy and legislative framework within which the Northern Ireland courts operate; Preparing legislation for which the Lord Chancellor is responsible in Northern Ireland; Providing legal advice to the Court Service; Providing the secretariat to Court Rules Committees.

Finance Division
Head of Division: David Thompson
Providing a wide range of corporate support services for the Judiciary and staff in the Court Service including commercial contracts and estates management services; Finance and resource management; Managing funds lodged in court on behalf of minors and patients, through the Court Funds Office; The provision of internal risk management and assurance services.

Public Funded Legal Services
Head of Division: Paul Andrews
Reform of public funded Legal Services; Sponsorship of the Northern Ireland Legal Services Commission; Formulating and implementing legal aid policy.

Tribunal Reform
Head of Division: Siobhan Broderick
Provide administrative support for the Northern Ireland Court Service tribunals and bring forward proposals for the reform of tribunals with the view ot establishing a unified tribunal service for Northern Ireland.

SCOTLAND

COURT OF SESSION

Parliament House, Parliament Square, Edinburgh EH1 1RQ
Tel: 0131-225 2595   Fax: 0131-240 6755
Rutland Exchange: 549306 Edinburgh-36
Legal Post: LP1

HIGH COURT OF JUSTICIARY

Justiciary Office, Lawnmarket, Edinburgh EH1 2NS
Tel: 0131-225 2595   Fax: 0131-240 6915
Rutland Exchange: 549307 Edinburgh-36
Legal Post: LP1

The Lord President and Lord Justice General: The Rt. Hon. Lord Hamilton

INNER HOUSE – *First Division*

The Lord President (The Rt. Hon. Lord Hamilton)

The Rt. Hon. Lord Nimmo Smith
The Rt. Hon. Lord Philip
The Rt. Hon. Lord Kingarth
The Hon. Lord Eassie

Second Division

The Lord Justice Clerk (The Rt. Hon. Lord Gill)

The Rt. Hon. Lord Osborne
The Rt. Hon. Lord MacFadyen
The Rt. Hon. Lord Abernethy
The Rt. Hon. Lord Johnston
The Hon. Lady Paton

OUTER HOUSE

The Hon. Lord Dawson
The Hon. Lord Reed
The Hon. Lord Wheatley
The Hon. Lord Carloway
The Hon. Lord Clarke
The Rt. Hon. the Lord Hardie
The Rt. Hon. the Lord Mackay of Drumadoon
The Hon. Lord McEwan
The Hon. Lord Menzies
The Hon. Lord Drummond Young
The Hon. Lord Emslie
The Hon. Lady Smith

The Hon. Lord Brodie
The Hon. Lord Bracadale
The Hon. Lady Dorrian
The Hon. Lord Hodge
The Hon. Lord Macphail
The Hon. Lord Glennie
The Hon. Lord Kinclaven
The Hon. Lord Turnbull
The Hon. Lady Clark of Calton
The Hon. Lord Brailsford
The Hon. Lord Uist
The Hon. Lord Malcolm

SCOTTISH EXECUTIVE JUSTICE DEPARTMENT

Head of Department: Robert Gordon
www.scotland.gov.uk

Civil and International Group
Head of Group: Micheline Brannan
Civil Justice Division
   Division Head: Paul Cackette
   St. Andrews House, Regent Road, Edinburgh EH1 3DG
   Telephone: 0131 244 4821   Fax: 0131 244 4848   DX 557 007

Courts Group
Head of Group: Robert Gordon
Judicial Appointments and Finance Division
   Division Head: John L. Anderson
   Telephone: 0131 221 6801   Fax: 0131 221 6895

Hayweight House, 23 Lauriston Street, Edinburgh EH3 9DQ
Telephone: 0131 229 9200   DX ED 545307

SCOTTISH COURT SERVICE
www.scotcourts.gov.uk
Hayweight House, 23 Lauriston Street, Edinburgh EH3 9DQ
Tel: 0131-229 9200   Fax: 0131-221 6895   DX 545309

Chief Executive: Mrs. Eleanor Emberson
Director of Field Services: Eric McQueen
Director of Policy and Strategy Alistair Sim
Director of Operational Support: Gordon Waks

CROWN COURTS

ENGLAND AND WALES

> Please note that as from 1st April 2007 Her Majesty's Courts Service was restructured in England and Wales. Information on Her Majesty's Courts Service, including a comprehensive list of Regional and Area Directors, can be found below.

NOTE: First Tier centres deal with both High Court civil cases and Crown Court criminal cases and are served by High Court and Circuit Judges. Second Tier centres deal with criminal cases only, but are served both by High Court and Circuit Judges. Third Tier centres deal with criminal cases only and are served only by Circuit Judges.

MIDLANDS REGION

PRESIDING JUDGES: The Rt. Hon. Lord Justice Leveson, Senior Presiding Judge
The Hon. Mr. Justice Gibbs
The Hon. Mr. Justice Treacy

FAMILY DIVISION LIAISON JUDGE:
The Hon. Mr. Justice Hedley

CHANCERY SUPERVISING JUDGE:
The Hon. Mr. Justice Hart

CIRCUIT JUDGES:

Her Honour Judge			Fisher	His Honour Judge		Gregory
His	"	"	Pyke	"	"	Everard
"	"	"	Chapman	"	"	Pearce-Higgins, Q.C.
"	"	"	Matthews	"	"	Bellamy
Her	"	"	Alton	"	"	Morrison OBE, Q.C.
His	"	"	Orme	"	"	Styler
"	"	"	Hodson	"	"	Cavell
"	"	"	D. Hamilton	"	"	Geddes
"	"	"	McCarthy	"	"	Rubery
"	"	"	McCreath	"	"	Eades
"	"	"	Warner	"	"	Mitchell
"	"	"	MacDuff, Q.C.	"	"	McEvoy, Q.C.
"	"	"	Marten Coates	"	"	Tonking
Her	"	"	Hindley, Q.C.	Her	"	Hughes
"	"	"	Deeley	His	"	Rundell
His	"	"	Griffith-Jones	"	"	Glenn
"	"	"	Eccles, Q.C.	"	"	Brunning
"	"	"	Oliver-Jones, Q.C.	"	"	Jenkins
"	"	"	McKenna	"	"	Orrell
"	"	"	Onions	"	"	Morrell
"	"	"	Collis	"	"	Pugsley
Her	"	"	Kirkham	"	"	Bray
His	"	"	Faber	"	"	Hammond
"	"	"	Norris, Q.C.	"	"	Bennett
"	"	"	Alexander, Q.C.	"	"	O'Rorke
"	"	"	Webb	"	"	Heath
"	"	"	Dudley	"	"	Inglis
"	"	"	Challinor	"	"	Machin
"	"	"	Cardinal	"	"	Wait
"	"	"	Ross	"	"	Teare

CROWN COURTS

His Honour Judge	Tony Mitchell
"	"	"	A. Hamilton
"	"	"	Stokes, Q.C.
"	"	"	Wide, Q.C.
"	"	"	Metcalf
"	"	"	Waine
Her	"	"	Hampton
"	"	"	Butler, Q.C.
His	"	"	Burgess
"	"	"	Milmo, Q.C.
"	"	"	Pert, Q.C.

His Honour Judge	Head
"	"	"	Price
"	"	"	Lea
Her	"	"	Swindells, Q.C.
His	"	"	Plunkett
"	"	"	Maxwell
Her	"	"	Thomas
His	"	"	Duggan
"	"	"	Clearly
"	"	"	Mithani

REGIONAL DIRECTOR:
Mr Alan Eccles,
6th Floor,
Temple Court,
34 Bull Street,
Birmingham B4 6WF
  Tel: 0121 250 6162
  Fax: 0121 250 6166
  DX 701993 BIRMINGHAM 7

AREA DIRECTORS:

Birmingham, Coventry, Solihull & Warwickshire
Kelvin Launchbury,
Area Director's Office,
3rd Floor,
Temple Court,
35 Bull Street,
Birmingham B4 6LG
  Tel: 0121 681 3201
  Fax: 0121 250 6154
  DX 701993 BIRMINGHAM 7

Black Country, Staffordshire & West Mercia
Peter Hammersley,
Area Director's Office,
1st Floor,
Victoria Park House,
2-9 Victoria Road,
Stafford ST16 2AV
  Tel: 01785 218360
  Fax: 01785 241643

Derbyshire & Nottinghamshire
Mark Swales,
Area Director's Office,
Nottingham Magistrates' Court,
Carrington Street,
Nottingham NG2 1EE
  Tel: 0115 955 8301
  Fax: 0115 955 8177
  DX 719030 NOTTINGHAM 32

Lincolnshire, Leicestershire & Rutland and Northamptonshire
Richard Redgrave

CROWN COURTS

Court Index – Midlands Region

Court Code	Town Name	Court Type	Area	Page No
2047	Ashby-de-la-Zouch L.J.A.	Magistrates	12	62
127	Birmingham	County	10	9
0404	Birmingham	Crown	10	43
2908	Birmingham L.J.A.	Magistrates	10	13
138	Boston	County	12	10
2073	Boston L.J.A.	Magistrates	12	62
2074	Bourne and Stamford L.J.A.	Magistrates	12	62
1840	Bromsgrove and Redditch L.J.A.	Magistrates	13	16
155	Burton upon Trent	County	13	13
158	Buxton	County	11	13
2799	Central and South West Staffordshire L.J.A.	Magistrates	13	16
171	Chesterfield	County	11	15
2321	Corby L.J.A.	Magistrates	12	63
180	Coventry	County	10	17
0417	Coventry	Crown	10	46
2910	Coventry District L.J.A.	Magistrates	10	13
2322	Daventry L.J.A.	Magistrates	12	63
185	Derby	County	11	18
0419	Derby	Crown	11	46
189	Dudley	County	13	18
2911	Dudley L.J.A.	Magistrates	13	17
2076	Elloes L.J.A.	Magistrates	12	63
197	Evesham	County	13	19
2075	Gainsborough L.J.A.	Magistrates	12	63
205	Grantham	County	12	21
2077	Grantham L.J.A.	Magistrates	12	64
220	Hereford	County	13	23
0762	Hereford	Crown	13	48
1841	Herefordshire L.J.A.	Magistrates	13	17
1430	High Peak L.J.A.	Magistrates	11	42
236	Kettering	County	12	25
2323	Kettering L.J.A.	Magistrates	12	64
237	Kidderminster	County	13	25
1842	Kidderminster L.J.A.	Magistrates	13	17
244	Leicester	County	12	27
0430	Leicester	Crown	12	50
2048	Leicester L.J.A.	Magistrates	12	64
249	Lincoln	County	12	27
0432	Lincoln	Crown	12	50
2079	Lincoln District L.J.A.	Magistrates	12	64
2049	Loughborough L.J.A.	Magistrates	12	65

CROWN COURTS

Court Code	Town Name	Court Type	Area	Page No
257	Ludlow	County	13	32
263	Mansfield	County	11	33
2566	Mansfield L.J.A.	Magistrates	11	42
2050	Market Bosworth L.J.A.	Magistrates	12	65
2051	Market Harborough and Lutterworth L.J.A.	Magistrates	12	65
2045	Melton, Belvoir and Rutland L.J.A.	Magistrates	12	65
268	Melton Mowbray	County	12	34
276	Newark	County	11	36
2567	Newark and Southwell L.J.A.	Magistrates	11	42
282	Northampton	County	12	37
0442	Northampton	Crown	12	55
2325	Northampton L.J.A.	Magistrates	12	66
1432	North East Derbyshire and Dales L.J.A.	Magistrates	11	43
2791	North Staffordshire L.J.A.	Magistrates	13	18
286	Nottingham	County	11	38
0444	Nottingham	Crown	11	55
2568	Nottingham L.J.A.	Magistrates	11	43
287	Nuneaton	County	10	38
289	Oswestry	County	13	38
306	Redditch	County	13	41
311	Rugby	County	10	42
322	Shrewsbury	County	13	44
0452	Shrewsbury	Crown	13	57
3278	Shrewsbury and North Shropshire L.J.A.	Magistrates	13	18
324	Skegness	County	12	44
2082	Skegness L.J.A.	Magistrates	12	66
2080	Sleaford L.J.A.	Magistrates	12	66
2916	Solihull L.J.A.	Magistrates	10	14
2860	South East Staffordshire L.J.A.	Magistrates	13	19
1428	Southern Derbyshire L.J.A.	Magistrates	11	43
1843	South Worcestershire L.J.A.	Magistrates	13	19
333	Stafford	County	13	46
0455	Stafford	Crown	13	58
338	Stoke on Trent	County	13	46
0456	Stoke on Trent	Crown	13	58
339	Stourbridge	County	13	47
2912	Stourbridge and Halesowen L.J.A.	Magistrates	13	20
340	Stratford upon Avon	County	10	47
2909	Sutton Coldfield L.J.A.	Magistrates	10	14
346	Tamworth	County	13	48
364	Telford	County	13	48
3276	Telford and South Shropshire L.J.A.	Magistrates	13	20

CROWN COURTS

Court Code	Town Name	Court Type	Area	Page No
3282	Telford and South Shropshire L.J.A.	Magistrates	13	20
2327	Towcester L.J.A.	Magistrates	12	66
358	Walsall	County	13	50
2917	Walsall and Aldridge L.J.A.	Magistrates	13	21
2914	Warley L.J.A.	Magistrates	13	21
361	Warwick	County	10	50
0463	Warwick	Crown	10	60
2904	Warwickshire L.J.A.	Magistrates	10	15
363	Wellingborough	County	12	51
2328	Wellingborough L.J.A.	Magistrates	12	67
2915	West Bromwich L.J.A.	Magistrates	13	21
2078	Wolds L.J.A.	Magistrates	12	67
378	Wolverhampton	County	13	52
0421	Wolverhampton	Crown	13	60
2919	Wolverhampton L.J.A.	Magistrates	13	21
380	Worcester	County	13	52
0466	Worcester	Crown	13	60
382	Worksop	County	11	53
2569	Worksop and Retford L.J.A.	Magistrates	11	44

CROWN COURTS

NORTH EAST REGION

PRESIDING JUDGES:
The Rt. Hon. Lord Justice Leveson, Senior Presiding Judge
The Hon. Mr. Justice Peregrine Simon
The Hon. Mr. Justice Wilkie

FAMILY DIVISION LIAISON JUDGE:
The Hon. Mr. Justice Bodey

CHANCERY SUPERVISING JUDGE:
The Hon. Mr. Justice Patten

CIRCUIT JUDGES:

His Honour Judge	D. Hodson	Her Honour Judge	J. P. Moir
" " "	P. J. Fox, Q.C.	His " "	M. J. A. Murphy, Q.C.
" " "	D. M. A. Bryant	" " "	P. J. B. Armstrong
" " "	M. T. Cracknell	" " "	G. Cliffe
" " "	P. M. L. Hoffman	" " "	K. M. P. Macgill
" " "	P. J. H. Langan, Q.C.	Her " "	A. C. Finnerty
" " "	J. W. M. Bullimore	His " "	T. Hewitt
" " "	M. K. Mettyear	" " "	J. H. Reddihough
" " "	A. N. J. Briggs	Her " "	J. Shipley
" " "	T. W. Barber	" " "	E. A. Carr, Q.C.
" " "	M. L. Cartlidge	His " "	A. T. Lancaster
" " "	S. P. Grenfell	" " "	P. H. F. Jones
" " "	A. G. McCallum	Her " "	B. M. Bolton
" " "	E. J. Faulks	His " "	J. Spencer, Q.C.
" " "	G. H. Kamil	" " "	P. C. Benson
" " "	R. M. Scott	" " "	L. D. Hull
Her " "	J. Davies	" " "	T. M. Walsh
His " "	P. J. Cockroft	" " "	R. Ibbotson
" " "	J. D. G. Walford	" " "	M. G. C. Moorhouse
" " "	R. P. Lowden	" " "	K. R. Keen, Q.C.
" " "	A. R. Goldsack, Q.C.	" " "	J. Dowse
" " "	P. E. Robertshaw	" " "	S. M. Spencer, Q.C.
" " "	D. R. Wood	" " "	S. W. Lawler, Q.C.
" " "	J. S. Wolstenholme	" " "	J. S. H. Stewart, Q.C.
" " "	R. J. Moore	" " "	J. T. Milford, Q.C.
" " "	R. A. Grant	" " "	S. M. Jack
" " "	I. J. Dobkin	Her " "	S. E. M. Cahill, Q.C.
" " "	P. H. Bowers	His " "	S. J. Ashurst
" " "	M. J. Taylor	" " "	R. E. Thorn, Q.C.
" " "	R. Bartfield	" " "	G. Robinson
" " "	L. Spittle	Her " "	J. C. Kershaw, Q.C.
" " "	J. A. Swanson	His " "	M. J. Evans
" " "	C. O. J. Behrens	" " "	J. A. Taylor
" " "	D. P. Hunt	" " "	J. D. Durham Hall, Q.C.
" " "	C. T. Walton	" " "	R. G. Kaye, Q.C.
" " "	G. Whitburn, Q.C.	" " "	G. C. Marson, Q.C.
" " "	S. J. Gullick	Her " "	P. Belcher
" " "	T. S. A. Hawkesworth, Q.C.	His " "	C. Prince

CROWN COURTS

REGIONAL DIRECTOR:
Mr Stephen Caven,
18th Floor,
West Riding House,
Albion Street,
Leeds LS1 5AA
   Tel: 0113 251 1242
   Fax: 0113 251 1248
DX 724960 LEEDS 56

AREA DIRECTORS:

Cleveland, Durham & Northumbria
Sheila Proudlock,
Area Director's Office,
P.O. Box 168,
Old Elvet,
Durham DH1 3FE
   Tel: 0191 384 4455
   Fax: 0191 375 1833

North & West Yorkshire
Dyfed Foulkes,
Area Director's Office,
Colbeck House,
Bradford Road,
Birstall,
Batley WF17 9NR
   Tel: 01924 424030
   Fax: 01924 427910

Humber & South Yorkshire
Paul Bradley,
Area Director's Office,
Sheffield Combined Court,
Family Hearing Centre,
48 West Bar,
Sheffield S3 8PH
   Tel: 0114 201 1140
   Fax: 0114 201 1150
DX 302028 SHEFFIELD 6

Court Index – North East Region

Court Code	Town Name	Court Type	Area	Page No
2347	Alnwick L.J.A.	Magistrates	4	31
118	Barnsley	County	6	7
2770	Barnsley L.J.A.	Magistrates	6	57
2996	Batley and Dewsbury L.J.A.	Magistrates	5	88
2348	Berwick-upon-Tweed L.J.A.	Magistrates	4	31
1942	Beverley and the Wolds L.J.A.	Magistrates	6	57
128	Bishop Auckland	County	4	9
141	Bradford	County	5	11
0402	Bradford	Crown	5	43
2978	Bradford L.J.A.	Magistrates	5	88
1941	Bridlington L.J.A.	Magistrates	6	57
2997	Calderdale L.J.A.	Magistrates	5	89
177	Consett	County	4	16
183	Darlington	County	4	17
186	Dewsbury	County	5	18
187	Doncaster	County	6	18
0420	Doncaster	Crown	6	46
2771	Doncaster L.J.A.	Magistrates	6	58

CROWN COURTS

Court Code	Town Name	Court Type	Area	Page No
190	Durham	County	4	19
0422	Durham	Crown	4	47
202	Gateshead	County	4	20
2850	Gateshead L.J.A.	Magistrates	4	31
1928	Goole and Howdenshire L.J.A.	Magistrates	6	58
208	Great Grimsby	County	6	21
0425	Great Grimsby	Crown	6	48
1940	Grimsby and Cleethorpes L.J.A.	Magistrates	6	58
212	Halifax	County	5	22
214	Harrogate	County	5	22
2527	Harrogate L.J.A.	Magistrates	5	89
215	Hartlepool	County	4	22
1247	Hartlepool L.J.A.	Magistrates	4	32
2854	Houghton-le-Spring L.J.A.	Magistrates	4	32
228	Huddersfield	County	5	24
2987	Huddersfield L.J.A.	Magistrates	5	89
1943	Hull and Holderness L.J.A.	Magistrates	6	58
234	Keighley	County	5	25
2979	Keighley L.J.A.	Magistrates	5	89
239	Kingston upon Hull	County	6	26
0403	Kingston upon Hull	Crown	6	49
1248	Langbaurgh East L.J.A.	Magistrates	4	32
243	Leeds	County	5	26
0429	Leeds	Crown	5	49
2992	Leeds District L.J.A.	Magistrates	5	90
270	Middlesbrough	County	4	34
273	Morpeth and Berwick	County	4	35
278	Newcastle upon Tyne	County	4	36
0439	Newcastle upon Tyne	Crown	4	54
2851	Newcastle upon Tyne L.J.A.	Magistrates	4	33
2543	Northallerton and Richmond L.J.A.	Magistrates	5	90
1583	North Durham L.J.A.	Magistrates	4	33
1903	North Lincolnshire L.J.A.	Magistrates	6	59
283	North Shields	County	4	37
2852	North Tyneside District L.J.A.	Magistrates	4	34
297	Pontefract	County	5	40
2994	Pontefract L.J.A.	Magistrates	5	90
310	Rotherham	County	6	42
2772	Rotherham L.J.A.	Magistrates	6	59
318	Scarborough	County	5	43
2536	Scarborough L.J.A.	Magistrates	5	90
319	Scunthorpe	County	6	43

CROWN COURTS

Court Code	Town Name	Court Type	Area	Page No
2537	Selby L.J.A.	Magistrates	5	91
320	Sheffield	County	6	44
0451	Sheffield	Crown	6	57
2773	Sheffield L.J.A.	Magistrates	6	59
325	Skipton	County	5	44
2538	Skipton L.J.A.	Magistrates	5	91
1584	South Durham L.J.A.	Magistrates	4	34
2349	South East Northumberland L.J.A.	Magistrates	4	35
331	South Shields	County	4	45
2853	South Tyneside District L.J.A.	Magistrates	4	35
343	Sunderland	County	4	47
2855	Sunderland L.J.A.	Magistrates	4	36
0460	Teesside	Crown	4	59
1249	Teesside L.J.A.	Magistrates	4	36
2346	Tynedale L.J.A.	Magistrates	4	36
357	Wakefield	County	5	50
2995	Wakefield L.J.A.	Magistrates	5	91
386	York	County	5	53
0467	York	Crown	5	60
2541	York L.J.A.	Magistrates	5	91

CROWN COURTS

NORTH WEST REGION

PRESIDING JUDGES:
  The Rt. Hon. Lord Justice Leveson, Senior Presiding Judge
  The Hon. Mr. Justice McCombe
  The Hon. Mr. Justice David Clarke

FAMILY DIVISION LIAISON JUDGE:
  The Hon. Mr. Justice Ryder

VICE CHANCELLOR OF THE COUNTY PALATINE OF LANCASTER:
  The Hon. Mr. Justice Patten

CIRCUIT JUDGES:

His Honour Judge Maddison (The Hon. Recorder of Manchester)	His Honour Judge	Swift
His Honour Judge Globe, Q.C. (The Hon. Recorder of Liverpool)	" " "	Lewis
His Honour Judge Russell, Q.C. (The Hon. Recorder of Preston)	" " "	Bloom, Q.C.
His Honour Judge Hammond	" " "	Baker
" " " Robert Brown	" " "	Henshell
" " " Duncan	" " "	Phillips
" " " Elgan Edwards, D.L.	" " "	Blake
" " " Kevin Barnett	" " "	Lyon
" " " Caulfield	" " "	Iain Hamilton
Her " " Elizabeth Steel, D.L.	" " "	Atherton
His " " Appleton	Her " "	Gilmour, Q.C.
" " " Gilliland, Q.C.	His " "	Kushner, Q.C.
" " " Mackay	Her " "	Mark Brown
" " " Holloway	His " "	Watson
" " " Clifton	" " "	Harris, Q.C.
" " " Tetlow	" " "	Badley
" " " Trigger	" " "	Lever
" " " Roberts	" " "	Raynor, Q.C.
" " " Macmillan	" " "	Lowcock
" " " Charles James	" " "	Boulton
" " " Earnshaw	" " "	Sycamore
" " " Peter Smith	Her " "	Case
Her " " Daley	" " "	Nicholas Woodward
His " " Geake	His " "	Newton
" " " Allweis	" " "	Roddy
" " " Halbert	" " "	Steiger, T.D., Q.C.
" " " Holman	" " "	Armitage, Q.C.
" " " Morris	" " "	Jeffrey Lewis
" " " Hale	" " "	Knopf
Her " " Eaglestone	" " "	Rumbelow, Q.C.
His " " Stephen Clarke	" " "	Cornwall
" " " Lakin	" " "	Goldstone, Q.C.
" " " Slinger	" " "	Byrne
" " " George	Her " "	Rudland
" " " Ensor	His " "	Forrester
" " " Mort	" " "	Appleby
" " " Hegarty, Q.C.	" " "	Stewart, Q.C.
" " " Phipps	" " "	Warnock
" " " Roger Dutton	" " "	Batty, Q.C.
" " " Adrian Smith	" " "	Gilbart, Q.C.
	" " "	Foster, Q.C.
	" " "	Anthony Gee, Q.C.
	Her " "	de Haas, Q.C.

CROWN COURTS

His Honour Judge Clayson
" " " Hernandez
Her " " Lunt
His " " Fletcher
" " " Thomas, Q.C.
" " " Platts
" " " Hodge, Q.C.
Her " " Nield
His " " Aubery, Q.C.

His Honour Judge Pelling, Q.C.
" " " Wright
" " " Wallwork
" " " Woolman
" " " Teague
" " " Khokhar
" " " Morrow
" " " Everett

REGIONAL DIRECTOR:
Mrs Chris Mayer, C.B.E.,
4th Floor,
15 Quay Street,
Manchester M60 9FD
  Tel: 0161 833 1004/5
  Fax: 0161 832 8596
  DX 724780 Manchester 44

AREA DIRECTORS:

Cheshire & Merseyside
Shaun McNally,
Area Director's Office,
1st Floor,
Queen Elizabeth II Law Courts,
Derby Square,
Liverpool L2 1XA
  Tel: 0151 330 9605
  Fax: 0151 236 5180
  DX 702600 LIVERPOOL 5

Greater Manchester
Richard Knott,
Area Director's Office,
15 Quay Street,
Manchester M60 9FD
  Tel: 0161 833 1005
  Fax: 0161 831 6329
  DX 724780 MANCHESTER 44

Cumbria & Lancashire
Gill Hague,
Area Director's Office,
Sessions House,
Lancaster Road,
Preston PR1 2PD
  Tel: 01772 272820
  Fax: 01772 272821
  DX 724880 PRESTON 21

Court Index – North West Region

Court Code	Town Name	Court Type	Area	Page No
103	Accrington	County	1	5
106	Altrincham	County	2	6
120	Barrow-in-Furness	County	1	7
0751	Barrow-in-Furness	Crown	1	42
126	Birkenhead	County	3	8
130	Blackburn	County	1	9
2012	Blackburn, Darwen and Ribble Valley L.J.A.	Magistrates	1	37
131	Blackpool	County	1	9
137	Bolton	County	2	10
0470	Bolton	Crown	2	43

CROWN COURTS

Court Code	Town Name	Court Type	Area	Page No
1731	Bolton L.J.A.	Magistrates	2	51
154	Burnley	County	1	12
0409	Burnley	Crown	1	44
2014	Burnley, Pendle and Rossendale L.J.A.	Magistrates	1	37
156	Bury	County	2	13
1732	Bury L.J.A.	Magistrates	2	51
165	Carlisle	County	1	14
0412	Carlisle	Crown	1	45
1322	Carlisle and District L.J.A.	Magistrates	1	38
170	Chester	County	3	15
0415	Chester	Crown	3	45
1188	Chester, Ellesmere Port and Neston L.J.A.	Magistrates	3	27
174	Chorley	County	1	16
1998	Chorley L.J.A.	Magistrates	1	38
1747	City of Salford L.J.A.	Magistrates	2	51
181	Crewe	County	3	17
1324	Eden L.J.A.	Magistrates	1	38
1398	Furness and District L.J.A.	Magistrates	1	38
1992	Fylde Coast L.J.A.	Magistrates	1	39
1177	Halton L.J.A.	Magistrates	3	27
2010	Hyndburn L.J.A.	Magistrates	1	39
235	Kendal	County	1	25
2266	Knowsley, L.J.A.	Magistrates	3	27
0767	Knutsford	Crown	3	49
242	Lancaster	County	1	26
0768	Lancaster	Crown	1	49
2002	Lancaster L.J.A.	Magistrates	1	39
245	Leigh	County	2	27
251	Liverpool	County	3	28
0433	Liverpool	Crown	3	50
2267	Liverpool L.J.A.	Magistrates	3	28
260	Macclesfield	County	3	33
1178	Macclesfield L.J.A.	Magistrates	3	28
262	Manchester	County	2	33
1733	Manchester City L.J.A.	Magistrates	2	52
0435	Manchester (Crown Square)	Crown	2	53
0436	Manchester (Minshull Street)	Crown	2	54
275	Nelson	County	1	36
2269	North Sefton District L.J.A.	Magistrates	3	28
284	Northwich	County	3	37
288	Oldham	County	2	38
1734	Oldham L.J.A.	Magistrates	2	52

CROWN COURTS

Court Code	Town Name	Court Type	Area	Page No
2003	Ormskirk L.J.A.	Magistrates	1	40
292	Penrith	County	1	39
303	Preston	County	1	41
0448	Preston	Crown	1	56
2005	Preston L.J.A.	Magistrates	1	40
304	Rawtenstall	County	1	41
1750	Rochdale, Middleton and Heywood L.J.A.	Magistrates	2	52
312	Runcorn	County	3	42
315	St Helens	County	3	43
2268	St Helens L.J.A.	Magistrates	3	28
316	Salford	County	2	43
1187	South Cheshire L.J.A.	Magistrates	3	29
1323	South Lakeland L.J.A.	Magistrates	1	40
330	Southport	County	3	45
2007	South Ribble, L.J.A.	Magistrates	1	40
2270	South Sefton District L.J.A.	Magistrates	3	29
336	Stockport	County	2	46
1739	Stockport L.J.A.	Magistrates	2	52
112	Tameside	County	2	48
1748	Tameside L.J.A.	Magistrates	2	53
1742	Trafford L.J.A.	Magistrates	2	53
1179	Vale Royal L.J.A.	Magistrates	3	29
360	Warrington	County	3	50
0462	Warrington	Crown	3	59
1180	Warrington L.J.A.	Magistrates	3	29
1325	West Allerdale and Keswick L.J.A.	Magistrates	1	41
373	Whitehaven	County	1	52
1375	Whitehaven L.J.A.	Magistrates	1	41
374	Wigan	County	2	52
1749	Wigan and Leigh L.J.A.	Magistrates	2	53
2271	Wirral L.J.A.	Magistrates	3	30

CROWN COURTS

SOUTH EAST REGION

PRESIDING JUDGES:
The Hon. Mr. Justice Gross, Senior Presiding Judge
The Hon. Mr. Justice Calvert-Smith
The Hon. Mr. Justice Bean
The Hon. Mr. Cooke

FAMILY DIVISION LIAISON JUDGES:
The Hon. Mrs. Justice Pauffley DBE
The Hon. Mr. Justice Macur DBE
The Hon. Mr. Justice Hedley

CHANCERY SUPERVISING JUDGE:
The Right Hon. Sir Andrew Morritt CVO

CIRCUIT JUDGES:

His Honour Judge C. D. Compston
" " " Jack D. Morton
Her " " M. F. Norrie
His " " J. Hall
" " " M. F. Addison
" " " P. C. Clegg
" " " C. J. M. Tyrer
" " " A. G. Y. Thorpe
" " " P. W. O'Brien
" " " J. D. Farnworth
" " " S. Coltart
" " " R. G. Brown
" " " P. N. De Mille
" " " A. W. P. King
" " " Charles Harris, Q.C.
" " " J. E. Devaux
" " " S. P. Sleeman
" " " G. S. Barham
Her " " N. Pearce
His " " T. G. E. Corrie
" " " J. F. Crocker
" " " M. Baker, Q.C.
" " " P. H. Downes
" " " D. M. Cryan
Her " " M. S. Mowat
His " " A. R. Scott-Gall
" " " R. Hayward
" " " P. Curl
" " " J. M. Haworth
Her " " C. Ludlow
His " " R. A. Barrat, Q.C.
" " " C. J. B. Kemp
" " " M. P. Yelton
" " " N. J. Coleman
" " " J. R. Reid, Q.C.
" " " A. R. Webb
" " " D. Serota, Q.C.
" " " D. Worsley

His Honour Judge A. Patience, Q.C.
" " " W. G. Hawkesworth
Her " " Z. P. Smith
His " " B. M. McIntyre
" " " P. G. Dedman
" " " C. A. Critchlow
" " " K. J. M. Hollis
" " " G. B. Breen
Her " " J. A. Williams
His " " A. M. Darroch
" " " N. A. McKittrick
Her " " I. M. Plumstead
His " " C. Ball Q.C.
" " " N. C. Van der Bijl
" " " D. J. Rennie
Her " " M. T. Catterson
His " " G. S. Murdoch, Q.C.
" " " J. P. Burke, Q.C.
" " " R. Hayward Smith, Q.C.
" " " A. I. Niblett
" " " J. R. T. Rylance
" " " G. Gypps
" " " D. N. Goodin
" " " C. Gratwicke
" " " C. R. Mitchell
" " " D. W. Caddick
" " " D. G. P. Turner, Q.C.
" " " J. S. Richards
" " " J. Carey
" " " R. J. S. Foster
" " " M. E. M. Brooke, Q.C.
" " " M. N. O'Sullivan
" " " A. Goldstaub, Q.C.
Her " " K. P. Cox
His " " P. Jacobs
" " " R. C. Elly
" " " P. J. Thompson
" " " M. L. S. Cripps

CROWN COURTS

His Honour Judge			J. F. Holt
Her	"	"	S. Coates
His	"	"	M. G. Anthony
"	"	"	A. R. Campbell
"	"	"	M. Horowitz, Q.C.
"	"	"	J. P. V. Bevan, Q.C.
"	"	"	A. E. M. Cooper
"	"	"	C. J. Blackett
"	"	"	R. J. Simpkiss
"	"	"	M. Kay, Q.C.
"	"	"	M. H. Lawson, Q.C.
"	"	"	D. Mitchell
"	"	"	P. R. Statman
"	"	"	D. Inman
"	"	"	A. W. Poole King
"	"	"	M. A. Everall, Q.C.
Her Honour Judge			B. Mensah (Miss)
His	"	"	R. B. Newton
Her	"	"	D. F. Taylor
His	"	"	C. A. MacDonald
"	"	"	P. J. Nathan
"	"	"	P. J. Fenn
"	"	"	P. M. Wright
"	"	"	M. A. Hughes
"	"	"	J. C. Plumstead
"	"	"	S. C. Warner
Her	"	"	V. L. Hammerton
His	"	"	W. R. Wood, Q.C.
"	"	"	N. A. Stewart
"	"	"	C. T. J. Joseph
"	"	"	G. Risius

REGIONAL DIRECTOR:
Mr Keith Budgen,
3rd Floor,
Rose Court,
2 Southwark Bridge,
London SE1 9HS
   Tel: 020 7921 2020
   Fax: 020 7921 2017
DX 154262 SOUTHWARK 12

AREA DIRECTORS:

Bedfordshire, Essex & Hertfordshire
Mike Littlewood,
Area Director's Office,
1st Floor,
Steeple House,
Church Lane,
Chelmsford,
Essex CM1 1NA
   Tel: 01245 287974
   Fax: 01245 314369
DX 97375 CHELMSFORD 3

Cambridgeshire, Norfolk & Suffolk
Pauline Cornford,
Area Director's Office,
1st Floor,
The Courthouse,
Old Bury Road,
Thetford IP24 3AQ
   Tel: 01842 757300
   Fax: 01842 763084

Kent
Dave Weston,
Area Director's Office,
Gail House,
Lower Stone Street,
Maidstone ME15 6NB
   Tel: 01622 680050
   Fax: 01622 680078
DX 152300 MAIDSTONE 19

Surrey & Sussex
Julia Eeles,
Area Director's Office,
The Court House,
Friar's Walk,
Lewes,
East Sussex BN7 2PG
   Tel: 01273 409160
   Fax: 01273 409161
DX 3110 LEWES

CROWN COURTS

Thames Valley
Jonathon Lane,
Area Director's Office,
Magistrates' Court,
Walton Street,
Aylesbury,
Bucks. HP21 7QZ
  Tel: 01296 554350

Court Index – South East Region

Court Code	Town Name	Court Type	Area	Page No
111	Ashford	County	20	6
113	Aylesbury	County	22	6
0401	Aylesbury	Crown	22	42
114	Banbury	County	22	7
153	Basildon	County	18	8
0461	Basildon	Crown	18	42
124	Bedford	County	18	8
1051	Bedford and Mid Bedfordshire L.J.A.	Magistrates	18	8
150	Brighton	County	21	12
157	Bury St Edmunds	County	19	13
0754	Bury St Edmunds	Crown	19	44
162	Cambridge	County	19	14
0410	Cambridge	Crown	19	44
1165	Cambridge L.J.A.	Magistrates	19	22
163	Canterbury	County	20	14
0479	Canterbury	Crown	20	44
1129	Central Buckinghamshire L.J.A.	Magistrates	22	96
1892	Central Hertfordshire L.J.A.	Magistrates	18	8
1960	Central Kent L.J.A.	Magistrates	20	60
1442	Central Norfolk L.J.A.	Magistrates	19	22
167	Chelmsford	County	18	15
0414	Chelmsford	Crown	18	45
172	Chichester	County	21	16
0416	Chichester	Crown	21	46
176	Colchester	County	18	16
184	Dartford	County	20	18
1072	East Berkshire L.J.A.	Magistrates	22	96
191	Eastbourne	County	21	19
1166	East Cambridgeshire L.J.A.	Magistrates	19	22
1888	East Hertfordshire L.J.A.	Magistrates	18	9
1957	East Kent L.J.A.	Magistrates	20	61
196	Epsom	County	21	19
1167	Fenland L.J.A.	Magistrates	19	23

CROWN COURTS

Court Code	Town Name	Court Type	Area	Page No
1443	Great Yarmouth L.J.A.	Magistrates	19	23
211	Guildford	County	21	21
0474	Guildford	Crown	21	48
213	Harlow	County	18	22
216	Hastings	County	21	22
218	Haywards Heath	County	21	23
221	Hertford	County	18	23
223	High Wycombe	County	22	23
225	Hitchin	County	18	24
227	Horsham	County	21	24
229	Huntingdon	County	19	24
1168	Huntingdonshire L.J.A.	Magistrates	19	23
233	Ipswich	County	19	25
0426	Ipswich	Crown	19	48
238	King's Lynn	County	19	25
0765	King's Lynn	Crown	19	49
247	Lewes	County	21	27
0431	Lewes	Crown	21	50
256	Lowestoft	County	19	32
258	Luton	County	18	32
0476	Luton	Crown	18	53
1055	Luton and South Bedfordshire L.J.A.	Magistrates	18	9
261	Maidstone	County	20	33
0434	Maidstone	Crown	20	53
267	Medway	County	20	34
1612	Mid-North Essex L.J.A.	Magistrates	18	10
1610	Mid-South Essex L.J.A.	Magistrates	18	10
388	Milton Keynes	County	22	35
1124	Milton Keynes L.J.A.	Magistrates	22	97
277	Newbury	County	22	36
1613	North-East Essex L.J.A.	Magistrates	18	10
2863	North East Suffolk L.J.A.	Magistrates	19	23
2775	Northern Oxfordshire L.J.A.	Magistrates	22	97
1889	North Hertfordshire L.J.A.	Magistrates	18	11
1966	North Kent L.J.A. (Dartford)	Magistrates	20	61
1966	North Kent L.J.A. (Medway)	Magistrates	20	61
1444	North Norfolk L.J.A.	Magistrates	19	24
2849	North Surrey L.J.A.	Magistrates	21	92
1619	North-West Essex L.J.A.	Magistrates	18	11
2857	North West Surrey L.J.A.	Magistrates	21	93
285	Norwich	County	19	38
0443	Norwich	Crown	19	55

CROWN COURTS

Court Code	Town Name	Court Type	Area	Page No
1445	Norwich L.J.A.	Magistrates	19	24
291	Oxford	County	22	39
0445	Oxford	Crown	22	56
2777	Oxford L.J.A.	Magistrates	22	98
294	Peterborough	County	19	39
0473	Peterborough	Crown	19	56
1162	Peterborough L.J.A.	Magistrates	19	24
305	Reading	County	22	41
0449	Reading	Crown	22	57
1076	Reading L.J.A.	Magistrates	22	98
307	Reigate	County	21	41
313	St Albans	County	18	42
0450	St Albans	Crown	18	57
327	Slough	County	22	45
1629	South-East Essex L.J.A.	Magistrates	18	12
2866	South East Suffolk L.J.A.	Magistrates	19	25
2856	South East Surrey L.J.A.	Magistrates	21	93
329	Southend	County	18	45
0772	Southend	Crown	18	58
2774	Southern Oxfordshire L.J.A.	Magistrates	22	98
1446	South Norfolk L.J.A.	Magistrates	19	25
1626	South-West Essex L.J.A.	Magistrates	18	12
2848	South West Surrey L.J.A.	Magistrates	21	93
334	Staines	County	21	46
2950	Sussex (Central) L.J.A.	Magistrates	21	94
2948	Sussex (Eastern) L.J.A.	Magistrates	21	94
2947	Sussex (Northern) L.J.A.	Magistrates	21	95
2949	Sussex (Western) L.J.A.	Magistrates	21	95
348	Thanet	County	20	48
355	Tunbridge Wells	County	20	49
362	Watford	County	18	50
1075	West Berkshire L.J.A.	Magistrates	22	99
1893	West Hertfordshire L.J.A.	Magistrates	18	12
1447	West Norfolk L.J.A.	Magistrates	19	25
2867	West Suffolk L.J.A.	Magistrates	19	26
838	Worthing	County	21	53
1130	Wycombe and Beaconsfield L.J.A.	Magistrates	22	99

CROWN COURTS

LONDON REGION

PRESIDING JUDGES:
The Hon. Mr. Justice Gross, Lead Presiding Judge
The Hon. Mr. Justice Calvert-Smith
The Hon. Mr. Justice Bean
The Hon. Mr. Justice Cooke

FAMILY DIVISION LIAISON JUDGES:
The Hon. Mrs. Justice Pauffley DBE
The Hon. Mr. Justice Hedly
The Hon. Mr. Justice Macur DBE

CHANCERY SUPERVISING JUDGE:
Vice-Chancellor

CIRCUIT JUDGES:
Crown Court

His Honour Judge Ader
" " " Ainley
" " " Altman
" " " Ansell
Her " " Anwyl, Q.C.
His " " Bailey
" " " Barker, Q.C.
Her " " Barnes
His " " Beaumont, Q.C.
Her " " Bevington
His " " Bing
" " " Birtles
" " " Birts, Q.C.
" " " Blacksell, Q.C.
" " " Brasse
" " " Browne, Q.C.
" " " Burn
" " " Byers
" " " Andrew Campbell
" " " Quentin Campbell
" " " Carroll
" " " Chapple
" " " Clark
" " " Colgan
" " " Collender, Q.C.
" " " Coulson, Q.C.
Her " " Dangor
His " " Davis
" " " Dodgson
" " " Edwards
" " " Elwen
" " " Forrester
Her " " Freedman
His " " Gibson
Her " " Goddard, Q.C.

His Honour Judge Gordon
" " " Goymer
" " " Alan Greenwood
" " " Grobel
Her " " Guggenheim
His " " Hardy, Q.C.
" " " Harris
" " " Hawkins
" " " Haworth
" " " Higgins
" " " Hillen
" " " Hone, Q.C.
" " " Huskinson
" " " Issard-Davies
" " " Nicholas Jones
" " " Karsten, Q.C.
Her " " Karu
His " " Katkhuda
" " " Kennedy
" " " Khayat, Q.C.
" " " King
Her " " Knowles
His " " Kramer, Q.C.
" " " Lawrence
" " " Loraine-Smith
" " " Lowen
" " " Lyons, C.B.E.
" " " MacRae
" " " Madge
" " " Marron, Q.C.
" " " Martineau
" " " Matheson, Q.C.
Her " " Matthews, Q.C.
His " " McDowall
" " " McGregor-Johnson

CROWN COURTS

His Honour Judge	McKinnon	His Honour Judge	Radford
" " "	McMullen, Q.C.	" " "	Richardson
" " "	Fergus Mitchell	" " "	Rivlin, Q.C.
" " "	John Mitchell	" " "	Robbins
" " "	Mole, Q.C.	" " "	Jeremy Roberts, Q.C.
" " "	Christopher Moss, Q.C.	" " "	Mervyn Roberts
" " "	Moss	" " "	Roberts, Q.C.
" " "	Moss, Q.C.	" " "	Colin Smith, Q.C.
" " "	Peter Moss	" " "	Smith, Q.C.
" " "	Ronald Moss	" " "	Smith
" " "	Norris	" " "	Stephens
" " "	Norris, O.B.E.	" " "	Stone, Q.C.
" " "	O'Mahony	" " "	Stow, Q.C.
" " "	Paget, Q.C.	" " "	Tain
" " "	Pardoe, Q.C.	" " "	Tanzer
" " "	Pawlak	Her " "	Tapping
" " "	Pearl	" " "	Taylor
Her " "	Patricia Pearl	His " "	Testar
" " "	Pearlman	" " "	Tilling
His " "	Philpot	" " "	Van der Werff
" " "	Pillay	" " "	Wadsworth, Q.C.
" " "	Pitman	" " "	Wakefield
" " "	Pitts	" " "	Waller
" " "	Pontius	" " "	Welchman
" " "	Pratt	" " "	Wilkinson
" " "	John Price	" " "	Winstanley
" " "	Nicholas Price, Q.C.	" " "	Worsley, Q.C.
" " "	Price	" " "	Zeidman, Q.C.
" " "	Price, Q.C.		

County Court:

His Honour Judge	Atkins	His Honour Judge	Lindsay, Q.C.
" " "	Williams Barnett, Q.C.	" " "	Mackie, C.B.E., Q.C.
" " "	Behar	Her " "	Marshall, Q.C.
" " "	Collins, C.B.E.	" " "	Mayer
" " "	Copley	His " "	Hugh Morgan
" " "	Cowell	" " "	Oppenheimer
" " "	Dean, Q.C.	" " "	David Pearl
" " "	Ellis	" " "	Platt
Her " "	Faber	" " "	Polden
His " "	Fysh, Q.C.	" " "	Riddell
Her " "	Hallon	" " "	Ryland
" " "	Hamilton, Q.C.	" " "	Simpson
His " "	Hornby	Her " "	Sally Williams
" " "	Knight, Q.C.	His " "	Stuart-Brown
" " "	Latham	" " "	Wulwik

CROWN COURTS

DIRECTOR OF THE ROYAL COURTS OF JUSTICE:
Alastair Clegg,
Director's Office,
TM8.09,
Royal Courts of Justice,
Strand,
London WC2A 2LL
  Tel: 020 7947 6534
  Fax: 020 7947 6666

REGIONAL DIRECTOR:
Kevin Pogson, C.B.E.,
2nd Floor,
Rose Court,
2 Southwark Bridge,
London SE1 9HS
  Tel: 020 7921 2010
  Fax: 0870 739 4469
  DX 154261 SOUTHWARK 12

AREA DIRECTORS:

Civil & Family
Linda Lennon,
Area Director's Office,
Rose Court,
2 Southwark Bridge,
London SE1 9HS
  Tel: 020 7921 2174
  Fax: 020 7921 2004
  DX 154261 SOUTHWARK 12

Central & South London (Crime)
Sarah McAdam,
Area Director's Office,
2nd Floor,
Rose Court,
2 Southwark Bridge,
London SE1 9HS
  Tel: 020 7921 2014
  Fax: 020 7921 2080
  DX 154261 SOUTHWARK 12

North & West London (Crime)
Sandra Aston,
Area Director's Office,
2nd Floor,
Rose Court,
2 Southwark Bridge,
London SE1 9HS
  Tel: 020 7921 2013
  Fax: 020 7921 2030
  DX 154261 SOUTHWARK 12

Court Index – London Region

Court Code	Town Name	Court Type	Area	Page No
2723	Acton	Magistrates	24	78
2814	Barking	Magistrates	24	75
117	Barnet	County	25	28
2728	Bexley	Magistrates	23	69
0428	Blackfriars	Crown	23	51
140	Bow	County	25	29
2762	Brent	Magistrates	24	76
144	Brentford	County	25	29
2769	Brentford	Magistrates	24	82

CROWN COURTS

Court Code	Town Name	Court Type	Area	Page No
152	Bromley	County	25	29
2727	Bromley	Magistrates	23	70
2656	Camberwell Green	Magistrates	23	73
0413	Central Criminal	Crown	23	51
372	Central London	County	25	29
2631	City of London	Magistrates	23	70
2660	City of Westminster	Magistrates	23	71
321	Clerkenwell & Shoreditch	County	25	30
182	Croydon	County	25	30
0418	Croydon	Crown	23	51
2732	Croydon	Magistrates	23	71
2734	Ealing	Magistrates	24	77
194	Edmonton	County	25	30
2757	Enfield	Magistrates	24	78
2769	Feltham	Magistrates	24	82
2643	Greenwich	Magistrates	23	72
2742	Haringey	Magistrates	24	80
0468	Harrow	Crown	24	51
2760	Harrow	Magistrates	24	80
1837	Havering	Magistrates	24	81
2741	Hendon	Magistrates	24	76
2663	Highbury Corner	Magistrates	24	77
231	Ilford	County	25	30
0440	Inner London	Crown	23	51
6700	Inner London FPC	Magistrates	25	87
0475	Isleworth	Crown	24	52
240	Kingston upon Thames	County	25	30
0427	Kingston upon Thames	Crown	24	52
2812	Kingston upon Thames	Magistrates	24	83
241	Lambeth	County	25	31
266	Mayor's and City of London	County	25	31
2815	Redbridge	Magistrates	24	85
2768	Richmond upon Thames	Magistrates	24	85
387	Romford	County	25	31
0453	Snaresbrook	Crown	24	52
0471	Southwark	Crown	23	52
2649	South Western	Magistrates	24	86
2721	Stratford	Magistrates	24	84
2733	Sutton	Magistrates	23	74
2650	Thames	Magistrates	24	79
2651	Tower Bridge	Magistrates	23	74
356	Uxbridge	County	25	31

CROWN COURTS

Court Code	Town Name	Court Type	Area	Page No
2766	Uxbridge	Magistrates	24	81
2813	Waltham Forest	Magistrates	24	86
359	Wandsworth	County	25	31
368	West London	County	25	31
2658	West London	Magistrates	24	79
375	Willesden	County	25	32
2763	Wimbledon	Magistrates	24	84
0469	Wood Green	Crown	24	53
379	Woolwich	County	25	32
0472	Woolwich	Crown	23	53
2643	Woolwich	Magistrates	23	72

CROWN COURTS

HMCS WALES

PRESIDING JUDGES:
>The Hon. Mr. Justice Roderick Evans, Senior Presiding Judge
>The Hon. Mr. Justice Nigel Davis

FAMILY DIVISION LIAISON JUDGE:
>The Hon. Mr. Justice Roderic Wood

CHANCERY SUPERVISING JUDGE:
>The Hon. Mr. Justice Lewison

CIRCUIT JUDGES:

His Honour Judge	J. B. S. Diehl, Q.C.		His Honour Judge	Gerald A. L. Price, Q.C.
"	"	"	Burr	"	"	"	D. W. Morgan
"	"	"	Philip Price, Q.C.	"	"	"	Merfyn Hughes, Q.C.
"	"	"	David Morris	"	"	"	Philip Richards
"	"	"	Crispin Masterman	"	"	"	Michael Farmer, Q.C.
"	"	"	Curran	"	"	"	C. Llewellyn-Jones, Q.C.
"	"	"	Kevin Barnett	"	"	"	Eleri Rees
"	"	"	Gaskell	Her	"	"	Isabel Parry
"	"	"	Furness	His	"	"	S. J. Hopkins, Q.C.
"	"	"	John Michael Thomas	"	"	"	K. G. Thomas
			Rogers, Q.C.	"	"	"	Neil Bidder, Q.C.
"	"	"	R. Philip Hughes	"	"	"	Dafydd Hughes
"	"	"	D. Wyn Richards	"	"	"	G. Hickinbottom
"	"	"	Nicholas Mordaunt	"	"	"	D. Wyn Rees
			Chambers, Q.C.	"	"	"	C. J. Vosper, Q.C.

HMCS, DIRECTOR FOR WALES:
>Mr Nick Chibnall,
>Director for Wales Office,
>Churchill House,
>Churchill Way,
>Cardiff, CF10 2HH
> Tel: 029 2041 5505
> Fax: 029 2041 5511
>DX 121723 CARDIFF 9

CROWN COURTS

AREA DIRECTORS:

Mid & West Wales
Luigi Strinati,
Area Director's Office,
The Old Vicarage,
Picton Terrace,
Carmarthen SA31 1BJ
 Tel: 01267 221658
 Fax: 01267 221812
DX 99570 CARMARTHEN 2

South East Wales
Alan Davies,
Area Director's Office,
47 Charles Street,
Cardiff CF10 2GD
 Tel: 029 2030 0250
 Fax: 029 2030 0240

North Wales
Clare Pillman,
Area Director's Office,
The Law Courts,
Civic Centre,
Mold,
Flintshire,
North Wales CH7 1AE
 Tel: 01352 707400
 Fax: 01352 707409
DX 702521 MOLD 2

Court Index – HMCS Wales

Court Code	Town Name	Court Type	Area	Page No
101	Aberdare	County	9	5
102	Aberystwyth	County	8	5
132	Blackwood	County	9	10
143	Brecknock	County	8	11
146	Bridgend	County	9	11
159	Caernarfon	County	7	13
0755	Caernarfon	Crown	7	44
164	Cardiff	County	9	14
0411	Cardiff	Crown	9	45
3348	Cardiff L.J.A.	Magistrates	9	109
166	Carmarthen	County	8	15
0756	Carmarthen	Crown	8	45
3138	Carmarthen L.J.A.	Magistrates	8	100
3135	Ceredigion L.J.A.	Magistrates	8	101
3062	Conwy L.J.A.	Magistrates	7	106
178	Conwy and Colwyn	County	7	17
3262	Cynon Valley L.J.A.	Magistrates	9	109
3350	De Brycheiniog L.J.A.	Magistrates	8	101
3061	Denbighshire L.J.A.	Magistrates	7	106
3140	Dinefwr L.J.A.	Magistrates	8	102
0758	Dolgellau	Crown	7	46
3059	Flintshire L.J.A.	Magistrates	7	107
3211	Gwent L.J.A.	Magistrates	9	110
3244	Gwynedd L.J.A.	Magistrates	7	107

CROWN COURTS

Court Code	Town Name	Court Type	Area	Page No
217	Haverfordwest	County	8	23
0761	Haverfordwest	Crown	8	48
253	Llanelli	County	8	28
3122	Llanelli L.J.A.	Magistrates	8	102
254	Llangefni	County	7	28
269	Merthyr Tydfil	County	9	34
0437	Merthyr Tydfil	Crown	9	54
3264	Merthyr Tydfil L.J.A.	Magistrates	9	110
3265	Miskin L.J.A.	Magistrates	9	110
271	Mold	County	7	35
0438	Mold	Crown	7	54
3355	Montgomeryshire L.J.A.	Magistrates	8	103
274	Neath Port Talbot	County	8	35
3359	Neath Port Talbot L.J.A.	Magistrates	8	103
3266	Newcastle and Ogmore L.J.A.	Magistrates	9	111
280	Newport (Gwent)	County	9	37
0441	Newport (South Wales)	Crown	9	55
3356	Pembrokeshire L.J.A.	Magistrates	8	104
298	Pontypool	County	9	40
299	Pontypridd	County	9	40
3351	Radnorshire and North Brecknock L.J.A.	Magistrates	8	104
308	Rhyl	County	7	42
344	Swansea	County	8	47
0457	Swansea	Crown	8	58
3360	Swansea L.J.A.	Magistrates	8	105
3349	Vale of Glamorgan L.J.A.	Magistrates	9	111
366	Welshpool and Newtown	County	8	51
0774	Welshpool	Crown	8	60
384	Wrexham	County	7	53
3058	Wrexham Maelor L.J.A.	Magistrates	7	107
3238	Ynys Mon/Anglesey L.J.A.	Magistrates	7	108

CROWN COURTS

SOUTH WEST REGION

PRESIDING JUDGES:
    The Rt. Hon. Lord Justice Leveson, Senior Presiding Judge
    The Hon. Mr. Justice Owen
    The Hon. Mr. Justice Royce

FAMILY DIVISION LIAISON JUDGE:
    The Hon. Mr. Justice Coleridge

CHANCERY SUPERVISING JUDGE:
    The Hon. Mr. Justice Lewison

CIRCUIT JUDGES:

His Honour Judge T. Crowther, Q.C.	His Honour Judge T. Longbotham
" " " M. J. L. Brodrick	" " " Lord Meston, Q.C.
" " " J. Rucker	" " " J. R. Jarvis
" " " R. D. Bursell, Q.C.	" " " R. C. B. Wade
" " " S. K. O'Malley, DL	" " " D. I. H. Tyzack, Q.C.
" " " D. L. Griffiths	" " " M. K. Harington
" " " T. J. Milligan	" " " A. M. Havelock-Allan, Q.C.
Her " " Linda Davies	" " " C. Leigh, Q.C.
" " " Susan P. Darwall-Smith, DL	" " " F. Gilbert, Q.C.
His " " S. C. Darwall-Smith	" " " N. Vincent
Her " " C. M. A. Hagen	" " " I. Hughes, Q.C.
His " " G. H. Jones	" " " A. D. Hope
" " " J. M. Burford, Q.C.	" " " J. Tabor, Q.C.
" " " R. M. Shawcross	" " " G. Boney, Q.C.
" " " J. F. Beashel	" " " R. Hetherington
" " " G. W. A. Cottle	" " " J. M. Harrow
" " " J. Foley	" " " T. G. Cowling
" " " J. D. Griggs	" " " P. Wassall
" " " J. S. Wiggs	" " " A. J. Barnett
" " " A. Rutherford, DL	" " " J. W. Dixon
Her " " J. Bonvin	" " " P. Lambert
His " " J. G. Boggis, Q.C.	" " " I. Pearson
" " " John O Neligan	" " " R. Bromilow
" " " Richard Price	" " " C. Harvey-Clark, Q.C.
" " " K. C. Cutler	Her " " Miranda Robertshaw
" " " P. Darlow	His " " N. Marsdon
" " " R. Bond	" " " M. Picton
" " " P. R. Barclay	" " " D. Field
" " " D. K. Ticehurst	" " " G. White
" " " M. W. Roach	

CROWN COURTS

REGIONAL DIRECTOR:
Mr Peter Risk,
5th Floor,
Greyfriars,
Lewins Mead,
Bristol BS1 2NR
  Tel: 0117 9103635
  Fax: 0117 9103650
  DX 95908 BRISTOL 3

AREA DIRECTORS:

Avon & Somerset
Rod White,
Area Director's Office,
PO Box 484,
Queensway House,
Weston-Super-Mare,
Somerset BS23 9BJ
  Tel: 01934 528500
  Fax: 01934 528520
  DX 152360 WESTON SUPER MARE 5

Devon & Cornwall
David Gentry,
Area Director's Office,
Trevecca,
Culverland Road,
Liskeard PL14 6RF
  Tel: 01579 325325
  Fax: 01579 325300

Dorset, Gloucestershire & Wiltshire
Rod Brummitt,
Area Director's Office,
The Law Courts,
Park Road,
Poole,
Dorset BH15 2RH
  Tel: 01202 711810
  Fax: 01202 747255
  DX 98700 POOLE 4

Hampshire & Isle of Wight
Stephen Williamson,
Area Director's Office,
The Court House,
Elmleigh Road,
Havant,
Hampshire PO9 2AL
  Tel: 023 9249 2024
  Fax: 023 9247 5356

Court Index – South West Region

Court Code	Town Name	Court Type	Area	Page No
104	Aldershot and Farnham	County	17	5
119	Barnstaple	County	15	7
0750	Barnstaple	Crown	15	42
122	Basingstoke	County	17	8
123	Bath	County	14	8
1022	Bath and Wansdyke L.J.A.	Magistrates	14	5
136	Bodmin	County	15	10
139	Bournemouth	County	16	10
0406	Bournemouth	Crown	16	43
151	Bristol	County	14	12
0408	Bristol	Crown	14	44
1013	Bristol L.J.A.	Magistrates	14	5
1292	Central Devon L.J.A.	Magistrates	15	45
168	Cheltenham	County	16	15
0407	Dorchester	Crown	16	47
	Dorset Combined Family Panel	Magistrates	16	48
5522/5523	Dorset Combined Youth Panel	Magistrates	16	48

CROWN COURTS

Court Code	Town Name	Court Type	Area	Page No
1289	East Cornwall L.J.A.	Magistrates	15	45
1522	East Dorset L.J.A.	Magistrates	16	48
198	Exeter	County	15	20
0423	Exeter	Crown	15	47
203	Gloucester	County	16	20
0424	Gloucester	Crown	16	47
1698	Gloucestershire L.J.A.	Magistrates	16	49
5698	Gloucestershire Youth Court	Magistrates	16	49
1945	Isle of Wight L.J.A.	Magistrates	17	54
2715	Mendip L.J.A.	Magistrates	14	5
1779	New Forest L.J.A.	Magistrates	17	54
279	Newport (Isle of Wight)	County	17	36
0478	Newport (Isle of Wight)	Crown	17	55
1021	North Avon L.J.A.	Magistrates	14	6
1291	North Devon L.J.A.	Magistrates	15	46
1780	North East Hampshire L.J.A.	Magistrates	17	55
1023	North Somerset L.J.A.	Magistrates	14	6
1781	North West Hampshire L.J.A.	Magistrates	17	55
3026	North West Wiltshire L.J.A.	Magistrates	16	49
293	Penzance	County	15	39
296	Plymouth	County	15	39
0446	Plymouth	Crown	15	56
1290	Plymouth District L.J.A.	Magistrates	15	46
300	Poole	County	16	40
302	Portsmouth	County	17	40
0447	Portsmouth	Crown	17	56
317	Sailsbury	County	16	43
0480	Salisbury	Crown	16	57
2706	Sedgemoor L.J.A.	Magistrates	14	6
328	Southampton	County	17	45
0454	Southampton	Crown	17	58
1775	Southampton L.J.A.	Magistrates	17	56
1293	South Devon L.J.A.	Magistrates	15	46
1782	South East Hampshire L.J.A.	Magistrates	17	55
3027	South East Wiltshire L.J.A.	Magistrates	16	50
1783	South Hampshire L.J.A.	Magistrates	17	56
2714	South Somerset L.J.A.	Magistrates	14	7
345	Swindon	County	16	47
0458	Swindon	Crown	16	59
3015	Swindon L.J.A.	Magistrates	16	50
347	Taunton	County	14	48
0459	Taunton	Crown	14	59

CROWN COURTS

Court Code	Town Name	Court Type	Area	Page No
2709	Taunton Deane and West Somerset L.J.A.	Magistrates	14	7
352	Torquay and Newton Abbot	County	15	49
353	Trowbridge	County	16	49
354	Truro	County	15	49
0477	Truro	Crown	15	59
1288	West Cornwall L.J.A.	Magistrates	15	47
1523	West Dorset L.J.A.	Magistrates	16	50
370	Weston-Super-Mare	County	14	51
371	Weymouth	County	16	51
376	Winchester	County	17	52
0465	Winchester	Crown	17	60
385	Yeovil	County	14	53

CROWN COURTS

HER MAJESTY'S COURT SERVICE ESTATE BY REGION AND AREA

North West Region
1   Cumbria and Lancashire
2   Greater Manchester
3   Cheshire and Merseyside

North East Region
4   Cleveland, Durham and Northumbria
5   North and West Yorkshire
6   Humber and South Yorkshire

HMCS Wales
7   North Wales
8   Mid and West Wales
9   South East Wales

Midlands Region
10   Birmingham, Coventry, Solihull and Warwickshire
11   Derbyshire and Nottinghamshire
12   Lincolnshire, Leicestershire & Rutland and Northamptonshire
13   Black Country, Staffordshire and West Mercia

South West Region
14   Avon & Somerset
15   Devon & Cornwall
16   Dorset, Gloucestershire and Wiltshire
17   Hampshire and The Isle of Wight

South East Region
18   Bedfordshire, Essex and Hertfordshire
19   Cambridgeshire, Norfolk and Suffolk
20   Kent
21   Surrey and Sussex
22   Thames Valley

London Region
23   Central and South (Crime)
24   North and West (Crime)
25   Civil and Family

CROWN COURTS

CROWN COURTS

Court No	Town and Region	Tier	Court Manager and Court Offices	Court Houses
0468	**ACTON,** (CLOSED)			

0401	**AYLESBURY**
	
	SE (22)
		3	R. Ward,
			County Hall,
			Market Square,
			Aylesbury, Bucks. HP20 1XD
			  Tel: 01296 434401
			  Fax: 01296 435665
			DX 97400 AYLESBURY 2
				County Hall,
				Aylesbury, Bucks

0750	**BARNSTAPLE**
	
	SW (15)
		3	Tony Hammond,
			Exeter Crown & County Court,
			Southernhay Gardens,
			Exeter EX1 1UH
			  Tel: 01392 415300
			    (General Enquiries)
			    01392 415330
			    (Crown Enquiries)
			    01392 415332
			    (Crown Listing)
			    01392 415313
			    (Customer Service Officer)
			  Fax: 01392 415642
			    (General Enquiries)
			    01392 415644
			    (Crown Enquiries)
			    01392 415644
			    (Crown Listing)
			    01392 415642
			    (Customer Service Officer)
			DX 98440 EXETER 2
				The Civic Centre,
				Barnstaple
				  Tel: 01271 373286
				  (when Court sitting only)

0751	**BARROW-IN-
	FURNESS**
	
	NW (1)
		3	Alan Thompson,
			Preston Combined Court Centre,
			The Law Courts,
			Openshaw Place,
			Ring Way,
			Preston PR1 2LL
			  Tel: 01772 844700
			  Fax: 01772 844759
			DX 702660 PRESTON 5
				Barrow Courthouse,
				Abbey Road,
				Barrow-in-Furness,
				Cumbria
				  Tel: 01229 820161

0461	**BASILDON**
	
	SE (18)
		3	Jeannine North,
			Basildon Combined Court,
			The Gore,
			Basildon,
			Essex SS14 2BU
			  Tel: 01268 458000
			  Fax: 01268 458100
			DX 97633 BASILDON 5
				The Gore,
				Basildon

CROWN COURTS

Court No	Town and Region	Tier	Court Manager and Court Offices	Court Houses
0403	**BEVERLEY**		(CLOSED)	
0404	**BIRMINGHAM** M (10)	1	Mr. A. T. Draper, Queen Elizabeth II Law Courts, 1 Newton Street, Birmingham B4 7NA Tel: 0121-681 3300 3304 (Listing) Fax: 0121-681 3370 DX 702033 BIRMINGHAM 8	Queen Elizabeth II Law Courts, 1 Newton Street, Birmingham
0405	**BODMIN**		(CLOSED) see TRURO	
0470	**BOLTON** NW (2)	3	T. Anderson, Bolton Combined Court Centre, The Law Courts, Blackhorse Street, Bolton BL1 1SU Tel: 01204 392881 Fax: 01204 363204 (Crown Office) 01204 373706 (County Office) DX 702610 BOLTON 3	The Law Courts, Blackhorse Street, Bolton
0406	**BOURNEMOUTH** SW (16)	3	D. Daly, Bournemouth Crown and County Court, Courts of Justice, Deansleigh Road, Bournemouth BH7 7DS Tel: 01202 502800 Fax: 01202 502801 DX 98420 BOURNEMOUTH 4	Courts of Justice, Deansleigh Road, Bournemouth
0402	**BRADFORD** NE (5)	2	A. Marshall, Bradford Combined Court Centre, Bradford Law Courts, Exchange Square, Drake Street, Bradford, W. Yorks. BD1 1JA Tel: 01274 840274 Fax: 01274 843510 DX 702083 BRADFORD 2	Bradford Law Courts, Exchange Square, Drake Street, Bradford
0753	**BRIGHTON,** (CLOSED) see LEWES			

CROWN COURTS

Court No	Town and Region	Tier	Court Manager and Court Offices	Court Houses

0408	**BRISTOL**
	
	 SW (14)
		1	Miss D. Starkey, O.B.E.,
			 The Law Courts,
			 Small Street,
			 Bristol BS1 1DA
			   Tel: 0117 976 3030
			   Fax: 0117 976 3026
			     (General Office)
			   Fax: 0117 976 3074
			     (Listing Office)
			 DX 78128 BRISTOL
				(1) The Law Courts,
				     Small Street

0409	**BURNLEY**
	
	 NW (1)
		3	Mrs. M. McGuinness,
			 Burnley Combined
			   Court Centre,
			 The Law Courts,
			 Hammerton Street,
			 Burnley, Lancs. BB11 1XD
			   Tel: 01282 416899
			   Fax: 01282 414911
			 DX 724940 Burnley 4
				The Law Courts,
				 Hammerton Street,
				 Burnley

0754	**BURY ST. EDMUNDS**
	
	 SE (19)
		3	T. Rose,
			 The Court House,
			 1 Russell Road,
			 Ipswich,
			 Suffolk IP1 2AG
			   Tel: 01473 228585
			   Fax: 01473 228560
			 DX 729480 IPSWICH 19
				Shire Hall,
				 Bury St. Edmunds,
				 Suffolk

0755	**CAERNARFON**
	
	 WAL (7)
		1	Mrs. C. Chesters,
			 The Law Courts,
			 County Civi Centre,
			 Mold CH7 1AE
			   Tel: 01352 753874
			   Fax: 01352 707340
				Castle Ditch,
				 Caernarfon
				   Tel: 01286 675753
				   Fax: 01286 678201

0410	**CAMBRIDGE**
	
	 SE (19)
		1	R. W. Gardner,
			 83 East Road,
			 Cambridge CB1 1BT
			   Tel: 01223 488321
			   Fax: 01223 488333
			 DX 97365 CAMBRIDGE 2
				83 East Road, Cambridge

0479	**CANTERBURY**
	
	 SE (20)
		3	Mr. G. Downer,
			 Canterbury Combined Court
			   Centre,
			 The Law Courts,
			 Chaucer Road,
			 Canterbury, Kent CT1 1ZA
			   Tel: 01227 819200
			   Fax: 01227 819329
			 DX 99710 CANTERBURY 3
				The Law Courts,
				 Chaucer Road,
				 Canterbury

CROWN COURTS

Court No	Town and Region	Tier	Court Manager and Court Offices	Court Houses
0411	**CARDIFF** WAL (9)	1	Lynne Mills, The Law Courts, Cathays Park, Cardiff CF10 3PG Tel: 029 2041 4400 Fax: 029 2041 4441 DX 99450 CARDIFF 5	The Law Courts, Cathays Park, Cardiff
0412	**CARLISLE** NW (1)	1	Mrs. A. Robinson, Carlisle Combined Court Centre, Courts of Justice, Earl Street, Carlisle CA1 1DJ Tel: 01228 520619 Fax: 01228 590588 DX 65331 CARLISLE 2	Courts of Justice, Earl Street, Carlisle
0756	**CARMARTHEN** WAL (8)	2	Mrs. L. M. Vincent, The Law Courts, St. Helens Road, Swansea SA1 4PF Tel: 01792 637000 Fax: 01792 637049 DX 99540 SWANSEA 4	The Guildhall, Camarthen
0413	**CENTRAL CRIMINAL COURT,** see LONDON Region, p 51 *post*			
0414	**CHELMSFORD** SE (18)	1	Mrs. J. Woodley, P.O. Box 9, New Street, Chelmsford CM1 1EL Tel: 01245 603000 Fax: 01245 603011 (General Office) 603020 (List Office) 603110 (Court Clerks) DX 97375 CHELMSFORD 3	New Street, Chelmsford
0415	**CHESTER** NW (3)	1	Mrs. K. Gallimore, The Castle, Chester CH1 2AN Tel: 01244 317606 Fax: 01244 356731 (General Office) 01244 350773 (Listing Office) DX 702527 CHESTER 5	The Castle, Chester

CROWN COURTS

Court No	Town and Region	Tier	Court Manager and Court Offices	Court Houses

0416	**CHICHESTER**
	
	SE (21)
		3	J. D. Betts,
			Chichester Combined
			   Court Centre,
			Southgate, Chichester,
			W. Sussex PO19 1SX
			   Tel: 01243 520742
			     (General Office)
			     01243 520741
			     (Lists Office)
			   Fax: 01243 538252
			DX 97460 CHICHESTER 2
				The Courthouse,
				Southgate,
				Chichester, W. Sussex

0417	**COVENTRY**
	
	M (10)
		3	Mrs. J. Barton,
			Coventry Combined
			   Court Centre,
			140 Much Park Street,
			Coventry CV1 2SN
			   Tel: 024 7653 6166
			   Fax: 024 7625 1083
			DX 701580 COVENTRY 5
				140 Much Park Street,
				Coventry

0419	**DERBY**
	
	M (11)
		3	Isabel Syred,
			Derby Combined
			   Court Centre,
			Morledge, Derby DE1 2XE
			   Tel: 01332 622600
			   Fax: 01332 622543
			DX 724060 DERBY 21
				Derby Combined Court
				   Centre,
				Morledge,
				Derby

0757	**DEVIZES**		(CASES DEALT WITH AT SWINDON)	

0758	**DOLGELLAU**
	
	WAL (7)
		3	Mrs. C. Chesters,
			The Law Courts,
			County Civic Centre,
			Mold CH7 1AE
			   Tel: 01352 707340
			   Fax: 01352 753874
				The County Hall,
				Dolgellau, Gwynedd
				   Tel: 01341 423451
				   Fax: 01341 423081

0420	**DONCASTER**
	
	NE (6)
		3	Mrs. M. Ellis,
			Crown Court,
			College Road,
			Doncaster, S. Yorks.
			DN1 3HS
			   Tel: 01302 322211
			   Fax: 01302 329471
			DX 703001 DONCASTER 5
				Crown Court,
				College Road,
				Doncaster

CROWN COURTS

Court No	Town and Region	Tier	Court Manager and Court Offices	Court Houses

0407	**DORCHESTER**
	
	SW (16)
		2	Mrs. S. A. Allport,
			Weymouth and Dorchester
			  Combined Court Centre,
			Westwey House,
			Westwey Road,
			Weymouth, Dorset DT4 8TE
			  Tel: 01305 752510
			  Fax: 01305 788293
			DX 98820 WEYMOUTH 3
				County Hall,
				Dorchester
				  Tel: 01305 265867
				  (not continuously
				  manned)

0421	**DUDLEY**		(CLOSED)	

0422	**DURHAM**
	
	NE (4)
		3	C. Raeburn,
			The Law Courts,
			Old Elvet,
			Durham DH1 3HW
			  Tel: 0191-386 6714
			  Fax: 0191-383 0605
			DX 65112 DURHAM 4
				The Law Courts,
				Old Elvet,
				Durham

0423	**EXETER**
	
	SW (15)
		1	Tony Hammond,
			Exeter Crown & County Court,
			Southernhay Gardens,
			Exeter EX1 1UH
			  Tel: 01392 415300
			    (General Enquiries)
			  01392 415330
			    (Crown Enquiries)
			  01392 415332
			    (Crown Listing)
			  01392 415313
			    (Customer Service Officer)
			  Fax: 01392 415642
			    (General Enquiries)
			  01392 415644
			    (Crown Enquiries)
			  01392 415644
			    (Crown Listing)
			  01392 415642
			    (Customer Service Officer)
			DX 98440 EXETER 2
				Southernhay Gardens,
				Exeter

0424	**GLOUCESTER**
	
	SW (16)
		2	Mrs. C. Banks,
			Criminal Court Offices,
			2nd Floor,
			Southgate House,
			Southgate Street,
			Gloucester GL1 1UB
			  Tel: 01452 420100
			  Fax: 01452 833555
			DX 98660 GLOUCESTER 5
				Longsmith Street,
				Gloucester

CROWN COURTS

Court No	Town and Region	Tier	Court Manager and Court Offices	Court Houses

0425	**GREAT GRIMSBY**
	
	NE (6)
		3	Mrs. S. Booth,
			Great Grimsby Combined
			Court Centre,
			Town Hall Square, Grimsby,
			North East Lincolnshire
			DN31 1HX
			  Tel: 01472 265250
			  Fax: 01472 265251
			DX 702007 GRIMSBY 3
				The Combined Court
				  Centre,
				Town Hall Square,
				Grimsby

0474	**GUILDFORD**
	
	SE (21)
		3	Mrs. G. Cook,
			Bedford Road,
			Guildford,
			Surrey GU1 4ST
			  Tel: 01483 468500
			  Fax: 01483 579545
			DX 97862 GUILDFORD 5
				Bedford Road,
				Guildford

0761	**HAVERFORDWEST**
	
	WAL (8)
		3	Mrs. L. M. Vincent,
			The Law Courts,
			St. Helens Road,
			Swansea SA1 4PF
			  Tel: 01792 637000
			  Fax: 01792 637049
			DX 99540 SWANSEA 4
				Penffynnon,
				Hawthorn Rise, Dyfed
				SA61 3BQ

0762	**HEREFORD**
	
	M (13)
		3	Mrs. J. Lloyd,
			Worcester Combined Court
			Centre,
			Shire Hall,
			Foregate Street,
			Worcester WR1 1EQ
			  Tel: 01905 730800
			  Fax: 01905 730810
			DX 721120 WORCESTER 11
				Shire Hall,
				Hereford
				  Tel: 01432 276118
				  Fax: 01432 274350

	HOVE, see LEWES			
0763	**HUDDERSFIELD**		(CLOSED)	
0440	**INNER LONDON SESSIONS HOUSE,** see LONDON REGION, p 51 *post*			

0426	**IPSWICH**
	
	SE (19)
		2	T. Rose,
			The Court House,
			1 Russell Road,
			Ipswich,
			Suffolk IP1 2AG
			  Tel: 01473 228585
			  Fax: 01473 228560
			DX 729480 IPSWICH 19
				The Court House,
				1 Russell Road,
				Ipswich

0475	**ISLEWORTH,** see LONDON REGION, p 52 *post*			

CROWN COURTS

Court No	Town and Region	Tier	Court Manager and Court Offices	Court Houses
0764	**KENDAL**		(CLOSED)	
0765	**KING'S LYNN** SE (19)	3	T. M. Room, Norwich Combined Court Centre, The Law Courts, Bishopgate, Norwich NR3 1UR Tel: 01603 728200 Fax: 01603 760863 DX 97385 NORWICH 5	The Court House, College Lane, King's Lynn, Norfolk Tel: 01553 760847 Fax: 01553 772873

0403	**KINGSTON-UPON-HULL**
	NE (6)
		2	B. Hunter,
			Kingston-upon-Hull Combined
			Court Centre,
			Lowgate, Hull HU1 2EZ
			Tel: 01482 586161
			         585328 (Bailiffs)
			Fax: 01482 588527
			         585328 (Bailiffs)
			DX 703010 HULL 5
				Kingston-upon-Hull
				Combined Court
				Centre,
				Lowgate, Hull

0427	**KINGSTON-UPON-THAMES,** see LONDON REGION, p 52 post			
0428	**KNIGHTSBRIDGE** – renamed BLACKFRIARS – see page 51			
0767	**KNUTSFORD** NW (3)	3	Mrs. K. Gallimore, The Castle, Chester CH1 2AN Tel: 01244 317606 Fax: 01244 350773 DX 702527 CHESTER 5	The Sessions House, Toft Road, Knutsford Tel: 01565 624020 624029 Fax: 01565 652454
0768	**LANCASTER** NW (1)	3	Alan Thompson, Preston Combined Court Centre, The Law Courts, Openshaw Place, Ring Way, Preston PR1 2LL Tel: 01772 844700 Fax: 01772 844759 DX 702660 PRESTON 5	The Castle, Lancaster Tel: 01524 32454
0429	**LEEDS** NE (5)	1	Leeds Combined Court Centre, The Court House, 1 Oxford Row, Leeds LS1 3BG Tel: 0113 306 2800 DX 703016 LEEDS 6	Leeds Combined Court Centre, The Court House, 1 Oxford Row, Leeds Coverdale House, 13-15 East Parade, Leeds LS1 4BJ Tel: 0113 242 8555

CROWN COURTS

Court No	Town and Region	Tier	Court Manager and Court Offices	Court Houses

0430	**LEICESTER**
	
	M (12)
		2	Robin Cook,
			90 Wellington Street,
			Leicester LE1 6HG
			  Tel: 0116 222 5800
			  Fax: 0116 222 5888/9
			  DX 10880 LEICESTER 3
				90 Wellington Street,
				Leicester

0431	**LEWES**
	
	SE (21)
		1	Mr. D. Manning,
			Lewes Combined Court
			  Centre,
			The Law Courts,
			High Street,
			Lewes, E. Sussex BN7 1YB
			  Tel: 01273 480400
			  Fax: 01273 485269
			  DX 97395 LEWES 4
				The Law Courts,
				High Street,
				Lewes, E. Sussex
				
				sittings also at
				
				Hove Court Centre,
				The Court House,
				Lansdowne Road,
				Hove,
				East Sussex BN3 3BN
				  Tel: 01273 229200
				  Fax: 01273 229229
				  DX 99402 HOVE 3
				
				Brighton Magistrates
				  Court,
				Edward Street,
				Brighton BN2 0LG
				  Tel: 01273 670888
				  Fax: 01273 790260

0432	**LINCOLN**
	
	M (12)
		1	H. Morgan,
			Lincoln Crown Court,
			The Castle,
			Castle Hill,
			Lincoln LN1 3GA
			  Tel: 01522 525222
			  Fax: 01522 543962
			  DX 722500 LINCOLN 11
				The Castle, Castle Hill,
				Lincoln

0433	**LIVERPOOL**
	
	NW (3)
		1	B. R. Wilson,
			Liverpool Crown Court,
			The Queen Elizabeth II Law
			  Courts,
			Derby Square,
			Liverpool L2 1XA
			  Tel: 0151-473 7373
			  Fax: 0151-258 1587
			  DX 740880 LIVERPOOL 22
				The Queen Elizabeth II
				  Law Courts,
				Derby Square,
				Liverpool

CROWN COURTS

Court No	Town and Region	Tier	Court Manager and Court Offices	Court Houses
			GREATER LONDON	
0468	**ACTON**		(CLOSED)	
0428	**BLACKFRIARS** (formerly Knightsbridge) LON (23)	3	Miss. M. Reed, 1-15 Pocock Street, London SE1 0BJ Tel: 020 7922 5800 Fax: 020 7922 5815 (List Office) 020 7922 5827 (General Office) DX 400800 LAMBETH 3	Pocock Street SE1
0413	**CENTRAL CRIMINAL COURT** LON (23)	2	Carole Read, Central Criminal Court, Old Bailey, London EC4M 7EH Tel: 020 7248 3277 Fax: 020 7192 2242 DX 46700 OLD BAILEY	Central Criminal Court, Old Bailey, London EC4
0418	**CROYDON** LON (23)	3	M. Taylor, Croydon Crown Court, The Law Courts, Altyre Road, Croydon CR9 5AB Tel: 020 8410 4700 Fax: 020 8781 1007 DX 97473 CROYDON 6	The Law Courts, Altyre Road, Croydon
0468	**HARROW** LON (24)	3	Mr. Neil Parker, Harrow Crown Court, Hailsham Drive, off Headstone Drive, Harrow, Middlesex HA1 4TU Tel: 020 8424 2294 Fax: 020 8424 2209 DX 97335 HARROW 5	Harrow Crown Court, Hailsham Drive, Harrow
0440	**INNER LONDON SESSIONS HOUSE** LON (23)	3	Steve Turnbull, Sessions House, Newington Causeway, London SE1 6AZ Tel: 020 7234 3100 Fax: 020 7234 3222 DX 97345 SOUTHWARK 3	(1) Sessions House, Newington Causeway, London SE1 6AZ (2) Swan Street, London SE1

CROWN COURTS

Court No	Town and Region	Tier	Court Manager and Court Offices	Court Houses
0475	**ISLEWORTH** LON (24)	3	Paul Jabbal, 36 Ridgeway Road, Isleworth TW7 5LP Tel: 020 8380 4500 Fax: 020 8568 5368 (General Office) 020 8758 2717 (List Office) DX 97420 ISLEWORTH 1	Ridgeway Road, Isleworth
0427	**KINGSTON UPON THAMES** LON (24)	3	Mr. Sean O'Brien, 6-8 Penrhyn Road, Kingston upon Thames KT1 2BB Tel: 020 8240 2500 Fax: 020 8240 2675 DX 97430 KINGSTON UPON THAMES 2 E-mail: kingston.crn.cm@courtservice.gsi.gov.uk	Crown Court, 6-8 Penrhyn Road, Kingston upon Thames
0428	**KNIGHTSBRIDGE** – renamed BLACKFRIARS – see page 51			
0464	**MIDDLESEX GUILDHALL** (CLOSED)			
	NEWINGTON CAUSEWAY, see INNER LONDON SESSIONS HOUSE (p 51 ante)			
0453	**SNARESBROOK** LON (24)	3	Mr. Stuart Hill, Snaresbrook Crown Court, 75 Hollybush Hill, Snaresbrook, London E11 1QW Tel: 020 8530 0000 (Switchboard) 020 8530 0234 (List Office) Fax: 020 8530 0073 020 8530 0071 (List Office) DX 98240 WANSTEAD 2	Snaresbrook Crown Court, 75 Hollybush Hill, Snaresbrook, London E11 1QW
0471	**SOUTHWARK** LON (23)	3	1 English Grounds, (off Battlebridge Lane), Southwark, London SE1 2HU Tel: 020 7522 7200 Fax: 020 7522 7300 DX 39913 LONDON BRIDGE SOUTH	1 English Grounds, Southwark

CROWN COURTS

Court No	Town and Region	Tier	Court Manager and Court Offices	Court Houses
0469	**WOOD GREEN** LON (24)	3	Mr. Phil Joseph, Wood Green Crown Court, Woodall House, Lordship Lane, Wood Green, London N22 5LF Tel: 020 8826 4100 Fax: 020 8826 4222 DX 130346 WOOD GREEN 3	Wood Green Crown Court, Woodall House, Lordship Lane, Wood Green, London N22 5LF
0472	**WOOLWICH** LON (23)	3	Michelle Penn, Woolwich Crown Court, 2 Belmarsh Road, London SE28 0EY Tel: 020 8312 7000 Fax: 020 8312 7078 DX 117650 WOOLWICH 7	Woolwich Crown Court, 2 Belmarsh Road, London SE28
0476	**LUTON** SE (18)	2	Ms. Therese Curran, Luton Crown Court, 7 George Street, Luton LU1 2AA Tel: 01582 522000 Fax: 01582 522001 01582 522026 (List Office) DX 120500 LUTON 6	Luton Crown Court, 7 George Street, Luton LU1 2AA
0434	**MAIDSTONE** SE (20)	2	Mr. C. Kreffer, Maidstone Combined Court Centre, The Law Courts, Barker Road, Maidstone, Kent ME16 8EQ Tel: 01622 202000 Fax: 01622 202001 DX 130065 MAIDSTONE 7	Law Courts, Barker Road, Maidstone
0435	**MANCHESTER (CROWN SQUARE)** NW (2)	1	Miss A. Bradley, Courts of Justice, Crown Square, Manchester M3 3FL Tel: 0161-954 1800 Fax: 0161-954 1705 DX 702538 MANCHESTER 11 Customer Service: Tel: 0161 954 1702/1703 Fax: 0161 954 1701 E-mail: manchester.enquiries@manchester.crowncourt.gsi.gov.uk	Courts of Justice, Crown Square, Manchester M3 3FL Tel: 0161-954 1800.

CROWN COURTS

Court No	Town and Region	Tier	Court Manager and Court Offices	Court Houses

0436	**MANCHESTER (MINSHULL STREET)**
	
	NW (2)
		3	Ian Jordan,
			The Crown Court at
			  Manchester,
			Minshull Street,
			Manchester M1 3FS
			  Tel: 0161-954 7500
			  Fax: 0161-954 7600
			DX 724860 MANCHESTER 43
				The Crown Court at
				  Manchester,
				Minshull Street,
				Manchester

0437	**MERTHYR TYDFIL**
	
	WAL (9)
		2	(Vacant),
			Merthyr Tydfil Combined
			  Court Centre,
			The Law Courts,
			Glebeland Place,
			Merthyr Tydfil,
			Mid Glam. CF47 8BH
			  Tel: 01685 358222
			  Fax: 01685 359727
			DX 99582 MERTHYR TYDFIL -2
				The Law Courts,
				Glebeland Place,
				Merthyr Tydfil

	MIDDLESBROUGH, see TEESSIDE			

0438	**MOLD**
	
	WAL (7)
		1	Mrs. C. Chesters,
			The Law Courts,
			County Civic Centre,
			Mold CH7 1AE
			  Tel: 01352 707340
			  Fax: 01352 753874
				The Law Courts,
				County Civic Centre,
				Mold, Clwyd CH7 1AE
				  Tel: 01352 707340
				  Fax: 01352 753874

0439	**NEWCASTLE UPON TYNE**
	
	NE (4)
		1	Ruth Parker,
			Newcastle upon Tyne
			  Combined Court Centre,
			The Law Courts, Quayside,
			Newcastle upon Tyne
			NE1 3LA
			  Tel: 0191-201 2000
			  Fax: 0191-201 2001
			DX 65127 NEWCASTLE UPON TYNE 2
				(1) The Law Courts,
				    Quayside,
				    Newcastle upon Tyne
				(2) The Moot Hall,
				    Newcastle upon Tyne
				    Tel: 0191-261 5100

	NEWINGTON CAUSEWAY, see INNER LONDON SESSIONS HOUSE (p 51 ante)			

CROWN COURTS

Court No	Town and Region	Tier	Court Manager and Court Offices	Court Houses

0441	**NEWPORT (South Wales)**
	
	WAL (9)
		2	Margaret Lewis
			  (Officer in charge),
			Crown Court,
			Faulkner Road,
			Newport, South Wales
			NP20 4PR
			  Tel: 01633 266211
			  Fax: 01633 216824
			DX 99460 NEWPORT 3
			(Court Manager – L. Mills
			  based at Cardiff)
			E-Mail:
			newport.crn.cm@hmcourts-service.gsi.gov.uk
				Crown Court,
				Faulkner Road,
				Newport

0478	**NEWPORT, I.O.W.**
	
	SW (17)
		3	S. Crow,
			Newport, I.O.W.
			Crown and County Courts,
			The Law Courts,
			Quay Street,
			Newport, I.O.W. PO30 5YT
			  Tel: 01983 535100
			  Fax: 01983 554977
			DX 98460 NEWPORT (I.O.W.) 2
				The Law Courts,
				Quay Street,
				Newport, I.O.W.

0442	**NORTHAMPTON**
	
	M (12)
		2	L. Handshaw,
			Northampton Combined
			  Court Centre,
			85/87 Lady's Lane,
			Northampton NN1 3HQ
			  Tel: 01604 470400
			  Fax: 01604 232398
			DX 725380 NORTHAMPTON 21
				Combined Court Centre,
				85/87 Lady's Lane,
				Northampton

0443	**NORWICH**
	
	SE (19)
		1	T. M. Room,
			Norwich Combined
			  Court Centre.
			The Law Courts,
			Bishopgate,
			Norwich NR3 1UR
			  Tel: 01603 728200
			  Fax: 01603 760863
			DX 97385 NORWICH 5
				The Law Courts,
				Bishopgate,
				Norwich

0444	**NOTTINGHAM**
	
	M (11)
		1	Mrs. P. Gamble,
			Nottingham Crown Court,
			The Law Courts,
			60 Canal Street,
			Nottingham NG1 7EL
			  Tel: 0115 910 3551
			                3556 (Listing)
			  Fax: 0115 910 3599
			DX 702383 NOTTINGHAM 7
				The Law Courts,
				60 Canal Street.
				Nottingham

CROWN COURTS

Court No	Town and Region	Tier	Court Manager and Court Offices	Court Houses

0445	**OXFORD**
	
	SE (22)
		1	Mrs. G. Henley,
			Oxford Combined Court Centre,
			St. Aldates,
			Oxford OX1 1TL
			  Tel: 01865 264200
			  Fax: 01865 790773 (Civil)
			         01865 264253 (Criminal)
			DX 96450 OXFORD 4
				The Court House,
				St. Aldates,
				Oxford

0473	**PETERBOROUGH**
	
	SE (19)
		3	Sue Clarke,
			Peterborough Combined
			  Court Centre,
			Crown Buildings,
			Rivergate,
			Peterborough PE1 1EJ
			  Tel: 01733 349161
			  Fax: 01733 557348
			DX 702302 PETERBOROUGH 8
				Crown Buildings,
				Rivergate,
				Peterborough

0446	**PLYMOUTH**
	
	SW (15)
		2	Plymouth Combined Court
			  Centre,
			The Law Courts,
			Armada Way,
			Plymouth PL1 2ER
			  Tel: 01752 677400
			    (Court Manager)
			    01752 677480
			    (Crown Court Office)
			  Fax: 01752 208286 (Civil)
			         208292 (Crown)
			         677498 (Bailiff)
			DX 98470 PLYMOUTH 7
				The Law Courts,
				Armada Way,
				Plymouth

0447	**PORTSMOUTH**
	
	SW (17)
		3	P. Bray,
			Portsmouth Combined Court
			  Centre,
			The Courts of Justice,
			Winston Churchill Avenue,
			Portsmouth, Hants. PO1 2EB
			  Tel: 023 9289 3000
			  Fax: 023 9282 6385
			DX 98490 PORTSMOUTH 5
				The Courts of Justice,
				Winston Churchill Avenue,
				Portsmouth
				  Tel: 023 9289 3000

0448	**PRESTON**
	
	NW (1)
		1	Alan Thompson,
			Preston Combined
			  Court Centre,
			The Law Courts,
			Openshaw Place,
			Ring Way,
			Preston PR1 2LL
			  Tel: 01772 844700
			  Fax: 01772 844759
			DX 702660 PRESTON 5
				The Law Courts,
				Openshaw Place,
				Ring Way,
				Preston
				
				The Sessions House,
				Lancaster Road,
				Preston

CROWN COURTS

Court No	Town and Region	Tier	Court Manager and Court Offices	Court Houses

0449	**READING**
	
	SE (22)
		2	Mrs. S. Heath,
			Old Shire Hall,
			The Forbury,
			Reading,
			Berks. RG1 3EH
			  Tel: 0118 967 4400
			    (Switchboard)
			  Fax: 0118 967 4444
			  Tel: 0118 967 4441/2/3
			    (List Office)
			DX 97440 READING 5
				Old Shire Hall,
				The Forbury,
				Reading

0450	**ST. ALBANS**
	
	SE (18)
		2	S. Moran,
			The Court Building,
			Bricket Road,
			St. Albans,
			Herts. AL1 3JW
			  Tel: 01727 753220
			  Fax: 01727 753221
			DX 99700 ST. ALBANS 3
				The Court Building,
				Bricket Road,
				St. Albans

0480	**SALISBURY**
	
	SW (16)
		3	Mrs. Alison Cannon,
			Salisbury Combined Court
			  Centre,
			Courts of Justice,
			Alexandra House,
			St. John Street,
			Salisbury, Wilts. SP1 2PN
			  Tel: 01722 325444
			  Fax: 01722 412991
			DX 98500 SALISBURY 2
				Courts of Justice,
				Alexandra House,
				St. John Street,
				Sailsbury

0451	**SHEFFIELD**
	
	NE (6)
		1	D. Crossfield,
			Sheffield Combined Court
			  Centre,
			The Law Courts,
			50 West Bar,
			Sheffield S3 8PH
			  Tel: 0114 281 2400
			  Fax: 0114 281 2425
			DX 703028 SHEFFIELD 6
				The Law Courts,
				50 West Bar,
				Sheffield

0452	**SHREWSBURY**
	
	M (13)
		2	Mrs. D. Marrow,
			The Shire Hall,
			Abbey Foregate,
			Shrewsbury SY2 6LU
			  Tel: 01743 260820
			  Fax: 01743 244236
			DX 702022 SHREWSBURY 2
				The Shire Hall,
				Abbey Foregate,
				Shrewsbury

0453	**SNARESBROOK,** see LONDON REGION, p 52 ante			

CROWN COURTS

Court No	Town and Region	Tier	Court Manager and Court Offices	Court Houses

0454	**SOUTHAMPTON**
	
	SW (17)
		3	Mrs. H. Williams,
			Southampton Combined
			  Court Centre,
			The Courts of Justice,
			London Road,
			Southampton SO15 2XQ
			  Tel: 023 8021 3200
			  Fax: 023 8021 3222 (County Court)
			       023 8021 3234 (Crown Court)
			       023 8021 3232 (Civil Listing)
			DX 111000 SOUTHAMPTON 11
				The Courts of Justice,
				London Road,
				Southampton

0772	**SOUTHEND**
	
	SE (18)
		3	Jeannine North,
			Basildon Combined Court,
			The Gore,
			Basildon,
			Essex SS14 2BU
			  Tel: 01268 458000
			  Fax: 01268 458100
			DX 97633 BASILDON 5
				The Court House,
				Victoria Avenue,
				Southend-on-Sea,
				SS2 6EG
				  Tel: 01268 458000
				  Fax: 01268 458100

0471	**SOUTHWARK,** see LONDON REGION, p 52 ante			

0455	**STAFFORD**
	
	M (13)
		1	Ilse Tivenan,
			Stafford Combined
			  Court Centre,
			Victoria Square,
			Stafford ST16 2QQ
			  Tel: 01785 610730
			  Fax: 01785 213250
			DX 703190 STAFFORD 4
				Combined Court Centre,
				Victoria Square,
				Stafford

0456	**STOKE-ON-TRENT**
	
	M (13)
		3	Mrs. S. Hooper,
			Stoke-on-Trent Combined
			  Court Centre,
			Bethesda Street,
			Hanley,
			Stoke-on-Trent, Staffs
			ST1 3BP
			  Tel: 01782 854000
			  Fax: 01782 854021
			DX 703360 HANLEY 3
				Bethesda Street,
				Hanley,
				Stoke-on-Trent

0457	**SWANSEA**
	
	WAL (8)
		1	Mrs. L.M. Vincent,
			The Law Courts,
			St. Helens Road,
			Swansea SA1 4PF
			  Tel: 01792 637000
			  Fax: 01792 637049
			DX 99540 SWANSEA 4
				(1) The Law Courts,
				    St. Helens Road,
				    Swansea
				(2) The Law Courts,
				    The Guildhall,
				    Swansea

CROWN COURTS

Court No	Town and Region	Tier	Court Manager and Court Offices	Court Houses

0458	**SWINDON**
	
	SW (16)
		3	Mrs. L. Thompson,
			Swindon Combined
			   Court Centre,
			The Law Courts,
			Islington Street,
			Swindon, Wilts. SN1 2HG
			   Tel: 01793 690500
			   Fax: 01793 690535
			DX 98430 SWINDON 5
				The Law Courts,
				Islington Street,
				Swindon

0459	**TAUNTON**
	
	SW (14)
		3	Mr. R. Cousins,
			Taunton Crown Court,
			Shire Hall, Taunton,
			Somerset TA1 4EU
			   Tel: 01823 281100
			   Fax: 01823 322116
			DX 98411 TAUNTON 2
				Shire Hall,
				Taunton

0460	**TEESSIDE**
	
	NE (4)
		1	E. Short,
			Teesside Combined Court
			   Centre,
			Russell Street,
			Middlesbrough,
			Cleveland TS1 2AE
			   Tel: 01642 340000
			   Fax: 01642 340002
			DX 65152 MIDDLESBROUGH 2
				Russell Street,
				Middlesbrough

0477	**TRURO**
	
	SW (15)
		1	Mr. P. Rodda,
			Truro Crown Court,
			Courts of Justice,
			Edward Street, Truro TR1 2PB
			   Tel: 01872 222328
			   Fax: 01872 261550
			DX 135396 TRURO 2
				Courts of Justice,
				Edward Street,
				Truro

0461	**WAKEFIELD**		(CLOSED)	
0773	**WALSALL**		(CLOSED)	

0462	**WARRINGTON**
	
	NW (3)
		2	Mr. G. A. Allman,
			The Law Courts,
			Legh Street,
			Warrington,
			Cheshire WA1 1UR
			   Tel: 01925 256700
			   Fax: 01925 413335 (County)
			        01925 256762 (Crown)
			DX 702501 WARRINGTON 3
				Legh Street,
				Warrington

CROWN COURTS

Court No	Town and Region	Tier	Court Manager and Court Offices	Court Houses

0463	**WARWICK**
	
	M (10)
		1	Mrs. J. A. Beckett,
			Warwick Combined
			  Court Centre,
			Northgate South Side,
			Warwick CV34 4RB
			  Tel: 01926 495428
			  Fax: 01926 474227
			  DX 701964 WARWICK 2
				Shire Hall,
				Northgate Street,
				Warwick

0774	**WELSHPOOL**
	
	WAL (8)
		2	Mrs. C. Chesters,
			The Law Courts,
			County Civic Centre,
			Mold CH7 1AE
			  Tel: 01352 707340
			  Fax: 01352 753874
				Town Hall,
				Welshpool, Powys
				SY2 7TQ
				  Tel: 01938 553144

0465	**WINCHESTER**
	
	SW (17)
		1	Mrs. L. Nother,
			Winchester Combined Court
			  Centre,
			The Law Courts,
			Winchester, Hants. SO23 9EL
			  Tel: 01962 814100
			  Fax: 01962 853821
			  DX 98520 WINCHESTER 3
				The Law Courts,
				Winchester

0421	**WOLVERHAMPTON**
	
	M (13)
		2	Mrs. T. Herbert,
			Wolverhampton Combined
			  Court Centre,
			Pipers Row,
			Wolverhampton,
			W. Mids. WV1 3LQ
			  Tel: 01902 481000
			  Fax: 01902 481001
			  DX 702019 WOLVERHAMPTON 4
				Combined Court Centre,
				Pipers Row,
				Wolverhampton

0469	**WOOD GREEN,** see LONDON REGION, p 53 ante			

0466	**WORCESTER**
	
	M (13)
		2	Mrs. J. Lloyd,
			Worcester Combined Court
			  Centre,
			Shire Hall,
			Foregate Street,
			Worcester WR1 1EQ
			  Tel: 01905 730800
			  Fax: 01905 730810
			  DX 721120 WORCESTER 11
				Shire Hall,
				Foregate Street,
				Worcester

0467	**YORK**
	
	NE (5)
		2	Miss. W. Forsdyke,
			The Castle,
			York YO1 9WZ
			  Tel: 01904 645121
			              654482
			  Fax: 01904 611689
			  DX 65162 YORK 3
				The Castle,
				York

CROWN COURTS

NORTHERN IRELAND

DIRECTOR:

David A. Lavery,
Court Service Headquarters,
Windsor House,
9-15 Bedford Street,
Belfast BT2 7LT
Tel: 028 9032 8594
Fax: 028 9024 1360

CROWN COURTS

Town	Court Offices	Court Houses
ANTRIM	The Courthouse, 30 Castle Way, Antrim BT41 4AQ Tel: 028 9446 2661 Fax: 028 9446 3301 DX 3452 NR ANTRIM E-mail: antrim_courthouse@courtsni.gov.uk	The Courthouse, Castle Way, Antrim
ARMAGH	Armagh Court Office, The Courthouse, The Mall, Armagh, Co. Armagh BT61 9DJ Tel: 028 3752 2816 Fax: 028 3752 8194	Courthouse, The Mall, Armagh
BALLYMENA	Ballymena Court Office, The Courthouse, Albert Place, Ballymena, Co. Antrim BT43 5BS Tel: 028 2564 9416 Fax: 028 2565 5371	Courthouse, Albert Place, Ballymena The Courthosue, Castle Way, Antrim
BELFAST	Crown Court Office, Laganside Courts, 45 Oxford Street, Belfast BT1 3LL Tel: 028 9032 8594 Fax: 028 9024 2078	Laganside Courts, 45 Oxford Street, Belfast BT1 3LL
CRAIGAVON	Craigavon Court Office, The Courthouse, Central Way, Craigavon BT64 1AP Tel: 028 3834 1324 Fax: 028 3834 1243	Courthouse, Central Way, Craigavon

CROWN COURTS

Town	Court Offices	Court Houses
DOWNPATRICK	Downpatrick Court Office, The Courthouse, 21 English Street, Downpatrick BT30 6AD Tel: 028 4461 4621 Fax: 028 4461 3969	Courthouse, English Street, Downpatrick
DUNGANNON	The Courthouse, 46 Killyman Road, Dungannon BT71 6DE Tel: 028 8772 2992 Fax: 028 8772 8169	The Courthouse, Killyman Road, Dungannon
ENNISKILLEN	Enniskillen Court Office, The Courthouse, East Bridge Street, Enniskillen BT74 7BP Tel: 028 6632 2356 Fax: 028 6632 3636	Courthouse, East Bridge Street, Enniskillen
LONDONDERRY	Londonderry Court Office, The Courthouse, Bishop Street, Londonderry BT48 6PQ Tel: 028 7136 3448 Fax: 028 7137 2059	Courthouse, Bishop Street, Londonderry
NEWRY	The Courthouse, 23 New Street, Newry BT35 6JD Tel: 028 3025 2040 Fax: 028 3026 9830	The Courthouse, New Street, Newry
NEWTOWNARDS	Downpatrick Court Office, The Courthouse, 21 English Street, Downpatrick BT30 6AD Tel: 028 4461 4621 Fax: 028 4461 3969	Courthouse, English Street, Downpatrick
OMAGH	Omagh Court Office, The Courthouse, High Street, Omagh, Co. Tyrone BT78 1DU Tel: 028 8224 2056 Fax: 028 8225 1198	Courthouse, High Street, Omagh

CROWN COURT CODES
NUMERICAL INDEX
as from 1 January 1984

Code	Court	Code	Court	Code	Court
0401	Aylesbury	0435	Manchester (Crown Square)	0469	Wood Green
0402	Bedford (CLOSED)			0470	Bolton
0402	Bradford	0436	Manchester (Minshull Street)	0471	Southwark
0403	Beverley (CLOSED)			0472	Woolwich
0403	Kingston-upon-Hull	0437	Merthyr Tydfil	0473	Peterborough
0404	Birmingham	0438	Mold	0474	Guildford
0405	Bodmin (CLOSED)	0439	Newcastle-upon-Tyne	0475	Isleworth
0406	Bournemouth	0440	Newington Causeway (Inner London Sessions House)	0476	Luton
0407	Bradford (CLOSED)			0477	Truro
0407	Dorchester			0478	Newport (I.O.W.)
0408	Bristol	0441	Newport	0479	Canterbury
0409	Burnley	0442	Northampton	0480	Salisbury
0410	Cambridge	0443	Norwich	0750	Barnstaple
0411	Cardiff	0444	Nottingham	0751	Barrow-in-Furness
0412	Carlisle	0445	Oxford	0752	Birkenhead (CLOSED)
0413	Central Criminal Court (Old Bailey)	0446	Plymouth		
		0447	Portsmouth	0753	Brighton (CLOSED)
0414	Chelmsford	0448	Preston	0754	Bury St. Edmunds
0415	Chester	0449	Reading	0755	Caernarfon
0416	Chichester	0450	St. Albans	0756	Carmarthen
0417	Coventry	0451	Sheffield	0757	Devizes (CLOSED)
0418	Croydon	0452	Shrewsbury	0758	Dolgellau
0419	Derby	0453	Snaresbrook	0759	Dorchester
0420	Doncaster	0454	Southampton	0760	Gravesend (CLOSED)
0421	Dudley (CLOSED)	0455	Stafford		
0421	Wolverhampton	0456	Stoke-on-Trent	0761	Haverfordwest
0422	Durham	0457	Swansea	0762	Hereford
0423	Exeter	0458	Swindon	0763	Huddersfield (CLOSED)
0424	Gloucester	0459	Taunton		
0425	Great Grimsby	0460	Teesside	0764	Kendal (CLOSED)
0426	Ipswich	0461	Wakefield (CLOSED)	0765	Kings Lynn
0427	Kingston-upon-Thames	0461	Basildon (wef 2/1/96)	0766	Kingston-upon-Hull
		0462	Warrington	0767	Knutsford
0428	Blackfriars	0463	Warwick	0768	Lancaster
0429	Leeds	0464	Middlesex Guildhall	0769	Luton
0430	Leicester	0465	Winchester	0769	Mold
0431	Lewes	0466	Worcester	0772	Southend
0432	Lincoln	0467	York	0773	Walsall (CLOSED)
0433	Liverpool	0468	Acton (CLOSED)	0774	Welshpool
0434	Maidstone	0468	Harrow		

PART II

COUNTY COURTS

Page

England and Wales 5

Northern Ireland 55

Please note that as from 1st April 2007 Her Majesty's Courts Service was restructured in England and Wales. Information on Her Majesty's Courts Service, including a comprehensive list of Regional and Area Directors, can be found at the beginning of the Crown Courts Section in Part I.

PART II．

COUNTY COURTS

HER MAJESTY'S COURT SERVICE ESTATE BY REGION AND AREA

North West Region
1 Cumbria and Lancashire
2 Greater Manchester
3 Cheshire and Merseyside

North East Region
4 Cleveland, Durham and Northumbria
5 North and West Yorkshire
6 Humber and South Yorkshire

HMCS Wales
7 North Wales
8 Mid and West Wales
9 South East Wales

Midlands Region
10 Birmingham, Coventry, Solihull and Warwickshire
11 Derbyshire and Nottinghamshire
12 Lincolnshire, Leicestershire & Rutland and Northamptonshire
13 Black Country, Staffordshire and West Mercia

South West Region
14 Avon & Somerset
15 Devon & Cornwall
16 Dorset, Gloucestershire and Wiltshire
17 Hampshire and The Isle of Wight

South East Region
18 Bedfordshire, Essex and Hertfordshire
19 Cambridgeshire, Norfolk and Suffolk
20 Kent
21 Surrey and Sussex
22 Thames Valley

London Region
23 Central and South (Crime)
24 North and West (Crime)
25 Civil and Family

COUNTY COURTS

ENGLAND AND WALES

Court No	Location, Region and Additional Jurisdiction	Court Manager and Court Offices	Court House and District Judges
101	**ABERDARE** WAL (9) *Bankruptcy*	Mrs. Russell, The Court House, Cwmbach Road, Aberdare, Mid Glam. CF44 0JE Tel: 01685 888575 Fax: 01685 883413 DX 99600 ABERDARE 2	The Court House, Cwmbach Road, Aberdare District Judge: G. Sandercock
102	**ABERYSTWYTH** WAL (8) **District Registry** *Adoption Centre* *Bankruptcy* *Family Hearing Centre*	Miss K. A. Lewis, Edleston House, Queens Road, Aberystwyth, Ceredigion SY23 2HP Tel: 01970 636370 (Office) 636375 (Bailiffs) Fax: 01970 625985 DX 99560 ABERYSTWYTH 2	Edleston House, Queens Road, Aberystwyth District Judges: W. H. Godwin

103	**ACCRINGTON**
	
	NW (1)
	
	Divorce
		A. Szewczuk,
		Bradshawgate House,
		1 Oak Street,
		Accrington, Lancs.
		BB5 1EQ
		Tel: 01254 398173
		           237490
		           238061 (Bailiffs)
		Fax: 01254 393869
		DX 702645 ACCRINGTON 2
			1 Oak Street,
			Accrington
			
			District Judges:
			J. M. Geddes

104	**ALDERSHOT AND FARNHAM** SW (17) *Divorce*	Mr. M. Davidson, 78/82 Victoria Road, Aldershot, Hants. GU11 1SS Tel: 01252 796800 (General Enquiries) Fax: 01252 345705 DX 98530 ALDERSHOT 2	84-86 Victoria Road, Aldershot District Judges: D. J. Ackner D. J. James
105	**ALFRETON**	(CLOSED wef 16/2/96 – successor courts – Chesterfield, Derby, Mansfield and Nottingham)	
701	**ALNWICK**	(CLOSED wef 15/12/97 – successor court – Morpeth and Berwick)	

COUNTY COURTS

Court No	Location, Region and Additional Jurisdiction	Court Manager and Court Offices	Court House and District Judges

106	**ALTRINCHAM**
	
	NW (2)
	
	Divorce
		Mrs. J. Plunkett,
		P.O. Box 240,
		Trafford Courthouse,
		Ashton Lane,
		Sale, Cheshire M33 7WX
		  Tel: 0161 975 4760
		                  4762 (Bailiffs)
		  Fax: 0161 975 4761
		DX 708292 SALE 6
			Trafford Courthouse,
			Ashton Lane,
			Sale,
			Cheshire
			
			District Judges:
			  J. Horan
			  A. C. Brazier
			  J. R. Clegg
			  C. Osbourne
			  D. N. Gaunt
			  P. Dignan
			  I. Lettall

107	**AMERSHAM**	(CLOSED wef 9/1/95 – successor courts – Aylesbury, Hemel Hempstead, High Wycombe, Slough, Uxbridge and Watford)	
108	**AMMANFORD**	(CLOSED wef 27/3/97 – successor courts – Swansea, Carmarthen and Llanelli)	
109	**ANDOVER**	(CLOSED wef 30/6/97 – successor courts – Basingstoke, Salisbury and Winchester)	
110	**ASHBY-DE-LA-ZOUCH**	(CLOSED wef 1/10/84 – successor court – Burton-on-Trent)	

111	**ASHFORD**
	
	SE (20)
		Mrs. J. King,
		Ground Floor,
		The Court House,
		Tufton Street,
		Ashford, Kent
		TN23 1QQ
		  Tel: 01233 632464
		  Fax: 01233 612786
		DX 98060 ASHFORD (KENT) 3
			Ground Floor,
			The Court House,
			Tufton Street,
			Ashford
			
			District Judge:
			  L. Burgess

112	**ASHTON-UNDER-LYNE AND STALYBRIDGE** *renamed* **TAMESIDE**		
702	**AXMINSTER AND CHARD**	(CLOSED wef 5/12/94 – successor court – Yeovil)	

113	**AYLESBURY**
	
	SE (22)
	
	Bankruptcy
		Dawn Sellars,
		Second Floor,
		Heron House,
		49 Buckingham Street,
		Aylesbury, Bucks.
		HP20 2NQ
		  Tel: 01296 393498
		  Fax: 01296 397363
		DX 97820 AYLESBURY 3
			Heron House,
			49 Buckingham Street,
			Aylesbury HP20 2NQ
			
			District Judges:
			  P. Mostyn
			  R. Tetlow
			  N. Hickman

COUNTY COURTS

Court No	Location, Region and Additional Jurisdiction	Court Manager and Court Offices	Court House and District Judges
114	**BANBURY** **SE** (22) *Bankruptcy*	S. Mason, The Courthouse, Warwick Road, Banbury, Oxon OX16 2AW Tel: 01295 452090 452093 (Bailiffs) Fax: 01295 452051 DX 701967 BANBURY 2	The Courthouse, Warwick Road, Banbury *District Judges:* M. Payne V. Gatter R. Matthews A. Jenkins
115	**BANGOR**	(CLOSED wef 4/7/94 – successor court – Caernarfon)	
116	**BARGOED**	(CLOSED wef 29/12/95 – successor court – Blackwood)	
117	**BARNET**, *see* LONDON, p.28 post		
118	**BARNSLEY** **NE** (6) District Registry *Bankruptcy* *Family Hearing Centre*	Miss K. Angel, 12 Regent Street, Barnsley, S. Yorks. S70 2EW Tel: 01226 777550 Fax: 01226 779126 DX 702080 BARNSLEY 3	12 Regent Street, Barnsley *District Judges:* A. M. Babbington M. Mornington
119	**BARNSTAPLE** **SW** (15) District Registry *Bankruptcy* *Divorce* *Family Hearing Centre*	T. Jones, 7th Floor, Civic Centre, North Walk, Barnstaple, Devon EX31 1DY Tel: 01271 372252 340949 (Bailiffs) Fax: 01271 322968 DX 98560 BARNSTAPLE 2	7th Floor, Civic Centre, North Walk, Barnstaple *District Judge:* M. Read
120	**BARROW-IN-FURNESS** **NW** (1) **District Registry** *Bankruptcy* *Divorce*	Mrs. D. M. Postlethwaite, Law Courts, Abbey Road, Barrow-in-Furness, Cumbria LA14 5QX Tel: 01229 840370 840380 (Bailiffs) Fax: 01229 840371 DX 65210 BARROW-IN-FURNESS 2	*District Judge:* M. Rhodes
121	**BARRY**	(CLOSED wef 29/12/95 – successor court – Cardiff)	

COUNTY COURTS

Court No	Location, Region and Additional Jurisdiction	Court Manager and Court Offices	Court House and District Judges
153	**BASILDON** SE (18)	Jeannine North, Basildon Combined Court, The Gore, Basildon, Essex SS14 2BU Tel: 01268 458000 Fax: 01268 458100 DX 97633 BASILDON 5	The Gore, Basildon *District Judge:* J. I. Collier
122	**BASINGSTOKE** SW (17) **District Registry** *Family Hearing Centre*	Mr. Leo Ssebweze, 3rd Floor, Grosvenor House, Basing View, Basingstoke, Hants. RG21 4HG Tel: 01256 318200 Fax: 01256 318225 DX 98570 BASINGSTOKE 3	3rd Floor, Grosvenor House, Basing View, Basingstoke *District Judges:* D. Carney M. Cooper
123	**BATH** SW (14) **District Registry** *Bankruptcy* *Divorce* *Family Hearing Centre*	Ms. T. Ashley, 3rd & 4th Floor, Cambridge House, Henry Street, Bath BA1 1DJ Tel: 01225 310282 Fax: 01225 480915 DX 98580 BATH 2	3rd Floor, Cambridge House, Henry Street, Bath *District Judges:* M. Rutherford F. Goddard
124	**BEDFORD** SE (18) **District Registry** *Bankruptcy* *Divorce* *Family Hearing Centre*	May House, 29 Goldington Road, Bedford MK40 3NN Tel: 01234 760400 760402 (Bailiffs) Fax: 01234 327431 DX 97590 BEDFORD 3	May House, 29 Goldington Road, Bedford *District Judges:* K. Wilding P. R. Ayers
703	**BERWICK-UPON-TWEED**	(CLOSED wef 15/12/97 – successor court – Morpeth and Berwick)	
704	**BEVERLEY**	(CLOSED wef 1/1/93 – successor court – Kingston-upon-Hull)	
126	**BIRKENHEAD** NW (3) **District Registry** *Bankruptcy* *Divorce*	76 Hamilton Street, Birkenhead, Merseyside CH41 5EN Tel: 0151-666 5800 Fax: 0151-666 5873 DX 725000 BIRKENHEAD 10	76 Hamilton Street, Birkenhead *District Judges:* B. W. Travers M. I. Peake R. Smedley P. J. O'Neill M. A. Baker

COUNTY COURTS

Court No	Location, Region and Additional Jurisdiction	Court Manager and Court Offices	Court House and District Judges

127	**BIRMINGHAM CIVIL JUSTICE CENTRE AND FAMILY COURTS**
	
	M (10)
	
	District Registry
	Extended
	Chancery
	Mercantile
	Technology and Construction
	Bankruptcy
	Care Centre
	Race Relations
	Administrative Centre
		Helen Dickens,
		Priory Courts,
		33 Bull Street,
		Birmingham B4 6DS
		  Tel: 0121 681 4441 (Civil)
		      0121 250 6382 (Family)
		  Fax: 0121-681 3001
		      3002
		DX 701987 BIRMINGHAM 7
			33 Bull Street,
			Birmingham
			Fax: 0121-681 3001
			(Civil)
			0121 250 6386
			(Family)
			
			District Judges:
			  R. L. Cole
			  D. J. Owen
			  R. J. Savage
			  P. G. Dowling
			  D. J. O'Regan
			  V. Sehdev
			  A. Davies
			  D. Cooke
			  M. Asokan
			  S. Middleton
			  I. Knifton
			  R. Sheldrake
			  D. Maughan
			  D. Truman
			  J. George
			  M. Rogers
			  S. Dowding

128	**BISHOP AUCKLAND**
	
	NE (4)
	
	Divorce
		I. McNaughton,
		Woodhouse Close,
		Bishop Auckland,
		Co. Durham DL14 6LD
		  Tel: 01388 660251
		  Fax: 01388 660265
		DX 65100 BISHOP AUCKLAND 2
			Woodhouse Close,
			Bishop Auckland
			
			District Judges:
			  J. E. Mainwaring-
			    Taylor
			  P. W. J. Traynor
			  D. Robertson

129	**BISHOP'S STORTFORD**	(CLOSED wef 1/12/97 – successor courts – Cambridge, Harlow and Colchester)	

130	**BLACKBURN**
	
	NW (1)
	
	District Registry
	
	Bankruptcy
	Care Centre
	Family Hearing Centre
		J. Hodgkinson,
		64 Victoria Street,
		Blackburn, Lancs.
		BB1 6DJ
		  Tel: 01254 680640
		      680654
		      662657 (Bailiffs)
		      679694 (Family Listing)
		  Fax: 01254 692712
		DX 702650 BLACKBURN 4
			64 Victoria Street,
			Blackburn
			
			District Judges:
			  I. J. Pickup
			  R.H. Talbot
			  A. Jones

131	**BLACKPOOL**
	
	NW (1)
	
	District Registry
	
	Bankruptcy
	Divorce
		Mrs. J. Kelly,
		The Law Courts,
		Chapel Street,
		Blackpool, Lancs. FY1 5RJ
		  Tel: 01253 754020
		  Fax: 01253 295255
		DX 724900 BLACKPOOL 10
			The Law Courts,
			Chapel Street,
			Blackpool
			
			District Judges:
			  M. E. Buckley
			  R. Bryce
			  N. Law

COUNTY COURTS

Court No	Location, Region and Additional Jurisdiction	Court Manager and Court Offices	Court House and District Judges

132	**BLACKWOOD**
	
	 WAL (9)
	
	 District Registry
	
	 Bankruptcy
	 Divorce
		Huw Evans,
		 Blackwood Civil and Family Court,
		 8 Hall Street,
		 Blackwood
		 NP12 1NY
		   Tel: 01495 238200
		   Fax: 01495 238203
		 DX 99470 BLACKWOOD 2
			Civil and Family Court,
			 10 Hall Street,
			 Blackwood
			
			 District Judges:
			 A. Fraser
			 M. Phillips

133	**BLETCHLEY AND LEIGHTON BUZZARD** *renamed* MILTON KEYNES *q.v.*		
134	**BLOOMSBURY**, *see* LONDON		
705	**BLYTH**	(CLOSED wef 15/12/97 – successor court – Morpeth and Berwick)	

136	**BODMIN**
	
	 SW (15)
	
	 Divorce
		Mrs. J. Hick,
		 Cockswell House,
		 Market Street,
		 Bodmin, Cornwall
		 PL31 2HJ
		   Tel: 01208 74224
		   Fax: 01208 77255
		 DX 136846 BODMIN 2
			Cockswell House,
			 Market Street,
			 Bodmin
			
			 District Judges:
			 P. Mitchell
			 R. A. F. Griggs
			 L. Thomas

137	**BOLTON**
	
	 NW (2)
	
	 District Registry
	
	 Bankruptcy
	 Family Hearing
	   Centre
		T. Anderson,
		 Bolton Combined Court
		   Centre,
		 The Law Courts,
		 Blackhorse Street,
		 Bolton, Lancs. BL1 1SU
		   Tel: 01204 392881
		   Fax: 01204 373706
		 DX 702610 BOLTON 3
			The Law Courts,
			 Blackhorse Street,
			 Bolton
			
			 District Judges:
			 J. Shaw
			 C. M. Swindley
			 M. Haigh

138	**BOSTON**
	
	 M (12)
	
	 District Registry
	
	 Bankruptcy
	 Divorce
		D. J. Woodward,
		 Boston County Court,
		 55 Norfolk Street,
		 Boston, Lincs. PE21 6PE
		   Tel: 01205 366080 (Office)
		                 359665 (Bailiff)
		   Fax: 01205 311692
		 DX 701922 BOSTON 2
			Boston County Court,
			 55 Norfolk Street,
			 Boston
			
			 District Judges:
			 R. L. Hudson
			 R. J. Toombs

139	**BOURNEMOUTH**
	
	 SW (16)
	
	 District Registry
	
	 Bankruptcy
	 Care Centre
	 Family Hearing
	   Centre
		D. Daly,
		 Bournemouth Crown and
		   County Courts,
		 Courts of Justice,
		 Deansleigh Road,
		 Bournemouth
		 BH7 7DS
		   Tel: 01202 502800
		   Fax: 01202 502801
		 DX 98420 BOURNEMOUTH 4
			Courts of Justice,
			 Deansleigh Road,
			 Bournemouth
			
			 District Judges:
			 I. Weintroub
			 J. Hurley
			 P. Mildred
			 M. Dancey

COUNTY COURTS

Court No	Location, Region and Additional Jurisdiction	Court Manager and Court Offices	Court House and District Judges
140	**BOW,** see LONDON		

141	**BRADFORD**
	
	NE (5)
	
	District Registry
	
	Bankruptcy
	Family Hearing Centre
		T. Lyons,
		Bradford Combined Court Centre,
		The Law Courts,
		Exchange Square,
		Drake Street,
		Bradford, W. Yorks.
		BD1 1JA
		  Tel: 01274 840274
		  Fax: 01274 840275
		    (Civil Listing)
		      843510
		    (Criminal Listing)
		      843541
		    (Case Progression)
		DX 702083 BRADFORD 2
			The Law Courts,
			Exchange Square,
			Drake Street,
			Bradford
			
			District Judges:
			  P. E. Lawton
			  G.Y. Lingard
			  G. J. Edwards
			  N. Hickinbottom

142	**BRAINTREE**	(CLOSED wef 1/12/97 – successor courts Chelmsford, Harlow and Colchester)	

143	**BRECKNOCK**
	
	WAL (8)
	
	District Registry
	
	Divorce
		Ann Pritchard,
		Brecon Law Courts,
		Cambrian Way,
		Brecon, Powys
		LD3 7HR
		  Tel: 01874 622993
		  Fax: 01874 622441
		DX 124340 BRECON 2
			Brecon Law Courts,
			Cambrian Way,
			Brecon
			
			District Judge:
			  R. Singh, CBE

144	**BRENTFORD,** see LONDON		
145	**BRENTWOOD**	transferred to BASILDON wef 29/12/95 *see* p.8	

146	**BRIDGEND**
	
	WAL (9)
	
	District Registry
	
	Bankruptcy
	Divorce
		Caroline Bevan,
		Bridgend Law Courts,
		Sunnyside,
		Bridgend CF31 4AJ
		  Tel: 01656 673833
		  Fax: 01656 647124
		DX 99750 BRIDGEND 2
			Bridgend Law Courts,
			Sunnyside,
			Bridgend
			
			District Judge:
			  D. P. Jenkins

147	**BRIDGNORTH**	(CLOSED wef 1/10/84 – successor court – Wellington)	
148	**BRIDGWATER**	(CLOSED wef 20/12/99 – successor court – Taunton)	
149	**BRIDLINGTON**	(CLOSED wef 24/12/97 – successor court – Scarborough)	

COUNTY COURTS

Court No	Location, Region and Additional Jurisdiction	Court Manager and Court Offices	Court House and District Judges

150	**BRIGHTON**
	
	SE (21)
	
	District Registry
	
	Bankruptcy
	Care Centre
		Mr. D. Wraith,
		William Street,
		Brighton BN2 0RF
		  Tel: 01273 674421
		  Fax: 01273 602138
		  DX 98070 BRIGHTON 3
		
		Family Section and Care Centre at:
		Brighton County Court Family Centre,
		1 Edward Street,
		Brighton,
		East Sussex BN2 2JD
		  Tel: 01273 811333
		  Fax: 01273 607638
		  DX 142600 BRIGHTON 12
			William Street,
			Brighton
			
			District Judges:
			J. Merrick
			M. Fawcett
			P. Gamba
			T. McLoughlin
			J. Robinson
			C. Edwards

151	**BRISTOL**
	
	SW (14)
	
	District Registry
	  Extended
	  Chancery
	
	Bankruptcy
	Care Centre
	Family Hearing
	  Centre
	Mercantile Court
	Patent Court
	(Trademarks Act 1994 only)
	Race Relations
	Dissolution of Civil
	  Partnerships
	(Regional Court of Protection
	  Hearing Venue
	  from 1st October 2007)
		Mrs. C. Bodington,
		Greyfriars,
		Lewins Mead,
		Bristol BS1 2NR
		  Tel: 0117 910 6700
		  Fax: 0117 910 6729 (Civil)
		      0117 910 6727 (Diary Manager)
		      0117 910 6728 (Family)
		  DX 95903 BRISTOL 3
		
		E-mail: enquiries@bristol.countycourt.gsi.gov.uk
			The Guildhall,
			Small Street,
			Bristol
			
			District Judges:
			Mr. M. P. W. Daniel
			Ms. J. A. Exton
			Ms. L. Rowe
			Mr. B. J. Watson
			Ms. J. Exton
			Mr. R. J. Britton

152	**BROMLEY,** see LONDON		
153	**BASILDON,** see p.8		

154	**BURNLEY**
	
	NW (1)
	
	District Registry
	
	Bankruptcy
	Divorce
		Mrs. M. McGuinness,
		Burnley Combined
		  Court Centre,
		The Law Courts,
		Hammerton Street,
		Burnley, Lancs. BB11 1XD
		  Tel: 01282 416899
		  Fax: 01282 414911
		  DX 724940 BURNLEY 4
			The Law Courts,
			Hammmerton Street,
			Burnley
			
			District Judges:
			I. J. Pickup
			J. M. Geddes
			C. Freeman

COUNTY COURTS

Court No	Location, Region and Additional Jurisdiction	Court Manager and Court Offices	Court House and District Judges
155	**BURTON-UPON-TRENT** **M** (13) *Bankruptcy* *Divorce*	M. J. Underwood, 165 Station Street, Burton-upon-Trent, Staffs. DE14 1BP Tel: 01283 568241 Fax: 01283 517245 DX 702044 BURTON-ON-TRENT 3	165 Station Street, Burton-upon-Trent *District Judges:* A. A. Butler A. Stark
156	**BURY** **NW** (2) **District Registry** *Divorce* *Insolvency*	Mrs. C. Marsh, Tenters Street, Bury, Lancs. BL9 0HX Tel: 0161 447 8699 Fax: 0161-763 4995 DX 702615 BURY 2	Tenters Street, Bury *District Judges:* J. F. Duerden P. Wilby
157	**BURY ST. EDMUNDS** **SE** (19) District Registry *Bankruptcy* *Divorce*	Mrs. M. J. Rumsey, Triton House (Entrance B), St Andrews Street North, Bury St. Edmunds, Suffolk IP33 1TR Tel: 01284 753254 Fax: 01284 702687 DX 97640 BURY ST. EDMUNDS 3	Triton House (Entrance F), St. Andrews Street North, Bury St. Edmunds *District Judges:* E. R. W. Temple J. Kirby G. Pearl
158	**BUXTON** **M** (11)	Richard Taylor, Court House, Peak Buildings, Terrace Road, Buxton, Derbys SK17 6DY Tel: 01298 23734 Fax: 01298 28035 DX 701970 BUXTON 2	Court House, Peak Buildings, Terrace Road, Buxton *District Judge:* A. A. Butler A. G. Stark
159	**CAERNARFON** **WAL** (7) **District Registry** *Bankruptcy* *Care Centre* *Family Hearing* *Centre*	Mrs. A. W. Williams, Court House, Llanberis Road, Caernarfon, Gwynedd LL55 2DF Tel: 01286 684600 Fax: 01286 678965 DX 702483 CAERNARFON 2	Court House, Llanberis Road, Caernarfon *District Judges:* J. G. Thomas O. W. Williams
160	**CAERPHILLY**	(CLOSED wef 1/12/00 – successor courts – Cardiff, Blackwood)	
161	**CAMBORNE AND REDRUTH**	(CLOSED wef 24/12/98 – successor court – Penzance)	

COUNTY COURTS

Court No	Location, Region and Additional Jurisdiction	Court Manager and Court Offices	Court House and District Judges

162	**CAMBRIDGE**
	
	SE (19)
	
	District Registry
	
	Care Centre
	Family Hearing
	  Centre
	Insolvency
	Race Relations
	Trial Centre
		Mrs. E. Richardson,
		197 East Road,
		Cambridge CB1 1BA
		  Tel: 01223 224500
		  Fax: 01223 224590
		DX 97650 CAMBRIDGE 3
			197 East Road,
			Cambridge
			
			District Judges:
			R. H. L. Blomfield, T.D.
			E. R. W. Temple
			J. L. C. Kirby
			P. H. Pelly
			J. Taylor
			G. Pearl

163	**CANTERBURY**
	
	SE (20)
	
	District Registry
	
	Bankruptcy
	Care Centre
	Family Hearing
	  Centre
	Race Relations
	Trial Centre
		Mr. G. Downer,
		Canterbury Combined Court
		  Centre,
		Law Courts,
		Chaucer Road,
		Canterbury, Kent
		CT1 1ZA
		  Tel: 01227 819200
		  Fax: 01227 819283
		DX 99710 CANTERBURY 3
			Law Courts,
			Chaucer Road,
			Canterbury
			
			District Judges:
			R. Hicks
			N. E. Jackson
			W. Jackson

164	**CARDIFF**
	
	WAL (9)
	
	District Registry
	  Extended
	  Chancery
	
	Administrative Court
	Bankruptcy
	Care Centre
	Family Hearing
	  Centre
	Mercantile Court
	Race Relations
	Technology and
	  Construction Court
	Adoption Centre
		Neil Pring,
		Cardiff Civil Justice Centre,
		2 Park Street,
		Cardiff CF10 1ET
		  Tel: 029 2037 6400
		  Fax: 029 2037 6475
		DX 99500 CARDIFF 6
			2 Park Street,
			Cardiff
			
			District Judges:
			R. L. Hendicott
			A. T. North
			T. A. John
			G. H. F. Carson
			J. E. Regan
			C. R. Dawson

707	**CARDIGAN**	(CLOSED wef 29/12/95 – successor court – Carmarthen)	

165	**CARLISLE**
	
	NW (1)
	
	District Registry
	
	Bankruptcy
	Care Centre
	Race Relations
		The Court Manager,
		Carlisle Combined Court
		  Centre,
		Courts of Justice,
		Earl Street,
		Carlisle CA1 1DJ
		  Tel: 01228 528182
		  Fax: 01228 590588
		DX 65331 CARLISLE 2
			Courts of Justice,
			Earl Street,
			Carlisle
			
			District Judges:
			J. Park
			S. Smith

COUNTY COURTS

Court No	Location, Region and Additional Jurisdiction	Court Manager and Court Offices	Court House and District Judges

166	**CARMARTHEN**
	
	WAL (8)
	
	District Registry
	
	Bankruptcy
	Divorce
	Family Hearing Centre
		M. Thomas,
		The Old Vicarage,
		Picton Terrace,
		Carmarthen,
		Dyfed SA31 1BJ
		  Tel: 01267 228010
		  Fax: 01267 221844
		DX 99570 CARMARTHEN 2
			Guildhall,
			Carmarthen
			
			District Judge:
			  J. L. Davies

	CENTRAL LONDON, *see* LONDON		
	CHARD, *see* AXMINSTER AND CHARD		
	CHATHAM, *see* MEDWAY		

167	**CHELMSFORD**
	
	SE (18)
	
	District Registry
	
	Bankruptcy
	Care Centre
		Mrs. R. Goodall,
		London House,
		New London Road,
		Chelmsford, Essex CM2 0QR
		  Tel: 01245 264670
		        350718
		  Fax: 01245 496216
		DX 97660 CHELMSFORD 4
			London House,
			New London Road,
			Chelmsford
			
			District Judges:
			  E. Silverwood-Cope
			  W. F. Shanks
			  D. Hallett

168	**CHELTENHAM**
	
	SW (16)
	
	District Registry
	
	Bankruptcy
		Mrs. L. Overbury,
		c/o Kimbrose Way,
		Gloucester GL1 2DE
		  Tel: 01452 834991
		  Fax: 01452 834923
		DX 98660 GLOUCESTER 5
			The Court House,
			St George's Road,
			Cheltenham
			
			District Judges:
			  A. B. Thomas
			  P. Singleton

169	**CHEPSTOW**	(CLOSED wef 1/4/02 – successor court – Newport (Gwent)	

170	**CHESTER**
	
	NW (3)
	
	District Registry
	
	Bankruptcy
	Care Centre
	Civil Trial Centre
		C. C. Grant,
		Trident House,
		Little St. John Street,
		Chester CH1 1SN
		  Tel: 01244 404200
		        404222 (Bailiffs)
		  Fax: 01244 404300
		DX 702460 CHESTER 4
			Trident House,
			Little St. John Street,
			Chester
			
			District Judges:
			  S. G. Harrison
			  C. W. F. Newman
			  C. E. O'Leary

171	**CHESTERFIELD**
	
	M (11)
	
	District Registry
	
	Bankruptcy
	Divorce
		Mrs. K. Cook,
		St. Mary's Gate,
		Chesterfield, Derbys.
		S41 7TD
		  Tel: 01246 501200
		        501201 (Bailiffs)
		  Fax: 01246 501205
		DX 703160 CHESTERFIELD 3
			St. Mary's Gate,
			Chesterfield
			
			District Judges:
			  A. A. Butler
			  A. G. Stark
			  M. Wall

COUNTY COURTS

Court No	Location, Region and Additional Jurisdiction	Court Manager and Court Offices	Court House and District Judges

172	**CHICHESTER**
	
	SE (21)
	
	District Registry
	
	Family Hearing Centre
		J. D. Betts,
		Chichester Combined
		   Court Centre,
		Southgate,
		Chichester, W. Sussex
		PO19 1SX
		Tel: 01243 520700
		Fax: 01243 533756
		DX 97460 CHICHESTER 2
			(1) The Courthouse,
			    Southgate,
			    Chichester
			(2) Jays House,
			    St. Martin's Street,
			    Chichester
			
			District Judges:
			S. Levinson

173	**CHIPPENHAM**	(CLOSED wef 1/5/96 – successor courts – Swindon and Trowbridge)	
174	**CHORLEY** **NW** (1) *Divorce*	Mrs. J. Windle, 59 St. Thomas's Road, Chorley, Lancashire PR7 1JE Tel: 01257 262778 Fax: 01257 232843 DX 702655 CHORLEY 3	59 St. Thomas's Road, Chorley *District Judge:* M. Turner
	CIRENCESTER, *see* **SWINDON**		
175	**CLERKENWELL,** *see* **LONDON**		
176	**COLCHESTER** **SE** (18) District Registry *Bankruptcy* *Family Hearing* *Centre* *Trial Centre*	E. Appleby, Falkland House, 25 Southway, Colchester, Essex CO3 3EG Tel: 01206 717200 Fax: 01206 717250 DX 97670 COLCHESTER 3	Falkland House, 25 Southway, Colchester Trial Centre:- Norfolk House, 23 Southway, Colchester Tel: 01206 717234 Fax: 01206 717248 *District Judges:* C. B. Molle S. R. Mitchell
	COLWYN BAY, *see* **CONWY AND COLWYN**		
177	**CONSETT** **NE** (4) *Divorce*	Ian Sheel, Victoria Road, Consett, Durham DH8 5AU Tel: 01207 502854 Fax: 01207 582626 DX 65106 CONSETT 2	Victoria Road, Consett *District Judge:* D. Scott-Phillips

COUNTY COURTS

Court No	Location, Region and Additional Jurisdiction	Court Manager and Court Offices	Court House and District Judges

178	**CONWY AND COLWYN**
	
	WAL (7)
		Mr. P. Roberts,
		36 Princes Drive,
		Colwyn Bay
		LL29 8LA
		Tel: 01492 530807
		           534286 (Bailiffs)
		Fax: 01492 533591
		DX 702492 COLWYN BAY 2
			Circuit Judge Sittings:
			  Llangefni County
			  Court,
			  Glanhwfa Road,
			  Llangefni, Gwynedd
			District Judge Sittings:
			  36 Princes Drive,
			  Colwyn Bay
			
			District Judges:
			  O. W. Williams
			  H. Smart
			  J. Thomas

179	**CORBY**	(CLOSED wef 1/3/99 – successor courts – Kettering and Peterborough)	

180	**COVENTRY**
	
	M (10)
	
	District Registry
	
	Bankruptcy
	Care Centre
		Mrs. J. Barton,
		Coventry Combined Court Centre,
		140 Much Park Street,
		Coventry CV1 2SN
		Tel: 024 7653 6166
		Fax: 024 7652 0443
		DX 701580 COVENTRY 5
			140 Much Park Street,
			Coventry
			
			District Judges:
			  T. C. Cotterill
			  T. R. Ridgway
			  P. A. Kesterton
			  P. B. Waterworth
			  A. S. Jones
			  P. Sanghera

181	**CREWE**
	
	NW (3)
	
	District Registry
	
	Bankruptcy
	Family Hearing
	  Centre
		Mrs. S. Woodward,
		The Law Courts,
		Civic Centre,
		Crewe, Cheshire
		CW1 2DP
		Tel: 01270 539300
		Fax: 01270 216344
		DX 702504 CREWE 2
			The Law Courts,
			Civic Centre,
			Crewe
			
			District Judges:
			  C. Gilham
			  G. Little

182	**CROYDON,** *see* LONDON		

183	**DARLINGTON**
	
	NE (4)
	
	District Registry
	
	Bankruptcy
	Family Hearing
	  Centre
		Mrs. J. Beaty,
		Mrs. S. Dolphin,
		4 Coniscliffe Road,
		Darlington, Co. Durham
		DL3 7RL
		Tel: 01325 463224
		Fax: 01325 362829
		DX 65109 DARLINGTON 3
			4, Coniscliffe Road,
			Darlington
			
			District Judges:
			  J. Mainwaring-Taylor
			  P. Cuthbertson
			  R. Hall

COUNTY COURTS

Court No	Location, Region and Additional Jurisdiction	Court Manager and Court Offices	Court House and District Judges
184	**DARTFORD** **SE** (20) *Divorce* *Family Hearing* *Centre*	Mrs. C. S. Holder, Court House, Home Gardens, Dartford, Kent DA1 1DX Tel: 01322 629820 Fax: 01322 270902 DX 98090 DARTFORD 2	Court House, Home Gardens, Dartford District Judges: A. J. Blunsdon P. J. Glover A. Grand
185	**DERBY** **M** (11) **District Registry** *Bankruptcy* *Care Centre*	Isabel Syred, Derby Combined Court Centre, Morledge, Derby DE1 2XE Tel: 01332 622600 Fax: 01332 622543 DX 724060 DERBY 21	Combined Court Centre, Morledge, Derby District Judges: A. A. Butler D. Douce J. Booth A. G. Stark
	DEVIZES, *see* **TROWBRIDGE**		

186	**DEWSBURY**
	
	NE (5)
	
	District Registry
	
	Bankruptcy
	Family Hearing
	   Centre
		Mr. D. Corbishley,
		County Court House,
		Eightlands Road,
		Dewsbury, W. Yorks.
		WF13 2PE
		Tel: 01924 465860
		          466135
		Fax: 01924 456419
		DX 702086 DEWSBURY 2
			County Court House,
			Eightlands Road,
			Dewsbury
			
			District Judge:
			J. A. B. Buchan

187	**DONCASTER** **NE** (6) **District Registry** *Bankruptcy* *Family Hearing* *Centre*	Mrs. H. Hepworth, 74 Waterdale, Doncaster, S. Yorks. DN1 3BT Tel: 01302 381730 Fax: 01302 768090 DX 702089 DONCASTER 4	74 Waterdale, Doncaster District Judges: D. M. Stocken S. Rodgers P. Thompson
	DORCHESTER, *see* **WEYMOUTH**		
188	**DOVER**	(CLOSED wef 30/3/96 – successor court – Canterbury)	

189	**DUDLEY**
	
	M (13)
	
	District Registry
	
	Bankruptcy
	Divorce
	Family Hearing
	   Centre
		Mrs. S. Daniels,
		Harbour Buildings,
		Waterfront West,
		Brierley Hill,
		West Midlands
		DY5 1LN
		Tel: 01384 480799 (Court Office)
		          482201 (Bailiffs)
		Fax: 01384 482799
		DX 701949 DUDLEY 2
			Harbour Buildings,
			Waterfront West,
			Brierley Hill
			
			District Judges:
			R. J. Morton
			Miss. J. Ingram

COUNTY COURTS

Court No	Location, Region and Additional Jurisdiction	Court Manager and Court Offices	Court House and District Judges
190	**DURHAM** **NE** (4) **District Registry** *Bankruptcy* *Family Hearing Centre*	Mr. A. Plowman (Deputy), Hallgarth Street, Durham DH1 3RG Tel: 0191-386 5941 Fax: 0191-386 1328 DX 65115 DURHAM 5	Hallgarth Street, Durham *District Judges:* D. Scott-Phillips G. M. Marley
191	**EASTBOURNE** **SE** (21) **District Registry** *Bankruptcy* *Divorce*	Mrs. C. Price (Acting), The Law Courts, Old Orchard Road, Eastbourne, East Sussex BN21 4UN Tel: 01323 727518 Fax: 01323 649372	The Law Courts, Eastbourne *District Judge:* J. T. Robinson
192	**EAST GRINSTEAD**	(CLOSED wef 4/1/94 – successor courts – Haywards Heath and Tunbridge Wells)	
194	**EDMONTON,** *see* LONDON		
195	**ELLESMERE PORT**	(CLOSED wef 5/12/94 – successor court – Chester)	
196	**EPSOM** **SE** (21) *Divorce*	Mrs. A. Wright, The Parade, Epsom, Surrey KT18 5DN Tel: 01372 721801 Fax: 01372 726588 DX 97850 EPSOM 3	The Parade, Epsom *District Judges:* H. Letts D. Beck
197	**EVESHAM** **M** (13)	Mrs. J. Crelling, 1st Floor 87 High Street, Evesham, Worcs. WR11 4EE Tel: 01386 442287 (Office) Fax: 01386 49203 DX 701910 EVESHAM 3	87 High Street, Evesham *District Judge:* E. Dickinson

COUNTY COURTS

Court No	Location, Region and Additional Jurisdiction	Court Manager and Court Offices	Court House and District Judges

198	**EXETER**
	
	SW (15)
	
	District Registry
	
	Bankruptcy
	Family Hearing Centre
	Race Relations Care Centre
		Tony Hammond,
		Exeter Crown and County Court,
		Southernhay Gardens,
		Exeter, Devon
		EX1 1UH
		  Tel: 01392 415300 (General Enquiries)
		        415310 (Civil Listing DJ)
		        415350 (Civil Listing CJ)
		        415320 (Family)
		        415313 (Customer Service Officer)
		  Fax: 01392 415642 (General Enquiries)
		        415642 (Civil Listing DJ)
		        415645 (Civil Listing CJ)
		        415643 (Family)
		        415642 (Customer Service Officer)
		DX 98440 EXETER 2
			Southernhay Gardens, Exeter
			
			District Judges:
			  Miss A. J. Wainwright
			  A. Harvey
			  J. P. Crosse

	FARNHAM, see ALDERSHOT AND FARNHAM		
199	**FOLKESTONE**	(CLOSED wef 30/3/96 – successor court – Ashford)	
	FROME, see TROWBRIDGE		
201	**GAINSBOROUGH**	(CLOSED wef 1/1/93 – successor court – Lincoln)	

202	**GATESHEAD**
	
	NE (4)
	
	Divorce
		Ian Cuthbertson,
		5th Floor, Chad House,
		Tynegate Precinct,
		Sunderland Road,
		Gateshead, Tyne and Wear
		NE8 3HY
		  Tel: 0191-477 2445 (4 lines)
		        6858 (Bailiffs)
		  Fax: 0191-477 8562
		DX 65118 GATESHEAD 2
			5th Floor, Chad House,
			Tynegate Precinct,
			Sunderland Road,
			Gateshead
			
			District Judges:
			  D. Scott-Phillips
			  R. Howard

203	**GLOUCESTER**
	
	SW (16)
	
	District Registry
	
	Bankruptcy
	Family Hearing Centre
		Mrs. L. Overbury,
		Family and Civil Courts,
		County Court Offices,
		Kimbrose Way,
		Gloucester GL1 2DE
		  Tel: 01452 834900
		  Fax: 01452 834923
		DX 98660 GLOUCESTER 5
			Kimbrose Way, Gloucester
			
			District Judges:
			  A. B. Thomas
			  P. Singleton

COUNTY COURTS

Court No	Location, Region and Additional Jurisdiction	Court Manager and Court Offices	Court House and District Judges
204	**GOOLE**	(CLOSED wef 4/11/96 – successor court – Doncaster)	

205	**GRANTHAM**
	
	M (12)
		Mrs. T. Gray,
		Harlaxton Road,
		Grantham, Lincs.
		NG31 7SB
		   Tel: 01476 539030
		   Fax: 01476 539040
		DX 711102 GRANTHAM 4
			Harlaxton Road,
			Grantham
			
			District Judge:
			D. J. Maw
			D. J. Toombs

206	**GRAVESEND**
	
	SE (20)
		J. Burton,
		26 King Street,
		Gravesend, Kent
		DA12 2DU
		   Tel: 01474 321771
		   Fax: 01474 534811
		DX 98140 GRAVESEND 2
			26 King Street,
			Gravesend
			
			District Judge:
			A. J. Blunsdon

	NOTE: This building is only used for occasional hearings. Please direct all correspondence to Dartford County Court, see page 18.		
207	**GRAYS THURROCK**	(CLOSED wef 31/1/2000 – successor court – Basildon)	

208	**GREAT GRIMSBY**
	
	NE (6)
	
	District Registry
	
	Bankruptcy
	Divorce
	Family Hearing
	   Centre
		Mrs. S. Booth,
		Great Grimsby
		   Combined Court Centre,
		   Town Hall Square,
		Grimsby, North East Lincolnshire
		DN31 1HX
		   Tel: 01472 265200
		   Fax: 01472 265201
		DX 702007 GRIMSBY 3
			The Combined
			   Court Centre,
			Town Hall Square,
			Grimsby
			
			District Judges:
			J. S. Robinson
			S. Chesterfield
			B. J. Clark

209	**GREAT MALVERN**	(CLOSED wef 1/1/93 – successor court – Worcester)	
210	**GREAT YARMOUTH**	(CLOSED wef 31/1/2000 – successor court – Lowestoft, Norwich)	
	GRIMSBY, *see* **GREAT GRIMSBY**		

211	**GUILDFORD**
	
	SE (21)
	
	District Registry
	
	Adoption Centre
	Bankruptcy
	Care Centre
		Mrs. A. Wright,
		The Law Courts,
		Mary Road, Guildford,
		Surrey GU1 4PS
		   Tel: 01483 405300
		   Fax: 01483 300031 (Civil)
		                    405359 (Family)
		DX 97860 GUILDFORD 5
			The Law Courts,
			Mary Road,
			Guildford
			
			District Judges:
			H. A. J. Letts
			A. Levey
			D. Beck
			A. Raeside
			I. Kubiak
			R. Karp

COUNTY COURTS

Court No	Location, Region and Additional Jurisdiction	Court Manager and Court Offices	Court House and District Judges
212	**HALIFAX** **NE** (5) **District Registry** *Bankruptcy* *Family Hearing Centre*	Miss D. Halmshaw, Prescott Street, Halifax, W. Yorks. HX1 2JJ Tel: 01422 344700 (General Office) 369936 (Bailiffs – with Answerphone) Fax: 01422 360132 DX 702095 HALIFAX 2	Prescott Street, Halifax *District Judge:* I. F. Slim
	HANLEY, *see* STOKE-ON-TRENT		
213	**HARLOW** **SE** (18) **District Registry** *Divorce*	J. Goodwin, Gate House, The High, Harlow, Essex CM20 1UW Tel: 01279 443291/635628 Fax: 01279 451110 DX 97700 HARLOW 2	Gate House, The High, Harlow *District Judges:* W. F. Shanks P. H. Pelly G. Pearl A. Rowley
214	**HARROGATE** **NE** (5) **District Registry** *Bankruptcy* *Family Hearing Centre*	S. Kaye, 2 Victoria Avenue, Harrogate, N. Yorks. HG1 1EL Tel: 01423 503921 527732 (Bailiffs) Fax: 01423 528679 DX 702098 HARROGATE 3	2 Victoria Avenue, Harrogate *District Judge:* Helen Wood
215	**HARTLEPOOL** **NE** (4) **District Registry** *Divorce*	Susan Stamp, Law Courts, Victoria Road, Hartlepool TS24 8BS Tel: 01429 268198 Fax: 01429 862550 DX 65121 HARTLEPOOL 2	Law Courts, Victoria Road, Hartlepool *District Judges:* D. M. Robertson P. Traynor
216	**HASTINGS** **SE** (21) **District Registry** *Bankruptcy* *Divorce*	Mrs. J. D. Smith, Law Courts, Horntye Park, Bohemia Road, Hastings, E. Sussex TN34 1QX Tel: 01424 435128 445115 (Listing) 461966 (Bailiffs) Fax: 01424 421585 DX 98150 HASTINGS 2	Law Courts, Horntye Park, Bohemia Road, Hastings *District Judge:* D. C. Lamdin D. Pollard

COUNTY COURTS

Court No	Location, Region and Additional Jurisdiction	Court Manager and Court Offices	Court House and District Judges
217	**HAVERFORDWEST** **WAL** (8) **District Registry** *Bankruptcy* *Family Hearing Centre*	Mrs. M. Evans, Penffynnon, Hawthorn Rise, Haverfordwest, Pembs. SA61 2AX Tel: 01437 772060 772075 (Bailiffs) Fax: 01437 769222 DX 99610 HAVERFORDWEST 2	Penffynnon,, Hawthorn Rise, Haverfordwest District Judge: W. H. Godwin
218	**HAYWARDS HEATH** **SE** (21)	Miss K. Cockburn, Milton House, Milton Road, Haywards Heath, West Sussex RH16 1YZ Tel: 01444 447970 Fax: 01444 415282 DX 98160 HAYWARDS HEATH 3	Milton House, Milton Road, Haywards Heath District Judge: D. Pollard
219	**HEMEL HEMPSTEAD**	(CLOSED wef 24/12/98 – successor courts – Aylesbury, Luton and Watford)	
220	**HEREFORD** **M** (13) **District Registry** *Bankruptcy* *Divorce*	Mrs. S. Mower, First Floor, Barclays Bank Chambers, 1/3 Broad Street, Hereford HR4 9BA Tel: 01432 357233/264118 Fax: 01432 352593 DX 701904 HEREFORD 2	Shire Hall, Hereford District Judges: P. R. Mackenzie M. Parry
221	**HERTFORD** **SE** (18) *Bankruptcy* *Divorce*	Avril Powell, Sovereign House, Hale Road, Hertford SG13 8DY Tel: 01992 503954 503955 (Bailiffs) Fax: 01992 501274 DX 97710 HERTFORD 2	4th Floor, Sovereign House, Hale Road, Hertford District Judge: D. M. Eynon
713	**HEXHAM**	(CLOSED wef 4/1/94 – successor court – Newcastle-upon-Tyne)	
223	**HIGH WYCOMBE** **SE** (22)	Miss J. Leask, The Law Courts, Ground Floor, Easton Street, High Wycombe, Bucks. HP11 1LR Tel: 01494 651011 651038 (Bailiffs) Fax: 01494 651030 DX 97880 HIGH WYCOMBE 3	The Law Courts, Easton Street, High Wycombe District Judges: S. Jones T. Parker K. McCulloch P. Devlin
224	**HINCKLEY**	(CLOSED wef 1/10/84 – successor court – Nuneaton)	

COUNTY COURTS

Court No	Location, Region and Additional Jurisdiction	Court Manager and Court Offices	Court House and District Judges
225	**HITCHIN** SE (18) Family Hearing Centre	(Vacant), Park House, 1-12 Old Park Road, Hitchin, Herts. SG5 2JR Tel: 01462 443750 Fax: 01462 443758 DX 97720 HITCHIN 2	Park House, 1-12 Old Park Road, Hitchin District Judges: E. Willers G. B. Field
226	**HOLYWELL**	(CLOSED wef 7/9/98 – successor courts – Rhyl and Chester)	
227	**HORSHAM** SE (21) Divorce	Mary Hamilton, The Law Courts, Hurst Road, Horsham, Sussex RH12 2EU Tel: 01403 252474 Fax: 01403 258844 DX 98170 HORSHAM 2	The Law Courts, Hurst Road, Horsham District Judge: A. Taylor
228	**HUDDERSFIELD** NE (5) District Registry Bankruptcy Family Hearing Centre	D. Corbishley, County Court, Queensgate House, Queensgate, Huddersfield HD1 2RR Tel: 01484 421043 535085 Fax: 01484 426366 DX 703013 HUDDERSFIELD 2	County Court, Queensgate House, Queensgate, Huddersfield District Judges: J. E. Harrison R. Barraclough
	HULL, see KINGSTON UPON HULL		
229	**HUNTINGDON** SE (19)	Ground Floor, Godwin House, George Street, Huntingdon, Cambs. PE29 3BD Tel: 01480 450932 Fax: 01480 435397 DX 96650 HUNTINGDON 2	Godwin House, George Street, Huntingdon District Judges: R. Blomfield A. Wharton
230	**HYDE**	(CLOSED wef 31/1/87 – successor court – Tameside)	
231	**ILFORD,** see LONDON		
232	**ILKESTON**	(CLOSED wef 16/2/96 – successor courts – Derby and Nottingham)	

COUNTY COURTS

Court No	Location, Region and Additional Jurisdiction	Court Manager and Court Offices	Court House and District Judges
233	**IPSWICH** **SE** (19) **District Registry** *Bankruptcy* *Care Centre*	Mrs. M. Tibble, 8 Arcade Street, Ipswich, Suffolk IP1 1EJ Tel: 01473 214256 Fax: 01473 251797 DX 97730 IPSWICH 3	8 Arcade Street, Ipswich *District Judges:* Patrick Bazley White Ian Evans
234	**KEIGHLEY** **NE** (5) District Registry *Family Hearing* *Centre*	Debby Halmshaw, Yorkshire Bank Chambers, North Street, Keighley, W. Yorks. BD21 3SH Tel: 01535 602803 Fax: 01535 610549 DX 703007 KEIGHLEY 2	County Court House, North Street, Keighley *District Judge:* N. G. Hickinbottom
235	**KENDAL** **NW** (1) District Registry *Bankruptcy* *Divorce*	Mark P. Nicholson, The Court House, County Court, Burneside Road, Kendal LA9 4NF Tel: 01539 721218 Fax: 01539 733840 DX 63450 KENDAL 2	The Court House, County Court, Burneside Road, Kendal *District Judges:* R. M. Forrester M. Rhodes
236	**KETTERING** **M** (12)	Mrs. J. Gurney, Dryland Street, Kettering, Northants NN16 0BH Tel: 01536 512471 Fax: 01536 416857 DX 701886 KETTERING 2	Dryland Street, Kettering *District Judges:* D. Cernik P. McHale S. Watson I. Murdock
237	**KIDDERMINSTER** **M** (13) *Bankruptcy*	Mrs. A. Whattus, 10 Comberton Place, (off Comberton Hill), Kidderminster DY10 1QT Tel: 01562 822480 Fax: 01562 827809 DX 701946 KIDDERMINSTER 2	*District Judges:* A. Marston M. Nield
238	**KING'S LYNN** **SE** (19) District Registry *Bankruptcy* *Divorce* *Family Hearing* *Centre*	Mrs. H. D. Thomas, Chequer House, 12 King Street, King's Lynn, Norfolk PE30 1ES Tel: 01553 772067 Fax: 01553 769824 DX 97740 KING'S LYNN 2	Chequer House, 12 King Street, King's Lynn *District Judge:* B. J. Rutland

COUNTY COURTS

Court No	Location, Region and Additional Jurisdiction	Court Manager and Court Offices	Court House and District Judges

239	**KINGSTON-UPON-HULL**
	
	NE (6)
	
	District Registry
	
	Bankruptcy
	Care Centre
		B. Hunter,
		Kingston-upon-Hull Combined Court Centre,
		Lowgate,
		Hull HU1 2EZ
		Tel: 01482 586161
		        585328 (Bailiffs)
		Fax: 01482 588527
		        585328 (Bailiffs)
		DX 703010 HULL 5
			Kingston-upon-Hull Combined Court Centre,
			Lowgate, Hull
			
			District Judges:
			D. J. R. Weston
			I. L. Buxton
			I. P. Besford

240	**KINGSTON-UPON-THAMES,** *see* **LONDON**		
241	**LAMBETH,** *see* **LONDON**		
714	**LAMPETER**	(CLOSED wef 5/12/94 – successor courts – Aberystwyth and Carmarthen)	
242	**LANCASTER** **NW** (1) **District Registry** *Adoption Centre* *Bankruptcy* *Care Centre* *Trial Centre*	S. Sainsbury, 2nd Floor, Mitre House, Church Street, Lancaster, Lancs. LA1 1UZ Tel: 01524 68112 Fax: 01524 846478 DX 145880 LANCASTER 2	County Court, 2nd Floor, Mitre House, Church Street, Lancaster District Judges: R. Forrester M. Rhodes
715	**LAUNCESTON**	(CLOSED wef 5/12/95 – successor court – Bodmin)	

243	**LEEDS**
	
	NE (5)
	
	District Registry
	  Extended
	  Chancery
	
	Bankruptcy
	Care Centre
	Race Relations
	Mercantile
		Leeds Combined Court Centre,
		The Courthouse,
		1 Oxford Row,
		Leeds LS1 3BG
		Tel: 0113 306 2800
		DX 703016 LEEDS 6
			(1) Leeds Combined Court Centre,
			The Court House,
			1 Oxford Row,
			Leeds
			(2) Coverdale House
			13–15 East Parade,
			Leeds LS1 4BJ
			
			District Judges:
			P. G. Giles
			R. Jordan
			H. F. Heath
			S. Greenwood
			G. Lord
			I. Fairwood
			J. Flanagan
			S. Spencer
			A. Saffman
			H. Anderson

COUNTY COURTS

Court No	Location, Region and Additional Jurisdiction	Court Manager and Court Offices	Court House and District Judges
244	**LEICESTER** **M** (12) **District Registry** *Bankruptcy* *Care Centre*	Mrs. Pat Haynes, The Court House, 90 Wellington Street, Leicester LE1 6HG Tel: 0116 222 5700 Fax: 0116 222 5763 DX 17401 LEICESTER 3	The Court House, 90 Wellington Street, Leicester *District Judges:* R. P. Whitehurst R. J. Merriman L. Eaton V. Stamenkovich P. Atkinson
245	**LEIGH** **NW** (2) *Divorce*	M. Kingsford, 22 Walmesley Road, Leigh, Lancs. WN7 1YF Tel: 01942 673639 Fax: 01942 681216 DX 702555 LEIGH 2	County Court, 22 Walmesley Road, Leigh *District Judges:* E. Donnelly S. Jackson I. Sanderson
	LEIGHTON BUZZARD, *see* BLETCHLEY AND LEIGHTON BUZZARD		
246	**LEOMINSTER**	(CLOSED wef 1/10/84 – successor court – Hereford)	
247	**LEWES** **SE** (21)	Mr. D. Manning, Lewes Combined Court Centre, The Law Courts, High Street, Lewes, East Sussex BN7 1YB Tel: 01273 480400 Fax: 01273 485270 DX 97395 LEWES 4	Law Courts, High Street, Lewes *District Judge:* J. Merrick
248	**LICHFIELD**	(CLOSED wef 3/7/00 – successor courts – Burton upon Trent, Stafford, Tamworth, Walsall)	
249	**LINCOLN** **M** (12) **District Registry** *Adoption Centre* *Bankruptcy* *Care Centre* *Civil Trial Centre* *Family Hearing Centre*	H. Morgan, Lincoln County Court, 360 High Street, Lincoln LN5 7PS Tel: 01522 883000 Fax: 01522 883003 DX 703231 LINCOLN 6	360 High Street, Lincoln *District Judges:* A. Maw R. Hudson R. Toombs
	LISKEARD, *see* BODMIN		

COUNTY COURTS

Court No	Location, Region and Additional Jurisdiction	Court Manager and Court Offices	Court House and District Judges

251	**LIVERPOOL**
	
	NW (3)
	
	District Registry
	*Extended
	Chancery*
	
	*Bankruptcy
	Care Centre
	Family Hearing
	  Centre
	Divorce*
		J. Martin-Hall,
		Liverpool Civil and Family Courts,
		35 Vernon Street,
		Liverpool L2 2BX
		Tel: 0151 296 2200
		    2444 (Diary Manager Listing)
		    2406 (DJ Listing)
		    2460 (Family Listing)
		    2404 (Enforcements and Cash)
		    2408 (Family General)
		    2415 (Issue of New Claims)
		    2407 (Case Management)
		Fax: 0151 296 2201
		DX 702600 LIVERPOOL 5
			35 Vernon Street,
			Liverpool
			
			District Judges:
			G. Humphreys-Roberts
			Miss E. Johnson
			G. Fitzgerald
			J. Heyworth
			Mrs. S. Wright
			J. Clark
			R. Smedley
			Mrs. L. Sykes
			J. Henthorn
			J. Coffey
			P. Bellamy
			P. O'Neil
			M. Baker
			N. Harrison

143143	**LLANDRINDOD WELLS**	(CLOSED wef 29/12/95 – successor court – Brecknock)	
253	**LLANELLI** WAL (8) *Divorce*	Mrs. P. M. Jones, 2nd Floor, Court Buildings, Town Hall Square, Llanelli, Carms. SA15 3AL Tel: 01554 757171 Fax: 01554 758079 DX 99510 LLANELLI 2	2nd Floor, Court Buildings, Town Hall Square, Llanelli *District Judges:* Jane Garland-Thomas P. Llewelyn, O.B.E.
254	**LLANGEFNI** WAL (7) District Registry *Bankruptcy Family Hearing Centre*	Mrs. Ll. Roberts, County Court Buildings, Glanhwfa Road, Llangefni, Anglesey LL77 7EN Tel: 01248 750225 Fax: 01248 750778 DX 702480 LLANGEFNI 2	County Court Buildings, Llangefni *District Judges:* O. W. Williams J. G. Thomas H. Smart
	LONDON		
117	**Barnet** LON (25) *Divorce*	Mrs S. Mosley, St. Mary's Court, Regents Park Road, Finchley Central, London N3 1BQ Tel: 020 8343 4272 020 8371 7111 (family) Fax: 020 8343 1324 DX 122570 FINCHLEY (CHURCH END)	St. Mary's Court, Regents Park Road, Finchley Central, London N3 1BQ *District Judges:* S. Stephenson S. Gerlis M. Marin

COUNTY COURTS

Court No	Location, Region and Additional Jurisdiction	Court Manager and Court Offices	Court House and District Judges
	LONDON – *continued*		
134	**Bloomsbury**	(combined with Westminster County Court to form Central London County Court) wef 14/8/92	
140	**Bow** **LON** (25) *Family Hearing Centre*	Kerry Greenidge, 96 Romford Road, Stratford E15 4EG Tel: 020 8536 5200 Fax: 020 8503 1152 DX 97490 STRATFORD (LONDON) 2	96 Romford Road, Stratford *District Judges:* D. L. Millard N. Gregory D. J. Beattie D. J. Vokes D. J. Johns
144	**Brentford** **LON** (25) *Family Hearing Centre*	Miss S. Knight, Alexandra Road, High Street, Brentford, Middx. TW8 0JJ Tel: 020 8231 8940 (Gen. Enq) Fax: 020 8568 2401 DX 97840 BRENTFORD 2	Alexandra Road, High Street, Brentford *District Judges:* S. Plaskow J. Allen T. Jenkins
152	**Bromley** **LON** (25) *Family Hearing Centre*	Mr. L. Davies, Court House, College Road, Bromley, Kent BR1 3PX Tel: 020 8290 9620 (Main Switchboard) Fax: 020 8313 9624 DX 98080 BROMLEY 2	Court House, College Road, Bromley *District Judges:* A. Thomas T. Brett J. Wilkinson S. Burn

372	**Central London**
	LON (25)
	Race Relations
	Sex Discrimination
	
	(At the Central London Civil Justice Centre:)
	020 7917 7821
	Patents County Court
	The Business List
	The Chancery List
	Technical and Construction Court
		Mr. Michael Burke,
		13-14 Park Crescent,
		London W1N 4HT
		Tel: 020 7917 5000 (Switchboard)
		       7932 (Trial Centre)
		       5062 (Listing Officer)
		       5099 (Bailiffs)
		Fax: 020 7917 5014
		DX 97325 REGENTS PARK 2
			Central London Civil Justice Centre,
			26 Park Crescent,
			London W1N 4HT
			Fax: 020 7917 7940
			
			District Judges:
			I. Avent
			Mrs. S. Hasan
			Mrs M. Langley
			Mrs. R. Fine
			M. Gilchrist
			B. Lightman
			J. Taylor
			K. Price
			H. Silverman

COUNTY COURTS

Court No	Location, Region and Additional Jurisdiction	Court Manager and Court Offices	Court House and District Judges
	LONDON – *continued*		
321	**Clerkenwell and Shoreditch** **LON** (25)	Mrs. Sarah Christou, The Gee Street Courthouse, 29–41 Gee Street, London EC1V 3RE Tel: 020 7250 7200 Fax: 020 7250 7250 DX 121000 SHOREDITCH 2	29–41 Gee Street District Judges: S. Jackson H. Manners A. Armon-Jones E. Stary M. J. Haselgrove
182	**Croydon** **LON** (25) District Registry Bankruptcy Family Hearing Centre	Ms. F. Waller, Croydon County Court, The Law Courts, Altyre Road, Croydon CR9 5AB Tel: 020 8410 4797 Fax: 020 8760 0432 DX 97470 CROYDON 6	The Law Courts, Altyre Road, Croydon District Judges: N. G. Freeborough S. H. D. Fink B. R. J. Cole A. J. Mills M. Parker
194	**Edmonton** **LON** (25) Family Hearing Centre	Mrs. S. Bennett, Court House, 59 Fore Street, Upper Edmonton N18 2TN Tel: 020 8884 6500 Fax: 020 8803 0564 DX 136686 EDMONTON 3	Court House, 59 Fore Street, Upper Edmonton District Judges: L. Cohen G. Silverman S. Morley
231	**Ilford** **LON** (25) Family Hearing Centre	Mr. S. Liddiard, Buckingham Road, Ilford, Essex IG1 1BR Tel: 020 8477 1920 Fax: 020 8553 2824 DX 97510 ILFORD 3	Buckingham Road, Ilford District Judges: I. V. Sheratte H. E. Kemp
240	**Kingston-upon-Thames** **LON** (25) Bankruptcy Family Hearing Centre Civil Trial Centre	Mr. S. Pigott, County Court, St. James's Road, Kingston-upon-Thames, Surrey KT1 2AD Tel: 020 8972 8700 Fax: 020 8547 1426 DX 97890 KINGSTON-UPON-THAMES 3	County Court, St. James's Road, Kingston-upon-Thames District Judges: A. Sturdy S. Gold M. Stewart A. Nisa

COUNTY COURTS

Court No	Location, Region and Additional Jurisdiction	Court Manager and Court Offices	Court House and District Judges
	LONDON – *continued*		
241	**Lambeth** LON (25)	Mrs. Charmaine Thickins, Court House, Cleaver Street, Kennington Road SE11 4DZ Tel: 020 7091 4420 Fax: 020 7587 1951 DX 145020 KENNINGTON 2	Court House, Cleaver Street, Kennington Road SE11 4DZ *District Judges:* R. M. Jacey M. Zimmels A. Worthington M. Wakem
266	**The Mayor's and City of London** LON (25)	Mr. John Laverick, Guildhall Buildings, Basinghall Street, London EC2V 5AR Tel: 020 7796 5400 Fax: 020 7796 5424 DX 97520 MOORGATE (EC2)	Guildhall Buildings, Basinghall Street, London EC2V 5AR *District Judges:* R. Southcombe M. Trent
387	**Romford** LON (25) District Registry *Bankruptcy* *Family*	Mr. J. Ward, 2A Oaklands Avenue, Romford, Essex RM1 4DP Tel: 01708 775353 Fax: 01708 756653 DX 97530 ROMFORD 2	2A Oaklands Avenue, Romford *District Judges:* J. H. G. Chrispin R. W. Mullis T. P. Bowles
356	**Uxbridge** LON (25) *Divorce*	Sally Hook, 501 Uxbridge Road, Hayes, Middlesex UB4 8HL Tel: 020 8756 3520 Fax: 020 8561 2020 DX 44658 HAYES (Middlesex)	501 Uxbridge Road, Hayes *District Judges:* J. Banks A. Wicks
359	**Wandsworth** LON (25) *Family Jurisdiction*	Mrs. Tracey Wildash, 76/78 Upper Richmond Road, Putney SW15 2SU Tel: 020 8333 4351 Fax: 020 8877 9854 DX 97540 PUTNEY 2	76/78 Upper Richmond Road, Putney SW15 *District Judges:* I. G. Tilbury J. Gittens M. Walker E. Habershon
368	**West London** LON (25)	Mrs. Deb Wharton, Courthouse, 181 Talgarth Road, Hammersmith W6 8DN Tel: 020 8600 6868 Fax: 020 8600 6860 DX 97550 HAMMERSMITH 8	Courthouse, 181 Talgarth Road, Hammersmith W6 8DN *District Judges:* M. Nicholson A. Fraser

COUNTY COURTS

Court No	Location, Region and Additional Jurisdiction	Court Manager and Court Offices	Court House and District Judges
	LONDON – *continued*		
369	**Westminster**	(combined with Bloomsbury County Court to form Central London County Court) wef 14/8/92	
375	**Willesden** **LON** (25) *Family Hearing Centre*	(Vacant), 9 Acton Lane, Harlesden NW10 8SB Tel: 020 8963 8200 Fax: 020 8453 0946 DX 97560 HARLESDEN 2	9 Acton Lane, Harlesden District Judges: Anthony J. Morris Derek V. Steel Edward Cohen Carlos Dabezies
379	**Woolwich** **LON** (25)	Mrs. M. Millard, The Court House, 165 Powis Street SE18 6JW Tel: 020 8301 8700 Fax: 020 8316 4842 DX 123450 WOOLWICH 8	The Court House, Powis Street SE18 District Judge: Michael Lee Wendy Backhouse
255	**LOUGHBOROUGH**	(CLOSED wef 31/12/98 – successor courts – Derby, Leicester and Nottingham)	
256	**LOWESTOFT** **SE** (19) **District Registry** *Divorce*	Mrs. J. Fossey, Old Nelson Street, Lowestoft, Suffolk NR32 1HJ Tel: 01502 501060 Fax: 01502 513875 DX 97750 LOWESTOFT 2	Old Nelson Street, Lowestoft, Suffolk NR32 1HJ District Judge: M. Birchall
257	**LUDLOW** **M** (13)	The Guildhall, Mill Street, Ludlow, Shropshire SY8 1BB Tel: 01584 872091 Fax: 01584 877606 DX 702013 LUDLOW 2	The Guildhall, Mill Street, Ludlow, Shropshire SY8 1BB District Judge: A. W. Brown
258	**LUTON** **SE** (18) **District Registry** *Adoption Centre* *Bankruptcy* *Care Centre* *Divorce* *Family Hearing Centre* *Trial Centre*	Mrs. Julie McGrory, 5th Floor, Cresta House, Alma Street, Luton, Beds. LU1 2PU Tel: 01582 506700 506736 (Bailiff) 506703 (Family) Fax: 01582 506701 DX 97760 LUTON 4	2nd Floor, Cresta House, Alma Street, Luton District Judges: P. F. Hewetson-Brown M. M. Short P. S. Gill D. Eynon K. Wilding

COUNTY COURTS

Court No	Location, Region and Additional Jurisdiction	Court Manager and Court Offices	Court House and District Judges
260	**MACCLESFIELD** **NW** (3) **District Registry** *Bankruptcy* *Family Hearing Centre* *Designated Adoption Centre*	J. Moss, 2nd Floor, Silk House, Park Green, Macclesfield SK11 7NA Tel: 01625 412800 Fax: 01625 501262 DX 702498 MACCLESFIELD 3	2nd Floor, Silk House, Park Green, Macclesfield *District Judges:* A. A. Wallace T. R. M. Swan
261	**MAIDSTONE** **SE** (20) **District Registry** *Bankruptcy* *Family Hearing Centre*	Mr. C. Kreffer, Maidstone Combined Court Centre, The Law Courts, Barker Road, Maidstone, Kent ME16 8EQ Tel: 01622 202000 Fax: 01622 202002 DX 130065 MAIDSTONE 7	The Law Courts, Barker Road, Maidstone *District Judges:* Mrs. L. Burgess Miss E. Millward
719	**MALDON**	(CLOSED wef 30/6/92 – successor court – Chelmsford)	
720	**MALTON**	(CLOSED wef 4/1/94 – successor court – York)	

262	**MANCHESTER**
	
	NW (2)
	
	District Registry
	  Extended
	  Chancery/Mercantile
	
	Bankruptcy
	Care Centre
	Divorce
	Family Hearing Centre
	Race Relations
		Mrs. S. Brooks,
		County Court,
		Courts of Justice,
		Crown Square,
		Manchester M60 9DJ
		Tel: 0161-954 1800
		Fax: 0161-954 1661
		  (County Court Listing, Issue and Enforcement)
		0161-954 1662
		  (Family)
		0161-954 1667
		  (District Registry/Chancery)
		0161-834 5493
		  (Diary Manager)
			184-186 Deansgate,
			Manchester
			(No correspondence to above address)
			
			District Judges:
			J. M. Griffiths
			C. R. Fairclough
			E. R. Jones
			G. A. Needham
			J. J. B. Rawkins
			A. J. J. Harrison
			B. V. McGrath
			M. Gosnall
			Mrs. L. Stephens
			G. D. Smith
			P. Richmond
			C. Khan
			Mrs. B. Stonier

263	**MANSFIELD** **M** (11) **District Registry** *Family Hearing Centre*	Ms. H. Ellis, Beech House, 58 Commercial Gate, Mansfield, Notts. NG18 1EU Tel: 01623 656406 Fax: 01623 626561 DX 702180 MANSFIELD 3	Beech House, 58 Commercial Gate, Mansfield *District Judges:* J. Booth M. Wall

COUNTY COURTS

Court No	Location, Region and Additional Jurisdiction	Court Manager and Court Offices	Court House and District Judges
	MARGATE, see THANET		
264	**MARKET DRAYTON**	(CLOSED wef 27/10/95 – successor courts – Shrewsbury and Stoke on Trent)	
265	**MATLOCK**	(CLOSED wef 16/2/96 – successor courts – Burton, Chesterfield and Derby)	
266	**MAYOR'S AND CITY OF LONDON,** see LONDON		
267	**MEDWAY** **SE** (20) District Registry *Bankruptcy* *Care Centre*	Miss. C. Ross, Anchorage House, 47-67 High Street, Chatham, Kent ME4 4DW Tel: 01634 810720 Fax: 01634 811332 DX 98180 CHATHAM 4	Anchorage House, High Street, Chatham *District Judges:* G. A. Green I. M. Diamond G. Parnell
268	**MELTON MOWBRAY** **M** (12)	Mrs. A. L. Harrison, The Court House, Norman Way, Melton Mowbray, Leics. LE13 1NH Tel: 01664 485100 Fax: 01664 501869 DX 701937 MELTON MOWBRAY 2	The Court House, Norman Way, Melton Mowbray *District Judge:* V. Stamenkovich
269	**MERTHYR TYDFIL** **WAL** (9) **District Registry** *Bankruptcy*	Mrs. S. Cumpston, Merthyr Tydfil Combined Court Centre, The Law Courts, Glebeland Place, Merthyr Tydfil, Mid Glam. CF47 8BH Tel: 01685 358200 Fax: 01685 359727 DX 99582 MERTHYR TYDFIL 2	The Law Courts, Glebeland Place, Merthyr Tydfil *District Judge:* G. Sandercock J. Doel

270	**MIDDLESBROUGH**
	
	NE (4)
	
	District Registry
	
	Bankruptcy
	Care Centre
		E. Short,
		Teesside Combined Court
		  Centre,
		Russell Street,
		Middlesbrough,
		Cleveland TS1 2AE
		Tel: 01642 340000
		Fax: 01642 340002
		DX 65152 MIDDLESBROUGH 2
			Russell Street,
			Middlesbrough
			
			District Judges:
			J. E. Mainwaring-
			  Taylor
			D. Robertson
			P. W. J. Traynor
			P. Cuthbertson
			R. V. Hall
			C. A. Arkless
			J. P. Jackson

COUNTY COURTS

Court No	Location, Region and Additional Jurisdiction	Court Manager and Court Offices	Court House and District Judges
388	**MILTON KEYNES** **SE** (22) **District Registry** Bankruptcy Care Centre	Mrs. C. Marriott, 351 Silbury Boulevard, Witan Gate East, Central Milton Keynes MK9 2DT Tel: 01908 302800 (Civil Matters) 01908 302801 (Family Matters) Fax: 01908 230063 DX 136266 MILTON KEYNES 6	351 Silbury Boulevard, Milton Keynes District Judges: P. Mostyn R. Tetlow N. Hickman N. Brookes
271	**MOLD** **WAL** (7) Bankruptcy Civil	Law Courts, County Civic Centre, Mold, Flintshire CH7 1AE Tel: 01352 707330 Fax: 01352 707333 DX 702521 MOLD 2	Law Courts, County Civic Centre, Mold District Judges: V. Reeves C. G. Perry
272	**MONMOUTH**	(CLOSED wef 1/4/02 – successor court – Newport (Gwent))	

273	**MORPETH AND BERWICK**
	
	NE (4)
	
	Divorce
		Mrs. D. Thomas,
		Fountain House,
		Newmarket,
		Morpeth,
		Northumberland
		NE61 1LA
		Tel: 01670 512221
		Fax: 01670 504188
		DX 65124 MORPETH 2
			(1) Fountain House,
			    Newmarket, Morpeth
			(2) The Magistrates'
			    Court,
			    The Court House,
			    40 Church Street,
			    Berwick-upon-Tweed
			    TD15 1EA
			    Tel: 01289 305053
			    (Wed. only, 11 a.m.–
			    3 p.m.)
			
			District Judges:
			A. Powell
			P. Bullock
			M. Large
			R. Howard
			N. W. Goudie
			S. T. Alderson
			B. Stapely
			I. Atherton
			C. A. Arkless
			R. Loomba

274	**NEATH PORT TALBOT** **WAL** (8) Bankruptcy Divorce	Mrs. L. Pardoe, Forster Road, Neath, W. Glam. SA11 3BN Tel: 01639 642267 635088 (Bailiffs) Fax: 01639 633505 DX 99550 NEATH 2	Forster Road, Neath District Judge: J. Garland Thomas

COUNTY COURTS

Court No	Location, Region and Additional Jurisdiction	Court Manager and Court Offices	Court House and District Judges

275	**NELSON**
	
	NW (1)
	
	Divorce
		(Vacant),
		Phoenix Chambers,
		9/13 Holme Street,
		Nelson, Lancs.
		BB9 9SU
		  Tel: 01282 601177
		         619060 (Bailiff)
		  Fax: 01282 619557
		DX 702560 NELSON 2
			Phoenix Chambers,
			9/13 Holme Street,
			Nelson, Lancs.
			
			District Judges:
			J. M. Geddes

276	**NEWARK**
	
	M (11)
		R. Bumpsteed,
		The County Court,
		Crown Building,
		41 Lombard Street,
		Newark, Notts. NG24 1XB
		  Tel: 01636 703607
		  Fax: 01636 613726
		DX 701928 NEWARK 2
			The County Court,
			Crown Building,
			41 Lombard Street,
			Newark
			
			District Judges:
			A. Maw
			R. Toombs

277	**NEWBURY**
	
	SE (22)
	
	Bankruptcy
		Mrs. D. L. Bailey,
		The Courthouse,
		Mill Lane,
		Newbury,
		Berkshire RG14 5QS
		  Tel: 01635 642210
		  Fax: 01635 529580
		DX 30816 NEWBURY 1
			District Judges:
			G. Burgess
			J. R. Davidson
			S. Henson
			R. Henry
			C. Darbyshire

278	**NEWCASTLE UPON TYNE**
	
	NE (4)
	
	District Registry
	Extended
	Chancery
	
	Bankruptcy
	Care Centre
	Race Relations
		Ruth Parker,
		Newcastle upon Tyne
		  Combined Court Centre,
		The Law Courts,
		Quayside,
		Newcastle upon Tyne
		NE1 3LA
		  Tel: 0191-201 2000
		  Fax: 0191-201 2001
		DX 65128 NEWCASTLE UPON
		         TYNE 2
			The Law Courts,
			Quayside,
			Newcastle upon Tyne
			
			District Judges:
			P. Jackson
			P. Bullock
			R. Howard
			A. M. Large
			A. P. Powell
			S. T. Alderson
			N. W. Goudie
			R. Loomba
			I. D. Atherton
			B. D. Stapely
			P. Pescod

279	**NEWPORT (I.O.W.)**
	
	SW (17)
	
	District Registry
	
	Bankruptcy
	Divorce
		S. Crow,
		Newport (I.O.W.)
		  Crown and County Courts,
		The Law Courts,
		Quay Street,
		Newport, I.O.W. PO30 5YT
		  Tel: 01983 535100
		  Fax: 01983 821039
		DX 98460 NEWPORT (I.O.W.) 2
			The Law Courts,
			Quay Street,
			Newport, I.O.W.
			
			District Judge:
			M. H. Tennant

COUNTY COURTS

Court No	Location, Region and Additional Jurisdiction	Court Manager and Court Offices	Court House and District Judges
280	**NEWPORT (GWENT)** **WAL** (9) **District Registry** *Bankruptcy* *Care Centre* *Family Hearing Centre*	Mrs. Diana Edwards, Olympia House, 3rd Floor, Upper Dock Street, Newport, South Wales NP20 1PQ Tel: 01633 227150 Fax: 01633 263820 DX 99480 NEWPORT (SOUTH WALES) 4	The Concourse, Clarence House, Clarence Place, Newport, South Wales NP19 7AA *District Judges:* Rachel Evans A. J. P. Weaver
281	**NEWTON ABBOT**	(CLOSED wef 30/3/96 – amalgamated with Torquay)	
	NEWTOWN, see WELSHPOOL AND NEWTOWN		
722	**NORTHALLERTON**	(CLOSED wef 1/4/92 – successor court – Darlington)	
282	**NORTHAMPTON** **M** (12) **District Registry** *Bankruptcy* *Care Centre*	L. Handshaw, Northampton Combined Court Centre, 85/87 Lady's Lane, Northampton NN1 3HQ Tel: 01604 470400 Fax: 01604 232398 Fax: 01604 470445 (Family Section/Bankruptcy) DX 725380 NORTHAMPTON 21	Combined Court Centre, 85/87 Lady's Lane, Northampton *District Judges:* P. McHale K. Venables I. Murdoch S. Watson
283	**NORTH SHIELDS** **NE** (4) *Divorce*	Keith Swan, 2nd Floor, Kings Court, Earl Grey Way, Royal Quays, North Shields, Tyne & Wear NE29 6AR Tel: 0191 298 2339 Fax: 0191 298 2337 DX 65137 NORTH SHIELDS 2	2nd Floor, Kings Court, Earl Grey Way, North Shields *District Judges:* A. M. Large
284	**NORTHWICH** **WAL** (3)	Mrs. J. Johnson, The Court House, Chesterway, Northwich, Cheshire CW9 5ES Tel: 01606 338508 Fax: 01606 48740	The Court House, Chesterway, Northwich *District Judges:* G. W. Little C. F. Gilham

COUNTY COURTS

Court No	Location, Region and Additional Jurisdiction	Court Manager and Court Offices	Court House and District Judges

285	**NORWICH**
	
	SE (19)
	
	District Registry
	
	Bankruptcy
	Care Centre
	Family Hearing Centre
	Trial Centre
		Claire Bayley,
		Norwich Combined
		  Court Centre,
		The Law Courts,
		Bishopgate,
		Norwich NR3 1UR
		  Tel: 01603 728200
		  Fax: 01603 760863
		DX 97385 NORWICH 5
			The Law Courts,
			Bishopgate,
			Norwich
			
			District Judges:
			  Martyn Royall
			  R. G. Sparrow
			  B. I. Rutland
			  M. Birchall
			  D. N. Hayes
			  P. C. Rogers
			  Mrs. C. Hamilton

286	**NOTTINGHAM**
	
	M (11)
	
	District Registry
	
	Bankruptcy
	Care Centre
	Race Relations
		Mr. M. Lewis,
		Nottingham County Court,
		The Law Courts,
		60 Canal Street,
		Nottingham NG1 7EJ
		  Tel: 0115 910 3500
		  Fax: 0115 910 3510
		DX 702380 NOTTINGHAM 7
			The Law Courts,
			60 Canal Street,
			Nottingham
			
			District Judges:
			  C. M. Beale
			  D. S. Millard
			  B. J. Oliver
			  D. F. Reeson
			  J. Booth
			  S. Smith
			  M. Wall

287	**NUNEATON**
	
	M (10)
		S. Sephton,
		Warwickshire Justice Centre,
		Vicarage Street,
		Nuneaton CV11 4WX
		  Tel: 02476 482970
		  Fax: 02476 352835
		DX 701940 NUNEATON 2
			Warwickshire Justice
			  Centre,
			Vicarage Street,
			Nuneaton
			
			District Judge:
			  P. S. Sanghera

288	**OLDHAM**
	
	NW (2)
	
	District Registry
	
	Bankruptcy
	Divorce
	Family Hearing Centre
	Trial Centre
		Mrs. J. Webster,
		The County Court House,
		New Radcliffe Street,
		(off Rochdale Road),
		Oldham OL1 1NL
		  Tel: 0161-290 4200
		  Fax: 0161-290 4222
		DX 702595 OLDHAM 2
			The County Court
			  House,
			New Radcliffe Street,
			(off Rochdale Road),
			Oldham
			
			District Judges:
			  R. R. P. Ackroyd
			  P. S. Stockton
			  C. Fox
			  M. J. Simpson

289	**OSWESTRY**
	
	M (13)
		Cambrian Business Centre,
		Chester Street,
		Shrewsbury,
		Shropshire SY1 1NA
		  Tel: 01691 652127
		  Fax: 01691 671239
		DX 702047 SHREWSBURY 3
			The Court House,
			Holbache Road,
			Oswestry
			
			District Judge:
			  S. Rogers

290	**OTLEY**	(CLOSED wef 2/1/96 – successor courts – Bradford, Harrogate, Leeds and Skipton)	

COUNTY COURTS

Court No	Location, Region and Additional Jurisdiction	Court Manager and Court Offices	Court House and District Judges
291	**OXFORD** SE (22) **District Registry** *Bankruptcy* *Care Centre* *Family Hearing Centre* *Race Relations* *Trial Centre* *Divorce*	Mrs. G. Henley, Oxford Combined Court Centre, St. Aldates, Oxford OX1 1TL Tel: 01865 264200 Fax: 01865 790773 (Civil) 01865 264253 (Criminal) DX 96450 OXFORD 4	The Court House, St. Aldates, Oxford District Judges: A. Jenkins M. Payne R. Matthews V. Gatter
292	**PENRITH** NW (1) *Divorce*	Lindsay Allison, The Court House, Lowther Terrace, Penrith, Cumbria CA11 7QL Tel: 01768 862535 Fax: 01768 899700 DX 65207	The Court House, Lowther Terrace, Penrith District Judge: J. Park

293	**PENZANCE**
	
	SW (15)
	
	Divorce
		Mrs. L. Norman,
		Trevear,
		Alverton Terrace,
		Penzance, Cornwall
		TR18 4GH
		Tel: 01736 362987
		Fax: 01736 330595
		DX 136900 PENZANCE 2
			(1) Trevear,
			    Alverton Terrace,
			    Penzance
			(2) The Basset Centre,
			    Basset Road,
			    Camborne
			
			District Judges:
			P. Mitchell
			L. Thomas
			R. Griggs

294	**PETERBOROUGH** SE (19) **District Registry** *Bankruptcy* *Care Centre*	Sue Clarke, Peterborough Combined Court Centre, Crown Buildings, Rivergate, Peterborough PE1 1EJ Tel: 01733 349161 Fax: 01733 557348 DX 702302 PETERBOROUGH 8	Crown Buildings, Rivergate, Peterborough District Judges: A. Wharton S. Farquhar

296	**PLYMOUTH**
	
	SW (15)
	
	District Registry
	
	Bankruptcy
	Care Centre
		Plymouth Combined Court Centre,
		The Law Courts,
		Armada Way,
		Plymouth, Devon
		PL1 2ER
		Tel: 01752 677400
		      208286 (Civil)
		      677498 (Bailiffs)
		DX 98470 PLYMOUTH 7
			The Law Courts,
			Armada Way,
			Plymouth
			
			District Judges:
			A. D. Moon
			C. J. Tromans
			A. Walker

COUNTY COURTS

Court No	Location, Region and Additional Jurisdiction	Court Manager and Court Offices	Court House and District Judges

297	**PONTEFRACT**
	 NE (5)
	 District Registry
	 Family Hearing Centre
		S. Lally,
		 Horsefair House,
		 Horsefair,
		 Pontefract, W. Yorks.
		 WF8 1RJ
		   Tel: 01977 702357
		   Fax: 01977 600204
		 DX 703022 PONTEFRACT 2
			Horsefair House,
			 Horsefair,
			 Pontefract
			
			 District Judge:
			   R. Bedford

298	**PONTYPOOL**
	 WAL (9)
		Mrs. S. Wilcox,
		 Court Offices,
		 Park Road,
		 Riverside,
		 Pontypool, Torfaen
		 NP4 6NZ
		   Tel: 01495 762248
		   Fax: 01495 762467
		 DX 117500 PONTYPOOL 2
			Court Offices,
			 Park Road,
			 Riverside,
			 Pontypool
			
			 District Judge:
			   A. Weaver

299	**PONTYPRIDD**
	 WAL (9)
	 District Registry
	 Bankruptcy
	 Care Centre
	 Divorce
		Mrs. J. Jones,
		 The Courthouse,
		 Courthouse Street,
		 Pontypridd,
		 Mid Glamorgan
		 CF37 1JR
		   Tel: 01443 490800
		              490821/2 (Bailiffs)
		   Fax: 01443 480305
		 DX 99620 PONTYPRIDD 2
			The Courthouse,
			 Courthouse Street,
			 Pontypridd
			
			 District Judges:
			   G. Sandercock
			   J. M. Doel
			   T. M. Phillips

300	**POOLE**
	 SW (16)
		Mrs. J. Airth,
		 Law Courts,
		 Civic Centre,
		 Park Road, Poole
		 BN15 2NS
		   Tel: 01202 741150
		   Fax: 01202 747245
		 DX 98700 POOLE 4
			Law Courts,
			 Civic Centre,
			 Park Road, Poole
			
			 District Judge:
			   J. Freeman

301	**PORTHMADOG**	(CLOSED wef 4/7/94 – successor court – Caernarfon)	

302	**PORTSMOUTH**
	 SW (17)
	 District Registry
	 Admiralty
	 Bankruptcy
	 Care Centre
	 Family Hearing Centre
		P. Bray,
		 Portsmouth Combined Court
		   Centre,
		 The Courts of Justice,
		 Winston Churchill Avenue,
		 Portsmouth, Hants.
		 PO1 2EB
		   Tel: 023 9289 3000
		   Fax: 023 9282 6385
		 DX 98490 PORTSMOUTH 5
			The Courts of Justice,
			 Winston Churchill
			   Avenue,
			 Portsmouth
			
			 District Judges:
			   G. Cawood
			   P. Jolly
			   C. Ackroyd
			   R. Wilson
			   E. Manuel

PORT TALBOT, see NEATH AND PORT TALBOT

COUNTY COURTS

Court No	Location, Region and Additional Jurisdiction	Court Manager and Court Offices	Court House and District Judges
303	**PRESTON** **NW** (1) **District Registry** *Extended* *Chancery* *Bankruptcy* *Divorce*	Alan Thompson, Preston Combined Court Centre, The Law Courts, Openshaw Place, Ring Way, Preston PR1 2LL Tel: 01772 844700 Fax: 01772 844710 DX 702660 PRESTON 5	The Law Courts, Openshaw Place Ring Way, Preston District Judges: G. R. Ashton M. Turner P. Wheeler
304	**RAWTENSTALL** **NW** (1) *Divorce*	Miss. G. Clements, 1 Grange Street, Rawtenstall, Lancs. BB4 7RT Tel: 01706 214614 831044 (Bailiffs) Fax: 01706 219814 DX 702565 RAWTENSTALL 2	Court House, 1 Grange Street, Rawtenstall District Judges: J. M. Geddes
305	**READING** **SE** (22) **District Registry** *Bankruptcy* *Care Centre*	Mrs. L. Storey, 160-163 Friar Street, Reading RG1 1HE Tel: 0118 987 0500 Fax: 0118 987 0555 959 9827 DX 98010 READING 6	160-163 Friar Street, Reading District Judges: G. Burgess S. Henson J. R. Davidson R. Henry C. Darbyshire
306	**REDDITCH** **M** (13)	Mrs. L. Gailey, Court Office, 13 Church Road, Redditch, Worcs. B97 4AB Tel: 01527 67822 Fax: 01527 65791 DX 701880 REDDITCH 2	Court House, 13 Church Road, Redditch District Judges: M. Nield P. R. McKenzie
	REDHILL, *see* **REIGATE**		
	REDRUTH, *see* **CAMBORNE AND REDRUTH**		
307	**REIGATE** **SE** (21) *Divorce*	Mrs. S. McGinty (Acting), Law Courts, Hatchlands Road, Redhill, Surrey RH1 6BL Tel: 01737 763637 Fax: 01737 766917 DX 98020 REDHILL WEST	Law Courts, Hatchlands Road, Redhill District Judges: A. Levey H. A. J. Letts I. Kubiak A. Raeside D. Beck

COUNTY COURTS

Court No	Location, Region and Additional Jurisdiction	Court Manager and Court Offices	Court House and District Judges
308	**RHYL** **WAL** (7) **District Registry** Bankruptcy Care Centre Family Hearing Centre	S. Forsythe, The Courthouse, Clwyd Street, Rhyl, Denbighshire LL18 3LA Tel: 01745 352940 Fax: 01745 336726 DX 702489 RHYL 2	The Courthouse, Clwyd Street, Rhyl District Judges: O. W. Williams J. G. Thomas
309	**ROCHDALE**	(CLOSED wef 7/9/98 – successor courts – Oldham and Rawtenstall)	
387	**ROMFORD,** see LONDON		
310	**ROTHERHAM** **NE** (6) Family Hearing Centre	Mrs. S. Frost, Rotherham Law Courts, The Statutes, Off Main Street, Rotherham S60 1YW Tel: 01709 839339 Fax: 01709 370082 DX 703025 ROTHERHAM 4	Rotherham Law Courts, The Statutes, off Main Street, Rotherham District Judges: T. W. Hill K. Woodhead B. J. Clark
311	**RUGBY** **M** (10)	Sandra O'Neil (Acting), The New Courthouse, Newbold Road, Rugby CV21 2LQ Tel: 01788 542543 Fax: 01788 866004 DX 701934 RUGBY 2	The New Courthouse, Newbold Road, Rugby District Judge: Sanghera
312	**RUNCORN** **M** (3) Divorce	Mr. G. A. Allman, The Law Courts, Legh Street, Warrington, Cheshire WA1 1UR Tel: 01925 256700 Fax: 01925 413335 DX 702501 WARRINGTON 3	The Law Courts, Halton Lea, Runcorn District Judge: G. W. Little
313	**ST. ALBANS** **SE** (18) Bankruptcy	Jacqui Brownsell, Victoria House, 117 Victoria Street, St. Albans, Herts. AL1 3TJ Tel: 01727 856925 Fax: 01727 852484 DX 97770 ST. ALBANS 2	Victoria House, 117 Victoria Street, St. Albans District Judge: G. Field
314	**ST. AUSTELL**	(CLOSED wef 30/3/96 – successor courts – Bodmin and Truro)	

COUNTY COURTS

Court No	Location, Region and Additional Jurisdiction	Court Manager and Court Offices	Court House and District Judges
315	**ST. HELENS** NW (3) District Registry Divorce	Sheila Jones, 1st Floor, Rexmore House, Cotham Street, St. Helens, Merseyside WA10 1SE Tel: 01744 27544 759173 (Bailiffs (answerphone)) Fax: 01744 20484 DX 725020 ST HELENS 4	The Law Courts, Corporation Street, St. Helens District Judges: I. Bennett M. Peake I. R. Knifton

316	**SALFORD**
	
	NW (2)
	
	District Registry
	
	Bankruptcy
	Divorce
		Mr. M. Huddleston,
		Prince William House,
		Peel Cross Road,
		Salford, Lancashire M5 4RR
		Tel: 0161 745 7511
		     0161 742 9812 (Civil)
		                 9819 (Enforcement)
		                 9813 (Cash & Issue)
		Fax: 0161 745 7202
		DX 702630 SALFORD 5
			Prince William House,
			Peel Cross Road,
			Salford, Lancashire
			M5 4RR
			
			District Judges:
			D. B. Chapman
			M. Hovington
			A. Obodai

317	**SALISBURY**
	
	SW (16)
	
	District Registry
	
	Bankruptcy
	Divorce
	Family Hearing
	   Centre
		Mrs. Alison Cannon,
		Salisbury Combined
		   Court Centre,
		Courts of Justice,
		Alexandra House,
		St. John Street,
		Salisbury, Wilts. SP1 2PN
		Tel: 01722 325444
		Fax: 01722 412991
		DX 98500 SALISBURY 2
			Courts of Justice,
			Alexandra House,
			St. John Street,
			Salisbury
			
			District Judges:
			N. J. Murphy
			D. Asplin

318	**SCARBOROUGH** NE (5) District Registry Bankruptcy Family Hearing Centre	I. Marshall, Pavilion House, Valley Bridge Road, Scarborough, N. Yorks YO11 2JS Tel: 01723 366361 Fax: 01723 501992 DX 65140 SCARBOROUGH 2	Pavilion House, Valley Bridge Road, Scarborough District Judge: R. N. Hill
319	**SCUNTHORPE** NE (6) District Registry Bankruptcy Divorce	Miss. M. A. McElhinney, Scunthorpe Court Centre, Corporation Road, Scunthorpe, N. Lincs. DN15 6QB Tel: 01724 281100 Fax: 01724 281890 DX 742212 SCUNTHORPE 10	Scunthorpe Court Centre, Corporation Road, Scunthorpe District Judges: J. S. Robinson S. Chesterfield
723	**SEVENOAKS**	(CLOSED wef 5/4/94 – successor court – Tunbridge Wells)	
724	**SHAFTESBURY**	(CLOSED wef 5/12/94 – successor court – Yeovil)	

COUNTY COURTS

Court No	Location, Region and Additional Jurisdiction	Court Manager and Court Offices	Court House and District Judges
725	**SHEERNESS**	(CLOSED wef 5/4/94 – successor court – Sittingbourne)	
320	**SHEFFIELD** **NE** (6) **District Registry** *Bankruptcy* *Care Centre*	D. Crossfield, Sheffield Combined Court Centre, The Law Courts, 50 West Bar, Sheffield S3 8PH Tel: 0114 281 2400 Fax: 0114 281 2425 DX 703028 SHEFFIELD 6	The Law Courts, 50 West Bar, Sheffield *District Judges:* D. Kirkham D. A. Oldham P. Mort C. J. Birkby T. W. Hill Mrs. M. Young
321	**SHOREDITCH,** *see* **LONDON**		
322	**SHREWSBURY** **M** (13) **District Registry** *Bankruptcy* *Divorce*	Miss. C. Thompson, 4th Floor, Cambrian Business Centre, Chester Street, Shrewsbury SY1 1NA Tel: 01743 289069 Fax: 01743 237954 DX 702047 SHREWSBURY 3	3rd Floor, Cambrian Business Centre, Chester Street, Shrewsbury *District Judges:* S. Rogers A. W. Brown
323	**SITTINGBOURNE**	CLOSED wef 30/3/96 – successor courts – Maidstone and Medway)	

324	**SKEGNESS**
	
	M (12)
		D. J. Woodward,
		c/o Boston County Court,
		55 Norfolk Street,
		Boston,
		Lincolnshire PE21 6PE
		  Tel: 01205 366080
		  Fax: 01205 311692
		DX 701922 BOSTON 2
			The Court House,
			Park Avenue,
			Skegness
			
			District Judge:
			A. R. Maw

325	**SKIPTON** **NE** (5) *Family Hearing* *Centre*	Miss. Dawn Marie Shie (Acting), The Law Courts, Otley Street, Skipton, N. Yorks. BD23 1RH Tel: 01756 692650 Fax: 01756 692655 DX 703031 SKIPTON 2	The Law Courts, Otley Street, Skipton *District Judges:* J. A. B. Buchan G. Y. Lingard
326	**SLEAFORD**	(CLOSED wef 16/2/96 – successor courts – Boston, Grantham, Lincoln and Newark)	

COUNTY COURTS

Court No	Location, Region and Additional Jurisdiction	Court Manager and Court Offices	Court House and District Judges
327	**SLOUGH** **SE** (22) *Bankruptcy* *Family Hearing Centre*	Mrs. P. Hazell, The Law Courts, Windsor Road, Slough SL1 2HE Tel: 01753 690300 Fax: 01753 575990 DX 98030 SLOUGH 3	The Law Courts, Windsor Road, Slough District Judge: S. Jones T. Parker K. McCulloch P. Devlin
328	**SOUTHAMPTON** **SW** (17) **District Registry** *Bankruptcy* *Family Hearing Centre* *Race Relations*	Mrs. Helen Williams, Southampton Combined Court Centre, The Courts of Justice, London Road, Southampton, Hants. SO15 2XQ Tel: 023 8021 3200 Fax: 023 8021 3222 (County Court) 023 8021 3234 (Crown Court) 023 8021 3232 (Listing) 023 8021 3227 (Bailiffs) DX 111000 SOUTHAMPTON 11	The Courts of Justice, London Road, Southampton District Judges: M. H. Tennant J. D. Ainsworth R. Naylor J. S. Sparrow
329	**SOUTHEND** **SE** (18) **District Registry** *Trial Centre* *Bankruptcy* *Family Hearing Centre*	Mrs. C. Wallner, County Court, Tylers House, Tylers Avenue, Southend-on-Sea, Essex SS1 2AW Tel: 01702 601991 Fax: 01702 603090 DX 97780 SOUTHEND ON SEA 2	Tylers House, Tylers Avenue, Southend-on-Sea District Judges: C. B. Chandler R. D. Dudley A. Rowley L. Grosse
330	**SOUTHPORT** **NW** (3) **District Registry** *Divorce*	Mr. Philip Green, Duke's House, 34 Hoghton Street, Southport, Merseyside PR9 0PU Tel: 01704 531541 535027 (Bailiffs' Office) Fax: 01704 542487 DX 702580 SOUTHPORT 2	Duke's House, 34 Hoghton Street, Albert Road, Southport District Judges: P. Bellamy G. A. Humphreys-Roberts
331	**SOUTH SHIELDS** **NE** (4) **District Registry** *Admiralty* *Divorce*	Carol Gallagher, South Tyneside Law Courts, Millbank, Secretan Way, South Shields, Tyne & Wear NE33 1RG Tel: 0191-456 3343 Fax: 0191-427 9503 DX 65143 SOUTH SHIELDS 3	Law Courts, Millbank, Secretan Way District Judges: D. E. Lascelles H. Scott-Phillips

COUNTY COURTS

Court No	Location, Region and Additional Jurisdiction	Court Manager and Court Offices	Court House and District Judges
332	**SPALDING**	(CLOSED wef 16/2/96 – successor courts – Boston, Grantham and Peterborough)	
333	**STAFFORD** **M** (13) **District Registry** *Bankruptcy* *Family Hearing Centre*	Ilse Tivenan, Stafford Combined Court Centre, Victoria Square, Stafford ST16 2QQ Tel: 01785 610730 Fax: 01785 213250 (County) DX 703190 STAFFORD 4	Combined Court Centre, Victoria Square, Stafford *District Judges:* J. I. Ilsley J. Jack
334	**STAINES** **SE** (21) *Divorce*	Mr. R. Lynch, The Law Courts, Knowle Green, Staines, Middx. TW18 1XH Tel: 01784 459175 Fax: 01784 460176 DX 98040 STAINES 2	The Law Courts, Knowle Green, Staines *District Judges:* V. S. Batcup R. Karp
335	**STAMFORD**	(CLOSED wef 1/10/84 – successor court – Peterborough)	
336	**STOCKPORT** **NW** (2) **District Registry** *Bankruptcy* *Family Hearing Centre*	Janette Plunkett, 'Heron House', Wellington Street, Stockport, Cheshire SK1 3DJ Tel: 0161-474 7707 Fax: 0161-476 3129 DX 702621 STOCKPORT 4	'Heron House', Wellington Street, Stockport *District Judges:* A. J. C. Brazier J. Clegg J. P. Horan P. S. Dignan I. Lettall
337	**STOCKTON-ON-TEES**	(CLOSED wef 2/11/94 – resited to form Teeside Combined Court Centre)	
338	**STOKE-ON-TRENT** **M** (13) **District Registry** *Bankruptcy* *Care Centre*	Mrs. S. Hooper, Stoke-on-Trent Combined Court Centre, Bethesda Street, Hanley, Stoke-on-Trent, Staffs. ST1 3BP Tel: 01782 854 000 Fax: 01782 854 046 854 014 DX 703360 HANLEY 3	Bethesda Street, Hanley, Stoke-on-Trent *District Judges:* L. Schroeder J. I. Ilsley J. Jack P. Rank R. Chapman

COUNTY COURTS

Court No	Location, Region and Additional Jurisdiction	Court Manager and Court Offices	Court House and District Judges
339	**STOURBRIDGE** **M** (13) *Bankruptcy*	Mrs. S. M. Daniels, 7 Hagley Road, Stourbridge, W. Mids. DY8 1QL Tel: 01384 394232 440182 (Bailiffs only) Fax: 01384 441736 DX 701889 STOURBRIDGE 2	Hagley Road, Stourbridge *District Judges:* S. Dowding J. George
340	**STRATFORD-UPON-AVON** **M** (10)	Mrs. J. George, 5 Elm Court, Arden Street, Stratford-upon-Avon, Warwickshire CV37 6PA Tel: 01789 293056 Fax: 01789 414973 DX 701998 STRATFORD-UPON-AVON 1	5 Elm Court, Arden Street, Stratford-upon-Avon CV37 6PA *District Judge:* A. Jones
341	**STROUD**	(CLOSED wef 4/7/94 – successor court – Gloucester)	
342	**SUDBURY**	(CLOSED wef 5/4/94 – successor courts – Bury St. Edmunds, Braintree, Colchester and Ipswich)	
343	**SUNDERLAND** **NE** (4) **District Registry** *Bankruptcy* *Care Centre*	Mrs. A. Neary, The Court House, 44 John Street, Sunderland SR1 1RB Tel: 0191-568 0750 Minicom: 0191 478 1476 Fax: 0191-514 3028 DX 65149 SUNDERLAND 2	The Court House, John Street, Sunderland *District Judges:* D. Lascelles D. Scott-Phillips G. Marley B. Stapely
344	**SWANSEA** **WAL** (8) **District Registry** *Bankruptcy* *Care Centre* *Family Hearing Centre* *Civil Justice Centre*	Miss M. Edwards, M.B.E., Caravella House, Quay West,, Quay Parade, Swansea SA1 1SP Tel: 01792 510350 Fax: 01792 473520 DX 99740 SWANSEA 5	Caravella House, Quay West, Quay Parade, Swansea *District Judges:* T. J. Lewis P. Evans P. Llewellyn, O.B.E.

345	**SWINDON**
	
	SE (16)
	
	District Registry
	
	Bankruptcy
	Care Centre
	Family Hearing Centre
		Mrs. L. Thompson,
		Swindon Combined
		  Court Centre,
		The Law Courts,
		Islington Street,
		Swindon, Wilts. SN1 2HG
		Tel: 01793 690500 (General Enquiries)
		Fax: 01793 690555
		DX 98430 SWINDON 5
			(1) The Law Courts,
			    Islington Street,
			    Swindon
			(2) Court House,
			    The Forum,
			    Cirencester
			
			District Judges:
			D. Adam
			B. Carron

COUNTY COURTS

Court No	Location, Region and Additional Jurisdiction	Court Manager and Court Offices	Court House and District Judges
112	**TAMESIDE** NW (2) *Bankruptcy* *Divorce*	Mr. Patrick Ward, P.O. Box 166 Henry Square, Ashton-under-Lyne, Lancashire OL6 7TP Tel: 0161 331 5614 Fax: 0161 331 5649	Henry Square, Ashton-under-Lyne District Judges: C. Osborne P. S. Stockton R. R. P. Ackroyd C. Fox
346	**TAMWORTH** M (13)	Miss S. Howis, Mrs. R. Bolton, The Precinct, Lower Gungate, Tamworth, Staffs. B79 7AJ Tel: 01827 62664 55011 (Bailiffs) Fax: 01827 65289 DX 702016 TAMWORTH 2	The Precinct, Lower Gungate, Tamworth District Judge: R. Chapman

347	**TAUNTON**
	
	SW (14)
	
	District Registry
	
	Bankruptcy
	Care Centre
	Family Hearing
	* Centre*
	Trial Centre
		Miss. M. Dell,
		Taunton County Court,
		Shire Hall,
		Taunton,
		Somerset TA1 4EU
		Tel: 01823 281110
		Fax: 01823 351337
		DX 98410 TAUNTON 2
			(1) Shire Hall,
			    Taunton
			(2) Bridgwater
			    Magistrates' Court,
			    The Courthouse,
			    Northgate,
			    Bridgwater,
			    Somerset TA1 4EU
			
			District Judges:
			D. White
			Miss J. M. R. Dowell

364	**TELFORD** M (13) *Adoption Centre* *Care Centre* *Trial Centre* *Divorce*	Mrs. I. Wetherburn, Telford County Court, Telford Square, Malinsgate, Town Centre, Telford, Shropshire TF3 4JP Tel: 01952 238280 Fax: 01952 291601 DX 701976 TELFORD 3	Telford Square, Malinsgate, Telford District Judges: S. Rogers R. D. Chapman J. A. Jack
348	**THANET** SE (20) **District Registry** *Divorce*	Brett Stevenson, The Court House, 2nd Floor, Cecil Square, Margate, Kent CT9 1RL Tel: 01843 221722 Fax: 01843 222730 DX 98210 CLIFTONVILLE 2	The Court House, 2nd Floor, Cecil Square, Margate District Judges: R. Hicks G. Parnell N. Jackson W. Jackson

COUNTY COURTS

Court No	Location, Region and Additional Jurisdiction	Court Manager and Court Offices	Court House and District Judges
350	**THORNE**	(CLOSED wef 4/1/94 – successor court – Doncaster)	
351	**TONBRIDGE**	(CLOSED wef 1/10/84 – successor court – Tunbridge Wells)	
727	**TODMORDEN**	(CLOSED wef 28/10/91 – successor court – Halifax)	

352	**TORQUAY AND NEWTON ABBOT**
	
	SW (15)
	
	District Registry
	
	Bankruptcy
	Divorce
		Mrs. Debbie Crispin,
		The Willows,
		Nicholson Road,
		Torquay,
		Devon TQ2 7AZ
		  Tel: 01803 616791
		      01803 617031 (Listing)
		  Fax: 01803 616795
		DX 98740 TORQUAY 4
			Nicholson Road,
			Torquay
			
			District Judges:
			  Mrs. B. G. Meredith
			  Mr. S. W. Arnold

353	**TROWBRIDGE**
	
	SW (16)
	
	Divorce
		Mrs. M. D. Hamnett,
		Ground Floor,
		Clarks Mill,
		Stallard Street,
		Trowbridge,
		Wilts. BA14 8DB
		  Tel: 01225 752101
		      893012/3 (Bailiffs)
		  Fax: 01225 776638
		DX 98750 TROWBRIDGE 2
			District Judges:
			  M. Rutherford
			  F. Goddard
			  D. Asplin

354	**TRURO**
	
	SW (15)
	
	District Registry
	
	Bankruptcy
	Care Court
	  Family Hearing
	  Centre
		Mr. P. Rodda,
		Truro County Court,
		Courts of Justice,
		Edward Street,
		Truro,
		Cornwall TR1 2PB
		  Tel: 01872 222340
		  Fax: 01872 222348
		DX 135396 TRURO 2
			Courts of Justice,
			Edward Street,
			Truro
			
			District Judges:
			  P. Mitchell
			  R. Griggs
			  L. Thomas

355	**TUNBRIDGE WELLS**
	
	SE (20)
	
	District Registry
	
	Bankruptcy
	Divorce
		Mrs. S. Collins,
		Merevale House,
		42-46 London Road,
		Tunbridge Wells,
		Kent TN1 1DP
		  Tel: 01892 515515
		  Fax: 01892 513676
		DX 98220 TUNBRIDGE WELLS 3
			1st Floor,
			Merevale House,
			42-46 London Road,
			Tunbridge Wells
			
			District Judges:
			  C. J. Lethem
			  T. P. McLoughlin
			  D. Hebblethwaite
			  A. Grand

356	**UXBRIDGE,** see LONDON		

COUNTY COURTS

Court No	Location, Region and Additional Jurisdiction	Court Manager and Court Offices	Court House and District Judges

357	**WAKEFIELD**
	
	NE (5)
	
	District Registry
	
	Bankruptcy
	Family Hearing
	Centre
		Mrs. S. Lally,
		Crown House,
		127 Kirkgate,
		Wakefield, W. Yorks.
		WF1 1JW
		Tel: 01924 370268
		         291257 (Bailiffs)
		         299161 (Court Manager)
		Fax: 01924 200818
		DX 703040 WAKEFIELD 3
			Crown House,
			127 Kirkgate,
			Wakefield
			
			District Judge:
			M. Glentworth

358	**WALSALL** **M** (13) **District Registry** *Bankruptcy* *Family Hearing* *Centre*	Mr. A. Bennett, Bridge House, Bridge Street, Walsall, W. Mids. WS1 1JQ Tel: 01922 728855 Fax: 01922 728891 DX 701943 WALSALL 2	Bridge House, Bridge Street, Walsall *District Judges:* S. Gailey S. Middleton R. Hearne M. Anson M. Ellery
359	**WANDSWORTH,** *see* LONDON		
360	**WARRINGTON** **NW** (3) **District Registry** *Bankruptcy* *Care Centre* *Family Hearing* *Centre*	Mr. G. A. Allman, Law Courts, Legh Street, Warrington WA1 1UR Tel: 01925 256700 Fax: 01925 413335 DX 702501 WARRINGTON 3	Law Courts, Legh Street, Warrington *District Judges:* Mrs. H. Dawson G. Perry
361	**WARWICK** **M** (10) *Bankruptcy*	Mrs. J. A. Beckett, Warwick Combined Court Centre, Northgate South Side, Warwick CV34 4RB Tel: 01926 492276 Fax: 01926 411855 DX 701964 WARWICK 2	Shire Hall, Northgate Street, Warwick *District Judge:* A. S. Jones
362	**WATFORD** **SE** (18) *Care Centre* *Family Proceedings* *Court*	Mrs. Y. McKenna-Young, Cassiobury House, 11-19 Station Road, Watford, Herts. WD17 1EZ Tel: 01923 699400/1 Fax: 01923 251317 DX 122740 WATFORD 5	Cassiobury House, 11-19 Station Road, Watford *District Judges:* R. A. Davis P. Carr J. Rhodes S. Sethi

COUNTY COURTS

Court No	Location, Region and Additional Jurisdiction	Court Manager and Court Offices	Court House and District Judges
363	**WELLINGBOROUGH** **M** (12)	Mrs. Joanne Gurney, Lothersdale House, West Villa Road, Wellingborough, Northants NN8 4NF Tel: 01933 226168 Fax: 01933 272977 DX 701883 WELLINGBOROUGH 2	Lothersdale House, West Villa Road, Wellingborough District Judges: P. McHale I. Murdoch
364	**WELLINGTON** renamed TELFORD COUNTY COURT, *q.v.* (Shropshire)		
	WELLS, *see* BRISTOL		
366	**WELSHPOOL AND NEWTOWN** **WAL** (8) **District Registry** *Bankruptcy* *Family Hearing Centre*	Mrs. E. McCarthy, The Mansion House, 24 Severn Street, Welshpool, Powys SY21 7UX Tel: 01938 552004 Fax: 01938 555395 DX 702524 WELSHPOOL 2	The Mansion House, 24 Severn Street, Welshpool District Judges: V. Reeves G. Perry
367	**WEST BROMWICH**	(CLOSED wef 24/12/98 – successor courts – Birmingham, Dudley and Walsall)	
368	**WEST LONDON,** *see* LONDON		
369	**WESTMINSTER,** *see* LONDON		
370	**WESTON-SUPER-MARE** **SW** (14) *Divorce*	K. Dunn, The Hedges, St. Georges, Weston-Super-mare BS22 7BB Tel: 01934 626967 627787 Fax: 01934 643028	The Hedges, St. Georges, Weston-super-Mare District Judge: P. Corrigan

371	**WEYMOUTH**
	
	SW (16)
	
	District Registry
	
	Bankruptcy
	Divorce
	Family Hearing Centre
		Mrs. S. A. Allport,
		Weymouth & Dorchester
		  Combined Court Centre,
		Westwey House.
		Westwey Road,
		Weymouth, Dorset
		DT4 8TE
		Tel: 01305 752510
		Fax: 01305 788293
		DX 98820 WEYMOUTH 3
			(1) Westwey House,
			    Westwey Road,
			    Weymouth
			(2) County Hall,
			    Dorchester
			
			District Judge:
			J. Freeman

730	**WHITBY**	(CLOSED wef 4/1/94 – successor court – Scarborough)	

COUNTY COURTS

Court No	Location, Region and Additional Jurisdiction	Court Manager and Court Offices	Court House and District Judges
373	**WHITEHAVEN** NW (1) **District Registry** *Bankruptcy* *Divorce*	Mrs. C. Andrews, Old Town Hall, Duke Street, Whitehaven, Cumbria CA28 7NU Tel: 01946 67788 Fax: 01946 691219 DX 63990 WHITEHAVEN 2	Old Town Hall, Duke Street, Whitehaven *District Judge:* J. K. Park
374	**WIGAN** NW (2) **District Registry** *Bankruptcy* *Divorce*	M. A. Williams, Crawford Street, Wigan, Lancs. WN1 1NG Tel: 01942 246481 Fax: 01942 829164	Crawford Street, Wigan *District Judges:* E. Donnelly S. Jackson I. Sanderson
375	**WILLESDEN,** see LONDON		
376	**WINCHESTER** SW (17) **District Registry** *Bankruptcy* *Divorce*	Mrs. L. Nother, Winchester Combined Court Centre, The Law Courts, Winchester, Hants. SO23 9EL Tel: 01962 814100 Fax: 01962 853821 DX 98520 WINCHESTER 3	The Law Courts, Winchester *District Judge:* N. J. Murphy
377	**WISBECH**	(CLOSED wef 29/9/95 – successor court – King's Lynn)	
378	**WOLVERHAMPTON** M (13) **District Registry** *Bankruptcy* *Care Centre*	Mrs. G. Pedder, Wolverhampton Combined Court Centre, Pipers Row, Wolverhampton, W. Mids. WV1 3LQ Tel: 01902 481000 Fax: 01902 481001 DX 702019 WOLVERHAMPTON 4	Combined Court Centre, Pipers Row, Wolverhampton *District Judge:* R. Hearne
379	**WOOLWICH,** see LONDON		
380	**WORCESTER** M (13) **District Registry** *Bankruptcy* *Care Centre* *Trial Centre*	Mrs. J. Lloyd, Worcester Combined Court Centre, Shirehall, Foregate Street, Worcester WR1 1EQ Tel: 01905 730800 Fax: 01905 730801 DX 721120 WORCESTER 11	Shirehall, Foregate Street, Worcester *District Judges:* E. Dickinson M. Parry A. Marston P. Mackenzie M. Nield
381	**WORKINGTON**	(CLOSED wef 2/1/01 – successor court – Whitehaven)	

COUNTY COURTS

Court No	Location, Region and Additional Jurisdiction	Court Manager and Court Offices	Court House and District Judges
382	**WORKSOP** **M** (11)	P. Smith, 8 Slack Walk, Worksop, Notts. S80 1LN Tel: 01909 472358 Fax: 01909 530181 DX 702190 WORKSOP 2	8 Slack Walk, Worksop *District Judges:* R. L. Hudson S. C. W. Smith
383	**WORTHING** **SE** (21) **District Registry** *Divorce*	B. D. Hollingdale, The Law Courts, Christchurch Road, Worthing, West Sussex BN11 1JD Tel: 01903 221920 Fax: 01903 235559 DX 98230 WORTHING 4	Law Courts, Christchurch Road, Worthing *District Judge:* C. Edwards
384	**WREXHAM** **WAL** (7) **District Registry** *Bankruptcy* *Family Hearing Centre* *Race Relations*	Miss L. A. Hyde, 2nd Floor, Crown Buildings, 31 Chester Street, Wrexham, Clwyd LL13 8XN Tel: 01978 296140 Fax: 01978 290677 DX 721921 WREXHAM 4	2nd Floor, Crown Buildings, 31 Chester Street, Wrexham *District Judges:* G. Perry V. Reeves
385	**YEOVIL** **SW** (14) **District Registry** *Bankruptcy* *Divorce* *Family Hearing Centre*	The Court Manager, 22 Hendford, Yeovil, Somerset BA20 2QD Tel: 01935 382150 Fax: 01935 410004 DX 98830 YEOVIL 2	22 Hendford, Yeovil *District Judge:* B. J. A. Smith
386	**YORK** **NE** (5) **District Registry** *Bankruptcy* *Care Centre*	Mrs. J. Hunter, Piccadilly House, 55 Piccadilly, York YO1 9WL Tel: 01904 688550 Fax: 01904 679963 DX 65165 YORK 4	Piccadilly House, 55 Piccadilly, York *District Judges:* P. J. E. Wildsmith M. F. Handley
387	**ROMFORD,** *see* p.31		
388	**MILTON KEYNES,** *see* p.35		
701	**ALNWICK**	(CLOSED wef 15/12/97 – successor courts – Morpeth and Berwick)	

COUNTY COURTS

Court No	Location, Region and Additional Jurisdiction	Court Manager and Court Offices	Court House and District Judges
702	**AXMINSTER AND CHARD**	(CLOSED wef 5/12/94 – successor court – Yeovil)	
703	**BERWICK-UPON-TWEED**	(CLOSED wef 15/12/97 – successor court – Morpeth and Berwick)	
704	**BEVERLEY**	(CLOSED wef 1/1/93 – successor court – Kingston-upon-Hull)	
705	**BLYTH**	(CLOSED wef 15/12/97 – successor courts – Morpeth and Berwick)	
707	**CARDIGAN**	(CLOSED wef 29/12/95 – successor court – Carmarthen)	
713	**HEXHAM**	(CLOSED wef 4/1/94 – successor court – Newcastle-upon-Tyne)	
714	**LAMPETER**	(CLOSED wef 5/12/94 – successor courts – Aberystwyth and Carmarthen)	
715	**LAUNCESTON**	(CLOSED wef 5/12/94 – successor court – Bodmin)	
719	**MALDON**	(CLOSED wef 30/6/92 – successor court – Chelmsford)	
720	**MALTON**	(CLOSED wef 4/1/94 – successor court – York)	
722	**NORTHALLERTON**	(CLOSED wef 1/4/92 – successor court – Darlington)	
723	**SEVENOAKS**	(CLOSED wef 5/4/94 – successor court – Tunbridge Wells)	
724	**SHAFTESBURY**	(CLOSED wef 5/12/94 – successor court – Yeovil)	
725	**SHEERNESS**	(CLOSED wef 5/4/94 – sucessor court – Sittingbourne)	
727	**TODMORDEN**	(CLOSED wef 28/10/91 – successor court – Halifax)	
730	**WHITBY**	(CLOSED wef 4/1/94 – successor court – Scarborough)	

COUNTY COURTS

NORTHERN IRELAND

Division	Court Offices and Business Manager	Court House
ARDS	Mrs. V. Brennan, Newtownards Court Office, The Courthouse, Regent Street, Newtownards, Co Down BT23 4LP Tel: 028 9181 4343 Fax: 028 9181 8024	Courthouse, Regent Street, Newtownards
ARMAGH AND SOUTH DOWN	Mrs. G. Campbell, Armagh Court Office, The Courthouse, The Mall, Armagh, Co Armagh BT61 9DJ Tel: 028 3752 2816 Fax: 028 3752 8194	Courthouse, Armagh
BELFAST (Belfast Recorder's Court)	Mr. K. Barr, Business Manager, Belfast Combined Courts, Laganside Courts, 45 Oxford Street, Belfast BT1 3LL Tel: 028 9072 4515 Fax: 028 9031 5219	Laganside Courts, 45 Oxford Street, Belfast Old Town Hall, Victoria Street, Belfast
FERMANAGH AND TYRONE	Mr. N. Elliott, Omagh Court Office, The Courthouse, High Street, Omagh, Co Tyrone BT78 1DU Tel: 028 8224 2056 Fax: 028 8225 1198	Courthouse, Omagh
LONDONDERRY (Londonderry Recorder's Court)	Miss. M. W. McKeegan, Londonderry Court Office, The Courthouse, Bishop Street, Londonderry BT48 6PQ Tel: 028 7136 3448 Fax: 028 7137 2059	Courthouse, Londonderry

COUNTY COURTS

Division	Court Offices and Business Manager	Court House
ANTRIM	Mrs. S. Hughes, Chief Clerk, Ballymena Court Office, The Courthouse, Albert Place, Ballymena, Co Antrim BT43 5BS Tel: 028 2564 9416 Fax: 028 2565 5371	Courthouse, Albert Place, Ballymena
CRAIGAVON	Miss. M. Elliott, Craigavon Court Office, The Courthouse, Central Way, Craigavon BT64 1AP Tel: 028 3834 1324 Fax: 028 3834 1243	Courthouse, Craigavon Courthouse, Lisburn

PART III

COURTS OF SUMMARY JURISDICTION

MAGISTRATES' COURTS

	Page
ENGLAND	5
WALES	100
NORTHERN IRELAND	113

SHERIFFS COURTS AND DISTRICT COURTS IN SCOTLAND ... 119
With Numerical Indices of Court Codes

GAZETTEER OF PLACES IN THE GREATER LONDON AREA ... 153

NUMERICAL INDEX TO COURT CODES of Courts of ... 159
Summary Jurisdiction in ENGLAND AND WALES

ALPHABETICAL INDEX TO COURTS OF SUMMARY JURISDICTION. 205
Including reference to Court Codes

LIST OF ABBREVIATIONS
used in Part III of this Directory

Accts.	Accounts	HMCE	Her Majesty's Customs and Excise
Admin.	Administration		
Adop.	Adoption		
Arrs.	Arrears	Juv.	Juvenile
BGL	Betting and Gaming Licensing	Lic.	Licensing
		LVL	Local Vehicle Licensing
Ccl.	Council	Misc.	Miscellaneous
CPS	Crown Prosecution Service	Mtce.	Maintenance
Ct.	Court	Mtwy.	Motorway
CT	Council Tax		
		NP	Non-Police
Dflt.	Default		
Dir.	Directions	PS	Petty Sessions
Dom.	Domestic	PTR	Pre-trial Review
EAH	Early Administrative Hearing	SDVC	Special Domestic Violence Court
EFH	Early First Hearing		
Enf.	Enforcement		
Enq.	Enquiries	TS	Transfer Sessions
FDir.	Family Directions		
FPC	Family Proceedings Court	VC	Video Court
Genl.	General	YC	Youth Court

HER MAJESTY'S COURT SERVICE ESTATE BY REGION AND AREA

North West Region

1. Cumbria and Lancashire
2. Greater Manchester
3. Cheshire and Merseyside

North East Region

4. Cleveland, Durham and Northumbria
5. North and West Yorkshire
6. Humber and South Yorkshire

HMCS Wales

7. North Wales
8. Mid and West Wales
9. South East Wales

Midlands Region

10. Birmingham, Coventry, Solihull and Warwickshire
11. Derbyshire and Nottinghamshire
12. Lincolnshire, Leicestershire & Rutland and Northamptonshire
13. Black Country, Staffordshire and West Mercia

South West Region

14. Avon & Somerset
15. Devon & Cornwall
16. Dorset, Gloucestershire and Wiltshire
17. Hampshire and The Isle of Wight

South East Region

18. Bedfordshire, Essex and Hertfordshire
19. Cambridgeshire, Norfolk and Suffolk
20. Kent
21. Surrey and Sussex
22. Thames Valley

London Region

23. Central and South (Crime)
24. North and West (Crime)
25. Civil and Family

SOUTH WEST REGION

AVON AND SOMERSET

Area Director: Rod White, Area Director's Office, PO Box 484, Queensway House, Weston Super Mare, Somerset BS23 9BJ. Tel: 01934 528500   Fax: 01934 528520
DX 152360 WESTON SUPER MARE 5

Adult Court No	Name of Court and Clerk/Legal Adviser		Normal Times and Places of Courts	
1022	**BATH AND WANSDYKE L.J.A.**			
	Mrs. E. A. Laken, Magistrates' Court, P.O. Box 3835, North Parade Road, Bath BA1 5XL	Adult – Daily, 10 a.m. and 2.15 p.m.	Magistrates' Court, North Parade Road, Bath	
		YC – Thursday, 10 a.m.	Do.	
	Tel: 01225 463281			
	Fax: 01225 420255	FPC – Wednesday, 10 a.m.	Do.	
	DX 138142 BATH 5			
	E-mail: av-bath.mc@hmcourts-service.gsi.gov.uk			
1013	**BRISTOL L.J.A.**			
	D. M. Speed, M.A., Magistrates' Court, Marlborough Street, Bristol BS1 3MU	Adult – Daily, 10 a.m.	Marlborough Street, Bristol	
		YC – Monday, Wednesday, Thursday and Friday, 10 a.m.	Do.	
	Tel: 0117 943 5100			
	Fax: 0117 925 0443	FPC – Tuesday and Wednesday, 10 a.m.	Do.	
	DX 78126 BRISTOL			
	E-mail: av-bristol.mc@hmcourts-service.gsi.gov.uk			
2715	**MENDIP L.J.A.**			
	Mrs E. A. Laken, Magistrates' Court, P.O. Box 3835, North Parade Road, Bath BA1 5XL	Adult – Monday, 10 a.m.	The Court House, Oakfield Road, Frome	
		Thursday, 10 a.m.	The Court House, Oakfield Road, Frome	
		YC – Two in four Wednesdays in month, 10 a.m.	The Court House, Oakfield Road, Frome	
	Tel: 01225 463281			
	Fax: 01225 420255	FPC – One in four Wednesdays in month, 10 a.m.	Town Hall, Wells	
	DX 138142 BATH 5	One in four Wednesdays in month, 10 a.m.	The Court House, Oakfield Road, Frome	
	E-mail: av-bath.mc@hmcourts-service.gsi.gov.uk			

AVON AND SOMERSET

Adult Court No	Name of Court and Clerk/Legal Adviser	Normal Times and Places of Courts	
1021	**NORTH AVON L.J.A.**		
	Mrs. E. A. Laken, Barrister, Magistrates' Court, Kennedy Way, Yate, South Gloucestershire BS37 4PY	Adult – Daily, 10 a.m. and 2.15 p.m.	Magistrates' Court, Kennedy Way, Yate
		YC – Tuesday, 10 a.m.	Do.
		FPC – Thursday, 10 a.m.	Do.
	Tel: 01454 310505 01454 338201 (Family) 01454 338200 (Enforcement)		
	Fax: 01454 319404 (General and Family)		
	DX 47260 YATE		
	E-mail: AV-yate.mc@hmcourts-service.gsi.gov.uk		
1023	**NORTH SOMERSET L.J.A.**		
	T. G. Moore, LL.M., B.A., North Somerset Courthouse, The Hedges, St Georges, Weston-super-Mare BS22 7BB	Adult – Monday, Tuesday, Wednesday, Thursday and Friday, 10 a.m.	North Somerset Courthouse, The Hedges, St Georges, Weston-super-Mare
		YC – Wednesday, 10 a.m.	Do.
	Tel: 01934 528500	FPC – Thursday, 2 p.m.	Do.
	Fax: 01934 528599		
	DX 152361 WSM5		
	E-mail: av-weston.mc@hmcourts-service.gsi.gov.uk		
2706	**SEDGEMOOR L.J.A.**		
	T. G. Moore, LL.M., B.A., The Court House, Northgate, Bridgwater, Somerset TA6 3YL	Adult – Monday, Tuesday, Wednesday, Thursday and Friday, 10 a.m.	Court House, Northgate, Bridgwater
		YC – Friday, 10 a.m.	Do.
	Tel: 01823 257084		
	Fax: 01823 335195	FPC – Tuesday, 10 a.m.	Do.
	DX 122473 TAUNTON 7		
	E-mail: av-taunton.mc@hmcourts-service.gsi.gov.uk		

AVON AND SOMERSET

Adult
Court *Name of Court and*
No *Clerk/Legal Adviser*   *Normal Times and Places of Courts*

2714 SOUTH SOMERSET L.J.A.

T. G. Moore, LL.M., B.A.,	Adult – Monday, Tuesday and Thursday, 10 a.m.	The Law Courts, Petters Way, Yeovil
The Law Courts, Petters Way, Yeovil, Somerset	YC – Wednesday, 10 a.m.	Do.
BA20 1SW	FPC – Wednesday, 10 a.m.	Do.
Tel: 01935 426281	Dom – Tuesday, 10 a.m.	Do.
Fax: 01935 431022	Trials – Tuesday and friday (and as required), 10 a.m.	Do.
DX 100537 YEOVIL		

E-mail: av-yeovil.mc@hmcourts-service.gsi.gov.uk

2709 TAUNTON DEANE AND WEST SOMERSET L.J.A.

T. G. Moore, LL.M., B.A., Magistrates' Court, St. John's Road, Taunton, Somerset TA1 4AX	Adult – Monday, Tuesday, Wednesday, Thursday and Friday, 10 a.m.	Magistrates' Court, St. John's Road, Taunton
		Townsend Road, Minehead
Tel: 01823 257084	YC – Every first, third, fourth and fifth Tuesday in month, 10 a.m.	Magistrates' Court, St. John's Road, Taunton
Fax: 01823 335195		
DX 122473 TAUNTON 7	Second Tuesday in month	Townsend Road, Minehead
	FPC – Every first, third, fourth and fifth Tuesday in month, 10 a.m.	Magistrates' Court, St. John's Road, Taunton
	Second Tuesday in month	Townsend Road, Minehead

E-mail: av-taunton.mc@hmcourts-service.gsi.gov.uk

SOUTH EAST REGION

BEDFORDSHIRE, ESSEX AND HERTFORDSHIRE

Area Director: Mike Littlewood, Area Director's Office, 1st Floor, Steeple House, Church Lane, Chelmsford, Essex CM1 1NA. Tel: 01245 287974 Fax: 01245 341369
DX 97375 CHELMSFORD 3

NOTE: With effect from November 2007 the Area Director's Office will be located at Priory Place, Chelmsford, Essex CM1 0PP.

Head of Legal Services (Bedfordshire): David Gibbs, South Bedfordshire Magistrates' Court, Stewart Street, Luton LU1 5BL. Tel: 01582 524200 Fax: 01582 524252
DX 151660 LUTON 16

Head of Legal Services (Essex): T. Szagun, Osprey House, Hedgerows Business Park, Colchester Road, Springfield, Chelmsford, Essex CM2 5PF.
Tel: 01245 313500 Fax: 01245 313399 DX 151020 CHELMSFORD 17

Adult Court No	Name of Court and Clerk/Legal Adviser	Normal Times and Places of Courts	
1051	**BEDFORD AND MID BEDFORDSHIRE L.J.A.**		
	L. Ladlow, 3 St Paul's Square, Bedford MK40 1SQ Tel: 01234 319100 Fax: 01234 319114 DX 729420 BEDFORD 10	Adult – Every day, 10 a.m.	Shire Hall, Bedford
		YC – Wednesday, 10 a.m.	Do.
		FPC – Friday, 10 a.m.	Do.
1892	**CENTRAL HERTFORDSHIRE L.J.A.**		
	David Gibbs, The Court House, Civic Centre, St. Peter's Street, St. Albans, Herts. AL1 3LB Tel: 01727 816834/37 (Court Support) 816832 (Family) 01923 699412 (Fines) Fax: 01727 816829 DX 6172 ST. ALBANS	Adult – Monday to Friday, 10 a.m.	Court House, Civic Centre, St. Albans
		YC – Thursday, 10 a.m.	Do.
		FPC – Wednesdays, 10 a.m.	Do.
		Fines – Thursdays, 10 a.m.	Do.

BEDFORDSHIRE, ESSEX AND HERTFORDSHIRE

Adult Court No	Name of Court and Clerk/Legal Adviser	Normal Times and Places of Courts	

1888 EAST HERTFORDSHIRE L.J.A.

Paul Fellingham,
Bayley House,
Sish Lane,
Stevenage,
Herts. SG1 3SS

Adult – Monday to Friday, 10 a.m.   Shire Hall, Fore Street, Hertford

Tel: 01438 730412 (Admin)
01923 699412 (Family)
01438 730400 (Payments Central Accounting Unit)
01438 730415 (Legal Aid Processing Unit)
01923 297540 (Central Enforcement Unit)

YC – Tuesday, 10 a.m.   Do.

Fax: 01438 730413 (Admin)
01923 251317 (Family)
01438 730407 (Central Accounting Unit)
01438 730417 (Legal Aid Processing Unit)
01923 297555 (Central Enforcement Unit)

Fines – Tuesdays, 10 a.m.   Do.

DX 122187 OLD STEVENAGE

1055 LUTON AND SOUTH BEDFORDSHIRE L.J.A.

Mrs. L. Ladlow,
South Bedfordshire Magistrates' Courts,
Stuart Street,
Luton, Beds. LU1 5BL

Adult – Daily, 10.00 a.m.   Luton Magistrates' Court, Stuart Street, Luton

YC – Tuesday (and as required), 10 a.m.   Do

Tel: 01582 524200
Fax: 01582 524252

FPC – Wednesday 10 a.m. (and as required)   Do

E-mail: loraine.ladlow@hmcourts-service.gsi.gov.uk

DX 151660 LUTON 16

CENTRAL PAYMENTS UNIT

Bedfordshire Magistrates' Court,
PO Box 936,
Luton
LU1 5TJ

Tel: 01582 524200

BEDFORDSHIRE, ESSEX AND HERTFORDSHIRE

Adult
Court Name of Court and
No   Clerk/Legal Adviser   Normal Times and Places of Courts

1612 MID-NORTH ESSEX L.J.A.

I. C. Gill,   Adult – Daily, 10 a.m.   The Magistrates' Court,
Osprey House,   Shire Hall, Tindal Square,
Hedgerows Business Park,   Chelmsford
Colchester Road,   Wednesday, Thursday and   The Court House, Newland
Springfield,   Friday, 10 a.m.   Street, Witham
Chelmsford,
Essex CM2 5PF   YC – Tuesday, 10 a.m.   The Court House, Newland
                                                                      Street, Witham
Tel: 01245 313300
                                     FPC – Friday, 10 a.m.   The Magistrates' Court,
Fax: 01245 313553   Shire Hall, Tindal Square,
                                                                      Chelmsford

DX 151020 CHELMSFORD 17

NOTE: All payments and account queries, including Transfer of Fine Orders and Fixed Penalty Registrations should be sent to the Central Accounts and Enforcement Office. Write to Central accounts and Enforcement Office, The Court House, 80 Victoria Avenue, Southend-on-Sea, Essex SS2 6EU.   Tel: 01702 283830   Fax: 01702 283898   DX 97585 SOUTHEND 3

1610 MID-SOUTH ESSEX L.J.A.

F. Garland-Collins,   Adult – Daily, 10 a.m.   The Court House, Great
Osprey House,   Oaks, Basildon
Hedgerows Business Park,
Colchester Road,   YC – Tuesday, 10 a.m.   Do.
Springfield,
Chelmsford,
Essex CM2 5PF   FPC – 3rd and 4th Monday,   Do.
                                           1st, 2nd and 3rd Wednesday
Tel: 01245 313300   and 4th and 5th Friday, 10 a.m.

Fax: 01245 313397

DX 151020 CHELMSFORD 17

NOTE: All payments and account queries, including Transfer of Fine Orders and Fixed Penalty Registrations should be sent to the Central Accounts and Enforcement Office. Write to Central accounts and Enforcement Office, The Court House, 80 Victoria Avenue, Southend-on-Sea, Essex SS2 6EU.   Tel: 01702 283830   Fax: 01702 283898   DX 97585 SOUTHEND 3

1613 NORTH-EAST ESSEX L.J.A.

A. D. Whitehead,   Adult – Daily, 10 a.m.   Town Hall, High Street,
Osprey House,   Colchester
Hedgerows Business Park,   Monday, Tuesday, Thursday   363 Main Road, Dovercourt,
Colchester Road,   and Friday, 10 a.m.   Harwich
Springfield,
Chelmsford,   YC – Wednesday, 10 a.m.   363 Main Road, Dovercourt,
Essex CM2 5PF   Harwich
                                     FPC – 2nd and 5th Monday and   Colchester County Court,
Tel: 01245 313300   1st, 4th and 5th Wedneday, Falkland House,
Fax: 01245 313396   10 a.m.   25 Southway,
                                                                      Colchester CO3 3EG

DX 151020 CHELMSFORD 17

NOTE: All payments and account queries, including Transfer of Fine Orders and Fixed Penalty Registrations should be sent to the Central Accounts and Enforcement Office. Write to Central accounts and Enforcement Office, The Court House, 80 Victoria Avenue, Southend-on-Sea, Essex SS2 6EU.   Tel: 01702 283830   Fax: 01702 283898   DX 97585 SOUTHEND 3

BEDFORDSHIRE, ESSEX AND HERTFORDSHIRE

Adult Court No	Name of Court and Clerk/Legal Adviser	Normal Times and Places of Courts	

1889 NORTH HERTFORDSHIRE L.J.A.

Paul Fellingham,
Bayley House,
Sish Lane,
Stevenage,
Herts. SG1 3SS

Adult – Monday, Tuesday, Wednesday, Thursday and Friday, 10 a.m.

The Court House, Danesgate, Stevenage

Tel: 01438 730412 (Admin)
01923 699412 (Family)
01438 730400 (Central Accounting Unit)
01438 730415 (Legal Aid)
01923 297540 (Central Enforcement Unit)

YC – Wednesday, 10 a.m.

Do.

Fax: 01438 730413 (Admin)
01923 251317 (Family)
01438 730407 (Central Accounting Unit)
01438 730417 (Legal Aid)
01923 297555 (Central Enforcement Unit)

Fines – Wednesday, 10 a.m. Court

Do.

DX 122187 OLD STEVENAGE

1619 NORTH-WEST ESSEX L.J.A.

I. C. Gill,
Osprey House,
Hedgerows Business Park,
Colchester Road,
Springfield,
Chelmsford,
Essex CM2 5PF

Adult – Monday, Tuesday, Wednesday and Thursday, 10 a.m.

The Court House, Harlow

Monday, Tuesday, and 2nd and 4th Wednesday, 10 a.m.

The Court House, Epping

Tel: 01245 313300

YC – Friday, 10 a.m.

The Court House, Harlow

Fax: 01245 313398

FPC – Thursday, 10 a.m.

The Court House, Harlow

DX 151020 CHELMSFORD 17

NOTE: All payments and account queries, including Transfer of Fine Orders and Fixed Penalty Registrations should be sent to the Central Accounts and Enforcement Office. Write to Central accounts and Enforcement Office, The Court House, 80 Victoria Avenue, Southend-on-Sea, Essex SS2 6EU. Tel: 01702 283830 Fax: 01702 283898 DX 97585 SOUTHEND 3

BEDFORDSHIRE, ESSEX AND HERTFORDSHIRE

Adult Court No	Name of Court and Clerk/Legal Adviser	Normal Times and Places of Courts	

1629 SOUTH-EAST ESSEX L.J.A.

A. D. Whitehead, Osprey House, Hedgerows Business Park, Colchester Road, Springfield, Chelmsford, Essex CM2 5PF	Adult – Daily, 10 a.m.	The Court House, 80 Victoria Avenue, Southend-on-Sea
	YC – Wednesday, 10 a.m.	Do.
Tel: 01245 313300	FPC – Tuesday and Thursday, 10 a.m.	Do.
Fax: 01245 313392		
DX 151020 CHELMSFORD 17		

NOTE: All payments and account queries, including Transfer of Fine Orders and Fixed Penalty Registrations should be sent to the Central Accounts and Enforcement Office. Write to Central accounts and Enforcement Office, The Court House, 80 Victoria Avenue, Southend-on-Sea, Essex SS2 6EU. Tel: 01702 283830   Fax: 01702 283898   DX 97585 SOUTHEND 3

1626 SOUTH-WEST ESSEX L.J.A.

F. Garland-Collins, Osprey House, Hedgerows Business Park, Colchester Road, Springfield, Chelmsford, Essex CM2 5PF	Adult – Daily, 10 a.m.	Grays Magistrates' Court, The Court House, Orsett Road, Grays
	YC – Friday, 10 a.m.	Do.
Tel: 01245 313300		
Fax: 01245 313397		
DX 151020 CHELMSFORD 17		

NOTE: All payments and account queries, including Transfer of Fine Orders and Fixed Penalty Registrations should be sent to the Central Accounts and Enforcement Office. Write to Central accounts and Enforcement Office, The Court House, 80 Victoria Avenue, Southend-on-Sea, Essex SS2 6EU. Tel: 01702 283830   Fax: 01702 283898   DX 97585 SOUTHEND 3

1893 WEST HERTFORDSHIRE L.J.A.

David Gibbs, The Court House, Clarendon Road, Watford, Herts. WD17 1ST	Adult – Monday to Friday, 10 a.m. and 2 p.m.	The Court House, Clarendon Road, Watford
	Monday, Tuesday, Thursday and Friday, 10 a.m. and 2 p.m.	The Court House, Dacorum Way, Hemel Hempstead
Tel: 01923 297500	YC – Wednesday, 10 a.m. and 2 p.m.	Do.
Fax: 01923 297528		
Minicom: 01992 556532	FPC – Thursday, 10 a.m. and 2 p.m.	Do.
DX 51509 WATFORD 2	Fines – Monday (fortnightly), 10 a.m.	The Court House, Clarendon Road, Watford
	Monday (fortnightly), 10 a.m.	The Court House, Dacorum Way, Hemel Hempstead

MIDLANDS REGION

BIRMINGHAM, COVENTRY, SOLIHULL AND WARWICKSHIRE

Area Director: Kelvin Launchbury, Area Director's Office, 3rd Floor, Temple Court, 35 Bull Street, Bimingham, B4 6LG.   Tel: 0121 681 3201   Fax: 0121 250 6154
DX 701993 BIRMINGHAM 7

Central Fines Unit: Victoria Law Courts, Corporation Street, Birmingham B4 6QA. Tel: 0121 212 6690

Adult Court No	Name of Court and Clerk/Legal Adviser		Normal Times and Places of Courts
2908	**BIRMINGHAM L.J.A.**		
	Anthony R. Heath, M.A., O.B.E., Solicitor, Victoria Law Courts, Corporation Street, Birmingham B4 6QA	Adult – Daily, 10 a.m. and 2 p.m.	Victoria Law Courts, Corporation Street, Birmingham
	Tel: 0121 212 6600 250 6189/6193 (Family Courts Centre)	YC – Daily, 10 a.m. and 2 p.m.	Youth Courts, Steelhouse Lane, Birmingham (correspondence to Victoria Law Courts)
	Fax: 0121 212 6771 (Post-Court) 0121 212 6613 (Listing Pre-Court) 0121 250 6183 (Family Courts Centre)	FPC – Daily, 10 a.m. and 2 p.m.	Birmingham Family Courts Centre, Level 5, Priory Courts, Bull Street, Birmingham B4 6JX
	DX 715206 BIRMINGHAM 39 (Central Finance Unit) DX 715207 BIRMINGHAM 39 (Listing Pre and Post Court Offices) DX 715205 BIRMINGHAM 39 (Finance)		
2910	**COVENTRY DISTRICT L.J.A.**		
	Anthony R. Heath, M.A., O.B.E. Magistrates' Court, Little Park Street, Coventry CV1 2SQ Tel: 024-7663 0666	Adult – Daily, Monday to Friday, 10 a.m.	Magistrates' Court, Little Park Street, Coventry
		YC – Daily, Monday to Friday, 10 a.m. Wednesday and Thursday, 2 p.m.	Do. Do.
	Fax: 024 7650 0699 DX 701583 COVENTRY 5	FPC – Daily, 10 a.m.	Do.
	NOTE: All payments, account enquiries and correspondence, including Transfer of Fine Orders and Fixed Penalty Registrations, should now be forwarded to the Central Finance Unit, Department 05CY, Victoria Law Courts, Corporation Street, Birmingham B4 6QF		

BIRMINGHAM, COVENTRY, SOLIHULL AND WARWICKSHIRE

Adult Court No	Name of Court and Clerk/Legal Adviser		Normal Times and Places of Courts	
2916	**SOLIHULL L.J.A.**			
	Anthony R. Heath, M.A., O.B.E.	Adult	– Daily, 10 a.m. and 2 p.m.	The Court House, Solihull
	The Court House, Homer Road, Solihull, W. Midlands B91 3RD	YC	– Monday, 10 a.m. Tuesday and Thursday, 10 a.m. and 2 p.m.	Do.
	Tel: 0121-705 8101	FPC	– Monday, Wednesday and Friday, 10 a.m.	Do.
	Fax: 0121-711 2045			
	DX 708350 SOLIHULL 14			
	NOTE: All payments, account enquiries and correspondence, including Transfer of Fine Orders and Fixed Penalty Registrations, should now be forwarded to The Central Finance Unit, Department 08SL, Victoria Law Courts, Corporation Street, Birmingham B4 6QF			
2909	**SUTTON COLDFIELD L.J.A.**			
	Anthony R. Heath, M.A., O.B.E. The Court House, Lichfield Road, Sutton Coldfield, W. Midlands B74 2NS	Adult	– Monday, Tuesday, Wednesday, Thursday and Friday, 10 a.m. and 2.15 p.m.	The Court House, Lichfield Road, Sutton Coldfield
		YC	– Monday and Wednesday, 10 a.m. and 2.15 p.m.	Do.
	Tel: 0121-354 7777	FPC	– Friday 10 a.m. and 2.15 p.m.	Do.
	Fax: 0121-355 0547			
	DX 708310 SUTTON COLDFIELD 6			

BIRMINGHAM, COVENTRY, SOLIHULL AND WARWICKSHIRE

Adult Court No	Name of Court and Clerk/Legal Adviser	Normal Times and Places of Courts	
2904	**WARWICKSHIRE L.J.A.**		
	Justices' Clerk Magistrates' Court, PO Box 10, Leamington Spa, CV31 9ET	Adult – Monday to Friday, 10 a.m.	The Courthouse, 5 Newbold Road, Rugby CV21 2RN*
		Monday to Friday, 10 a.m.	Warwickshire Justice Centre, PO Box 3878, Vicarage Street, Nuneaton CV11 4WX
	Tel: 01926 429133	Monday to Friday, 10 a.m.	The Courthouse, Rother Street, Stratford-upon-Avon CV37 6JJ*
	Fax: 01926 426217		
	DX 11874 LEAMINGTON SPA 1		
		YC – Tuesday, 10 a.m.	The Courthouse, Rother Street, Stratford-upon-Avon CV37 6JJ*
		Friday, 10 a.m.	The Courthouse, 5 Newbold Road Rugby CV21 2RN*
		Wednesday, 10 a.m.	Warwickshire Justice Centre, PO Box 3878, Vicarage Street, Nuneaton CV11 4WX
		FPC – Monday, 10 a.m.	The Courthouse, Rother Street, Stratford-upon-Avon CV37 6JJ*
		First and third Thursday in month, 10 a.m.	The Courthouse, 5 Newbold Road, Rugby CV21 2RN*
		Friday, 10 a.m.	Warwickshire Justice Centre, PO Box 3878, Vicarage Street, Nuneaton CV11 4WX

* NOTE: There are no offices at these Courts. The Criminal and Youth Courts for Warwickshire are administered from Leamington Spa and Family, Accounts and Enforcement are administered from Nuneaton.

MIDLANDS REGION

BLACK COUNTRY, STAFFORDSHIRE AND WEST MERCIA

Area Director: Peter Hammersley, Area Director's Office, 1st Floor, Victoria Park House, 2-9 Victoria Road, Stafford ST16 2AV. Tel: 01785 218360 Fax: 01785 241643

Adult Court No	Name of Court and Clerk/Legal Adviser		Normal Times and Places of Courts	
1840	**BROMSGROVE AND REDDITCH L.J.A.**			
	Phillip Hines, Solicitor, D.M.S., The Magistrates' Courts, Comberton Place, Kidderminster, Worcestershire DY10 1QQ	Adult –	Monday, Tuesday, Wednesday and Friday, 10 a.m. and 2 p.m.	Magistrates' Court, Grove Street, Redditch
		YC –	Thursday, 10 a.m.	Do.
		FPC –	Friday, 10 a.m.	Do.
	Tel: 01562 514000 Fax: 01562 514097	Enf. –	Wednesday, 10 a.m. (fortnightly)	Do.

NOTE: All payments to be sent to the West Mercia Accounts Centre at Kidderminster (see above)

TRANSFER OF FINE ACCOUNTS should be sent to the following address: The Magistrates' Court, Comberton Place, Kidderminster DY10 1QQ

All enquiries relating to Enforcement of accounts should be made to West Mercia Fine Enforcement Centre, Telford (see p. 20)

All enquiries and correspondence relating to Family Proceedings should be directed to the West Mercia Family Centre at Kidderminster (see above)

2799	**CENTRAL AND SOUTH WEST STAFFORDSHIRE L.J.A.**			
	D. R. Goodman, Justices' Clerk's Office, The Court House, South Walls, Stafford ST16 3DW	Adult –	Monday, Tuesday, Wednesday, Thursday and Friday, 10 a.m.	The Court House, South Walls, Stafford
			Monday, Tuesday, Wednesday, Thursday and Friday, 10 a.m.	The Court House, Wolverhampton Road, Cannock
	Tel: 01785 223144 Fax: 01785 258508 DX 14575 STAFFORD-1	YC –	Tuesday and Thursday, 10 a.m.	The Court House, South Walls, Stafford
			Wednesday, 10 a.m.	The Court House, Wolverhampton Road, Cannock
		FPC –	Wednesday, 10 a.m.	The Court House, South Walls, Stafford
		Enf. –	Monday, 10 a.m. (fortnightly)	Do.
			Friday, 10 a.m.	The Court House, Wolverhampton Road, Cannock
			Private Prosecutions: Thursday, 10 a.m.	The Court House, South Walls, Stafford

BLACK COUNTRY, STAFFORDSHIRE AND WEST MERCIA

Adult Court No	Name of Court and Clerk/Legal Adviser	Normal Times and Places of Courts	

2911 DUDLEY L.J.A.

John E. Griffin, Magistrates' Clerk's Office, Magistrates' Courts, The Inhedge, Dudley DY1 1RY	Adult – Monday to Friday inclusive, 10 a.m. and 2 p.m.	Magistrates' Courts, The Inhedge, Dudley
	YC – Tuesday and Thursday, 10 a.m. and 2 p.m.	Do.
Tel: 01384 211411 Fax: 01384 211415 DX 12769	FPC – Monday, Wednesday and Friday, 10 a.m. and 2 p.m.	Do.

1841 HEREFORDSHIRE L.J.A.

Richard Burton, Solicitor, D.M.S., B.A. (Hons), The Magistrates' Court, Bath Street, Hereford HR1 2HE	Adult – Daily, 10 a.m.	The Court House, Bath Street, Hereford
	YC – Tuesday, 10 a.m.	Do.
	FPC – Thursday, 10 a.m.	Do.
Tel: 01562 514000 Fax: 01562 514111	Enf. – Monday, 10 a.m. and 2 p.m.	Do.

NOTE: All payments to be sent to the West Mercia Accounts Centre at Kidderminster (see p. 16)
TRANSFER OF FINE ACCOUNTS should be sent to the following address: The Magistrates' Court, Comberton Place, Kidderminster DY10 1QQ
All enquiries relating to Enforcement of accounts should be made to West Mercia Fine Enforcement Centre, Telford (see p. 20)
All enquiries and correspondence relating to Family Proceedings should be directed to the West Mercia Family Centre at Kidderminster (see p. 16)

1842 KIDDERMINSTER L.J.A.

Phillip Hines, Solicitor, D.M.S., The Magistrates' Courts Comberton Place, Kidderminster, Worcestershire DY10 1QQ	Adult – Monday, Tuesday, Thursday and Friday, 10 a.m. and 2 p.m.	Comberton Place, Kidderminster
	YC – Wednesday, 10 a.m.	Do.
	FPC – Monday, 10 a.m.	Do.
Tel: 01562 514000 Fax: 01562 514097	Enf. – Thursday, 10 a.m. (fortnightly)	Do.

NOTE: All payments to be sent to the West Mercia Accounts Centre at Kidderminster (see p. 16)
TRANSFER OF FINE ACCOUNTS should be sent to the following address: The Magistrates' Court, Comberton Place, Kidderminster DY10 1QQ
All enquiries relating to Enforcement of accounts should be made to West Mercia Fine Enforcement Centre, Telford (see p. 20)
All enquiries and correspondence relating to Family Proceedings should be directed to the West Mercia Family Centre at Kidderminster (see p. 16)

BLACK COUNTRY, STAFFORDSHIRE AND WEST MERCIA

Adult Court No	Name of Court and Clerk/Legal Adviser	Normal Times and Places of Courts	

2791 NORTH STAFFORDSHIRE L.J.A.

D. R. Goodman, Justices' Clerk's Office, Baker Street, Fenton, Stoke-on-Trent, Staffs. ST4 3BX	Adult – Daily, 10 a.m. and 2 p.m. Daily, 10 a.m.	The Court House, Albert Square, Fenton, Stoke-on-Trent The Court House, Ryecroft, Newcastle-under-Lyme	

Tel: 01782 845353
Fax: 01782 744782
DX 700402 FENTON
	YC – Daily, 10 a.m.
	FPC – Monday, Wednesday and
	      Friday, and occasional
	      Thursdays, 10 a.m.
		Do.
		Do.	

3278 SHREWSBURY & NORTH SHROPSHIRE L.J.A.

Sean Currie,
  Barrister, B.A. (Hons),
  M.B.A., Assoc., C.I.P.D.,
Court Office,
Preston Street,
Shrewsbury SY2 5NX
	Adult – Monday, Tuesday,
	       Wednesday and Thursday,
	       10 a.m.
	Tuesday, 10 a.m.
	
	Wednesday, 10 a.m.
		The Court House,
		  Preston Street,
		  Shrewsbury
		The Court House, Holbache
		  Road, Oswestry
		The Court House, Cheshire
		  Street, Market Drayton

Tel: 01743 458500
    (Switchboard)
          458503
    (Court Support)
	VC – Tuesday, 10 a.m.	The Court House, Preston
		  Street, Shrewsbury

Fax: 01743 458502	YC – Monday, 10 a.m.
	
	Thursday, 10 a.m.
	
	Friday, 10 a.m.
		The Court House, Holbache
		  Road, Oswestry
		The Court House, Cheshire
		  Street, Market Drayton
		The Court House, Preston
		  Street, Shrewsbury

	FPC – Thursday, 10 a.m. Enf. – As required	Do.

BLACK COUNTRY, STAFFORDSHIRE AND WEST MERCIA

Adult Court No	Name of Court and Clerk/Legal Adviser		Normal Times and Places of Courts
2860	**SOUTH EAST STAFFORDSHIRE L.J.A.**		
	D. R. Goodman, Justices' Clerk's Office, The Court House, South Walls, Stafford ST16 3DW	Adult – Monday, Tuesday, Wednesday and Thursday, 10 a.m. Daily, 10 a.m.	The Court House, Spinning School Lane, Tamworth Magistrates' Court, Horninglow Street, Burton-upon-Trent
	Tel: 01785 223144		
	Fax: 01785 258508 DX 14575 STAFFORD-1	YC – Friday, 10 a.m. Wednesday, 10 a.m.	The Court House, Spinning School Lane, Tamworth Magistrates' Court, Horninglow Street, Burton-upon-Trent
		FPC – Thursday, 10 a.m. Every 3rd Monday	The Court House, Spinning School Lane, Tamworth Magistrates' Court, Horninglow Street, Burton-upon-Trent
		Enf – Tuesday	The Court House, Spinning School Lane, Tamworth
		Council Tax Tuesday, 2 p.m.	Do.
		Enf – Monday (fortnightly), 10 a.m.	Magistrates' Court, Horninglow Street, Burton-upon-Trent
		Private Procecutions Monday 10 a.m.	Do.
1843	**SOUTH WORCESTERSHIRE L.J.A.**		
	J. N. Stephenson, Solicitor, M.B.A., Magistrates' Court, Castle Street, Worcester WR1 3QZ	Adult – Daily, 10 a.m.	Magistrates' Courts, Castle Street, Worcester
		YC – Weekly Wednesday, 10 a.m.	Do.
		FPC – Weekly Monday and Tuesday, 10 a.m.	Do.
	Tel: 01905 743200 Fax: 01905 743346	Enf. – Fortnightly Tuesday, 10 a.m.	Do.

NOTE: All payments to be sent to the West Mercia Accounts Centre at Kidderminster (see p. 16)
TRANSFER OF FINE ACCOUNTS should be sent to the following address: The Magistrates' Court, Comberton Place, Kidderminster DY10 1QQ
All enquiries relating to Enforcement of accounts should be made to West Mercia Fine Enforcement Centre, Telford (see p. 20)
All enquiries and correspondence relating to Family Proceedings should be directed to the West Mercia Family Centre at Kidderminster (see p. 16)

BLACK COUNTRY, STAFFORDSHIRE AND WEST MERCIA

Adult Court No	Name of Court and Clerk/Legal Adviser	Normal Times and Places of Courts	
2912	**STOURBRIDGE AND HALESOWEN L.J.A.**		
	John E. Griffin, Magistrates' Clerk's Office, Magistrates' Court, The Inhedge, Dudley, W. Midlands DY1 1RY	Adult – Daily, 10 a.m. and 2 p.m.	Magistrates' Court, Laurel Lane, Halesowen
		YC – Wednesday, 10 a.m. and 2 p.m.	Do.
	Tel: 01384 211411		
	Fax: 01384 211415		
3276	**TELFORD & SOUTH SHROPSHIRE L.J.A.**		
	Anita Bickerdike, Solicitor, LL.B., M.B.A., Court Office, Telford Square, Malinsgate, Telford TF3 4HX	Adult – Wednesday, Thursday, and second Friday in month, 10 a.m.	The Guildhall, Mill Street, Ludlow
	Tel: 01952 204500 (Switchboard)		
	Fax: 01952 204554		
	NOTE: All payments to be sent to the West Mercia Accounts Centre at Kidderminster (see p. 16) TRANSFER OF FINE ACCOUNTS should be sent to the following address: The Magistrates' Court, Comberton Place, Kidderminster DY10 1QQ All enquiries relating to Enforcement of accounts should be made to West Mercia Fine Enforcement Centre, Telford (see above) All enquiries and correspondence relating to Family Proceedings should be directed to the West Mercia Family Centre at Kidderminster (see p. 16)		
3282	**TELFORD & SOUTH SHROPSHIRE L.J.A.**		
	Anita Bickerdike, LL.B., M.B.A., Court Office, Telford Square, Malinsgate, Telford TF3 4HX	Adult – Daily, 10 a.m. and 2 p.m.	Magistrates' Court, Telford Square, Malinsgate, Telford
		YC – Monday, Wednesday and Friday, 10 a.m.	Do.
		FPC – Tuesday and Thursday, 10 a.m.	Do.
	Tel: 01952 204500 (Switchboard)		
	Fax: 01952 204554		
	NOTE: All payments to be sent to the West Mercia Accounts Centre at Telford (see p. 16) TRANSFER OF FINE ACCOUNTS should be sent to the following address: The Magistrates' Court, Telford Square, Malinsgate, Telford TF3 4HX All enquiries relating to Enforcement of accounts should be made to West Mercia Fine Enforcement Centre, Telford (see above) All enquiries and correspondence relating to Family Proceedings should be directed to the West Mercia Family Centre at Kidderminster (see p. 16)		

BLACK COUNTRY, STAFFORDSHIRE AND WEST MERCIA

Adult Court No	Name of Court and Clerk/Legal Adviser	Normal Times and Places of Courts	
2917	**WALSALL AND ALDRIDGE L.J.A.**		
	John R. Griffin, Magistrates' Court, Stafford Street, Walsall WS2 8HA Tel: 01922 638222 Fax: 01922 635657 DX 12118 WALSALL 1	Adult – Monday to Friday, 10 a.m.	Magistrates' Court, Stafford Street, Walsall
		YC – Thursday and Friday, 10 a.m.	Do.
		FPC – Wednesday, Thursday, Friday, 10 a.m.	The Court House, Rookery Lane, Aldridge
		SDVC– Monday, 10 a.m.	Magistrates' Court, Stafford Street, Walsall
2914	**WARLEY L.J.A.**		
	John E. Griffin, The Court House, Oldbury Ringway, Oldbury, W. Midlands B69 4JN Tel: 0121-511 2222 Fax: 0121-544 8492 DX 708330 OLDBURY 3	Adult – Daily, 10 a.m. and 2 p.m.	The Court House, Oldbury
		YC – Tuesday and Thursday, 10 a.m. and 2 p.m.	Do.
		FPC – Monday, Wednesday and Friday, 10 a.m. and 2 p.m.	Do.
		Directions Appointments Monday and Tuesday, 2 p.m.	Do.
		Fine Enf. – Monday, 10 a.m. and Friday, 2 p.m.	Do.
2915	**WEST BROMWICH L.J.A.**		
	John E. Griffin, Warley Magistrates' Court, Oldbury Ringway B69 4JN Tel: 0121 511 2222 Fax: 0121-544 8492 DX 708330 OLDBURY 3	Adult – Daily, 10 a.m. and 2 p.m.	Law Courts, Lombard Street West, West Bromwich
		YC – Monday, 10 a.m. Wednesday, 10 a.m. and 2 p.m.	Do.
		Fine Enf. – Wednesday, 2 p.m.	Do.
2919	**WOLVERHAMPTON L.J.A.**		
	John E. Griffin, Law Courts, North Street, Wolverhampton WV1 1RA Tel: 01902 773151 Fax: 01902 427875 DX 10419	Adult – Monday to Friday, 10 a.m.	The Law Courts, North Street, Wolverhampton
		YC – Monday, Thursday and Friday, 10 a.m.	Do.
		FPC – Monday, Wednesday, Thursday and Friday, 10 a.m.	Do.
		Fine Dflt – Thursday, 10 a.m.	Do.

SOUTH EAST REGION

CAMBRIDGESHIRE, NORFOLK AND SUFFOLK

Area Director: Pauline Cornford, Area Director's Office, 1st Floor, The Courthouse, Old Bury Road, Thetford, Norfolk IP24 3AQ. Tel: 01842 757300 Fax: 01842 763084

Adult Court No	Name of Court and Clerk/Legal Adviser		Normal Times and Places of Courts	
1165	**CAMBRIDGE L.J.A.**			
	T. M. Daber, LL.B., The Courthouse, 43 Hauxton Road, Trumpington, Cambridge CB2 2EY Tel: 0845 310 0575 Fax: 01223 844980 DX 131966 CAMBRIDGE 6	Adult – YC – FPC –	Daily, 10 a.m. (Combined with East Cambridgeshire L.J.A.) Wednesday, 10 a.m. (Combined with East Cambridgeshire, Peterborough, Huntingdon and Wisbech L.J.As) Monday, 10 a.m.	The Courthouse, Trumpington, Cambridge Do. Do.
1442	**CENTRAL NORFOLK L.J.A.**			
	The Court House, College Lane, King's Lynn, Norfolk PE30 1PQ Tel: 01553 770120 Fax: 01553 775098 DX 57807 KING'S LYNN E-mail: kingslynn.court@hmcourts-service.gsi.gov.uk	Adult – YC – FPC –	Tuesday and Friday, 10 a.m. (Combined with South Norfolk and West Norfolk) Wednesday, 10 a.m. Specified dates – please contact Court Office (Combined with South Norfolk and West Norfolk) Specified dates – please contact Court Office	Court House, Swaffham Do. Do.
1166	**EAST CAMBRIDGESHIRE L.J.A.**			
	T. M. Daber, LL.B., The Courthouse, 43 Hauxton Road, Trumpington, Cambridge CB2 2EY Tel: 0845 310 0575 Fax: 01223 844980 DX 131966 CAMBRIDGE 6	Adult – YC – FPC –	Tuesday and Thursday, 10 a.m. (Combined with Cambridge L.J.A.) Second Thursday in month (Combined with Cambridge, Peterborough, Huntingdon and Wisbech L.J.As) As required	Sessions House, Lynn Road, Ely Do. Do.

CAMBRIDGESHIRE, NORFOLK AND SUFFOLK

Adult Court No	Name of Court and Clerk/Legal Adviser	Normal Times and Places of Courts	
1167	**FENLAND L.J.A.**		
	T. M. Daber, LL.B., Magistrates' Court, Bridge Street, Peterborough PE1 1ED	Adult – Tuesday, 10 a.m. Wednesday, 10 a.m.	Court House, Wisbech
	Tel: 0845 310 0575 Fax: 01733 313749	YC – (Combined with Huntingdonshire and Peterborough L.J.As) Every two weeks on a Thursday or Friday, 10 a.m. and one Thursday or Friday a month (trial court only).	Do.
	DX 742250 PETERBOROUGH 23		
1443	**GREAT YARMOUTH L.J.A.**		
	Magistrates' Courthouse, North Quay, Great Yarmouth, Norfolk NR30 1PW	Adult – Weekdays, 10 a.m. and 2.15 p.m.	Magistrates' Courthouse, North Quay, Great Yarmouth
	Tel: 01493 849800	YC – (Combined with North Norfolk) Thursday, 10 a.m.	Do.
	Fax: 01493 852169	FPC – (Combined with North Norfolk) Wednesday, 10 a.m.	Do.
	DX 139400 GREAT YARMOUTH 3		
	E-mail: greatyarmouth.court@hmcourts-service.gsi.gov.uk		
1168	**HUNTINGDONSHIRE L.J.A.**		
	T. M. Daber, LL.B., Magistrates' Court, Bridge Street, Peterborough PE1 1ED	Adult – Monday, Tuesday, Wednesday, Thursday and Friday, 10 a.m.	Town Hall, Huntingdon
	Tel: 0845 310 0575 Fax: 01733 313749	YC – (Combined with Fenland and Peterborough L.J.As) Tuesday, 10 a.m.	Do.
	DX 742250 PETERBOROUGH 23		
2863	**NORTH EAST SUFFOLK L.J.A.**		
	Christopher F. Bowler, LL.B., The Magistrates' Court, Old Nelson Street, Lowestoft, Suffolk NR32 1HJ	Adult – Daily, 10 a.m. Monday, Tuesday, Wednesday and Thursday, 2.15 p.m.	The Magistrates' Court, Old Nelson Street, Lowestoft
	Tel: 01502 501060	YC – Friday, 10 a.m.	Do.
	Fax: 01502 513875	FPC – Wednesday, 10 a.m.	Do.
	DX 41219 LOWESTOFT		
	NOTE: All Transfer of Fine Orders (TFOs) should be addressed to the Centralised TFO Office at North East Suffolk Magistrates Court.		

CAMBRIDGESHIRE, NORFOLK AND SUFFOLK

Adult Court No	Name of Court and Clerk/Legal Adviser	Normal Times and Places of Courts	

1444 NORTH NORFOLK L.J.A.

Magistrates' Courthouse, North Quay, Great Yarmouth, Norfolk NR30 1PW	Adult – Monday and Thursday, 10 a.m.	The Court House, Holt Road, Cromer
Tel: 01493 849800 Fax: 01493 852169	YC – (Combined with Great Yarmouth) Tuesday (every three weeks), 10 a.m.	Do.
	FPC – (Combined with Great Yarmouth)	Magistrates' Courthouse, North Quay, Great Yarmouth

DX 139400 GREAT YARMOUTH 3

E-mail: greatyarmouth.court@hmcourts-service.gsi.gov.uk

NOTE: All Transfer of Fine Orders (TFOs) should be addressed to the Centralised TFO Office at North East Suffolk Magistrates Court.

1445 NORWICH L.J.A.

The Magistrates' Court, Bishopgate, Norwich NR3 1UP	Adult – Daily, 10 a.m. and 2.15 p.m.	The Magistrates' Court, Bishopgate, Norwich
Tel: 01603 679500	PTR – Friday, 10 a.m.	
	YC – Daily, (Criminal), 10 a.m.	Do.
Fax: 01603 663263	FPC – Monday and Wednesday, 2 p.m.	Do.
DX 97389 NORWICH 5	Tuesday, Thursday and Friday. 10 a.m.	

E-mail: norwich.court@hmcourts-service.gsi.gov.uk

1162 PETERBOROUGH L.J.A.

T. M. Daber, LL.B., Magistrates' Court, Bridge Street, Peterborough PE1 1ED	Adult – Daily, 10 a.m.	Magistrates' Court, Bridge Street, Peterborough
Tel: 0845 310 0575 Fax: 01733 313749	YC – (Combined with Fenland and Huntingdonshire L.J..As) Monday, Tuesday and Thursday, 10 a.m.	Do.
	FPC – Monday, 2 p.m. Wednesday and Friday, 10 a.m.	Do.

DX 742250 PETERBOROUGH 23

CAMBRIDGESHIRE, NORFOLK AND SUFFOLK

Adult Court No	Name of Court and Clerk/Legal Adviser		Normal Times and Places of Courts
2866	**SOUTH EAST SUFFOLK L.J.A.**		
	Christopher F. Bowler, LL.B., The Magistrates' Court, Elm Street, Ipswich, Suffolk IP1 2AP	Adult – Daily, 10 a.m. and Monday, Tuesday and Wednesday, 2.15 p.m.	The Magistrates' Court, Elm Street, Ipswich
	Tel: 01473 217261	YC – Tuesday and Thursday, 10 a.m.	Do.
	Fax: 01473 231249	FPC – Wednesday, 2.15 p.m.	Do.
	DX 3232 IPSWICH		
	NOTE: All Transfer of Fine Orders (TFOs) should be addressed to the Centralised TFO Office at North East Suffolk Magistrates Court.		
1446	**SOUTH NORFOLK L.J.A.**		
	The Court House, College Lane, King's Lynn, Norfolk PE30 1PQ	Adult – Monday and Thursday and Wednesday, 10 a.m. (3 week cycle commencing Week 3)	Court House, Thetford
	Tel: 01553 770120	YC – (Combined with Central Norfolk and West Norfolk) Wednesday, 10 a.m. Specified dates – please contact Court Office	Do.
	Fax: 01553 775098 DX 57807 KING'S LYNN		
		FPC – Specified dates – please contact Court Office	Do.
	E-mail: kingslynn.court@hmcourts-service.gsi.gov.uk		
1447	**WEST NORFOLK L.J.A.**		
	The Court House, College Lane, King's Lynn, Norfolk PE30 1PQ	Adult – Daily (except Saturday), 10 a.m.	The Court House, College Lane, King's Lynn
	Tel: 01553 770120	YC – (Combined with Central Norfolk and South Norfolk) Tuesday, 10 a.m.	Do.
	Fax: 01553 775098 DX 57807 KING'S LYNN	FPC – Second Wednesday in month, 10 a.m.	Do.
	E-mail: kingslynn.court@hmcourts-service.gsi.gov.uk		

CAMBRIDGESHIRE, NORFOLK AND SUFFOLK

Adult Court No	Name of Court and Clerk/Legal Adviser	Normal Times and Places of Courts	
2867	**WEST SUFFOLK L.J.A.**		
	Christopher F. Bowler, LL.B., Shire Hall, Bury St. Edmunds, Suffolk IP33 1HF	Adult – Monday, Tuesday, Wednesday and Friday, 10 a.m.	The Court House, Acton Lane, Sudbury
		Monday, Tuesday, Thursday and Friday 10 a.m.	The Court House, Queensway, Mildenhall
	Tel: 01284 352300	Monday, Tuesday, Thursday and Friday, 10 a.m.	The Courthouse, Shire Hall, Bury St. Edmunds
	Fax: 01284 352345	YC – (West Suffolk Combined Youth Court)	
		Tuesday (fortnightly), 10 a.m.	The Court House, Acton Lane, Sudbury
		Wednesday (weekly), 10 a.m.	The Courthouse, Shire Hall, Bury St. Edmunds
		FPC – Monday (weekly)	Do.
		Thursday and Friday (every other month), 10 a.m.	The Court House, Acton Lane, Sudbury
			The Court House, Queensway, Mildenhall
		Fines – Monday (monthly), 2.15 p.m.	The Courthouse, Shire Hall, Bury St. Edmunds
		As required	The Court House, Acton Lane, Sudbury
		As required	The Court House, Queensway, Mildenhall

NOTE: All Transfer of Fine Orders (TFOs) should be addressed to the Centralised TFO Office at North East Suffolk Magistrates Court.

NORTH WEST REGION

CHESHIRE AND MERSEYSIDE

Area Director: Shaun McNally, Area Director's Office, 1st Floor, Queen Elizabeth II Law Courts, Derby Square, Liverpool L2 1XA. Tel: 0151 330 9605
Fax: 0151 236 5180   DX 740880 L22

Fines Unit (Cheshire): The Accounts Enforcement Central Payments Office, PO Box 104, Runcorn, Cheshire WA7 2GE. Fax: 01928 703356

Fines Unit (Merseyside): 35 Vernon Street, Liverpool L2 2BX. Tel: 0151 296 2300

Adult Court No	Name of Court and Clerk/Legal Adviser	Normal Times and Places of Courts	
1188	**CHESTER, ELLESMERE PORT AND NESTON L.J.A.**		
	Clerk to the Justices, Chester Magistrates' Court, Grosvenor Street, Chester CH1 2XA	Adult – Monday to Friday, 10 a.m.	Chester Magistrates' Court, Grosvenor Street, Chester
		YC – Tuesday and Thursday, 10 a.m.	Do.
	Tel: 0870 1626261	FPC – Wednesday, 10 a.m.	Do.
	Fax: 01244 405843		
	TFO/FPRC and Account/Enforcement Enquiries to Central Payments Office, P.O. Box 103, Runcorn, Cheshire WA7 2GD Tel: 0870 1626261		
1177	**HALTON L.J.A.**		
	Justices Clerk, Winmarleigh Street, Warrington, Cheshire WA1 1PB	Adult – Monday to Friday, 10 a.m.	Court House, Halton Lea, Runcorn
		YC – Thursday, 10 a.m.	Do.
	Tel: 0870 1626261	FPC – Monday, 10 a.m.	Court House, Kingsway, Widnes
	Fax: 01925 231284		
	DX 17793 WARRINGTON 1		
	TFO/FPRC and Account/Enforcement Enquiries to Central Payments Office, P.O. Box 101, Runcorn, Cheshire WA7 2GA Tel: 0870 1626261		
2266	**KNOWSLEY L.J.A.**		
	N. H. Draper, The Court House, Corporation Street, St. Helens, Merseyside WA10 1SZ	Adult – Monday, Tuesday, Wednesday, Thursday and Friday, 9.30 a.m. and 2 p.m.	Court House, Lathom Road, Huyton
		YC – Tuesday, Thursday and Friday, 9.30 a.m.	Do.
	Tel: 01744 620244	Wednesday, 2.15 p.m.	Do.
	Fax: 0151-449 2841	FPC – Monday to Friday, 10 a.m. and 2 p.m.	Civil and Family Courts, 35 Vernon Street, Liverpool L2 2BX
	DX 19488 ST HELENS		
	TFO/FPRC and Account/Enforcement Enquiries to County Payments and Enforcement Centre, P.O. Box 827, Liverpool L69 3FD. Tel: 0151 296 2300.		

CHESHIRE AND MERSEYSIDE

Adult Court No	Name of Court and Clerk/Legal Adviser	Normal Times and Places of Courts	

2267 LIVERPOOL L.J.A.

N. H. Draper, City Magistrates' Courts, Dale Street, Liverpool L2 2JQ Tel: 0151-243 5500 Fax: 0151-243 5555 DX 707900 LIVERPOOL 8	Adult – Monday to Friday, 10 a.m. and 2 p.m.	Magistrates' Courts, Dale Street, Liverpool
	YC – Monday to Friday, 10 a.m. and 2 p.m.	Youth Courts, Hatton Garden, Liverpool
	FPC – Monday to Friday, 10 a.m. and 2 p.m.	Civil and Family Courts, 35 Vernon Street, Liverpool L2 2BX

NOTE: With effect from 26th November 2007 the Youth Courts will move to QEII Law Courts, Derby Square, Liverpool L2 1XA.

TFO/FPRC and Account/Enforcement Enquiries to County Payments and Enforcement Centre, P.O. Box 827, Liverpool L69 3FD. Tel: 0151 293 8301/02/03/04.

1178 MACCLESFIELD L.J.A.

Justices' Clerk's Office, The Court House, Chester Way, Northwich, Cheshire CW9 5ES Tel: 0870 1626261 Fax: 01606 48740	Adult – Monday, Wednesday, Thursday and Friday, 10 a.m.	The Law Courts, Hibel Road, Macclesfield
	YC – Tuesday, 10 a.m.	Do.
	FPC – Alternate Tuesdays, 10 a.m.	Do.

TFO/FPRC and Account/Enforcement Enquiries to Central Payments Office, P.O. Box 102, Runcorn, Cheshire WA7 2GB   Tel: 0870 1626261

2269 NORTH SEFTON DISTRICT L.J.A.

N. H. Draper, The Court House, Merton Road, Bootle, Merseyside L20 3XX Tel: 0151 933 6999 Fax: 0151 922 4285	Adult – Daily, 10 a.m. and 2 p.m.	Law Courts, Albert Road, Southport
	YC – Tuesday, 10 a.m. and 2 p.m. Friday, 10 a.m.	Do.

TFO/FPRC and Account/Enforcement Enquiries to County Payments and Enforcement Centre, P.O. Box 827, Liverpool L69 3FD. Tel: 0151 293 8301/02/03/04.

2268 ST. HELENS L.J.A.

N. H. Draper, The Court House, Corporation Street, St. Helens, Merseyside WA10 1SZ Tel: 01744 620244 Fax: 01744 759697 (Secretariat) DX 19488 ST. HELENS	Adult – Every weekday, 9.30 a.m. and 2.15 p.m.	The Court House, St. Helens
	YC – Monday, Tuesday and Thursday, 9.30 a.m.	Do.
	Thursday, 2.15 p.m.	Do.
	FPC – Monday to Friday, 10 a.m and 2 p.m.	Civil and Family Courts, 35 Vernon Street, Liverpool L2 2BX

TFO/FPRC and Account/Enforcement Enquiries to County Payments and Enforcement Centre, P.O. Box 827, Liverpool L69 3FD. Tel: 0151 296 2300.

CHESHIRE AND MERSEYSIDE

Adult Court No	Name of Court and Clerk/Legal Adviser	Normal Times and Places of Courts	

1187 SOUTH CHESHIRE L.J.A.

Vacant, Law Courts, Civic Centre, Crewe, Cheshire CW1 2DT	Adult – Monday, Tuesday, Wednesday and Friday, 10 a.m. and 2 p.m.	Law Courts, Civic Centre, Crewe
	YC – Thursday, 10 a.m. and 2 p.m.	Do.
Tel: 0870 1626261 Fax: 01270 589357	FPC – Thursday, 10 a.m.	Do.

TFO/FPRC and Account/Enforcement Enquiries to Central Payments Office, P.O. Box 102, Runcorn, Cheshire WA7 2GB   Tel: 0870 1626261

2270 SOUTH SEFTON DISTRICT L.J.A.

N. H. Draper, The Magistrates' Court, Court Buildings, Merton Road, Bootle, Merseyside L20 3XX	Adult – Monday to Friday, 10 a.m. and 2 p.m.	Magistrates' Courts, Merton Road, Bootle
	YC – Monday, Thursday and Friday, 10 a.m.	Do.
Tel: 0151-933 6999 Fax: 0151-922 4285 DX 707620 BOOTLE	Monday, Tuesday, Wednesday, Thursday and Friday, 2 p.m.	Do.

TFO/FPRC and Account/Enforcement Enquiries to County Payments and Enforcement Centre, P.O. Box 827, Liverpool L69 3FD.   Tel: 0151 293 8301/02/03/04.

1179 VALE ROYAL L.J.A.

Justices' Clerk's Office, The Court House, Chester Way, Northwich, Cheshire CW9 5ES	Adult – Monday to Friday, 10 a.m.	Court House, Chester Way, Northwich
	YC – Wednesday, 10 a.m.	Do.
Tel: 0870 1626261 Fax: 01606 48740	FPC – Alternate Thursdays, 10 a.m.	Do.

TFO/FPRC and Account/Enforcement Enquiries to Central Payments Office, P.O. Box 103, Runcorn, Cheshire WA7 2GD   Tel: 0870 1626261

1180 WARRINGTON L.J.A.

Justices Clerk, Winmarleigh Street, Warrington, Cheshire WA1 1PB	Adult – Monday to Friday, 10 a.m.	The Court House, Arpley Street, Warrington
	YC – Thursday, 10 a.m.	Do.
Tel: 0870 1626261 Fax: 01925 231284 DX 17793 WARRINGTON 1	FPC – Thursday, 10 a.m.	Do.

TFO/FPRC and Account/Enforcement Enquiries to Central Payments Office, P.O. Box 101, Runcorn, Cheshire WA7 2GA   Tel: 0870 1626261

CHESHIRE AND MERSEYSIDE

Adult Court No	Name of Court and Clerk/Legal Adviser		Normal Times and Places of Courts	
2271	**WIRRAL L.J.A.**			
	N. H. Draper, The Sessions Courts, Chester Street, Birkenhead, Merseyside CH41 5HW	MC	– Daily, 10 a.m. and 2 p.m.	Birkenhead
	Tel: 0151-285 4100	YC	– Daily, 10 a.m. and 2 p.m.	Do.
	Fax: 0151-285 4111			
	DX 17888 BIRKENHEAD			
	TFO/FPRC and Account/Enforcement Enquiries to County Payments and Enforcement Centre, P.O. Box 827, Liverpool L69 3FD. Tel: 0151 296 2300.			

NORTH EAST REGION

CLEVELAND, DURHAM AND NORTHUMBRIA

Area Director: Sheila Proudlock, Area Director's Office, P.O. Box 168, Old Elvet, Durham DH1 3FE. Tel: 0191 384 4455 Fax: 0191 375 1833

Adult Court No	Name of Court and Clerk/Legal Adviser	Normal Times and Places of Courts	
2347	**ALNWICK L.J.A. (formerly Coquetdale Division)**		
	D. Pryer, MCMI, First CPD Prudhoe Street, Alnwick, Northumberland NE66 1UJ Tel: 01665 602727 Fax: 01665 510247	Adult – Wednesday and Friday, 10 a.m.	The Court House, Prudhoe Street, Alnwick
		YC – Mondays, alternating with FPC, 10 a.m.	Do.
		FPC – Mondays, alternating with YC, 10 a.m.	Do.
	For the Centralised Accounts Office, *see* South East Northumberland L.J.A.		
2348	**BERWICK-UPON-TWEED L.J.A.**		
	D. Pryer, MCMI, The Courthouse, 40 Church Street, Berwick-upon-Tweed, Northumberland TD15 1DX Tel: 01289 306885 Fax: 01289 302735	Adult – Tuesday and Thursday, 10 a.m.	Court House, Church Street, Berwick-upon-Tweed
		YC – Mondays, alternating with FPC, 10 a.m.	Do.
		FPC – Mondays, alternating with YC, 10 a.m.	Do.
2850	**GATESHEAD DISTRICT L.J.A.**		
	C. J. Livesley, B.A.(Hons), Gateshead Magistrates' Court, Warwick Street, Gateshead, Tyne and Wear NE8 1DT Tel: 0191-477 5821 Fax: 0191-478 7825 DX 742120 GATESHEAD 6	Adult – Monday, Tuesday, Wednesday, Thursday and Friday, 10 a.m.	The Magistrates' Court, Warwick Street, Gateshead
		Private – Tuesday, 10 a.m. Prosecutions	Do.
		YC – Tuesday, 10 a.m.	The Magistrates Court, Larch Road, Blaydon
		FPC – Monday, 10 a.m.	Do.
		Enf. – Tuesday, 10 a.m.	The Magistrates' Court, Warwick Street, Gateshead
		Trials – Wednesday, Thursday and Friday, 10 a.m.	The Magistrates' Court, Larch Road, Blaydon
	For the Centralised Accounts Office, *see* Newcastle upon Tyne L.J.A.		

CLEVELAND, DURHAM AND NORTHUMBRIA

Adult Court No	Name of Court and Clerk/Legal Adviser	Normal Times and Places of Courts	

1247 HARTLEPOOL L.J.A.

Siân E. Jones,	Adult – Daily, 10 a.m. and	The Law Courts, Victoria
The Law Courts,	2.15 p.m.	Road, Hartlepool
Victoria Road,		
Hartlepool		
TS24 8AG	YC – Thursday, 10 a.m. and	Do.
Tel: 01429 271451	2.15 p.m.	
(4 lines)		
230605/6		
(Fines)		
230601/2	FPC – Tuesday, 10 a.m.	Do.
(Admin)		

Fax: 01429 866696

DX 68706 HARTLEPOOL 2

E-mail: postboxHP@hmcourts-service.gsi.gov.uk

2854 HOUGHTON-LE-SPRING L.J.A.

S. P. Rowbottom,	Adult – Monday, Wednesday,	Magistrates' Court,
Barrister, LL.B.(Hons),	Thursday and Friday,	Houghton-le-Spring
M.B.A.	10 a.m.	
Justices' Clerk's Office,	Monday, Wednesday and	
The Villa, Dairy Lane,	Thursday, 2 p.m.	
Houghton-le-Spring,		
Tyne and Wear	YC – Tuesday, 10 a.m.	Magistrates' Court,
DH4 5BL		Houghton-le-Spring
Tel: 0191-514 1621	FPC – Monday, Wednesday, Thursday	Do.
Fax: 0191-584 5809/	and Friday, 10 a.m. and	
565 8564	2 p.m.	

DX 65306 HOUGHTON-LE-SPRING

For the Centralised Accounts Office, see Sunderland L.J.A.

1248 LANGBAURGH EAST L.J.A.

Siân E. Jones LL.B.	Adult – Daily, 10 a.m. and Monday	The Court House, Church
	to Thursday, 2.15 p.m.	Lane, Guisborough
	YC – see 1249 TEESSIDE L.J.A.	
	FPC – see 1249 TEESSIDE L.J.A.	

All correspondence and telephone calls to 1249 TEESSIDE DIVISION.

CLEVELAND, DURHAM AND NORTHUMBRIA

Adult Court No	Name of Court and Clerk/Legal Adviser	Normal Times and Places of Courts	

2851 NEWCASTLE UPON TYNE L.J.A.

Mrs. Rosemary Watson, LL.B., Magistrates' Courts, P.O. Box 839, Market Street, Newcastle upon Tyne NE99 1AU	Adult –	Monday to Friday, 10 a.m., 11 a.m., 12 noon and 2.15 p.m.	Market Street, Newcastle upon Tyne
		Monday, 10 a.m.	West Avenue, Gosforth, Newcastle upon Tyne
		Saturdays and Bank Holidays, 10 a.m.	Market Street, Newcastle upon Tyne
Tel: 0191-232 7326	YC –	Wednesday, 10 a.m., 11 a.m. and 2.15 p.m.	Magistrates' Courts, West Avenue, Gosforth, Newcastle upon Tyne
Fax: 0191-221 0025		First and third Tuesday in month, 10 a.m.	
DX 61098 NEWCASTLE UPON TYNE		Friday, 10 a.m., 11 a.m. and 2.15 p.m.	
		Tuesday, 10 a.m., 11 a.m. and 12 noon	Market Street, Newcastle upon Tyne
	FPC –	Thursday, 10 a.m. and every fourth Tuesday in month, 10 a.m.	Magistrates' Courts, West Avenue, Gosforth, Newcastle upon Tyne

E-mail: no-newcastle@hmcourts-service.gsi.gov.uk

1583 NORTH DURHAM L.J.A.

Miss L. E. Brenkley, Solicitor, Magistrates' Court, Newcastle Road, Chester-le-Street, Co. Durham DH3 3UA	Adult –	Monday, Tuesday, Wednesday, Thursday and Friday, 10 a.m.	Magistrates' Courts, St Aidan's Way, Peterlee
		Monday, Tuesday, Thursday and Friday, 10 a.m.	Magistrates' Court, Ashdale Road, Consett
DX 721663 CHESTER-LE-STREET 2	YC –	Wednesday and Friday, 10 a.m.	Do.
Central Admin. Office Tel: 0191 387 0700 Fax: 0191 387 0746		Thursday, 10 a.m.	Magistrates' Court, St Aidan's Way, Peterlee
	FPC –	Tuesday and Thursday, 10 a.m.	Magistrates' Court, Old Elvet, Durham
		Private Prosecutions: Monday, Wednesday and Friday, 10 a.m.	Do.

CLEVELAND, DURHAM AND NORTHUMBRIA

Adult
Court Name of Court and
No   Clerk/Legal Adviser   Normal Times and Places of Courts

2852 NORTH TYNESIDE DISTRICT L.J.A.

Mrs. Rosemary Watson, LL.B., Clerk to the Justices, The Courthouse, Tynemouth Road, North Shields, Tyne and Wear NE30 1AG	Adult – Monday, Tuesday, Wednesday, Thursday and Friday, 10 a.m. and 2 p.m.	The Court House, Tynemouth Road, North Shields
	YC – Monday, Tuesday and Friday, 10 a.m. and 2 p.m.	Do.
Tel: 0191-296 0099 (Clerk/General Office) 0191-296 0055 (Fines/Accounts) 0191-298 2322 (Family Proceedings)	FPC – Monday to Friday, 9.30 a.m. and 2 p.m.	Hearing and administration at Kings Court, Earl Grey Way, Royal Quays, North Shields
Fax: 0191-296 2478		

For the Centralised Accounts Office, *see* South Tyneside District L.J.A.

1584 SOUTH DURHAM L.J.A.

Miss L. E. Brenkley, Solicitor, Magistrates' Court, Central Avenue, Newton Aycliffe, Co. Durham DL5 5RT	Adult – Tuesday and Friday	Magistrates' Court, Woodhouse Close, Bishop Auckland
	Weekdays, 10 a.m.	Magistrates' Court, Central Avenue, Newton Aycliffe
DX 63808 NEWTON AYCLIFFE	Tuesday and Thursday	Magistrates' Court, Parkgate, Darlington
Central Admin. Office Tel: 01325 318114	YC – Wednesday, 10 a.m.	Magistrates' Court, Woodhouse Close, Bishop Auckland
Fax: 01325 327697 (General)	Monday, 10 a.m.	Magistrates' Court, Central Avenue, Newton Aycliffe
01325 327699 (Listing)	Friday, 10 a.m.	Magistrates' Court, Parkgate, Darlington
	FPC – Monday, 10 a.m.	Do.
	Tuesday, 10 a.m.	Magistrates' Court, Central Avenue, Newton Aycliffe
	Wednesday, 10 a.m.	Magistrates' Court, Parkgate, Darlington
	Private Prosecutions: Monday, Thursday and Friday, 10 a.m.	Magistrates' Court, Woodhouse Close, Bishop Auckland

CLEVELAND, DURHAM AND NORTHUMBRIA

Adult Court No	Name of Court and Clerk/Legal Adviser		Normal Times and Places of Courts	
	Central Finance Unit *(for North & South Durham)* PO Box 107, Darlington DL1 1ZD DX 712818 DARLINGTON 8 Tel: 01325 376670 (Payments) 01325 376671 (Enforcement) 01325 376672 (Fixed Penalty) 01325 376673 (Licensing) Fax: 01325 376639	Fines Mtce.	Thursday Wednesday, p.m. (fortnightly) Fortnightly on Friday	Magistrates' Court, Parkgate, Darlington Magistrates' Court, Parkgate, Darlington Magistrates' Court, Old Elvet, Durham
2349	**SOUTH EAST NORTHUMBERLAND L.J.A.**			
	D. Pryer, MCMI, Finst CPD, Magistrates' Clerk's Office, The Law Courts, Bedlington, Northumberland NE22 7LX Tel: 01670 531100 Fax: 01670 820133 DX 62705 BEDLINGTON	Adult – YC – FPC –	Monday, Tuesday, Wednesday, Thursday and Friday, 10 a.m. Friday, 10 a.m. Thursday, 10 a.m.	The Law Courts, Bedlington Do. Do.
2853	**SOUTH TYNESIDE DISTRICT L.J.A.**			
	C. J. Livesley, B.A.(Hons), South Tyneside Magistrates' Court, Millbank, Secretan Way, South Shields NE33 1RG Tel: 0191-455 8800 427 4410 (Fines & Fees) 427 4400 (Criminal & Road Traffic Proceedings) 427 4420 (Family Proceedings) 427 4404 (Legal Aid) Fax: 0191-427 4499 DX 68670 SOUTH SHIELDS 6	Adult – YC – FPC – Dir. – CT –	Daily, 10 a.m. and 2 p.m. Private Prosecutions Friday, 10 a.m. and 2 p.m. Monday, 10 a.m. Wednesday, 10 a.m. and 2 p.m. Thursday, 10 a.m. and 2 p.m. 3 out of 4 Tuesdays, 2 p.m. Enforcement: Fines: Tuesday, 10 a.m. Maintenance Arrears: Thursday, 10 a.m. Alternate Tuesdays, 10 a.m.	South Tyneside Magistrates' Court, Millbank, Secretan Way, South Shields Do. Do. Do. Do. Do. Do.

CLEVELAND, DURHAM AND NORTHUMBRIA

Adult Court No	Name of Court and Clerk/Legal Adviser	Normal Times and Places of Courts	
2855	**SUNDERLAND L.J.A.**		
	S. P. Rowbottom, Barrister, LL.B.(Hons), M.B.A., Magistrates' Courts, Gillbridge Avenue, Sunderland SR1 3AP	Adult – Daily, 10 a.m.	Magistrates' Courts, Gillbridge Avenue, Sunderland
		YC – Thursday, 10 a.m.	Do.
	Tel: 0191-514 1621	FPC – Tuesday and Friday, 10 a.m.	Do.
	Fax: 0191-565 8564		
	DX 67757 SUNDERLAND 1		
1249	**TEESSIDE L.J.A.**		
	Siân E. Jones LL.B., Teesside Law Courts, Victoria Square, Middlesbrough TS1 2AS	Adult – Every week day, 10 a.m. and 2.15 p.m.	Magistrates' Court, Teesside Law Courts, Victoria Square, Middlesbrough
	Tel: 01642 240301	YC – Every weekday, 10 a.m. and 2.15 p.m.	Youth Court, Teeside Law Courts, Albert Road, Middlesbrough
	Fax: 01642 224010		
		FPC – Every weekday, 10 a.m. and 2.15 p.m.	Do.
	DX 60562 MIDDLESBROUGH		
	E-mail: postbox@hmcourts-service.gsi.gov.uk		
2346	**TYNEDALE L.J.A.**		
	D. Pryer, MCMI, The Court House, Beaumont Street, Hexham, Northumberland NE46 3NB	Adult – Tuesday, Wednesday, Thursday and Friday, 10 a.m.	Court House, Beaumont Street, Hexham
		YC – Monday, 10 a.m.	Do.
	Tel: 01434 603248	FPC – Fourth Wednesday in month, 10 a.m.	Do.
	Fax: 01434 609378		
	DX 68720		
	For the Centralised Accounts Office, see South East Northumberland L.J.A.		

NORTH WEST REGION

CUMBRIA AND LANCASHIRE

Area Director: Gill Hague, Area Director's Office, Sessions House, Lancaster Road, Preston, Lancashire PR1 2PD. Tel: 01772 272820 Fax: 01772 272821 DX 724880 PRESTON 21

Lancashire Central Fixed Penalty Office: P.O. Box 268, Blackburn, BB1 2WD
Tel: 01254 299940 Fax: 01254 583451

Cumbria Central Payments Unit (including Fixed Penalty Office): Burnside Road, Kendal Tel: 01539 720478 Fax: 01539 740502

Adult Court No	Name of Court and Clerk/Legal Adviser	Normal Times and Places of Courts	
2012	**BLACKBURN, DARWEN AND RIBBLE VALLEY L.J.A.**		
	John Robinson, Court House, Northgate, Blackburn, Lancs. BB2 1AF	Adult – Monday, Tuesday, Wednesday, and Friday, 10 a.m. and 2 p.m.	Court House, Northgate, Blackburn
	Tel: 01254 687500 687510 (Collecting Office)	YC – Thursday 10 a.m. and 2 p.m.	Do.
		Comb. Monday, 10 a.m.	Law Courts, Manchester Road, Accrington
		FPC (3 sittings per month)	
	Fax: 01254 687524 687520 (Fines Office)	Enf – Monday and Wednesday, 2 p.m.	Court House, Northgate, Blackburn
2014	**BURNLEY, PENDLE AND ROSSENDALE L.J.A.**		
	John Robinson, Justices' Clerk's Office, P.O. Box 64, Colne Road, Reedley, Nr. Burnley, Lancs. BB10 2NQ	Adult – Monday to Friday, 10 a.m.	Court House, Parker Lane, Burnley
		Monday and Wednesday, 10 a.m.	Court House, off Haslingden Road, Rawtenstall, Rossendale
		YC – Monday 10 a.m.	Court House, Colne Road, Reedley, near Burnley
	Tel: 01282 610000	Tuesday, 10 a.m.	Court House, off Haslingden Road, Rawtenstall, Rossendale
	Fax: 01282 610034 or 01282 610057		
	DX 741470 BURNLEY 7	FPC – Friday 10 a.m.	Court House, Colne Road, Reedley, near Burnley

CUMBRIA AND LANCASHIRE

Adult Court No	Name of Court and Clerk/Legal Adviser	Normal Times and Places of Courts	
1322	**CARLISLE AND DISTRICT L.J.A.**		
	C. J. Armstrong, B.A., North Cumbria Magistrates' Court, Rickergate, Carlisle, Cumbria CA3 8QH	Adult – Monday, Tuesday, Thursday and Friday, 10 a.m.	The Court House, Rickergate, Carlisle
		YC – Wednesday, 10 a.m.	Do.
	Tel: 01228 518800 Fax: 01228 518844	FPC – Wednesday, 10 a.m.	Do.
	DX 63018 CARLISLE		
	E-mail: cumbria.north.magistrates@hmcourts-service.gsi.gov.uk		
1998	**CHORLEY L.J.A.**		
	John Robinson, Court House, St. Thomas's Square, Chorley, Lancs. PR7 1DS	Adult – Monday, Wednesday, Thursday and Friday, 9.30 a.m. Wednesday, 2 p.m.	Court House, St. Thomas's Square, Chorley
		YC – Tuesday, 9.30 a.m.	Do.
	Tel: 01257 225000 Fax: 01257 261948	FPC – Friday (fortnightly), 9.30 a.m.	Court House, Lancastergate, Leyland
	DX 707530 CHORLEY 5	Enf. – Thursday, 9.30 a.m.	Court House, St. Thomas's Square, Chorley
1324	**EDEN L.J.A.**		
	C. J. Armstrong, B.A., North Cumbria Magistrates' Court, Rickergate, Carlisle, Cumbria CA3 8QH	Adult – Monday, Wednesday and Friday, 10 a.m.	Court House, Lowther Terrace, Penrith
		YC – Thursdays (fortnightly), 10 a.m.	Do.
	Tel: 01228 518800 Fax: 01228 518844	FPC – Wednesday, 10 a.m. (combined with Carlisle and District L.J.A.)	The Courthouse, Rickergate, Carlisle
	DX 63018 CARLISLE		
	E-mail: cumbria.north.magistrates@hmcourts-service.gsi.gov.uk		
1398	**FURNESS AND DISTRICT L.J.A.**		
	C. J. Armstrong, B.A., South Cumbria Magistrates' Court, Abbey Road, Barrow-in-Furness, Cumbria LA14 5QX	Adult – Monday, Tuesday and Thursday, 10 a.m. and 2 p.m.	Magistrates' Court, Abbey Road, Barrow-in-Furness
		YC – Fridays, 10 a.m.	Do.
		FPC – Wednesday, 10 a.m.	Do.
	Tel: 01229 820161 Fax: 01229 870287	Enf – Alternate Wednesdays, 10 a.m. or 2 p.m.	Do.
		Non Police Prosecutions – Wednesdays, 10 a.m. and 2 p.m.	
	DX 65211 BARROW-IN-FURNESS		
	E-mail: cumbria.south.magistrates@hmcourts-service.gsi.gov.uk		

CUMBRIA AND LANCASHIRE

Adult Court No	Name of Court and Clerk/Legal Adviser	Normal Times and Places of Courts	
1992	**FYLDE COAST L.J.A.**		
	John Robinson, The Law Courts, Civic Centre, Chapel Street, Blackpool, Lancs. FY1 5RH	Adult – Monday to Friday, 10 a.m. Monday, Tuesday, Wednesday, Thursday and Friday, 2 p.m.	Chapel Street, Blackpool
	Tel: 01253 757000 757040 (Fines Office)	Monday to Friday, 10 a.m. Monday, Tuesday, Wednesday, Thursday and Friday, 2 p.m.	11 The Esplanade, Fleetwood, Lancs. FY7 6AT
		YC – Monday to Friday, 10 a.m.	Chapel Street, Blackpool
	Fax: 01253 757024 757014	Tuesday, 10 a.m.	11 The Esplanade, Fleetwood, Lancs. FY7 6AT
		FPC – Friday, 10 a.m.	Chapel Street, Blackpool
		Wednesday, 10 a.m.	11 The Esplanade, Fleetwood, Lancs. FY7 6AT
2010	**HYNDBURN L.J.A.**		
	John Robinson, Court House, Northgate, Blackburn, Lancs. BB2 1AF	Adult – Monday, Wednesday, Thursday and Friday, 10 a.m. Wednesday and Friday, 2 p.m.	Law Courts, Manchester Road, Accrington Do.
	Tel: 01254 687500 687510 (Fines Office)	YC – Tuesday, 10 a.m. Comb. FPC – Monday, 10 a.m. (3 sittings per month)	Do. Do.
	Fax: 01254 687524 687520 (Fines office)	Enf. – Thursday 2 p.m.	Do.
2002	**LANCASTER L.J.A.**		
	John Robinson, Magistrates' Court, George Street, Lancaster LA1 1XZ	Adult – Monday, Tuesday, Wednesday, Thursday and Friday, 10 a.m. and 2 p.m.	Magistrates' Court, George Street, Lancaster
	Tel: 01524 597000 Fax: 01524 597024	YC – Tuesday and Thursday, 10 a.m. and 2 p.m.	Do.
		FPC – Wednesday, 10 a.m. and 2 p.m.	Do.
		Non-Police Prosecutions – Wednesday, 10 a.m. and Friday, 2 p.m.	–

NOTE: All fines and maintenance correspondence and enquiries to Preston L.J.A.

CUMBRIA AND LANCASHIRE

Adult Court No	Name of Court and Clerk/Legal Adviser	Normal Times and Places of Courts	
2003	**ORMSKIRK L.J.A.**		
	John Robinson, Court House, St. Thomas's Square, Chorley, Lancs. PR7 1DS	Adult – Monday, Tuesday, and Friday, 9.30 a.m. Friday, 2 p.m.	The Court House, Derby Street, Ormskirk
		NP – Thursday, 2 p.m.	
	Tel: 01257 225000	YC – Thursday, 9.30 a.m.	Do.
	Fax: 01257 261948	FPC – Wednesday (fortnightly), 9.30 a.m.	Do.
	DX 707530 CHORLEY 5	Enf. – Monday, 9.30 a.m.	Do.
	NOTE: Please send all correspondence to Chorley Magistrates' Court.		
2005	**PRESTON L.J.A.**		
	John Robinson, Magistrates' Court, P.O. Box 52, Lawson Street, Preston, Lancs. PR1 2RD	Adult – Monday, Tuesday, Wednesday, Thursday and Friday, 10 a.m. and 2 p.m.	Magistrates' Court, Lawson Street, Preston
	Tel: 01772 208000 208002 (Accounts)	YC – Monday, Tuesday, Wednesday, Thursday and Friday, 10 a.m.	Do.
		FPC – Tuesday 2 p.m. Friday, 10 a.m.	Do.
	Fax: 01772 208026		
1323	**SOUTH LAKELAND L.J.A.**		
	C. J. Armstrong, B.A. South Cumbria, Magistrates' Court, Abbey Road, Barrow-in-Furness, Cumbria LA14 5QX	Adult – Monday, Tuesday and Thursday, 10 a.m. and 2 p.m.	The Court House, Burneside Road, Kendal
		YC – Wednesday, 10.30 a.m.	Do.
	Tel: 01229 820161	FPC – Second and fourth Friday in month, 10.30 a.m.	Do.
	Fax: 01229 870287		
	DX 65211 BARROW-IN-FURNESS		
	E-mail: cumbria.south.magistrates@hmcourts-service.gsi.gov.uk		
2007	**SOUTH RIBBLE L.J.A.**		
	John Robinson, Court House, St. Thomas's Square, Chorley, Lancs. PR7 1DS	Adult – Monday and Thursday, 9.30 a.m. Thursday, 2 p.m.	Court House, Lancastergate, Leyland
		NP – Tuesday and Wednesday, 2 p.m.	Do.
	Tel: 01257 225000	YC – Wednesday, 9.30 a.m.	Do.
	Fax: 01257 261948	FPC – Friday (fortnightly), 9.30 a.m.	Do.
	DX 707530 CHORLEY 5	Enf. – Tuesdays, 9.30 a.m.	Do.
	NOTE: Please send all correspondence to Chorley Magistrates' Court.		

CUMBRIA AND LANCASHIRE

Adult Court No	Name of Court and Clerk/Legal Adviser	Normal Times and Places of Courts	

1325 WEST ALLERDALE AND KESWICK L.J.A.

C. J. Armstrong, B.A., West Cumbria Magistrates' Courts, Hall Park, Ramsay Brow, Workington, Cumbria CA14 4AS	Adult – Monday, Wednesday, Thursday and Friday, 10 a.m.	West Cumbria Magistrates' Courts, Ramsay Brow, Workington
	YC – Wednesday, 10 a.m. (combined with Whitehaven L.J.A.)	Do.
Tel: 01900 62244	FPC – Tuesday, fortnightly, 10 a.m. (combined with Whitehaven L.J.A.)	Do.
Fax: 01900 68644		
DX 68690 WORKINGTON 4		
E-mail: cumbria.west.magistrates@hmcourts-service.gsi.gov.uk		

1375 WHITEHAVEN L.J.A.

C. J. Armstrong, B.A., West Cumbria Magistrates' Courts, Hall Park, Ramsay Brow, Workington, Cumbria CA14 4AS	Adult – Monday, Wednesday and Friday, 10 a.m.	Magistrates' Court, Catherine Street, Whitehaven
	YC – Tuesday, 10 a.m. (combined with West Allerdale and Keswick L.J.A.)	Do.
Tel: 01900 62244	FPC – Thursday, fortnightly, 10 a.m. (combined with West Allerdale and Keswick L.J.A.)	Do.
Fax: 01900 68644		
DX 68690 WORKINGTON 4		
E-mail: cumbria.west.magistrates@hmcourts-service.gsi.gov.uk		

MIDLANDS REGION

DERBYSHIRE AND NOTTINGHAMSHIRE

Area Director: Mark Swales, Area Director's Office, Nottingham Magistrates' Court, Carrington Street, Nottingham NG2 1EE. Tel: 0115 955 8301 Fax: 0115 955 8177
DX 719030 NOTTINGHAM 32

Adult Court No	Name of Court and Clerk/Legal Adviser		Normal Times and Places of Courts
1430	**HIGH PEAK L.J.A.**		
	Miss D. Windsor-Bush, Peak Buildings, Terrace Road, Buxton, Derbyshire SK17 6DY	Adult – Monday and Wednesday, 10 a.m. (except Bank Holidays) Tuesday 10 a.m.	Court House, Peak Buildings, Terrace Road, Buxton
	Tel: 01298 23951 (General Enquiries)	YC – On Thursdays at 10 a.m. – dates specified annually	Do.
	Fax: 01298 26031	FPC – On Fridays at 10 a.m. – dates specified annually	Do.
	DX 26745 BUXTON		
	NOTE: All enquiries re payment of fines and maintenance and all transfer of fine orders should be directed to Southern Derbyshire Magistrates' Court.		
2566	**MANSFIELD L.J.A.**		
	G. B. Hooper, LL.B. (Hons.), Mansfield Magistrates' Court, Rosemary Street, Mansfield, Notts. NG19 6EE	Adult – Daily, 10 a.m. and 2.15 p.m.	Mansfield Magistrates' Court, Rosemary Street, Mansfield
		YC – Tuesday and Thursday, 10 a.m.	Do.
	Tel: 01623 451500		
	Fax: 01623 451648	FPC – Friday, 10 a.m.	Do.
	DX 179560 MANSFIELD 9		
2567	**NEWARK AND SOUTHWELL L.J.A.**		
	G. B. Hooper, LL.B. (Hons.), The Court House, Magnus Street, Newark, Notts. NG24 1LD	Adult – Monday, Wednesday, Thursday and Friday, 10 a.m. Wednesday, 2.15 p.m.	The Court House, Magnus Street, Newark
	Tel: 01636 688200	YC – Tuesday, 10 a.m.	Do.
	Fax: 01636 688222	FPC – Every second Thursday, 10 a.m.	Do.
	DX 11836(1) NEWARK 1		

DERBYSHIRE AND NOTTINGHAMSHIRE

Adult Court No	Name of Court and Clerk/Legal Adviser		Normal Times and Places of Courts	
1432	**NORTH EAST DERBYSHIRE AND DALES L.J.A.**			
	Miss D. Windsor-Bush, Court House, Tapton Lane, Chesterfield, Derbyshire S41 7TW	Adult – Daily, 10 a.m.	Court House, Tapton Lane, Chesterfield	
		YC – Tuesday and Friday, 10 a.m.	Do.	
	Tel: 01246 224040 (General Enquiries)	FPC – Thursday, 10 a.m.	Do.	
	Fax: 01246 246492			
	DX 742041 CHESTERFIELD 7			
2568	**NOTTINGHAM L.J.A.**			
	G. B. Hooper, LL.B. (Hons.), Nottingham Magistrates' Court, Carrington Street, Nottingham NG2 1EE	Adult – Daily, 10 a.m. and 2.15 p.m. Occasional courts, 10 a.m.	Nottingham Magistrates' Court, Carrington Street, Nottingham NG2 1EE	
		YC – Daily, 10 a.m. and 2.15 p.m.	Do.	
	Tel: 0115 955 8111	FPC – Monday, 2.15 p.m. Wednesday, 10 a.m. and 2.15 p.m. Thursday and Friday, 10 a.m.	Do.	
	Fax: 0115 955 8139			
	DX 719030 NOTTINGHAM 32			
1428	**SOUTHERN DERBYSHIRE L.J.A.**			
	Nigel E. Hallam, The Court House, St. Mary's Gate, Derby DE1 3JR	Adult – Daily, 10 a.m. and 2.15 p.m.	The Court House, St Mary's Gate, Derby	
		Tuesday, Wednesday and Thursday, 10 a.m. & 2.15 p.m.	The Court House, Pimlico, Ilkeston	
	Tel: 01332 362000			
	Fax: 01332 333183	YC – Daily, 10 a.m. & 2.15 p.m.	The Court House, St. Mary's Gate, Derby	
	DX 707570 DERBY 8	FPC – Tuesday, Wednesday and Thursday, 10 a.m. & 2.15 p.m.	Do.	
		Thursday, 10 a.m.	The Court House, Pimlico, Ilkeston	

DERBYSHIRE AND NOTTINGHAMSHIRE

Adult Court No	Name of Court and Clerk/Legal Adviser	Normal Times and Places of Courts	
2569	**WORKSOP AND RETFORD L.J.A.**		
	G. B. Hooper, LL.B. (Hons.), The Court House, 30 Potter Street, Worksop, Notts. S80 2AJ	Adult – Monday and Wednesday, 10 a.m. and 2.15 p.m. Friday, 10 a.m., and occasionally 2.15 p.m.	The Court House, Potter Street, Worksop
		Monday and Wednesday, 10 a.m. and Thursday, 10 a.m. and 2.15 p.m.	The Court House, Exchange Street, Retford
	Tel: 01909 486111		
	Fax: 01909 473521	YC – Alternate Tuesdays, 10 a.m. and 2.15 p.m.	The Court House, Potter Street, Worksop
	DX 12229 WORKSOP 1		The Court House, Exchange Street, Retford
		FPC – Alternate Tuesdays, 10 a.m. and 2.15 p.m.	The Court House, Potter Street, Worksop
		Thursday, three weeks out of four, 10 a.m.	The Court House, Potter Street, Worksop

SOUTH WEST REGION

DEVON AND CORNWALL

Area Director: David Gentry, Area Director's Office, Trevecca, Culverland Road, Liskeard, PL14 6RF. Tel: 01579 325325   Fax: 01579 325300

Fixed Penalty Office: PO Box 76, Plymouth, Devon PL1 2YN. Tel: 01752 675444   Fax: 01752 269492   DX 98470 PLYMOUTH 7

Adult Court No	Name of Court and Clerk/Legal Adviser	Normal Times and Places of Courts	
1292	**CENTRAL DEVON L.J.A.**		
	A. E. Mimmack, LL.B., M.Sc., Barrister, Central Devon Magistrates' Courts, Southernhay Gardens, Exeter EX1 1UH	Adult – Daily, 10 a.m.	Court House, Heavitree Road, Exeter
		Monday, 10 a.m.	Court House, Exeter Hill, Cullompton
		Wednesday, 10 a.m.	The Court House, Dowell Street, Honiton
		YC – Wednesday, Thursday and Friday, 10 a.m.	Court House, Heavitree Road, Exeter
		FPC – Tuesday and Thursday, 10 a.m.	Crown and County Buildings, Southernhay Gardens, Exeter
	Tel: 01392 415594 (Admin) 415560 (Finance) 415325 (Family)		Court House, Exeter Hill, Cullompton
	Fax: 01392 415593 DX 98440 EXETER 2		The Court House, Dowell Street, Honiton
1289	**EAST CORNWALL L.J.A.**		
	N. J. Lord, Barrister, The Magistrates' Courts, PO Box 2, Launceston Road, Bodmin, Cornwall PL31 1XQ	Adult – Every Tuesday, Wednesday, Thursday and Friday, 10 a.m.	The Court House, Launceston Road, Bodmin
		Monday and Wednesday, 10 a.m.	The Court House, Ground Floor, Trevecca, Liskeard
		Tuesday, 10 a.m.	The Court House, Dunheved Road, Launceston
	Tel: 01208 262700 Fax: 01208 77198	YC – Monday, 10 a.m.	The Court House, Launceston Road, Bodmin
		FPC – Selected Thursdays, 10 a.m. Thursday, 10 a.m.	Do. The Court House, Ground Floor, Trevecca, Liskeard
		Enf. – Alternate Thursdays, 10 a.m.	The Court House, Launceston Road, Bodmin

NOTE: All payments, correspondence and enquiries should be addressed to the court office at Bodmin.

DEVON AND CORNWALL

Adult Court No	Name of Court and Clerk/Legal Adviser	Normal Times and Places of Courts	
1291	**NORTH DEVON L.J.A.**		
	A. E. Mimmack, LL.B., M.Sc., Barrister, The Law Courts, Civic Centre, Barnstaple, Devon EX31 1DX	Adult – Daily, 10 a.m.	The Law Courts, Civic Centre, Barnstaple
		YC – Tuesday, 10 a.m.	The Law Courts, Civic Centre, Barnstaple
	Tel: 01271 340410	FPC – Thursday, 10 a.m.	Do.
	Fax: 01271 340415		
1290	**PLYMOUTH DISTRICT L.J.A.**		
	T. A. M. Smith, B.A., Solicitor, Magistrates' Court, St. Andrew Street, Plymouth PL1 2DP	Adult – Daily, 10 a.m. and 2 p.m.	Magistrates' Court, St. Andrew Street, Plymouth
		YC – Daily, 10 a.m. and 2 p.m.	Do.
	Tel: 01752 206200	FPC – Monday, 2 p.m. Wednesday, 10 a.m. and 2 p.m. Friday, 10 a.m.	Do.
	Fax: 01752 206194		
1293	**SOUTH DEVON L.J.A.**		
	T. A. M. Smith, B.A., Solicitor, First Floor, Riviera House, Nicholson Road, Torquay, Devon TQ2 7TT	Adult – Daily 10 a.m.	The Court House, Union Street, Torquay
		Wednesday, 10 a.m.	The Court House, Ashburton Road, Totnes
		Monday, Tuesday, Thursday and Friday, 10 a.m.	Court House, Newton Abbot
		YC – Wednesday, 10 a.m.	Do.
		FPC – Monday and Tuesday, 10 a.m. Every second Thursday, 10 a.m.	The Court House, Ashburton Road, Totnes
	Tel: 01803 612211 01803 618625 (Family) 01803 618621 (Fines) 01803 618633 (Betting and Gaming)		
	Fax: 01803 618618		

DEVON AND CORNWALL

Adult Court No	Name of Court and Clerk/Legal Adviser	Normal Times and Places of Courts	
1288	**WEST CORNWALL L.J.A.**		
	N. J. Lord, Barrister, P.O. Box 60, Truro TR1 2HQ	Adult – Daily, 10 a.m.	The Court House, Tremorvah Wood Lane, Mitchell Hill, Truro
	Tel: 01872 321900 (General Enquiries) 01872 321950 (Fines/Maintenance/Family)	Thursday, 10 a.m.	Magistrates' Court, The Basset Centre, Basset Road, Camborne
		Tuesdays (as required), 10 a.m.	The Guildhall, Penzance
	Fax: 01872 276227 DX 140880 TRURO 5	Quarterly, 10 a.m.	Old Wesleyan Chapel, Garrison Lane, Hugh Town, St Marys, Isles of Scilly
		YC – Friday, 10 a.m.	The Court House, Tremorvah Wood Lane, Mitchell Hill, Truro
		As required	Magistrates' Court, The Basset Centre, Basset Road, Camborne
		As required	The Guildhall, Penzance
		FPC – As required	Magistrates' Court, The Basset Centre, Basset Road, Camborne
		As required	The Guildhall, Penzance
	E-mail: westcornwall@hmcourts-service.gsi.gov.uk		

SOUTH WEST REGION

DORSET, GLOUCESTERSHIRE AND WILTSHIRE

Area Director: Rod Brummitt, Area Director's Office, The Law Courts, Park Road, Poole, Dorset BH15 2RH. Tel: 01202 711810   Fax: 01202 747245   DX 98700 POOLE 4

Adult Court No	Name of Court and Clerk/Legal Adviser	Normal Times and Places of Courts	
	DORSET COMBINED FAMILY PANEL		
	Mrs. R. V. Davies, The Law Courts, Park Road, Poole, Dorset BH15 2RH	Wednesday and Alternate Fridays, 10 a.m.	The Family Court Suite at The Law Courts, Stafford Road, Bournemouth
	Tel: 01202 711872	Alternate Mondays, 10 a.m.	The Law Courts, Westwey Road, Weymouth
	Fax: 01202 711996 DX 123822 POOLE 7	Every fourth Thursday, 10 a.m.	The Court House, Salisbury Road, Blandford Forum
5522/ 5523	**DORSET COMBINED YOUTH PANEL**		
	Mrs. R. V. Davies, The Law Courts, Westwey Road, Weymouth, Dorset DT4 8BS	Monday, and Thursday, 10 a.m.	The Law Courts, Park Road, Poole
		Wednesday, 10 a.m.	The Law Courts, Westwey Road, Weymouth
	Tel: 01305 783891 Fax: 01305 761418 DX 98820 WEYMOUTH 3		
1522	**EAST DORSET L.J.A.**		
	Mrs. R. V. Davies, The Law Courts, Stafford Road, Bournemouth, Dorset BH1 1LA	Adult – Daily, 10 a.m.	The Law Courts, Stafford Road, Bournemouth
		Monday, Tuesday and Thursday, 10 a.m.	The Law Courts, Hanham Road, Wimborne
	Tel: 01202 745309 Fax: 01202 711999 DX 123822 POOLE 7	As required	The Law Courts, Worgret Road, Wareham
		Tuesday, Wedneday and Friday, 10 a.m.	The Law Courts, Park Road, Poole
		YC – See Dorset Combined Youth Panel	
		FPC – See Dorset Combined Family Panel	

DORSET, GLOUCESTERSHIRE AND WILTSHIRE

Adult Court No	Name of Court and Clerk/Legal Adviser		Normal Times and Places of Courts
1698	**GLOUCESTERSHIRE L.J.A.**		
	Mr. M. T. Seath, P.O. Box 9051, Gloucester GL1 2XG		
	Cheltenham Courthouse	Adult – Monday, Tuesday, Wednesday, Thursday and Friday, 10 a.m. and 2 p.m.	Magistrates' Court, St George's Road, Cheltenham
	Cirencester Courthouse		The Courthouse, The Forum, Cirencester
	Coleford Courthouse		The Courthouse, Gloucester Road, Coleford
	Gloucester Courthouse	Adult – Monday, Tuesday, Wednesday and Friday, 10 a.m. and 2 p.m.	The Courthouse, Barbican Way, Gloucester
	Stroud Courthouse	Adult – Monday, Tuesday, Wednesday, Thursday and Friday, 10 a.m. and 2 p.m.	The Courthouse, Parliament Street, Stroud
	NOTE: For enquiries and correspondence please see Gloucestershire contact details.		
5698	**GLOUCESTERSHIRE YOUTH COURT**		
	Mr. M. T. Seath, P.O. Box 9051, Gloucester GL1 2XG	YC – County Panel Tuesday, 10 a.m.	The Courthouse, Parliament Street, Stroud
		Thursday, 10 a.m.	The Courthouse, Barbican Way, Gloucester
	FAMILY PROCEEDINGS SECTION		
	PO Box 9050, Gloucester GL1 2WG	FPC – County Panel Tuesday, Wednesday and Thursday	Kimbrose Way, Gloucester
	NOTE: For enquiries and correspondence please see Gloucestershire contact details.		
3026	**NORTH WEST WILTSHIRE L.J.A.**		
	D. L. Brewer, B.A., Barrister, The Court House, Pewsham Way, Chippenham, Wilts. SN15 3BF	Adult – Monday to Friday, 10 a.m.	The Court House, Pewsham Way, Chippenham
		YC – Wednesday, 10 a.m.	The Court House, Pewsham Way, Chippenham
	Tel: 01249 463473	Friday, 10 a.m.	Do.
	Fax: 01249 444319 DX 34213 CHIPPENHAM	Fine – Fortnightly, 10 a.m. Dflt	The Court House, Pewsham Way, Chippenham

DORSET, GLOUCESTERSHIRE AND WILTSHIRE

Adult Court No	Name of Court and Clerk/Legal Adviser	Normal Times and Places of Courts	
3027	**SOUTH EAST WILTSHIRE L.J.A.**		
	D. L. Brewer, B.A., Barrister, Magistrates' Court, Administration Office, 43/55 Milford Street, Salisbury, Wilts. SP1 2BP Tel: 01722 333225 Fax: 01722 413395 DX 58022 SALISBURY	Adult – Monday and Tuesday, 10 a.m. Monday, Wednesday and Friday, 10 a.m.	The Courthouse, Northgate Gardens, Off Northgate Street, Devizes Guildhall, Market Square, Salisbury
		YC – Tuesday, 10 a.m.	Guildhall, Market Square, Salisbury
		FPC – As required As required	The Courthouse, Northgate Gardens, off Northgate Street, Devizes Guildhall, Market Square, Salisbury
		Enf. CT – Monday, once a month, 12 noon Monday, once a month, 10 a.m.	The Courthouse, Northgate Gardens, off Northgate Street, Devizes Guildhall, Market Square, Salisbury
3015	**SWINDON L.J.A.**		
	D. L. Brewer, B.A., Barrister, Swindon Magistrates' Court, Princes Street, Swindon, Wilts. SN1 2JB Tel: 01793 699800 Fax: 01793 433740 DX 118725 SWINDON 7	Adult – Daily, 10 a.m. and 2 p.m.	Swindon Magistrates' Court
		YC – Monday and Wednesday, 10 a.m. and 2 p.m.	Do.
		FPC – Tuesday (every eight weeks), 10 a.m. and 2 p.m.	Do.
1523	**WEST DORSET L.J.A.**		
	Mrs. R. V. Davies, The Law Courts, Westwey Road, Weymouth, Dorset DT4 8BS Tel: 01305 783891 Fax: 01305 761418 DX 98820 WEYMOUTH 3	Adult – Monday, Tuesday, Thursday and Friday, 10 a.m.	The Law Courts, Westwey Road, Weymouth
		Wednesday, 10 a.m.	The Law Courts, Salisbury Road, Blandford Forum
		Every fourth Tuesday, 10 a.m.	The Court House, Mountfield, Bridport
		YC – See Dorset Combined Youth Panel	
		FPC – See Dorset Combined Family Panel	

NORTH WEST REGION

GREATER MANCHESTER

Area Director: Richard Knott, Area Director's Office, 15 Quay Street, Manchester M60 9FD. Tel: 0161 833 1005 Fax: 0161 831 6329
DX 724780 MANCHESTER 44

Adult Court No	Name of Court and Clerk/Legal Adviser		Normal Times and Places of Courts	
1731	**BOLTON L.J.A.**			
	David Greensmith, P.O. Box 24, The Courts, Civic Centre, Le Mans Crescent, Bolton BL1 1QX	Adult – Monday, Tuesday, Thursday and Friday, 10 a.m. and 2. p.m.	The Courts, Civic Centre, Bolton	
		YC – Wednesday and Friday, 10 a.m. and 2 p.m.	Do.	
	Tel: 01204 558200	FPC – Monday and Thursday, 10 a.m. and 2 p.m.	Do.	
	Fax: 01204 364373 (Genl) 394669 (Private)			
	DX 707360/61/62 BOLTON 6			
1732	**BURY L.J.A.**			
	David Greensmith, Magistrates' Court, The Courthouse, Tenters Street, Bury BL9 0HX	Adult – Monday to Friday (inclusive), 10 a.m. and 2 p.m.	Magistrates' Court, Tenters Street, Bury	
		YC – Thursday, 10 a.m. and 2 p.m.	Do.	
	Tel: 0161-447 8600	FPC – Tuesday, 10 a.m. and 2 p.m.	Do.	
	Fax: 0161-447 8630	Directions appointments – Tuesday mornings	Do.	
	DX 707370 BURY 4			
1747	**CITY OF SALFORD L.J.A.**			
	David Greensmith, Magistrates' Court, Bexley Square, Salford M3 6DJ	Adult – Daily, 10 a.m. and 2 p.m.	Magistrates' Court, Bexley Square, Salford	
	Tel: 0161-834 9457	YC – Tuesday and Thursday, 10 a.m.	Do.	
	Fax: 0161-839 1806 (Admin) 0161-831 9561 (Family & Fines)	FPC – Wednesday and Friday, 10 a.m.	Do.	
		Dir. – Wednesday 2 p.m.	Do.	
	DX 708270 SALFORD 8			

GREATER MANCHESTER

Adult Court No	Name of Court and Clerk/Legal Adviser	Normal Times and Places of Courts	
1733	**MANCHESTER CITY L.J.A.**		
	David Greensmith, City Magistrates' Court, Crown Square, Manchester M60 1PR	Adult – Daily, 10 a.m.	Magistrates' Court, Crown Square, Manchester
	Tel: 0161-830 4200	YC – Daily, 10 a.m.	Do.
	Fax: 0161-830 4210 (Pre-court) 0161-830 4225 (Enforcement)	FPC – Daily, 10 a.m.	Do.
1734	**OLDHAM L.J.A.**		
	David Greensmith, Magistrates' Court, St. Domingo Place, West Street, Oldham OL1 1QE	Adult – Monday, Tuesday, Wednesday and Thursday, 10 a.m. and 2 p.m. Friday, 10 a.m.	Magistrates' Court, St. Domingo Place, Oldham
	Tel: 0161-620 2331	YC – Friday, 10 a.m. and 2 p.m.	Do.
	Fax: 0161-652 0172 DX 708252	FPC – Monday, Tuesday, Wednesday and Thursday, 10 a.m. and 2 p.m.	Do.
1750	**ROCHDALE, MIDDLETON AND HEYWOOD L.J.A.**		
	Frederick Wood, The Court House, P.O. Box 8, Town Meadows, Rochdale OL16 1AR,	Adult – Monday, Tuesday, Wednesday, Thursday and Friday, 10 a.m. Monday, Tuesday, Wednesday Thursday and Friday, 2 p.m.	The Court House, Town Meadows, Rochdale
	Tel: 01706 514800 Fax: 01706 514850	YC – Wednesday and Thursday, 10 a.m. and 2 p.m.	Do.
		FPC – Monday, 10 a.m. and 2 p.m.	Do.
1739	**STOCKPORT L.J.A.**		
	David Greensmith, The Courthouse, Stockport Magistrates' Court, P.O. Box 155, Edward Street, Stockport SK1 3NF	Adult – Monday, Tuesday, Wednesday, Thursday and Friday, 10 a.m. and 2 p.m.	The Courthouse, Edward Street, Stockport
		YC – Wednesday and Friday	Do.
	Tel: 0161-477 2020 Fax: 0161-474 1115	FPC – Tuesday and Thursday, 10 a.m.	Do.

GREATER MANCHESTER

Adult Court No	Name of Court and Clerk/Legal Adviser	Normal Times and Places of Courts	
1748	**TAMESIDE L.J.A.**		
	David Greensmith, Magistrates' Court, Henry Square, Ashton-under-Lyne OL6 7TP	Adult – Monday, Tuesday, Wednesday, Thursday and Friday, 10 a.m.	Magistrates' Court, Henry Square, Ashton-under-Lyne
	Tel: 0161-330 2023	YC – Tuesday and Thursday, 10 a.m.	Do.
	Fax: 0161-343 1498	FPC – Friday, 10 a.m.	Do.
1742	**TRAFFORD L.J.A.**		
	David Greensmith, Magistrates' Court, P.O. Box 13, Ashton Lane, Sale, Cheshire M33 7NR	Adult – Daily, 10 a.m.	Magistrates' Court, Ashton Lane, Sale
	Tel: 0161-976 3333	YC – Tuesday, Wednesday and Thursday, 10 a.m.	Do.
	Fax: 0161-975 4673	FPC – Monday, 10 a.m.	Do.
	DX 708290 SALE 6		
1749	**WIGAN AND LEIGH L.J.A.**		
	David Greensmith, Magistrates' Court, Darlington Street, Wigan WN1 1DW	Adult – Monday to Friday, 10 a.m. and 2 p.m.	Darlington Street, Wigan
	Tel: 01942 405405 405439 (Fines and Fees)	YC – Tuesday and Thursday, 10 a.m. and 2 p.m.	Do.
	405433 (Family Court Office)	FPC – Wednesday, 10 a.m. and 2 p.m.	Do.
		FDir. – Wednesday, 10 a.m.	Do.
	Fax: 01942 405444/69		

SOUTH WEST REGION

HAMPSHIRE AND THE ISLE OF WIGHT

Area Director: Stephen Williamson, The Court House, Elmleigh Road, Havant, Hampshire PO9 2AL. Tel: 02392 492024   Fax: 02392 475356

Adult Court No	Name of Court and Clerk/Legal Adviser		Normal Times and Places of Courts	
1945	**ISLE OF WIGHT L.J.A.**			
	J. S. W. Black, LL.M., F.C.I.P.D., Solicitor, The Magistrates' Court, The Law Courts, Quay Street, Newport, Isle of Wight PO30 5YT	Adult	– Monday, Tuesday, Thursday and Friday, 9.30 a.m.	Magistrates' Court, The Law Courts, Quay Street, Newport, I.O.W.
		YC	– Wednesday and alternate Mondays, 9.30 a.m.	Do.
	Tel: 01983 535100	FPC	– Wednesday, 9.30 a.m.	Do.
	Fax: 01983 554977			
1779	**NEW FOREST L.J.A.**			
	J. S. W. Black, LL.M., F.C.I.P.D., Solicitor, Southampton Magistrates' Court, 100 The Avenue, Southampton SO17 1EY	Adult	– Monday to Friday, 10 a.m. and 2 p.m.	The Court House, Pike's Hill, Lyndhurst
	Tel: 023 8038 4200			
	Fax: 023 8038 4201 4202 (Financial Services) 4203 (Court Services) 4204 (Scheduling) 4205 (Family)	YC	– (Combined with Southampton L.J.A., see p. 56)	Southampton Magistrates' Court, 100 The Avenue, Southampton
	DX 135986 SOUTHAMPTON 32			
		FPC	– (Combined with Southampton L.J.A., see p. 56)	Southampton Magistrates' Court, 100 The Avenue, Southampton

HAMPSHIRE AND THE ISLE OF WIGHT

Adult Court No	Name of Court and Clerk/Legal Adviser	Normal Times and Places of Courts	

1780 NORTH EAST HAMPSHIRE L.J.A.

J. S. W. Black, LL.M., F.C.I.P.D., Solicitor,
The Court House,
Civic Centre,
Aldershot, Hants.
GU11 1NY

Tel: 01252 366000
       366033
     (Accounts)

Fax: 01252 330877

DX 145110
ALDERSHOT 4

Adult – Monday, Tuesday, Wednesday, Thursday and Friday, 10 a.m. and 2 p.m.

As required

YC – (Combined panel with North West Hampshire)
Alternate Mondays, 10 a.m. and 2 p.m.
Wednesday, 10 a.m. and 2 p.m.

FPC – As required

As required

The Court House, Civic Centre, Aldershot

The Court House, Normandy Street, Alton

The Court House, Normandy Street, Alton
The Court House, London Road, Basingstoke

The Court House, Normandy Street, Alton

The Court House, West Street, Andover

All correspondence to Civic Centre.

1781 NORTH WEST HAMPSHIRE L.J.A.

J. S. W. Black, LL.M., F.C.I.P.D., Solicitor,
The Court House,
London Road,
Basingstoke, Hants.
RG21 4AB

Tel: 01252 366000

Fax: 01256 811447

DX 145110
ALDERSHOT 4

Adult – Monday, Tuesday, Thursday and Friday, 10 a.m. and 2 p.m.

As required

YC – (Combined panel with North East Hampshire)
Wednesday, 10 a.m.

Alternate Friday, 10 a.m.

FPC – As required

The Court House, London Road, Basingstoke

The Court House, West Street, Andover

The Court House, London Road, Basingstoke

The Court House, West Street, Andover

The Court House, West Street, Andover

All correspondence to Civic Centre.

1782 SOUTH EAST HAMPSHIRE L.J.A.

J. S. W. Black, LL.M., F.C.I.P.D., Solicitor,
The Law Courts,
Winston Churchill Avenue,
Portsmouth, Hants.
PO1 2DQ

Tel: 023 9281 9421

Fax: 023 9229 3085

DX 98494 PORTSMOUTH 5

Adult – Daily (except Saturday), 10 a.m.

YC – (Combined with South Hampshire L.J.A.)
Daily (except Saturday), 10 a.m.

FPC – (Combined with South Hampshire L.J.A.)
Monday, Wednesday and Thursday, 10 a.m.

The Law Courts, Winston Churchill Avenue, Portsmouth

The Court House, Trinity Street, Fareham, Hants.

The Law Courts, Winston Churchill Avenue, Portsmouth

HAMPSHIRE AND THE ISLE OF WIGHT

Adult Court No	Name of Court and Clerk/Legal Adviser		Normal Times and Places of Courts	
1783	**SOUTH HAMPSHIRE L.J.A.**			
	J. S. W. Black, LL.M., F.C.I.P.D., Solicitor, The Law Courts, Winston Churchill Avenue, Portsmouth, Hants. PO1 2DQ	Adult –	Daily (except Saturday), 10 a.m.	The Court House, Trinity Street, Fareham, Hants
		YC –	(Combined with South East Hampshire L.J.A.) Daily (except Saturday), 10 a.m.	Do.
	Tel: 023 9281 9421 Fax: 023 9229 3085			
		FPC –	(Combined with South East Hampshire L.J.A.) Monday, Wednesday and Thursday, 10 a.m.	The Law Courts, Winston Churchill Avenue, Portsmouth
	DX 98494 PORTSMOUTH 5			
1775	**SOUTHAMPTON L.J.A.**			
	J. S. W. Black, LL.M., F.C.I.P.D., Solicitor, Southampton Magistrates' Court, 100 The Avenue, Southampton SO17 1EY	Adult –	Monday to Friday, 10 a.m. and 2 p.m.	Southampton Magistrates' Court, 100 The Avenue, Southampton
	Tel: 023 8038 4200 Fax: 023 8038 4201 4202 (Financial Services)	YC –	Monday to Friday, 10 a.m. and 2 p.m.	Do.
	4203 (Court Services) 4204 (Scheduling) 4205 (Family)	FPC –	First and third Monday, Wednesday and Friday, 10 a.m. and 2 p.m. Second and fourth Thursdays, 10 a.m. and 2 p.m.	Do.
	DX 135986 SOUTHAMPTON 32			

NORTH EAST REGION

HUMBER AND SOUTH YORKSHIRE

Area Director: Paul Bradley, Sheffield Combined Court, Family Hearing Centre, 48 West Bar, Sheffied S3 8PH. Tel: 0114 201 1140 Fax: 0114 201 1150
DX 302028 SHEFFIELD 6

Adult Court No	Name of Court and Clerk/Legal Adviser	Normal Times and Places of Courts	
2770	**BARNSLEY L.J.A.**		
	Debbie Conway, District Legal Director, Court House, P.O. Box 17, Barnsley, S. Yorks. S70 2DW	Adult – Monday to Friday, 10 a.m. and 2.15 p.m.	Court House, Westgate, Barnsley
		YC – Tuesday and Friday, 10 a.m. Thursday and Friday, 2 p.m.	Do.
		FPC – Monday and Wednesday, 10 a.m.	Do.
	Tel: 01226 320032 Criminal Listing 320013 Administration general enquiries 320001/320015 Fines 320005/320053 Family and Maintenance 320024 Legal Aid 320023 Legal Advisers 320010 Licensing 320000 Main switchboard		
	Fax: 01226 320044 Administration 320043 Finance		
	DX 12279 BARNSLEY 1		
1942	**BEVERLEY AND THE WOLDS L.J.A.**		
	Mrs. T. S. Brown, Bench Legal Manager, Beverley Magistrates' Court, Champney Road, Beverley, E. Yorkshire HU17 9EJ	Adult – Daily, 9.30 a.m.	The Court House, Champney Road, Beverley
		YC – Tuesday, 10.30 a.m.	Do.
		FPC – Monday, 9.30 a.m.	Do.
	Tel: 01482 861607	Non-CPS – Wednesday, 9.30 a.m.	Do.
	Fax: 01482 882004		
1941	**BRIDLINGTON L.J.A.**		
	Mrs. T. S. Brown, Bench Legal Manager, Beverley Magistrates' Court, Champney Road, Beverley, E. Yorkshire HU17 9EJ	Adult – Daily, 9.30 a.m.	The Court House, Quay Road, Bridlington
		YC – Thursday, 10.30 a.m.	Do.
		FPC – Wednesday, 9.30 a.m.	Do.
	Tel: 01482 861607	Non-CPS – Thursday, 9.30 a.m.	Do.
	Fax: 01482 882004		

HUMBER AND SOUTH YORKSHIRE

Adult Court No	Name of Court and Clerk/Legal Adviser	Normal Times and Places of Courts	
2771	**DONCASTER L.J.A.**		
	Richard Hazell, District Legal Director, P.O. Box 49, The Law Courts, College Road, Doncaster, S. Yorks. DN1 3HT Tel: 01302 366711 Fax: 01302 347359 DX 12574 DONCASTER	Adult – Monday, Tuesday, Wednesday, Thursday and Friday, 10 a.m. and 2.15 p.m. YC – Tuesday and Thursday, 10 a.m. and 2.15 p.m. FPC – Tuesday, Wednesday, Thursday and Friday, 10 a.m. (or at any other time by special arrangement)	The Law Courts, College Road, Doncaster The Law Courts, College Road, Doncaster The Law Courts, College Road, Doncaster
1928	**GOOLE AND HOWDENSHIRE L.J.A.**		
	Mrs. T. S. Brown, Bench Legal Manager, Beverley Magistrates' Court, Champney Road, Beverley, E. Yorkshire HU17 9EJ Tel: 01482 861607 Fax: 01482 882004	Adult – Tuesday and Friday, 9.30 a.m. YC – Wednesday, 10.30 a.m. FPC – Monday, 9.30 a.m. Non-CPS – Thursday, 9.30 a.m.	The Court House, Estcourt Terrace, Goole Do. Do. Do.
1940	**GRIMSBY AND CLEETHORPES L.J.A.**		
	Mr. Michael Draper, Bench Legal Manager, Victoria Street, Grimsby, N.E. Lincs. DN31 1PD Tel: 01472 320444 Fax: 01472 320440 DX 707680 GRIMSBY 5	Adult – Monday to Friday, 9.30 a.m. Monday, Tuesday, Wednesday and Thursday, 2.15 p.m. YC – Monday, 9.30 a.m. and 2.15 p.m. and Wednesday and Friday, 9.30 a.m. and 2.15 p.m. FPC – Wednesday, 9.30 a.m.	Magistrates' Court, Victoria Street, Grimsby Do. Do.
	The financial section has been re-located to North Lincolnshire Magistrates' Court. All correspondence should be addressed to the Grimsby & Scunthorpe Magistrates' Courts, Central Finance Unit, Corporation Road, Scunthorpe, North Lincolnshire DN15 6QB		
1943	**HULL AND HOLDERNESS L.J.A.**		
	Mrs. Karen Clark, Bench Legal Manager, P.O. Box 2, Market Place, Kingston upon Hull HU1 2AD Tel: 01482 328914 Fax: 01482 219790 DX 742160 HULL 20	Adult – Daily, 10 a.m. YC – Daily, 10 a.m. FPC – Daily, 10 a.m.	Law Courts, Market Place, Kingston upon Hull Do. Do.

HUMBER AND SOUTH YORKSHIRE

Adult
Court *Name of Court and*
No *Clerk/Legal Adviser*   *Normal Times and Places of Courts*

1903	**NORTH LINCOLNSHIRE L.J.A.**		
	Mr. Mike Prudom, Bench Legal Manager, Court Centre Office, Corporation Road, Scunthorpe DN15 6QB	Adult – Daily, 9.30 a.m. and 2.15 p.m.	Scunthorpe Court Centre, Laneham Street, Scunthorpe
		YC – Thursday, 9.30 a.m. and 2.15 p.m.	Do.
	Tel: 01724 281100	FPC – Friday, 9.30 a.m. and 2.15 p.m.	Do.
	Fax: 01724 281890		
	DX 742212 SCUNTHORPE 10		
2772	**ROTHERHAM L.J.A.**		
	Christopher G. O'Dowd, District Legal Director, The Statutes, P.O. Box 15, Rotherham, S. Yorks. S60 1YW	Adult – Monday to Friday, 10 a.m. and 2.15 p.m. Saturday, 10 a.m.	The Statutes, Rotherham
		YC – Monday, Tuesday and Thursday, 10 a.m. and 2.15 p.m.	Do.
	Tel: 01709 839339		
	Fax: 01709 370082	FPC – Tuesday 10 a.m. and 2.15 p.m. Wednesday, 10 a.m.	Do.
	DX 12619 ROTHERHAM		
2773	**SHEFFIELD L.J.A.**		
	Miss Elizabeth Fisher, District Legal Director, Magistrates' Court, Castle Street, Sheffield S3 8LU	Adult – Monday to Friday, 10 a.m. and 2.15 p.m.	Magistrates' Court, Castle Street, Sheffield
		YC – Monday to Friday, 10 a.m. and 2.15 p.m.	Do.
	Tel: 0114 276 0760	FPC – Monday, Tuesday and Thursday, 2.15 p.m. Wednesday and Friday, 10 a.m. (or at any other time by special arrangement)	Do.
	Fax: 0114 272 0129		
	DX 10599 SHEFFIELD 1		

SOUTH EAST REGION

KENT

Area Director: Dave Weston, Area Director's Office, Gail House, Lower Stone Street, Maidstone ME15 6NB. Tel: 01622 680050 Fax: 01622 680078 DX 152300 MAIDSTONE 19

Fixed Penalty Office: Phoenix House, PO Box 925, 2-8 London Road, Maidstone, ME16 8YA Tel: 01622 656380

East Kent Finance Centre: The Magistrates' Court, Pencester Road, Dover CT16 1BS. Tel: 01304 218600 Fax: 01304 211815 DX 6306 DOVER

West Kent Finance Centre: Gail House, Lower Stone Street, Maidstone ME15 6NB. Tel: 01622 680070 Fax: 01622 680079 DX 152300 MAIDSTONE 19

Adult Court No	Name of Court and Clerk/Legal Adviser	Normal Times and Places of Courts	
1960	**CENTRAL KENT L.J.A.**		
	M. Q. Morton, Barrister, Clerk to the Justices, The Courthouse, Palace Avenue, Maidstone, Kent ME15 6LL	Adult – Monday, Tuesday, Wednesday, Thursday, Friday, 10 a.m.	The Courthouse, Palace Avenue, Maidstone, Kent ME15 6LL
	Tel: 01622 671041	YC – Monday, 10 a.m.	Do.
	Fax: 01622 691800	FPC – Wednesday and Friday, 10 a.m.	Do.
		Adult – Monday, Tuesday, Wednesday, Thursday, Friday, 10 a.m.	The Courthouse, Park Road, Sittingbourne, Kent ME10 1DP
		YC – Thursday, 10 a.m.	Do.
		FPC – Friday, 10 a.m.	Do.
		Adult – Monday, Tuesday, Wednesday, Thursday, Friday, 10 a.m.	The Courthouse, Morewood Close, London Road, Sevenoaks TN13 2HT
		YC – Thursday, 10 a.m.	Do.
		FPC – First, Third and Fifth, Monday in the month, 10 a.m.	Do.
	DX 51954 MAIDSTONE 2		

KENT

Adult Court No	Name of Court and Clerk/Legal Adviser	Normal Times and Places of Courts	
1957	**EAST KENT L.J.A.**		
	Court Admin Office, The Magistrates' Court, Pencester Road, Dover, Kent CT16 1BS		
	Tel: 01304 218600		
	Fax: 01304 213819 (Admin)		
	DX 6306 DOVER		
	Ashford Courthouse	Adult – Daily, 10 a.m.	The Magistrates' Courts, Tufton Street, Ashford
	Canterbury Courthouse	Adult – Monday, Wednesday, Thursday and Friday, 10 a.m.	The Magistrates' Court, Broad Street, Canterbury
		YC – Tuesday, 10 a.m.	Do.
		FPC – Wednesday, 10 a.m.	Do.
	Dover Courthouse	Adult – Monday, Thursday, and occasional Fridays, 10 a.m.	The Magistrates' Court, Pencester Road, Dover
	Folkestone Courthouse	Adult – Daily, 10 a.m.	The Law Courts, Castle Hill Avenue, Folkestone
		YC – Tuesday, 10 a.m.	Do.
		FPC – Friday, 10 a.m.	Do.
	Margate Courthouse	Adult – Monday, Tuesday, Thursday and Friday, 10 a.m.	The Court House, Cecil Square, Margate CT9 1RL
		YC – Wednesday, 10 a.m.	Do
		FPC – Monday, 10 a.m.	Do.
1966	**NORTH KENT L.J.A. (DARTFORD)**		
	Court Admin Office, P.O. Box CH 4,	Adult – Daily, 10 a.m. and 2 p.m.	Sessions House, Highfield Road, Dartford DA12 2JW
	The Court House, The Brook, Chatham, Kent ME4 4JZ	YC – Tuesday, 10 a.m. and 2 p.m.	Sessions House, Highfield Road, Dartford DA12 2JW
	Tel: 01634 830232	FPC – Wednesday, Thursday and Friday, 10 a.m. and 2 p.m.	The Court House, The Brook, Chatham
	Fax: 01634 847400		
	DX 98183 CHATHAM 4		
1966	**NORTH KENT L.J.A. (MEDWAY)**		
	Court Admin Office, P.O. Box CH 4,	Adult – Daily, 10 a.m. and 2 p.m.	The Court House, The Brook, Chatham
	The Court House, The Brook, Chatham, Kent ME4 4JZ	YC – Tuesday, 10 a.m. and 2 p.m.	Do.
	Tel: 01634 830232	FPC – Wednesday, Thursday and Friday, 10 a.m. and 2 p.m.	Do.
	Fax: 01634 847400		
	DX 98183 CHATHAM 4		

MIDLANDS REGION

LINCOLNSHIRE, LEICESTERSHIRE AND RUTLAND AND NORTHAMPTONSHIRE

Area Director: Richard Redgrave

Adult Court No	Name of Court and Clerk/Legal Adviser	Normal Times and Places of Courts	
2047	**ASHBY-DE-LA-ZOUCH L.J.A.**		
	Nick Watson, The Court House, Upper Bond Street, Hinckley, Leicestershire LE10 1NZ	Adult – Tuesday and Thursday, 10 a.m. and 2 p.m.	Court House, Vaughan Street, Coalville
		YC – (Combined Youth Panel for Leicestershire) Monday, 10 a.m.	Do.
	Tel: 01455 623000 Fax: 01455 623020	FPC – 1st, 3rd and 5th Wednesday of month, 10 a.m. and 2 p.m.	Do.
2073	**BOSTON L.J.A.**		
	Paul Wydell, The Court House, Park Avenue, Skegness, Lincs. PE25 1BH	Adult – Monday, Wednesday and Friday, 10 a.m.	Sessions House, Boston
	Tel: 01754 898848 896447 (Family Admin)	YC – Alternate Thursdays, 10 a.m.	Do.
	01522 528218 (Fines) Fax: 01754 767318 DX 27511 SKEGNESS	FPC – (combined with Skegness L.J.A. and Wolds L.J.A.) Alternate Thursdays, 10 a.m.	Do.
2074	**BOURNE AND STAMFORD L.J.A.**		
	St. John Pilkington, Justices' Clerk's Office, Harlaxton Road, Grantham, Lincs. NG31 7SB	Adult – Mondays, 10 a.m. Thursdays, 10 a.m. 2nd Wednesday in month (private prosecutions)	Town Hall, Bourne Town Hall, Bourne Town Hall, Bourne
	Tel: 01476 563438	YC – Second and fourth Monday in month, 2 p.m.	Town Hall, Bourne
	Fax: 01476 567200 DX 711100 GRANTHAM 4	FPC – Second Friday in month, 10 a.m.	Do.

LINCOLNSHIRE, LEICESTERSHIRE and RUTLAND and NORTHAMPTONSHIRE

Adult Court No	Name of Court and Clerk/Legal Adviser	Normal Times and Places of Courts	
2321	**CORBY L.J.A.**		
	N. M. Clarke, Regent's Pavilion, Summerhouse Road, Moulton Park, Northampton NN3 6AS	Adult – Thursday and Friday, 10 a.m.	The Court House, Elizabeth Street, Corby
	Tel: 01604 497000	FPC – Alternate Wednesdays, 10 a.m.	Do.
	Fax: 01604 497010 497020		
	DX 151720 NORTHAMPTON 27		
2322	**DAVENTRY L.J.A.**		
	N. M. Clarke, Regent's Pavilion, Summerhouse Road, Moulton Park, Northampton NN3 6AS	Adult – Tuesday, 10 a.m.	The Court House, New Street, Daventry
	Tel: 01604 497000		
	Fax: 01604 497010 497020		
	DX 151720 NORTHAMPTON 27		
2076	**ELLOES L.J.A.**		
	St. John Pilkington, Justices' Clerk's Office, Harlaxton Road, Grantham, Lincs. NG31 7SB	Adult – Tuesday and Thursday, 10 a.m.	Sessions House, Spalding
		YC – First and third Wednesday in month, 10 a.m.	Do.
	Tel: 01476 563438		
	Fax: 01476 567200	FPC – Monday twice monthly, 10 a.m.	Do.
	DX 711100 GRANTHAM 4		
2075	**GAINSBOROUGH L.J.A.**		
	P. J. Veits, Magistrates' Clerk's Office, The Court House, 358 High Street, Lincoln LN5 7QA	Adult – Monday, Tuesday and Friday, 10 a.m. and 2 p.m.	Court House, Roseway, Gainsborough
		YC – (combined with Lincoln District L.J.A.)	The Court House, 358 High Street, Lincoln
	Tel: 01522 528218		
	Fax: 01522 525832	FPC – (combined with Lincoln District L.J.A.)	Do.
	DX 703232 LINCOLN 6		

LINCOLNSHIRE, LEICESTERSHIRE and RUTLAND and NORTHAMPTONSHIRE

Adult Court No	Name of Court and Clerk/Legal Adviser		Normal Times and Places of Courts	
2077	**GRANTHAM L.J.A.**			
	St. John Pilkington, Justices' Clerk's Office, Harlaxton Road, Grantham, Lincs. NG31 7SB	Adult –	Monday, Wednesday, Thursday and Friday, 10 a.m.	Magistrates' Court, Harlaxton Road, Grantham
	Tel: 01476 563438	YC –	Tuesday and Friday, alternate weeks, 10 a.m.	Do.
	Fax: 01476 567200 DX 711100 GRANTHAM 4	FPC –	Tuesday, twice monthly, 10 a.m.	Do.
2323	**KETTERING L.J.A.**			
	N. M. Clarke, Regent's Pavilion, Summerhouse Road, Moulton Park, Northampton NN3 6AS	Adult –	Wednesday, 10 a.m.	The Court House, London Road, Kettering
		YC –	Monday, 10 a.m.	Do.
	Tel: 01604 497000 Fax: 01604 497010 497020 DX 151720 NORTHAMPTON 27	FPC –	Alternate Thursdays, 10 a.m.	Do.
2048	**LEICESTER L.J.A.**			
	Nick Watson, 15 Pocklingtons Walk, Leicester LE1 6BT	Adult –	Daily (except Saturday), 9.30 a.m.	15 Pocklingtons Walk, Leicester
	Tel: 0116 255 3666 Fax: 0116 254 5851	YC –	Tuesday Wednesday and Friday, 9.30 a.m. and 2.15 p.m.	Do.
	DX 10828 LEICESTER 1	FPC –	Monday and Thursday, 9.30 a.m. and 2 p.m.	90 Wellington Street, Leicester LE1 6HG
		Enf. –	Daily (except Saturday), 9.30 a.m.	15 Pocklingtons Walk, Leicester
2079	**LINCOLN DISTRICT L.J.A.**			
	P. J. Veits, Magistrates' Clerk's Office, The Court House, 358 High Street, Lincoln LN5 7QA	Adult –	Each weekday, 10 a.m. Each weekday (except third Friday in month), 2.15 p.m.	The Court House, 358 High Street, Lincoln
	Tel: 01522 528218 Fax: 01522 525832 DX 703232 LINCOLN 6	YC –	(combined with Gainsborough L.J.A.) Tuesday, 10 a.m. and 2.15 p.m. Thursday, 10 a.m. and 2.15 p.m.	Do.
		FPC –	(combined with Gainsborough L.J.A.) Monday, Wednesday and Friday, 10.30 a.m.	Do.

LINCOLNSHIRE, LEICESTERSHIRE and RUTLAND and NORTHAMPTONSHIRE

Adult Court No	Name of Court and Clerk/Legal Adviser	Normal Times and Places of Courts	
2049	**LOUGHBOROUGH L.J.A.**		
	Nick Watson, The Court House, Woodgate, Loughborough, Leics. LE11 2XB Tel: 01509 215715 Fax: 01509 261714 DX 716116 LOUGHBOROUGH 4	Adult – Monday, Wednesday and Friday, 10 a.m. and 2 p.m. and Tuesday, 2 p.m. YC – (Combined with Melton, Belvoir and Rutland L.J.A.) Thursday, 10 a.m. and 2 p.m. FPC – Tuesday, 10 a.m.	The Court House, Woodgate, Loughborough Do. Do.
2050	**MARKET BOSWORTH L.J.A.**		
	Nick Watson, The Court House, Upper Bond Street, Hinckley, Leicestershire LE10 1NZ Tel: 01455 623000 Fax: 01455 623020	Adult – Monday, Wednesday, and Friday, 10 a.m. and 2 p.m. YC – (Combined Youth Panel for Leicestershire) Tuesday, 10 a.m. and 2 p.m. FPC – 2nd and 4th Wednesday of month, a.m. only 2nd Thursday of month, all day	Court House, Upper Bond Street, Hinckley Do. Do.
2051	**MARKET HARBOROUGH AND LUTTERWORTH L.J.A.**		
	Nick Watson, 15 Pocklingtons Walk, Leicester LE1 6BT Tel: 0116 255 3666 Fax: 0116 254 5851 DX 10828 LEICESTER 1	Adult – Tuesday and Thursday, 10 a.m. YC – Tuesday, Wednesday and Friday, 9.30 a.m. and 2.15 p.m. Enf. Ct. – Tuesday and Thursday, 10 a.m.	Court House, Doddridge Road, Market Harborough 15 Pocklingtons Walk, Leicester Court House, Doddridge Road, Market Harborough
2045	**MELTON, BELVOIR AND RUTLAND L.J.A.**		
	Nick Watson, The Court House, Woodgate, Loughborough, Leics. LE11 2XB Tel: 01509 215715 Fax: 01509 261714 DX 716116 LOUGHBOROUGH 4	Adult – First Monday in month, 10 a.m. and 2 p.m. Tuesday and Thursday, 10 a.m. and 2 p.m. YC – (Combined with Loughborough L.J.A.) First, third and fifth Wednesday in month, 10 a.m. FPC – Friday, 10 a.m.	The Council Chambers, Catmose, Oakham Court House, Norman Way, Melton Mowbray Do. Do.

LINCOLNSHIRE, LEICESTERSHIRE and RUTLAND and NORTHAMPTONSHIRE

Adult Court No	Name of Court and Clerk/Legal Adviser		Normal Times and Places of Courts	
2325	**NORTHAMPTON L.J.A.**			
	N. M. Clarke, Regent's Pavilion, Summerhouse Road, Moulton Park, Northampton NN3 6AS	Adult	– Monday to Friday, 10 a.m.	The Court House, Campbell Square, Northampton
		YC	– Monday and Wednesday, 10 a.m.	Do.
	Tel: 01604 497000			
	Fax: 01604 497010 497020	FPC	– Tuesday, 10 a.m.	Do.
	DX 151720 NORTHAMPTON 27			
2082	**SKEGNESS L.J.A. (formerly Spilsby and Skegness Division)**			
	Paul Wydell, The Court House, Park Avenue, Skegness, Lincs. PE25 1BH	Adult	– Alternate Mondays, 10 a.m. Tuesday, Thursday and Friday, 10 a.m.	Court House, Park Avenue, Skegness
	Tel: 01754 898848 896447 (Family Admin) 01522 528218 (Fines)	YC	– (combined with Wolds L.J.A.) Wednesday	Do.
		FPC	– (combined with Boston L.J.A. and Wolds L.J.A.) Alternate Tuesdays, 10 a.m.	Do.
	Fax: 01754 767318			
	DX 27511 SKEGNESS			
2080	**SLEAFORD L.J.A.**			
	St. John Pilkington, Justices' Clerk's Office, Harlaxton Road, Grantham, Lincs. NG31 7SB	Adult	– Tuesday, 10 a.m. First Wednesday in month, 10 a.m. (Private Prosecutions and Enforcement)	Sessions House, Sleaford
	Tel: 01476 563438	YC	– Second Tuesday in month, 2.15 p.m.	Do.
	Fax: 01476 567200			
	DX 711100 GRANTHAM 4	FPC	– Third Wednesday in month, 2.15 p.m.	Do.
2327	**TOWCESTER L.J.A.**			
	N. M. Clarke, Regent's Pavilion, Summerhouse Road, Moulton Park, Northampton NN3 6AS	Adult	– Friday, 10 a.m.	The Court House, Watling Street West, Towcester
	Tel: 01604 497000			
	Fax: 01604 497010 497020			
	DX 151720 NORTHAMPTON 27			

LINCOLNSHIRE, LEICESTERSHIRE and RUTLAND and NORTHAMPTONSHIRE

Adult
Court *Name of Court and*
No *Clerk/Legal Adviser*   *Normal Times and Places of Courts*

2328 WELLINGBOROUGH L.J.A.

N. M. Clarke,	Adult – Monday and Tuesday,	The Court House, Midland
Regent's Pavilion,	10 a.m.	Road, Wellingborough
Summerhouse Road,		
Moulton Park,		
Northampton NN3 6AS		
Tel: 01604 497000	FPC – Friday, 10 a.m.	Do.
Fax: 01604 497010		
497020		
DX 151720 NORTHAMPTON 27		

2078 WOLDS L.J.A.

Paul Wydell,	Adult – Thursday, 10 a.m.	The Sessions House,
The Court House,		Eastgate, Louth
Park Avenue,		
Skegness, Lincs.		
PE25 1BH	YC – (combined with Skegness	
Tel: 01754 898848	L.J.A.)	
896447		
(Family Admin)	FPC – (combined with Boston L.J.A.	
01522 528218 (Fines)	and Skegness L.J.A.)	
	Alternate Tuesdays, 10 a.m.	Court House, Park Avenue,
Fax: 01754 767318		Skegness
DX 27511 SKEGNESS		

LONDON REGION

LONDON REGION

Regional Director: Kevin Pogson, C.B.E., 2nd Floor, Rose Court, 2 Southwark Bridge, London SE1 9HS   Tel: 020 7921 2010/2005   Fax: 0870 739 4469
DX 154261 SOUTHWARK 12
E-mail: london@hmcourts-service.gsi.gov.uk

AREAS AND LOCAL JUSTICE AREAS IN THE GREATER LONDON COMMISSION AREA

Page

Central and South London (Crime)
- Bexley L.J.A. 69
- Bromley L.J.A. 70
- City of London L.J.A. 70
- City of Westminster L.J.A. 71
- Croydon L.J.A. 71
- Greenwich and Lewisham L.J.A. 72
- Lambeth and Southwark L.J.A. 73
- Sutton L.J.A. 74

North and West London (Crime)
- Barking L.J.A. 75
- Barnet L.J.A. 76
- Brent L.J.A. 76
- Camden and Islington L.J.A. 77
- Ealing L.J.A. 77
- Enfield L.J.A. 78
- Hackney and Tower Hamlets L.J.A. 79
- Hammersmith and Fulham, and Kensington and Chelsea L.J.A. 79
- Haringey L.J.A. 80
- Harrow L.J.A. 80
- Havering L.J.A. 81
- Hillingdon L.J.A. 81
- Hounslow L.J.A. 82
- Kingston-upon-Thames L.J.A. 83
- Merton L.J.A. 84
- Newham L.J.A. 84
- Redbridge L.J.A. 85
- Richmond-upon-Thames L.J.A. 85
- Waltham Forest L.J.A. 86
- Wandsworth L.J.A. 86

Civil and Family
- Inner London Family Proceedings Court 87

Inner London Youth Courts
- Camden, Hackney, Islington, Tower Hamlets and City 83
- Greenwich, Lewisham and Southwark 73
- Hammersmith and Fulham, Kensington and Chelsea and Westminster 83
- Lambeth and Wandsworth 83

The Board of Green Cloth Verge of the Palaces 87

LONDON REGION

LONDON – CENTRAL AND SOUTH (CRIME)

Area Director: Sarah McAdam, Area Director's Office, 2nd Floor, Rose Court, 2 Southwark Bridge, London SE1 9HS. Tel: 020 7921 2014 Fax: 020 7921 2080 DX 154261 SOUTHWARK 12

Central Clerkship: 65 Romney Street, London SW1P 3RD. Fax: 020 7805 1002 DX 120554 VICTORIA 6

Justices' Clerk: Beverley Morse. Tel: 020 7805 1015

Area Operations Manager: John Wheatle. Tel: 020 7805 1131

South East Clerkship: 1 London Road, Bromley BR1 1RA. Fax: 020 8272 9111 DX 119601 BROMLEY 8

Justices' Clerk: Kevin Griffiths. Tel: 020 8272 9101

Area Operations Manager: Pak-Yee Chan. Tel: 020 8272 9102

Adult Court No	Name of Court/ Bench Legal Manager/ Bench Office Manager		Normal Times and Places of Courts

BEXLEY L.J.A.

2728 BEXLEY MAGISTRATES' COURT

Bench Legal Manager: Stephen McAllister,
Bench Office Manager: Stephen Ironmonger,
Bexley Magistrates' Court,
Norwich Place,
Bexleyheath,
Kent DA6 7NB
Tel: 020 8304 5211
Fax: 020 8303 6849
DX 100150 BEXLEYHEATH 3

Adult	– Monday, Tuesday, Thursday and Friday, 9.30 a.m.	Norwich Place, Bexleyheath
YC	– Monday and Wednesday, 9.30 a.m.	Do.
FPC	– Wednesday, 9.30 a.m.	Do.

From 1st October 2007 all Transfer of Fine Orders, Crown Court Orders and Fixed Penalty Registrations will be administered by the Central Accounts Office. Write to Central Accounting Office, PO Box 31090, London SW1P 3WQ.
Tel: 0845 940 0111 (public) 020 7805 1055 (HMCS staff only)
DX 120554 VICTORIA 6
E-mail: correspondence.cao@hmcourts-service.gsi.gov.uk

LONDON – CENTRAL AND SOUTH (CRIME)

Adult Court No	Name of Court/ Bench Legal Manager/ Bench Office Manager		Normal Times and Places of Courts	

BROMLEY L.J.A.

2727 BROMLEY MAGISTRATES' COURT

Bench Legal Manager:
  Valerie Morgan,
Bench Office Manager:
  Keith Davis,
The Court House,
London Road,
Bromley, Kent
BR1 1RA

Adult – Every day, Monday to Friday, 10 a.m. and 2.15 p.m.   The Court House, London Road, Bromley

YC – Tuesday and Friday, 10 a.m.   Do.

FPC – Wednesday and Thursday, 10 a.m.   Do.

Tel: 0845 601 3600
    020 8437 3503 (Legal Aid)
    020 8437 3500 (Listing)
    020 8437 3502 (Licensing)
    020 8437 3510 (Post Court)
    020 8437 3515 (Family)

Fax: 020 8437 3506

DX 119601 BROMLEY 8

From 1st October 2007 all Transfer of Fine Orders, Crown Court Orders and Fixed Penalty Registrations will be administered by the Central Accounts Office. Write to Central Accounting Office, PO Box 31090, London SW1P 3WQ.
Tel: 0845 940 0111 (public) 020 7805 1055 (HMCS staff only)
DX 120554 VICTORIA 6
E-mail: correspondence.cao@hmcourts-service.gsi.gov.uk

CITY OF LONDON L.J.A.

2631 CITY OF LONDON MAGISTRATES' COURT

Bench Legal Manager:
  Martin Vose,
Bench Office Manager:
  Paul Hutchinson,
1 Queen Victoria Street,
London EC4N 4XY

Adult – Monday to Friday, 10.30 a.m.   1 Queen Victoria Street, London EC4N 4XY

Tel: 020 7332 1830
           1838

Fax: 020 7332 1493

DX 98943 CHEAPSIDE 2

From 1st October 2007 all Transfer of Fine Orders, Crown Court Orders and Fixed Penalty Registrations will be administered by the Central Accounts Office. Write to Central Accounting Office, PO Box 31090, London SW1P 3WQ.
Tel: 0845 940 0111 (public) 020 7805 1055 (HMCS staff only)
DX 120554 VICTORIA 6
E-mail: correspondence.cao@hmcourts-service.gsi.gov.uk

LONDON – CENTRAL AND SOUTH (CRIME)

| Adult Court No | Name of Court/ Bench Legal Manager/ Bench Office Manager | Normal Times and Places of Courts |

CITY OF WESTMINSTER L.J.A.

2660 CITY OF WESTMINSTER MAGISTRATES' COURT

Bench Legal Manager:
  Jeffrey Bryer, Judith Melnick,
Bench Office Manager:
  Jenny Taylor,
Horseferry Road Magistrates' Court,
70 Horseferry Road
SW1P 2AX

Adult – Weekdays 10 a.m. to 5 p.m.

FPC – See p.87

70 Horseferry Road
SW1P 2AX

Tel: 020 7805 1151 (Legal Aid Representation Order Enquiries)
   020 7805 1144 (Listing)
   020 7805 1171 (Applications)
   020 7805 1173 (Applications)
   020 7805 1159 (Post Court/Resulting)

Fax: 020 7805 1193

DX 120551 VICTORIA 6

CENTRAL ACCOUNTING OFFICE
All administrative enquiries about fines and maintenance orders should be addressed to Central Accounting Office. This includes Transfer of Fine Orders (TFOs) and any sums enforceable as a legal aid contribution that would ordinarily be sent to Bow Street Magistrates' Court or Horseferry Road Magistrates' Court. Write to Central Accounting Office, Dept. 2660, P.O. Box 31089, London SW1P 3WP   Tel: 0845 940 0111 Monday to Friday.
DX 120554 VICTORIA 6
NOTE: Matters involving Maintenance Enforcement should be addressed to Central Accounting Office, Matrimonial Department, P.O. Box 31093, London SW1P 3WP

CROYDON L.J.A.

2732 CROYDON MAGISTRATES' COURT

Bench Legal Manager:
  David Richmond,
Bench Office Manager:
  Peter Lumm,
The Magistrates' Court,
Barclay Road,
Croydon CR9 3NG

Adult – Daily (except Saturdays), 10 a.m. and 2.15 p.m.

YC – Daily (except Saturdays), 10 a.m.

FPC – Daily (except Wednesday and Saturday), 10 a.m.

The Magistrates' Court,
 Barclay Road, Croydon

Youth Court, Barclay Road, Croydon

The Magistrates' Court,
 Barclay Road, Croydon

Tel: 020 8603 0452 (Fines)
   8603 0431/0443 (Maint.)
   8603 0438 (Listing)

Fax: 020 8680 9801

DX 97474 CROYDON 6

From 1st October 2007 all Transfer of Fine Orders, Crown Court Orders and Fixed Penalty Registrations will be administered by the Central Accounts Office. Write to Central Accounting Office, PO Box 31090, London SW1P 3WQ.
Tel: 0845 940 0111 (public) 020 7805 1055 (HMCS staff only)
DX 120554 VICTORIA 6
E-mail: correspondence.cao@hmcourts-service.gsi.gov.uk

LONDON – CENTRAL AND SOUTH (CRIME)

Adult Court No	Name of Court/ Bench Legal Manager/ Bench Office Manager		Normal Times and Places of Courts

GREENWICH AND LEWISHAM L.J.A.

2643 GREENWICH MAGISTRATES' COURT

Bench Legal Manager:
 Keith Burman,
Bench Office Manager:
 Keith Reed,
9 Blackheath Road,
Greenwich
SE10 8PE

Adult – Weekdays, 10 a.m.
 to 5 p.m.
Saturdays, 10 a.m.
 to 1 p.m.

YC – See p.73

FPC – See p.87

(1) 9 Blackheath Road,
 Greenwich SE10 8PG
(2) Belmarsh Magistrates'
 Court, 4 Belmarsh Road,
 London SE28 0HA

Tel: 020 8276 1334 (Cash and Licensing)
 020 8276 1347/1325 (Resulting)
 020 8276 1351 (Representation Orders)
 020 8276 1341 (Listing)
 020 8276 1359 (Committals/Appeals)
 020 8271 9089/9 (Belmarsh Magistrates' Court)

Fax: 020 8276 1397 (Cash and Licensing)
 020 8276 1346 (Resulting)
 020 8276 1398 (Charges)
 020 8276 1399 (Summonses)

DX 35203 GREENWICH WEST

CENTRAL ACCOUNTING OFFICE
All administrative enquiries about fines and maintenance orders should be addressed to Central Accounting Office. This includes Transfer of Fine Orders (TFOs) and any sums enforceable as a legal aid contribution that would ordinarily be sent to Greenwich Magistrates' Court or Woolwich Magistrates' Court. Write to Central Accounting Office, Dept. 2643, P.O. Box 31090, London SW1P 3WQ   Tel: 0845 940 0111 Monday to Friday.
DX 120554 VICTORIA 6
NOTE: Matters involving Maintenance Enforcement should be addressed to Central Accounting Office, Matrimonial Department, P.O. Box 310939 London SW1P 3WP

2643 WOOLWICH MAGISTRATES' COURT

Post as for Greenwich
Tel: as for Greenwich
Fax: as for Greenwich

Adult – Weekdays, 10 a.m.
 to 4.30 p.m.

YC – See p.73

FPC – See p.87

Market Street, Woolwich
SE18 6QY

CENTRAL ACCOUNTING OFFICE
All administrative enquiries about fines and maintenance orders should be addressed to Central Accounting Office. This includes Transfer of Fine Orders (TFOs) and any sums enforceable as a legal aid contribution that would ordinarily be sent to Greenwich Magistrates' Court or Woolwich Magistrates' Court. Write to Central Accounting Office,
Dept. 2643, P.O. Box 31090, London SW1P 3WQ   Tel: 0845 940 0111 Monday to Friday.
DX 120554 VICTORIA 6
NOTE: Matters involving Maintenance Enforcement should be addressed to Central Accounting Office, Matrimonial Department, P.O. Box 31093, London SW1P 3WP

LONDON – CENTRAL AND SOUTH (CRIME)

Adult Court No	Name of Court/ Bench Legal Manager/ Bench Office Manager		Normal Times and Places of Courts

INNER LONDON YOUTH COURTS

The Inner London Youth Courts have been devolved to four Youth Court centres.

Communications and enquiries should be addressed as follows:

6656 Greenwich, Lewisham & Southwark Youth Courts:

Assistant Justices Clerk, (Youth Justice),
Uzma Qureshi,
Inner London Youth Courts Centre 2,
Camberwell Green Magistrates' Court,
D'Eynsford Road SE5 7UP
Tel: 020 7805 9844
Fax: 020 7805 3899

LAMBETH AND SOUTHWARK L.J.A.

2656 CAMBERWELL GREEN MAGISTRATES' COURT

Bench Legal Manager:
  Thirza Mullins,
Bench Office Manager:
  Manjit Birak,
15 D'Eynsford Road,
Camberwell Green
SE5 7UP

Adult – Weekdays, 9.15 a.m. to 5 p.m.

YC – 9.15 a.m. to 5 p.m.
See p.83

FPC – See p.87

15 D'Eynsford Road,
Camberwell Green
SE5 7UP

Tel: 0845 601 3600
  020 7805 9802/3 (Secretaries' Office)
  020 7805 9852
  and 9843 (Legal Aid)
  020 7805 9841/2 (Listing)
  020 7805 9851 (Licensing)
  020 7805 9858 (Post Court/Resulting)
  020 7805 9844 (Youth Court Listing)

Fax: 020 7805 9896

DX 35305 CAMBERWELL GREEN

CENTRAL ACCOUNTING OFFICE

All administrative enquiries about fines and maintenance orders should be addressed to Central Accounting Office. This includes Transfer of Fine Orders (TFOs) and any sums enforceable as a legal aid contribution that would ordinarily be sent to Camberwell Green Magistrates' Court or Tower Bridge Magistrates' Court. Write to Central Accounting Office, Dept. 2656, P.O. Box 31090, London SW1P 3WQ   Tel: 0845 940 0111 Monday to Friday. DX 120554 VICTORIA 6

NOTE: Matters involving Maintenance Enforcement should be addressed to Central Accounting Office, Matrimonial Department, P.O. Box 31093, London SW1P 3WP

LONDON – CENTRAL AND SOUTH (CRIME)

Adult Court No	Name of Court/ Bench Legal Manager/ Bench Office Manager		Normal Times and Places of Courts

2651 TOWER BRIDGE MAGISTRATES' COURT

Bench Legal Manager:
 Thirza Mullins,
Bench Office Manager:
 Manjit Birak,
c/o 15 D'Eynsford Road,
Camberwell Green
SE5 7UP

Adult – Weekdays only,
 9.30 a.m. to 4.30 p.m.

211 Tooley Street SE1

Tel: 020 7805 6705/6

Fax: 020 7805 6718

DX 35305 CAMBERWELL GREEN

CENTRAL ACCOUNTING OFFICE
All administrative enquiries about fines and maintenance orders should be addressed to Central Accounting Office. This includes Transfer of Fine Orders (TFOs) and any sums enforceable as a legal aid contribution that would ordinarily be sent to Camberwell Green Magistrates' Court or Tower Bridge Magistrates' Court. Write to Central Accounting Office, Dept. 2656, P.O. Box 31090, London SW1P 3WQ   Tel: 0845 940 0111 Monday to Friday. DX 120554 VICTORIA 6
NOTE: Matters involving Maintenance Enforcement should be addressed to Central Accounting Office, Matrimonial Department, P.O. Box 31093, London SW1P 3WP

SUTTON L.J.A.

2733 SUTTON MAGISTRATES' COURT

Bench Legal Manager:
 Jane Austin,
Bench Office Manager:
 Peter Lumm,
The Court House,
Shotfield,
Wallington, Surrey
SM6 0JA

Adult – Monday to Friday, 10 a.m. and 2 p.m.

The Court House, Shotfield, Wallington

YC – Tuesday, 10 a.m. and 2 p.m.

Do.

Tel: 020 8770 5950

FPC – Wednesday and Friday, 10 a.m. and 2 p.m.

Do.

Fax: 020 8770 5977

DX 59957 WALLINGTON

From 1st October 2007 all Transfer of Fine Orders, Crown Court Orders and Fixed Penalty Registrations will be administered by the Central Accounts Office. Write to Central Accounting Office, PO Box 31090, London SW1P 3WQ.
Tel: 0845 940 0111 (public) 020 7805 1055 (HMCS staff only)
DX 120554 VICTORIA 6
E-mail: correspondence.cao@hmcourts-service.gsi.gov.uk

LONDON REGION

LONDON – NORTH AND WEST (CRIME)

Area Director: Sandra Aston, Area Director's Office, 2nd Floor, Rose Court, 2 Southwark Bridge, London SE1 9HS. Tel: 020 7921 2013   Fax: 020 7921 2080   DX 154261 SOUTHWARK 12

North West Clerkship: Brent Magistrates' Court, 448 High Road, London NW10 2DZ.
Tel: 020 8965 0555   Fax: 020 8955 0543   DX 110850 WILLESDEN 2

Justices' Clerk: Gaynor Houghton-Jones

Area Operations Manager: Ewan McEwan

North East Clerkship: Thames Magistrates' Court, 58 Bow Road, London E3 4DJ.
Tel: 0845 601 3600   Fax: 020 8271 1251   DX 55654 BOW

Justices' Clerk: Tom Ring

Area Operations Manager: Jenny Francis

South West Clerkship: West London Magistrates' Court, 181 Talgarth Road, London W6 8DN. Tel: 0845 601 3600   Fax: 020 8700 9344   DX 124800 HAMMERSMITH 8

Justices' Clerk: Julien Vantyghem

Acting Area Operations Manager: Richard Tulloch

Adult Court No	Name of Court/ Bench Legal Manager/ Bench Office Manager	Normal Times and Places of Courts	

BARKING L.J.A.

2814 BARKING MAGISTRATES' COURT

Bench Legal Manager: Judith Francis,
Bench Office Manager: Kim Weatherley,
The Court House,
East Street,
Barking, Essex
IG11 8EW

Tel: 0845 601 3600

Fax: 020 8273 2739

DX 131527 ROMFORD 8

Adult – Daily, Monday to Friday, 10 a.m.   Court House, Barking

YC – Monday and Thursday, 10 a.m.   Do.

CENTRAL ACCOUNTING OFFICE
All administrative enquiries about fines and maintenance orders should be addressed to Central Accounting Office. This includes Transfer of Fine Orders (TFOs) and any sums enforceable as a legal aid contribution that would ordinarily be sent to this Court. Write to Central Accounting Office, Dept. 2650, P.O. Box 31092, London SW1P 3WS
Tel: 0845 940 0111 Monday to Friday.   DX 120554 VICTORIA 6
NOTE: Matters involving Maintenance Enforcement should be addressed to Central Accounting Office, Matrimonial Department, P.O. Box 31093, London SW1P 3WP
NOTE: Please send all correspondence to Havering Magistrates' Court, Main Road, Romford, Essex RM1 3BH.

LONDON – NORTH AND WEST (CRIME)

Adult Court No	Name of Court/ Bench Legal Manager/ Bench Office Manager		Normal Times and Places of Courts	

BARNET L.J.A.

2741 HENDON MAGISTRATES' COURT

Bench Legal Manager:
  Michael Steere,
Bench Office Manager:
  Maureen Stankiewicz
The Court House,
The Hyde,
Hendon,
London NW9 7BY

Tel: 020 8441 9042

Fax: 020 8441 6753

Adult – Monday to Friday, 10 a.m. and 2 p.m — The Court House, Hendon

YC – Wednesday and Friday, 10 a.m. and 2 p.m — The Court House, Hendon

North London FPC – Monday to Friday, 10 a.m. and 2 p.m. — Barnet County Court, St. Mary's Court, Regents Park Road, London N3 1BQ

NOTE: From 1st October 2007 all Transfer of Fine Orders, Crown Court Orders and Fixed Penalty Registrations will be administered by the Central Accounts Office.
Write to Central Accounting Office, PO Box 31090, London SW1P 3WQ.
Tel: 0845 940 0111 (public)   020 7805 1055 (HMCS staff only)   DX 120554 VICTORIA 6
E-mail: correspondence.cao@hmcourts-service.gsi.gov.uk

BRENT L.J.A.

2762 BRENT MAGISTRATES' COURT

Bench Legal Manager:
  Margaret O'Keefe,
Bench Office Manager:
  Kim Leech,
Brent Magistrates' Court,
448 High Road
NW10 2DZ

Tel: 020 8955 0555

Fax: 020 8955 0543

Minicom: 020 8955 0550

DX 110850 WILLESDEN 2

Adult – Monday to Friday, 10 a.m. Saturday, 10 a.m. — 448 High Road NW10

YC – Monday, Wednesday and Friday, 10 a.m. — Do.

FPC – Tuesday and Thursday, 10 a.m. — Do.

NOTE: From 1st October 2007 all Transfer of Fine Orders, Crown Court Orders and Fixed Penalty Registrations will be administered by the Central Accounts Office.
Write to Central Accounting Office, PO Box 31090, London SW1P 3WQ.
Tel: 0845 940 0111 (public)   020 7805 1055 (HMCS staff only)   DX 120554 VICTORIA 6
E-mail: correspondence.cao@hmcourts-service.gsi.gov.uk

LONDON – NORTH AND WEST (CRIME)

Adult Court No	Name of Court/ Bench Legal Manager/ Bench Office Manager		Normal Times and Places of Courts	

CAMDEN AND ISLINGTON L.J.A.

2663 HIGHBURY CORNER MAGISTRATES' COURT

Bench Legal Manager:
   Robert Allan,
Bench Office Manager:
   Sandra Crozier,
51 Holloway Road
N7 8JA

Adult – Weekdays and Saturdays, 10 a.m. to 5 p.m.

YC – See p.83

FPC – See p.87

51 Holloway Road N7

Tel: 0845 601 3600 (General Enquiries)
   020 7506 3151 (Legal Aid)
   020 7506 3143 (Listing)
   020 7506 3128 (Licensing)
   020 7506 3156 (Post Court/Resulting)

Fax: 020 7506 3191

DX 51855 HIGHBURY

CENTRAL ACCOUNTING OFFICE
All administrative enquiries about fines and maintenance orders should be addressed to Central Accounting Office. This includes Transfer of Fine Orders (TFOs) and any sums enforceable as a legal aid contribution that would ordinarily be sent to this Court. Write to Central Accounting Office, Dept. 2663, P.O. Box 31091, London SW1P 3WR
Tel: 0845 940 0111 Monday to Friday.   DX 120554 VICTORIA 6
NOTE: Matters involving Maintenance Enforcement should be addressed to Central Accounting Office, Matrimonial Department, P.O. Box 31093, London SW1P 3WP

EALING L.J.A.

2734 EALING MAGISTRATES' COURT

Bench Legal Manager:
   Christopher Jordan,
Bench Office Manager:
   Andrew Whaley,
The Court House,
Green Man Lane,
Ealing,
London W13 0SD

Adult – Monday to Friday, 10 a.m. and 2 p.m.
Saturday (as necessary), 10 a.m.

The Court House, Green Man Lane, Ealing W13 0SD

Tel: 0845 601 3600

Fax: 020 8437 4777

DX 5166 EALING

NOTE: From 1st October 2007 all Transfer of Fine Orders, Crown Court Orders and Fixed Penalty Registrations will be administered by the Central Accounts Office.
Write to Central Accounting Office, PO Box 31090, London SW1P 3WQ.
Tel: 0845 940 0111 (public)   020 7805 1055 (HMCS staff only)   DX 120554 VICTORIA 6
E-mail: correspondence.cao@hmcourts-service.gsi.gov.uk

LONDON – NORTH AND WEST (CRIME)

Adult Court No	Name of Court/ Bench Legal Manager/ Bench Office Manager		Normal Times and Places of Courts
2723	**ACTON MAGISTRATES' COURT**		
	Bench Legal Manager: Christopher Jordan, Bench Office Manager: Andrew Whaley, The Court House, Winchester Street, Acton W3 8PB	Adult – Monday to Friday, 10 a.m. and 2 p.m.	The Court House, Winchester Street, Acton W3
		YC – Tuesday, 10 a.m.	Do.
	Tel: 0845 601 3600 Fax: 020 8437 4626	FPC – Friday, 10 a.m.	
	DX 5166 EALING		

Please send all correspondence to Ealing Magistrates' Court.

NOTE: From 1st October 2007 all Transfer of Fine Orders, Crown Court Orders and Fixed Penalty Registrations will be administered by the Central Accounts Office.
Write to Central Accounting Office, PO Box 31090, London SW1P 3WQ.
Tel: 0845 940 0111 (public)   020 7805 1055 (HMCS staff only)   DX 120554 VICTORIA 6
E-mail: correspondence.cao@hmcourts-service.gsi.gov.uk

ENFIELD L.J.A.

2757	**ENFIELD MAGISTRATES' COURT**		
	Bench Legal Manager: Stephen Carroll, Bench Office Manager: Teresa Wright (Acting), The Court House, Lordship Lane, Tottenham, London N17 6RT	Adult – Monday, Tuesday, Thursday and Friday, 10 a.m. and 2 p.m.	The Court House, Lordship Lane, Tottenham N17
		YC – Wednesday, 10 a.m. and 2 p.m.	Do.
	Tel: 020 8808 5411 Fax: 020 8885 4343	North– Monday to Friday, 10 a.m. London and 2 p.m. FPC	Barnet County Court, St. Mary's Court, Regents Park Road, London N3 1BQ
	DX 134490 TOTTENHAM 3		

NOTE: From 1st October 2007 all Transfer of Fine Orders, Crown Court Orders and Fixed Penalty Registrations will be administered by the Central Accounts Office.
Write to Central Accounting Office, PO Box 31090, London SW1P 3WQ.
Tel: 0845 940 0111 (public)   020 7805 1055 (HMCS staff only)   DX 120554 VICTORIA 6
E-mail: correspondence.cao@hmcourts-service.gsi.gov.uk

LONDON – NORTH AND WEST (CRIME)

Adult Court No	Name of Court/ Bench Legal Manager/ Bench Office Manager		Normal Times and Places of Courts

HACKNEY AND TOWER HAMLETS L.J.A.

2650 THAMES MAGISTRATES' COURT

Bench Legal Manager: James Mulreany,
Bench Office Manager: Tina Lane, 58 Bow Road E3 4DJ

Adult – Weekdays, 9 a.m. to 5 p.m.

YC – Weekdays, 9 a.m. to 5 p.m.

Thames Magistrates' Court, 58 Bow Road E3 4DJ

Do.

Tel: 020 8271 1232/3/4 (Legal Representation)
    020 8271 1200 (Listing)
    020 8271 1239/40 (Licensing)
    020 8271 1259 (Post Court/Resulting)
    0845 601 3600 (Switchboard)

Fax: 020 8271 1251 (Listing)
    020 8271 1241 (Licensing)
    020 8271 1263 (Post Court/Resulting)

DX 55654 BOW

CENTRAL ACCOUNTING OFFICE
All administrative enquiries about fines and maintenance orders should be addressed to Central Accounting Office. This includes Transfer of Fine Orders (TFOs) and any sums enforceable as a legal aid contribution that would ordinarily be sent to this Court. Write to Central Accounting Office, Dept. 2650, P.O. Box 31092, London SW1P 3WS
Tel: 0845 940 0111 Monday to Friday.   DX 120554 VICTORIA 6
NOTE: Matters involving Maintenance Enforcement should be addressed to Central Accounting Office, Matrimonial Department, P.O. Box 31093, London SW1P 3WP

HAMMERSMITH AND FULHAM, AND KENSINGTON AND CHELSEA L.J.A.

2658 WEST LONDON MAGISTRATES' COURT

Bench Legal Manager: Clive McIntyre,
Bench Office Manager: Peter Bridges,
181 Talgarth Road W6 8DN

Adult – Weekdays, 9 a.m. to 4.30 p.m.
Saturdays, 9 a.m. to 1 p.m.

YC – See p.83
FPC – See p.30

181 Talgarth Road W6

Tel: 020 8700 9368/9369 (Licensing)
    020 8700 9353/9354 (Legal Aid)
    020 8700 9350 (Listing)
    020 8700 9360 (Post Court/Resulting)

Fax: 020 8700 9344 (Listing)
    020 8700 9366 (Legal Aid/Licensing)
    020 8700 9355 (Post Court)

DX 124800 HAMMERSMITH 8

CENTRAL ACCOUNTING OFFICE
All administrative enquiries about fines and maintenance orders should be addressed to Central Accounting Office. This includes Transfer of Fine Orders (TFOs) and any sums enforceable as a legal aid contribution that would ordinarily be sent to this Court. Write to Central Accounting Office, Dept. 2658, P.O. Box 31089, London SW1P 3WP
Tel: 0845 940 0111 Monday to Friday.   DX 120554 VICTORIA 6
NOTE: Matters involving Maintenance Enforcement should be addressed to Central Accounting Office, Matrimonial Department, P.O. Box 31093, London SW1P 3WP

LONDON – NORTH AND WEST (CRIME)

Adult Court No	Name of Court/ Bench Legal Manager/ Bench Office Manager	Normal Times and Places of Courts

HARINGEY L.J.A.

2742 HARINGEY MAGISTRATES' COURT

Bench Legal Manager:
  Robert Allan,
Bench Office Manager:
  Teresa Wright,
The Court House,
Bishops Road,
Archway Road,
Highgate,
London N6 4HS

Tel: 0845 601 3600

Fax: 020 8273 3838
  (Highgate)
  020 8365 0436
  (Tottenham)

DX 123550 HIGHGATE 3

Adult – Monday, Tuesday, Wednesday and Friday, 10 a.m. and 2 p.m. — The Court House, Bishops Road, Archway Road, Highgate N6

Monday, Tuesday, Wednesday, Thursday and Friday, 10 a.m. and 2 p.m. — The Court House, Lordship Lane, Tottenham N17

YC – Thursday, 10 a.m. and 2 p.m. — The Court House, Highgate

North-London FPC – Weekdays, 10 a.m. and 2 p.m. — Barnet Civil and Family Court Centre, St Mary's Court, Regents Park Road, Finchley Central N3 1BQ

NOTE: From 1st October 2007 all Transfer of Fine Orders, Crown Court Orders and Fixed Penalty Registrations will be administered by the Central Accounts Office.
Write to Central Accounting Office, PO Box 31090, London SW1P 3WQ.
Tel: 0845 940 0111 (public)   020 7805 1055 (HMCS staff only)   DX 120554 VICTORIA 6
E-mail: correspondence.cao@hmcourts-service.gsi.gov.uk

HARROW L.J.A.

2760 HARROW MAGISTRATES' COURT

Bench Legal Manager:
  Pauline Calderato,
Bench Office Manager:
  Helen Mascurine
  (Acting),
P.O. Box 164,
Court House,
Rosslyn Crescent,
Wealdstone,
Harrow, Middlesex
HA1 2JY

Tel: 020 8427 5146
  020 8490 1414 (Fines)
  020 8490 1423 (Legal Representation)
  020 8490 1422

Fax: 020 8863 9518

DX 30451 HARROW 3

Adult – Monday, Wednesday, Thursday and Friday, 10 a.m. and 2 p.m. — Court House, Rosslyn Crescent, Wealdstone, Harrow

YC – Tuesday, 10 a.m. and 2 p.m. — Do.

NOTE: From 1st October 2007 all Transfer of Fine Orders, Crown Court Orders and Fixed Penalty Registrations will be administered by the Central Accounts Office.
Write to Central Accounting Office, PO Box 31090, London SW1P 3WQ.
Tel: 0845 940 0111 (public)   020 7805 1055 (HMCS staff only)   DX 120554 VICTORIA 6
E-mail: correspondence.cao@hmcourts-service.gsi.gov.uk

LONDON – NORTH AND WEST (CRIME)

Adult Court No	Name of Court/ Bench Legal Manager/ Bench Office Manager		Normal Times and Places of Courts

HAVERING L.J.A.

1837 HAVERING MAGISTRATES' COURT

Bench Legal Manager:
 Melinda Hunt
Bench Office Manager:
 Kim Weatherley,
Magistrates' Court,
Main Road,
Romford, Essex
RM1 3BH

Adult – Daily — Magistrates' Court, Main Road, Romford

YC – Wednesday, 10 a.m. and 2 p.m. — Do.

FPC – Wednesday, 10 a.m. and 2 p.m. — Do.

Tel: 0845 601 3600 (Switchboard)

Fax: 01708 794270

DX 131527 ROMFORD 8

CENTRAL ACCOUNTING OFFICE
All administrative enquiries about fines and maintenance orders should be addressed to Central Accounting Office. This includes Transfer of Fine Orders (TFOs) and any sums enforceable as a legal aid contribution that would ordinarily be sent to this Court. Write to Central Accounting Office, Dept. 2650, P.O. Box 31092, London SW1P 3WS
Tel: 0845 940 0111 Monday to Friday.   DX 120554 VICTORIA 6
NOTE: Matters involving Maintenance Enforcement should be addressed to Central Accounting Office, Matrimonial Department, P.O. Box 31093, London SW1P 3WP

HILLINGDON L.J.A.

2766 UXBRIDGE MAGISTRATES' COURT

Bench Legal Manager:
 Margaret O'Keeffe,
Bench Office Manager:
 John Millward,
The Court House,
Harefield Road,
Uxbridge, Middlesex
UB8 1PQ

Adult – Daily, 10 a.m. — The Court House, Harefield Road, Uxbridge

YC – Monday and Thursday — Do.

FPC – Wednesday, 10 a.m. — Do.

Tel: 01895 814646 (Switchboard)
         208410 (Family)
         208408/407/419 (Fines Enquiries)
         208416/417/418 (Listing)
         208415 (Licensing)

Fax: 01895 274280

DX 149720 UXBRIDGE 4

NOTE: From 1st October 2007 all Transfer of Fine Orders, Crown Court Orders and Fixed Penalty Registrations will be administered by the Central Accounts Office.
Write to Central Accounting Office, PO Box 31090, London SW1P 3WQ.
Tel: 0845 940 0111 (public)   020 7805 1055 (HMCS staff only)   DX 120554 VICTORIA 6
E-mail: correspondence.cao@hmcourts-service.gsi.gov.uk

LONDON – NORTH AND WEST (CRIME)

Adult Court No	Name of Court/ Bench Legal Manager/ Bench Office Manager		Normal Times and Places of Courts

HOUNSLOW L.J.A.

2769 BRENTFORD MAGISTRATES' COURT

Bench Legal Manager:
Jane Lynam,
Bench Office Manager:
Stephanie Potter,
Magistrates' Court,
Market Place,
Brentford, Middlesex
TW8 8EN

Tel: 020 8917 3400

Fax: 020 8917 3448

Minicom: 020 8917 3438

DX 133823 FELTHAM 3

Adult – Wednesday, Thursday and Friday, 10 a.m. and 2.15 p.m.
Saturday and Bank Holidays (as necessary) by arrangement

YC – Monday and Tuesday, 10 a.m. and 2.15 p.m.

FPC – Thursday, 10 a.m.

Magistrates' Court, Market Place, Brentford

Do.

Richmond Magistrates' Court, Parkshot, Richmond

NOTE: From 1st October 2007 all Transfer of Fine Orders, Crown Court Orders and Fixed Penalty Registrations will be administered by the Central Accounts Office.
Write to Central Accounting Office, PO Box 31090, London SW1P 3WQ.
Tel: 0845 940 0111 (public)   020 7805 1055 (HMCS staff only)   DX 120554 VICTORIA 6
E-mail: correspondence.cao@hmcourts-service.gsi.gov.uk

2769 FELTHAM MAGISTRATES' COURT

Bench Legal Manager:
Jane Lynam,
Bench Office Manager:
Stephanie Potter,
Magistrates' Court,
Hanworth Road,
Feltham, Middlesex
TW13 5AF

Tel: 020 8917 3400

Fax: 020 8917 3527

DX 133821 FELTHAM 3

Adult – Monday to Friday, 10 a.m. and 2.15 p.m.
Saturday and Bank Holidays (as necessary) by arrangement

Magistrates' Court, Hanworth Road, Feltham

NOTE: From 1st October 2007 all Transfer of Fine Orders, Crown Court Orders and Fixed Penalty Registrations will be administered by the Central Accounts Office.
Write to Central Accounting Office, PO Box 31090, London SW1P 3WQ.
Tel: 0845 940 0111 (public)   020 7805 1055 (HMCS staff only)   DX 120554 VICTORIA 6
E-mail: correspondence.cao@hmcourts-service.gsi.gov.uk

LONDON – NORTH AND WEST (CRIME)

Adult Court No	Name of Court/ Bench Legal Manager/ Bench Office Manager		Normal Times and Places of Courts

INNER LONDON YOUTH COURTS

The Inner London Youth Courts have been devolved to four Youth Court centres.

Communications and enquiries should be addressed as follows:

6649 Lambeth and Wandsworth Youth Courts (Balham Youth Court):
Assistant Justices Clerk, (Youth Justice), Frances Searle, Inner London Youth Courts Centre 4, 217 Balham High Road, London SW17 7BS
Tel: 020 7805 1452
Fax: 020 7805 1437

6658 Hammersmith & Fulham, Kensington & Chelsea and Westminster Youth Courts:
Assistant Justices Clerk, (Youth Justice), Clive McIntyre, Inner London Youth Courts Centre 3, West London Magistrates' Court, 181 Talgarth Road W6 8DN
Tel: 020 8700 9344
Fax: 020 8700 9350

6650 Camden, Hackney, Islington, Tower Hamlets and City Youth Courts:
Assistant Justices Clerk, (Youth Justice), Ms. Laura Huntley, Inner London Youth Courts Centre 1, Thames Magistrates' Court, 58 Bow Road E3 4DJ
Tel: 020 8271 1217
Fax: 020 8271 1251/1230/1208

KINGSTON-UPON-THAMES L.J.A.

2812 KINGSTON-UPON-THAMES MAGISTRATES' COURT

Bench Legal Manager:
   Susan Graham,
Guildhall,
Kingston-upon-Thames,
Surrey KT1 1EU
Tel: 020 8481 6565
   (General Office)
   8271 2313
   (Accounts)
Fax: 020 8481 6556
   (General Office)

Adult	– Every day, 10 a.m.	The Guildhall, Kingston-upon-Thames
YC	– Tuesday and Wednesday, 10 a.m.	Do.
FPC	– Thursday, 10 a.m.	Do.

DX 119975 KINGSTON-UPON-THAMES 6

NOTE: From 1st October 2007 all Transfer of Fine Orders, Crown Court Orders and Fixed Penalty Registrations will be administered by the Central Accounts Office.
Write to Central Accounting Office, PO Box 31090, London SW1P 3WQ.
Tel: 0845 940 0111 (public)   020 7805 1055 (HMCS staff only)   DX 120554 VICTORIA 6
E-mail: correspondence.cao@hmcourts-service.gsi.gov.uk

LONDON – NORTH AND WEST (CRIME)

Adult Court No	Name of Court/ Bench Legal Manager/ Bench Office Manager		Normal Times and Places of Courts

MERTON L.J.A.

2763 WIMBLEDON MAGISTRATES' COURT

Bench Legal Manager:
Andrew Nicholson,
Courthouse Operations Manager:
Damian Farnan,
The Law Courts,
Alexandra Road,
Wimbledon SW19 7JP

Tel: 020 8946 8622

Fax: 020 8946 7030

DX 116610 WIMBLEDON 4

Adult – Daily (Monday to Friday), 10 a.m. and 2 p.m.

YC – Monday and Thursday, 10 a.m.

FPC – Daily (Monday to Friday), 10 a.m.

The Law Courts, Alexandra Road, Wimbledon SW19

Do.

Do.

NOTE: From 1st October 2007 all Transfer of Fine Orders, Crown Court Orders and Fixed Penalty Registrations will be administered by the Central Accounts Office. Write to Central Accounting Office, PO Box 31090, London SW1P 3WQ.
Tel: 0845 940 0111 (public)   020 7805 1055 (HMCS staff only)   DX 120554 VICTORIA 6
E-mail: correspondence.cao@hmcourts-service.gsi.gov.uk

NEWHAM L.J.A.

2721 STRATFORD MAGISTRATES' COURT

Bench Legal Manager:
Kevin McHale,
Bench Office Manager:
Mark Smith,
Magistrates' Court,
389-397 High Street,
London E15 4SB

Tel: 0845 601 3600

Fax: 0208 437 6010

Minicom: 020 8534 7966

DX 5417 STRATFORD

Adult – Monday to Friday, 10 a.m. to 4 p.m. (Trials and sentencing held throughout the week)

YC – First appearances – Wednesday, 10 a.m. to 4 p.m.
(Trials held throughout the week)
Sentencing – Thursdays, 10 a.m. to 4 p.m.

Remand and Trial Courts – Daily, 10 a.m. and 2 p.m.

FPC – Daily, 10 a.m.

SDVC– Tuesday

The Courthouse, 389-397 High Street, London E15

Do.

Do.

Do.

Do.

CENTRAL ACCOUNTING OFFICE
All administrative enquiries about fines and maintenance orders should be addressed to Central Accounting Office. This includes Transfer of Fine Orders (TFOs) and any sums enforceable as a legal aid contribution that would ordinarily be sent to this Court. Write to Central Accounting Office, Dept. 2650, P.O. Box 31092, London SW1P 3WS
Tel: 0845 940 0111 Monday to Friday.   DX 120554 VICTORIA 6
NOTE: Matters involving Maintenance Enforcement should be addressed to Central Accounting Office, Matrimonial Department, P.O. Box 31093, London SW1P 3WP

LONDON – NORTH AND WEST (CRIME)

Adult Court No
Name of Court/ Bench Legal Manager/ Bench Office Manager
Normal Times and Places of Courts

REDBRIDGE L.J.A.

2815 REDBRIDGE MAGISTRATES' COURT

Bench Legal Manager:
 Brian Gilbert,
Bench Office Manager:
 Carol Lewis,
850 Cranbrook Road,
Barkingside,
Ilford, Essex
IG6 1HW

Tel: 0845 601 3600

Fax: 020 8437 6561

DX 99327 BARKINGSIDE

Adult – Monday to Friday, 10 a.m. and 2 p.m.

YC – Tuesday and Friday, 10 a.m. (Remands and Sentencing) Wednesday, 10 a.m. (Sentencing)

FPC – Monday and Thursday, 10 a.m. and 2 p.m.

The Court House,
850 Cranbrook Road,
Barkingside, Ilford

Do.

Do.

CENTRAL ACCOUNTING OFFICE
All administrative enquiries about fines and maintenance orders should be addressed to Central Accounting Office. This includes Transfer of Fine Orders (TFOs) and any sums enforceable as a legal aid contribution that would ordinarily be sent to this Court. Write to Central Accounting Office, Dept. 2650, P.O. Box 31092, London SW1P 3WS
Tel: 0845 940 0111 Monday to Friday.   DX 120554 VICTORIA 6
NOTE: Matters involving Maintenance Enforcement should be addressed to Central Accounting Office, Matrimonial Department, P.O. Box 31093, London SW1P 3WP

RICHMOND-UPON-THAMES L.J.A.

2768 RICHMOND-UPON-THAMES MAGISTRATES' COURT

Bench Legal Manager:
 (Vacant),
Bench Office Manager:
 Jeannie Lombardi,
The Court House,
Parkshot,
Richmond, Surrey
TW9 2RF

Tel: 020 8271 2300

Fax: 020 8271 2330

DX 100257 RICHMOND 2

Adult – Daily, 10 a.m.

YC – Tuesday, 10 a.m.

FPC – Tuesday and Thursday, 10 a.m.

The Court House, Parkshot, Richmond

Do.

Do.

NOTE: From 1st October 2007 all Transfer of Fine Orders, Crown Court Orders and Fixed Penalty Registrations will be administered by the Central Accounts Office.
Write to Central Accounting Office, PO Box 31090, London SW1P 3WQ.
Tel: 0845 940 0111 (public)   020 7805 1055 (HMCS staff only)   DX 120554 VICTORIA 6
E-mail: correspondence.cao@hmcourts-service.gsi.gov.uk

LONDON – NORTH AND WEST (CRIME)

Adult Name of Court/
Court Bench Legal Manager/
No Bench Office Manager   *Normal Times and Places of Courts*

WALTHAM FOREST L.J.A.

2813 WALTHAM FOREST MAGISTRATES' COURT

Bench Legal Manager: Huw Richards, *Bench Office Manager:* Carol Lewis (Acting), The Court House, 1 Farnan Avenue, Walthamstow E17 4NX	Adult – Daily, 10 a.m.	Court House, 1 Farnan Avenue, Walthamstow
	YC – Wednesday, 10 a.m. and alternate Tuesdays and Thursdays, 2 p.m.	Do.
Tel: 0845 601 3600	FPC – Wednesday, 10 a.m.	Do.

Fax: 020 8527 9063

DX 99327 BARKINGSIDE

CENTRAL ACCOUNTING OFFICE
All administrative enquiries about fines and maintenance orders should be addressed to Central Accounting Office. This includes Transfer of Fine Orders (TFOs) and any sums enforceable as a legal aid contribution that would ordinarily be sent to this Court. Write to Central Accounting Office, Dept. 2650, P.O. Box 31092, London SW1P 3WS
Tel: 0845 940 0111 Monday to Friday.   DX 120554 VICTORIA 6
NOTE: Matters involving Maintenance Enforcement should be addressed to Central Accounting Office, Matrimonial Department, P.O. Box 31093, London SW1P 3WP

WANDSWORTH L.J.A.

2649 SOUTH WESTERN MAGISTRATES' COURT

Bench Legal Manager: Denise Duncan *Bench Office Manager:* Jan Hartnett, 176A Lavender Hill SW11	Adult – Weekdays, 9 a.m. to 4.30 p.m.	Lavender Hill SW11
	YC – See p.83	
	FPC – See p.87	

Tel: 020 7805 1462 (Finance and Resources)
     020 7805 1453 (Legal Aid)
     020 7805 1444-7 (Listing)
     020 7805 1470 (Licensing)
     020 7805 1459 (Post Court/Resulting)
     020 8271 2210 (Balham Youth Court)
     020 7805 1452 (Youth Listing)

Fax: 020 7805 1448 (Main)
          1461 (Listing)
          1437 (Youth Listing)

DX 58559 CLAPHAM JUNCTION

CENTRAL ACCOUNTING OFFICE
All administrative enquiries about fines and maintenance orders should be addressed to Central Accounting Office. This includes Transfer of Fine Orders (TFOs) and any sums enforceable as a legal aid contribution that would ordinarily be sent to this Court. Write to Central Accounting Office, Dept. 2649, P.O. Box 31091, London SW1P 3WR
Tel: 0845 940 0111 Monday to Friday.   DX 120554 VICTORIA 6
NOTE: Matters involving Maintenance Enforcement should be addressed to Central Accounting Office, Matrimonial Department, P.O. Box 31093, London SW1P 3WP

LONDON REGION

LONDON – CIVIL AND FAMILY

Area Director: Linda Lennon, Area Director's Office, Rose Court, 2 Southwark Bridge, London SE1 9HS. Tel: 020 7927 2174 Fax: 020 7921 2004 DX 154269 SOUTHWARK 12

NOTE: Area Director Linda Lennon is responsible for all County Courts and Civil business. See the County Courts in London for more information.

Adult Court No	Name of Court/ Bench Legal Manager/ Bench Office Manager	Normal Times and Places of Courts
6700	**INNER LONDON FAMILY PROCEEDINGS COURT**	
	Justices' Clerk: Audrey Damazer, *Bench Legal Manager:* Maurine Lewin, *Bench Office Manager:* Gary Waple, Inner London Family Proceedings Court, 59/65 Wells Street, London W1A 3AE Tel: 020 7805 3400 Fax: 020 7805 3490 DX 89268 SOHO SQUARE	Family – Weekdays, 9 a.m. to 5 p.m. 59/65 Wells Street, London W1A 3AE

THE BOARD OF GREEN CLOTH VERGE OF THE PALACES

Board of Green Cloth,
Buckingham Palace SW1

SPECIAL JURISDICTION
(for Gaming)
Six courts a year on
Wednesday, 11.30 a.m.

Clerk to the Board,
T. C. O'Maoileoin, BA, Solicitor Advocate and Barrister,
c/o Davenport Lyons Solicitors,
30 Old Burlington Street,
London
W1S 3NL

Tel: 020 7468 5562
Fax: 020 7434 5562
DX 37233 PICCADILLY 1

NORTH EAST REGION

NORTH AND WEST YORKSHIRE

Area Director: Dyfed Foulkes, Area Director's Office, Colbeck House, Bradford Road, Birstall, Batley WF17 9NR. Tel: 01924 424030   Fax: 01924 427910

Collection & Enforcement Centre (West Yorkshire): PO Box 135, Morley LS27 7ZT.
Tel: 0113 307 6600

Central Finance Office (North Yorkshire): PO Box 87, Northallerton DL7 8GF.
Tel: 01609 783539   Fax: 01609 760918

Adult Court No	Name of Court and Clerk/Legal Adviser	Normal Times and Places of Courts	
2996	**BATLEY AND DEWSBURY L.J.A.**		
	The Court House, Grove Street, Dewsbury, W. Yorks. WF13 1JP	Adult – Daily, 10 a.m. and 2 p.m.	Grove Street, Dewsbury
		YC – Monday and Thursday, 10 a.m. and 2 p.m. Wednesday, 2 p.m.	Do.
		FPC – Five sittings every month, 10 a.m.	Do.
	Tel: 01924 468287 0113 307 6600 (Collection and Enforcement Centre)		
	Fax: 01924 430483		

NOTE: All fines and fees accounts and documentation should be forwarded to P.O. Box 135, Morley LS27 7ZT.

2978	**BRADFORD L.J.A.**		
	The Court Office, P.O. Box 187, The Tyrls, Bradford, W. Yorks. BD1 1JL	Adult – Each weekday, 10 a.m. and 2.15 p.m.	The Tyrls, Bradford
		YC – Each weekday, 10.30 a.m. and 2.15 p.m.	Do.
	Tel: 01274 390111 Fax: 01274 391731	FPC – Monday, 10 a.m. and 2.15 p.m. Friday, 2.15 p.m.	Do.
		Wednesday, 10 a.m. and 2.15 p.m.	Bradford Road, Bingley
		Dir. Hgs. – Tuesday, 10 a.m. (Public) Friday, 10 a.m. (Private)	The Tyrls, Bradford

NOTE: All fines and fees accounts and documentation should be forwarded to P.O. Box 135, Morley LS27 7ZT.

NORTH AND WEST YORKSHIRE

Adult Court No	Name of Court and Clerk/Legal Adviser	Normal Times and Places of Courts	

2997 CALDERDALE L.J.A.

Gordon M. Airy, Legal Adviser, The Court Office, P.O. Box 32, Harrison Road, Halifax, W. Yorks. HX1 2AN	Adult – Daily, 10 a.m.	Harrison Road, Halifax
	YC – Monday and Wednesday, 10 a.m.	Do.
Tel: 01422 360695	FPC – Tuesday and Thursday, 10 a.m.	Do.
Fax: 01422 347874		

NOTE: All fines and fees accounts and documentation should be forwarded to P.O. Box 135, Morley LS27 7ZT.

2527 HARROGATE L.J.A.

(Vacant), The Court House, P.O. Box 72, Victoria Avenue, Harrogate HG1 1LS	Adult – Monday, Tuesday, Wednesday, Thursday and Friday, 10 a.m.	Court House, Victoria Avenue, Harrogate
	YC – (Combined with Skipton L.J.A.) Wednesday, 10 a.m.	Do.
	FPC – (Combined with Skipton L.J.A.) Monday, 10 a.m.	Do.

Tel: 01423 722000
       722002 (Maintenance Office)

Fax: 01423 722001

DX 11972 HARROGATE 1

2987 HUDDERSFIELD L.J.A.

The Court Office, Civic Centre, Huddersfield HD1 2NH	Adult – Daily, 10 a.m. and 2. p.m.	Court House, Civic Centre, Huddersfield
Tel: 01484 423552	YC – Monday, Tuesday and Thursday, 10 a.m. and 2 p.m.	Do.
Fax: 01484 430085	FPC – Wednesday, 10 a.m. and 2 p.m., and Thursday, 10 a.m.	Do.

NOTE: All fines and fees accounts and documentation should be forwarded to P.O. Box 155, Morley LS27 7ZR.

2979 KEIGHLEY L.J.A.

The Court Office, Bradford Road, Bingley, W. Yorks. BD16 1YA	Adult – Each weekday, 10 a.m. and 2 p.m.	Bradford Road, Bingley
	YC – Friday, 10 a.m.	Do.
Tel: 01274 568411	FPC – (Combined with Bradford)	
Fax: 01274 551289		

NOTE: All fine and fees accounts and documentation should be forwarded to P.O. Box 135, Morley LS27 7ZT.

NORTH AND WEST YORKSHIRE

Adult Court No	Name of Court and Clerk/Legal Adviser	Normal Times and Places of Courts	

2992 LEEDS DISTRICT L.J.A.

The Court House,
P.O. Box No. 97,
Westgate,
Leeds LS1 3JP

Tel: 0113 245 9653
Fax: 0113 244 4700

Adult – Daily, 10 a.m. and 2 p.m.   Westgate, Leeds

YC – Daily, 10 a.m.   Do.

FPC – Daily, 10 a.m.   Do.

NOTE: All fines and fees accounts and documentation should be forwarded to P.O. Box 145, Morley LS27 7ZS.

2543 NORTHALLERTON AND RICHMOND L.J.A.

(Vacant),
Clerk to the Justices,
3 Racecourse Lane,
Northallerton,
N. Yorks. DL7 8QZ

Tel: 01609 788200
(General Enquiries)
01609 788201
(Lic. and family enquiries)

Fax: 01609 783509

DX 69143 NORTHALLERTON

Adult – Monday, Wednesday, Thursday and Friday, 10 a.m.   3 Racecourse Lane, Northallerton

YC – Tuesday, 10 a.m.   Do.

FPC – Alternate Mondays, 10 a.m.   Do.

Central Finance Office for North Yorkshire   PO Box 87, Northallerton DL7 8GF
Tel: 01609 783539   Fax: 01609 760918

2994 PONTEFRACT L.J.A.

The Court Office,
Front Street,
Pontefract, W. Yorks.
WF8 1BW

Tel: 01977 691600
Fax: 01977 691610

Adult – Monday, Tuesday, Wednesday and Friday, 10 a.m. and 2 p.m.   Front Street, Pontefract

YC – Thursday, 10 a.m.   Do.

FPC – Wednesday and Friday, 10 a.m.   Do.

NOTE: All fines and fees accounts and documentation should be forwarded to P.O. Box 155, Morley LS27 7ZR.

2536 SCARBOROUGH L.J.A.

Mrs. A. C. Gardner
(Acting),
Law Courts,
Northway,
Scarborough,
N. Yorks. YO12 7AE

Tel: 01723 505000
Fax: 01723 353250
DX 68893

Adult – Mondays, Wednesdays, Thursdays and Fridays, 10 a.m. and 2.00 p.m.   Northway, Scarborough

Monday to Thursday, 10 a.m.   Law Courts, Waterstead Lane, Whitby

YC – Tuesdays, 10 a.m.   Northway, Scarborough

FPC – Thursdays, 10 a.m.   Scarborough County Court, Valley Bridge Road, Scarborough

NORTH AND WEST YORKSHIRE

Adult Court No	Name of Court and Clerk/Legal Adviser	Normal Times and Places of Courts	
2537	**SELBY L.J.A.**		
	Mrs. Christine Gardner (Acting), Law Courts, Clifford Street, York YO1 9RE	Adult – Tuesday, Wednesday, Thursday and Friday, 10 a.m.	Court House, New Lane, Selby
	Tel: 01904 615200	YC – Three Mondays per month, 10 a.m. (combined with York L.J.A.)	Do.
	Fax: 01904 615201 DX 61573 YORK 1	FPC – One Monday per month, 10 a.m. (combined with York L.J.A.)	Do.
2538	**SKIPTON L.J.A. (formerly Staincliffe Division)**		
	Magistrates' Court Office, Skipton Law Courts, Otley Street, Skipton, N. Yorks. BD23 1RQ	Adult – Wednesday and Friday, 10 a.m.	Skipton Law Courts, Otley Street, Skipton
	Tel: 01756 692670	YC – (Combined with Harrogate L.J.A.) Second and fourth Monday in month, 10 a.m.	Do.
	Fax: 01756 701169 DX 703031 SKIPTON 2	FPC – (Combined with Harrogate L.J.A.) Monday, once per month, 10 a.m.	Do.
2995	**WAKEFIELD L.J.A.**		
	Ray Goodman, District Legal Director, The Court Office, Cliff Parade, Wakefield WF1 2TW	Adult – Monday, Tuesday, Thursday and Friday, 10 a.m. and 2 p.m.	Court House, Cliff Parade, Wakefield
	Tel: 01924 231100	YC – Wednesday, 10 a.m. and 2 p.m.	Do.
	Fax: 01924 231146 DX 708370 WAKEFIELD	FPC – Tuesday, 10 a.m.	Do.
	NOTE: All fines and fees accounts and documentation should be forwarded to P.O. Box 155, Morley LS27 7ZR.		
2541	**YORK L.J.A.**		
	Mrs. Christine Gardner (Acting), Law Courts, Clifford Street, York YO1 9RE	Adult – Weekdays, 10 a.m.	Law Courts, Clifford Street, York
	Tel: 01904 615200	YC – Tuesday, 10 a.m. (combined with Selby L.J.A.)	Do.
	Fax: 01904 615201 DX 61573 YORK 1	FPC – Wednesday, 10 a.m. (combined with Selby L.J.A.)	Do.

SOUTH EAST REGION

SURREY AND SUSSEX

Area Director: Julia Eels, Area Director's Office, The Court House, Friar's Walk, Lewes, East Sussex BN7 2PG. Tel: 01273 409160   Fax: 01273 409161   DX 3110 LEWES

Director of Legal Services: Based at Area Director's office.

Central Finance Unit (West): Mid-Sussex Magistrates' Court, Bolnore Road, Haywards health RH16 4BA. Tel: 01444 472661   Fax: 01444 472633
DX 135596 HAYWARDS HEATH 6

Central Finance Unit (East): Brighton Magistrates' Court, The Law Courts, Edward Street, Brighton BN2 0LG.   Tel: 01273 811660   Fax: 01273 811773
DX 153460 BRIGHTON 17

Central Enforcement Office (West): Worthing Magistrates' Court, The Law Courts, Christchurch Road, Worthing BN11 1JE.   Tel: 01903 534833   Fax: 01903 820074   DX 98233 WORTHING 4

Central Enforcement Office (East): Brighton Magistrates' Court, The Law Courts, Edward Street, Brighton BN2 0LG. Tel: 01273 811670   Fax: 01273 811771
DX 153460 BRIGHTON 17

Adult Court No	Name of Court and Clerk/Legal Adviser	Normal Times and Places of Courts	
2849	**NORTH SURREY L.J.A.**		
	J. V. R. Baker, P.O. Box 5, The Law Courts, Knowle Green, Staines, Middlesex TW18 1XR	Adult – Daily, 10 a.m.	The Law Courts, Knowle Green, Staines
	Tel: 01784 459261	YC – Wednesday, 10 a.m.	Do.
	Fax: 01784 459826 (Office) 466257 (Ushers) 462870 (Family) **(Family Administration Unit for the County)** DX 98045 STAINES 2	FPC – Tuesday, 10 a.m.	Do.

SURREY AND SUSSEX

Adult Court No	Name of Court and Clerk/Legal Adviser	Normal Times and Places of Courts	
2857	**NORTH WEST SURREY L.J.A.**		
	J. V. R. Baker, The Court House, Station Approach, Woking, Surrey GU22 7YL	Adult – Daily, 10 a.m.	Court House, Station Approach, Woking
	Tel: 01483 714950	YC – Wednesday and Thursday, 10 a.m.	Do.
	Fax: 01483 712500 (Office) 712501 (Ushers)	FPC – Tuesday, 10 a.m.	The Law Courts, Knowle Green, Staines
	DX 135090 WOKING 5		
2856	**SOUTH EAST SURREY L.J.A.**		
	J. V. R. Baker, Director of Legal Services (Justices' Clerk) The Law Courts, Hatchlands Road, Redhill, Surrey RH1 6DH	Adult – Daily, 10 a.m.	The Law Courts, Hatchlands Road, Redhill
	Tel: 01737 765581	YC – Wednesday, 10 a.m.	Do.
	Fax: 01737 778372 (Office) 764972 (Ushers)	FPC – Wednesday, 10 a.m.	Magistrates' Court, London Road, Dorking
	DX 98021 REDHILL WEST		
2848	**SOUTH WEST SURREY L.J.A.**		
	J. V. R. Baker, P.O. Box 36, Guildford, Surrey GU1 4AS	Adult – Daily, 10 a.m.	Magistrates' Court, Mary Road, Guildford
	Tel: 01483 405300	YC – Thursday, 10 a.m.	Do.
	Fax: 01483 449208 (Office) 405375 (Ushers)	FPC – Wednesday, 10 a.m.	Do.
	DX 97865 GUILDFORD 5		

SURREY AND SUSSEX

Adult Court No	Name of Court and Clerk/Legal Adviser	Normal Times and Places of Courts	
2950	**SUSSEX (CENTRAL) L.J.A.**		
	P. T. A. Vahey, M.B.A., Barrister, Brighton and Lewes Magistrates' Court, The Law Courts, Edward Street, Brighton BN2 0LG	Adult – Monday to Friday, 10 a.m. and 2.15 p.m.	Law Courts, Edward Street, Brighton
		YC – Monday and Friday, 10 a.m. and 2.15 p.m.	Brighton Youth and Family Suite, John Street, Brighton
		FPC – Monday, Tuesday, Wednesday and Thursday, 10 a.m. and 2.15 p.m.	Do.
		Adult – Monday to Friday, 10 a.m. and 2.15 p.m.	The Court House, Friars Walk, Lewes
		YC – Thursday, 10 a.m. and 2.15 p.m.	Do.
		FPC – Friday, 10 a.m. and 2.15 p.m.	Do.
	Tel: 01273 670888 (General Enquiries) 811620 (Listing) 811630 (Family) 811640 (Court Support) 811660 (Accounts) 811670 (Enforcement) 811700 (Fixed Penalty)		
	Fax: 01273 811770 (Listing and Court Support) 811771 (Enforcement) 811772 (Licensing/Legal Aid) 811773 (Accounts) 811627 (Family)		
	DX 153460 BRIGHTON 17		
2948	**SUSSEX (EASTERN) L.J.A.**		
	P. T. A. Vahey, M.B.A., Barrister, Eastbourne Magistrates' Court, Old Orchard Road, Eastbourne BN21 4UN	Adult – Monday to Friday, 10 a.m. and 2.15 p.m.	The Law Courts, Old Orchard Road, Eastbourne
		YC – Tuesday, 10 a.m. and Wednesday, 2.15 p.m.	Do.
	Tel: 01323 727518 Fax: 01323 649372	FPC – Thursday and Friday, 10 a.m. and 2.15 p.m.	Do.
	Hastings Magistrates' Court, The Law Courts, Horntye Park, Bohemia Road, Hastings TN34 1ND	Adult – Monday to Friday, 10 a.m. and 2.15 p.m.	The Law Courts, Horntye Park, Bohemia Road, Hastings
		YC – Thursday, 2.15 p.m. and Friday, 10 a.m. and 2.15 p.m.	Do.
	Tel: 01424 437644 Fax: 01424 429878	FPC – Tuesday, Wednesday and Thursday, 10 a.m. and 2.15 p.m.	Do.

SURREY AND SUSSEX

Adult Court No	Name of Court and Clerk/Legal Adviser	Normal Times and Places of Courts	

2947 SUSSEX (NORTHERN) L.J.A.

P. T. A. Vahey, M.B.A., Barrister, *(Crawley, Horsham and Mid Sussex Magistrates' Courts)* Bolnore Road, Haywards Heath RH16 4BA	Adult – Weekdays, 10 a.m.		The Court House, County Buildings, Woodfield Road, Crawley
	YC	– Tuesday, 10 a.m.	Do.
	FPC	– Thursday, 10 a.m.	Do.
	VC	– Wednesday, 9.30 a.m. and Thursday, 2.15 p.m.	Magistrates' Court, Bolnore Road, Haywards Health
	YC	– Monday, 10 a.m.	Do.
	FPC	– Wednesday, 10 a.m.	Do.
	YC	– Friday, 10 a.m.	Magistrates' Court, Hurst Road, Horsham
	FPC	– Monday, 10 a.m.	Do.

Tel: 01444 417611 (Main Swichboard)
       472662 (Family Section)
   01903 534833 (Enforcement Section)

Fax: 01444 472639 (Court Support and Listing)
         472638 (Family Section)
   01903 820074 (Enforcement Section)

DX 135596 HAYWARDS HEATH 6

2949 SUSSEX (WESTERN) L.J.A.

P. T. A. Vahey, M.B.A., Barrister, Worthing Magistrates' Court, The Law Courts, P.O. Box 199, Christchurch Road, Worthing BN11 1JE	Adult – Monday to Friday, 10 a.m.		The Law Courts, Christchurch Road, Worthing
	YC	– Tuesday, 10 a.m. and Thursdays, 10 a.m.	Do.
	FPC	– Tuesday, 10 a.m.	Do.

Tel: 01903 210981 (General Enquiries)
         543833 (Enforcement Section)
         534828 (Listing)

Fax: 01903 820746 (General Enquiries)
         534839 (Listing)
         820074 (Enforcement)

DX 98233 WORTHING 4

Chichester Magistrates' Court, 6 Market Avenue, Chichester PO19 1YE	Adult – Monday to Friday, 10 a.m.		Magistrates' Court, 6 Market Avenue, Chichester
	YC	– Wednesday and Friday, 10 a.m.	Do.
	FPC	– Monday and Thursday, 10 a.m.	Do.

Tel: 01243 817000 (General Enquiries)
         817006 (Family Section)

Fax: 01243 533655

DX 97463 CHICHESTER 2

SOUTH EAST REGION

THAMES VALLEY

Area Director: Jonathon Lane, Area Director's Office, Magistrates' Court, Walton Street, Aylesbury, Bucks. HP21 7QZ. Tel: 01296 554350 (Switchboard)

Adult Court No	Name of Court and Clerk/Legal Adviser		Normal Times and Places of Courts	
1129	**CENTRAL BUCKINGHAMSHIRE L.J.A.**			
	Philip J. Knowles, LL.B., D.M.S. Magistrates' Court, Walton Street, Aylesbury, Bucks. HP21 7QZ	Adult –	Monday, Tuesday, Wednesday, Thursday and Friday, 10 a.m.	Magistrates Court, Walton Street, Aylesbury
			Monday, Wednesday and Thursday, 10 a.m.	Magistrates' Court, King George VI Road, Amersham
	Tel: 01296 554350 (General Enquiries) 01296 554333 (Listing) 01908 302800 (Family)	YC –	Tuesday and Friday, 10 a.m.	Magistrates' Court, Walton Street, Aylesbury
	Fax: 01296 554320 01908 230063	FPC –	Wednesday, 10 a.m. Friday, 10 a.m. once a month	Magistrates' Court, Walton Street, Aylesbury

NOTE: All payments and account enquiries to be made to Thames Valley Central Payments Office, P.O. Box 269, Bicester OX25 4ZF. Tel: 0870 240 5995

1072	**EAST BERKSHIRE L.J.A.**			
	Miss G. M. Andrews, Justices' Clerk's Office, Law Courts, Chalvey Park, off Windsor Road, Slough SL1 2HJ	Adult –	Daily, 10 a.m.	Law Courts, Chalvey Park, off Windsor Road, Slough
			Daily, 10 a.m.	Court House, Town Square, Bracknell
	Tel: 0870 2412820 (General Enquiries)	YC –	Tuesday and Thursday, 10 a.m.	Bridge Road, Maidenhead
	Fax: 01753 232190 DX 98033 SLOUGH 3	FPC –	Friday: For listing contact Reading County Court on 01189 870542	

NOTE: All payments and account enquiries to be made to Thames Valley Central Payments Office, P.O. Box 268, Bicester OX25 4ZE. Tel: 0870 240 5995

THAMES VALLEY

Adult
Court *Name of Court and*
No *Clerk/Legal Adviser*   *Normal Times and Places of Courts*

1124 MILTON KEYNES L.J.A.

Philip J. Knowles, LL.B., D.M.S., *Deputy*: Marcia Davis, Barrister 301 Silbury Boulevard, Witan Gate East, Milton Keynes MK9 2AJ	Adult – Daily, 10 a.m.	Magistrates' Court, 301 Silbury Bvd., Witan Gate East, Milton Keynes
	YC – Every Tuesday and Thursday, 10 a.m.	Do.
Tel: 0870 2412819 01908 451125 (Listing) 01908 451150 (Family & Liquor Licensing)	FPC – Every Monday and Thursday, 10 a.m.	Do.
Fax: 01908 451146 DX 54462 MILTON KEYNES	(Licensing Committee 2nd Wednesday in month, 10 a.m.)	
Thames Valley Central Payments Office P.O. Box 269, Bicester OX25 4ZF		
Tel: 0870 240 5995		

2775 NORTHERN OXFORDSHIRE L.J.A.

Mrs. Susan Lutter, Magistrates' Clerk's Office, The Court House, Warwick Road, Banbury, Oxon. OX16 2AW	Adult – Monday to Friday, 10 a.m.	Court House, Warwick Road, Banbury
	Monday, 10 a.m.	The Court House, Welch Way, Witney
	YC – Thursday, 10 a.m. (Combined with Oxford and Southern Oxfordshire L.J.As)	Court House, Warwick Road, Banbury
Tel: 01295 452000		
Fax: 01295 452050 DX 701968 BANBURY 2	FPC – (Combined with Oxford and Southern Oxfordshire L.J.As) First, third Wednesday in month, 10 a.m.	Court House, Warwick Road, Banbury
	Fourth Monday in month, 10 a.m.	The Court House, Welch Way, Witney

NOTE: All correspondence to the Banbury Courthouse, Warwick Road, Banbury, Oxon. OX16 2AW.

THAMES VALLEY

Adult Court No	Name of Court and Clerk/Legal Adviser	Normal Times and Places of Courts	
2777	**OXFORD L.J.A.**		
	Mrs. Susan Lutter, The Court House, P.O. Box 37, Speedwell Street, Oxford OX1 1RZ Tel: 0870 241 2808 (General Enquiries) Fax: 01865 448024 DX 96452 OXFORD 4	Adult – Monday, Tuesday, Thursday and Friday, 10 a.m. YC – (Combined with Northern Oxfordshire and Southern Oxfordshire L.J.As) Wednesday, 10 a.m. FPC – (Combined with Northern Oxfordshire and Southern Oxfordshire L.J.As) Wednesday, 10 a.m.	The Court House, Speedwell Street, Oxford The Youth Court, The Court House, Speedwell Street, Oxford The Court House, Speedwell Street, Oxford
1076	**READING L.J.A.**		
	Miss G. M. Andrews, Miss J. Sprott (Court Manager), Magistrates' Courts, Civic Centre, Reading RG1 7TQ Tel: 01189 801800 (Court) 801872 (Family Court) Fax: 01189 801873 DX 151160 READING 25	Adult – Daily, 10 a.m. YC – (Combined with West Berkshire L.J.A.) Monday, Tuesday and Friday, 10 a.m. FPC – (Combined with West Berkshire L.J.A.) Wednesday, 10 a.m.	Magistrates' Courts, Civic Centre, Reading Do. Do.
2774	**SOUTHERN OXFORDSHIRE L.J.A. (formerly Abingdon, Didcot and Wantage Division)**		
	Mrs. Susan Lutter, The Court House, P.O. Box 37, Speedwell Street, Oxford OX1 1RZ Tel: 0870 241 2808 (General Enquiries) Fax: 01865 448024 DX 96452 OXFORD 4	Adult – Monday and Thursday, 10 a.m. and 2 p.m. YC – (Combined with Northern Oxfordshire and Oxford L.J.As) Friday, 10 a.m. FPC – (Combined with Northern Oxfordshire and Oxford L.J.As) Third Monday in month, 10 a.m.	The Court House, Mereland Road, Didcot Do. Do.

THAMES VALLEY

Adult Court No	Name of Court and Clerk/Legal Adviser	Normal Times and Places of Courts	

1075 WEST BERKSHIRE L.J.A.

Miss G. M. Andrews,
Miss J. Sprott
(Court Manager),
The Magistrates' Court,
Civic Centre,
Reading RG1 7TQ

Tel: 01189 801800
      (Court)
    801872
    (Family Court)

Fax: 01189 801873

DX 151160 READING 25

Adult – Wednesday, Thursday and Friday, 10 a.m.   The Court House, Mill Lane, Newbury

YC – (Combined with Reading L.J.A.) Monday, 10 a.m.   Do.

FPC – (Combined with Reading L.J.A.) Tuesday, 10 a.m.   Do.

1130 WYCOMBE AND BEACONSFIELD L.J.A.

Philip J. Knowles,
  LL.B., D.M.S., Barrister
Deputy:
Mrs. Susan P. Walton,
  D.M.S., Solicitor
Law Courts,
Easton Street,
High Wycombe, Bucks.
HP11 1LR

Tel: 01494 651035
    (General)
  0870 2405995
    (Fines etc.)

Fax: 01494 651030

DX 97883 HIGH WYCOMBE 3

Email: wycombe.magistrates@hmcourts-service.gsi.gov.uk

Adult – Daily, 10 a.m.   Law Courts, Easton Street, High Wycombe

Monday, 10 a.m.   Magistrates' Court, King George V Road, Amersham

FPC – Every Thursday, 10 a.m.   Law Courts, Easton Street, High Wycombe

YC – Every Tuesday and Friday, 10 a.m.   Do.

NOTE: All payments and account enquiries to be made to Thames Valley Central Payments Office, P.O. Box 269, Bicester OX25 4ZF. Tel: 0870 240 5995

HMCS WALES

MID AND WEST WALES

Area Director: Luigi Stranati, Area Director's Office, The Old Vicarage, Picton Terrace, Carmarthen SA31 1BJ. Tel: 01267 221658   Fax: 01267 221812
DX 99570 CARMARTHEN 2

Adult Court No	Name of Court and Clerk/Legal Adviser	Normal Times and Places of Courts	
3138	**CARMARTHEN L.J.A.**		
	Stephen J. T. Whale, M.B.A., Magistrates' Clerk's Office, Town Hall Square, Llanelli, Carmarthenshire SA15 3AW	Adult – Monday, Tuesday, Wednesday and Thursday, 9.30 a.m.	The Shire Hall, Carmarthen
		YC – Friday, 10 a.m.	Do.
	Tel: 01554 757201 757203	FPC – First Monday, 2.00 p.m.	Do.
	Fax: 01554 759669	Enf. – Second Monday, 9.30 a.m.	Do.
	DX 99512 LLANELLI 2		
	CENTRAL FINANCE OFFICE Penffynnon, Hawthorn Rise, Haverfordwest SA61 2AZ		
	Tel: 01437 771200		
	Fax: 01437 771201		
	DX 99613 HAVERFORDWEST 2		

All payment and account enquiries should be made to the Central Finance Office, Penffynnon, Hawthorn Rise, Haverfordwest, Pembrokeshire SA61 2AZ.

Please note: Transfer of Fine Orders (TFOs) should be sent to the Central Finance Office address.
Matters involving Maintenance Enforcement should be addressed to individual Court Offices.

MID AND WEST WALES

Adult Court No	Name of Court and Clerk/Legal Adviser	Normal Times and Places of Courts	
3135	**CEREDIGION L.J.A.**		
	Stephen J. T. Whale, M.B.A., Magistrates' Court's Office, 21 Alban Square, Aberaeron, Ceredigion SA46 0DB	Adult – Each Monday, Wednesday and Friday, 9.30 a.m.	Swyddfa'r Sir, Aberystwyth
		Each Thursday and Friday, 9.30 a.m.	Court House, Priory Street, Cardigan
		YC – Every first and third Tuesday, 9.30 a.m.	Swyddfa'r Sir, Aberystwyth
		Second and fourth Tuesday in month, 9.30 a.m.	Court House, Priory Street, Cardigan
	Tel: 01545 570886	FPC – First Thursday in month, 9.30 a.m.	Swyddfa'r Sir, Aberystwyth
	Fax: 01545 570295		
	DX 92405 ABERAERON	Enf. – First Tuesday, 9.30 a.m.	Court House, Priory Street, Cardigan
		Second Tuesday, 9.30 a.m.	Swyddfa'r Sir, Aberystwyth

CENTRAL FINANCE OFFICE – p. 100

All payment and account enquiries should be made to the Central Finance Office, Penffynnon, Hawthorn Rise, Haverfordwest, Pembrokeshire SA61 2AZ.

Please note: Transfer of Fine Orders (TFOs) should be sent to the Central Finance Office address.
Matters involving Maintenance Enforcement should be addressed to individual Court Offices.

3350	**DE BRYCHEINIOG L.J.A.**		
	Stephen J. T. Whale, M.B.A., Brecon Law Courts, Cambrian Way, Brecon, Powys LD3 7HR	Adult – Monday, Tuesday and Thursday, 9.30 a.m.	Brecon Law Courts, Cambrian Way, Brecon
		YC – (Combined with Radnorshire and North Brecknock L.J.A.) Friday, 9.30 a.m.	Do.
	Tel: 01874 622993	FPC – First Friday in month, 9.30 a.m.	Do.
	Fax: 01874 622441		
	DX 124340 BRECON 2	Enf. – Second Friday in month, 9.30 a.m.	Do.

CENTRAL FINANCE OFFICE – see p. 100 ante

All payment and account enquiries should be made to the Central Finance Office, Penffynnon, Hawthorn Rise, Haverfordwest, Pembrokeshire SA61 2AZ.

Please note: Transfer of Fine Orders (TFOs) should be sent to the Central Finance Office address.
Matters involving Maintenance Enforcement should be addressed to individual Court Offices.

MID AND WEST WALES

Adult Court No	Name of Court and Clerk/Legal Adviser	Normal Times and Places of Courts	

3140 DINEFWR L.J.A.

Stephen J. T. Whale, M.B.A., Magistrates' Clerk's Office, Town Hall Square, Llanelli, Carmarthenshire SA15 3AW	Adult – Monday, Tuesday and Thursday, 9.30 a.m. Wednesday, 9.30 a.m.	The Court House, Margaret Street, Ammanford Magistrates' Court, Town Hall Square, Llanelli
	YC – Second and fourth Tuesday, 9.30 a.m.	The Court House, Margaret Street, Ammanford
Tel: 01554 757201 757203	FPC – Second and fourth Monday (fortnightly), 1.45 p.m.	Do.
Fax: 01554 759669 DX 99512 LLANELLI 2	ENF – Second Monday, 9.30 a.m.	Do.

CENTRAL FINANCE OFFICE – see p. 100 ante

All payment and account enquiries should be made to the Central Finance Office, Penffynnon, Hawthorn Rise, Haverfordwest, Pembrokeshire SA61 2AZ.

Please note: Transfer of Fine Orders (TFOs) should be sent to the Central Finance Office address.
Matters involving Maintenance Enforcement should be addressed to individual Court Offices.

3122 LLANELLI L.J.A.

Stephen J. T. Whale, M.B.A., Magistrates' Clerk's Office, Town Hall Square, Llanelli, Carmarthenshire SA15 3AW	Adult – Monday, Wednesday, Thursday and Friday, 9.30 a.m.	Magistrates' Court, Town Hall Square, Llanelli
	YC – Tuesday, 9.30 a.m.	Do.
Tel: 01554 757201 757203	FPC – First and third Tuesday, 9.30 a.m.	Do.
Fax: 01554 759669 DX 99512 LLANELLI 2	ENF – First Monday, 9.30 a.m.	Do.

CENTRAL FINANCE OFFICE – see p. 100 ante

All payment and account enquiries should be made to the Central Finance Office, Penffynnon, Hawthorn Rise, Haverfordwest, Pembrokeshire SA61 2AZ.

Please note: Transfer of Fine Orders (TFOs) should be sent to the Central Finance Office address.
Matters involving Maintenance Enforcement should be addressed to individual Court Offices.

MID AND WEST WALES

Adult Court No	Name of Court and Clerk/Legal Adviser	Normal Times and Places of Courts	

3355 MONTGOMERYSHIRE L.J.A.

Stephen J. T. Whale, M.B.A.,	Adult –	Thursday, 10 a.m.	The Magistrates' Court, Llandrindod Wells
P.O. Box 105, Mansion House, 24 Severn Street, Welshpool,		Monday, Tuesday and Wednesday, 10 a.m.	Mansion House, Welshpool
	YC –	Wednesday, 10 a.m.	Mansion House, Welshpool
Powys SY21 7UX	FPC –	Fourth Friday in month, 10 a.m.	Mansion House, 24 Severn Street, Welshpool
Tel: 01938 555968 Fax: 01938 554593	Misc. –	Third Friday in month, 10 a.m.	Do.
DX 702535 WELSHPOOL 2	Enf. –	First Friday in month, 10 a.m.	Do.

CENTRAL FINANCE OFFICE – see p. 100 ante

All payment and account enquiries should be made to the Central Finance Office, Penffynnon, Hawthorn Rise, Haverfordwest, Pembrokeshire SA61 2AZ.

Please note: Transfer of Fine Orders (TFOs) should be sent to the Central Finance Office address.
Matters involving Maintenance Enforcement should be addressed to individual Court Offices.

3359 NEATH PORT TALBOT L.J.A.

J. P. F. Hehir, B.A., M.B.A., Solicitor	Adult –	Monday, Wednesday and Friday, 10 a.m. and 2.15 p.m.	The Court House, Fairfield Way, Neath
Magistrates' Clerk's Office, Fairfield Way, Neath, W. Glam. SA11 1RF		Tuesday and Thursday, 10 a.m. and 2.15 p.m.	The Court House, Cramic Way, Port Talbot
	YC –	Tuesday, 10 a.m.	The Court House, Fairfield Way, Neath
Tel: 01639 765900 Fax: 01639 765954		Friday, 10 a.m.	The Court House, Cramic Way, Port Talbot
	FPC –	Thursday, 10 a.m.	The Court House, Fairfield Way, Neath

NOTE: All fine payments and account enquiries should be made to the central Finance Unit, Cramic Way, Port Talbot SA13 1RU   Tel:01639 889494

MID AND WEST WALES

Adult Court No | *Name of Court and Clerk/Legal Adviser* | *Normal Times and Places of Courts*

3356 PEMBROKESHIRE L.J.A.

Stephen J. T. Whale, M.B.A.,
Magistrates' Courts
Penffynnon,
Hawthorn Rise,
Haverfordwest,
Pembrokeshire
SA61 2AZ

Tel: 01437 772090
   01437 771200 (Fines)

Fax: 01437 768662

DX 99613 HAVERFORDWEST 2

Adult – Monday, Tuesday, Wednesday and Thursday, 9.30 a.m.

YC – Every Friday, 9.30 a.m.

FPC – Second and fourth Friday in month, 9.30 a.m.

Enf. – First and third Friday in month, 9.30 a.m.

Magistrates' Courts, Penffynnon, Hawthorn Rise, Haverfordwest SA61 2AZ

Do.

Do.

Do.

CENTRAL FINANCE OFFICE – see p. 100 ante

All payment and account enquiries should be made to the Central Finance Office, Penffynnon, Hawthorn Rise, Haverfordwest, Pembrokeshire SA61 2AZ.

Please note: Transfer of Fine Orders (TFOs) should be sent to the Central Finance Office address.
Matters involving Maintenance Enforcement should be addressed to individual Court Offices.

3351 RADNORSHIRE AND NORTH BRECKNOCK L.J.A. *(formerly LLANDRINDOD WELLS DIVISION)*

Stephen J. T. Whale, M.B.A.,
Brecon Law Courts,
Cambrian Way,
Brecon,
Powys LD3 7HR

Tel: 01874 622993

Fax: 01874 622441

DX 124340 BRECON 2

Adult – Wednesday and Friday, 9.30 a.m.

YC – (Combined with De Brycheiniog L.J.A.) Friday, 9.30 a.m.

FPC – Third Tuesday in month, 9.30 a.m.

Enf. – Fourth Tuesday in month, 9.30 a.m.

The Magistrates' Court, Llandrindod Wells

Brecon Law Courts, Cambrian Way, Brecon

The Magistrates' Court, Llandrindod Wells

Do.

CENTRAL FINANCE OFFICE – see p. 100 ante

All payment and account enquiries should be made to the Central Finance Office, Penffynnon, Hawthorn Rise, Haverfordwest, Pembrokeshire SA61 2AZ.

Please note: Transfer of Fine Orders (TFOs) should be sent to the Central Finance Office address.
Matters involving Maintenance Enforcement should be addressed to individual Court Offices.

MID AND WEST WALES

Adult Court No	Name of Court and Clerk/Legal Adviser	Normal Times and Places of Courts	
3360	**SWANSEA L.J.A.**		
	J. S. Barron, Magistrates' Court, Grove Place, Swansea SA1 5DB	Adult – Daily, 10 a.m. and 2.15 p.m.	Magistrates' Court, Grove Place, Swansea
		YC – Daily, 10 a.m.	Magistrates' Court, Dynevor Place, Swansea
	Tel: 01792 478300	FPC – Monday and Friday, 2.15 p.m. Alternate Tuesdays and Wednesdays, 2.15 p.m.	Do.
	Fax: 01792 651066		

NOTE: All fine payments and account enquiries should be made to the central Finance Unit, Cramic Way, Port Talbot SA13 1RU   Tel:01639 889494

HMCS WALES

NORTH WALES

Area Director: Clare Pillman, Area Director's Office, The Law Courts, Civic Centre, Mold, Flintshire, North Wales CH7 1AE. Tel: 01352 707400 Fax: 01352 707409 DX 702521 MOLD 2

Central Fines Office: The Courthouse, Grove Road, Denbigh LL16 3UU. Tel: 01745 812683

Adult Court No	Name of Court and Clerk/Legal Adviser	Normal Times and Places of Courts	
3062	**CONWY L.J.A.**		
	I. W. Thomas, LL.B., The Courthouse, Conwy Road, Llandudno LL30 1GA	Adult – Monday, Tuesday, Wednesday, Thursday and Friday (with Wednesday remand prisoners), 10 a.m.	The Courthouse, Conwy Road, Llandudno
	Tel: 01492 871333	YC – Tuesday and Thursday, 10 a.m.	Do.
	Fax: 01492 872321 (Admin) 01492 879203 (Listing)	FPC – First and third Wednesday in month, 10 a.m.	Do.
	DX 11365 LLANDUDNO	BGL – First Tuesday in January, April, July and October, 10 a.m.	Do.
	NOTE: All payments and account enquiries should be made to the Central Finance Office, The Courthouse, Grove Road, Denbigh LL16 3UU. Tel: 01745 812683.		
3061	**DENBIGHSHIRE L.J.A.**		
	I. W. Thomas, LL.B., The Courthouse, Conwy Road, Llandudno LL30 1GA	Adult – Monday, Tuesday, Wednesday, Thursday and Friday, 10 a.m.	The Courthouse, Victoria Road, Prestatyn
	Tel: 01492 871333	10 a.m. (remand prisoners)	Do.
	Fax: 01492 872321 (Admin) 01492 879203 (Listing)	Monday, Tuesday and first and third Thursday in month, 10 a.m.	The Courthouse, Grove Road, Denbigh
		YC – Wednesday and Friday, 10 a.m.	The Courthouse, Victoria Road, Prestatyn
	DX 11365 LLANDUDNO	First and third Thursday in month, 10 a.m.	The Courthouse, Grove Road, Denbigh
		FPC – Second and fourth Thursday in month, 10 a.m.	The Court House, Victoria Road, Prestatyn
		BGL – First Tuesday in January, April, July and October, 10 a.m.	Do.
	NOTE: All payments and account enquiries should be made to the Central Finance Office, The Courthouse, Grove Road, Denbigh LL16 3UU. Tel: 01745 812683.		

NORTH WALES

Adult Court No	Name of Court and Clerk/Legal Adviser	Normal Times and Places of Courts	

3059	**FLINTSHIRE L.J.A.**		
	I. W. Thomas, LL.B., Justices' Clerk's Office, Law Courts, Bodhyfryd, Wrexham LL12 7BP	Adult – Monday, Tuesday Wednesday and Thursday, 10 a.m.	The Law Courts, Mold
		YC – Friday, 10 a.m.	Do.
	Tel: 01978 310106 317407 (Listing)	FPC – Wednesday, 10 a.m.	Do.
	Fax: 01978 358213		
	DX 721923 WREXHAM 4		

NOTE: All payments and account enquiries should be made to the Central Finance Office, The Courthouse, Grove Road, Denbigh LL16 3UU. Tel: 01745 812683.

3244	**GWYNEDD L.J.A.**		
	I. W. Thomas, LL.B., Magistrates' Clerk's Office, 10/12 Market Street, Caernarfon, Gwynedd LL55 1RT	Adult – Monday and Wednesday, 10 a.m.	The County Hall, Caernarfon
		Friday, 10 a.m.	Shire Hall, Llangefni
		Thursday, 10 a.m.	The Shire Hall, Dolgellau
	Tel: 01286 675200 675288	Wednesday, 10 a.m.	The Court House, Pwllheli
	Fax: 01286 678691	YC – Twice monthly, alternate Tuesdays	The County Hall, Caernarfon
		Twice monthly	The Shire Hall, Dolgellau
		Twice monthly	The Court House, Pwllheli
		FPC – Monthly, variable	The County Court Buildings, Caernarfon
		Betting and Gaming – Jan, April, July and Oct	ring for details
	DX 713562 CAERNARFON 5		

NOTE: All payments and account enquiries should be made to the Central Finance Office, The Courthouse, Grove Road, Denbigh LL16 3UU. Tel: 01745 812683.

3058	**WREXHAM MAELOR L.J.A.**		
	I. W. Thomas, LL.B., Justices' Clerk's Office, Law Courts, Bodhyfryd, Wrexham LL12 7BP	Adult – Every weekday, 10 a.m.	Law Courts, Bodhyfryd, Wrexham
		YC – Tuesday, 10 a.m.	Do.
	Tel: 01978 310106 317407 (Listing)	FPC – Friday, 10 a.m.	Do.
	Fax: 01978 358213	Lic. – Monthly, Thursday	Do.
	DX 721923 WREXHAM 4		

NOTE: All payments and account enquiries should be made to the Central Finance Office, The Courthouse, Grove Road, Denbigh LL16 3UU. Tel: 01745 812683.

NORTH WALES

Adult Court No	Name of Court and Clerk/Legal Adviser	Normal Times and Places of Courts		
3238	**YNYS MON/ANGLESEY L.J.A.**			
	I. W. Thomas, LL.B., Magistrates' Clerk's Office, 10/12 Market Street, Caernarfon, Gwynedd LL55 1RT	Adult – Monday and Thursday, 10 a.m.		Shire Hall, Llangefni
			Tuesday, 10 a.m.	Law Courts, Holyhead
		YC	– Twice monthly, alternate Tuesdays	Shire Hall, Llangefni
	Tel: 01286 675200 675288		Monthly, variable	Law Courts, Holyhead
	Fax: 01286 678691	FPC	– Monthly, variable	Law Courts, Holyhead only
		Betting and Gaming – Jan, April, July and Oct.		ring for details
	DX 713562 CAERNARFON 5			

NOTE: All payments and account enquiries should be made to the Central Finance Office, The Courthouse, Grove Road, Denbigh LL16 3UU. Tel: 01745 812683.

HMCS WALES

SOUTH EAST WALES

Area Director: Alan Davies, Area Director's Office, 47 Charles Street, Cardiff, CF10 2GD.
Tel: 029 2030 0250   Fax: 029 2030 0240

NOTE With effect from 2008 the Area Director's Office will be located at Churchill House, Cardiff CF10 2HH.

Adult Court No	Name of Court and Clerk/Legal Adviser		Normal Times and Places of Courts	
3348	**CARDIFF L.J.A.**			
	Martyn Waygood, LL.B., M.B.A., The Magistrates' Court, Fitzalan Place, Cardiff CF24 0RZ	Adult –	Monday to Friday, 10 a.m. and 2.15 p.m. Saturday, 9.30 a.m.	Magistrates' Court, Cardiff
		YC –	Daily, 10 a.m.	Do.
		FPC –	Tuesday and Wednesday, 10 a.m. and any other day as required	Do.
	Tel: 029 2046 3040 2047 4317 (Family) 2047 4342 (Licensing) 2047 4350 (Listing)			
	Fax: 029 2046 0264 (Listing/Licensing/Results/Family/Representation) 2045 6224 (Clerk to the Justices)			
	NOTE: All fine payments and account enquiries should be made to the central Finance Unit, Cramic Way, Port Talbot SA13 1RU Tel:01639 889494			
3262	**CYNON VALLEY L.J.A.**			
	Steve Miller, The Court House, Cwmbach Road, Aberdare CF44 0NW	Adult –	Monday, Wednesday and Friday, 10 a.m.	The Court House, Cwmbach Road, Aberdare
		YC –	Tuesday, 10 a.m.	Do.
	Tel: 01685 721731 Fax: 01685 723919	FPC –	Thursday, 10 a.m.	Do.
	NOTE: All fine payments and account enquiries should be made to the central Finance Unit, Cramic Way, Port Talbot SA13 1RU Tel:01639 889494			

SOUTH EAST WALES

Adult Court No	Name of Court and Clerk/Legal Adviser	Normal Times and Places of Courts	
3211	**GWENT L.J.A.**		
	E. J. Harding, P.O. Box 85, Cwmbran NP44 1WY Tel: 01633 645000 Fax: 01633 645177 DX 43665 CWMBRAN	Adult – Daily (except Saturday) Tuesday, Wednesday and Thursday, 10 a.m. Monday and Friday, 10 a.m. Daily (except Saturday), 10 a.m. Monday, Tuesday and Thursday, 10 a.m.	Magistrates' Court, Civic Centre, Newport Magistrates' Court, Tudor Street, Abergavenny Magistrates' Court, Tudor Road, Cwmbran The Court House, Mountain Road, Caerphilly The Court House, Springbank, Abertillery
		YC – Tuesday, Wednesday and Thursday, 10 a.m.	Magistrates' Court, Tudor Road, Cwmbran
		FPC – Wednesday, 10 a.m. Friday, 10 a.m.	County Court, Pontypool The Court House, Springbank, Abertillery
3264	**MERTHYR TYDFIL L.J.A.**		
	Steve Miller, Magistrates' Court, Law Courts, Glebeland Place, Merthyr Tydfil CF47 8BU Tel: 01685 721731 Fax: 01685 723919	Adult – Monday, Tuesday and Thursday, 10 a.m. YC – Friday, 10 a.m. FPC – Wednesday, 10 a.m.	Law Courts, Merthyr Tydfil Do. Do.
	NOTE: All fine payments and account enquiries should be made to the central Finance Unit, Cramic Way, Port Talbot SA13 1RU Tel:01639 889494		
3265	**MISKIN L.J.A.**		
	Steve Miller, Magistrates' Clerk's Office, Union Street, Pontypridd CF37 1SD Tel: 01443 480750 (General Office) Fax: 01443 485472	Adult – Monday, Wednesday, Thursday and Friday, 10 a.m. Monday, Tuesday, Thursday and Friday, 10 a.m. YC – Wednesday, 10 a.m. FPC – Tuesday, 10 a.m.	Union Street, Pontypridd The Courthouse, Llwynypia The Courthouse, Llwynypia The Courthouse, Pontypridd
	NOTE: All fine payments and account enquiries should be made to the central Finance Unit, Cramic Way, Port Talbot SA13 1RU Tel:01639 889494		

SOUTH EAST WALES

Adult Court No	Name of Court and Clerk/Legal Adviser	Normal Times and Places of Courts	
3266	**NEWCASTLE AND OGMORE L.J.A.**		
	Anthony R. Seculer, The Magistrates' Court, The Law Courts, Sunnyside, Bridgend CF31 4AJ	Adult – Tuesday, Wednesday, Thursday and Friday, 10 a.m.	Magistrates' Court, Sunnyside, Bridgend
		YC – Monday, 10 a.m.	Do.
	Tel: 01656 673800 Fax: 01656 668981	FPC – Friday, 10 a.m.	Do.
	NOTE: All fine payments and account enquiries should be made to the central Finance Unit, Cramic Way, Port Talbot SA13 1RU Tel:01639 889494		
3349	**VALE OF GLAMORGAN L.J.A.**		
	Anthony R. Seculer, Magistrates' Court, Thompson Street, Barry, Vale of Glam. CF63 4SX	Adult – Monday, Tuesday, Wednesday and Friday, 10 a.m.	Magistrates' Court, Thompson Street, Barry
		YC – Thursday, 9.30 a.m.	Do.
	Tel: 01446 737491 Fax: 01446 732743	FPC – Tuesday, 10 a.m.	Do.
	NOTE: All fine payments and account enquiries should be made to the central Finance Unit, Cramic Way, Port Talbot SA13 1RU Tel:01639 889494		

NORTHERN IRELAND

Adult Court No	Name of Court and Clerk/Legal Adviser	Normal Times and Places of Courts	
9001	**ANTRIM**		
	Mrs B. McLernon, Antrim Court Office, The Courthouse, 30 Castle Way, Antrim BT41 4AQ	Adult – Tuesday, 10 a.m. and 1st and 5th Monday, 10 a.m.	Antrim
		VC – Tuesday, 9.30 a.m.	Do.
		YC – 2nd and 4th Thursday, 10 a.m.	Do.
	Tel: 028 9446 2661	Dom – 3rd Monday, 10 a.m.	Do.
	Fax: 028 9446 3301	Dept – 1st Monday, 10 a.m.	Do.
9002	**ARDS**		
	Mrs. D. Thompson, Newtownards Court Office,	Adult – 2nd, 4th and 5th Monday and every Tuesday, 10.30 a.m.	Newtownards
	The Courthouse, Regent Street,	VC – Friday, 10 a.m.	Do.
	Newtownards BT23 4LP	YC – 2nd and 4th Thursday, 10.30 a.m.	Do.
	Tel: 028 9181 4343 Fax: 028 9181 8024	FPC – 1st, 2nd, 3rd and 4th Monday, Wednesday and Thursday, 10.30 a.m.	Do.
		Dom – 1st and 3rd Thursday, 10.30 a.m.	Do.
9003	**ARMAGH**		
	Mrs. G. Campbell, Armagh Court Office,	Adult – Every Tuesday, 10.30 a.m.	Armagh
	The Courthouse,	VC – Tuesday, 10 a.m.	Do.
	The Mall, Armagh BT61 9DJ	YC – 2nd Friday, 10.30 a.m.	Do.
	Tel: 028 3752 2816	Dom – 4th Friday, 10.30 a.m.	Do.
	Fax: 028 3752 8194	Dept – 3rd Friday	Do.
9004	**BALLYMENA**		
	Mrs. S. Hughes, Ballymena Court Office, The Courthouse,	Adult – 2nd and 4th Tuesdays, 5th Wednesday and every Thursday, 10 a.m.	Ballymena
	Albert Place, Ballymena, Co. Antrim	YC – 1st and 3rd Tuesday, 10 a.m.	Do.
	BT43 5BS Tel: 028 2564 9416 Fax: 028 2565 5371	FPC – Every Wednesday, 10 a.m. 2nd and 4th Monday, 10 a.m. 1st Thursday, 10 a.m. 3rd Thursday, 10 a.m.	Ballymena Coleraine Antrim Larne
		Dom – 2nd and 4th Monday, 10 a.m.	Ballymena
		Dept – 4th Tuesday	Do.

9005 **BALLYMONEY** – combined with COLERAINE and MOYLE to form **The Petty Sessions District of NORTH ANTRIM**, q.v.

NORTHERN IRELAND

Adult Court No	Name of Court and Clerk/Legal Adviser	Normal Times and Places of Courts	
9006	**BANBRIDGE**		
	Mrs. G. Campbell, Banbridge Court Office, The Courthouse, 23 New Street, Newry BT35 6JD Tel: 028 4062 3622 Fax: 028 4062 3059	Adult – 1st, 3rd and 4th Thursdays, 10.30 a.m. YC and Dom – 3rd Monday, 10.30 a.m. Dept – 2nd Thursday	Newry Do. Do.
9007	**BELFAST AND NEWTOWNABBEY**		
9008 **9009**	Mr. K. Barr, Laganside Courts, 45 Oxford Street, Belfast BT1 3LL Tel: 028 9023 2721 Fax: 028 9031 5219	Adult – Each weekday, 10.30 a.m. VC – Each Weekday, 10 a.m. Youth VC – Wednesday, 10 a.m. YC – Every Monday, Wednesday and Friday, excluding 5th Friday of the month, 10.30 a.m. FPC – Every Monday, Tuesday, 10 a.m. Thursday and Friday, 10.30 a.m. Dom – Every Wednesday, 1st Tuesday and 3rd Tuesday, 10.30 a.m. Dept – Every Tuesday	Laganside Courts, 45 Oxford Street, Belfast BT1 3LL Belfast Do. Old Town Hall Building, 80 Victoria Street, Belfast BT1 3FA Do. Do. Do. Do.
9010	**CARRICKFERGUS & NEWTOWNABBEY** – renamed **NEWTOWNABBEY** – see p.117		
9012	**CASTLEREAGH**		
	Mrs. D. Thompson, Newtownards Court Office, The Courthouse, Regent Street, Newtownards BT23 4LP Tel: 028 9181 4343 Fax: 028 9181 8024	Adult – 1st and 3rd Wednesdays and every Friday, 10.30 a.m. VC – Friday, 10 a.m. YC – 2nd and 4th Thursday, 10.30 a.m. Dom – 2nd Wednesday, 10.30 a.m.	Newtownards Do. Do. Do.
9014	**COLERAINE** – combined with BALLYMONEY and MOYLE to form **The Petty Sessions District of NORTH ANTRIM,** q.v.		
9015	**COOKSTOWN** – combined with DUNGANNON to form **The Petty Sessions District of EAST TYRONE,** q.v.		

NORTHERN IRELAND

Adult Court No	Name of Court and Clerk/Legal Adviser	Normal Times and Places of Courts	
9016	**CRAIGAVON**		
9017	Miss. Margaret Elliott, Craigavon Court Office, The Courthouse, Central Way, Craigavon BT64 1AP Tel: 028 3834 1324 Fax: 028 3834 1243	Adult – 5th Mondays, 4th and 5th Wednesday and every Thursday and Friday, 10.30 a.m.	Craigavon
		VC – Thursday, 10 a.m.	Do.
		YC – 2nd Tuesday, 10.30 a.m. and 4th Monday, 10.30 a.m.	Do.
		FPC – 1st and 3rd Monday, 10.30 a.m.	Do.
		3rd Wednesday, 10.30 a.m.	The Courthouse, Railway Street, Lisburn
		Dom – 1st and 3rd Wednesday, 10.30 a.m.	Craigavon
		Dept – 2nd Monday	Do.
9018	**DOWN**		
	Mr. R. Kernaghan, Downpatrick Court Office, The Courthouse, English Street, Downpatrick BT30 6AD Tel: 028 4461 4621 Fax: 028 4461 3969	Adult – Every Thursday, 10.30 a.m. 2nd and 4th Monday, 10.30 a.m.	Downpatrick Newcastle (at Downpatrick)
		VC – Thursday, 9.30am	Downpatrick
		YC – 1st and 3rd Tuesday, 10.30 a.m.	Do.
		Dom – 3rd Monday, 10.30 a.m.	Do.
		Dept – 1st Monday	Do.
9019	**DUNGANNON** – combined with COOKSTOWN to form **The Petty Sessions District of EAST TYRONE,** see below		
	EAST TYRONE		
	Mrs. L. Dripps, Dungannon Court Office, The Courthouse, 46 Killyman Road, Dungannon BT71 6FG Tel: 028 8772 2992 Fax: 028 8772 8169	Adult – 4th Monday, 5th Tuesday, every Wednesday, and every Friday, 10.30 a.m.	Dungannon
		Dept – 2nd Monday, 10.30 a.m.	Do.
		YC – 1st and 3rd Tuesday, 10.30 a.m.	Do.
		Dom – 2nd Tuesday, 10.30 a.m.	Do.
		FPC – 2nd and 5th Thursday, 10.30 a.m.	Do.

NORTHERN IRELAND

Adult Court No	Name of Court and Clerk/Legal Adviser	Normal Times and Places of Courts	
9020	**FERMANAGH**		
	Mr. N. Elliott, Deputy Principal, Mrs. Clare Deazley, Office Manager Enniskillen Court Office, The Courthouse, East Bridge Street, Enniskillen BT74 7BP Tel: 028 6632 2356 Fax: 028 6632 3636	Adult – Every Monday, 10 a.m. 1st, 2nd and 3rd Wednesdays, 10 a.m. 2nd Tuesday, 10 a.m. YC – 4th Wednesday, 10 a.m. Dom – 2nd Thursday, 10.30 a.m. Dept – 2nd Monday	Enniskillen Do. Do. Do.
9024	**LARNE**		
	Miss. Avril Finlay, Larne Court Office, The Courthouse, Victoria Road, Larne BT40 1RN Tel: 028 2827 2927 Fax: 028 2827 6414	Adult – 2nd, 3rd, 4th and 5th Friday, 10 a.m. YC – 4th Thursday, 10 a.m. FPC – 3rd Thursday, 10 a.m. Dom – 2nd Thursday, 10 a.m. Dept – 1st Friday	Larne Do. Do. Do. Do.
9025	**LIMAVADY**		
	Mrs. P. McCourt, Limavady Court Office, The Courthouse, Main Street, Limavady BT49 0EY Tel: 028 7772 2688 Fax: 028 7776 8794	Adult – 1st, 2nd, 4th and 5th Wednesday, 10 a.m. Dept – 3rd Wednesday	Limavady Do.
9026	**LISBURN**		
	Mr. C. Cromie, Lisburn Court Office, The Courthouse, Railway Street, Lisburn BT28 1XR Tel: 028 9267 5336 Fax: 028 9260 4107	Adult – Every Monday, Tuesday, 5th Wednesday, and 5th Thursday, 10.30 a.m. 2nd and 4th Fridays, 10.30 a.m. VC – Tuesday, 10 a.m. YC – 1st and 3rd Wednesday, 10.30 a.m. Dom – 1st and 3rd Thursday, 10.30 a.m. Dept – 4th Thursday	Lisburn Hillsborough at Lisburn Do. Hillsborough and Lisburn Lisburn Lisburn

NORTHERN IRELAND

Adult Court No	Name of Court and Clerk/Legal Adviser	Normal Times and Places of Courts	
9028	**LONDONDERRY**		
	Miss M. W. McKeegan, Court Administrator, Londonderry Court Office, The Courthouse, Bishop Street, Londonderry BT48 6PQ	Adult – 1st, 2nd, 3rd and 5th Monday, 1st, 3rd, 4th and 5th Tuesday, 5th Wednesday, 1st, 2nd, 4th and 5th Thursday, and every Friday, 10. a.m.	Londonderry
	Tel: 028 7136 3448 Fax: 028 7137 2059	YC – 1st, 2nd and 3rd Wednesday, 10 a.m.	Do.
		FPC – 2nd Tuesday, 4th Wednesday and every Friday, 10 a.m.	Do.
		Dom – 4th Monday, 10 a.m.	Do.
		Dept – 3rd Thursday	Do.
9029	**MAGHERAFELT**		
	Mrs. S. McCollum, Magherafelt Court Office, The Courthouse, Hospital Road, Magherafelt BT45 5DG	Adult – 1st and 4th Monday, 10 a.m. 1st, 2nd, 3rd and 4th Tuesday, 10 a.m.	Magherafelt Do.
	Tel: 028 7963 2121 Fax: 028 7963 4063	YC and Dom – 3rd Monday, 10 a.m. (Youth) 11.00 a.m. (Domestic)	Do.
		Dept – 1st Monday	Do.
9030	**MOYLE** – combined with COLERAINE and BALLYMONEY to form **The Petty Sessions District of NORTH ANTRIM**, q.v.		
9032	**NEWRY AND MOURNE**		
	Mrs. G. Campbell, Newry House Court Office, The Courthouse, 23 New Street, Newry BT35 6JD	Adult – 1st, 2nd, 4th and 5th Monday, every Wednesday, 5th Thursday and Friday, 10.30 a.m.	Newry
		VC – Wednesday, 10 a.m.	Do.
	Tel: 028 3025 2040 Fax: 028 3026 9830	YC – 1st and 3rd Friday, 10.30 a.m.	Do.
		FPC – 2nd Monday and 1st, 2nd, 3rd and 4th Tuesday, 10.30 a.m.	Do.
		Dom – 2nd and 4th Friday, 10.30 a.m.	Do.
9033	**NEWTOWNABBEY** – (CLOSED – Business transferred to BELFAST AND NEWTOWN ABBEY see p. 114)		

NORTHERN IRELAND

Adult Court No	Name of Court and Clerk/Legal Adviser	Normal Times and Places of Courts	
	NORTH ANTRIM		
	Mrs. S. Hughes, Coleraine Court Office, The Courthouse, 46A Mountsandel Road, Coleraine, Co. Londonderry BT52 1NY	Adult – Every Monday, 10 a.m. 1st Wednesday, 10 a.m. 2nd, 3rd and 4th Fridays, 10 a.m.	Coleraine
		YC – 2nd and 4th Wednesday, 10 a.m.	Do.
	Tel: 028 7034 3437	Dom – 1st and 3rd Thursday, 10 a.m.	Do.
	Fax: 028 7032 0156	Dept – 1st Friday	Do.
9034	**NORTH DOWN**		
	Mrs. V. Brennan, Bangor Court Office, The Courthouse, 6 Quay Street, Bangor BT20 5ED	Adult – Every Wednesday and 1st, Friday, 10.30 a.m.	Bangor
		YC – 2nd and 4th Tuesday, 10.30 a.m.	The Courthouse, Regent Street, Newtonards
	Tel: 028 9147 2626	Dom – 2nd and 4th Fridays, 10.30 a.m.	Bangor
	Fax: 028 9127 2667	Dept – 3rd and 5th Fridays	Do.
9035	**OMAGH**		
	Mrs. R. Crockett, Omagh Court Office, The Courthouse, High Street, Omagh BT78 1DU	Adult – Every Tuesday, 4th Friday, 5th Wednesday and 5th Thursday, 10 a.m.	Omagh
	Tel: 028 8224 2056 Fax: 028 8225 1198	FPC – 1st, 3rd and 4th Thursday, 10.30 a.m.	Do.
		YC – 3rd Wednesday, 10 a.m.	Do.
		YC and Dom – 1st Friday, 10 a.m.	Do.
		Dept – 2nd Friday	Do.
9036	**STRABANE**		
	Mrs. A. Hall, Strabane Court Office, The Courthouse, Derry Road, Strabane BT82 8DT	Adult – 5th Wednesday, 10 a.m. 1st, 3rd, 4th and 5th Thursday, 10 a.m. 1st, 2nd and 4th Friday, 10 a.m.	Strabane
	Tel: 028 7138 2544 Fax: 028 7138 3209	YC and Dom – 3rd Friday, 10 a.m. (Youth), 11 a.m. (Domestic)	Do.
		Dept – 2nd Thursday	Do.

COURTS OF SUMMARY, CIVIL AND SOLEMN CRIMINAL JURISDICTION

SCOTLAND

	Page
SHERIFFDOM OF GRAMPIAN, HIGHLANDS AND ISLANDS	120
SHERIFFDOM OF TAYSIDE, CENTRAL AND FIFE	128
SHERIFFDOM OF LOTHIAN AND BORDERS	133
SHERIFFDOM OF GLASGOW AND STRATHKELVIN	138
SHERIFFDOM OF NORTH STRATHCLYDE	140
SHERIFFDOM OF SOUTH STRATHCLYDE, DUMFRIES AND GALLOWAY	145

SCOTLAND

SHERIFFDOM OF GRAMPIAN, HIGHLAND AND ISLANDS

Sheriff Principal: Sir Stephen S. T. Young, BT, Q.C.

Adult Court No	Name of Court District and Clerks/Legal Advisors		Normal Times of Courts
9701	**ABERDEEN SHERIFF COURT DISTRICT**		
	Sheriff Clerk: F. Hendry, Sheriff Court House, Castle Street, Aberdeen AB10 1WP Tel: 01224 657200 Fax: 01224 657234 DX 61 ABERDEEN	CRIMINAL COURT:	Daily, 10 a.m.
		CIVIL COURT:	Wednesday, 9.45 a.m.
		FAMILY COURT & CHILD WELFARE HEARINGS/CHILD WELFARE HEARINGS:	Alternate Fridays, 9.45 a.m.
		SUMMARY CAUSES AND SMALL CLAIMS COURT:	Thursday, 10 a.m.
		COMMERCIAL COURT:	Tuesday, 10 a.m.
9400	**City of Aberdeen District Court**		
	Clerk of District Court: Jane G. MacEachran, Queen Street, Aberdeen AB10 1AQ Tel: 01224 522760 Fax: 01224 646895 DX 529450 ABERDEEN 9	DISTRICT COURT:	Monday, Wednesday, Thursday and Friday, 10 a.m.
		CUSTODY COURT:	Tuesday, 11.30 a.m.
9407	**The District Court of Aberdeenshire at Inverurie**		
	Depute Clerk of District Court: Kay M. Polson, LL.B. (Hons), N.P., Council Offices, Gordon House, Blackhall Road, Inverurie AB51 3WA Tel: 01467 620981 Fax: 01467 623329 Legal Post: LP-3 INVERURIE	DISTRICT COURT Wyness Hall, Jackson Street, Inverurie AB51 3QB	Wednesday 10. a.m. One Thursday in month, 10 a.m. (Means inquiry only)
9711	**BANFF SHERIFF COURT DISTRICT**		
	Sheriff Clerk Depute: David Altman, Sheriff Court House, Banff AB45 1AU Tel: 01261 812140 Fax: 01261 818394 DX 521325 BANFF	CRIMINAL COURT:	As and when required
		ORDINARY COURT:	Alternate Tuesdays, 10 a.m.
		SUMMARY CAUSES COURT:	Alternate Tuesdays, 11 a.m.
		SMALL CLAIMS COURT:	Alternate Tuesdays, 11 a.m.

GRAMPIAN, HIGHLAND AND ISLANDS

Adult Court No	Name of Court District and Clerks/Legal Advisors		Normal Times of Courts
9405	**The District Court of Aberdeenshire at Banff**		
	Depute Clerk of District Court: Colin D. Campbell, St. Leonards, Sandyhill Road, Banff AB45 1BH Tel: 01261 813314 Fax: 01261 815664 Legal Post: LP-6 BANFF	DISTRICT COURT: Sheriff Court House, Low Street, Banff	Wednesday every two weeks, 10 a.m.
9721	**DINGWALL SHERIFF COURT DISTRICT**		
	Sheriff Clerk: M. McBey, Sheriff Court House, Dingwall IV15 9QX Tel: 01349 863153 Fax: 01349 863153 DX 520584 DINGWALL Legal Post: LP-4 DINGWALL	CRIMINAL COURT: ORDINARY COURT: SUMMARY CAUSE COURT:	Every second Thursday, and as required Every second Thursday, 10 a.m. Every second Thursday, 10 a.m.
9500	**Highland District Court at Dingwall**		
	Clerk of District Court: Shona Pottinger, Council Offices, High Street, Dingwall IV15 9QN Tel: 01349 863381	DISTRICT COURT: Sheriff Court House, Ferry Road, Dingwall	Tuesday, three weekly or as required, 10 a.m.
9722	**DORNOCH SHERIFF COURT DISTRICT**		
	Sheriff Clerk Depute: Sheriff Court House, Dornoch IV25 3SD Tel: 01862 810224 Fax: 01862 810224 E-mail: dornoch@scotcourts.gov.uk Legal Post: LP-2 DORNOCH	CRIMINAL COURT: ORDINARY COURT: SUMMARY CAUSES COURT:	Every fourth Monday, 10.15 a.m. Every fourth Monday, 10.15 a.m. Every fourth Monday, 10.15 a.m.
9501	**Highland District Court at Dornoch**		
	Depute Clerk of District Court: (Vacant), Main Street, Golspie, Sutherland KW10 6RB Tel: 01408 635200 Fax: 01408 633120	DISTRICT COURT:	Seven courts per year, 11 a.m.

GRAMPIAN, HIGHLAND AND ISLANDS

Adult Court No	Name of Court District and Clerks/Legal Advisors		Normal Times of Courts
9742	**ELGIN SHERIFF COURT DISTRICT**		
	Sheriff Clerk: Frances MacPherson, Sheriff Court House, Elgin IV30 1BU	CRIMINAL COURT:	Cited Cases: Monday, 10 a.m. As and when required, other days
	Tel: 01343 542505 Fax: 01343 559715	ORDINARY COURT:	Fortnightly on Tuesday, 10.30 a.m.
		SUMMARY CAUSE COURT:	Fortnightly on Tuesday, 10 a.m.
	DX 520652 ELGIN		
	Legal Post: LP-8 ELGIN		
	E-mail: elginsc@scotcourts.gov.uk		
9522	**Moray District Court at Elgin**		
	Clerk of District Court: Roderick D. Burns, Council Headquarters, High Street, Elgin IV30 1BX	DISTRICT COURT:	Tuesday, 10 a.m.
	Tel: 01343 563013		
	Fax: 01343 540183		
	DX 520666 ELGIN		
9753	**FORT WILLIAM SHERIFF COURT DISTRICT**		
	Sheriff Clerk Depute and Auditor of Court: Steve McKenna, Sheriff Court House, High Street, Fort William PH33 6EE	CRIMINAL COURT:	Twice monthly on a Thursday, 10 a.m.
		ORDINARY COURT:	Fourth Friday in each month, 10 a.m.
	Tel: 01397 702087 Fax: 01397 706214	SUMMARY CAUSES COURT:	Do.
	DX 531405 FORT WILLIAM		
	Legal Post: LP-2 FORT WILLIAM		
	E-mail: fortwilliam@scotcourts.gov.uk		
9502	**Highland District Court at Fort William**		
	Depute Clerk of District Court: K. D. Falconer, Lochaber House, High Street, Fort William PH33 6EL	DISTRICT COURT:	First Wednesday in month, 10 a.m.
	Tel: 01397 703881		
	Fax: 01397 704016		
	DX LP-6 FORT WILLIAM		

GRAMPIAN, HIGHLAND AND ISLANDS

Adult Court No	Name of Court District and Clerks/Legal Advisors		Normal Times of Courts
9781	**INVERNESS SHERIFF COURT DISTRICT**		
	Sheriff Clerk and Auditor of Court: Mrs. Audrey E. Bayliss, Sheriff Court House, Inverness IV2 3EG	CRIMINAL COURT:	Daily, 10 a.m. (except Tuesday, 10 a.m. and 10.30 a.m.)
		ORDINARY COURT:	Alternate Wednesdays, 10 a.m.
	Tel: 01463 230782	SUMMARY CAUSES COURT: The Castle, Inverness	Alternate Wednesdays, 10 a.m.
	Fax: 01463 710602		
	DX IN25		
	Legal Post: LP-15		
	E-mail: inverness@scotcourts.gov.uk		
9503	**Highland District Court at Inverness**		
	Depute Clerk of District Court: D. R. Somerville, LL.B.N.P., Town House, Inverness IV1 1JJ	DISTRICT COURT: The North Tower, The Castle, Inverness	Monday, 10 a.m. Friday, 10 a.m.
	Tel: 01463 724231		
	Fax: 01463 724302		
	E-mail: laura-beth.scally@highland.gov.uk		
9504	**Highland District Court at Kingussie**		
	Depute Clerk of District Court: Catrionna B. Macdonald, Ruthven Road, Kingussie PH21 1EJ	DISTRICT COURT: Talla Nan Ros, King Street, Kingussie	Wednesdays, 10 a.m. on a 4 weekly basis
	Tel: 01540 664521		
	Fax: 01540 661004		
9505	**Highland District Court at Nairn**		
	Depute Clerk of District Court: Catriona Macdonald, The Court House, High Street, Nairn IV12 4AU	DISTRICT COURT:	Wednesdays, 10 a.m. on a 4 weekly basis
	Tel: 01667 458515		
	Fax: 01667 452056		

GRAMPIAN, HIGHLAND AND ISLANDS

Adult Court No	Name of Court District and Clerks/Legal Advisors		Normal Times of Courts
9805	**KIRKWALL SHERIFF COURT DISTRICT**		
	Sheriff Clerk Depute: Anne P. Moore, Sheriff Court House, Kirkwall KW15 1PD	CRIMINAL COURT:	Every second Wednesday, 10 a.m. and as and when required
		ORDINARY COURT:	Every second Tuesday, 10 a.m.
	Tel: 01856 872110 Fax: 01856 874835	SUMMARY CAUSES AND SMALL CLAIMS COURT:	Every second Tuesday, 10 a.m.
	No District Court in Kirkwall		
9812	**LERWICK SHERIFF COURT DISTRICT**		
	Sheriff Clerk Depute: Christina Bardsley, Sheriff Court House, Lerwick ZE1 0HD	CRIMINAL COURT:	As and when required
		ORDINARY COURT:	Every second Tuesday, 10 a.m.
	Tel: 01595 693914 Fax: 01595 693340	SUMMARY CAUSES COURT:	Every second Tuesday, 10 a.m.
	E-mail: lerwick@scotcourts.gov.uk		
	No District Court in Lerwick		
9814	**LOCHMADDY SHERIFF COURT DISTRICT**		
	Sheriff Clerk Depute: Miss M. Campbell, Sheriff Court House, Lochmaddy HS6 5AE	CRIMINAL COURT:	As and when required
		ORDINARY COURT:	Every fourth Tuesday, 10.30 a.m.
	Tel: 01478 612191 Fax: 01876 500432	SUMMARY CAUSES COURT:	Every fourth Tuesday, 10.30 a.m.
9854	**PETERHEAD SHERIFF COURT DISTRICT**		
	Sheriff Clerk: R. Cantwell, Sheriff Court House, Queen Street, Peterhead AB42 1TP Tel: 01779 476676 Fax: 01779 472435 DX 521376 PETERHEAD Legal Post: LP-3 PETERHEAD	CRIMINAL COURT:	Intermediate Diet Court: Every second Wednesday, 10 a.m. Criminal Court: Every Thursday, 10 a.m. Trials Court: Every second Monday, Tuesday and Friday, 9.30 a.m. Custody Court: Daily, 12 p.m.
		ORDINARY COURT:	Every alternate Friday, 9.45 a.m.
		SUMMARY CAUSES COURT:	Every alternate Friday, 2.15 p.m.

GRAMPIAN, HIGHLAND AND ISLANDS

Adult Court No	Name of Court District and Clerks/Legal Advisors		Normal Times of Courts
9408	**The District Court of Aberdeenshire at Peterhead**		
	Depute Clerk of District Court: Colin D. Campbell, St. Leonards, Sandyhill Road, Banff AB45 1BH	DISTRICT COURT: Sheriff Court House, Queen Street, Peterhead	Monday and Tuesday, approximately every two weeks, 10 a.m.
	Tel: 01261 813314		
	Fax: 01261 815664		
	Legal Post: LP-6 BANFF		
9855	**PORTREE SHERIFF COURT DISTRICT**		
	Sheriff Clerk Depute: Miss M. Campbell, Sheriff Court House, Portree IV51 9EH	CRIMINAL COURT:	As and when required
		ORDINARY COURT:	Every fourth Monday, 11 a.m.
	Tel: 01478 612191 Fax: 01478 613203	SUMMARY CAUSES COURT:	Every fourth Monday, 11 a.m.
9506	**Highland District Court at Portree**		
	Depute Clerk of District Court: Alaisdair H. Mackenzie, Tigh Na Sgire, Park Lane, Portree, Isle of Skye IV51 9GP	DISTRICT COURT:	Every fourth Wednesday, 10 a.m. and as required
	Tel: 01478 613826 613820		
	Fax: 01478 613828		
9873	**STONEHAVEN SHERIFF COURT DISTRICT**		
	Sheriff Clerk: Andrew H. Hempseed, Sheriff Court House, Stonehaven AB39 2JH	CRIMINAL COURT:	Alternate Wednesdays, 10 a.m.
		ORDINARY COURT:	Alternate Thursdays, 10 a.m.
	Tel: 01569 762758 Fax: 01569 762132	SUMMARY CAUSES COURT AND SMALL CLAIMS COURT:	Alternate Thursdays, 10 a.m. (same days as Ordinary Court)
	DX 521023 STONEHAVEN		
	Legal Post: LP-3 STONEHAVEN		
	E-mail: stonehaven@scotcourts.gov.uk.		

GRAMPIAN, HIGHLAND AND ISLANDS

Adult Court No	Name of Court District and Clerks/Legal Advisors		Normal Times of Courts
9409	**The District Court of Aberdeenshire at Stonehaven**		
	Depute Clerk of District Court: James S. McPherson, Viewmount, Arduthie Road, Stonehaven AB39 2DQ	DISTRICT COURT: Sheriff Court House, Stonehaven	Every third Tuesday, 10 a.m. plus as and when required
	Tel: 01569 768257		
	Fax: 01569 768259		
	Legal Post: LP-5 STONEHAVEN		
9874	**STORNOWAY SHERIFF COURT DISTRICT**		
	Sheriff Clerk Depute: Kenneth Finnie, Sheriff Court House, 9 Lewis Street, Stornoway HS1 2JF	CRIMINAL COURT:	As and when required
		ORDINARY COURT:	Alternate Thursdays, 10 a.m.
	Tel: 01851 702231	SUMMARY CAUSES COURT:	Alternate Thursdays, 10 a.m.
	Fax: 01851 704296		
9584	**Western Isles District Court at Stornoway**		
	Clerk of District Court: Lesley Ann McDonald, Council Offices, Sandwick Road, Stornoway HS1 2BW	DISTRICT COURT: Sheriff Court House, Lewis Street, Stornoway, Isle of Lewis HS1 2JF	Usually every fourth Tuesday, 10 a.m. (and additionally as required)
	Tel: 01851 709263		
	Fax: 01851 709390		
9881	**TAIN SHERIFF COURT DISTRICT**		
	Sheriff Clerk Depute: R. M. Hughes, Sheriff Court House, Tain IV19 1AB	CRIMINAL COURT:	Trials Court: As and when required Cited Court: Every second Monday, 10 a.m.
	Tel: 01862 892518		
	Fax: 01862 892518	ORDINARY COURT:	Every fourth Thursday, 10.00 a.m.
		SUMMARY CAUSES COURT:	Every fourth Thursday, 11.00 a.m.
9509	**Highland District Court at Tain**		
	Clerk of District Court: Shona Pottinger, Council Offices, High Street, Dingwall IV15 9QN	DISTRICT COURT: Sheriff Court House, Tain	Thursday monthly or as required, 10 a.m.
	Tel: 01349 863381		

GRAMPIAN, HIGHLAND AND ISLANDS

Adult Court No	*Name of Court District and Clerks/Legal Advisors*		*Normal Times of Courts*
9891	**WICK SHERIFF COURT DISTRICT**		
	Sheriff Clerk Depute: Janet McEwan, Sheriff Court House, Wick KW1 4AJ	CRIMINAL COURT:	Cited Cases: Every second Friday, 10 a.m. Others: As and when required other days
	Tel: 01955 602846	ORDINARY COURT:	Every second Friday, 10 a.m.
	Fax: 01955 602846	SUMMARY CAUSES COURT:	Every second Friday, 10 a.m.
9508	**Highland District Court at Wick**		
	Depute Clerk of District Court: Fiona Sinclair, Council Offices, Market Square, Wick KW1 4AB	DISTRICT COURT: Sheriff Court Wick	Every fourth Tuesday, 10.15 a.m.
	Tel: 01955 607705		
	Fax: 01955 603021		

SHERIFFDOM OF TAYSIDE, CENTRAL AND FIFE

Sheriff Principal: R. A. Dunlop, Q.C.

Adult Court No	Name of Court District and Clerks		Normal Times of Courts
9703	**ALLOA SHERIFF COURT DISTRICT**		
	Sheriff Clerk: L. Reid, Sheriff Court House, Mar Street, Alloa FK10 1HR Tel: 01259 722734 212981 Fax: 01259 219470 DX 560433 ALLOA Legal Post: LP-3 ALLOA	CRIMINAL COURT: ORDINARY COURT: SUMMARY CAUSES COURT: SMALL CLAIMS COURT:	As and when required Fortnightly on Fridays, 10 a.m. Fortnightly on Fridays, 10 a.m. Fortnightly on Fridays, 10 a.m.
9440	**Clackmannanshire District Court at Alloa**		
	Clerk of District Court: Jacqueline M. McGuire, 14 Bank Street, Alloa FK10 1HP Tel: 01259 720872 Fax: 01259 720891 Legal Post: LP-9 ALLOA	DISTRICT COURT:	Cited Diets: (held at 14 Bank Street, Alloa), Tuesday, 10 a.m. Means Court: Wednesday, 10.30 a.m.
9705	**ARBROATH SHERIFF COURT DISTRICT**		
	Sheriff Clerk: Stuart Munro, Sheriff Court House, Arbroath DD11 1HL Tel: 01241 876600 Fax: 01241 874413 DX 530442 ARBROATH Legal Post: LP-3 ARBROATH	CRIMINAL COURT: ORDINARY COURT: SMALL CLAIMS AND SUMMARY CAUSES COURT:	Monday to Thursday, 10 a.m. Monday, 10 a.m. Monday, 10 a.m.
9415	**Angus District Court at Arbroath**		
	Clerk of District Court: Sheona C. Hunter, Angus House, Orchardbank Business Park, Forfar DD8 1AN Tel: 01307 461460 Fax: 01307 476299 DX 530678 FORFAR	DISTRICT COURT: Arbroath	Friday, 10 a.m.

TAYSIDE, CENTRAL AND FIFE

Adult Court No	Name of Court District and Clerks		Normal Times of Courts
9717	**CUPAR SHERIFF COURT DISTRICT**		
	Sheriff Clerk: C. L. Donald, Sheriff Court House, Cupar KY15 4LX	CRIMINAL COURT:	As and when required
		ORDINARY COURT:	Wednesday (fortnightly), 10 a.m.
	Tel: 01334 652121 Fax: 01334 656807	SUMMARY CAUSES/SMALL CLAIMS COURT:	Wednesday (fortnightly), 11 a.m.
	DX 560545 CUPAR		
	Legal Post: LP-11 CUPAR		
9485	**Fife District Court at Cupar**		
	Depute Clerk of District Court: Steven Paterson, Fife House, North Street, Glenrothes KY7 5LT	DISTRICT COURT:	Friday, 10 a.m.
	Tel: 01592 414003		
	Fax: 01592 414016		
9726	**DUNDEE SHERIFF COURT DISTRICT**		
	Sheriff Clerk: R. McMillan, Sheriff Court House, Dundee DD1 9AD	CRIMINAL COURT:	Daily, 9.30 a.m.
		MATRIMONIAL COURT	Tuesday, 10 a.m.
	Tel: 01382 229961 Fax: 01382 318222	ORDINARY COURT:	Thursday, 10 a.m.
		SUMMARY CAUSES/ SMALL CLAIMS COURT:	Monday, 9.30 a.m.
	DX DD33 DUNDEE		
	Legal Post: LP-21 Dundee		
9456	**City of Dundee District Court**		
	Clerk of District Court: Patricia McIlquham, LL.B., 6 West Bell Street, Dundee DD1 9RD	CRIMINAL COURT:	Monday, Wednesday and Friday, 10 a.m. and 2 p.m. Tuesday and Thursday, 10 a.m. Means Enquiry Court: Twice monthly on a Tuesday, 2.30 p.m.
	Tel: 01382 432190		
	Fax: 01382 432195		

TAYSIDE, CENTRAL AND FIFE

Adult Court No	Name of Court District and Clerks		Normal Times of Courts

9727 DUNFERMLINE SHERIFF COURT DISTRICT

Sheriff Clerk:
J. Murphy,
Sheriff Court House,
1-6 Carnegie Drive,
Dunfermline
KY12 7HJ

Tel: 01383 724666

Fax: 01383 621205

CRIMINAL COURT: Daily, 10 a.m.

ORDINARY COURT: Every second Wednesday, 10 a.m.

SMALL CLAIMS COURT: Every second Friday, 10.15 a.m.

SUMMARY CAUSE COURT: Every second Friday, 9.45 a.m.

DX DF17 DUNFERMLINE

Legal Post: LP-5 DUNFERMLINE

E-mail: dunfermline@scotcourts.gov.uk

9486 Fife District Court at Dunfermline

Depute Clerk of District Court:
Mrs. Anne McCamley,
Fife House,
North Street,
Glenrothes
KY7 5LT

Tel: 01592 414260/007

Fax: 01592 414016

DISTRICT COURT: Monday and Tuesday, 10 a.m.

9751 FALKIRK SHERIFF COURT DISTRICT

Sheriff Clerk:
Mrs. Pamela McFarlane,
Sheriff Court House,
Camelon,
Falkirk FK1 4AR

Tel: 01324 620822

Fax: 01324 678238

CRIMINAL COURT: Daily

ORDINARY COURT: Wednesday, 10 a.m.

SUMMARY CAUSES COURT: Wednesday, 9.30 a.m.

SMALL CLAIMS COURT: Wednesday, 9.30 a.m.

DX FA17 FALKIRK

Legal Post: LP 2 FALKIRK

9482 Falkirk District Court

Clerk of District Court:
Rosemary Glackin,
Municipal Buildings,
Falkirk FK1 5RS

Tel: 01324 506072

Fax: 01324 506122

Legal Post: LP-1 FALKIRK 2

DISTRICT COURT:

Pleading Diets:
Tuesday, 10 a.m.
Means Court:
Wednesday, 2 p.m.
Trials:
Thursday, 11 a.m.
Intermediate Diets:
Thursday, 10 a.m.

TAYSIDE, CENTRAL AND FIFE

Adult Court No	Name of Court District and Clerks		Normal Times of Courts
9752	**FORFAR SHERIFF COURT DISTRICT**		
	Sheriff Clerk: Mike Herbertson, Sheriff Court House, Market Street, Forfar DD8 3LA	CRIMINAL COURT:	Thursday, 10 a.m. and as and when required
		ORDINARY COURT:	Wednesday, 10 a.m.
	Tel: 01307 462186	SUMMARY CAUSES COURT:	Wednesday, 9.45 a.m.
	Fax: 01307 462268	SMALL CLAIMS COURT:	Wednesday, 9.45 a.m.
	DX 530674 FORFAR		
	E-mail: mherbertson@scotcourts.gov.uk		
9417	**Angus District Court at Forfar**		
	Clerk of District Court: Sheona C. Hunter, Angus House, Orchardbank Business Park, Forfar DD8 1AN	DISTRICT COURT: Forfar	First and third Wednesday in month, 10 a.m.
	Tel: 01307 461460		
	Fax: 01307 476299		
	DX 530678 FORFAR		
9803	**KIRKCALDY SHERIFF COURT DISTRICT**		
	Sheriff Clerk: S. Walker, Sheriff Court House, Whytescauseway, Kirkcaldy KY1 1XQ	CRIMINAL COURT:	Daily, 10 a.m.
		ORDINARY COURT:	Each alternate Friday, 9.30 a.m.
		OPTIONS HEARINGS:	Each alternate Friday, 9.30 a.m.
	Tel: 01592 260171 Fax: 01592 642361	CHILD WELFARE HEARINGS:	Each Wednesday, 9.30 a.m.
		SUMMARY CAUSES AND SMALL CLAIMS COURT:	Each alternate Friday, 12 noon
		SUMMARY CAUSE HERITABLE COURT:	Each alternate Friday, 2 p.m.
	DX KY17 KIRKCALDY		
	Legal Post: LP-7 KIRKCALDY		
	E-mail: kirkcaldy@scotcourts.gov.uk		
9487	**Fife District Court at Kirkcaldy**		
	Deputy Clerk of District Court: Kimberley Robertson, Fife House, North Street, Glenrothes KY7 5LT	DISTRICT COURT:	Monday and Thursday, 10 a.m.
	Tel: 01592 416595/120		
	Fax: 01592 414016		

TAYSIDE, CENTRAL AND FIFE

Adult Court No	Name of Court District and Clerks		Normal Times of Courts
9853	**PERTH SHERIFF COURT DISTRICT**		
	Sheriff Clerk: Mr. A. Nicol, Sheriff Court House, Perth PH2 8NL Tel: 01738 620546 Fax: 01738 623601 DX PE20 PERTH Legal Post: LP-8 PERTH	CRIMINAL COURT: ORDINARY COURT: SUMMARY CAUSES AND SMALL CLAIMS COURT:	As and when required Wednesday, 10 a.m. Friday, 9.30 a.m.
9538	**Perth and Kinross District Court at Perth**		
	Clerk of District Court: I. T. Innes, 16 Tay Street, Perth PH1 5LQ Tel: 01738 475149 Fax: 01738 475160 Legal Post: LP-16 E-mail: districtcourt@pkc.gov.uk	DISTRICT COURT: Perth	Tuesday, Wednesday and Friday. Other weekdays as required
9872	**STIRLING SHERIFF COURT DISTRICT**		
	Sheriff Clerk: Maureen McLean, Sheriff Court House, Stirling FK8 1NH Tel: 01786 462191 Fax: 01786 470456 DX ST15 STIRLING Legal Post: LP-6 STIRLING	CRIMINAL COURT: ORDINARY COURT: SUMMARY CAUSES COURT: HERITABLE COURT: SMALL CLAIMS COURT:	As and when required Alternate Tuesdays, 10 a.m. Alternate Tuesdays, 10 a.m. Alternate Tuesdays, 11 a.m. Alternate Tuesdays, 10 a.m.
9572	**Stirling District Court**		

	Clerk of District Court:
	Peter Broadfoot,
	Old Viewforth,
	Stirling FK8 2ET
	Tel: 01786 443288 ⎱ Direct
	       443299 ⎬ lines
	       443443 ⎰
	Fax: 01786 442966
	Legal Post: LP-1 STIRLING 2
		DISTRICT COURT:
		Spittal Street,
		Stirling
			Tuesday, 10 a.m.

SHERIFFDOM OF LOTHIAN AND BORDERS

Sheriff Principal: E. F. Bowen, Q.C.

Adult Court No	Name of Court District and Clerks		Normal Times of Courts
9729	**DUNS SHERIFF COURT DISTRICT**		
	Sheriff Clerk: (Vacant), Sheriff Court House, Jedburgh TD8 6AR	CRIMINAL COURT:	Wednesdays, 10.30 a.m.
		ORDINARY COURT:	Alternate Wednesdays, 10.30 a.m.
	Tel: 01835 863231 Fax: 01835 864110 DX 581222 JEDBURGH Legal Post: LP-3 JEDBURGH E-mail: jedburgh@scotcourts.gov.uk	SUMMARY CAUSES COURT:	Alternate Wednesdays, 10.30 a.m.
9550	**Scottish Borders District Court at Duns**		
	Clerk of District Court: Ian Wilkie, Council Offices, 8 Newtown Street, Duns TD11 3DT	DISTRICT COURT: Duns	Alternate Tuesdays, 10 a.m. (Additional sittings as required)
	Tel: 01361 882600 Fax: 01361 886111 Legal Post: LP-3 DUNS		
9741	**EDINBURGH SHERIFF COURT DISTRICT**		
	Sheriff Clerk: David Shand, Sheriff Court House, 27 Chambers Street, Edinburgh EH1 1LB	CRIMINAL COURT:	As and when required (daily from 10 a.m.)
		ORDINARY COURT: and OPTIONS COURT:	Daily at 10 a.m.
	Tel: 0131 225 2525 Fax: 0131 225 4422	SUMMARY CAUSES COURT:	Tuesday and Friday, 10 a.m.
		SMALL CLAIMS – PRELIMINARY HEARINGS:	Tuesday, 10 a.m.

(Fax) 0131 225 8899 (Civil Section, Summary Causes and Small Claims Section)
    0131 226 6569 (Criminal Section)
    0131 225 4422 (Admin.)
    0131 247 2569 (Cashiers Section)
    0131 247 2850 (Commissary Section)

DX 550308 ED 37 (Admin/Crime/Cash)
    550312 ED 37 (Civil)
    550313 ED37 (Commissary)

    Legal Post: LP-2 EDINBURGH 10

LOTHIAN AND BORDERS

Adult Court No	Name of Court District and Clerks		Normal Times of Courts

9478 City of Edinburgh District Court

Clerk of District Court:
Gill Lindsay,
1 Parliament Square,
Edinburgh
EH1 1RF

DISTRICT COURT:

Monday to Friday, 10 a.m.

Tel: 0131 529 4173 (Fines and Fixed Penalties)
      0131 529 4543 (Fines Enforcement)
      0131 529 4161 (Court Hearings)

Fax: 0131-529 4191

Legal Post: LP-5 EDINBURGH-8

9518 Midlothian District Court at Loanhead

Clerk of District Court:
N. Grieve,
Midlothian Council,
PO Box 28929,
Dalkeith EH22 1WU

DISTRICT COURT:
Loanhead

Tuesday, 10 a.m.

Tel: 0131 271 3585
            3586

Fax: 0131 271 3252

9771 HADDINGTON SHERIFF COURT DISTRICT

Sheriff Clerk:
I. Munro,
Sheriff Court House,
Haddington
EH41 3HN

CRIMINAL COURT:

Wednesday to Friday

ORDINARY COURT:

Monday (fortnightly), 10 a.m.

Tel: 01620-822325
          822936

SUMMARY CAUSES COURT:

Monday (fortnightly), 10 a.m.

Fax: 01620-826350

DX 540732 HADDINGTON

E-mail: haddington@scotcourts.gov.uk

9470 East Lothian District Court at Haddington

Clerk of District Court:
I. A. Forrest,
John Muir House,
Brewery Park,
Haddington EH41 3HA

DISTRICT COURT:
Haddington

Tuesday, 10 a.m.

Tel: 01620 827389
            827221 (General Enquiries)

Fax: 01620 827253

Legal Post: LP-4 HADDINGTON

LOTHIAN AND BORDERS

Adult Court No	Name of Court District and Clerks		Normal Times of Courts
9791	**JEDBURGH SHERIFF COURT DISTRICT**		
	Sheriff Clerk: (Vacant), Sheriff Court House, Jedburgh TD8 6AR	CRIMINAL COURT:	Thursday, 10 a.m.
		ORDINARY COURT:	Alternate Thursdays, 10 a.m.
	Tel: 01835 863231	SUMMARY CAUSES COURT:	Alternate Thursdays, 10 a.m.
	Fax: 01835 864110		
	DX 581222 JEDBURGH		
	Legal Post: LP-3 JEDBURGH		
	E-mail: jedburgh@scotcourts.gov.uk		
9551	**Scottish Borders District Court at Jedburgh**		
	Clerk of District Court: Ian Wilkie, Council Offices, High Street, Hawick TD9 9EF	DISTRICT COURT: Jedburgh	Alternate Tuesdays, 10 a.m. Additional sittings when required
	Tel: 01450 375991		
	Fax: 01450 364711		
	Legal Post: LP-5 HAWICK		
9813	**LINLITHGOW SHERIFF COURT DISTRICT**		
	Sheriff Clerk: D. G. Lynn, Sheriff Court House, Linlithgow EH49 7EQ	CRIMINAL COURT:	Daily, 10 a.m.
		ORDINARY COURT:	Wednesday, 10 a.m.
	Tel: 01506 842922	SMALL CLAIMS/SUMMARY CAUSES COURT:	Alternate Thursdays, 10 a.m.
	Fax: 01506 848457		
	DX 540881 LINLITHGOW		
	Legal Post: LP-2 LINLITHGOW		
	E-mail: linlithgow@scotcourts.gov.uk		
9815	**LIVINGSTON SHERIFF COURT DISTRICT**		
	Sheriff Clerk: D. G. Lynn, Sheriff Court House, Linlithgow EH49 7EQ	CRIMINAL TRIALS:	Monday, Wednesday, Thursday and Friday, 10 a.m.
	Tel: 01506 462118	UNDERTAKING COURT:	Tuesday, 10 a.m.
	Fax: 01506 417312		
	NOTE: All correspondence and enquiries should be addressed to Linlithgow		

LOTHIAN AND BORDERS

Adult Court No	Name of Court District and Clerks		Normal Times of Courts
9580	**West Lothian District Court at Livingston**		
	Clerk of District Court: M. G. McCann, MA, LL.B., District Courthouse, Civic Square, Almondvale Boulevard, Livingston EH54 6QZ	DISTRICT COURT:	Pleas and Intermediate Diets: Tuesday, 10 a.m. Trials: Thursday, 10 a.m. Means Court: Monday, 10 a.m.
	Tel: 01506 777474		
	Fax: 01506 773663		
	Legal Post: LP-3 LIVINGSTON		
	E-mail: districtcourt@westlothian.gov.uk		
9852	**PEEBLES SHERIFF COURT DISTRICT**		
	Sheriff Clerk Depute: Heather Johnston, Sheriff Court House, Peebles, P.O. Box 23713	CRIMINAL COURT: Sitting in Scottish Borders Council Offices, Rosetta Road, Peebles	Alternate Wednesdays, 10 a.m.
	Tel: 01721 720204	ORDINARY COURT: Sitting in Scottish Borders Council Offices, Rosetta Road, Peebles	Alternate Wednesdays, 10 a.m.
	Fax: 0131 247 2850	SUMMARY CAUSES COURT: Sitting in Scottish Borders Council Offices, Rosetta Road, Peebles	Alternate Wednesdays, 10 a.m.
	DX 540971 PEEBLES		
	Legal Post: LP-5 PEEBLES		
9552	**Scottish Borders District Court at Peebles**		
	Clerk of District Court: Ian Wilkie, Council Offices, Rosetta Road, Peebles EH45 8HG	DISTRICT COURT:	Thursdays, monthly, 10 a.m.
	Tel: 01721 720153		
	Fax: 01721 726311		
	Legal Post: LP-6 PEEBLES		

LOTHIAN AND BORDERS

Adult
Court
No   *Name of Court District and Clerks*   *Normal Times of Courts*

9871 SELKIRK SHERIFF COURT DISTRICT

Sheriff Clerk Depute: M. McCabe, Sheriff Court House, Selkirk TD7 4LE Tel: 01750 21269	CRIMINAL COURT: ORDINARY COURT:	Monday, 10 a.m., Alternate Tuesdays, 10 a.m. Alternate Tuesdays, 10 a.m. during session
Fax: 01750 22884	SUMMARY CAUSES COURT:	Alternate Tuesdays, 10 a.m. during session
	SMALL CLAIMS COURT:	Alternate Tuesdays, 10 a.m. during session

DX 581011 SELKIRK

Legal Post: LP-2 SELKIRK

E-mail: selkirk@scotcourts.gov.uk

9553 Scottish Borders District Court at Selkirk

Clerk of District Court: Ian Wilkie, Council Chambers, Albert Place, Galashiels TD1 3DL	DISTRICT COURT: Selkirk	Alternate Thursdays, 10 a.m. during session, and as and when required at other times

Tel: 01896 754751

Fax: 01896 662711

Legal Post: LP-8 GALASHIELS

SHERIFFDOM OF GLASGOW AND STRATHKELVIN

Sheriff Principal: James A. Taylor

Adult Court No	Name of Court District and Clerks/Legal Advisors		Normal Times of Courts
9761	**GLASGOW AND STRATHKELVIN SHERIFF COURT**		
	Deputy Director of Field Services: David Forrester, Sheriff Court House, 1 Carlton Place, Glasgow G5 9DA	TRIAL COURTS:	Monday to Friday, 10 a.m.
		CRIMINAL CUSTODY COURT:	Monday to Friday, 2 p.m.
	Sheriff Clerk: Steve Bain	SUMMARY CAUSES – MISCELLANEOUS PAYMENTS COURT:	Alternate Wednesdays, 10 a.m.
	Tel: 0141-429 8888		
	Fax: 0141 418 5244 DX 551020 GLASGOW (Admin)	HERITABLE COURT:	Tuesday, 10 a.m. (3 days per month)
	Fax: 0141 418 5247 DX 551021 GLASGOW (Criminal Office)	SMALL CLAIMS COURT:	Thursday, 10 a.m. (3 days per month)
	Fax: 0141 418 5248 DX 551024 GLASGOW (Civil Office)	PARTY LITIGANTS COURT:	Thursday, 12 noon (3 days per month)
	Fax: 0141 418 5186 DX 551023 GLASGOW (Commissary/ Summary Cause)	DEBTORS COURT/ MISCELLANEOUS CIVIL COURT:	Monday, 10 a.m.
		OPTIONS HEARINGS:	Tuesday to Friday, 10 a.m.
	Fax: 0141 418 5270 DX 551021 GLASGOW (Cashier)	MOTIONS COURT:	Tuesday to Friday, 11.30 a.m.,
	All departments located as above		
9495	**City of Glasgow District Court**		
	Clerk of District Court: Mrs. P. Wallace, LL.B., 21 St. Andrew's Street, Glasgow G1 5PW	DISTRICT COURT:	Monday to Friday, 9.30 a.m. and 2 p.m.
	Tel: 0141-287 5415 (Fines) 0141-287 5055 (Enquiries) 0141-287 5132 (Court)		
	Fax: 0141-552 7895 (Enquiries) 0141-287 3874		

GLASGOW AND STRATHKELVIN

Adult Court No	Name of Court District and Clerks/Legal Advisors		Normal Times of Courts
9465	**East Dunbartonshire District Court at Kirkintilloch**		
	Clerk of District Court: Diane I. Campbell, LL.B.(Hons), Tom Johnston House, Civic Way, Kirkintilloch, Glasgow G66 4TJ	DISTRICT COURT: 21 Southbank Road, Kirkintilloch G66 1NH	Every second and fourth Tuesday, 10 a.m. and 2 p.m. Every third Wednesday, 10 a.m. and 2 p.m. (except July)
	Tel: 0141-578 8000		
	Fax: 0141-578 8117		
	Legal Post: LP-7 KIRKINTILLOCH		
9565	**South Lanarkshire District Court at East Kilbride**		
	Clerk of District Court: Sandra Dickson, M.A., LL.B., Civic Centre, East Kilbride G74 1AB	DISTRICT COURT:	Tuesday, 10 a.m. Cited Court: Fourth Thursday of each month, 11 a.m. Means Court: Fourth Thursday of each month, 11 a.m.
	Tel: 01355 806474 806483		
	Fax: 01355 248847		
	E-mail: dclr@southlanarkshire.gov.uk		
9568	**South Lanarkshire District Court at Rutherglen**		
	Clerk of District Court: Sandra Dickson, M.A., LL.B., Town Hall, 139 Main Street, Rutherglen G73 2JJ	DISTRICT COURT:	Thursday 9.30 a.m. Means Court: Thursday, 9.30 a.m. fortnightly and as and when required
	Tel: 0141 613 5730		
	Fax: 0141 613 5734		
	E-mail: frances.joyce@southlanarkshire.gov.uk		

SHERIFFDOM OF NORTH STRATHCLYDE

Sheriff Principal: B. A. Kerr, Q.C.

Adult Court No	Name of Court District and Clerks		Normal Times of Courts
9716	**CAMPBELTOWN SHERIFF COURT DISTRICT**		
	Sheriff Clerk Depute: Mrs. E. Harvey, Sheriff Court House, Castlehill, Campbeltown PA28 6AN Tel: 01586 552503 Fax: 01586 554967	CRIMINAL COURT: ORDINARY COURT: SUMMARY CAUSE COURT:	As and when required Every fourth Friday, 10 a.m. Every fourth Friday, 10 a.m.
9426	**Argyll and Bute District Court at Campbeltown**		
	Clerk of District Court: Susan Mair, LL.B., Kilmory, Lochgilphead PA31 8RT Tel: 01546 604340 Fax: 01546 604373	DISTRICT COURT: Sheriff Court House, Castlehill, Campbeltown	Every fourth Tuesday, 10 a.m.
9723	**DUMBARTON SHERIFF COURT DISTRICT**		
	Sheriff Clerk: Kenneth Carter, Sheriff Court House, Dumbarton G82 1QR Tel: 01389 763266 Fax: 01389 764085 DX 597 DUMBARTON	CRIMINAL COURT: ORDINARY COURT: SUMMARY CAUSE COURT:	Daily Thursday, (weekly) 10 a.m. Wednesday, (fortnighly) 10 a.m.
9428	**Argyll and Bute District Court at Helensburgh**		
	Clerk of District Court: Susan Mair, LL.B., Kilmory, Lochgilphead PA31 8RT Tel: 01546 604340 Fax: 01546 604373	DISTRICT COURT: 1 East Princes Street, Helensburgh	Every third Wednesday, 10 a.m., and other days dependent on business

NORTH STRATHCLYDE

Adult Court No | *Name of Court District and Clerks* | *Normal Times of Courts*

9466 East Dunbartonshire District Court at Milngavie

Clerk of District Court:
Diane I. Campbell,
 LL.B.(Hons.),
Tom Johnston House,
Civic Way,
Kirkintilloch,
Glasgow G66 4TJ

Tel: 0141-578 8000

Fax: 0141-578 8117

Legal Post: LP-7 KIRKINTILLOCH

DISTRICT COURT:
Milngavie Town Hall,
 71 Station Road,
 Milngavie G62

Every first and third Tuesday in month 10 a.m. (except in month of July)

9575 West Dunbartonshire District Court at Clydebank

Clerk of District Court:
Stephen B. Brown,
 LL.B., Dip.L.P.,
Council Offices,
Garshake Road,
Dumbarton G82 3PU

Tel: 01389 737000

Fax: 01389 737870

DISTRICT COURT:
Town Hall,
49 Dumbarton Road,
Clydebank G81 1UE

Monday, 10 a.m.
 (except second and fourth Monday in month)
Thursday, 10 a.m.

9576 West Dunbartonshire District Court at Dumbarton

Clerk of District Court:
Stephen B. Brown,
 LL.B., Dip.L.P.,
Council Offices,
Garshake Road,
Dumbarton G82 3PU

Tel: 01389 737000

Fax: 01389 737870

DISTRICT COURT:
Municipal Buildings,
Station Road,
Dumbarton G82 1QE

Wednesday, 10 a.m.
Friday, 10 a.m.
 (except third Wednesday of each month)

9728 DUNOON SHERIFF COURT DISTRICT

Sheriff Clerk Depute:
Kim Wilson,
Sheriff Court House,
Dunoon PA23 8BQ

Tel: 01369 704166

Fax: 01369 702191

DX 591655 DUNOON

CRIMINAL COURT:

ORDINARY COURT:

SUMMARY CAUSES COURT:

As and when required

Every alternate Tuesday, 10 a.m.

Every alternate Tuesday, 11 a.m.

NORTH STRATHCLYDE

Adult Court No	Name of Court District and Clerks		Normal Times of Courts

9427 Argyll and Bute District Court at Dunoon

Clerk of District Court:
Susan Mair, LL.B.,
Kilmory,
Lochgilphead
PA31 8RT

DISTRICT COURT:
Sheriff Court House,
George Street,
Dunoon

Every third Friday, 10.30 a.m.

Tel: 01546 604340

Fax: 01546 604373

9429 Argyll and Bute District Court at Lochgilphead

Clerk of District Court:
Susan Mair, LL.B.,
Kilmory,
Lochgilphead PA31 8RT

DISTRICT COURTS:
Court House,
Lochnell Street,
Lochgilphead

Every fourth Tuesday, 10 a.m.

Tel: 01546 604340

Fax: 01546 604373

9762 GREENOCK SHERIFF COURT DISTRICT

Sheriff Clerk:
J. Blackstock,
Sheriff Court House,
1 Nelson Street,
Greenock PA15 1TR

CRIMINAL COURT: As and when required

ORDINARY COURT: Monday, 10 a.m.

Tel: 01475 787073

SUMMARY CAUSES COURT: Every Monday, 11 a.m.

Fax: 01475 729746

DX GR16 GREENOCK

Legal Post: LP-5 GREENOCK 1

9514 Inverclyde District Court at Greenock

Clerk of District Court:
Elaine Paterson,
Municipal Buildings,
Greenock PA15 1LX

DISTRICT COURT:

Monday, Wednesday and Thursday, 10 a.m. and otherwise as required

Tel: 01475 712126

Fax: 01475 712181

DX GR11 GREENOCK

9801 KILMARNOCK SHERIFF COURT DISTRICT

Sheriff Clerk:
A. Johnston,
Sheriff Court House,
Kilmarnock KA1 1ED

CRIMINAL COURT: As and when required

ORDINARY COURT: Wednesday, 10 a.m.

Tel: 01563 550024

SUMMARY CAUSES COURT AND SMALL CLAIMS COURT: Friday, 10 a.m.

Fax: 01563 543568

DX KK20 KILMARNOCK

Legal Post: LP-5 KILMARNOCK

E-mail: kilmarnock@scotcourts.gov.uk

NORTH STRATHCLYDE

Adult Court No	Name of Court District and Clerks		Normal Times of Courts
9461	**East Ayrshire District Court at Kilmarnock**		
	Clerk of Court: David Mitchell, Council Headquarters, London Road, Kilmarnock KA3 7BU	DISTRICT COURT: Court House, Council Offices, John Dickie Street, Kilmarnock	Monday, 10 a.m. Tuesday, 10 a.m.
	Tel: 01563 576078		
	Fax: 01563 576179		
	Legal Post: LP-18 KILMARNOCK		
9526	**North Ayrshire District Court at Irvine**		
	Clerk of District Court: Andrew Fraser, Town House, High Street, Irvine KA12 0AZ	DISTRICT COURT:	Wednesday and Thursday, 10 a.m. First and second Tuesday in each month, 10 a.m.
	Tel: 01294 279275		
	Fax: 01294 312170		
9841	**OBAN SHERIFF COURT DISTRICT**		
	Sheriff Clerk Depute: Graham Whitelaw, Sheriff Court House, Oban PA34 4AL	CRIMINAL COURT: ORDINARY COURT:	As and when required Third Wednesday in month, 10 a.m.
	Tel: 01631 562414 Fax: 01631 562037	SUMMARY CAUSES COURT:	Third Wednesday in month, 10 a.m.
	DX OB8 OBAN		
	Legal Post: LP-4 OBAN		
	E-mail: oban@scotcourts.gov.uk		
9430	**Argyll and Bute District Court at Oban**		
	Clerk of District Court: Susan Mair, LL.B., Kilmory, Lochgilphead PA31 8RT	DISTRICT COURT: Sheriff Court House, Albany Street, Oban	Every fourth Thursday, 10 a.m.
	Tel: 01546 604340		
	Fax: 01546 604373		
9851	**PAISLEY SHERIFF COURT DISTRICT**		
	Sheriff Clerk: Christine Cockburn, Sheriff Court House, St. James' Street, Paisley PA3 2HW	CRIMINAL COURT: ORDINARY COURT:	Daily Monday, 10 a.m.
	Tel: 0141-887 5291 Fax: 0141-887 6702	SUMMARY CAUSE COURT:	Friday, 9.30 a.m.
	DX PA48 PAISLEY		
	E-mail: paisley@scotcourts.gov.uk		

NORTH STRATHCLYDE

Adult Court No	Name of Court District and Clerks		Normal Times of Courts
9474	**East Renfrewshire District Court at Giffnock**		
	Clerk of District Court: Mrs. J. A. C. Leonard, LL.B., Council Headquarters, Eastwood Park, Rouken Glen Road, Giffnock, East Renfrewshire G46 6UG	DISTRICT COURT: Court House, Braidholm Road, Giffnock	Friday, 10 a.m.
	Tel: 0141-577 3014/3825		
	Fax: 0141-577 3834		
	DX 501600 GIFFNOCK		
9542	**Renfrewshire District Court at Paisley**		
	Clerk of District Court: Kenneth Graham, LL.B., Dip.L.P, North Building, Cotton Street, Paisley PA1 1TT	DISTRICT COURT: Location: Court Building, Mill Street, Paisley	Cited Court: Monday and Tuesday, 10 a.m. Custody Court: Wednesday and Friday, 12 noon Means Court: Monday, 2 p.m. Trials: Thursday, 10 a.m.
	Tel: 0141-840 3296		
	Fax: 0141-840 3200		
	DX 590702 PAISLEY 3		
9861	**ROTHESAY SHERIFF COURT DISTRICT**		
	Sheriff Clerk: Janet Blackstock, (Greenock), Sheriff Court House, Rothesay PA20 9HA	CRIMINAL COURT:	Monday (and at Greenock Sheriff Court all other days)
		ORDINARY COURT:	Alternate Mondays, 10 a.m.
	Tel: 01700 502982 01475 787073		
	Fax: 01700 504112	SUMMARY CAUSES COURT:	Alternate Mondays, 10 a.m.
	DX GR16 GREENOCK		
	Legal Post: LP-5 GREENOCK 1		
	All administration for Rothesay Sheriff Court is conducted by Greenock Sheriff Court.		

SHERIFFDOM OF SOUTH STRATHCLYDE, DUMFRIES AND GALLOWAY

Sheriff Principal: Brian A. Lockhart

Adult Court No	Name of Court District and Clerks		Normal Times of Courts
9702	**AIRDRIE SHERIFF COURT DISTRICT**		
	Sheriff Clerk: J. Hamilton, Sheriff Court House, Graham Street, Airdrie ML6 6EE Tel: 01236 751121 Fax: 01236 747497 DX 570416 AIRDRIE Legal Post: LP-7 AIRDRIE E-mail: airdrie@scotcourts.gov.uk	CRIMINAL COURT: CIVIL COURT: SUMMARY CAUSES COURT:	Daily Thursday, 10 a.m. Every second Tuesday, 10 a.m.
9530	**North Lanarkshire District Court at Coatbridge**		
	Clerk of District Court: June Murray, LL.B., M.N.P., P.O. Box 14, Civic Centre, Motherwell ML1 1TW Tel: 01698 302222 Fax: 01698 302211 DX 1700 MOTHERWELL 2	DISTRICT COURT: 453 Main Street, Coatbridge Tel: 01236 431141 Fax: 01236 431141 Fines Office: Tel: 01236 812482 Fax: 01236 812483	Monday, Wednesday and Thursday, 10 a.m. Tuesday and Friday, as required
9531	**North Lanarkshire District Court at Cumbernauld**		
	Clerk of District Court: Jane Murray, LL.B., M.N.P., P.O. Box 14, Civic Centre, Motherwell ML1 1TW Tel: 01698 302222 Fax: 01698 302211	DISTRICT COURT: Bron Way, Cumbernauld Tel: 01236 616393 Fax: 01236 616393	Tuesday 10 a.m. Friday, 10 a.m.
9704	**AYR SHERIFF COURT DISTRICT**		
	Sheriff Clerk: Mrs. O. McShane, Sheriff Court House, Ayr KA7 1EE Tel: 01292 268474 Fax: 01292 292249 DX AY16 AYR	CRIMINAL COURT: ORDINARY COURT: SUMMARY CAUSES COURT: SMALL CLAIMS COURT:	Daily Every Thursday, 10 a.m. Every second Friday, 10 a.m. Every second Friday, 10 a.m.

SOUTH STRATHCLYDE, DUMFRIES AND GALLOWAY

Adult Court No	Name of Court District and Clerks		Normal Times of Courts
9460	**East Ayrshire District Court at Cumnock**		
	Clerk of District Court: David Mitchell, Council Headquarters, London Road, Kilmarnock KA3 7BU Tel: 01563 576078 Fax: 01563 576179 Legal Post: LP-18 KILMARNOCK	DISTRICT COURT: Court House, Ayr Road, Cumnock	Pleas: First and third Wednesday in month, 2 p.m. Trials: First, and third Friday in month, 10 a.m.
9560	**South Ayrshire District Court at Ayr**		
	Clerk of District Court: Dan Russell, Court House, 29 New Bridge Street, Ayr KA7 1JX Tel: 01292 617645 Fax: 01292 283695	DISTRICT COURT: 29 New Bridge Street, Ayr	Pleas: Second and fourth Wednesday in month, 9.30 a.m. Trials: First Tuesday in month, 10 a.m., every Thursday 9.30 a.m., and first Friday in month, 10 a.m.
9561	**South Ayrshire District Court at Girvan**		
	Clerk of District Court: Dan Russell, Court House, 29 New Bridge Street, Ayr KA7 1JX Tel: 01292 617645 Fax: 01292 283695	DISTRICT COURT: Court House, Knockcushan Street, Girvan	Last Friday in month, 10 a.m. Second Tuesday in month, 10 a.m.
9724	**DUMFRIES SHERIFF COURT DISTRICT**		
	Sheriff Clerk: Miss Eso Young, Sheriff Court House, Dumfries DG1 2AN Tel: 01387 262334 Fax: 01387 262357 DX 580617 DUMFRIES	CRIMINAL COURT: MOTION ROLL/ OPTIONS HEARING: SUMMARY CAUSES COURT: SMALL CLAIMS COURT:	Daily, 10 a.m. Thursday, 11 a.m. Every 4th Thursday, 10 a.m. Every 4th Thursday, 10 a.m.
9445	**Dumfries and Galloway District Court at Annan**		
	Clerk of District Court: Alex Haswell, Council Offices, High Street, Annan, Dumfriesshire DG12 6AQ Tel: 01387 260000 Fax: 01461 207029	DISTRICT COURT:	First and third Wednesday of each month, 10 a.m. Additional courts as required

SOUTH STRATHCLYDE, DUMFRIES AND GALLOWAY

Adult Court No   *Name of Court District and Clerks*   *Normal Times of Courts*

9446 Dumfries and Galloway District Court at Dumfries

Clerk of District Court:
Alex Haswell,
Municipal Chambers,
Buccleuch Street,
Dumfries DG1 2AD

DISTRICT COURT: Thursday, 10 a.m.

Tel: 01387 245923
       245922

Fax: 01387 252978

9449 Dumfries and Galloway District Court at Sanquhar – CLOSED – successor court – Dumfries

9772 HAMILTON SHERIFF COURT DISTRICT

Sheriff Clerk:
Fiona Petrie,
Sheriff Court House,
Beckford Street,
Hamilton ML3 0BT

CRIMINAL COURT: Daily

Tel: 01698 282957

Fax: 01698 201365
       (Criminal)
       201366
       (Fines)

Civil Department,
Birnie House,
Caird Park,
Hamilton Business Park,
Caird Street,
Hamilton ML3 0AL

OPTIONS HEARING: Tuesday and Thursday, 10 a.m.

SUMMARY CAUSES COURT: Monday, 10 a.m.

Tel: 01698 201375

SMALL CLAIMS COURT: Thursday, 10 a.m.

Fax: 01698 284870

DX HA16 HAMILTON

Legal Post: LP-4 HAMILTON 2

E-mail: hamilton@scotcourts.gov.uk

9532 North Lanarkshire District Court at Motherwell

Clerk of District Court:
June Murray, LL.B.,
M.N.P.,
P.O. Box 14,
Civic Centre,
Motherwell ML1 1TW

DISTRICT COURT:
Civic Centre,
Motherwell ML1 1TW
Tel: 01698 302267
Fax: 01698 302339

Trials:
  Monday, Wednesday, Thursday and Friday, 10 a.m.
Cited Court:
  Tuesday, 10 a.m.

Tel: 01698 302222

Fax: 01698 302211

DX 1700 MOTHERWELL 2

SOUTH STRATHCLYDE, DUMFRIES AND GALLOWAY

Adult Court No	Name of Court District and Clerks		Normal Times of Courts

9566 South Lanarkshire District Court at Hamilton

Clerk of District Court:
Sandra Dickson, M.A., LL.B.,
District Court House,
Campbell Street,
Hamilton ML3 6AT

Tel: 01698 527111

Fax: 01698 426128

E-mail: dclr@southlanarkshire.gov.uk

DISTRICT COURT:

Trials:
Monday and Friday,
9.30 a.m.
Cited Court:
Wednesday, 9.30 a.m.
Means Court:
Wednesday, 11 a.m.
(as required)

9804 KIRKCUDBRIGHT SHERIFF COURT DISTRICT

Sheriff Clerk Depute:
D. R. S. Hood,
Sheriff Court House,
Kirkcudbright
DG6 4JW

Tel: 01557 330574

Fax: 01557 331764

DX 580812 KIRKCUDBRIGHT

Legal Post: LP-2 KIRKCUDBRIGHT

CRIMINAL COURT:

ORDINARY COURT:

SMALL CLAIMS COURT:
SUMMARY CAUSES COURT:

Every Thursday and as and when required

Every Thursday

Second and fourth Thursday in month, 10 a.m.

9447 Dumfries and Galloway District Court at Kirkcudbright

Clerk of District Court:
Alex Haswell,
Council Offices,
Sun Street,
Stranraer DG9 7JJ

Tel: 01776 702151

Fax: 01776 704819

DISTRICT COURT:

Every fourth Friday
10 a.m.

9811 LANARK SHERIFF COURT DISTRICT

Sheriff Clerk:
John G. Foy,
Sheriff Court House,
24 Hope Street,
Lanark ML11 7NE

Tel: 01555 661531

Fax: 01555 664319

DX 570832 LANARK

Legal Post: LP-2 LANARK

CRIMINAL COURT:

ORDINARY COURT:

SUMMARY CAUSES COURT:

Monday 2 p.m.
Tuesday to Friday, 12.30 p.m.

Every second Tuesday,
10.30 a.m.

Every second Tuesday,
10 a.m.

SOUTH STRATHCLYDE, DUMFRIES AND GALLOWAY

Adult Court No	Name of Court District and Clerks		Normal Times of Courts
9567	**South Lanarkshire District Court at Lanark**		
	Clerk of District Court: Sandra Dickson, MA., LL.B., Council Offices, South Vennel, Lanark ML11 7JT	DISTRICT COURT:	Every Monday 10 a.m. Means Court: 9.30 a.m. as and when required
	Tel: 0845 7406080		
	Fax: 01555 673262		
	E-mail: loraine.parker@southlanarkshire.gov.uk		
9875	**STRANRAER SHERIFF COURT DISTRICT**		
	Sheriff Clerk: B. J. Lindsay, Sheriff Court House, Stranraer DG9 7AA	CRIMINAL COURT:	Tuesday, 10 a.m.
	Tel: 01776 702138 706135	SUMMARY CAUSES COURT:	Second and fourth Friday in month, 10 a.m.
	Fax: 01776 706792		
	DX 581261 STRANRAER		
	Legal Post: LP-2 STRANRAER		
9450	**Dumfries and Galloway District Court at Stranraer**		
	Clerk of District Court A. Haswell, Council Offices, Sun Street, Stranraer DG9 7JJ	DISTRICT COURT:	First and third Thursday in month, 10 a.m.
	Tel: 01776 702151		
	Fax: 01776 704819		

INDEX

NUMERICAL INDEX OF COURT CODES FOR SHERIFF COURT DISTRICTS

Court No		Page
9701	Aberdeen	120
9702	Airdrie	145
9703	Alloa	128
9704	Ayr	145
9705	Arbroath	128
9711	Banff	120
9716	Campbeltown	140
9717	Cupar	129
9721	Dingwall	121
9722	Dornoch	121
9723	Dumbarton	140
9724	Dumfries	146
9726	Dundee	129
9727	Dunfermline	130
9728	Dunoon	141
9729	Duns	133
9741	Edinburgh	133
9742	Elgin	122
9751	Falkirk	130
9752	Forfar	131
9753	Fort William	122
9761	Glasgow and Strathkelvin	138
9762	Greenock	142
9771	Haddington	134
9772	Hamilton	147

Court No		Page
9781	Inverness	123
9791	Jedburgh	135
9801	Kilmarnock	142
9803	Kirkcaldy	131
9804	Kirkcudbright	148
9805	Kirkwall	124
9811	Lanark	148
9812	Lerwick	124
9813	Linlithgow	135
9814	Lochmaddy	124
9815	Livingston	135
9841	Oban	143
9851	Paisley	143
9852	Peebles	136
9853	Perth	132
9854	Peterhead	124
9855	Portree	125
9861	Rothesay	144
9871	Selkirk	137
9872	Stirling	132
9873	Stonehaven	125
9874	Stornoway	126
9875	Stranraer	149
9881	Tain	126
9891	Wick	127

INDEX

NUMERICAL INDEX OF COURT CODES FOR DISTRICT COURTS
in use prior to 1 September 1998

Court No		Page
9900	Aberdeen (City of) DC	120
9901	Angus DC at Arbroath	128
	Angus DC at Forfar	131
9902	Dumfries and Galloway DC at Annan	146
9903	Argyll and Bute DC at Campbeltown	140
	Argyll and Bute DC at Dunoon	142
	Argyll and Bute DC at Helensburgh	140
	Argyll and Bute DC at Lochgilphead	142
	Argyll and Bute DC at Oban	143
9904	Highland DC at Kingussie	123
9905	Aberdeenshire DC at Banff	121
	Aberdeenshire DC at Peterhead	125
9906	East Dunbartonshire DC at Milngavie	141
9907	Scottish Borders DC at Duns	133
9908	Highland DC at Wick	127
9909	Clackmannanshire DC at Alloa	128
9910	West Dunbartonshire DC at Clydebank	141
9911	North Lanarkshire DC at Cumbernauld	145
9912	East Ayrshire DC at Cumnock	146
9913	North Ayrshire DC at Irvine	143
9914	West Dunbartonshire DC at Dumbarton	141
9915	Dundee, (City of) DC	129
9916	Fife DC at Dunfermline	130
9917	South Lanarkshire DC at East Kilbride	139
9918	East Lothian DC at Haddington	134
9919	East Renfrewshire DC at Giffnock	144
9920	Edinburgh, (City of) DC	134
9921	Scottish Borders DC at Selkirk (Ettrick & Lauderdale Division)	137
9922	Falkirk DC	130
9923	Glasgow, (City of) DC	138
9924	Aberdeenshire DC at Inverurie	120
9925	South Lanarkshire DC at Hamilton	148
9926	Inverclyde DC at Greenock	142
9927	Highland DC at Inverness	123
9928	East Ayrshire DC at Kilmarnock	143
9929	Aberdeenshire DC at Stonehaven	126
9930	Fife DC at Kirkcaldy	131
9931	South Ayrshire DC at Ayr	146
	South Ayrshire DC at Girvan	146
9932	South Lanarkshire DC at Lanark	149
9933	Highland DC at Fort William	122
9934	Midlothian DC at Loanhead	134
9935	North Lanarkshire DC at Coatbridge	145
9936	Moray DC at Elgin	122
9937	North Lanarkshire DC at Motherwell	147
9938	Highland DC at Nairn	123
9939	Dumfries and Galloway DC at Dumfries	147
	Dumfries and Galloway DC at Sanquhar (CLOSED)	147
9940	Fife DC at Cupar	129
9941	Perth and Kinross DC at Perth	132
9942	Renfrewshire DC at Paisley	144
9943	Highland DC at Dingwall	121
9944	Scottish Borders DC at Jedburgh (Roxburgh Division)	135
9945	Highland DC at Portree	125
9946	Dumfries and Galloway DC at Kirkcudbright	148
9947	Stirling DC	132
9948	East Dunbartonshire DC at Kirkintilloch	139
9949	Highland DC at Dornoch	121
9950	Scottish Borders DC at Peebles (Tweeddale Division)	136
9951	West Lothian DC at Livingston	136
9952	Western Isles DC at Stornoway	126
9953	Dumfries and Galloway DC at Stranraer	149

INDEX

NUMERICAL INDEX OF COURT CODES FOR DISTRICT COURTS
as from 1 September 1998

Court No		Page
9400	Aberdeen (City of) DC	120
9405	Aberdeenshire DC at Banff	121
9407	Aberdeenshire DC at Inverurie	120
9408	Aberdeenshire DC at Peterhead	125
9409	Aberdeenshire DC at Stonehaven	126
9415	Angus DC at Arbroath	128
9417	Angus DC at Forfar	131
9426	Argyll & Bute DC at Campbeltown	140
9427	Argyll & Bute DC at Dunoon	142
9428	Argyll & Bute DC at Helensburgh	140
9429	Argyll & Bute DC at Lochgilphead	142
9430	Argyll & Bute DC at Oban	143
9440	Clackmannanshire DC at Alloa	128
9445	Dumfries and Galloway DC at Annan	146
9446	Dumfries and Galloway DC at Dumfries	147
9447	Dumfries and Galloway DC at Kirkcudbright	148
9449	Dumfries and Galloway DC at Sanquhar (CLOSED)	147
9450	Dumfries and Galloway DC at Stranraer	149
9456	Dundee, (City of) DC	129
9460	East Ayrshire DC at Cumnock	146
9461	East Ayrshire DC at Kilmarnock	143
9465	East Dunbartonshire DC at Kirkintilloch	139
9466	East Dunbartonshire DC at Milngavie	141
9470	East Lothian DC at Haddington	134
9474	East Renfrewshire DC at Giffnock	144
9478	Edinburgh (City of) DC	134
9482	Falkirk DC	130
9485	Fife DC at Cupar	129
9486	Fife DC at Dunfermline	130
9487	Fife DC at Kirkcaldy	131
9495	Glasgow (City of) DC	138
9500	Highland DC at Dingwall	121
9501	Highland DC at Dornoch	121
9502	Highland DC at Fort William	122
9503	Highland DC at Inverness	123
9504	Highland DC at Kingussie	123
9505	Highland DC at Nairn	123
9506	Highland DC at Portree	125
9508	Highland DC at Wick	127
9509	Highland DC at Tain	126
9514	Inverclyde DC at Greenock	142
9518	Midlothian DC at Loanhead	134
9522	Moray DC at Elgin	122
9526	North Ayrshire DC at Irvine	143
9530	North Lanarkshire DC at Coatbridge	145
9531	North Lanarkshire DC at Cumbernauld	145
9532	North Lanarkshire DC at Motherwell	147
9538	Perth & Kinross DC at Perth	132
9542	Renfrewshire DC at Paisley	144
9550	Scottish Borders DC at Duns	133
9551	Scottish Borders DC at Jedburgh	135
9552	Scottish Borders DC at Peebles	136
9553	Scottish Borders DC at Selkirk	137
9560	South Ayrshire DC at Ayr	146
9561	South Ayrshire DC at Girvan	146
9565	South Lanarkshire DC at East Kilbride	139
9566	South Lanarkshire DC at Hamilton	148
9567	South Lanarkshire DC at Lanark	149
9568	South Lanarkshire DC at Rutherglen	139
9572	Stirling DC	132
9575	West Dunbartonshire DC at Clydebank	141
9576	West Dunbartonshire DC at Dumbarton	141
9580	West Lothian DC at Livingston	136
9584	Western Isles DC at Stornoway	126

GAZETTEER OF PLACES IN THE GREATER LONDON AREA

indicating the appropriate Local Justice Area or Magistrates' Court
(See pages 68 to 86)

Note: Where the names of two Courts are given, this indicates that the place named falls across the boundary of a Court area and an address within that place may lie within the jurisdiction of either Court. In such cases, it is recommended that advice should be sought from the Warrant Officer of one of the Courts in question.

Place	Adult Area/Court
A	
Abbey Wood	{ Bexley / Greenwich }
Acton	Ealing
Addington	Croydon
Addiscombe	Croydon
Alexandra Park	Haringey
Alperton	Brent
Anerley	Bromley
Arkley	Barnet
B	
Balham	South Western
Barking	Barking and Dagenham
Barkingside	Redbridge
Barnes	Richmond-upon-Thames
Barnet	Barnet
Barnehurst	Bexley
Battersea	South Western
Beckenham	Bromley
Becton	Newham
Beacontree	{ Barking and Dagenham / Redbridge }
Beddington	Sutton
Bedfont, East	Feltham
Bellingham	Greenwich
Belmont	Sutton
Belsize Park	Highbury Corner
Belvedere	Bexley
Bermondsey	Tower Bridge
Berryland	Kingston-upon-Thames
Bethnal Green	Highbury Corner
Bexley	Bexley
Bexleyheath	Bexley
Bickley	Bromley
Biggin Hill	Bromley
Blackfen	Bexley
Blackheath	Greenwich
Bounds Green	Haringey
Bow	Thames

Place	Adult Area/Court
Bowes Park	Enfield
Brent	Brent
Brentford	Hounslow
Brixton	Camberwell
Brockley	Tower Bridge
Bromley-by-Bow	Thames
Bromley	Bromley
Brondesbury Park	Brent
Brook Green	West London
Broom Hill	Bromley
Burnt Oak	Barnet
Bushey Park	Richmond-upon-Thames
C	
Camberwell	Camberwell
Camden Town	Highbury Corner
Canning Town	Newham
Canon's Park	Harrow
Carshalton	Sutton
Carshalton Beeches	Sutton
Catford	Greenwich
Chadwell Heath	{ Barking and Dagenham / Redbridge }
Chapel End	Waltham Forest
Charlton	{ Greenwich / Woolwich }
Cheam	Sutton
Chelsea	Horseferry Road
Chelsfield	Bromley
Chessington	Kingston-upon-Thames
Child's Hill	Barnet
Chingford	Waltham Forest
Chipping Barnet	Barnet
Chislehurst	Bromley
Chiswick	Hounslow
Church End	Barnet
Clapham	South Western
Clerkenwell	Highbury Corner
Cockfosters	{ Barnet / Enfield }

GAZETTEER OF PLACES IN GREATER LONDON

Place	Adult Area/Court
Collindale	Barnet
Collier Road	Havering
Colliers Wood	Merton
Colney Hatch	Barnet
Coney Hall	Bromley
Coombe	Kingston-upon-Thames
Corbets Tey	Havering
Cottenham Park	Merton
Coulsdon	Croydon
Cowley	Hillingdon
Cranford	Hounslow
Cranham	Havering
Crayford	Bexley
Cricklewood	{ Barnet / Brent }
Crofton Park	Tower Bridge
Crouch End	Haringey
Croydon	Croydon
Crystal Palace	{ Bromley / Camberwell / Croydon }
Cudham	Bromley
Custom House	Newham

D

Place	Adult Area/Court
Dagenham	Barking and Dagenham
Dalston	Highbury Corner
Dartmouth Park	Highbury Corner
Denmark Hill	Camberwell
Deptford	Tower Bridge
Dollis Hill	Brent
Downe	Bromley
Downham	Greenwich
Dulwich	Camberwell

E

Place	Adult Area/Court
Ealing	Ealing
Earls Court	West London
Earlsfield	South Western
East Acton	Ealing
East Barnet	Barnet
East Bedfont	Hounslow
Eastcote	Hillingdon
East Croydon	Croydon
East Dulwich	Camberwell
East Finchley	Barnet
East Ham	Newham
East Sheen	Richmond-upon-Thames
East Wickham	Bexley
Eden Park	Bromley
Edgware	Barnet
Edmonton	Enfield
Elmers End	Bromley
Elm Park	Havering
Elstree	Barnet
Eltham	Woolwich
Emerson Park	Havering
Enfield	Enfield
Erith	Bexley

F

Place	Adult Area/Court
Farnborough	Bromley
Feltham	Hounslow
Finchley	Barnet
Finsbury	Highbury Corner
Finsbury Park	{ Highbury Corner / Haringey }
Foots Cray	Bexley
Forest Gate	Newham
Forest Hill	Greenwich
Fortis Green	Haringey
Friern Barnet	Barnet
Fulham	West London
Fulwell	Richmond-upon-Thames

G

Place	Adult Area/Court
Gants Hill	Redbridge
Gidea Park	Havering
Golders Green	Barnet
Goodmayes	Redbridge
Green Street Green	Bromley
Greenford	Ealing
Greenhill	Harrow
Greenwich	Greenwich
Grove Park	Greenwich
Gunnersbury	{ Ealing / Hounslow }

H

Place	Adult Area/Court
Hackbridge	Sutton
Hackney	Highbury Corner
Hacton	Havering
Hadley	Barnet
Hadley Wood	Enfield
Haggerston	Highbury Corner
Hainault	Redbridge
Hale End	Waltham Forest
Ham	Richmond-upon-Thames

154

GAZETTEER OF PLACES IN GREATER LONDON

Place	Adult Area/Court
Hammersmith	West London
Hampstead	Highbury Corner
Hampstead Garden Suburb	Barnet
Hampton	Richmond-upon-Thames
Hampton Hill	Richmond-upon-Thames
Hampton Wick	Richmond-upon-Thames
Hanwell	Ealing
Hanworth	Hounslow
Harefield	Hillingdon
Haringey	Haringey
Harlesden	Brent
Harlington	Hillingdon
Harmondsworth	Hillingdon
Harold Hill	Havering
Harold Wood	Havering
Harringay	Haringey
Harrow	Harrow
Harrow-on-the-Hill	Harrow
Harrow Weald	Harrow
Hatch End	Harrow
Havering-atte-Bower	Havering
Havering	Havering
Hayes (Kent)	Bromley
Hayes (Middx.)	Hillingdon
Headstone	Harrow
Hendon	Barnet
Herne Hill	Camberwell
Heston	Hounslow
Higham Hill	Waltham Forest
Highams Park	Waltham Forest
Highbury	Highbury Corner
Highbury Vale	Highbury Corner
Highgate	Haringey
Hillingdon	Hillingdon
Holborn	Highbury Corner
Holland Park	Marylebone
Holloway	Highbury Corner
Homerton	Highbury Corner
Honor Oak	Camberwell / Greenwich
Hook	Kingston-upon-Thames
Hornchurch	Havering
Hornsey	Haringey
Hounslow	Hounslow

I

Place	Adult Area/Court
Ickenham	Hillingdon
Ilford	Redbridge
Isle of Dogs	Thames
Isleworth	Hounslow
Islington	Highbury Corner

K

Place	Adult Area/Court
Kenley	Croydon
Kennington	Horseferry Road
Kensal Green	Marylebone / Brent
Kensal Rise	Brent
Kensington	Horseferry Road
Kentish Town	Highbury Corner
Kenton	Brent
Keston	Bromley
Kevingtown	Bromley
Kew	Richmond-upon-Thames
Kidbrooke	Greenwich
Kilburn	Highbury Corner / Brent
Kingsbury	Brent
Kingsbury Green	Brent
Kingsland	Highbury Corner
Kingston-upon-Thames	Kingston-upon-Thames

L

Place	Adult Area/Court
Lambeth	Camberwell
Lamorbey	Bexley
Lampton	Hounslow
Lansbury	Thames
Lee	Greenwich
Lewisham	Greenwich
Leyton	Waltham Forest
Leytonstone	Waltham Forest
Limehouse	Thames
Locksbottom	Bromley
London Airport Heathrow (North)	Hillingdon
London Airport Heathrow (South)	Hounslow
London Docks	Thames / Newham
Lower Clapton	Highbury Corner
Lower Edmonton	Enfield
Lower Holloway	Highbury Corner
Lower Sydenham	Greenwich

M

Place	Adult Area/Court
Manor Park	Newham
Marks Gate	Barking

GAZETTEER OF PLACES IN GREATER LONDON

Place	Adult Area/Court
Merton	Merton
Mill Hill	Barnet
Millwall	Thames
Mitcham	Merton
Morden	Merton
Mortlake	Richmond-upon-Thames
Motspur Park	{ Kingston-upon Thames / Merton }
Mottingham	{ Bromley / Woolwich }
Muswell Hill	Haringey

N

Place	Adult Area/Court
Neasden	Brent
New Addington	Croydon
New Barnet	Barnet
Newbury Park	Redbridge
New Charlton	Greenwich
New Cross	Greenwich
New Eltham	Woolwich
New Malden	Kingston-upon-Thames
Newham	Newham
Newington	{ Camberwell / Tower Bridge }
Newington Green	Highbury Corner
New Southgate	Enfield
Norbiton	Kingston-upon-Thames
Norbury	Croydon
North Cray	Bexley
North End	Bexley
Northfield	Ealing
North Finchley	Barnet
North Harrow	Harrow
North Kensington	Marylebone
North Ockenden	Havering
Northolt	Ealing
Northolt Airport	Hillingdon
Northolt R.A.F.	Hillingdon
Northumberland Heath	Bexley
Northwood	Hillingdon
North Woolwich	Newham
Norwood Green	Ealing
Notting Hill	Marylebone
Nunhead	Camberwell

O

Place	Adult Area/Court
Old Brompton	Horseferry Road
Old Ford	Thames
Orpington	Bromley
Osterley	Hounslow

P

Place	Adult Area/Court
Paddington	Marylebone
Palmers Green	Enfield
Park Royal	{ Ealing / Brent }
Parsons Green	West London
Peckham	{ Camberwell / Tower Bridge }
Penge	Bromley
Perivale	Ealing
Perry Hill	Greenwich
Perry Vale	Greenwich
Petersham	Richmond-upon-Thames
Petts Wood	Bromley
Pinner	Harrow
Plaistow	Newham
Plumstead	Woolwich
Ponders End	Enfield
Poplar	Thames
Pratt's Bottom	Bromley
Purley	Croydon
Purley Oaks	Croydon
Putney	South Western

R

Place	Adult Area/Court
R.A.F. Northolt	Hillingdon
Rainham	Havering
Rayners Lane	Harrow
Raynes Park	Merton
Redbridge	Redbridge
Richmond-upon-Thames	Richmond-upon-Thames
Roehampton	South Western
Romford	Havering
Rotherhithe	Tower Bridge
Roundshaw	Sutton
Roxeth	Harrow
Ruislip	Hillingdon
Rush Green	{ Barking and Dagenham / Redbridge }

S

Place	Adult Area/Court
St. Helier	Sutton
St. John's Wood	{ Highbury Corner / Marylebone }
St. Margarets	Richmond-upon-Thames

GAZETTEER OF PLACES IN GREATER LONDON

Place	Adult Area/Court
St. Mary Cray	Bromley
St. Paul's Cray	Bromley
Sanderstead	Croydon
Selhurst	Croydon
Selsdon	Croydon
Seven Kings	Redbridge
Shadwell	Thames
Shepherds Bush	West London
Shirley	Croydon
Shooters Hill	Woolwich
Shoreditch	{ Highbury Corner / Thames }
Shortlands	Bromley
Sidcup	Bexley
Silvertown	Newham
Slade Green	Bexley
Snaresbrook	Redbridge
Southall	Ealing
Southborough	Kingston-upon-Thames
Southborough (Kent)	Bromley
South Croydon	Croydon
Southfields	{ South Western / Merton }
Southgate	Enfield
South Harrow	Harrow
South Hornchurch	Havering
South Lambeth	Camberwell
South Norwood	Croydon
South Ruislip	Hillingdon
South Tottenham	Haringey
Southwark	Tower Bridge
South Woodford	Redbridge
Stanford Hill	Highbury Corner
Stanmore	Harrow
Stepney	Thames
Stoke Newington	Highbury Corner
Stonebridge	Brent
Stratford	Newham
Stratford New Town	Newham
Strawberry Hill	Richmond-upon-Thames
Streatham	Camberwell
Stroud Green	{ Highbury Corner / Haringey }
Sudbury	Brent
Summerstown	{ Camberwell / South Western }
Surbiton	Kingston-upon-Thames
Surrey Docks	Tower Bridge
Sutton	Sutton
Swiss Cottage	Highbury Corner
Sydenham	Greenwich

T

Place	Adult Area/Court
Teddington	Richmond-upon-Thames
Thamesmead	{ Bexley / Woolwich }
Thornton Heath	Croydon
Tolworth	Kingston-upon-Thames
Tooting	South Western
Tottenham	Haringey
Totteridge	Barnet
Tower Hamlets	Thames
Tufnell Park	Highbury Corner
Tulse Hill	Camberwell
Twickenham	Richmond-upon-Thames

U

Place	Adult Area/Court
Upminster	Havering
Upper Clapton	Highbury Corner
Upper Edmonton	{ Enfield / Haringey }
Upper Holloway	Highbury Corner
Upper Norwood	{ Camberwell / Croydon }
Upper Sydenham	Greenwich
Upton Park	Newham
Uxbridge	Hillingdon

V

Place	Adult Area/Court
Victoria	Bow Street
Victoria Park	{ Highbury Corner / Thames }

W

Place	Adult Area/Court
Waddon	Croydon
Walham Green	West London
Wallington	Sutton
Walthamstow	Waltham Forest
Walworth	{ Camberwell / Tower Bridge }
Wandsworth	South Western
Wanstead	Redbridge
Wapping	Thames
Wealdstone	Harrow
Welling	Bexley
Wembley	Brent
Wennington	Havering

GAZETTEER OF PLACES IN GREATER LONDON

Place	Adult Area/Court
West Croydon	Croydon
West Drayton	Hillingdon
West Dulwich	Camberwell
West Ham	Newham
West Hampstead	Highbury Corner
West Harrow	Harrow
West Heath	Bexley
West India Docks	Thames
West Norwood	Camberwell
West Ruislip	Hillingdon
West Wickham	Bromley
Whetstone	Barnet
Whitechapel	Thames
Whitton	Richmond-upon-Thames
Willesden	Brent
Willesden Green	Brent
Wimbledon	Merton
Winchmore Hill	Enfield
Woodford	Redbridge
Woodford Bridge	Redbridge
Woodford Green	Redbridge
Woodford Wells	Redbridge
Wood End	Hillingdon
Wood Green	Haringey
Woodside	Croydon
Woolwich	Woolwich
Worcester Park	Sutton

Y

Place	Adult Area/Court
Yeading	Ealing / Hillingdon
Yiewsley	Hillingdon

NUMERICAL INDEX TO COURT CODES OF COURTS OF SUMMARY JURISDICTION IN ENGLAND AND WALES

(For NORTHERN IRELAND see p.113; For SCOTLAND see p.120)

ENGLAND

1012 **BATH DIVISION** – *combined with 1018 WANSDYKE DIVISION to form* **1022 BATH AND WANSDYKE DIVISION**

1013 **BRISTOL L.J.A.** – *see* **AVON AND SOMERSET** .... p. 5

1014 **LAWFORD'S GATE DIVISION** – *combined with 1016 SODBURY DIVISION to form* **1020 AVON NORTH DIVISION**

1015 **LONG ASHTON DIVISION** – *combined with 1019 WESTON-SUPER-MARE DIVISION to form* **1023 WOODSPRING DIVISION**

1016 **SODBURY DIVISION** – *combined with 1014 LAWFORD'S GATE DIVISION to form* **1020 AVON NORTH DIVISION**

1017 **THORNBURY DIVISION** – *combined with 1020 AVON NORTH DIVISION to form* **1021 NORTH AVON DIVISION**

1018 **WANSDYKE DIVISION** – *combined with 1012 BATH DIVISION to form* **1022 BATH AND WANSDYKE DIVISION**

1019 **WESTON-SUPER-MARE DIVISION** – *combined with 1015 LONG ASHTON DIVISION to form* **1023 WOODSPRING DIVISION**

1020 **AVON NORTH DIVISION** – *combined with 1017 THORNBURY DIVISION to form* **1021 NORTH AVON DIVISION**

1021 **NORTH AVON L.J.A.** – *see* **AVON AND SOMERSET** .... p. 6

1022 **BATH AND WANSDYKE L.J.A.** – *see* **AVON AND SOMERSET** .... p. 5

1023 **NORTH SOMERSET L.J.A.** – *see* **AVON AND SOMERSET** .... p. 6

1050 **AMPTHILL DIVISION** – *combined with 1051 BEDFORD DIVISION, 1052 BIGGLESWADE DIVISION, 1053 DUNSTABLE DIVISION (Part) and 1054 LEIGHTON BUZZARD DIVISION (Part) to form* **1051 BEDFORD AND MID BEDFORDSHIRE DIVISION**

1051 **BEDFORD DIVISION** – *(formerly North Bedfordshire Division) combined with 1050 AMPTHILL DIVISION, 1052 BIGGLESWADE DIVISION, 1053 DUNSTABLE DIVISION (Part) and 1054 LEIGHTON BUZZARD DIVISION (Part) to form* **1051 BEDFORD AND MID BEDFORDSHIRE DIVISION**

1051 **BEDFORD AND MID BEDFORDSHIRE L.J.A.** – *see* **BEDFORDSHIRE, ESSEX AND HERTFORDSHIRE** .... p. 8

1052 **BIGGLESWADE DIVISION** – *combined with 1050 AMPTHILL DIVISION, 1051 BEDFORD DIVISION, 1053 DUNSTABLE DIVISION (Part) and 1054 LEIGHTON BUZZARD DIVISION (Part) to form* **1051 BEDFORD AND MID BEDFORDSHIRE DIVISION**

ENGLAND

1053 DUNSTABLE DIVISION – Parish of Harlington combined 1050 AMPTHILL DIVISION, 1051 BEDFORD DIVISION, 1052 BIGGLESWADE DIVISION and 1054 LEIGHTON BUZZARD DIVISION (Part) to form **1051 BEDFORD AND MID BEDFORDSHIRE DIVISION**
Remaining parishes combined with 1054 LEIGHTON BUZZARD (Part) and 1055 LUTON DIVISION to form **1055 LUTON AND SOUTH BEDFORDSHIRE DIVISION**

1054 LEIGHTON BUZZARD DIVISION – Part combined with 1050 AMPTHILL DIVISION, 1051 BEDFORD DIVISION, 1052 BIGGLESWADE DIVISION, 1053 DUNSTABLE DIVISION (Parish of Harlington) to form **1051 BEDFORD AND MID BEDFORDSHIRE DIVISION**
Remainder combined with 1053 DUNSTABLE DIVISION (except Harlington) and 1055 LUTON DIVISION to form **1055 LUTON AND SOUTH BEDFORDSHIRE DIVISION**

1055 LUTON DIVISION – combined with 1053 DUNSTABLE DIVISION, (except Harlington), and 1054 LEIGHTON BUZZARD DIVISION to form **1055 LUTON AND SOUTH BEDFORDSHIRE DIVISION**

1055 LUTON AND SOUTH BEDFORDSHIRE L.J.A. – see **BEDFORDSHIRE, ESSEX AND HERTFORDSHIRE** .... p. 9

1065 BRADFIELD AND SONNING DIVISION – combined with 1071 READING DIVISION to form **1076 READING AND SONNING DIVISION**

1066 FOREST DIVISION – combined with 1068 MAIDENHEAD DIVISION, 1072 SLOUGH DIVISION and 1074 WINDSOR DIVISION to form **1072 EAST BERKSHIRE DIVISION**

1067 HUNGERFORD AND LAMBOURN DIVISION – combined with 1069 NEWBURY DIVISION to form **1075 WEST BERKSHIRE DIVISION**

1068 MAIDENHEAD DIVISION – combined with 1066 FOREST DIVISION, 1072 SLOUGH DIVISION and 1074 WINDSOR DIVISION to form **1072 EAST BERKSHIRE DIVISION**

1069 NEWBURY DIVISION – combined with 1067 HUNGERFORD AND LAMBOURN DIVISION to form **1075 WEST BERKSHIRE DIVISION**

1070 NEW WINDSOR DIVISION – combined with 1073 WINDSOR COUNTY DIVISION to form **1074 WINDSOR DIVISION**

1071 READING DIVISION – combined with 1065 BRADFIELD AND SONNING DIVISION to form **1076 READING AND SONNING DIVISION**

1072 SLOUGH DIVISION – combined with 1066 FOREST DIVISION, 1068 MAIDENHEAD DIVISION and 1074 WINDSOR DIVISION to form **1072 EAST BERKSHIRE DIVISION**

1072 EAST BERKSHIRE L.J.A. – see **THAMES VALLEY** .... p. 96

1073 WINDSOR COUNTY DIVISION – combined with 1070 NEW WINDSOR DIVISION to form **1074 WINDSOR DIVISION**

1074 WINDSOR DIVISION – combined with 1066 FOREST DIVISION, 1068 MAIDENHEAD DIVISION and 1072 SLOUGH DIVISION to form **1072 EAST BERKSHIRE DIVISION**

1075 WEST BERKSHIRE L.J.A. – see **THAMES VALLEY** .... p. 99

1076 READING AND SONNING DIVISION – renamed **1076 READING P.S.A.**

1076 READING L.J.A. – see **THAMES VALLEY** .... p. 98

1110 AMERSHAM DIVISION – combined with 1115 CHESHAM DIVISION to form **1128 CHILTERN DIVISION**

1111 AYLESBURY DIVISION – combined with 1112 BRILL DIVISION and 1118 LINSLADE DIVISION to form **1125 AYLESBURY DIVISION**

ENGLAND

1112 **BRILL DIVISION** – *combined with 1111 AYLESBURY DIVISION and 1118 LINSLADE DIVISION to form* **1125 AYLESBURY DIVISION**

1113 **BUCKINGHAM DIVISION** – *combined with 1122 WINSLOW DIVISION to form* **1126 BUCKINGHAM DIVISION**

1114 **BURNHAM DIVISION** – *combined with 1127 WYCOMBE DIVISION to form* **1130 WYCOMBE AND BEACONSFIELD DIVISION**

1115 **CHESHAM DIVISION** – *combined with 1110 AMERSHAM DIVISION to form* **1128 CHILTERN DIVISION**

1116 **FENNY STRATFORD DIVISION** – *combined with 1120 NEWPORT PAGNELL DIVISION and 1121 STONY STRATFORD DIVISION to form* **1124 MILTON KEYNES DIVISION**

1117 **HIGH WYCOMBE DIVISION** – *combined with 1119 MARLOW DIVISION and 1123 WYCOMBE (COUNTY) DIVISION to form* **1127 WYCOMBE DIVISION**

1118 **LINSLADE DIVISION** – *combined with 1111 AYLESBURY DIVISION and 1112 BRILL DIVISION to form* **1125 AYLESBURY DIVISION**

1119 **MARLOW DIVISION** – *combined with 1117 HIGH WYCOMBE DIVISION and 1123 WYCOMBE (COUNTY) DIVISION to form* **1127 WYCOMBE DIVISION**

1120 **NEWPORT PAGNELL DIVISION** – *combined with 1116 FENNY STRATFORD DIVISION and 1121 STONY STRATFORD DIVISION to form* **1124 MILTON KEYNES DIVISION**

1121 **STONY STRATFORD DIVISION** – *combined with 1116 FENNY STRATFORD DIVISION and 1120 NEWPORT PAGNELL DIVISION to form* **1124 MILTON KEYNES DIVISION**

1122 **WINSLOW DIVISION** – *combined with 1113 BUCKINGHAM DIVISION to form* **1126 BUCKINGHAM DIVISION**

1123 **WYCOMBE (COUNTY) DIVISION** – *combined with 1117 HIGH WYCOMBE DIVISION and 1119 MARLOW DIVISION to form* **1127 WYCOMBE DIVISION**

1124 **MILTON KEYNES L.J.A.** – see **THAMES VALLEY** .... p. 97

1125 **AYLESBURY DIVISION** – *combined with 1126 BUCKINGHAM DIVISION and 1128 CHILTERN DIVISION to form* **1129 CENTRAL BUCKINGHAMSHIRE DIVISION**

1126 **BUCKINGHAM DIVISION** – *combined with 1125 AYLESBURY DIVISION and 1128 CHILTERN DIVISIION to form* **1129 CENTRAL BUCKINGHAMSHIRE DIVISION**

1127 **WYCOMBE DIVISION** – *combined with 1114 BURNHAM DIVISION to form* **1130 WYCOMBE AND BEACONSFIELD DIVISION**

1128 **CHILTERN DIVISION** – *combined with 1125 AYLESBURY DIVISION and 1126 BUCKINGHAM DIVISION to form* **1129 CENTRAL BUCKINGHAMSHIRE DIVISION**

1129 **CENTRAL BUCKINGHAMSHIRE L.J.A.** – see **THAMES VALLEY** .... p. 96

1130 **WYCOMBE AND BEACONSFIELD L.J.A.** – see **THAMES VALLEY** .... p. 99

1133 **ARRINGTON AND MELBOURN DIVISION** – *combined with 1134 BOTTISHAM DIVISION, 1159 CAXTON DIVISION and 1141 LINTON DIVISION to form* **1163 SOUTH CAMBRIDGESHIRE DIVISION**

1134 **BOTTISHAM DIVISION** – *combined with 1133 ARRINGTON AND MELBOURN DIVISION, 1141 LINTON DIVISION and 1159 CAXTON DIVISION to form* **1163 SOUTH CAMBRIDGESHIRE DIVISION**

1135 **CAMBRIDGE DIVISION** – *combined with 1137 CAXTON DIVISION to form* **1159 CAXTON DIVISION**

ENGLAND

1136 **CAMBRIDGE CITY DIVISION** – combined with 1163 SOUTH CAMBRIDGESHIRE DIVISION to form **1165 CAMBRIDGE DIVISION**

1137 **CAXTON DIVISION** – combined with 1135 CAMBRIDGE DIVISION to form **1159 CAXTON DIVISION**

1138 **ELY DIVISION** – combined with 1164 NEWMARKET DIVISION to form **1166 EAST CAMBRIDGESHIRE DIVISION**

1140 **HURSTINGSTONE DIVISION** – combined with 1157 HUNTINGDON AND NORMAN CROSS DIVISION and 1145 RAMSEY DIVISION to form **1161 HUNTINGDON DIVISION**

1141 **LINTON DIVISION** – combined with 1133 ARRINGTON AND MELBOURN DIVISION, 1134 BOTTISHAM DIVISION and 1159 CAXTON DIVISION to form **1163 SOUTH CAMBRIDGESHIRE DIVISION**

1142 **NEWMARKET DIVISION** – combined with part of 1134 BOTTISHAM DIVISION to form **1164 NEWMARKET (CAMBS) DIVISION**

1143 **NORMAN CROSS DIVISION** – see **1157 HUNTINGDON AND NORMAN CROSS**

1144 **NORTH WITCHFORD DIVISION** – combined with 1160 WISBECH DIVISION to form **1167 FENLAND DIVISION**

1145 **RAMSEY DIVISION** – combined with 1157 HUNTINGDON AND NORMAN CROSS DIVISION and 1140 HURSTINGSTONE DIVISION to form **1161 HUNTINGDON DIVISION**

1147 **TOSELAND DIVISION** – combined with 1161 HUNTINGDON DIVISION to form **1168 HUNTINGDONSHIRE DIVISION**

1148 **WHITTLESEY DIVISION** – combined with 1158 SOKE OF PETERBOROUGH DIVISION to form **1162 PETERBOROUGH DIVISION**

1149 **WISBECH (BOROUGH) DIVISION** – combined with 1150 WISBECH (ISLE) DIVISION to form **1160 WISBECH DIVISION**

1150 **WISBECH (ISLE) DIVISION** – combined with 1149 WISBECH (BOROUGH) DIVISION to form **1160 WISBECH DIVISION**

1157 **HUNTINGDON AND NORMAN CROSS DIVISION** – combined with 1140 HURSTINGSTONE DIVISION and 1145 RAMSEY DIVISION to form **1161 HUNTINGDON DIVISION**

1158 **SOKE OF PETERBOROUGH DIVISION** – combined with 1148 WHITTLESEY DIVISION to form **1162 PETERBOROUGH DIVISION**

1159 **CAXTON DIVISION** – combined with 1133 ARRINGTON AND MELBOURN DIVISION, 1134 BOTTISHAM DIVISION AND 1141 LINTON DIVISION to form **1163 SOUTH CAMBRIDGESHIRE DIVISION**

1160 **WISBECH DIVISION** – combined with 1144 NORTH WITCHFORD DIVISION to form **1167 FENLAND DIVISION**

1161 **HUNTINGDON DIVISION** – combined with 1147 TOSELAND DIVISION to form **1168 HUNTINGDONSHIRE DIVISION**

1162 **PETERBOROUGH L.J.A.** – see **CAMBRIDGESHIRE, NORFOLK AND SUFFOLK** . p. 24

1163 **SOUTH CAMBRIDGESHIRE DIVISION** – combined with 1136 CAMBRIDGE CITY DIVISION to form **1166 EAST CAMBRIDGESHIRE DIVISION**

1164 **NEWMARKET (CAMBS) DIVISION** – combined with 1138 ELY DIVISION to form **1166 EAST CAMBRIDGESHIRE DIVISION**

1165 **CAMBRIDGE L.J.A.** – see **CAMBRIDGESHIRE, NORFOLK AND SUFFOLK** .... p. 22

1166 **EAST CAMBRIDGESHIRE L.J.A.** – see **CAMBRIDGESHIRE, NORFOLK AND SUFFOLK** .... p. 22

ENGLAND

1167 FENLAND L.J.A. – see CAMBRIDGESHIRE, NORFOLK AND SUFFOLK .... p. 23

1168 HUNTINGDONSHIRE L.J.A. – see CAMBRIDGESHIRE, NORFOLK AND SUFFOLK .... p. 23

1173 CHESTER P.S.A. – combined with 1176 ELLESMERE PORT AND NESTON P.S.A. to form **1188 CHESTER, ELLESMERE PORT AND NESTON P.S.A.**

1174 CONGLETON DIVISION – combined with 1175 CREWE AND NANTWICH DIVISION to form **1187 SOUTH CHESHIRE DIVISION**

1175 CREWE AND NANTWICH DIVISION – combined with 1174 CONGLETON DIVISION to form **1187 SOUTH CHESHIRE DIVISION**

1176 ELLESMERE PORT AND NESTON P.S.A. – combined with 1173 CHESTER P.S.A. to form **1188 CHESTER, ELLESMERE PORT AND NESTON P.S.A.**

1177 HALTON L.J.A. – see CHESHIRE AND MERSEYSIDE .... p. 27

1178 MACCLESFIELD L.J.A. – see CHESHIRE AND MERSEYSIDE .... p. 28

1179 VALE ROYAL L.J.A. – see CHESHIRE AND MERSEYSIDE .... p. 29

1180 WARRINGTON L.J.A. – see CHESHIRE AND MERSEYSIDE .... p. 29

1187 SOUTH CHESHIRE L.J.A. – see CHESHIRE AND MERSEYSIDE .... p. 29

1188 CHESTER, ELLESMERE PORT AND NESTON L.J.A. – see CHESHIRE AND MERSEYSIDE .... p. 27

1247 HARTLEPOOL L.J.A. – see CLEVELAND, DURHAM AND NORTHUMBRIA ..... p. 32

1248 LANGBAURGH EAST L.J.A. – see CLEVELAND, DURHAM AND NORTHUMBRIA .... p. 32

1249 TEESSIDE L.J.A. – see CLEVELAND, DURHAM AND NORTHUMBRIA .... p. 36

1260 BODMIN AND TRIGG DIVISION – combined with 1269 LESNEWTH DIVISION, 1273 POWDER TYWARDREATH DIVISION and 1278 WADEBRIDGE DIVISION to form **1279 BODMIN DIVISION**

1261 DUNHEVED DIVISION – combined with 1276 STRATTON DIVISION to form **1284 DUNHEVED AND STRATTON DIVISION**

1262 EAST MIDDLE DIVISION – combined with 1265 EAST SOUTH DIVISION and 1270 LISKERRETT DIVISION to form **1280 SOUTH EAST CORNWALL DIVISION**

1263 EAST PENWITH P.S.A. –combined with 1268 ISLES OF SCILLY P.S.A., PENWITH P.S.A., FALMOUTH AND KERRIER P.S.A., 1282 TRURO AND SOUTH POWDER P.S.A. and the parishes of Cubert and St.Newlyn East in 1274 PYDAR P.S.A. to form **1288 WEST CORNWALL P.S.A.**

1264 EAST POWDER P.S.A. – combined with 1274 PYDAR P.S.A. (except the parishes of Cubert and St.Newlyn East), 1279 BODMIN P.S.A., 1284 DUNHEVED AND STRATTON., and 1280 SOUTH EAST CORNWALL to form **1289 EAST CORNWALL P.S.A.**

1265 EAST SOUTH DIVISION – combined with 1262 EAST MIDDLE DIVISION and 1270 LISKERRETT DIVISION to form **1280 SOUTH EAST CORNWALL DIVISION**

1266 FALMOUTH DIVISION – combined with 1271 PENRYN DIVISION to form **1281 FALMOUTH-PENRYN DIVISION**

1267 HELSTON AND KERRIER DIVISION – combined with 1281 FALMOUTH-PENRYN DIVISION to form **1283 FALMOUTH AND KERRIER DIVISION**

1268 ISLES OF SCILLY P.S.A. – combined with 1272 PENWITH P.S.A., 1283 FALMOUTH AND KERRIER P.S.A., 1282 TRURO AND SOUTH POWDER P.S.A., and the Parishes of Cuber and St.Newlyn East in 1274 PYDAR P.S.A. to form **1288 WEST CORNWALL P.S.A.**

ENGLAND

1269 **LESNEWTH DIVISION** – combined with 1260 BODMIN AND TRIGG DIVISION, 1273 POWDER TYWARDREATH DIVISION and 1278 WADEBRIDGE DIVISION to form **1279 BODMIN DIVISION**

1270 **LISKERRETT DIVISION** – combined with 1262 EAST MIDDLE DIVISION and 1265 EAST SOUTH DIVISION to form **1280 EAST CORNWALL DIVISION**

1271 **PENRYN DIVISION** – combined with 1266 FALMOUTH DIVISION to form **1281 FALMOUTH-PENRYN DIVISION**

1272 **PENWITH P.S.A.** – combined with 1268 ISLES OF SCILLY P.S.A., 1263 EAST PENWITH P.S.A., 1283 FALMOUTH AND KERRIER P.S.A., 1282 TRURO AND SOUTH POWDER P.S.A. and the Parishes of Cubert and St.Newlyn East in 1274 PYDAR P.S.A. to form **1288 WEST CORNWALL DIVISION**

1273 **POWDER TYWARDREATH DIVISION** – combined with 1260 BODMIN AND TRIGG DIVISION, 1269 LESNEWTH DIVISION and 1278 WADEBRIDGE DIVISION to form **1279 BODMIN DIVISION**

1274 **PYDAR P.S.A.** – Parishes of Cubert and St.Newlyn East combined with 1268 ISLES OF SCILLY P.S.A., 1272 PENWITH P.S.A., 1263 EAST PENWITH P.S.A., 1283 FALMOUTH AND KERRIER P.S.A. and 1282 TRURO AND SOUTH POWDER P.S.A. to form **1288 WEST CORNWALL P.S.A.** Remainder combined with 1279 BODMIN P.S.A., 1264 EAST POWDER P.S.A. 1284 DUNHEVED AND STRATTON P.S.A., and 1280 SOUTH EAST CORNWALL P.S.A. to form **1289 EAST CORNWALL P.S.A.**

1275 **SOUTH POWDER DIVISION** – combined with 1277 TRURO AND WEST POWDER DIVISION to form **1282 TRURO AND SOUTH POWDER DIVISION**

1276 **STRATTON DIVISION** – combined with 1261 DUNHEVED DIVISION to form **1284 DUNHEVED AND STRATTON DIVISION**

1277 **TRURO AND WEST POWDER DIVISION** – combined with 1275 SOUTH POWDER DIVISION to form **1282 TRURO AND SOUTH POWDER DIVISION**

1278 **WADEBRIDGE DIVISION** – combined with 1260 BODMIN AND TRIGG DIVISION, 1269 LESNEWTH DIVISION and 1273 POWDER TYWARDREATH DIVISION to form **1279 BODMIN DIVISION**

1279 **BODMIN P.S.A.** – combined with 1274 PYDAR P.S.A. (except the parishes of Cubert and St.Newlyn East) 1264 EAST POWDER P.S.A., 1284 DUNHEVED AND STRATTON P.S.A. and 1280 SOUTH EAST CORNWALL to form **1289 EAST CORNWALL**

1280 **SOUTH EAST CORNWALL P.S.A.** – combined with 1274 PYDAR P.S.A. (except the parishes of Cubert and St.Newlyn East), 1279 BODMIN P.S.A., 1264 EAST POWDER P.S.A. and 1284 DUNHEVED AND STRATTON P.S.A. to form **1289 EAST CORNWALL P.S.A.**

1281 **FALMOUTH-PENRYN DIVISION** – combined with 1267 HELSTON AND KERRIER DIVISION to form **1283 FALMOUTH AND KERRIER DIVISION**

1282 **TRURO AND SOUTH POWDER P.S.A.** – combined with 1268 ISLES OF SCILLY P.S.A., 1272 PENWITH P.S.A., 1263 EAST PENWITH P.S.A., 1283 FALMOUTH AND KERRIER P.S.A. and the Parishes of Cubert and St.Newlyn East in 1274 PYDAR P.S.A. to form **1288 WEST CORNWALL P.S.A.**

1283 **FALMOUTH AND KERRIER P.S.A.** – combined with 1268 ISLES OF SCILLY P.S.A., 1272 PENWITH P.S.A., 1263 EAST PENWITH P.S.A., 1282 TRURO AND SOUTH POWDER P.S.A. and the Parishes of Cuber and St.Newlyn East in 1274 PYDAR P.S.A. to form **1288 WEST CORNWALL P.S.A.**

1284 **DUNHEVED AND STRATTON P.S.A.** – combined with 1274 PYDAR P.S.A. (except the parishes of Cubert and St.Newlyn East) 1279 BODMIN P.S.A., 1263 EAST POWDER P.S.A. and 1280 SOUTH EAST CORNWALL P.S.A. to form **1289 EAST CORNWALL P.S.A.**

ENGLAND

1288	WEST CORNWALL L.J.A. – see **DEVON AND CORNWALL**	p. 47
1289	EAST CORNWALL L.J.A. – see **DEVON AND CORNWALL**	p. 45
1290	PLYMOUTH DISTRICT L.J.A. – see **DEVON AND CORNWALL**	p. 46
1291	NORTH DEVON L.J.A. – see **DEVON AND CORNWALL**	p. 46
1292	CENTRAL DEVON L.J.A. – see **DEVON AND CORNWALL**	p. 45
1293	SOUTH DEVON L.J.A. – see **DEVON AND CORNWALL**	p. 46
1322	CARLISLE AND DISTRICT L.J.A. – see **CUMBRIA AND LANCASHIRE**	p. 38
1323	SOUTH LAKELAND L.J.A. – see **CUMBRIA AND LANCASHIRE**	p. 40
1324	EDEN L.J.A. – see **CUMBRIA AND LANCASHIRE**	p. 38
1325	WEST ALLERDALE AND KESWICK L.J.A. – see **CUMBRIA AND LANCASHIRE**	p. 41
1360	**ALSTON DIVISION** – combined with 1373 PENRITH DIVISION to form **1378 PENRITH AND ALSTON DIVISION**	
1361	**AMBLESIDE AND WINDERMERE DIVISION** – combined with 1367 HAWKSHEAD DIVISION to form **1381 SOUTH LAKES DIVISION**	
1362	**BARROW-IN-FURNESS DIVISION** – combined with 1363 BOOTLE DIVISION to form **1380 BARROW WITH BOOTLE DIVISION**	
1363	**BOOTLE DIVISION** – combined with 1362 BARROW-IN-FURNESS DIVISION to form **1380 BARROW WITH BOOTLE DIVISION**	
1364	**CARLISLE P.S.A.** – combined with 1376 WIGTON P.S.A. to form **1322 CARLISLE AND DISTRICT P.S.A.**	
1365	**COCKERMOUTH DIVISION** – combined with 1371 MARYPORT DIVISION and 1377 WORKINGTON DIVISION to form **1379 WEST ALLERDALE DIVISION**	
1366	**EAST WARD DIVISION** – combined with portions of 1374 WEST WARD DIVISION to form **1383 APPLEBY DIVISION**	
1367	**HAWKSHEAD DIVISION** – combined with 1361 AMBLESIDE AND WINDERMERE DIVISION to form **1381 SOUTH LAKES DIVISION**	
1368	**KENDAL DIVISION** – combined with 1370 LONSDALE WARD DIVISION to form **1382 KENDAL AND LONSDALE DIVISION**	
1369	**KESWICK P.S.A.** – (except for the Parish of Threlkeld) combined with 1379 WEST ALLERDALE P.S.A. to form **1325 WEST ALLERDALE AND KESWICK P.S.A.**	
1370	**LONSDALE WARD DIVISION** – combined with 1368 KENDAL DIVISION to form **1382 KENDAL AND LONSDALE DIVISION**	
1371	**MARYPORT DIVISION** – combined with 1365 COCKERMOUTH DIVISION and 1377 WORKINGTON DIVISION to form **1379 WEST ALLERDALE DIVISION**	
1372	**NORTH LONSDALE DIVISION** – combined with 1380 BARROW WITH BOOTLE DIVISION to form **1398 FURNESS AND DISTRICT DIVISION**	
1373	**PENRITH DIVISION** – combined with 1360 ALSTON DIVISION to form **1378 PENRITH AND ALSTON DIVISION**	
1374	**WEST WARD DIVISION** abolished – part absorbed into **1383 APPLEBY DIVISION** and remainder into **1384 PENRITH AND ALSTON DIVISION**	
1375	WHITEHAVEN L.J.A. – see **CUMBRIA AND LANCASHIRE**	p. 41
1376	**WIGTON P.S.A.** – combined with 1364 CARLISLE P.S.A. to form **1322 CARLISLE AND DISTRICT P.S.A.**	
1377	**WORKINGTON DIVISION** – combined with 1365 COCKERMOUTH DIVISION and 1371 MARYPORT DIVISION to form **1379 WEST ALLERDALE DIVISION**	

ENGLAND

1378 **PENRITH AND ALSTON DIVISION** – *combined with portions of 1374 WEST WARD DIVISION to form* **1384 PENRITH AND ALSTON DIVISION**

1379 **WEST ALLERDALE P.S.A.** – *combined with 1369 KESWICK P.S.A. (except for the Parish of Threlkeld) to form* **1325 WEST ALLERDALE AND KESWICK P.S.A.**

1380 **BARROW WITH BOOTLE DIVISION** – *combined with portions of 1372 NORTH LONSDLAE DIVISION to form* **1398 FURNESS AND DISTRICT DIVISION**

1381 **SOUTH LAKES P.S.A.** – *combined with 1382 KENDAL AND LONSDALE P.S.A. to form* **1323 SOUTH LAKELAND P.S.A.**

1382 **KENDAL AND LONSDALE P.S.A.** – *combined with 1381 SOUTH LAKES P.S.A. to form* **1323 SOUTH LAKELAND P.S.A.**

1383 **APPLEBY P.S.A.** – *combined with 1384 PENRITH AND ALSTON P.S.A. and the Parish of Threlkeld in 1369 KESWICK P.S.A. to form* **1324 EDEN P.S.A.**

1384 **PENRITH AND ALSTON P.S.A.** – *combined with 1383 APPLEBY P.S.A. and the Parish of Threlkeld in 1369 KESWICK P.S.A. to form* **1324 EDEN P.S.A.**

1385 **NORWICH DIVISION** – *subjected to boundary adjustments and renumbered* **1445 NORWICH DIVISION**

1386 **DOWNHAM MARKET DIVISION** – *combined with 1389 FAKENHAM DIVISION, 1394 HUNSTANTON DIVISION and 1392 KING'S LYNN DIVISION to form (after boundary adjustment)* **1447 WEST NORFOLK DIVISION**

1387 **DISS DIVISION** – *combined with 1396 THETFORD DIVISION to form* **1446 SOUTH NORFOLK DIVISION**

1388 **EAST DEREHAM DIVISION** – *combined with 1395 SWAFFHAM DIVISION and 1390 WYMONDHAM DIVISION to form* **1442 CENTAL NORFOLK DIVISION**

1389 **FAKENHAM DIVISION** – *combined with 1386 DOWNHAM MARKET DIVISION, 1394 HUNSTANTON DIVISION and 1392 KING'S LYNN DIVISION to form (after boundary adjustment)* **1447 WEST NORFOLK DIVISION**

1390 **WYMONDHAM DIVISION** – *combined with 1388 EAST DEREHAM DIVISION and 1395 SWAFFHAM DIVISION to form* **1442 CENTRAL NORFOLK DIVISION**

1391 **GREAT YARMOUTH DIVISION** – *subjected to boundary adjustments and renumbered* **1443 GREAT YARMOUTH DIVISION**

1392 **KING'S LYNN DIVISION** – *combined with 1386 DOWNHAM MARKET DIVISION, 1398 FAKENHAM DIVISION and 1394 HUNSTANTON DIVISION to form (after boundary adjustment)* **1447 WEST NORFOLK DIVISION**

1393 **CROMER DIVISION** – *combined with 1397 NORTH WALSHAM DIVISION to form (after boundary adjustment)* **1444 NORTH NORFOLK DIVISION**

1394 **HUNSTANTON DIVISION** – *combined with 1386 DOWNHAM MARKET DIVISION, 1389 FAKENHAM DIVISION and 1392 KING'S LYNN DIVISION to form (after boundary adjustment)* **1447 WEST NORFOLK DIVISION**

1395 **SWAFFHAM DIVISION** – *combined with 1388 EAST DEREHAM DIVISION and 1390 WYMONDHAM DIVISION to form* **1442 CENTRAL NORFOLK DIVISION**

1396 **THETFORD DIVISION** – *combined with 1387 DISS DIVISION to form* **1446 SOUTH NORFOLK DIVISION**

1397 **NORTH WALSHAM DIVISION** – *combined with 1393 CROMER DIVISION to form (after boundary adjustment)* **1444 NORTH NORFOLK DIVISION**

1398 **FURNESS AND DISTRICT L.J.A.** – *see* **CUMBRIA AND LANCASHIRE** . . . . p. 38

1414 **ALFRETON DIVISION** – *combined with 1417 BELPER DIVISION to form (after boundary adjustments)* **1426 ALFRETON AND BELPER DIVISION**

ENGLAND

1415 **ASHBOURNE DIVISION** – combined with 1416 BAKEWELL DIVISION and 1424 MATLOCK DIVISION to form (after boundary adjustments) **1428 WEST DERBYSHIRE DIVISION**

1416 **BAKEWELL DIVISION** – combined with 1415 ASHBOURNE DIVISION and 1424 MATLOCK DIVISION to form (after boundary adjustments) **1428 WEST DERBYSHIRE DIVISION**

1417 **BELPER DIVISION** – combined with 1414 ALFRETON DIVISION to form (after boundary adjustments) **1426 ALFRETON AND BELPER DIVISION**

1418 **CHESTERFIELD P.S.A.** – combined with Part of 1420 WEST DERBYSHIRE to form **1432 NORTH EAST DERBYSHIRE AND DALES P.S.A.**

1419 **DERBY DIVISION** – combined with 1420 DERBY COUNTY AND APPLETREE DIVISION and 1425 SOUTH DERBYSHIRE DIVISION to form (after boundary adjustments) **1427 DERBY AND SOUTH DERBYSHIRE DIVISION**

1420 **DERBY COUNTY AND APPLETREE DIVISION** – combined with 1419 DERBY DIVISION and 1425 SOUTH DERBYSHIRE DIVISION to form (after boundary adjustments) **1427 DERBY AND SOUTH DERBYSHIRE DIVISION**

1421 **GLOSSOP P.S.A.** – combined with 1422 HIGH PEAK P.S.A. to form **HIGH PEAK P.S.A.**

1422 **HIGH PEAK P.S.A.** – combined with 1421 GLOSSOP P.S.A. to form **HIGH PEAK P.S.A.**

1423 **ILKESTON DIVISION** – combined with 1426 ALFRETON AND BELPER DIVISION to form **1429 EAST DERBYSHIRE DIVISION**

1424 **MATLOCK DIVISION** – combined with 1415 ASHBOURNE DIVISION and 1416 BAKEWELL DIVISION to form (after boundary adjustments) **1428 WEST DERBYSHIRE DIVISION**

1425 **SOUTH DERBYSHIRE DIVISION** – combined with 1419 DERBY DIVISION and 1420 DERBY COUNTY AND APPLETREE DIVISION to form (after boundary adjustments) **1427 DERBY AND SOUTH DERBYSHIRE DIVISION**

1426 **ALFRETON AND BELPER DIVISION** – combined with 1423 ILKESTON DIVISION to form **1429 EAST DERBYSHIRE DIVISION**

1427 **DERBY AND SOUTH DERBYSHIRE P.S.A.** – combined with Part of 1428 WEST DERBYSHIRE P.S.A. to form **1431 DERBY AND SOUTH DERBYSHIRE P.S.A.**

1428 **SOUTHERN DERBYSHIRE L.J.A.** – see **DERBYSHIRE AND NOTTINGHAMSHIRE** .... p. 43

1429 **EAST DERBYSHIRE P.S.A.** combined with 1431 DERBY AND SOUTH DERBYSHIRE P.S.A. to form **1431 SOUTHERN DERBYSHIRE P.S.A.**

1430 **HIGH PEAK L.J.A.** – see **DERBYSHIRE AND NOTTINGHAMSHIRE** .... p. 42

1431 **DERBY AND SOUTH DERBYSHIRE P.S.A.** – combined with 1429 EAST DERBYSHIRE P.S.A. to form **1428 SOUTHERN DERBYSHIRE P.S.A.**

1432 **NORTH EAST DERBYSHIRE AND DALES L.J.A.** – see **DERBYSHIRE AND NOTTINGHAMSHIRE** .... p. 43

1442 **CENTRAL NORFOLK L.J.A.** – see **CAMBRIDGESHIRE, NORFOLK AND SUFFOLK** .... p. 22

1443 **GREAT YARMOUTH L.J.A.** – see **CAMBRIDGESHIRE, NORFOLK AND SUFFOLK** .... p. 23

1444 **NORTH NORFOLK L.J.A.** – see **CAMBRIDGESHIRE, NORFOLK AND SUFFOLK** .... p. 24

1445 **NORWICH L.J.A.** – see **CAMBRIDGESHIRE, NORFOLK AND SUFFOLK** ...... p. 24

ENGLAND

1446	SOUTH NORFOLK L.J.A. – see **CAMBRIDGESHIRE, NORFOLK AND SUFFOLK**	p. 25
1447	WEST NORFOLK L.J.A. – see **CAMBRIDGESHIRE, NORFOLK AND SUFFOLK**	p. 25

1475 **AXMINSTER DIVISION** – *combined with 1481 HONITON DIVISION to form* **1493 AXMINSTER AND HONITON DIVISION**

1476 **BARNSTAPLE DIVISION** – *combined with 1486 SOUTH MOLTON DIVISION to form* **1494 BARNSTAPLE AND SOUTH MOLTON DIVISION**

1477 **BIDEFORD AND GREAT TORRINGTON P.S.A.** – *combined with part of 1495 WEST DEVON P.S.A. and 1494 BARNSTAPLE AND SOUTH MOLTON P.S.A. (except Chawleigh, Eggesford and Thelbridge) to form* **1291 NORTH DEVON P.S.A.**

1478 **CULLOMPTON P.S.A.** – *combined with Chawleigh, Eggesford and Thelbridge in 1494 BARNSTAPLE AND SOUTH MOLTON, Part of 1495 WEST DEVON P.S.A., 1493 AXMINSTER AND HONITON P.S.A., 1478 CULLOMPTON P.S.A., 1489 TIVERTON P.S.A., 1497 EXETER AND WONFORD P.S.A. and 1480 EXMOUTH P.S.A. to form* **1292 CENTRAL DEVON P.S.A.**

1479 **EXETER DIVISION** – *combined with 1492 WONFORD DIVISION to form* **1497 EXETER AND WONFORD DIVISION**

1480 **EXMOUTH P.S.A.** – *combined with Chawleigh, Eggesford and Thelbridge in 1494 BARNSTAPLE AND SOUTH MOLTON P.S.A., Part of 1495 WEST DEVON P.S.A., 1493 AXMINSTER AND HONITON P.S.A., 1478 CULLOMPTON P.S.A., 1489 TIVERTON P.S.A., and 1497 EXETER AND WONFORD P.S.A. to form* **1292 CENTRAL DEVON P.S.A.**

1481 **HONITON DIVISION** – *combined with 1475 AXMINSTER DIVISION to form* **1493 AXMINSTER AND HONITON DIVISION**

1482 **KINGSBRIDGE DIVISION** – *combined with 1485 PLYMPTON DIVISION and 1491 TOTNES DIVISION to form* **1496 SOUTH HAMS DIVISION**

1483 **OKEHAMPTON DIVISION** – *combined with 1487 TAVISTOCK DIVISION to form* **1495 WEST DEVON DIVISION**

1484 **PLYMOUTH P.S.A.** – *combined with part of 1495 WEST DEVON P.S.A. to form* **1290 PLYMOUTH DISTRICT P.S.A.**

1485 **PLYMPTON DIVISION** – *combined with 1482 KINGSBRIDGE DIVISION and 1491 TOTNES DIVISION to form* **1496 SOUTH HAMS DIVISION**

1486 **SOUTH MOLTON DIVISION** – *combined with 1476 BARNSTAPLE DIVISION to form* **1494 BARNSTAPLE AND SOUTH MOLTON DIVISION**

1487 **TAVISTOCK DIVISION** – *combined with 1476 OKEHAMPTON DIVISION to form* **1495 WEST DEVON DIVISION**

1488 **TEIGNBRIDGE P.S.A.** – *combined with 1496 SOUTH HAMS P.S.A. and 1490 TORBAY P.S.A. to form* **1293 SOUTH DEVON P.S.A.**

1489 **TIVERTON P.S.A.** – *combined with Chawleigh, Eggesford and Thelbridge in 1494 BARNSTAPLE AND SOUTH MOLTON P.S.A., Part of 1495 WEST DEVON P.S.A. 1493 AXMINSTER AND HONITON P.S.A., 1478 CULLOMPTON P.S.A., 1497 EXETER AND WOMFORD P.S.A. and 1480 EXMOUTH P.S.A. to form* **1292 CENTRAL DEVON P.S.A.**

1490 **TORBAY P.S.A.** – *combined with 1488 TEIGNBRIDGE P.S.A. and 1496 SOUTH HANTS P.S.A. to form* **1293 SOUTH DEVON P.S.A.**

1491 **TOTNES DIVISION** – *combined with 1482 KINGSBRIDGE DIVISION and 1485 PLYMPTON DIVISION to form* **1496 SOUTH HAMS DIVISION**

1492 **WONFORD DIVISION** – *combined with 1479 EXETER DIVISION to form* **1497 EXETER AND WONFORD DIVISION**

ENGLAND

1493 **AXMINSTER AND HONITON P.S.A.** – *combined with Chwleigh, Eggesford and Thelbridge in 1494 BARNSTAPLE AND SOUTH MOLTON P.S.A., Part of 1495 WEST DEVON P.S.A., 1478 CULLOMPTON P.S.A., 1489 TIVERTON P.S.A., 1497 EXETER AND WONFORD P.S.A. to form* **1292 CENTRAL DEVON P.S.A.**

1494 **BARNSTAPLE AND SOUTH MOLTON P.S.A.** (except Chawleigh, Eggesford and Thelbridge) *combined with 1477 BIDEFORD AND GREAT TORRINGTON P.S.A. and Part of 1495 WEST DEVON P.S.A. to form* **1291 NORTH DEVON P.S.A.**Chawleigh, Eggesford and Thelbridge *combined with part of 1495 WEST DEVON P.S.A. and 1493 AXMINSTER AND HONNINGTON P.S.A., 1478 CULLOMPTON P.S.A., 1489 TIVERTON P.S.A., 1497 EXETER AND WONFORD P.S.A. and 1480 EXMOUTH P.S.A. to form* **1292 CENTRAL DEVON P.S.A.**

1495 **WEST DEVON P.S.A.** – *Part combined with 1484 PLYMOUTH P.S.A. to form* **1290 PLYMOUTH P.S.A.** *Part combined with 1477 BIDEFORD AND GREAT TORRINGTON P.S.A. and 1494 BARNSTAPLE AND SOUTH MOLTON P.S.A. (except Chawleigh, Eggesford and Thelbridge) to form* **1291 NORTH DEVON P.S.A.**, *and remaining part combined with Chawleigh, Eggesford and Thelbridgein 1494 BARNSTAPLE AND SOUTH MOLTON P.S.A. together with 1493 AXMINSTER AND HONITON P.S.A., 1478 CULLOMPTON P.S.A., 1489 TIVERTON P.S.A., 1479 EXETER AND WONFORD P.S.A. and* **1480 EXMOUTH P.S.A.** *to form* **1292 CENTRAL DEVON**

1496 **SOUTH HAMS P.S.A.** – *combined with 1488 TEIGNBRIDGE P.S.A. and 1490 TORBAY P.S.A. to form* **1293 SOUTH DEVON P.S.A.**

1497 **EXETER AND WONFORD P.S.A.** – *combined with Chawleigh, Eggesford and Thelbridge in 1494 BARNSTAPLE AND SOUTH MOLTON P.S.A., Part of 1495 WEST DEVON P.S.A., 1493 AXMINSTER AND HONITON P.S.A., 1478 CULLOMPTON P.S.A., 1489 TIVERTON P.S.A., 1497 EXETER AND WONFORD P.S.A. and EXMOUTH P.S.A. to form* **1292 CENTRAL DEVON P.S.A.**

1500 **BLANDFORD DIVISION** – *combined with 1508 STURMINSTER DIVISION to form (after boundary adjustments)* **1512 BLANDFORD AND STURMINSTER DIVISION**

1501 **BOURNEMOUTH DIVISION** – *combined with 1503 CHRISTCHURCH DIVISION to form* **1514 BOURNEMOUTH AND CHRISTCHURCH DIVISION**

1502 **BRIDPORT DIVISION** – *combined with 1504 DORCHESTER DIVISION and 1507 SHERBORNE DIVISION to form* **1516 WEST DORSET DIVISION**

1503 **CHRISTCHURCH DIVISION** – *combined with 1501 BOURNEMOUTH DIVISION to form* **1514 BOURNEMOUTH AND CHRISTCHURCH DIVISION**

1504 **DORCHESTER DIVISION** – *combined with 1502 BRIDPORT DIVISION and 1507 SHERBORNE DIVISION to form* **1516 WEST DORSET DIVISION**

1505 **POOLE P.S.A.** – *combined with 1514 BOURNEMOUTH AND CHRISTCHURCH P.S.A. and 1515 CENTRAL DORSET P.S.A. (except for the area of the North Dorset District Council) to form* **1522 EAST DORSET P.S.A.**

1506 **SHAFTESBURY DIVISION** – *combined with 1508 STURMINSTER DIVISION to form* **1513 SHAFTESBURY DIVISION**

1507 **SHERBORNE DIVISION** – *combined with 1502 BRIDPORT DIVISION and 1504 DORCHESTER DIVISION to form* **1516 WEST DORSET DIVISION**

1508 **STURMINSTER DIVISION** – *abolished* – *majority absorbed into* **1512 BLANDFORD AND STURMINSTER DIVISION** *and remainder into* **1513 SHAFTESBURY DIVISION**

1509 **WAREHAM DIVISION** – *combined with 1512 BLANDFORD AND STURMINSTER DIVISION, 1513 SHAFTESBURY DIVISION and 1511 WIMBORNE DIVISION to form* **1515 CENTRAL DORSET DIVISION**

ENGLAND

1510 **WEYMOUTH AND PORTLAND P.S.A.** – combined with 1516 WEST DORSET DIVISION and the area of the North Dorset District Council within 1515 CENTRAL DORSET P.S.A. to form **1523 WEST DORSET P.S.A.**

1511 **WIMBORNE DIVISION** – combined with 1512 BLANDFORD AND STURMINSTER DIVISION, 1513 SHAFTESBURY DIVISION and 1509 WAREHAM DIVISION to form **1515 CENTRAL DORSET DIVISION**

1512 **BLANDFORD AND STURMINSTER DIVISION** – combined with 1513 SHAFTESBURY DIVISION, 1509 WAREHAM DIVISION and 1511 WIMBORNE DIVISION to form **1515 CENTRAL DORSET DIVISION**

1513 **SHAFTESBURY DIVISION** – combined with 1512 BLANDFORD AND STURMINSTER DIVISION, 1509 WAREHAM DIVISION and 1511 WIMBORNE DIVISION to form **1515 CENTRAL DORSET DIVISION**

1514 **BOURNEMOUTH AND CHRISTCHURCH P.S.A.** – combined with 1505 POOLE P.S.A. and 1515 CENTRAL DORSET P.S.A. (except for the area of North Dorset District Council) to form **1522 EAST DORSET P.S.A.**

1515 **CENTRAL DORSET P.S.A.** – (Except for the area of the North Dorset District Council) combined with 1514 BOURNEMOUTH AND CHRISTCHURCH P.S.A. and 1505 POOLE P.S.A. to form **1522 EAST DORSET P.S.A.** – The area of the North Dorset District Council combined with 1516 WEST DORSET P.S.A. and 1510 WEYMOUTH AND PORTLAND P.S.A. to form **1523 WEST DORSET P.S.A.**

1516 **WEST DORSET P.S.A.** – combined with 1510 WEYMOUTH AND PORTLAND P.S.A. and the area of the North Dorset District Council within 1515 CENTRAL DORSET P.S.A. to form **1523 WEST DORSET P.S.A.**

1522 **EAST DORSET L.J.A.** – see **DORSET, GLOUCESTERSHIRE AND WILTSHIRE** .. p. 48

1523 **WEST DORSET L.J.A.** – see **DORSET, GLOUCESTERSHIRE AND WILTSHIRE** .. p. 50

1576 **CHESTER-LE-STREET P.S.A.** – combined with 1579 DURHAM P.S.A., 1576 DERWENTSIDE P.S.A. and 1580 EASINGTON P.S.A. to form **1583 NORTH DURHAM P.S.A.**

1577 **DARLINGTON P.S.A.** – combined with 1581 SEDGFIELD P.S.A. and 1582 TEESDALE AND WEAR VALLEY to form **1584 SOUTH DURHAM P.S.A.**

1578 **DERWENTSIDE P.S.A.** – combined with 1579 DURHAM P.S.A., 1576 CHESTER-LE-STREET P.S.A. and 1580 EASINGTON P.S.A. to form **1583 NORTH DURHAM P.S.A.**

1579 **DURHAM P.S.A.** – combined with 1578 DERWENTSIDE P.S.A., 1576 CHESTER-LE-STREET P.S.A. and 1580 EASINGTON P.S.A. to form **1583 NORTH DURHAM P.S.A.**

1580 **EASINGTON P.S.A.** – combined with 1579 DURHAM P.S.A., 1578 DERWENTSIDE P.S.A. and 1576 CHESTER-LE-STREET P.S.A. to form **1583 NORTH DURHAM P.S.A.**

1581 **SEDGFIELD P.S.A.** – combined with 1577 DARLINGTON P.S.A. and 1582 TEESDALE AND WEAR VALLEY P.S.A. to form **1584 SOUTH DURHAM P.S.A.**

1582 **TEESDALE AND WEAR VALLEY P.S.A.** – combined with 1581 SEDGFIELD P.S.A. and 1577 DARLINGTON P.S.A. to **form 1584 SOUTH DURHAM P.S.A.**

1583 **NORTH DURHAM L.J.A.** – see **CLEVELAND, DURHAM AND NORTHUMBRIA** .. p. 33

1584 **SOUTH DURHAM L.J.A.** – see **CLEVELAND, DURHAM AND NORTHUMBRIA** .. p. 34

1595 **BATTLE AND RYE DIVISION** – combined with 1596 BEXHILL DIVISION and 1601 HASTINGS DIVISION to form **1606 HASTINGS AND ROTHER DIVISION**

1596 **BEXHILL DIVISION** – combined with 1595 BATTLE AND RYE DIVISION and 1601 HASTINGS DIVISION to form **1606 HASTINGS AND ROTHER DIVISION**

ENGLAND

1597	**BRIGHTON DIVISION** – combined with 1602 HOVE DIVISION to form **1604 BRIGHTON AND HOVE DIVISION**
1598	**CROWBOROUGH DIVISION** – combined with 1603 LEWES DIVISION to form **1607 LEWES AND CROWBOROUGH DIVISION**
1599	**EASTBOURNE DIVISION** – combined with 1600 HAILSHAM DIVISION to form **1605 EASTBOURNE AND HAILSHAM DIVISION**
1600	**HAILSHAM DIVISION** – combined with 1599 EASTBOURNE DIVISION to form **1605 EASTBOURNE AND HAILSHAM DIVISION**
1601	**HASTINGS DIVISION** – combined with 1595 BATTLE AND RYE DIVISION and 1596 BEXHILL DIVISION to form **1606 HASTINGS AND ROTHER DIVISION**
1602	**HOVE DIVISION** – combined with 1597 BRIGHTON DIVISION to form **1604 BRIGHTON AND HOVE DIVISION**
1603	**LEWES DIVISION** – combined with 1596 CROWBOROUGH DIVISION to form **1607 LEWES AND CROWBOROUGH DIVISION**
1604	**BRIGHTON AND HOVE P.S.A.** – combined with 1607 LEWES AND CROWBOROUGH P.S.A. to form **2950 SUSSEX (CENTRAL) P.S.A.**
1605	**EASTBOURNE AND HAILSHAM P.S.A.** – combined with 1606 HASTINGS AND ROTHER P.S.A. to form **2948 SUSSEX (EASTERN) P.S.A.**
1606	**HASTINGS AND ROTHER P.S.A.** – combined with 1605 EASTBOURNE AND HAILSHAM P.S.A. to form **2948 SUSSEX (EASTERN) P.S.A.**
1607	**LEWES AND CROWBOROUGH P.S.A.** – combined with 1604 BRIGHTON AND HOVE P.S.A. to form **2950 SUSSEX (CENTRAL) P.S.A.**
1610	**BASILDON DIVISION** (formerly Billericay Division) – renamed **MID-SOUTH ESSEX DIVISION**
1610	**MID-SOUTH ESSEX L.J.A.** – see **BEDFORDSHIRE, ESSEX AND HERTFORDSHIRE** . . . . p. 10
1611	**BRENTWOOD DIVISION** combined with 1626 THURROCK DIVISION to form **1626 SOUTH-WEST ESSEX DIVISION**
1612	**CHELMSFORD DIVISION** combined with 1630 MALDON AND WITHAM DIVISION and (after boundary adjustment) 1631 BRAINTREE AND HALSTEAD DIVISION to form **1612 MID-NORTH ESSEX DIVISION**
1612	**MID-NORTH ESSEX L.J.A.** – see **BEDFORDSHIRE, ESSEX AND HERTFORDSHIRE** . . . . p. 10
1613	**COLCHESTER DIVISION** – combined with 1620 HARWICH DIVISION, 1625 TENDRING DIVISION and part of 1631 BRAINTREE AND HALSTEAD DIVISION to form **1613 NORTH-EAST ESSEX DIVISION**
1613	**NORTH-EAST ESSEX L.J.A.** – see **BEDFORDSHIRE, ESSEX AND HERTFORDSHIRE** . . . . p. 10
1614	**DENGIE AND MALDON DIVISION** – combined with 1627 WITHAM DIVISION to form **1630 MALDON AND WITHAM DIVISION**
1615	**DUNMOW DIVISION** – combined with 1623 SAFFRON WALDEN DIVISION to form **1632 DUNMOW AND SAFFRON WALDEN DIVISION**
1616	**EPPING AND ONGAR DIVISION** – combined with 1632 DUNMOW AND SAFFRON WALDEN DIVISION and 1619 HARLOW DIVISION to form **1619 NORTH-WEST ESSEX DIVISION**
1617	**FRESHWELL AND SOUTH HINCKFORD DIVISION** – combined with 1628 HALSTEAD AND HEDINGHAM DIVISION to form **1631 BRAINTREE AND HALSTEAD DIVISION**

ENGLAND

1618	**HALSTEAD DIVISION** – combined with 1621 NORTH HINCKFORD DIVISION to form **1628 HALSTEAD AND HEDINGHAM DIVISION**
1619	**HARLOW DIVISION** – combined with 1616 EPPING AND ONGAR DIVISION and 1632 DUNMOW AND SAFFRON WALDEN DIVISION to form **1619 NORTH-WEST ESSEX DIVISION**
1619	**NORTH-WEST ESSEX L.J.A.** – see **BEDFORDSHIRE, ESSEX AND HERTFORDSHIRE** .... p. 11
1620	**HARWICH DIVISION** – combined with 1613 COLCHESTER DIVISION, 1625 TENDRING DIVISION and part of 1631 BRAINTREE AND HALSTEAD DIVISION to form **1613 NORTH-EAST ESSEX DIVISION**
1621	**NORTH HINCKFORD DIVISION** – combined with 1618 HALSTEAD DIVISION to form **1628 HALSTEAD AND HEDINGHAM DIVISION**
1622	**ROCHFORD DIVISION** – combined with 1624 SOUTHEND-ON-SEA DIVISION to form **1629 ROCHFORD AND SOUTHEND-ON-SEA DIVISION**
1623	**SAFFRON WALDEN DIVISION** – combined with 1615 DUNMOW DIVISION to form **1632 DUNMOW AND SAFFRON WALDEN DIVISION**
1624	**SOUTHEND-ON-SEA DIVISION** – combined with 1622 ROCHFORD DIVISION to form **1629 ROCHFORD AND SOUTHEND-ON-SEA DIVISION**
1625	**TENDRING DIVISION** – combined with 1613 COLCHESTER DIVISION, 1620 HARWICH DIVISION and part of BRAINTREE AND HALSTEAD DIVISION to form **1613 NORTH-EAST ESSEX DIVISION**
1626	**THURROCK DIVISION** – combined with 1611 BRENTWOOD DIVISION to form **1626 SOUTH-WEST ESSEX DIVISION**
1626	**SOUTH-WEST ESSEX L.J.A.** – see **BEDFORDSHIRE, ESSEX AND HERTFORDSHIRE** .... p. 12
1627	**WITHAM DIVISION** – combined with DENGIE AND MALDON DIVISION to form **1630 MALDON AND WITHAM DIVISION**
1628	**HALSTEAD AND HEDINGHAM DIVISION** – combined with 1617 FRESHWELL AND SOUTH HINCKFORD DIVISION to form **1631 BRAINTREE AND HALSTEAD DIVISION**
1629	**ROCHFORD AND SOUTHEND-ON-SEA DIVISION** renamed **SOUTH-EAST ESSEX DIVISION**
1629	**SOUTH-EAST ESSEX L.J.A.** – see **BEDFORDSHIRE, ESSEX AND HERTFORDSHIRE** .... p. 12
1630	**MALDON AND WITHAM DIVISION** combined with 1612 CHELMSFORD DIVISION and (after boundary adjustment) 1631 BRAINTREE AND HALSTEAD DIVISION to form **1612 MID-NORTH ESSEX DIVISION**
1631	**BRAINTREE AND HALSTEAD DIVISION** – combined (after boundary adjustment) with 1612 CHELMSFORD DIVISION AND 1630 MALDON AND WITHAM DIVISION to form **1612 MID-NORTH ESSEX DIVISION**
1632	**DUNMOW AND SAFFRON WALDEN DIVISION** – combined with 1616 EPPING AND ONGAR DIVISION and 1619 HARLOW DIVISION to form **1619 NORTH-WEST ESSEX DIVISION**
1670	**BERKELEY DIVISION** – combined with 1675 DURSLEY DIVISION to form **1691 BERKELEY AND DURSLEY DIVISION**
1671	**CAMPDEN DIVISION** – combined with 1682 NORTHLEACH DIVISION, 1983 STOW-ON-THE-WOLD DIVISION and 1688 WINCHCOMBE DIVISION to form **1694 NORTH COTSWOLD DIVISION**

ENGLAND

1672 **CHELTENHAM DIVISION** – combined with 1694 NORTH COTSWOLD DIVISION and 1686 TEWKSBURY DIVISION to form **1696 NORTH GLOUCESTERSHIRE DIVISION**

1673 **CIRENCESTER DIVISION** – combined with 1676 FAIRFORD DIVISION and 1685 TETBURY DIVISION to form **1689 CIRENCESTER, FAIRFORD AND TETBURY DIVISION**

1674 **COLEFORD DIVISION** – combined with 1679 LYDNEY DIVISION and 1681 NEWNHAM DIVISION to form **1695 FOREST OF DEAN DIVISION**

1675 **DURSLEY DIVISION** – combined with 1670 BERKELEY DIVISION to form **1691 BERKELEY AND DURSLEY DIVISION**

1676 **FAIRFORD DIVISION** – combined with 1673 CIRENCESTER DIVISION and 1685 TETBURY DIVISION to form **1689 CIRENCESTER, FAIRFORD AND TETBURY DIVISION**

1677 **GLOUCESTER (CITY) DIVISION** – combined with 1690 GLOUCESTER COUNTY DIVISION to form **1692 GLOUCESTER DIVISION**

1678 **GLOUCESTER (COUNTY) DIVISION** – combined with 1680 NEWENT DIVISION to form **1690 GLOUCESTER COUNTY DIVISION**

1679 **LYDNEY DIVISION** – combined with 1674 COLEFORD DIVISION and 1681 NEWNHAM DIVISION to form **1695 FOREST OF DEAN DIVISION**

1680 **NEWENT DIVISION** – combined with 1678 GLOUCESTER (COUNTY) DIVISION to form **1690 GLOUCESTER COUNTY DIVISION**

1681 **NEWNHAM DIVISION** – combined with 1674 COLEFORD DIVISION and 1679 LYDNEY DIVISION to form **1695 FOREST OF DEAN DIVISION**

1682 **NORTHLEACH DIVISION** – combined with 1671 CAMPDEN DIVISION, 1683 STOW-ON-THE-WOLD DIVISION and 1688 WINCHCOMBE DIVISION to form **1694 NORTH COTSWOLD DIVISION**

1683 **STOW-ON-THE-WOLD DIVISION** – combined with 1671 CAMPDEN DIVISION, 1682 NORTHLEACH DIVISION and 1688 WINCHCOMBE DIVISION to form **1694 NORTH COTSWOLD DIVISION**

1684 **STROUD DIVISION** – combined with 1691 BERKELEY AND DURSLEY DIVISION and 1687 WHITMINSTER DIVISION to form **1693 SOUTH GLOUCESTERSHIRE DIVISION**

1685 **TETBURY DIVISION** – combined with 1673 CIRENCESTER DIVISION and 1676 FAIRFORD DIVISION to form **1689 CIRENCESTER, FAIRFORD AND TETBURY DIVISION**

1686 **TEWKSBURY DIVISION** – combined with 1672 CHELTENHAM DIVISION and 1694 NORTH COTSWOLD DIVISION to form **1696 NORTH GLOUCESTERSHIRE DIVISION**

1687 **WHITMINSTER DIVISION** – combined with 1691 BERKELEY AND DURSLEY DIVISION and 1684 STROUD DIVISION to form **1693 SOUTH GLOUCESTERSHIRE DIVISION**

1688 **WINCHCOMBE DIVISION** – combined with 1671 CAMPDEN DIVISION, 1682 NORTHLEACH DIVISION and 1683 STOW-ON-THE-WOLD DIVISION to form **1694 NORTH COTSWOLD DIVISION**

1689 **CIRENCESTER, FAIRFORD AND TETBURY P.S.A.** – renamed and renumbered **1698 CIRENCESTER L.J.A.**

1690 **GLOUCESTER COUNTY DIVISION** – combined with 1677 GLOUCESTER (CITY) DIVISION to form **1692 GLOUCESTER DIVISION**

ENGLAND

1691	BERKELEY AND DURSLEY DIVISION – *combined with 1684 STROUD DIVISION and 1687 WHITMINSTER DIVISION to form* **1693 SOUTH GLOUCESTERSHIRE DIVISION**	
1692	GLOUCESTER P.S.A. – *renamed and renumbered* **1698 GLOUCESTERSHIRE L.J.A.**	
1693	SOUTH GLOUCESTERSHIRE P.S.A. – *renamed and renumbered* **1698 STROUD L.J.A.**	
1694	NORTH COTSWOLD DIVISION – *combined with 1672 CHELTENHAM DIVISION and 1686 TEWKSBURY DIVISION to form* **1696 NORTH GLOUCESTERSHIRE DIVISION**	
1695	FOREST OF DEAN P.S.A. – *renamed and renumbered* **1698 CIRENCESTER L.J.A.**	
1696	NORTH GLOUCESTERSHIRE P.S.A. – *renamed and renumbered* **1698 GLOUCESTERSHIRE L.J.A.**	
1698	GLOUCESTERSHIRE L.J.A. – *see* **DORSET, GLOUCESTERSHIRE AND WILTSHIRE**	p. 49
1731	BOLTON L.J.A. – *see* **GREATER MANCHESTER**	p. 51
1732	BURY L.J.A. – *see* **GREATER MANCHESTER**	p. 51
1733	MANCHESTER CITY L.J.A. – *see* **GREATER MANCHESTER**	p. 52
1734	OLDHAM L.J.A. – *see* **GREATER MANCHESTER**	p. 52
1735	MIDDLETON AND HEYWOOD DIVISION – *combined with 1736 ROCHDALE DIVISION to form* **1750 ROCHDALE, MIDDLETON AND HEYWOOD DIVISION**	
1736	ROCHDALE DIVISION – *combined with 1735 MIDDLETON AND HEYWOOD DIVISION to form* **1750 ROCHDALE, MIDDLETON AND HEYWOOD DIVISION**	
1737	ECCLES DIVISION – *combined with 1738 SALFORD DIVISION to form* **1747 CITY OF SALFORD DIVISION**	
1738	SALFORD DIVISION – *combined with 1737 ECCLES DIVISION to form* **1747 CITY OF SALFORD DIVISION**	
1739	STOCKPORT L.J.A. – *see* **GREATER MANCHESTER**	p. 52
1740	ASHTON-UNDER-LYNE DIVISION – *combined with 1741 SOUTH TAMESIDE DIVISION to form* **1748 TAMESIDE DIVISION**	
1741	SOUTH TAMESIDE DIVISION – *combined with 1740 ASHTON-UNDER-LYNE DIVISION to form* **1748 TAMESIDE DIVISION**	
1742	TRAFFORD L.J.A. – *see* **GREATER MANCHESTER**	p. 53
1743	LEIGH P.S.A. – *combined with 1746 WIGAN P.S.A. to form* **1749 WIGAN AND LEIGH P.S.A.**	
1744	MAKERFIELD DIVISION – *combined with 1745 WIGAN DIVISION to form* **1746 WIGAN DIVISION**	
1745	WIGAN DIVISION – *combined with 1744 MAKERFIELD DIVISION to form* **1746 WIGAN DIVISION**	
1746	WIGAN P.S.A. – *combined with 1743 LEIGH P.S.A. to form* **1749 WIGAN AND LEIGH P.S.A.**	
1747	CITY OF SALFORD L.J.A. – *see* **GREATER MANCHESTER**	p. 51
1748	TAMESIDE L.J.A. – *see* **GREATER MANCHESTER**	p. 53
1749	WIGAN AND LEIGH L.J.A. – *see* **GREATER MANCHESTER**	p. 53
1750	ROCHDALE, MIDDLETON AND HEYWOOD L.J.A. – *see* **GREATER MANCHESTER**	p. 52

ENGLAND

1760	**ALTON DIVISION** – *combined with 1771 PETERSFIELD DIVISION to form* **1778 ALTON AND PETERSFIELD DIVISION**	
1761	**ANDOVER DIVISION** – *combined with 1762 BASINGSTOKE DIVISION and 1777 WINCHESTER DIVISION to form* **1781 NORTH WEST HAMPSHIRE DIVISION**	
1762	**BASINGSTOKE DIVISION** – *combined with 1761 ANDOVER DIVISION and 1777 WINCHESTER DIVISION to form* **1781 NORTH WEST HAMPSHIRE DIVISION**	
1763	**DROXFORD DIVISION** – *combined with 1764 EASTLEIGH DIVISION, 1765 FAREHAM DIVISION and 1766 GOSPORT DIVISION to form* **1783 SOUTH HAMPSHIRE DIVISION**	
1764	**EASTLEIGH DIVISION** – *combined with 1763 DROXFORD DIVISION, 1765 FAREHAM DIVISION and 1766 GOSPORT DIVISION to form* **1783 SOUTH HAMPSHIRE DIVISION**	
1765	**FAREHAM DIVISION** – *combined with 1763 DROXFORD DIVISION, 1764 EASTLEIGH DIVISION and 1766 GOSPORT DIVISION to form* **1783 SOUTH HAMPSHIRE DIVISION**	
1766	**GOSPORT DIVISION** – *combined with 1763 DROXFORD DIVISION, 1764 EASTLEIGH DIVISION and 1765 FAREHAM DIVISION to form* **1783 SOUTH HAMPSHIRE DIVISION**	
1767	**HAVANT DIVISION** – *combined with 1772 PORTSMOUTH DIVISION to form* **1782 EAST HAMPSHIRE DIVISION**	
1768	**HYTHE DIVISION** – *combined with 1769 LYMINGTON DIVISION, 1773 RINGWOOD DIVISION, 1774 ROMSEY DIVISION and 1776 TOTTON AND NEW FOREST DIVISION to form* **1779 NEW FOREST DIVISION**	
1769	**LYMINGTON DIVISION** – *combined with 1768 HYTHE DIVISION, 1773 RINGWOOD DIVISION, 1774 ROMSEY DIVISION and 1776 TOTTON AND NEW FOREST DIVISION to form* **1779 NEW FOREST DIVISION**	
1770	**ODIHAM DIVISION** – *combined with 1778 ALTON AND PETERSFIELD DIVISION to form* **1780 NORTH EAST HAMPSHIRE DIVISION**	
1771	**PETERSFIELD DIVISION** – *combined with 1760 ALTON DIVISION to form* **1778 ALTON AND PETERSFIELD DIVISION**	
1772	**PORTSMOUTH DIVISION** – *combined with 1767 HAVANT DIVISION to form* **1782 SOUTH EAST HAMPSHIRE DIVISION**	
1773	**RINGWOOD DIVISION** – *combined with 1768 HYTHE DIVISION, 1769 LYMINGTON DIVISION, 1774 ROMSEY DIVISION and 1776 TOTTON AND NEW FOREST DIVISION to form* **1779 NEW FOREST DIVISION**	
1774	**ROMSEY DIVISION** – *combined with 1768 HYTHE DIVISION, 1769 LYMINGTON DIVISION, 1773 RINGWOOD DIVISION and 1776 TOTTON AND NEW FOREST DIVISION to form* **1779 NEW FOREST DIVISION**	
1775	**SOUTHAMPTON L.J.A.** – *see* **HAMPSHIRE & ISLE OF WIGHT**	p. 56
1776	**TOTTON AND NEW FOREST DIVISION** – *combined with 1768 HYTHE DIVISION, 1769 LYMINGTON DIVISION, 1773 RINGWOOD DIVISION and 1774 ROMSEY DIVISION to form* **1779 NEW FOREST DIVISION**	
1777	**WINCHESTER DIVISION** – *combined with 1761 ANDOVER DIVISION and 1762 BASINGSTOKE DIVISION to form* **1781 NORTH WEST HAMPSHIRE DIVISION**	
1778	**ALTON AND PETERSFIELD DIVISION** – *combined with 1770 ODIHAM DIVISION to form* **1780 NORTH EAST HAMPSHIRE DIVISION**	
1779	**NEW FOREST L.J.A.** – *see* **HAMPSHIRE & ISLE OF WIGHT**	p. 54
1780	**NORTH EAST HAMPSHIRE L.J.A.** – *see* **HAMPSHIRE & ISLE OF WIGHT**	p. 55
1781	**NORTH WEST HAMPSHIRE L.J.A.** – *see* **HAMPSHIRE & ISLE OF WIGHT**	p. 55

ENGLAND

1782	SOUTH EAST HAMPSHIRE L.J.A. – see **HAMPSHIRE & ISLE OF WIGHT**	p. 55
1783	SOUTH HAMPSHIRE L.J.A. – see **HAMPSHIRE & ISLE OF WIGHT**	p. 56
1837	HAVERING MAGISTRATES' COURT – see **GREATER LONDON**	p. 81
1840	BROMSGROVE AND REDDITCH L.J.A. – see **BLACK COUNTRY, STAFFORDSHIRE AND WEST MERCIA**	p. 16
1841	HEREFORDSHIRE L.J.A. – see **BLACK COUNTRY, STAFFORDSHIRE AND WEST MERCIA**	p. 17
1842	SEVERNMINSTER P.S.A. – *renamed* 1842 **KIDDERMINSTER P.S.A.**	
1842	KIDDERMINSTER L.J.A. – see **BLACK COUNTRY, STAFFORDSHIRE AND WEST MERCIA**	p. 17
1843	SOUTH WORCESTERSHIRE L.J.A. – see **BLACK COUNTRY, STAFFORDSHIRE AND WEST MERCIA**	p. 19
1845	BEWDLEY BOROUGH DIVISION – combined with 1862 STOURPORT DIVISION to form (after boundary adjustment) 1871 **BEWDLEY AND STOURPORT DIVISION**	
1846	BROMSGROVE DIVISION – (after boundary adjustment) combined with 1860 REDDITCH DIVISION to form 1840 **BROMSGROVE AND REDDITCH DIVISION**	
1847	BROMYARD DIVISION – abolished wef 1/1/88: Majority absorbed into 1868 NORTH HEREFORDSHIRE DIVISION and remainder into 1869 **SOUTH HEREFORDSHIRE DIVISION**	
1848	DORE AND BREDWARDINE DIVISION – abolished wef 1/1/88 and absorbed into 1869 SOUTH HEREFORDSHIRE DIVISION	
1849	DROITWICH DIVISION – combined with 1853 HUNDRED HOUSE DIVISION and 1866 WORCESTER (COUNTY) DIVISION to form (after boundary adjustment) 1872 **MID-WORCESTER DIVISION**	
1850	EVESHAM DIVISION – combined with 1859 PERSHORE DIVISION to form (after boundary adjustment) 1873 **VALE OF EVESHAM DIVISION**	
1851	CITY OF HEREFORD DIVISION – combined with 1868 NORTH HEREFORDSHIRE DIVISION and 1869 SOUTH HEREFORDSHIRE DIVISION to form 1841 **HEREFORDSHIRE DIVISION**	
1852	HEREFORD (COUNTY) DIVISION – abolished wef 1/1/88. Majority absorbed into 1869 SOUTH HEREFORDSHIRE DIVISION and remainder into 1868 **NORTH HEREFORDSHIRE DIVISION**	
1853	HUNDRED HOUSE DIVISION – combined with 1849 DROITWICH DIVISION and 1866 WORCESTER (COUNTY) DIVISION to form (after boundary adjustment) 1872 **MID-WORCESTERSHIRE DIVISION**	
1854	KIDDERMINSTER DIVISION – combined with 1871 BEWDLEY AND STOURPORT DIVISION to form 1842 **SEVERNMINSTER DIVISION**	
1855	KINGTON DIVISION – absorbed into 1868 **NORTH HEREFORDSHIRE DIVISION**	
1856	LEDBURY DIVISION – absorbed into 1869 **SOUTH HEREFORDSHIRE DIVISION**	
1857	LEOMINSTER AND WIGMORE DIVISION – absorbed into 1868 **NORTH HEREFORDSHIRE DIVISION**	
1858	MALVERN DIVISION – combined with 1864 UPTON-ON-SEVERN DISTRICT to form (after boundary adjustment) 1870 **MALVERN HILLS DIVISION**	
1859	PERSHORE DIVISION – combined with 1850 EVESHAM DIVISION to form (after boundary adjustment) 1873 **VALE OF EVESHAM DIVISION**	
1860	REDDITCH DIVISION – combined with 1846 BROMSGROVE DIVISION (after boundary adjustment) to form 1840 **BROMSGROVE AND REDDITCH DIVISION**	

ENGLAND

1861	**ROSS DIVISION** – *absorbed into* **1869 SOUTH HEREFORDSHIRE DIVISION**	
1862	**STOURPORT DIVISION** – *combined with* **1845 BEWDLEY BOROUGH DIVISION** *to form (after boundary adjustment)* **1871 BEWDLEY AND STOURPORT DIVISION**	
1863	**TENBURY DIVISION** – *absorbed into* **1868 NORTH HEREFORDSHIRE DIVISION**	
1864	**UPTON-ON-SEVERN DIVISION** – *combined with* **1858 MALVERN DIVISION** *to form (after boundary adjustment)* **1870 MALVERN HILLS DIVISION**	
1865	**CITY OF WORCESTER DIVISION** – *boundary with* **1866 WORCESTER (COUNTY) DIVISION** *adjusted to form* **1874 CITY OF WORCESTER DIVISION**	
1866	**WORCESTER (COUNTY) DIVISION** – *combined with* **1849 DROITWICH DIVISION** *and* **1853 HUNDRED HOUSE DIVISION** *to form (after boundary adjustment)* **1872 MID-WORCESTERSHIRE DIVISION**	
1867	**WORCESTER (COUNTY) DIVISION (MOTORWAY)** – *abolished*	
1868	**NORTH HEREFORDSHIRE DIVISION** – *combined with* **1851 CITY OF HEREFORD DIVISION** *and* **1869 SOUTH HEREFORDSHIRE DIVISION** *to form* **1841 HEREFORDSHIRE DIVISION**	
1869	**SOUTH HEREFORDSHIRE DIVISION** – *combined with* **1851 CITY OF HEREFORD DIVISION** *and* **1868 HEREFORDSHIRE DIVISION** *to form* **1841 HEREFORDSHIRE DIVISION**	
1870	**MALVERN HILLS DIVISION** – *combined with* **1872 MID-WORCESTERSHIRE DIVISION** *(after boundary adjustment),* **1873 VALE OF EVESHAM DIVISION** *and* **1874 CITY OF WORCESTER DIVISION** *to form* **1843 SOUTH WORCESTERSHIRE DIVISION**	
1871	**BEWDLEY AND STOURPORT DIVISION** – *combined with* **1854 KIDDERMINSTER DIVISION** *to form* **1842 SEVERNMINSTER DIVISION**	
1872	**MID-WORCESTERSHIRE DIVISION** – *(after boundary adjustment) combined with* **1870 MALVERN HILLS DIVISION, 1873 VALE OF EVESHAM DIVISION** *and* **1874 CITY OF WORCESTER DIVISION** *to form* **1843 SOUTH WORCESTERSHIRE DIVISION**	
1873	**VALE OF EVESHAM DIVISION** – *combined with* **1870 MALVERN HILLS DIVISION, 1872 MID-WORCESTERSHIRE DIVISION** *(after boundary adjustment) and* **CITY OF WORCESTER DIVISION** *to form* **1843 SOUTH WORCESTERSHIRE DIVISION**	
1874	**CITY OF WORCESTER DIVISION** – *combined with* **1870 MALVERN HILLS DIVISION, 1872 MID-WORCESTERSHIRE DIVISION** *(after boundary adjustment) and* **1873 VALE OF EVESHAM DIVISION** *to form* **1843 SOUTH WORCESTERSHIRE DIVISION**	
1875	**BISHOP'S STORTFORD DIVISION** *combined with* **1877 CHESHUNT DIVISION** *and* **1888 HERTFORD AND WARE DIVISION** *to form* **1888 EAST HERTFORDSHIRE DIVISION**	
1876	**BUNTINGFORD DIVISION** – *combined with* **1888 HERTFORD AND WARE**	
1877	**CHESHUNT DIVISION** – *combined with* **1875 BISHOP'S STORTFORD DIVISION** *and* **1888 HERTFORD AND WARE DIVISION** *to form* **1888 EAST HERTFORDSHIRE DIVISION**	
1878	**DACORUM P.S.A.** – *combined with* **1886 WATFORD P.S.A.** *to form* **1893 WEST HERTFORDSHIRE P.S.A.**	
1879	**HATFIELD DIVISION** – *combined with* **1887 WELWYN DIVISION** *to form* **1890 MID HERTFORDSHIRE DIVISION**	
1881	**HITCHIN DIVISION** – *combined with* **1882 ODSEY DIVISION** *to form* **1889 NORTH HERTFORDSHIRE DIVISION**	

ENGLAND

1882 **ODSEY DIVISION** – combined with HITCHIN DIVISION to form **1889 NORTH HERTFORDSHIRE DIVISION**

1883 **ST. ALBANS P.S.A.** –combined with 1890 MID HERTFORDSHIRE P.S.A. to form **1892 CENTRAL HERTFORDSHIRE P.S.A.**

1884 **SOUTH MIMMS DIVISION** – abolished wef 3/9/93 and absorbed into **1877 CHESHUNT DIVISION and 1886 WATFORD DIVISION**

1885 **STEVENAGE DIVISION** – combined with 1889 North Hertfordshire Division to form one new division to be known as the **NORTH HERTFORDSHIRE DIVISION**

1886 **WATFORD P.S.A.** – (after boundary adjustment) combined with 1878 DACORUM P.S.A. to form **1893 WEST HERTFORDSHIRE P.S.A.**

1887 **WELWYN DIVISION** – combined with 1879 HATFIELD DIVISION to form **1890 MID HERTFORDSHIRE DIVISION**

1888 **HERTFORD AND WARE DIVISION** – combined with 1875 BISHOP'S STORTFORD DIVISION and 1877 CHESHUNT DIVISION to form **1888 EAST HERTFORDSHIRE DIVISION** (retaining existing Court Code No.)

1888 **EAST HERTFORDSHIRE L.J.A.** – see **BEDFORDSHIRE, ESSEX AND HERTFORDSHIRE** .... p. 9

1889 **NORTH HERTFORDSHIRE L.J.A.** – see **BEDFORDSHIRE, ESSEX AND HERTFORDSHIRE** .... p. 11

1890 **MID HERTFORDSHIRE P.S.A.** – combined with 1883 ST.ALBANS P.S.A. to form **1892 CENTRAL HERTFORDESHIRE P.S.A.**

1892 **CENTRAL HERTFORDSHIRE L.J.A.** – see **BEDFORDSHIRE, ESSEX AND HERTFORDSHIRE** .... p. 8

1893 **WEST HERTFORDSHIRE L.J.A.** – see **BEDFORDSHIRE, ESSEX AND HERTFORDSHIRE** .... p. 12

1901 **SOUTH HUNSLEY BEACON AND HOWDENSHIRE DIVISION** – Part combined with part of 1928 EPWORTH AND GOOLE DIVISION to form **1928 GOOLE AND HOWDENSHIRE DIVISION** and remainder becoming **1901 SOUTH HUNSLEY BEACON DIVISION**

1901 **SOUTH HUNSLEY BEACON P.S.A.** – combined with 1925 BEVERLEY P.S.A., parts of 1905 BAINTON, WILTON AND HOLME BEACON P.S.A. and parts of DICKERING AND NORTH HOLDERNESS P.S.A. to form **1942 BEVERLEY AND THE WOLDS P.S.A.**

1902 **SOUTH AND MIDDLE HOLDERNESS P.S.A.** – combined with 1933 KINGSTON UPON HULL P.S.A. to form **1943 HULL AND HOLDERNESS P.S.A.**

1903 **SCUNTHORPE, BRIGG AND BARTON DIVISION** – combined with part of 1928 EPWORTH AND GOOLE DIVISION to form **1903 NORTH LINCOLNSHIRE DIVISION**

1903 **NORTH LINCOLNSHIRE L.J.A.** – see **HUMBER AND SOUTH YORKSHIRE** .... p. 59

1904 **DICKERING AND NORTH HOLDERNESS P.S.A.** – Part combined with 1901 SOUTH HUNSLEY BEACON, 1925 BEVERLEY P.S.A. and part of 1905 BAINTON, WILTON AND HOLME BEACON P.S.A. to form **1942 BEVERLEY AND THE WOLDS P.S.A.** Remainder combined with remaining part of 1905 BAINTON WILTON AND HOLME P.S.A. to form **1941 BRIDLINGTON P.S.A.**

1905 **BAINTON, WILTON AND HOLME BEACON P.S.A.** – Part combined with 1901 SOUTH HUNSLEY BEACON P.S.A., 1925 BEVERLEY P.S.A. and part of 1904 DICKERING AND NORTH HOLDERNESS P.S.A. to form **1942 BEVERLEY AND THE WOLDS P.S.A.** Remainder combined with the remainder of DICKERING AND NORTH HOLDERNESS to form **1941 BRIDLINGTON P.S.A.**

ENGLAND

1923	**BAINTON BEACON DIVISION** – *combined with 1939 WILTON BEACON DIVISION and 1931 HOLME BEACON DIVISION to form* **1905 BAINTON, WILTON AND HOLME BEACON DIVISION**
1924	**BARTON-UPON-HUMBER DIVISION** – *combined with 1936 SCUNTHORPE DIVISION and 1926 BRIGG DIVISION to form* **1903 SCUNTHORPE, BRIGG AND BARTON DIVISION**
1925	**BEVERLEY P.S.A.** – *combined with 1901 SOUTH HUNSLEY BEACON P.S.A., part of 1905 BAINTON, WILTON AND HOLME BEACON P.S.A. and part of 1904 DICKERING AND NORTH HOLDERNESS P.S.A. to form* **1942 BEVERLEY AND THE WOLDS P.S.A.**
1926	**BRIGG DIVISION** – *combined with 1936 SCUNTHORPE DIVISION and 1924 BARTON-UPON-HUMBER DIVISION to form* **1903 SCUNTHORPE, BRIGG AND BARTON DIVISION**
1927	**DICKERING DIVISION** – *combined with 1935 NORTH HOLDERNESS DIVISION to form* **1904 DICKERING AND NORTH HOLDERNESS DIVISION**
1928	**EPWORTH AND GOOLE DIVISION** – *Part combined with 1903 SCUNTHORPE, BRIGG AND BARTON DIVISION to form* **1903 NORTH LINCOLNSHIRE DIVISION**; *Part combined with part of 1901 SOUTH HUNSLEY BEACON AND HOWDENSHIRE DIVISION to form* **1928 GOOLE AND HOWDENSHIRE DIVISION**
1928	**GOOLE AND HOWDENSHIRE L.J.A.** – *see* **HUMBER AND SOUTH YORKSHIRE** .... p. 58
1929	**GRIMSBY (BOROUGH) DIVISION** – *combined with 1930 CLEETHORPES DIVISION to form* **1940 GRIMSBY AND CLEETHORPES DIVISION**
1930	**GRIMSBY (COUNTY) DIVISION** – *renamed* **CLEETHORPES DIVISION**, *see below*
1930	**CLEETHORPES DIVISION** – *combined with 1929 GRIMSBY (BOROUGH) DIVISION to form* **1940 GRIMSBY AND CLEETHORPES DIVISION**
1931	**HOLME BEACON DIVISION** – *combined with 1923 BAINTON BEACON DIVISION and 1939 WILTON BEACON DIVISION to form* **1905 BAINTON, WILTON AND HOLME BEACON DIVISION**
1932	**HOWDENSHIRE DIVISION** – *combined with 1938 SOUTH HUNSLEY BEACON DIVISION to form* **1901 SOUTH HUNSLEY BEACON AND HOWDENSHIRE DIVISION**
1933	**KINGSTON UPON HULL P.S.A.** – *combined with 1902 SOUTH AND MIDDLE HOLDERNESS P.S.A. to form* **1943 HULL AND HOLDERNESS P.S.A.**
1934	**MIDDLE HOLDERNESS DIVISION** – *combined with 1937 SOUTH HOLDERNESS DIVISION to form* **1902 SOUTH AND MIDDLE HOLDERNESS DIVISION**
1935	**NORTH HOLDERNESS DIVISION** – *combined with 1927 DICKERING DIVISION to form* **1904 DICKERING AND NORTH HOLDERNESS DIVISION**
1936	**SCUNTHORPE DIVISION** – *combined with 1926 BRIGG DIVISION and 1924 BARTON-UPON-HUMBER DIVISION to form* **1903 SCUNTHORPE, BRIGG AND BARTON DIVISION**
1937	**SOUTH HOLDERNESS DIVISION** – *combined with 1934 MIDDLE HOLDERNESS DIVISION to form* **1902 SOUTH AND MIDDLE HOLDERNESS DIVISION**
1938	**SOUTH HUNSLEY BEACON DIVISION** – *combined with 1932 HOWDENSHIRE DIVISION to form* **1901 SOUTH HUNSLEY BEACON AND HOWDENSHIRE DIVISION**
1939	**WILTON BEACON DIVISION** – *combined with 1923 BAINTON BEACON DIVISION and 1931 HOLME BEACON DIVISION to form* **1905 BAINTON, WILTON AND HOLME BEACON DIVISION**

ENGLAND

1940	GRIMSBY AND CLEETHORPES L.J.A. – see HUMBER AND SOUTH YORKSHIRE	p. 58
1941	BRIDLINGTON L.J.A. – see HUMBER AND SOUTH YORKSHIRE	p. 57
1942	BEVERLEY AND THE WOLDS L.J.A. – see HUMBER AND SOUTH YORKSHIRE	p. 57
1943	HULL AND HOLDERNESS L.J.A. – see HUMBER AND SOUTH YORKSHIRE	p. 58
1945	ISLE OF WIGHT L.J.A. – see HAMPSHIRE & ISLE OF WIGHT	p. 54
1952	ASHFORD AND TENTERDEN DIVISION – combined with 1955 DOVER AND EAST KENT DIVISION and 1957 FOLKESTONE AND HYTHE DIVISION to form **1957 CHANNEL DIVISION**	
1953	CANTERBURY L.J.A. – combined with 1957 CHANNEL L.J.A. and 1968 THANET L.J.A. to form **1957 EAST KENT L.J.A.**	
1954	DARTFORD DIVISION – part combined with 1963 SEVENOAKS DIVISION, 1966 TUNBRIDGE WELLS AND CRANBROOK DIVISION and 1965 TONBRIDGE AND MALLING DIVISION (Part) to form **1963 WEST KENT DIVISION** – balance remains under existing Court Code of 1954	
1954	DARTFORD DIVISION – combined with 1958 GRAVESHAM DIVISION to form **1969 DARTFORD AND GRAVESHAM DIVISION**	
1955	DOVER AND EAST KENT DIVISION – combined with 1952 ASHFORD AND TENTERDEN DIVISION and 1957 FOLKESTONE AND HYTHE DIVISION to form **1957 CHANNEL DIVISION**	
1956	FAVERSHAM DIVISION – combined with 1964 SITTINGBOURNE DIVISION to form **1967 FAVERSHAM AND SITTINGBOURNE DIVISION**	
1957	FOLKESTONE AND HYTHE DIVISION – combined with 1952 ASHFORD AND TENTERDEN DIVISION and 1955 DOVER AND EAST KENT DIVISION to form **1957 CHANNEL DIVISION**	
1957	CHANNEL L.J.A. – combined with 1953 CANTERBURY L.J.A. and 1968 THANET L.J.A. to form **1957 EAST KENT L.J.A.**	
1957	EAST KENT L.J.A. – see KENT	p. 61
1958	GRAVESHAM DIVISION – combined with 1954 DARTFORD DIVISION to form **1969 DARTFORD AND GRAVESHAM DIVISION**	
1959	MAIDSTONE DIVISION – combined with 1965 TONBRIDGE AND MALLING DIVISION (Part) to form **1959 MID KENT DIVISION**	
1959	MID KENT – abolished and absorbed into **1960 CENTRAL KENT L.J.A.**	
1960	MARGATE DIVISION – combined with 1962 RAMSGATE DIVISION to form **1968 THANET DIVISION**	
1960	CENTRAL KENT L.J.A. – see KENT	p. 60
1961	MEDWAY – combined with 1969 DARTFORD AND GRAVESHAM P.S.A. to form **1966 NORTH KENT L.J.A.**	
1962	RAMSGATE DIVISION – combined with 1962 MARGATE DIVISION to form **1968 THANET DIVISION**	
1963	SEVENOAKS DIVISION – combined with 1965 TONBRIDGE AND MALLING DIVISION (Part), 1966 TUNBRIDGE WELLS AND CRANBROOK DIVISION and 1954 DARTFORD DIVISION (Part) to form **1963 WEST KENT DIVISION**	
1963	WEST KENT – abolished and absorbed into **1960 CENTRAL KENT L.J.A.**	
1964	SITTINGBOURNE DIVISION – combined with 1956 FAVERSHAM DIVISION to form **1967 FAVERSHAM AND SITTINGBOURNE DIVISION**	

ENGLAND

1965	**TONBRIDGE AND MALLING DIVISION** – part combined with 1959 MAIDSTONE DIVISION to form **1959 MID KENT DIVISION**: part combined with 1966 TUNBRIDGE WELLS AND CRANBROOK DIVISION, 1963 SEVENOAKS DIVISION and 1954 DARTFORD DIVISION (Part) to form **1963 WEST KENT DIVISION**
1966	**TUNBRIDGE WELLS AND CRANBROOK DIVISION** – combined with 1963 SEVENOAKS DIVISION, 1965 TONBRIDGE AND MALLING DIVISION (Part) and 1954 DARTFORD DIVISION (Part) to form **1963 WEST KENT DIVISION**
1966	**NORTH KENT L.J.A. (DARTFORD)** – see **KENT** .... p. 61
1966	**NORTH KENT L.J.A. (MEDWAY)** – see **KENT** .... p. 61
1967	**FAVERSHAM AND SITTINGBOURNE** – abolished and absorbed into **1960 CENTRAL KENT L.J.A.**
1968	**THANET L.J.A.** – combined with 1953 CANTERBURY L.J.A. and 1957 CHANNEL L.J.A. to form **1957 EAST KENT L.J.A.**
1969	**DARTFORD AND GRAVESEND P.S.A.** – combined with 1961 MEDWAY P.S.A. to form **1966 NORTH KENT L.J.A.**
1992	**FYLDE COAST L.J.A.** – see **CUMBRIA AND LANCASHIRE** .... p. 39
1994	**ACCRINGTON DIVISION** – combined with 1999 CHURCH DIVISION to form **2010 HYNDBURN DIVISION**
1995	**BLACKBURN DIVISION** – combined with 2000 DARWEN DIVISION and major part of 2008 RIBBLE VALLEY DIVISION to form **2012 BLACKBURN, DARWEN AND RIBBLE VALLEY DIVISION**
1996	**BLACKPOOL DIVISION** – combined with 2001 FYLDE DIVISION to form **1996 BLACKPOOL AND FYLDE DIVISION**
1996	**BLACKPOOL AND FYLDE P.S.A.** – combined with 2009 WYRE P.S.A. to form **1992 FLYDE COAST P.S.A.**
1997	**BURNLEY DIVISION** – combined with 2004 PENDLE DIVISION and part of 2008 RIBBLE VALLEY DIVISION to form **2011 BURNLEY AND PENDLE DIVISION**
1998	**CHORLEY L.J.A.** – see **CUMBRIA AND LANCASHIRE** .... p. 38
1999	**CHURCH DIVISION** – combined with 1994 ACCRINGTON DIVISION to form **2010 HYNDBURN DIVISION**
2000	**DARWEN DIVISION** – combined with 1925 BLACKBURN DIVISION and major part of 2008 RIBBLE VALLEY DIVISION to form **2012 BLACKBURN, DARWEN AND RIBBLE VALLEY DIVISION**
2001	**FYLDE DIVISION** – combined with 1996 BLACKPOOL DIVISION to form **1996 BLACKPOOL AND FYLDE DIVISION**
2002	**LANCASTER L.J.A.** – see **CUMBRIA AND LANCASHIRE** .... p. 39
2003	**ORMSKIRK L.J.A.** – see **CUMBRIA AND LANCASHIRE** .... p. 40
2004	**PENDLE DIVISION** – combined with 1997 BURNLEY DIVISION and part of 2008 RIBBLE VALLEY DIVISION to form **2011 BURNLEY AND PENDLE DIVISION**
2005	**PRESTON L.J.A.** – see **CUMBRIA AND LANCASHIRE** .... p. 40
2006	**ROSSENDALE P.S.A.** – combined with 2011 BURNLEY AND PENDLE P.S.A. to form **2014 BURNLEY, PENDLE AND ROSSENDALE P.S.A.**
2007	**SOUTH RIBBLE L.J.A.** – see **CUMBRIA AND LANCASHIRE** .... p. 40
2008	**RIBBLE VALLEY DIVISION** – abolished and absorbed into **2012 BLACKBURN, DARWEN AND RIBBLE VALLEY DIVISION, 2011 BURNLEY AND PENDLE DIVISION** and **2005 PRESTON DIVISION**

ENGLAND

2009	**WYRE P.S.A.** – *combined with 1996 BLACKPOOL AND FLYDE P.S.A. to form* **1992 FLYDE COAST P.S.A.**	
2010	**HYNDBURN L.J.A.** – *see* **CUMBRIA AND LANCASHIRE**	p. 39
2011	**BURNLEY AND PENDLE P.S.A.** – *combined with 2006 ROSSENDALE P.S.A. to form* **2014 BURNLEY, PENDLE AND ROSSENDALE P.S.A.**	
2012	**BLACKBURN, DARWEN AND RIBBLE VALLEY L.J.A.** – *see* **CUMBRIA AND LANCASHIRE**	p. 37
2014	**BURNLEY, PENDLE AND ROSSENDALE L.J.A.** – *see* **CUMBRIA AND LANCASHIRE**	p. 37
2038	**ASHBY-DE-LA-ZOUCH DIVISION** – *subjected to boundary adjustment and renumbered* **2047 ASHBY-DE-LA-ZOUCH DIVISION**	
2039	**LEICESTER (CITY) DIVISION** – *combined with 2040 LEICESTER (COUNTY) DIVISION to form (after boundary adjustment)* **2048 LEICESTER DIVISION**	
2040	**LEICESTER (COUNTY) DIVISION** – *combined with 2039 LEICESTER (CITY) DIVISION to form (after boundary adjustment)* **2048 LEICESTER DIVISION**	
2041	**LOUGHBOROUGH DIVISION** – *subjected to boundary adjustment and renumbered* **2049 LOUGHBOROUGH DIVISION**	
2042	**LUTTERWORTH DIVISION** – *combined with 2044 MARKET HARBOROUGH DIVISION to form (after boundary adjustment)* **2051 MARKET HARBOROUGH AND LUTTERWORTH DIVISION**	
2043	**MARKET BOSWORTH DIVISION** – *subjected to boundary adjustment and renumbered* **2050 MARKET BOSWORTH DIVISION**	
2044	**MARKET HARBOROUGH DIVISION** – *combined with 2042 LUTTERWORTH DIVISION to form (after boundary adjustment)* **2051 MARKET HARBOROUGH AND LUTTERWORTH DIVISION**	
2045	**MELTON AND BELVOIR DIVISION** – *combined with 2046 RUTLAND DIVISION to form* **2045 MELTON, BELVOIR AND RUTLAND DIVISION**	
2045	**MELTON, BELVOIR AND RUTLAND L.J.A.** – *see* **LINCOLNSHIRE, LEICESTERSHIRE & RUTLAND AND NORTHAMPTONSHIRE**	p. 65
2046	**RUTLAND DIVISION** – *combined with 2045 MELTON AND BELVOIR DIVISION to form* **2045 MELTON, BELVOIR AND RUTLAND DIVISION**	
2047	**ASHBY-DE-LA-ZOUCH L.J.A.** – *see* **LINCOLNSHIRE, LEICESTERSHIRE & RUTLAND AND NORTHAMPTONSHIRE**	p. 62
2048	**LEICESTER L.J.A.** – *see* **LINCOLNSHIRE, LEICESTERSHIRE & RUTLAND AND NORTHAMPTONSHIRE**	p. 64
2049	**LOUGHBOROUGH L.J.A.** – *see* **LINCOLNSHIRE, LEICESTERSHIRE & RUTLAND AND NORTHAMPTONSHIRE**	p. 65
2050	**MARKET BOSWORTH L.J.A.** – *see* **LINCOLNSHIRE, LEICESTERSHIRE & RUTLAND AND NORTHAMPTONSHIRE**	p. 65
2051	**MARKET HARBOROUGH AND LUTTERWORTH L.J.A.** – *see* **LINCOLNSHIRE, LEICESTERSHIRE & RUTLAND AND NORTHAMPTONSHIRE**	p. 65
2053	**ALFORD DIVISION** – *combined with 2064 LOUTH DIVISION and 2067 SPILSBY DIVISION to form* **2070 LOUTH DIVISION** *and* **2071 SPILSBY AND SKEGNESS DIVISION**	
2054	**BOSTON DIVISION** – *subjected to boundary adjustments and renumbered* **2073 BOSTON DIVISION**	
2055	**BOURNE DIVISION** – *combined with 2068 STAMFORD DIVISION to form* **2074 BOURNE AND STAMFORD DIVISION**	

ENGLAND

2056	**CAISTOR DIVISION** – *combined with 2079 LINCOLN DISTRICT DIVISION and 2081 MARKET RASEN DIVISION to form new* **2079 LINCOLN DISTRICT DIVISION**
2057	**EAST ELLOE DIVISION** – *combined with 2069 WEST ELLOE DIVISION to form (after boundary adjustment)* **2076 ELLOES DIVISION**
2058	**GAINSBOROUGH DIVISION** – *subjected to boundary adjustments and renumbered* **2075 GAINSBOROUGH DIVISION**
2059	**GRANTHAM DIVISION** – *subjected to boundary adjustments and renumbered* **2077 GRANTHAM DIVISION**
2060	**HORNCASTLE DIVISION** – *combined with 2070 LOUTH DIVISION to form (after boundary adjustments)* **2078 WOLDS DIVISION**
2061	**LINCOLN (CITY) DIVISION** – *combined with 2072 LINCOLN (COUNTY) DIVISION to form (after boundary adjustments)* **2079 LINCOLN DISTRICT DIVISION**
2062	**LINCOLN (KESTEVEN) DIVISION** – *combined with 2063 LINDSEY (LINCOLN AND WRAGBY) DIVISION to form* **2072 LINCOLN (COUNTY) DIVISION**
2063	**LINDSEY (LINCOLN AND WRAGBY) DIVISION** – *combined with 2062 LINCOLN (KESTEVEN) DIVISION to form* **2072 LINCOLN (COUNTY) DIVISION**
2064	**LOUTH DIVISION** – *combined with 2053 ALFORD DIVISION and 2067 SPILSBY DIVISION to form* **2070 LOUTH DIVISION** *and* **2071 SPILSBY AND SKEGNESS DIVISION**
2065	**MARKET RASEN DIVISION** – *subjected to boundary adjustments and renumbered* **2081 MARKET RASEN DIVISION**
2066	**SLEAFORD DIVISION** – *subjected to boundary adjustments and renumbered* **2080 SLEAFORD DIVISION**
2067	**SPILSBY DIVISION** – *combined with 2053 ALFORD DIVISION and 2064 LOUTH DIVISION to form* **2070 LOUTH DIVISION** *and* **2071 SPILSBY AND SKEGNESS DIVISION**
2068	**STAMFORD DIVISION** – *combined with 2055 BOURNE DIVISION to form* **2074 BOURNE AND STAMFORD DIVISION**
2069	**WEST ELLOE DIVISION** – *combined with 2057 EAST ELLOE DIVISION to form (after boundary adjustments)* **2076 ELLOES DIVISION**
2070	**LOUTH DIVISION** – *combined with 2060 HORNCASTLE DIVISION to form (after boundary adjustments)* **2079 WOLDS DIVISION**
2071	**SPILSBY AND SKEGNESS DIVISION** – *subjected to boundary adjustments and renumbered* **2082 SPILSBY AND SKEGNESS DIVISION**
2072	**LINCOLN (COUNTY) DIVISION** – *combined with 2061 LINCOLN (CITY) DIVISION to form (after boundary adjustments)* **2079 LINCOLN DISTRICT DIVISION**
2073	**BOSTON L.J.A.** – *see* **LINCOLNSHIRE, LEICESTERSHIRE & RUTLAND AND NORTHAMPTONSHIRE** .... p. 62
2074	**BOURNE AND STAMFORD L.J.A.** – *see* **LINCOLNSHIRE, LEICESTERSHIRE & RUTLAND AND NORTHAMPTONSHIRE** .... p. 62
2075	**GAINSBOROUGH L.J.A.** – *see* **LINCOLNSHIRE, LEICESTERSHIRE & RUTLAND AND NORTHAMPTONSHIRE** .... p. 63
2076	**ELLOES L.J.A.** – *see* **LINCOLNSHIRE, LEICESTERSHIRE & RUTLAND AND NORTHAMPTONSHIRE** .... p. 63
2077	**GRANTHAM L.J.A.** – *see* **LINCOLNSHIRE, LEICESTERSHIRE & RUTLAND AND NORTHAMPTONSHIRE** .... p. 64

ENGLAND

2078	WOLDS DIVISION – *combined with part of 2079 LINCOLN DISTRICT DIVISION to form enlarged* **2078 WOLDS DIVISION**	
2078	WOLDS L.J.A. – *see* **LINCOLNSHIRE, LEICESTERSHIRE & RUTLAND AND NORTHAMPTONSHIRE**	p. 67
2079	LINCOLN DISTRICT DIVISION – *part combined with 2078 WOLDS DIVISION to form enlarged* **2078 WOLDS DIVISION**; *remainder combined with 2056 CAISTOR DIVISION and 2081 MARKET RASEN DIVISION to form new* **2079 LINCOLN DISTRICT DIVISON**	
2079	LINCOLN DISTRICT L.J.A. – *see* **LINCOLNSHIRE, LEICESTERSHIRE & RUTLAND AND NORTHAMPTONSHIRE**	p. 64
2080	SLEAFORD L.J.A. – *see* **LINCOLNSHIRE, LEICESTERSHIRE & RUTLAND AND NORTHAMPTONSHIRE**	p. 66
2081	MARKET RASEN DIVISION – *combined with 2056 CAISTOR DIVISION and 2079 LINCOLN DISTRICT DIVISION to form new* **2079 LINCOLN DISTRICT DIVISION**	
2082	SPILSBY AND SKEGNESS DIVISION – *renamed* **SKEGNESS DIVISION**	
2082	SKEGNESS L.J.A. (formerly Spitsby and Skegness Division) – *see* **LINCOLNSHIRE, LEICESTERSHIRE & RUTLAND AND NORTHAMPTONSHIRE**	p. 66
2266	KNOWSLEY L.J.A. – *see* **CHESHIRE AND MERSEYSIDE**	p. 27
2267	LIVERPOOL L.J.A. – *see* **CHESHIRE AND MERSEYSIDE**	p. 28
2268	ST.HELENS L.J.A. – *see* **CHESHIRE AND MERSEYSIDE**	p. 28
2269	NORTH SEFTON DISTRICT L.J.A. – *see* **CHESHIRE AND MERSEYSIDE**	p. 28
2270	SOUTH SEFTON DISTRICT L.J.A. – *see* **CHESHIRE AND MERSEYSIDE**	p. 29
2271	WIRRAL L.J.A. – *see* **CHESHIRE AND MERSEYSIDE**	p. 30
2320	BRACKLEY DIVISION – *now amalgamated with* **2327 TOWCESTER DIVISION**	
2321	CORBY L.J.A. – *see* **LINCOLNSHIRE, LEICESTERSHIRE & RUTLAND AND NORTHAMPTONSHIRE**	p. 63
2322	DAVENTRY L.J.A. – *see* **LINCOLNSHIRE, LEICESTERSHIRE & RUTLAND AND NORTHAMPTONSHIRE**	p. 63
2323	KETTERING L.J.A. – *see* **LINCOLNSHIRE, LEICESTERSHIRE & RUTLAND AND NORTHAMPTONSHIRE**	p. 64
2324	MID NORTHANTS DIVISION – *part amalgamated with* **2322 DAVENTRY DIVISION**: – *part amalgamated with* **2327 TOWCESTER DIVISION**	
2325	NORTHAMPTON L.J.A. – *see* **LINCOLNSHIRE, LEICESTERSHIRE & RUTLAND AND NORTHAMPTONSHIRE**	p. 66
2326	OUNDLE AND THRAPSTON DIVISION – *part amalgamated with* **2321 CORBY DIVISION**: – *part amalgamated with* **2323 KETTERING DIVISION**: – *part amalgamated with* **2328 WELLINGBOROUGH DIVISION**	
2327	TOWCESTER L.J.A. – *see* **LINCOLNSHIRE, LEICESTERSHIRE & RUTLAND AND NORTHAMPTONSHIRE**	p. 66
2328	WELLINGBOROUGH L.J.A. – *see* **LINCOLNSHIRE, LEICESTERSHIRE & RUTLAND AND NORTHAMPTONSHIRE**	p. 67
2335	BAMBURGH WARD DIVISION – *combined with 2339 EAST COQUETDALE WARD DIVISION to form* **2345 BAMBURGH AND EAST COQUETDALE DIVISION**	
2336	BELLINGHAM DIVISION – *combined with 2341 HEXHAM DIVISION to form* **2346 TYNEDALE DIVISION**	
2337	BERWICK-UPON-TWEED DIVISION – *combined with 2340 GLENDALE WARD DIVISION to form* **2348 BERWICK-UPON-TWEED DIVISION**	

ENGLAND

2338	**BLYTH VALLEY DIVISION** – *combined with 2342 MORPETH WARD DIVISION and 2343 WANSBECK DIVISION to form* **2349 SOUTH EAST NORTHUMBERLAND DIVISION**	
2339	**EAST COQUETDALE WARD DIVISION** – *combined with 2335 BAMBURGH WARD DIVISION to form* **2345 BAMBURGH AND EAST COQUETDALE DIVISION**	
2340	**GLENDALE WARD DIVISION** – *combined with 2337 BERWICK-UPON-TWEED DIVISION to form* **2348 BERWICK-UPON-TWEED DIVISION**	
2341	**HEXHAM DIVISION** – *combined with 2336 BELLINGHAM DIVISION to form* **2346 TYNEDALE DIVISION**	
2342	**MORPETH WARD DIVISION** – *combined with 2338 BLYTH VALLEY DIVISION and 2343 WANSBECK DIVISION to form* **2349 SOUTH EAST NORTHUMBERLAND DIVISION**	
2343	**WANSBECK DIVISION** – *combined with 2338 BLYTH VALLEY DIVISION and 2342 MORPETH WARD DIVISION to form* **2349 SOUTH EAST NORTHUMBERLAND DIVISION**	
2344	**WEST COQUETDALE WARD DIVISION** – *combined with 2345 BAMBURGH AND EAST COQUETDALE DIVISION to form* **2347 COQUETDALE DIVISION**	
2345	**BAMBURGH AND EAST COQUETDALE DIVISION** – *combined with 2344 WEST COQUETDALE WARD DIVISION to form* **2347 COQUETDALE DIVISION**	
2346	**TYNEDALE L.J.A.** – see **CLEVELAND, DURHAM AND NORTHUMBRIA**	p. 36
2347	**ALNWICK L.J.A.** – *(formerly Coquetdale Division)* see **CLEVELAND, DURHAM AND NORTHUMBRIA**	p. 31
2348	**BERWICK-UPON-TWEED L.J.A.** – see **CLEVELAND, DURHAM AND NORTHUMBRIA**	p. 31
2349	**SOUTH EAST NORTHUMBERLAND L.J.A.** – see **CLEVELAND, DURHAM AND NORTHUMBRIA**	p. 35
2522	**ALLERTONSHIRE DIVISION** – *combined with 2523 BIRDFORTH DIVISION, 2528 GILLING EAST DIVISION (part), 2529 HALLIKELD DIVISION, 2530 HANG EAST DIVISION (part) and 2539 STOKESLEY DIVISION to form* **2543 NORTHALLERTON DIVISION**	
2523	**BIRDFORTH DIVISION** – *combined with 2522 ALLERTONSHIRE DIVISION, 2528 GILLING EAST DIVISION (part), 2529 HALLIKELD DIVISION, 2530 HANG EAST DIVISION (part) and 2539 STOKESLEY DIVISION to form* **2543 NORTHALLERTON DIVISION**	
2524	**BUCKROSE DIVISION** – *combined with 2542 MALTON DIVISION*	
2525	**BULMER EAST DIVISION** – *combined with 2526 BULMER WEST DIVISION to form* **2544 EASINGWOLD DIVISION**	
2526	**BULMER WEST DIVISION** – *combined with 2525 BULMER EAST DIVISION to form* **2544 EASINGWOLD DIVISION**	
2527	**CLARO DIVISION** – *abolished wef 1/1/97 and, after adjustment of boundaries with 2541 YORK division, reformed without change of Court Code Number.*	
2527	**CLARO DIVISION** – *combined with 2534 RIPON LIBERTY DIVISION, 2534 NORTHALLERTON DIVISION (part) and 2537 SELBY DIVISION (Parish of Wighill only) to form* **2527 HARROGATE DIVISION**	
2527	**HARROGATE L.J.A.** – see **NORTH AND WEST YORKSHIRE**	p. 89

ENGLAND

2528 **GILLING EAST DIVISION** – *part combined with 2522 ALLERTONSHIRE DIVISION, 2523 BIRDFORTH DIVISION, 2529 HALLIKELD DIVISION, 2530 HANG EAST DIVISION (part) and 2539 STOKESLEY DIVISION to form* **2543 NORTHALLERTON DIVISION:** – *part combined with 2530 HANG EAST DIVISION (part), 2531 HANG WEST DIVISION and 2533 RICHMOND AND GILLING WEST DIVISION to form* **2545 RICHMOND DIVISION**

2529 **HALLIKELD DIVISION** – *combined with 2522 ALLERTONSHIRE DIVISION, 2523 BIRDFORTH DIVISION, 2528 GILLING EAST DIVISION (part), 2530 HANG EAST DIVISION (part) and 2539 STOKESLEY DIVISION to form* **2543 NORTHALLERTON DIVISION**

2530 **HANG EAST DIVISION** – *part combined with 2522 ALLERTONSHIRE DIVISION, 2523 BIRDFORTH DIVISION, 2528 GILLING EAST DIVISION (part), 2529 HALLIKELD DIVISION and 2539 STOKESLEY DIVISION to form* **2543 NORTHALLERTON DIVISION:** – *part combined with 2528 GILLING EAST DIVISION (part), 2531 HANG WEST DIVISION and 2533 RICHMOND AND GILLING WEST DIVISION to form* **2545 RICHMOND DIVISION**

2531 **HANG WEST DIVISION** – *combined with 2528 GILLING EAST DIVISION (part), 2530 HANG EAST DIVISION (part), and 2533 RICHMOND AND GILLING WEST DIVISION to form* **2545 RICHMOND DIVISION**

2533 **RICHMOND AND GILLING WEST DIVISION** – *combined with 2528 GILLING EAST DIVISION (part), 2530 HANG EAST DIVISION (part), and 2531 HANG WEST DIVISION to form* **2545 RICHMOND DIVISION**

2534 **RIPON LIBERTY DIVISION** – *combined with 2527 CLARO DIVISION, 2543 NORTHALLERTON DIVISION (part) and 2537 SELBY DIVISION (Parish of Wighill only) to form* **2527 HARROGATE DIVISION**

2535 **RYEDALE DIVISION** – *combined with 2542 MALTON DIVISION to form* **2546 RYEDALE DIVISION**

2536 **SCARBOROUGH DIVISION** – *combined with 2540 WHITBY STRAND DIVISION, 2546 RYEDALE DIVISION and 2543 NORTHALLERTON DIVISION (part) to form* **2536 SCARBOROUGH DIVISION**

2536 **SCARBOROUGH L.J.A.** – see **NORTH AND WEST YORKSHIRE** .... p. 90

2537 **SELBY DIVISION** – *abolished wef 1/1/97 and, after adjustment of boundaries with 2541 YORK DIVISION, reformed without change of Court Code Number*

2537 **SELBY L.J.A.** – see **NORTH AND WEST YORKSHIRE** .... p. 91

2538 **SKIPTON L.J.A.** – see **NORTH AND WEST YORKSHIRE** .... p. 91

2539 **STOKESLEY DIVISION** – *combined with 2522 ALLERTONSHIRE DIVISION, 2523 BIRDFORTH DIVISION, 2528 GILLING EAST DIVISION (part), 2529 HALLIKELD DIVISION and 2530 HANG EAST DIVISION (part) to form* **2543 NORTHALLERTON DIVISION**

2540 **WHITBY STRAND DIVISION** – *combined with 2536 SCARBOROUGH DIVISION, 2546 RYEDALE DIVISION and 2543 NORTHALLERTON DIVISION (part) to form* **2536 SCARBOROUGH DIVISION**

2541 **YORK DIVISION** – *abolished wef 1/1/97 and, after adjustment of boundaries with 2527 CLARO DIVISION and 2537 SELBY DIVISION and absorbing part of 2544 EASINGWOLD DIVISION, reformed without change to Court Code Number*

2541 **YORK L.J.A.** – see **NORTH AND WEST YORKSHIRE** .... p. 91

2542 **MALTON DIVISION** – *combined with 2535 RYEDALE DIVISION to form* **2546 RYEDALE DIVISION**

2543 **NORTHALLERTON DIVISION** – *abolished wef 1/1/97 and reformed to include part of 2544 EASINGWOLD DIVISION, without change of Court Code Number*

ENGLAND

2543	**NORTHALLERTON DIVISION** – *part combined with 2527 CLARO DIVISION and 2534 RIPON DIVISION and 2537 SELBY DIVISION (part) to form* **2527 HARROGATE DIVISION:** – *part combined with 2536 SCARBOROUGH DIVISION, 2540 WHITBY STRAND DIVISION AND 2546 RYESDALE DIVISION to form* **2536 SCARBOROUGH DIVISION:** – *remainder combined with 2545 RICHMOND DIVISION to form* **2543 NORTHALLERTON AND RICHMOND DIVISION.**
2543	**NORTHALLERTON AND RICHMOND L.J.A.** – see **NORTH AND WEST YORKSHIRE** .... p. 90
2544	**EASINGWOLD DIVISION** – *abolished wef 1/1/97 – part combined with 2543 NORTHALLERTON DIVISION, part with 2546 RYEDALE DIVISION and part with 2541 YORK DIVISION*
2545	**RICHMOND DIVISION** – *combined with 2543 NORTHALLERTON DIVISION (part) to form* **2543 NORTHALLERTON AND RICHMOND DIVISION**
2546	**RYEDALE DIVISION** – *abolished wef 1/1/97 and reformed to include part of 2544 EASINGWOLD DIVISION, without change of Court Code Number*
2546	**RYEDALE DIVISION** – *combined with 2536 SCARBOROUGH DIVISION, 2540 WHITBY STRAND DIVISION and 2543 NORTHALLERTON DIVISION (part) to form* **2536 SCARBOROUGH DIVISION**
2552	**BINGHAM DIVISION** – *combined with 2557 NOTTINGHAM (CITY) DIVISION and 2558 NOTTINGHAM (COUNTY) DIVISION to form (after boundary adjustments)* **2568 NOTTINGHAM DIVISION**
2553	**EAST RETFORD P.S.A.** – *combined with 2560 WORKSOP P.S.A. to form* **2569 WORKSOP AND RETFORD P.S.A.**
2554	**MANSFIELD (BOROUGH) DIVISION** – *combined with 2555 MANSFIELD (COUNTY) DIVISION to form* **2566 MANSFIELD DIVISION**
2555	**MANSFIELD (COUNTY) DIVISION** – *combined with 2554 MANSFIELD (BOROUGH) DIVISION to form* **2566 MANSFIELD DIVISION**
2556	**NEWARK DIVISION** – *combined with 2559 SOUTHWELL DIVISION to form* **2567 NEWARK AND SOUTHWELL DIVISION**
2557	**NOTTINGHAM (CITY) DIVISION** – *combined with 2552 BINGHAM DIVISION and 2558 NOTTINGHAM (COUNTY) DIVISION to form (after boundary adjustments)* **2568 NOTTINGHAM DIVISION**
2558	**NOTTINGHAM (COUNTY) DIVISION** – *combined with 2552 BINGHAM DIVISION and 2557 NOTTINGHAM (CITY) DIVISION to form (after boundary adjustments)* **2568 NOTTINGHAM DIVISION**
2559	**SOUTHWELL DIVISION** – *combined with 2556 NEWARK DIVISION to form* **2567 NEWARK AND SOUTHWELL DIVISION**
2560	**WORKSOP P.S.A.** – *combined with 2553 EAST RETFORD P.S.A. to form* **2569 WORKSOP AND RETFORD P.S.A.**
2566	**MANSFIELD L.J.A.** – see **DERBYSHIRE AND NOTTINGHAMSHIRE** .... p. 42
2567	**NEWARK AND SOUTHWELL L.J.A.** – see **DERBYSHIRE AND NOTTINGHAMSHIRE** .... p. 42
2568	**NOTTINGHAM L.J.A.** – see **DERBYSHIRE AND NOTTINGHAMSHIRE** .... p. 43
2569	**WORKSOP AND RETFORD L.J.A.** – see **DERBYSHIRE AND NOTTINGHAMSHIRE** .... p. 44
2631	**CITY OF LONDON MAGISTRATES' COURT** – see **GREATER LONDON** .... p. 70
2641	**BOW STREET MAGISTRATES' COURT** – CLOSED
2642	**CLERKENWELL MAGISTRATES' COURT** – CLOSED

ENGLAND

2643	GREENWICH MAGISTRATES' COURT – see GREATER LONDON	p. 72
2643	WOOLWICH MAGISTRATES' COURT – see GREATER LONDON	p. 72
2644	MARLBOROUGH STREET MAGISTRATES' COURT – CLOSED	
2646	MARYLEBONE MAGISTRATES' COURT – CLOSED	
2648	OLD STREET MAGISTRATES' COURT – CLOSED	
2649	SOUTH WESTERN MAGISTRATES' COURT – see GREATER LONDON	p. 86
2650	THAMES MAGISTRATES' COURT – see GREATER LONDON	p. 79
2651	TOWER BRIDGE MAGISTRATES' COURT – see GREATER LONDON	p. 74
2652	WEST LONDON M.C. – combined with 2657 WALTON STREET M.C. to form **2658 WEST LONDON M.C.**	
2653	WOOLWICH MAGISTRATES' COURT – renumbered 2643 see **GREATER LONDON**	
2655	WELLS STREET MAGISTRATES' COURT – CLOSED	
2656	CAMBERWELL GREEN MAGISTRATES' COURT – see GREATER LONDON	p. 73
2657	WALTON STREET M.C. – combined with 2652 WEST LONDON M.C. to form **2658 WEST LONDON M.C.**	
2658	WEST LONDON MAGISTRATES' COURT – see GREATER LONDON	p. 79
2660	HORSEFERRY ROAD MAGISTRATES' COURT – renamed **CITY OF WESTMINSTER MAGISTRATES COURT**	
2660	CITY OF WESTMINSTER MAGISTRATES' COURT – see GREATER LONDON	p. 71
2663	HIGHBURY CORNER MAGISTRATES' COURT – see GREATER LONDON	p. 77
2665	**METROPOLITAN POLICE** (Fixed Penalty)	
2667	**ABINGDON (BOROUGH) DIVISION** – combined with 2668 ABINGDON (COUNTY) DIVISION to form **2681 ABINGDON DIVISION**	
2668	**ABINGDON (COUNTY) DIVISION** – combined with 2667 ABINGDON (BOROUGH) DIVISION to form **2681 ABINGDON DIVISION**	
2669	**BAMPTON EAST DIVISION** – combined with 2670 BAMPTON WEST DIVISION to form **2703 WITNEY DIVISION**	
2670	**BAMPTON WEST DIVISION** – combined with 2669 BAMPTON EAST DIVISION to form **2703 WITNEY DIVISION**	
2671	**BICESTER DIVISION** – subjected to boundary adjustment and renumbered **2776 BICESTER DIVISION**	
2672	**BULLINGDON DIVISION** – combined with 2680 WATLINGTON DIVISION to form **2717 EAST OXFORDSHIRE DIVISION**	
2673	**CHIPPING NORTON DIVISION** – combined with 2677 NORTH OXFORDSHIRE DIVISION to form **2702 NORTH OXFORDSHIRE AND CHIPPING NORTON DIVISION**	
2674	**FARINGDON DIVISION** – combined with 2679 WANTAGE DIVISION to form **2682 WANTAGE AND FARINGDON DIVISION**	
2675	**HENLEY DIVISION** – combined with 2717 EAST OXFORDSHIRE DIVISION to form **2719 THAME AND HENLEY DIVISION**	
2676	**MORETON AND WALLINGFORD DIVISION** – combined with 2682 WANTAGE AND FARINGDON DIVISION to form **2718 DIDCOT AND WANTAGE DIVISION**	

ENGLAND

2677	**NORTH OXFORDSHIRE DIVISION** – combined with 2673 CHIPPING NORTON DIVISION to form **2702 NORTH OXFORDSHIRE AND CHIPPING NORTON DIVISION**
2678	**OXFORD DIVISION** – subjected to boundary adjustment and renumbered **2777 OXFORD DIVISION**
2679	**WANTAGE DIVISION** – combined with 2674 FARINGDON DIVISION to form **2682 WANTAGE AND FARINGDON DIVISION**
2680	**WATLINGTON DIVISION** – combined with 2672 BULLINGDON DIVISION to form **2717 EAST OXFORDSHIRE DIVISION**
2681	**ABINGDON DIVISION** – combined with 2718 DIDCOT AND WANTAGE DIVISION to form (after boundary adjustment) **2774 ABINGDON, DIDCOT AND WANTAGE DIVISION**
2682	**WANTAGE AND FARINGDON DIVISION** – combined with 2676 MORETON AND WALLINGFORD DIVISION to form **2718 DIDCOT AND WANTAGE DIVISION**
2701	**WOODSTOCK DIVISION** – abolished and absorbed into **2775 BANBURY DIVISION, 2776 BICESTER DIVISION** and **2779 WITNEY DIVISION**
2702	**NORTH OXFORDSHIRE AND CHIPPING NORTON DIVISION** – abolished and absorbed into **2779 WITNEY DIVISION** and **2775 BANBURY DIVISION**
2703	**WITNEY DIVISION** – subjected to boundary adjustment and renumbered **2779 WITNEY DIVISION**
2704	**FROME DIVISION** – combined with 2707 SHEPTON MALLET DIVISION and 2710 WELLS DIVISION to form **2715 MENDIP DIVISION**
2705	**ILMINSTER DIVISION** – combined with 2708 SOMERTON DIVISION, 2712 WINCANTON DIVISION and 2713 YEOVIL DIVISION to form **2714 SOUTH SOMERSET DIVISION**
2706	**SEDGEMOOR L.J.A.** – see **AVON AND SOMERSET** .... p. 6
2707	**SHEPTON MALLET DIVISION** – combined with 2704 FROME DIVISION and 2710 WELLS DIVISION to form **2715 MENDIP DIVISION**
2708	**SOMERTON DIVISION** – combined with 2705 ILMINSTER DIVISION, 2712 WINCANTON DIVISION and 2713 YEOVIL DIVISION to form **2714 SOUTH SOMERSET DIVISION**
2709	**TAUNTON DEANE P.S.A.** – renamed **2709 TAUNTON DEANE AND WEST SOMERSET P.S.A.**
2709	**TAUNTON DEANE AND WEST SOMERSET L.J.A.** – see **AVON AND SOMERSET** .... p. 7
2710	**WELLS DIVISION** – combined with 2704 FROME DIVISION and 2707 SHEPTON MALLET DIVISION to form **2713 MENDIP DIVISION**
2711	**WEST SOMERSET P.S.A.** – absorbed into 2709 TAUNTON DEANE P.S.A. and renamed **2709 TAUNTON DEANE AND WEST SOMERSET P.S.A.**
2712	**WINCANTON DIVISION** – combined with 2705 ILMINSTER DIVISION, 2708 SOMERTON DIVISION and 2713 YEOVIL DIVISION to form **2714 SOUTH SOMERSET DIVISION**
2713	**YEOVIL DIVISION** – combined with 2705 ILMINSTER DIVISION, 2708 SOMERTON DIVISION and 2712 WINCANTON DIVISION to form **2714 SOUTH SOMERSET DIVISION**
2714	**SOUTH SOMERSET L.J.A.** – see **AVON AND SOMERSET** .... p. 7
2715	**MENDIP L.J.A.** – see **AVON AND SOMERSET** .... p. 5

ENGLAND

2717	EAST OXFORDSHIRE DIVISION – combined with 2675 HENLEY DIVISION to form **2719 THAME AND HENLEY DIVISION**	
2718	DIDCOT AND WANTAGE DIVISION – combined with 2681 ABINGDON DIVISION to form (after boundary adjustment) **2774 ABINGDON, DIDCOT AND WANTAGE DIVISION**	
2719	THAME AND HENLEY DIVISION – subjected to boundary adjustment and renumbered **2778 THAME AND HENLEY DIVISION**	
2721	STRATFORD MAGISTRATES' COURT –see GREATER LONDON	p. 84
2722	WEST HAM MAGISTRATES' COURT – CLOSED	
2723	ACTON MAGISTRATES' COURT –see GREATER LONDON	p. 78
2725	BARNET MAGISTRATES' COURT – CLOSED	
2726	BRENTFORD MAGISTRATES' COURT – renumbered 2769	
2727	BROMLEY MAGISTRATES' COURT – see GREATER LONDON	p. 70
2728	BEXLEY MAGISTRATES' COURT – see GREATER LONDON	p. 69
2731	WALLINGTON MAGISTRATES' COURT – combined with 2756 SUTTON M.C. to form **2733 SUTTON MAGISTRATES' COURT**	
2732	CROYDON MAGISTRATES' COURT – see GREATER LONDON	p. 71
2733	SUTTON MAGISTRATES' COURT – see GREATER LONDON	p. 74
2734	EALING MAGISTRATES' COURT – see GREATER LONDON	p. 77
2740	HAMPSTEAD MAGISTRATES' COURT – CLOSED	
2741	HENDON MAGISTRATES' COURT – see GREATER LONDON	p. 76
2742	HARINGEY MAGISTRATES' COURT – see GREATER LONDON	p. 80
2755	BEACONTREE MAGISTRATES' COURT – renamed and renumbered **2815 REDBRIDGE MAGISTRATES' COURT**	
2756	SUTTON MAGISTRATES' COURT – combined with 2731 WALLINGTON M.C. to form **2733 SUTTON M.C.**	
2757	ENFIELD MAGISTRATES' COURT – see GREATER LONDON	p. 78
2760	HARROW MAGISTRATES' COURT – see GREATER LONDON	p. 80
2762	BRENT MAGISTRATES' COURT – see GREATER LONDON	p. 76
2763	WIMBLEDON MAGISTRATES' COURT – see GREATER LONDON	p. 84
2766	UXBRIDGE MAGISTRATES' COURT – see GREATER LONDON	p. 81
2768	RICHMOND-UPON-THAMES MAGISTRATES' COURT – see GREATER LONDON	p. 85
2769	FELTHAM MAGISTRATES' COURT – see GREATER LONDON	p. 82
2769	BRENTFORD MAGISTRATES' COURT – see GREATER LONDON	p. 82
2770	BARNSLEY DISTRICT L.J.A. – see HUMBER AND SOUTH YORKSHIRE	p. 57
2771	DONCASTER L.J.A. – see HUMBER AND SOUTH YORKSHIRE	p. 58
2772	ROTHERHAM L.J.A. – see HUMBER AND SOUTH YORKSHIRE	p. 59
2773	SHEFFIELD L.J.A. – see HUMBER AND SOUTH YORKSHIRE	p. 59
2774	ABINGDON, DIDCOT AND WANTAGE DIVISION – renamed **2774 SOUTHERN OXFORDSHIRE DIVISION**	
2774	SOUTHERN OXFORDSHIRE L.J.A. (formerly Abingdon, Didcot and Wantage Division) – see THAMES VALLEY	p. 98

ENGLAND

2775	**BANBURY DIVISION** – combined with 2776 BICESTER DIVISION and 2779 WITNEY DIVISION to form **2775 NORTHERN OXFORDSHIRE DIVISION**
2775	**NORTHERN OXFORDSHIRE L.J.A.** – see **THAMES VALLEY** .... p. 97
2776	**BICESTER DIVISION** – combined with 2775 BANBURY DIVISION and 2779 WITNEY DIVISION to form **2775 NORTHERN OXFORDSHIRE DIVISION**
2777	**OXFORD DIVISION** – combined with 2778 THAME AND HENLEY DIVISION to form **2777 OXFORD P.S.A.**
2777	**OXFORD L.J.A.** – see **THAMES VALLEY** .... p. 98
2778	**THAME AND HENLEY DIVISION** – combined with 2777 OXFORD DIVISION to form **2777 OXFORD DIVISION**
2779	**WITNEY DIVISION** – combined with 2775 BANBURY DIVISION and 2776 BICESTER DIVISION to form **2775 NORTHERN OXFORDSHIRE DIVISION**
2780	**BURTON-UPON-TRENT P.S.A.** – combined with 2860 LICHFIELD AND TAMWORTH P.S.A. to form **2860 SOUTH EAST STAFFORDSHIRE P.S.A.**
2781	**CANNOCK DIVISION** – combined with 2789 SEISDON DIVISION to form **2859 CANNOCK AND SEISDON DIVISION**
2782	**CHEADLE DIVISION** – combined with 2784 LEEK DIVISION to form **2796 STAFFORDSHIRE MOORLANDS DIVISION**
2783	**ECCLESHALL DIVISION** – combined with 2790 STAFFORD DIVISION, 2792 STONE DIVISION and 2794 UTTOXETER DIVISION to form **2795 MID-STAFFORDSHIRE DIVISION**
2784	**LEEK DIVISION** – combined with 2782 CHEADLE DIVISION to form **2796 STAFFORDSHIRE MOORLANDS DIVISION**
2785	**LICHFIELD DIVISION** – combined with 2793 TAMWORTH DIVISION to form **2860 LICHFIELD AND TAMWORTH DIVISION**
2786	**NEWCASTLE-UNDER-LYME DIVISION** – combined with 2787 PIREHILL NORTH DIVISION to form **2797 NEWCASTLE-UNDER-LYME AND PIREHILL NORTH DIVISION**
2787	**PIREHILL NORTH DIVISION** – combined with 2786 NEWCASTLE-UNDER-LYME DIVISION to form **2797 NEWCASTLE-UNDER-LYME AND PIREHILL NORTH DIVISION**
2788	**RUGELEY DIVISION** – combined with 2795 MID STAFFORDSHIRE DIVISION to form **2799 MID STAFFORDSHIRE AND RUGELEY DIVISION**
2789	**SEISDON DIVISION** – combined with 2781 CANNOCK DIVISION to form **2859 CANNOCK AND SEISDON DIVISION**
2790	**STAFFORD DIVISION** – combined with 2792 STONE DIVISION, 2783 ECCLESHALL DIVISION and 2794 UTTOXETER DIVISION to form **2795 MID-STAFFORDSHIRE DIVISION**
2791	**STOKE-ON-TRENT P.S.A.** – combined with 2798 NORTH STAFFORDSHIRE P.S.A. to form **2791 NORTH STAFFORDSHIRE P.S.A.**
2791	**NORTH STAFFORDSHIRE L.J.A.** – see **BLACK COUNTRY, STAFFORDSHIRE AND WEST MERCIA** .... p. 18
2792	**STONE DIVISION** – combined with 2790 STAFFORD DIVISION, 2783 ECCLESHALL DIVISION and 2794 UTTOXETER DIVISION to form **2795 MID-STAFFORDSHIRE DIVISION**
2793	**TAMWORTH DIVISION** – combined with 2785 LICHFIELD DIVISION to form **2860 LICHFIELD AND TAMWORTH DIVISON**

ENGLAND

2794 **UTTOXETER DIVISION** – *combined with 2790 STAFFORD DIVISION, 2792 STONE DIVISION and 2793 ECCLESHALL DIVISION to form* **2795 MID-STAFFORDSHIRE DIVISION**

2795 **MID-STAFFORDSHIRE DIVISION** – *combined with 2788 RUGELEY DIVISION to form* **2799 MID STAFFORDSHIRE AND RUGELEY DIVISION**

2796 **STAFFORDSHIRE MOORLANDS DIVISION** – *combined with 2797 NEWCASTLE-UNDER-LYME AND PIREHILL NORTH DIVISION to form* **2798 NORTH STAFFORDSHIRE DIVISION**

2797 **NEWCASTLE-UNDER-LYME AND PIREHILL NORTH DIVISION** – *combined with 2796 STAFFORDSHIRE MOORLANDS DIVISION to form* **2798 NORTH STAFFORDSHIRE DIVISION**

2798 **NORTH STAFFORDSHIRE P.S.A.** – *combined with 2791 STOKE-ON-TRENT P.S.A. to form* **2791 NORTH STAFFORDSHIRE P.S.A.**

2799 **MID STAFFORDSHIRE AND RUGELEY P.S.A.** – *combined with 2859 CANNOCK AND SEISDON P.S.A. to form* **2799 CENTRAL AND SOUTH WEST STAFFORDSHIRE P.S.A.**

2799 **CENTRAL AND SOUTH WEST STAFFORDSHIRE L.J.A.** – *see* **BLACK COUNTRY, STAFFORDSHIRE AND WEST MERCIA** . . . . p. 16

2812 **KINGSTON-UPON-THAMES MAGISTRATES' COURT** – *see* **GREATER LONDON** . . . . p. 83

2813 **WALTHAM FOREST MAGISTRATES' COURT** – *see* **GREATER LONDON** . . . . p. 86

2814 **BARKING MAGISTRATES' COURT** – *see* **GREATER LONDON** . . . . p. 75

2815 **REDBRIDGE MAGISTRATES' COURT** – *see* **GREATER LONDON** . . . . p. 85

2816 **BECCLES DIVISION** – *combined with 2822 LOWESTOFT DIVISION and 2831 SAXMUNDHAM DIVISION to form* **2863 NORTH EAST SUFFOLK DIVISION**

2817 **BLYTHING DIVISION** – *combined with portions of 2819 HARTISMERE DIVISION to form* **2831 SAXMUNDHAM DIVISION**

2818 **FELIXSTOWE DIVISION** – *combined with 2829 WOODBRIDGE DIVISION to form* **2861 DEBEN DIVISION**

2819 **HARTISMERE DIVISION** – *abolished – part absorbed into* **2831 SAXMUNDHAM DIVISION,** *part into* **2832 ST. EDMUNDSBURY DIVISION** *and remainder into* **2833 STOW DIVISION**

2820 **IPSWICH DIVISION** – *combined with 2824 ORWELL DIVISION to form* **2830 IPSWICH DIVISION**

2821 **LACKFORD DIVISION** – *renamed* **MILDENHALL DIVISION** – *see below*

2821 **MILDENHALL DIVISION** – *combined with 2923 NEWMARKET DIVISION to form* **2862 NORTH WEST SUFFOLK DIVISION**

2822 **LOWESTOFT DIVISION** – *combined with 2816 BECCLES DIVISION and 2831 SAXMUNDHAM DIVISION to form* **2863 NORTH EAST SUFFOLK DIVISION**

2823 **NEWMARKET DIVISION** – *combined with 2021 MILDENHALL DIVISION to form* **2862 NORTH WEST SUFFOLK DIVISION**

2824 **ORWELL DIVISION** – *combined with 2820 IPSWICH DIVISION to form* **2830 IPSWICH DIVISION**

2825 **HAVERHILL DIVISION (formerly Risbridge Division)** – *combined with 2828 SUDBURY DIVISION to form* **2864 HAVERHILL AND SUDBURY DIVISION**

2826 **ST. EDMUNDSBURY DIVISION** – *combined with portions of 2819 HARTISMERE DIVISION to form* **2832 ST. EDMUNDSBURY DIVISION**

ENGLAND

2827	**STOW DIVISION** – combined with portions of 2819 HARTISMERE DIVISION to form **2833 STOW DIVISION (now renamed STOWMARKET DIVISION)**
2828	**SUDBURY DIVISION (formerly Sudbury and Cosford Division)** – combined with 2825 HAVERHILL DIVISION to form **2864 HAVERHILL AND SUDBURY DIVISION**
2829	**WOODBRIDGE DIVISION** – combined with 2818 FELIXSTOWE DIVISION to form **2861 DEBEN DIVISION**
2830	**IPSWICH P.S.A.** –combined with 2861 DEBEN P.S.A. to form **2866 SOUTH EAST SUFFOLK P.S.A.**
2831	**SAXMUNDHAM DIVISION** – combined with 2816 BECCLES DIVISION and 2822 LOWESTOFT DIVISION to form **2863 NORTH EAST SUFFOLK DIVISION**
2832	**ST. EDMUNDSBURY DIVISION** – combined with 2833 STOWMARKET DIVISION to form **2865 ST. EDMUNDSBURY AND STOWMARKET DIVISION**
2833	**STOWMARKET DIVISION (formerly Stow Division)** – combined with 2932 ST. EDMUNDSBURY DIVISION to form **2865 ST. EDMUNDSBURY AND STOWMARKET DIVISION**
2835	**CHERTSEY DIVISION** – combined with 2844 WOKING DIVISION (after boundary adjustment and including parts of 2838 ESHER AND WALTON DIVISION and 2839 FARNHAM DIVISION) to form **2846 NORTH WEST SURREY DIVISION**
2836	**DORKING DIVISION** – combined with 2840 GODSTONE DIVISION and 2842 REIGATE DIVISION to form **2847 SOUTH EAST SURREY DIVISION**
2837	**EPSOM DIVISION** – combined with 2843 STAINES AND SUNBURY DIVISION and part of 2838 EASHER AND WALTON DIVISION to form **2845 NORTH & EAST SURREY DIVISION**
2838	**ESHER AND WALTON DIVISION** – now absorbed into **2845 NORTH & EAST SURREY DIVISION** and **2846 NORTH WEST SURREY DIVISION**
2839	**FARNHAM DIVISION** – now absorbed into **2846 NORTH WEST SURREY DIVISION** and **2848 SOUTH WEST SURREY DIVISION**
2840	**GODSTONE DIVISION** – combined with 2836 DORKING DIVISION and 2842 REIGATE DIVISION to form **2847 SOUTH EAST SURREY DIVISION**
2841	**GUILDFORD DIVISION** – boundary adjusted to include part of 2844 WOKING DIVISION and part of 2839 FARNHAM DIVISION to form **2848 SOUTH WEST SURREY DIVISION**
2842	**REIGATE DIVISION** – combined with 2836 DORKING DIVISION and 2840 GODSTONE DIVISION to form **2847 SOUTH EAST SURREY DIVISION**
2843	**STAINES AND SUNBURY DIVISION** – combined with 2837 EPSOM DIVISION and part of 2838 ESHER AND WALTON DIVISION to form **2845 NORTH & EAST SURREY DIVISION**
2844	**WOKING DIVISION** – (after boundary adjustment and including parts of 2838 ESHER AND WALTON DIVISION and 2839 FARNHAM DIVISION) combined with 2835 CHERTSEY DIVISION to form **2846 NORTH WEST SURREY DIVISION**
2845	**NORTH & EAST SURREY DIVISION** boundary adjusted to include part of 2846 NORTH WEST SURREY TO FORM **2849 NORTH SURREY P.S.A.**
2846	**NORTH WEST SURREY DIVISION** boundary adjusted following absorption by NORTH SURREY of part of 2846 North West Surrey to form **2857 NORTH WEST SURREY P.S.A.**
2847	**SOUTH EAST SURREY DIVISION** boundary adjusted to include part of 2845 NORTH & EAST SURREY to form **2856 SOUTH EAST SURREY P.S.A.**
2848	**SOUTH WEST SURREY L.J.A.** – see **SURREY AND SUSSEX** . . . . p. 93
2849	**NORTH SURREY L.J.A.** – see **SURREY AND SUSSEX** . . . . p. 92

ENGLAND

2850	GATESHEAD L.J.A. – see **CLEVELAND, DURHAM AND NORTHUMBRIA**	p. 31
2851	NEWCASTLE-UPON-TYNE L.J.A. – see **CLEVELAND, DURHAM AND NORTHUMBRIA**	p. 33
2852	NORTH TYNESIDE DISTRICT L.J.A. – see **CLEVELAND, DURHAM AND NORTHUMBRIA**	p. 34
2853	SOUTH TYNESIDE DISTRICT L.J.A. – see **CLEVELAND, DURHAM AND NORTHUMBRIA**	p. 35
2854	HOUGHTON-LE-SPRING L.J.A. – see **CLEVELAND, DURHAM AND NORTHUMBRIA**	p. 32
2855	SUNDERLAND L.J.A. – see **CLEVELAND, DURHAM AND NORTHUMBRIA**	p. 36
2856	SOUTH EAST SURREY L.J.A. – see **SURREY AND SUSSEX**	p. 93
2857	NORTH WEST SURREY L.J.A. – see **SURREY AND SUSSEX**	p. 93
2859	**CANNOCK AND SEISDON P.S.A.** – combined with 2799 MID STAFFORDSHIRE AND RUGELEY P.S.A. to form **2799 CENTRAL AND SOUTH WEST STAFFORDSHIRE P.S.A.**	
2860	**LICHFIELD AND TAMWORTH P.S.A.** – combined with 2780 BURONT-UPON-TRENT P.S.A. to form **2860 SOUTH EAST STAFFORDSHIRE P.S.A.**	
2860	SOUTH EAST STAFFORDSHIRE L.J.A. – see **BLACK COUNTRY, STAFFORDSHIRE AND WEST MERCIA**	p. 19
2861	**DEBEN P.S.A.** – combined with 2830 IPSWICH P.S.A. to form **2866 SOUTH EAST SUFFOLK P.S.A.**	
2862	**NORTH WEST SUFFOLK P.S.A.** – combined with 2864 HAVERHILL AND SUDBURY P.S.A. and 2865 ST. EDMUNDSBURY AND STOWMARKET P.S.A. to form **2867 WEST SUFFOLK P.S.A.**	
2863	NORTH EAST SUFFOLK L.J.A. – see **CAMBRIDGESHIRE, NORFOLK AND SUFFOLK**	p. 23
2864	**HAVERHILL AND SUDBURY P.S.A.** – combined with 2862 NORTH WEST SUFFOLK P.S.A. and 2865 ST. EDMUNDSBURY AND STOWMARKET P.S.A. to form **2867 WEST SUFFOLK P.S.A.**	
2865	**ST. EDMUNDSBURY AND STOWMARKET P.S.A.** – combined with 2862 NORTH WEST SUFFOLK P.S.A. and 2864 HAVERHILL AND SUDBURY P.S.A. to form **2867 WEST SUFFOLK P.S.A.**	
2866	SOUTH EAST SUFFOLK L.J.A. – see **CAMBRIDGESHIRE, NORFOLK AND SUFFOLK**	p. 25
2867	WEST SUFFOLK L.J.A. – see **CAMBRIDGESHIRE, NORFOLK AND SUFFOLK**	p. 26
2893	**ALCESTER DIVISION** – combined with 2895 KINETON DIVISION, 2898 SHIPSTON-ON-STOUR DIVISION and 2900 STRATFORD-UPON-AVON DIVISION to form **2902 SOUTH WARWICKSHIRE DIVISION**	
2894	**ATHERSTONE AND COLESHILL P.S.A.** – combined with 2896 NENEATON P.S.A., 2897 RUGBY P.S.A., 2902 SOUTH WARWICKSHIRE P.S.A. and 2903 MID-WARWICKSHIRE P.S.A. to form **2904 WARWICKSHIRE P.S.A.**	
2895	**KINETON DIVISION** – combined with 2893 ALCESTER DIVISION, 2898 SHIPSTON-ON-STOUR DIVISION and 2900 STRATFORD-UPON-AVON DIVISION to form **2902 SOUTH WARWICKSHIRE DIVISION**	
2896	**NUNEATON P.S.A.** – combined with 2894 ATHERSTONE AND COLESHILL P.S.A., 2897 RUGBY P.S.A., 2902 SOUTH WARWICKSHIRE P.S.A. and 2903 MID-WARWICKSHIRE P.S.A. to form **2904 WARWICKSHIRE P.S.A.**	

ENGLAND

2897 **RUGBY P.S.A.** – *combined with 2894 ATHERSTONE AND COLESHILL P.S.A., 2896 NUNEATON P.S.A., 2902 SOUTH WARWICKSHIRE P.S.A. and 2903 MID-WARWICKSHIRE P.S.A. to form* **2904 WARWICKSHIRE P.S.A.**

2898 **SHIPSTON-ON-STOUR DIVISION** – *combined with 2893 ALCESTER DIVISION, 2895 KINETON DIVISION and 2900 STRATFORD-UPON-AVON DIVISION to form* **2902 SOUTH WARWICKSHIRE DIVISION**

2899 **SOUTHAM DIVISION** – *combined with 2901 WARWICK DIVISION to form* **2903 MID-WARWICKSHIRE DIVISION**

2900 **STRATFORD-UPON-AVON DIVISION** – *combined with 2893 ALCESTER DIVISION, 2895 KINETON DIVISION and 2898 SHIPSTON-ON-STOUR DIVISION to form* **2902 SOUTH WARWICKSHIRE DIVISION**

2901 **WARWICK DIVISION** – *combined with 2899 SOUTHAM DIVISION to form* **2903 MID-WARWICKSHIRE DIVISION**

2902 **SOUTH WARWICKSHIRE P.S.A.** – *combined with 2894 ATHERSTONE AND COLESHILL P.S.A., 2896 NUNEATON P.S.A., 2897 RUGBY P.S.A. and 2903 MID-WARWICKSHIRE P.S.A. to form* **2904 WARWICKSHIRE P.S.A.**

2903 **MID-WARWICKSHIRE P.S.A.** – *combined with 2894 ATHERSTONE AND COLESHILL P.S.A., 2896 NUNEATON P.S.A., 2897 RUGBY P.S.A. and 2902 SOUTH WARWICKSHIRE P.S.A. to form* **2904 WARWICKSHIRE P.S.A.**

2904 **WARWICKSHIRE L.J.A.** – *see* **BIRMINGHAM, COVENTRY, SOLIHULL AND WARWICKSHIRE** .... p. 15

2908 **BIRMINGHAM L.J.A.** – *see* **BIRMINGHAM, COVENTRY, SOLIHULL AND WARWICKSHIRE** .... p. 13

2909 **SUTTON COLDFIELD L.J.A.** – *see* **BIRMINGHAM, COVENTRY, SOLIHULL AND WARWICKSHIRE** .... p. 14

2910 **COVENTRY DISTRICT L.J.A.** – *see* **BIRMINGHAM, COVENTRY, SOLIHULL AND WARWICKSHIRE** .... p. 13

2911 **DUDLEY L.J.A.** – *see* **BLACK COUNTRY, STAFFORDSHIRE AND WEST MERCIA** .... p. 17

2912 **HALESOWEN DIVISION** – *combined with 2913 STOURBRIDGE DIVISION to form* **2912 STOURBRIDGE AND HALESOWEN DIVISION**

2912 **STOURBRIDGE AND HALESOWEN L.J.A.** – *see* **BLACK COUNTRY, STAFFORDSHIRE AND WEST MERCIA** .... p. 20

2913 **STOURBRIDGE DIVISION** – *combined with 2912 HALESOWEN DIVISION to form* **2912 STOURBRIDGE AND HALESOWEN DIVISION**

2914 **WARLEY L.J.A.** – *see* **BLACK COUNTRY, STAFFORDSHIRE AND WEST MERCIA** .... p. 21

2915 **WEST BROMWICH L.J.A.** – *see* **BLACK COUNTRY, STAFFORDSHIRE AND WEST MERCIA** .... p. 21

2916 **SOLIHULL L.J.A.** – *see* **BIRMINGHAM, COVENTRY, SOLIHULL AND WARWICKSHIRE** .... p. 14

2917 **WALSALL & ALDRIDGE L.J.A.** – *see* **BLACK COUNTRY, STAFFORDSHIRE AND WEST MERCIA** .... p. 21

2918 **WALSALL L.J.A.** – *combined with 2917 ALDRIDGE AND BROWNHILLS P.S.A. to form* **2917 WALSALL AND ALDRIDGE L.J.A.**

2919 **WOLVERHAMPTON L.J.A.** – *see* **BLACK COUNTRY, STAFFORDSHIRE AND WEST MERCIA** .... p. 21

ENGLAND

2927	**ARUNDEL P.S.A.** – *combined with 2937 WORTHING AND DISTRICT P.S.A. and 2936 CHICHESTER AND DISTRICT P.S.A. to form* **2949 SUSSEX (WESTERN) P.S.A.**	
2928	**CHICHESTER DIVISION** – *combined with 2931 MIDHURST DIVISION and 2933 PETWORTH DIVISION to form* **2936 CHICHESTER AND DISTRICT DIVISION**	
2929	**CRAWLEY P.S.A.** – *combined with 2930 HORSHAM P.S.A. and 2932 MID-SUSSEX P.S.A. to form* **2947 SUSSEX (NORTHERN) P.S.A.**	
2930	**HORSHAM P.S.A.** – *combined with 2929 CRAWLEY P.S.A. and 2932 MID-SUSSEX P.S.A. to form* **2947 SUSSEX (NORTHERN) P.S.A.**	
2931	**MIDHURST DIVISION** – *combined with 2928 CRAWLEY P.S.A. and 2930 HORSHAM DIVISION to form* **2947 SUSSEX (NORTHERN) P.S.A.**	
2932	**MID-SUSSEX P.S.A.** – *combined with 2929 CRAWLEY P.S.A. and 2930 HORSHAM DIVISION to form* **2947 SUSSEX (NORTHERN) P.S.A.**	
2933	**PETWORTH DIVISION** – *combined with 2928 CHICHESTER DIVISION and 2931 MIDHURST DIVISION to form* **2936 CHICHESTER AND DISTRICT DIVISION**	
2934	**STEYNING DIVISION** – *abolished w.e.f. 1 April 1996 and absorbed into* **2930 HORSHAM DIVISION and 2937 WORTHING AND DISTRICT DIVISION**	
2935	**WORTHING DIVISION** – *abolished w.e.f. 1 April 1996 and after adjustment of boundaries reconstituted as* **2937 WORTHING AND DISTRICT DIVISION**	
2936	**CHICHESTER AND DISTRICT P.S.A.** – *combined with 2927 ARUNDEL P.S.A. and 2937 WORTHING AND DISTRICT P.S.A. to form* **2949 SUSSEX (WESTERN) P.S.A.**	
2937	**WORTHING AND DISTRICT P.S.A.** – *combined with 2927 ARUNDEL P.S.A. and 2936 CHICHESTER AND DISTRICT P.S.A. to form* **2949 SUSSEX (WESTERN) P.S.A.**	
2947	**SUSSEX (NORTHERN) L.J.A.** – *see* **SURREY AND SUSSEX**	p. 95
2948	**SUSSEX (EASTERN) L.J.A.** – *see* **SURREY AND SUSSEX**	p. 94
2949	**SUSSEX (WESTERN) L.J.A.** – *see* **SURREY AND SUSSEX**	p. 95
2950	**SUSSEX (CENTRAL) L.J.A.** – *see* **SURREY AND SUSSEX**	p. 94
2978	**BRADFORD L.J.A.** – *see* **NORTH AND WEST YORKSHIRE**	p. 88
2979	**KEIGHLEY L.J.A.** – *see* **NORTH AND WEST YORKSHIRE**	p. 89
2980	**BRIGHOUSE DIVISION** – *combined with 2984 CALDER DIVISION and 2983 TODMORDEN DIVISION to form* **2997 CALDERDALE DIVISION**	
2981	**CALDER DIVISION** – *combined with 2982 HALIFAX DIVISION to form* **2984 CALDERDALE DIVISION**	
2982	**HALIFAX DIVISION** – *combined with 2981 CALDER DIVISION to form* **2984 CALDER DIVISION**	
2983	**TODMORDEN DIVISION** – *combined with 2980 BRIGHOUSE DIVISION and 2984 CALDER DIVISION to form* **2997 CALDERDALE DIVISION**	
2984	**CALDER DIVISION** – *combined with 2980 BRIGHOUSE DIVISION and 2983 TODMORDEN DIVISION to form* **2997 CALDERDALE DIVISION**	
2985	**BATLEY DIVISION** – *combined with 2986 DEWSBURY DIVISION to form* **2996 BATLEY AND DEWSBURY DIVISION**	
2986	**DEWSBURY DIVISION** – *combined with 2985 BATLEY DIVISION to form* **2996 BATLEY AND DEWSBURY DIVISION**	
2987	**HUDDERSFIELD L.J.A.** – *see* **NORTH AND WEST YORKSHIRE**	p. 89

ENGLAND

2988 **LEEDS P.S.A.** – combined with 2989 MORLEY P.S.A., 2990 PUDSEY AND OTLEY P.S.A. and 2991 SKYRACK AND WETHERBY P.S.A. to form **2992 LEEDS DISTRICT P.S.A.**

2989 **MORLEY P.S.A.** – combined with 2988 LEEDS P.S.A., 2990 PUDSEY AND OTLEY P.S.A., and 2991 SKYRACK AND WETHERBY P.S.A. to form **2992 LEEDS DISTRICT P.S.A.**

2990 **PUDSEY AND OTLEY P.S.A.** – combined with 2988 LEEDS P.S.A., 2989 MORLEY P.S.A. and 2991 SKYRACK AND WETHERBY P.S.A. to form **2992 LEEDS DISTRICT P.S.A.**

2991 **SKYRACK AND WETHERBY P.S.A.** – combined with 2988 LEEDS P.S.A., 2989 MORLEY P.S.A., 2990 PUDSEY AND OTLEY P.S.A. to form **2992 LEEDS DISTRICT P.S.A.**

2992 **LEEDS DISTRICT L.J.A.** – see **NORTH AND WEST YORKSHIRE** .... p. 90

2994 **PONTEFRACT L.J.A.** – see **NORTH AND WEST YORKSHIRE** .... p. 90

2995 **WAKEFIELD L.J.A.** – see **NORTH AND WEST YORKSHIRE** .... p. 91

2996 **BATLEY AND DEWSBURY L.J.A.** – see **NORTH AND WEST YORKSHIRE** ..... p. 88

2997 **CALDERDALE L.J.A.** – see **NORTH AND WEST YORKSHIRE** .... p. 89

3005 **BRADFORD-ON-AVON DIVISION** – combined with 3013 MELKSHAM DIVISION, 3017 TROWBRIDGE DIVISION, 3018 WARMINSTER DIVISION (most), 3019 WESTBURY DIVISION and 3020 WHORWELLSDOWN DIVISION to form **3024 WEST WILTSHIRE DIVISION**

3006 **CALNE DIVISION** – combined with 3007 CHIPPENHAM DIVISION, 3008 CRICKLADE DIVISION and 3011 MALMESBURY DIVISION to form **3022 NORTH WILTSHIRE DIVISION**

3007 **CHIPPENHAM DIVISION** – combined with 3006 CALNE DIVISION, 3008 CRICKLADE DIVISION and 3011 MALMESBURY DIVISION to form **3022 NORTH WILTSHIRE DIVISION**

3008 **CRICKLADE DIVISION** – combined with 3006 CALNE DIVISION, 3007 CHIPPENHAM DIVISION and 3011 MALMESBURY DIVISION to form **3022 NORTH WILTSHIRE DIVISION**

3009 **DEVIZES DIVISION** – (most) combined with 3010 EVERLEY AND PEWSEY DIVISION (most) and 3011 MARLBOROUGH DIVISION to form **3025 KENNET DIVISION**

3010 **EVERLEY AND PEWSEY DIVISION** – (most) combined with 3009 DEVIZES DIVISION (most) and 3011 MARLBOROUGH DIVISION to form **3025 KENNET DIVISION**

3011 **MALMESBURY DIVISION** – combined with 3006 CALNE DIVISION, 3007 CHIPPENHAM DIVISION and 3008 CRICKLADE DIVISION to form **3022 WILTSHIRE DIVISION**

3012 **MARLBOROUGH DIVISION** – combined with 3009 DEVIZES DIVISION (most) and 3010 EVERLEY AND PEWSEY DIVISION (most) to form **3025 KENNET DIVISION**

3013 **MELKSHAM DIVISION** – combined with 3005 BRADFORD-ON-AVON DIVISION, 3017 TROWBRIDGE DIVISION, 3016 WARMINSTER DIVISION (most), 3019 WESTBURY DIVISION and 3020 WHORWELLSDOWN DIVISION to form **3024 WEST WILTSHIRE DIVISION**

3014 **SALISBURY DIVISION** – combined with 3018 TISBURY AND MERE DIVISION and parts of 3009 DEVIZES DIVISION, 3010 EVERLEY AND PEWSEY DIVISION and 3018 WARMINSTER DIVISION to form **3023 SALISBURY DIVISION**

3015 **SWINDON L.J.A.** – see **DORSET, GLOUCESTERSHIRE AND WILTSHIRE** ...... p. 50

ENGLAND

3016 **TISBURY AND MERE DIVISION** – *combined with 3014 SALISBURY DIVISION and parts of 3009 DEVIZES DIVISION, 3010 EVERLEY AND PEWSEY DIVISION and 3018 WARMINSTER DIVISION to form* **3023 SALISBURY DIVISION**

3017 **TROWBRIDGE DIVISION** – *combined with 3005 BRADFORD-ON-AVON DIVISION, 3013 MELKSHAM DIVISION, 3018 WARMINSTER DIVISION (most), 3019 WESTBURY DIVISION and 3020 WHORWELLSDOWN DIVISION to form* **3024 WEST WILTSHIRE DIVISION**

3018 **WARMINSTER DIVISION** – *(most) combined with 3005 BRADFORD-ON-AVON DIVISION, 3013 MELKSHAM DIVISION, 3017 TROWBRIDGE DIVISION, 3019 WESTBURY DIVISION and 3020 WHORWELLSDOWN DIVISION to form* **3024 WEST WILTSHIRE DIVISION**

3019 **WESTBURY DIVISION** – *combined with 3005 BRADFORD-ON-AVON DIVISION, 3013 MELKSHAM DIVISION, 3017 TROWBRIDGE DIVISION, 3018 WARMINSTER DIVISION (most) and 3020 WHORWELLSDOWN DIVISION to form* **3024 WEST WILTSHIRE DIVISION**

3020 **WHORWELLSDOWN DIVISION** – *combined with 3005 BRADFORD-ON-AVON DIVISION, 3013 MELKSHAM DIVISION, 3017 TROWBRIDGE DIVISION 3018 WARMINSTER DIVISION (most) and 3019 WESTBURY DIVISION to form* **3024 WEST WILTSHIRE DIVISION**

3022 **NORTH WILTSHIRE DIVISION** – *combined with 3024 WEST WILTSHIRE DIVISION to form* **3026 NORTH WEST WILTSHIRE DIVISION**

3023 **SALISBURY DIVISION** – *combined with 3025 KENNET DIVISION to form* **3027 SOUTH EAST WILTSHIRE DIVISION**

3024 **WEST WILTSHIRE DIVISION** – *combined with 3022 NORTH WILTSHIRE DIVISION to form* **3026 NORTH WEST WILTSHIRE DIVISION**

3025 **KENNET DIVISION** – *combined with 3023 SALISBURY DIVISION to form* **3027 SOUTH EAST WILTSHIRE DIVISION**

3026 **NORTH WEST WILTSHIRE L.J.A.** – *see* **DORSET, GLOUCESTERSHIRE AND WILTSHIRE** .... p. 49

3027 **SOUTH EAST WILTSHIRE L.J.A.** – *see* **DORSET, GLOUCESTERSHIRE AND WILTSHIRE** .... p. 50

3274 **BRIDGNORTH L.J.A.** – *absorbed into* **3282 TELFORD & BRIDGNORTH L.J.A.**

3275 **DRAYTON L.J.A.** – *combined with 3277 OSWESTRY L.J.A. and 3279 SHREWSBURY L.J.A. to form* **3278 SHREWSBURY & NORTH SHROPSHIRE L.J.A**

3276 **TELFORD & SOUTH SHROPSHIRE L.J.A.** – *see* **BLACK COUNTRY, STAFFORDSHIRE AND WEST MERCIA** .... p. 20

3277 **OWESTRY L.J.A.** – *combined with 3275 DRAYTON L.J.A. and 3279 SHREWSBURY L.J.A. to form* **3278 SHREWSBURY & NORTH SHROPSHIRE L.J.A.**

3278 **SHREWSBURY & NORTH YORKSHIRE L.J.A.** – *see* **BLACK COUNTRY, STAFFORDSHIRE & WEST MERCIA** .... p. 18

3279 **SHREWSBURY L.J.A.** – *combined with 3275 DRAYTON L.J.A. and 3277 OSWESTRY L.J.A. to form* **3278 SHREWSBURY AND NORTH SHROPSHIRE L.J.A.**

3280 **THE WREKIN DIVISION** – *combined with 3278 SHIFNAL DIVISION and 3281 WENLOCK DIVISION to form* **3282 TELFORD DIVISION**

3281 **WENLOCK DIVISION** – *combined with 3278 SHIFNAL DIVISION and 3281 WENLOCK DIVISION to form* **3282 TELFORD DIVISION**

WALES

3282 TELFORD & SOUTH SHROPSHIRE L.J.A. – see **BLACK COUNTRY, STAFFORDSHIRE AND WEST MERCIA** .... p. 20

WALES

3051 BERWYN DIVISION – abolished – functions transferred to **3052 COLWYN DIVISION**, **3061 DENBIGHSHIRE DIVISION** or **3058 WREXHAM MAELOR DIVISION**

3052 COLWYN P.S.A. – combined with *3237 ABERCONWY P.S.A.* to form **3062 CONWY P.S.A.**

3053 DYFFRYN CLWYD DIVISION – part transferred to **3052 COLWYN DIVISION**, remainder combined with *3057 RHUDDLAN DIVISION*, *3051 BERWYN DIVISION (Part)* and *3052 COLWYN DIVISION (Part)* to form **3061 DENBIGHSHIRE DIVISION**

3054 FLINT DIVISION – combined with *3055 HAWARDEN DIVISION*, and *3056 MOLD DIVISION* to form (after boundary adjustment) **3059 FLINTSHIRE DIVISION**

3055 HAWARDEN DIVISION – combined with *3054 FLINT DIVISION* and *3056 MOLD DIVISION* to form (after boundary adjustment) **3059 FLINTSHIRE DIVISION**

3056 MOLD DIVISION – combined with *3054 FLINT DIVISION*, and *3055 HAWARDEN DIVISION* to form (after boundary adjustment) **3059 FLINTSHIRE DIVISION**

3057 RHUDDLAN DIVISION – combined with *3053 DYFFRYN CLWYD DIVISION (Part)*, *3051 BERWYN DIVISION (Part)* and *3052 COLWYN DIVISION (Part)* to form **3061 DENBIGHSHIRE DIVISION**

3058 WREXHAM MAELOR L.J.A. – see **NORTH WALES** .... p. 107

3059 FLINTSHIRE L.J.A. – see **NORTH WALES** .... p. 107

3060 ARFON P.S.A. – combined with *3236 DWYFOR P.S.A.* and *3239 MEIRIONNYDD P.S.A.* to form **3244 GWYNEDD P.S.A.**

3061 DENBIGHSHIRE L.J.A. – see **NORTH WALES** .... p. 106

3062 CONWY L.J.A. – see **NORTH WALES** .... p. 106

3109 ABERAERON DIVISION – combined with *3118 LAMPETER DIVISION* and *3121 LLANDYSSUL DIVISION* to form **3134 CEREDIGION GANOL DIVISION**

3110 ABERYSTWYTH DIVISION – combined with *3131 TREGARON DIVISION* to form **3135 GOGLEDD CEREDIGION DIVISION**

3111 AMMAN VALLEY DIVISION – combined with *3119 LLANDEILO DIVISION* and *3120 LLANDOVERY DIVISION (part)* to form **3140 DINEFWR DIVISION**

3112 CARDIGAN DIVISION – combined with *3128 RHYDLEWIS DIVISION* to form **3136 DE CEREDIGION DIVISION**

3113 CARMARTHEN DIVISION – combined with *3129 ST. CLEARS DIVISION* and *3132 WHITLAND DIVISION* to form **3138 CARMARTHEN SOUTH DIVISION**

3114 CEMAES DIVISION – combined with *3116 FISHGUARD DIVISION* to form **3141 GOGLEDD PRESELI DIVISION**

3115 DEWSLAND DIVISION – combined with *3117 HAVERFORDWEST DIVISION* to form **3133 DEWSLAND-HAVERFORDWEST DIVISION**

3116 FISHGUARD DIVISION – combined with *3114 CEMAES DIVISION* to form **3141 GOGLEDD PRESELI DIVISION**

3117 HAVERFORDWEST DIVISION – combined with *3115 DEWSLAND DIVISION* to form **3133 DEWSLAND-HAVERFORDWEST DIVISION**

WALES

3118	**LAMPETER DIVISION** – *combined with 3109 ABERAERON DIVISION and 3121 LLANDYSSUL DIVISION to form* **3134 CEREDIGION GANOL DIVISION**	
3119	**LLANDEILO DIVISION** – *combined with 3111 AMMAN VALLEY DIVISION and 3120 LLANDOVERY DIVISION (part) to form* **3140 DINEFWR DIVISION**	
3120	**LLANDOVERY DIVISION** – *part combined with 3111 AMMAN VALLEY DIVISION and 3119 LLANDEILO DIVISION to form* **3140 DINEFWR DIVISION** *and part combined with 3125 NEWCASTLE EMLYN DIVISION and PENCADER DIVISION to form* **3137 CARMARTHEN NORTH DIVISION**	
3121	**LLANDYSSUL DIVISION** – *combined with 3109 ABERAERON DIVISION and 3118 LAMPETER DIVISION to form* **3134 CEREDIGION DIVISION**	
3122	**LLANELLI L.J.A.** – see **MID AND WEST WALES**	p. 102
3123	**MILFORD HAVEN DIVISION** – *combined with 3133 DEWSLAND-HAVERFORDWEST DIVISION to form* **3139 CLEDDAU DIVISION**	
3124	**NARBERTH DIVISION** – *combined with 3126 PEMBROKE DIVISION and 3130 TENBY DIVISION to form* **3142 SOUTH PEMBROKESHIRE DIVISION**	
3125	**NEWCASTLE EMLYN DIVISION** – *combined with 3120 LLANDOVERY DIVISION (part) and 3127 PENCADER DIVISION to form* **3137 CARMARTHEN NORTH DIVISION**	
3126	**PEMBROKE DIVISION** – *combined with 3124 NARBERTH DIVISION and 3130 TENBY DIVISION to form* **3142 SOUTH PEMBROKESHIRE DIVISION**	
3127	**PENCADER DIVISION** – *combined with 3120 LLANDOVERY DIVISION (part) and 3125 NEWCASTLE EMLYN DIVISION to form* **3137 CARMARTHEN NORTH DIVISION**	
3128	**RHYDLEWIS DIVISION** – *combined with 3112 CARDIGAN DIVISION to form* **3136 DE CEREDIGION DIVISION**	
3129	**ST. CLEARS DIVISION** – *combined with 3113 CARMARTHEN DIVISION and 3132 WHITLAND DIVISION to form* **3138 CARMARTHEN SOUTH DIVISION**	
3130	**TENBY DIVISION** – *combined with 3124 NARBERTH DIVISION and 3126 PEMBROKE DIVISION to form* **3142 PEMBROKESHIRE DIVISION**	
3131	**TREGARON DIVISION** – *combined with 3110 ABERYSTWYTH DIVISION to form* **3135 GOGLEDD CEREDIGION DIVISION**	
3132	**WHITLAND DIVISION** – *combined with 3113 CARMARTHEN DIVISION and 3129 ST. CLEARS DIVISION to form* **3138 CARMARTHEN SOUTH DIVISION**	
3133	**DEWSLAND-HAVERFORDWEST DIVISION** – *combined with 3123 MILFORD HAVEN DIVISION to form* **3139 CLEDDAU DIVISION**	
3134	**CEREDIGION GANOL DIVISION** – *combined with 3135 GOGLEDD CEREDIGION DIVISION and 3136 DE CEREDIGION DIVISION to form* **3135 CEREDIGION DIVISION**	
3135	**GOGLEDD CEREDIGION DIVISION** – *combined with 3134 CEREDIGION GANOL DIVISION and 3136 DE CEREDIGION DIVISION to form* **3135 CEREDIGION DIVISION**	
3135	**CEREDIGION L.J.A.** – see **MID AND WEST WALES**	p. 101
3136	**DE CEREDIGION DIVISION** – *combined with 3134 CEREDIGION GANOL DIVISION and 3135 GOGLEDD CEREDIGION DIVISION to form* **3135 CEREDIGION DIVISION**	
3137	**CARMARTHEN NORTH DIVISION** – *combined with 3138 CARMARTHEN SOUTH DIVISION to form* **3138 CARMARTHEN DIVISION**	
3138	**CARMARTHEN SOUTH DIVISION** – *combined with 3137 CARMARTHEN NORTH DIVISION to form* **3138 CARMARTHEN DIVISION**	

WALES

3138	CARMARTHEN L.J.A. – see **MID AND WEST WALES**	p. 100

3139   CLEDDAU DIVISION combined with 3141 GOGLEDD PRESELI DIVISION to form **3139 NORTH PEMBROKESHIRE DIVISION**

3139   NORTH PEMBROKESHIRE L.J.A. – Combined with 3142 SOUTH PEMBROKESHIRE to form **3356 PEMBROKESHIRE L.J.A.**

3140	DINEFWR L.J.A. – see **MID AND WEST WALES**	p. 102

3141   GOGLEDD PRESELI DIVISION – combined with 3139 CLEDDAU DIVISION to form **3139 NORTH PEMBROKESHIRE DIVISION**

3142   SOUTH PEMBROKESHIRE L.J.A. – combined with 3139 NORTH PEMBROKESHIRE to form **3356 PEMBROKESHIRE L.J.A.**

3200   ABERGAVENNY DIVISION – combined with 3202 CWMBRAN DIVISION, 3203 CHEPSTOW DIVISION, 3204 MONMOUTH DIVISION, 3206 PONTYPOOL DIVISION and 3207 USK DIVISION to form **3208 EAST GWENT DIVISION**

3201   BEDWELLTY P.S.A. (except Llanelly Hill) – combined with 3263 LOWER RHYMNEY VALLEY P.S.A. and 3267 UPPER RHYMNEY VALLEY P.S.A. to form **3209 NORTH WEST GWENT P.S.A.**

3202   CWMBRAN DIVISION – combined with 3200 ABERGAVENNY DIVISION, 3203 CHEPSTOW DIVISION, 3204 MONMOUTH DIVISION, 3206 PONTYPOOL DIVISION and 3207 USK DIVISION to form **3208 EAST GWENT DIVISION**

3203   CHEPSTOW DIVISION – combined with 3200 ABERGAVENNY DIVISION, 3202 CWMBRAN DIVISION, 3204 MONMOUTH DIVISION, 3206 PONTYPOOL DIVISION and 3207 USK DIVISION to form **3208 EAST GWENT DIVISION**

3204   MONMOUTH DIVISION – combined with 3200 ABERGAVENNY DIVISION, 3202 CWMBRAN DIVISION, 3203 CHEPSTOW DIVISION, 3206 PONTYPOOL DIVISION and 3207 USK DIVISION to form **3208 EAST GWENT DIVISION**

3205   NEWPORT P.S.A. – combined with 3208 EAST GWENT P.S.A. (including Llanelly Hill) to form **3210 SOUTH EAST GWENT P.S.A.**

3206   PONTYPOOL DIVISION – combined with 3200 ABERGAVENNY DIVISION, 3202 CWMBRAN DIVISION, 3203 CHEPSTOW DIVISION, 3204 MONMOUTH DIVISION and 3207 USK DIVISION to form **3208 EAST GWENT DIVISION**

3207   USK DIVISION – combined with 3200 ABERGAVENNY DIVISION, 3202 CWMBRAN DIVISION, 3203 CHEPSTOW DIVISION, 3204 MONMOUTH DIVISION AND 3206 PONTYPOOL DIVISION to form **3208 EAST GWENT DIVISION**

3208   EAST GWENT P.S.A. – (including Llanelly Hill) combined with 3205 NEWPORT P.S.A. to form **3210 SOUTH EAST GWENT P.S.A.**

3209   NORTH WEST GWENT – combined with 3210 SOUTH EAST GWENT to form **3211 GWENT L.J.A.**

3210   SOUTH EAST GWENT – combined with 3209 NORTH WEST GWENT to form **3211 GWENT L.J.A.**

3211	GWENT L.J.A. – see **SOUTH EAST WALES**	p. 110

3220   ARDUDWY-IS-ARTRO DIVISION – combined with 3226 ESTIMANER DIVISION, 3230 PENLLYN DIVISION and 3233 TALYBONT DIVISION to form **3235 SOUTH MEIRIONNYDD DIVISION**

3221   NORTH MEIRIONNYDD DIVISION (formerly Ardudwy-uwch-Artro Division – combined with 3235 SOUTH MEIRIONNYDD DIVISION to form **3239 MEIRIONNYDD DIVISION**

3222   BANGOR DIVISION – combined with 3234 CAERNARFON DIVISION to form (after boundary adjustment) **3060 ARDON DIVISION**

WALES

3223	**CAERNARVON DIVISION** – *combined with 3227 GWYRFAI DIVISION to form* **3234 CAERNARFON AND GWYRFAI DIVISION**	
3224	**CONWY AND LLANDUDNO DIVISION** – *combined with 3228 NANT CONWY DIVISION to form* **3237 ABERCONWY DIVISION**	
3225	**EIFIONYDD DIVISION** – *combined with 3231 PWLLHELI DIVISION to form* **3236 EIFIONYDD AND PWLLHELI DIVISION**	
3226	**ESTIMANER DIVISION** – *combined with 3220 ARDUDWY-IS-ARTRO DIVISION, 3230 PENLLYN DIVISION and 3233 TALYBONT DIVISION to form* **3235 SOUTH MEIRIONNYDD DIVISION**	
3227	**GWYRFAI DIVISION** – *combined with 3223 CAERNARVON DIVISION to form* **3234 CAERNARFON AND GWYRFAI DIVISION**	
3228	**NANT CONWY DIVISION** – *combined with 3224 CONWY AND LLANDUDNO DIVISION to form* **3237 ABERCONWY DIVISION**	
3229	**NORTH ANGLESEY DIVISION** – *combined with 3232 SOUTH ANGLESEY DIVISION to form* **3238 YNYS MON/ANGLESEY DIVISION**	
3230	**PENLLYN DIVISION** – *combined with 3220 ARDUDWY-IS-ARTRO DIVISION, 3226 ESTIMANER DIVISION and 3233 TALYBONT DIVISION to form* **3235 SOUTH MEIRIONNYDD DIVISION**	
3231	**PWLLHELI DIVISION** – *combined with 3225 EIFIONYDD DIVISION to form* **3236 EIFIONYDD AND PWLLHELI DIVISION**	
3232	**SOUTH ANGLESEY DIVISION** – *combined with 3229 NORTH ANGLESEY DIVISION to form* **3238 YNYS MON/ANGLESEY DIVISION**	
3233	**TALYBONT DIVISION** – *combined with 3220 ARDUDWY-IS-ARTRO DIVISION, 3226 ESTIMANER DIVISION and 3230 PENLLYN DIVISION to form* **3235 SOUTH MEIRIONNYDD DIVISION**	
3234	**CAERNARFON AND GWYRFAI DIVISION** – *combined with 3222 BANGOR DIVISION to form (after boundary adjustment)* **3060 ARFON DIVISION**	
3235	**SOUTH MEIRIONNYDD DIVISION** – *combined with 3221 NORTH MEIRIONNYDD DIVISION to form* **3239 MEIRIONNYDD DIVISION**	
3236	**EIFIONYDD AND PWLLHELI DIVISION** *renamed* **DWYFOR DIVISION**	
3236	**DWYFOR P.S.A.** – *combined with 3060 ARFON P.S.A. and 3239 MEIRIONNYDD P.S.A. to form* **3244 GWYNEDD P.S.A.**	
3237	**ABERCONWY P.S.A.** – *combined with 3052 COLWYN P.S.A. to form* **3062 CONWY P.S.A.**	
3238	**YNYS MON/ANGLESEY L.J.A.** – *see* **NORTH WALES**	p. 108
3239	**MEIRIONNYD P.S.A.** – *combined with 3060 ARFON P.S.A. and 3236 DWYFOR P.S.A. to form* **3244 GWYNEDD P.S.A.**	
3244	**GWYNEDD L.J.A.** – *see* **NORTH WALES**	p. 107
3262	**CYNON VALLEY L.J.A.** – *see* **SOUTH EAST WALES**	p. 109
3263	**LOWER RHYMNEY VALLEY P.S.A.** – *combined with 3267 UPPER RHYMNEY VALLEY P.S.A. and 3201 BEDWELLTY P.S.A. (except Llanelly Hill) to form* **3209 NORTH WEST GWENT P.S.A.**	
3264	**MERTHYR TYDFIL L.J.A.** – *see* **SOUTH EAST WALES**	p. 110
3265	**MISKIN L.J.A.** – *see* **SOUTH EAST WALES**	p. 110
3266	**NEWCASTLE AND OGMORE L.J.A.** – *see* **SOUTH EAST WALES**	p. 111

WALES

3267	**UPPER RHYMNEY VALLEY P.S.A.** – *combined with 3263 LOWER RHYMNEY VALLEY P.S.A. AND 3201 BEDWELLTY P.S.A. (except Llanelly Hill) to form* **3209 NORTH WEST GWENT P.S.A.**	
3320	**BRECON DIVISION** – *combined with 3324 DEFYNOCK DIVISION to form* **3342 BRECON DIVISION**	
3321	**BUILTH DIVISION** – *combined with 3322 COLWYN DIVISION and 3335 PAINSCASTLE DIVISION to form* **3345 BUILTH DIVISION**	
3322	**COLWYN DIVISION** – *combined with 3321 BUILTH DIVISION and 3335 PAINSCASTLE DIVISION to form* **3345 BUILTH DIVISION**	
3323	**CRICKHOWELL DIVISION** – *combined with 3342 BRECON DIVISION (except for Ystradfellte) and 3338 TALGARTH DIVISION to form* **3350 BRECON DIVISION**	
3324	**DEFYNOCK DIVISION** – *combined with 3320 BRECON DIVISION to form* **3342 BRECON DIVISION**	
3325	**DEYTHEUR DIVISION** – *combined with 3328 LLANFYLLIN DIVISION and 3339 WELSHPOOL DIVISION to form* **3341 WELSHPOOL DIVISION**	
3326	**KNIGHTON DIVISION** – *combined with 3343 EAST RADNOR DIVISION to form* **3344 EAST RADNOR DIVISION**	
3327	**LLANDRINDOD WELLS DIVISION** – *combined with 3345 BUILTH DIVISION, 3344 EAST RADNOR DIVISION and 3337 RHAYADER DIVISION to form* **3351 LLANDRINDOD WELLS DIVISION**	
3328	**LLANFYLLIN DIVISION** – *combined with 3325 DEYTHEUR DIVISION and 3339 WELSHPOOL DIVISION to form* **3341 WELSHPOOL DIVISION**	
3329	**LLANIDLOES DIVISION** – *combined with 3347 NEWTOWN DIVISION to form* **3352 NEWTOWN DIVISION**	
3330	**MACHYNLLETH DIVISION** – *combined with 3352 NEWTOWN DIVISION to form* **3352 DE MALDWYN DIVISION** – *see above*	
3331	**MATHRAFAL DIVISION** – *combined with 3341 WELSHPOOL DIVISION to form* **3346 WELSHPOOL DIVISION**	
3332	**MONTGOMERY DIVISION** – *combined with 3334 NEWTOWN DIVISION to form* **3347 NEWTOWN DIVISION**	
3333	**NEW RADNOR DIVISION** – *combined with 3336 PRESTEIGNE DIVISION to form* **3343 EAST RADNOR DIVISION**	
3334	**NEWTOWN DIVISION** – *combined with 3332 MONTGOMERY DIVISION to form* **3347 NEWTOWN DIVISION**	
3335	**PAINSCASTLE DIVISION** – *combined with 3321 BUILTH DIVISION AND 3322 COLWYN DIVISION to form* **3345 BUILTH DIVISION**	
3336	**PRESTEIGNE DIVISION** – *combined with 3333 NEW RADNOR DIVISION to form* **3343 EAST RADNOR DIVISION**	
3337	**RHAYADER DIVISION** – *combined with 3345 BUILTH DIVISION, 3327 LLANDRINDOD WELLS DIVISION and 3344 EAST RADNOR DIVISION to form* **3351 LLANDRINDOD WELLS DIVISION**	
3338	**TALGARTH DIVISION** – *combined with 3342 BRECON DIVISION (except for Ystradfellte) and 3323 CRICKHOWELL DIVISION TO FORM* **3350 BRECON DIVISION**	
3339	**WELSHPOOL DIVISION** – *combined with 3325 DEYTHEUR DIVISION and 3328 LLANFYLLIN DIVISION to form* **3341 WELSHPOOL DIVISION**	
3340	**YSRTADGYNLAIS DIVISION** – *combined with 3350 BRECON DIVISION to form* **3350 DE BRYCHEINIOG DIVISION**	

WALES

3341	**WELSHPOOL DIVISION** – *combined with 3331 MATHRAFAL DIVISION to form* **3346 WELSHPOOL DIVISION**
3342	**BRECON DIVISION** – *(except for Ystradfellte) combined with 3323 CRICKHOWELL DIVISION and 3338 TALGARTH DIVISION to form* **3350 BRECON DIVISION**
3343	**EAST RADNOR DIVISION** – *combined with 3326 KNIGHTON DIVISION to form* **3344 EAST RADNOR DIVISION**
3344	**EAST RADNOR DIVISION** – *combined with 3345 BUILTH DIVISION, 3327 LLANDRINDOD WELLS DIVISION and 3337 RHAYADER DIVISION to form* **3351 LLANDRINDOD WELLS DIVISION**
3345	**BUILTH DIVISION** – *combined with 3327 LLANDRINDOD WELLS DIVISION, 3344 EAST RADNOR DIVISION and 3337 RHAYADER DIVISION to form* **3351 LLANDRINDOD WELLS DIVISION**
3346	**WELSHPOOL L.J.A.** – *combined with 3352 DE MALDWYN L.J.A. to form* **3355 MONTGOMERYSHIRE L.J.A.**
3347	**NEWTOWN DIVISION** – *combined with 3329 LLANIDLOES DIVISION to form* **3352 NEWTOWN DIVISION**
3348	**CARDIFF L.J.A.** – *see* **SOUTH EAST WALES** . . . . p. 109
3349	**VALE OF GLAMORGAN L.J.A.** – *see* **SOUTH EAST WALES** . . . . p. 111
3350	**BRECON DIVISION** – *combined with 3340 YSTRADGYNLAIS DIVISION to form* **3350 DE BRYCHEINIOG DIVISION**
3350	**DE BRYCHEINIOG L.J.A.** – *see* **MID AND WEST WALES** . . . . p. 101
3351	**LLANDRINDOD WELLS DIVISION** – *renamed* **RADNORSHIRE AND NORTH BRECKNOCK DIVISION**
3351	**RADNORSHIRE AND NORTH BRECKNOCK L.J.A.** – *see* **MID AND WEST** . . . . p. 104
3352	**NEWTOWN DIVISION** – *combined with 3330 MACHYNLLETH DIVISION to form* **3352 DE MALDWYN DIVISION**
3352	**DE MALDWYN L.J.A.** – *combined with 3346 WELSHPOOL L.J.A. to form* **3355 MONTGOMERYSHIRE L.J.A.**
3355	**MONTGOMERYSHIRE L.J.A.** – *see* **MID AND WEST WALES** . . . . p. 103
3356	**PEMBROKESHIRE L.J.A.** – *see* **MID AND WEST WALES** . . . . p. 104
3357	**PORT TALBOT DIVISION** – *combined with 3359 NEATH DIVISION to form* **3359 NEATH PORT TALBOT DIVISION**
3358	**LLIW VALLEY DIVISION** – *combined with 3360 SWANSEA DIVISION to form* **3360 SWANSEA COUNTY DIVISION**
3359	**NEATH DIVISION** – *combined with 3357 PORT TALBOT DIVISION to form* **3359 NEATH PORT TALBOT DIVISION**
3359	**NEATH PORT TALBOT L.J.A.** – *see* **MID AND WEST WALES** . . . . p. 103
3360	**SWANSEA DIVISION** – *combined with 3358 LLIW VALLEY DIVISION to form* **3360 SWANSEA COUNTY DIVISION**
3360	**SWANSEA L.J.A.** – *see* **MID AND WEST WALES** . . . . p. 105

INDEX TO COURTS OF SUMMARY JURISDICTION

	Ct No	Page		Ct No	Page
A			Ashton-under-Lyne	1740	174
Aberaeron	3109	199	Atherstone and Coleshill	2894	194
Aberconwy	3237	202	Avon North	1020	159
Aberdeen	9701	120	Axminster	1475	168
Aberdeen (City of) D.C.	9400	120	Axminster and Honiton	1493	169
Aberdeenshire D.C. at Banff	9405	121	Aylesbury	1111	160
Aberdeenshire D.C. at Inverurie	9407	120		1125	161
Aberdeenshire D.C. at Peterhead	9408	125	Ayr	9704	145
Aberdeenshire D.C. at Stonehaven	9409	126			
Abergavenny	3200	201	**B**		
Aberystwyth	3110	199	Bainton Beacon	1923	179
Abingdon	2681	189	Bainton, Wilton and Holme Beacon	1905	178
Abingdon (Borough)	2667	188	Bakewell	1416	167
Abingdon (County)	2668	188	Ballymena	9004	113
Abingdon, Didcot and Wantage	2774	190	Ballymoney	9005	113
Accrington	1994	181	Bamburgh and East Coquetdale	2345	185
Acton M.C.	2723	78	Bamburgh Ward	2335	184
Afan (renamed Port Talbot)	3357	204	Bampton East	2669	188
Airdrie	9702	145	Bampton West	2670	188
Alcester	2893	194	Banbridge	9006	114
Alford	2053	182	Banbury	2775	191
Alfreton	1414	166	Banff	9711	120
Alfreton and Belper	1426	167	Banff D.C.	9405	121
Allertonshire	2522	185	Bangor	3222	201
Alloa	9703	128	Barking M.C.	2814	75
Alnwick	2347	31	Barnet M.C.	2725	190
Alston	1360	165	Barnsley	2770	57
Alton	1760	175	Barnstaple	1476	168
Alton and Petersfield	1778	175	Barnstaple and South Molton	1494	169
Ambleside and Windermere	1361	165	Barrow-in-Furness	1362	165
Amersham	1110	160	Barrow with Bootle	1380	166
Amman Valley	3111	199	Barton-upon-Humber	1924	179
Ampthill	1050	159	Basildon	1610	171
Andover	1761	175	Basingstoke	1762	175
Anglesey	3238	108	Bath	1012	159
Angus D.C. at Arbroath	9415	128	Bath and Wansdyke	1022	5
Angus D.C. at Brechin	9416	131	Batley	2985	196
Angus D.C. at Forfar	9417	131	Batley and Dewsbury	2996	88
Annan D.C.	9445	146	Battle and Rye	1595	170
Antrim	9001	113	Beacontree (renamed Redbridge)	2755	190
Appleby	1383	166	Beccles	2816	192
Arbroath	9705	128	Bedford	1051	159
Ards	9002	113	Bedford and Mid Bedfordshire	1051	8
Ardudwy-is-Artro	3220	201	Bedwellty	3201	201
Arfon	3060	199	Belfast and Newtonabbey	9007	114
Argyll & Bute D.C. at Bowmore	9425	140	Bellingham	2336	184
Argyll & Bute D.C. at Campbeltown	9426	140	Belper	1417	167
Argyll & Bute D.C. at Dunoon	9427	142	Berkeley	1670	172
Argyll & Bute D.C. at Helensburgh	9428	140	Berkeley and Dursley	1691	174
Argyll & Bute at Lochgilphead	9429	142	Berwick-upon-Tweed	2337	184
Argyll & Bute D.C. at Oban	9430	143		2348	31
Armagh	9003	113	Berwyn	3051	199
Arrington and Melbourn	1133	161	Beverley	1925	179
Arundel	2927	196	Beverley and the Wolds	1942	57
Ashbourne	1415	167	Bewdley and Stourport	1871	177
Ashby-de-la-Zouch	2038	182	Bewdley Borough	1845	176
	2047	62	Bexhill	1596	170
Ashford and Tenterden	1952	180			

INDEX

	Ct No	Page
Bexley M.C.	2728	69
Bicester	2671 / 2776	188 / 191
Bideford and Great Torrington	1477	168
Biggleswade	1052	159
Billericay (renamed Basildon)	1610	171
Bingham	2552	187
Birdforth	2523	185
Birmingham	2908	13
Bishop's Stortford	1875	177
Blackburn	1995	181
Blackburn, Darwen and Ribble Valley	2012	37
Blackpool	1996	181
Blackpool and Fylde	1996	181
Blandford	1500	169
Blandford and Sturminster	1512	170
Blyth Valley	2338	185
Blything	2817	192
Board of Green Cloth Verge of the Palaces	—	87
Bodmin	1279	164
Bodmin and Trigg	1260	163
Bolton	1731	51
Bootle, Cumbria	1363	165
Bootle, M.C., Merseyside – See South Sefton L.J.A.	2270	29
Boston	2054 / 2073	182 / 62
Bottisham	1134	161
Bourne	2055	182
Bourne and Stamford	2074	62
Bournemouth	1501	169
Bournemouth and Christchurch	1514	170
Bow Street M.C.	2641	187
Brackley	2320	184
Bradfield and Sonning	1065	160
Bradford	2978	88
Bradford-on-Avon	3005	197
Braintree and Halstead	1631	172
Brecon	3320 / 3342 / 3350	203 / 204 / 204
Brent M.C.	2762	76
Brentford M.C.	2726 / 2769	190 / 82
Brentwood	1611	171
Bridgnorth	3274	198
Bridlington	1941	57
Bridport	1502	169
Brigg	1926	179
Brighouse	2980	196
Brighton	1597	171
Brighton and Hove	1604	171
Brill	1112	161
Bristol	1013	5
Bromley M.C.	2727	70
Bromsgrove	1846	176
Bromsgrove and Redditch	1840	16

	Ct No	Page
Bromyard	1847	176
Buckingham	1113 / 1126	161 / 161
Buckrose	2524	185
Builth	3321 / 3345	203 / 204
Bullingdon	2672	188
Bulmer East	2525	185
Bulmer West	2526	185
Buntingford	1876	177
Burnham	1114	161
Burnley	1997	181
Burnley and Pendle	2011	182
Burnley, Pendle and Rossendale	2014	37
Burton-upon-Trent	2780	191
Bury	1732	51

C

	Ct No	Page
Caernarfon and Gwyrfai	3234	202
Caernarvon	3223	202
Caistor	2056	183
Calder	2981 / 2984	196 / 196
Calderdale	2997	89
Calne	3006	197
Camberwell Green M.C.	2656	73
Cambridge	1135 / 1165	161 / 22
Cambridge City	1136	162
Camden Y.C.	6650	83
Campbeltown	9716	140
Campbeltown D.C.	9426	140
Campden	1671	172
Cannock	2781	191
Cannock and Seisdon	2859	194
Canterbury	1953	180
Cardiff	3348	109
Cardigan	3112	199
Carlisle	1364	165
Carlisle and District	1322	38
Carmarthen	3113 / 3138	199 / 100
Carmarthen North	3137	200
Carmarthen South	3138	200
Carrickfergus and Newtonabbey (renamed Newtownabbey)	9010	114
Castlereagh	9012	114
Caxton	1137 / 1159	162 / 162
Cemaes	3114	199
Central and South West Staffordshire	2799	16
Central Buckinghamshire	1129	96
Central Devon	1292	45
Central Dorset	1515	170
Central Hertfordshire	1892	8
Central Kent	1960	60
Central Norfolk	1442	22

INDEX

	Ct No	Page
Ceredigion	3135	101
Ceredigion Ganol	3134	200
Channel	1957	180
Cheadle	2782	191
Chelmsford	1612	171
Cheltenham	1672	173
Chepstow	3203	201
Chertsey	2835	193
Chesham	1115	161
Cheshunt	1877	177
Chester	1173	163
Chester, Ellesmere Port and Neston	1188	27
Chester-le-Street	1576	170
Chesterfield	1418	167
Chichester	2928	196
Chichester and District	2936	196
Chiltern	1128	161
Chippenham	3007	197
Chipping Norton	2673	188
Chorley	1998	38
Christchurch	1503	169
Church	1999	181
Cirencester	1673	173
Cirencester, Fairford and Tetbury	1689	173
City of Hereford	1851	176
City of London M.C.	2631	70
City of Salford	1747	51
City of Westminster	2660	71
City of Worcester	1865	177
	1874	177
Clackmannanshire D.C. at Alloa	9440	128
Claro	2527	185
Cleddau	3139	201
Cleethorpes	1930	179
Clerkenwell M.C.	2642	187
Clydebank D.C.	9575	141
Coatbridge D.C.	9530	145
Cockermouth	1365	165
Colchester	1613	171
Coleford	1674	173
Coleraine	9014	114
Colwyn (Clwyd)	3052	199
Colwyn (Powys)	3322	203
Congleton	1174	163
Conwy	3062	106
Conwy and Llandudno	3224	202
Cookstown	9015	114
Coquetdale (renamed Alnwick)	2347	31
Corby	2321	63
Coventry	2910	13
Craigavon	9016	115
Crawley	2929	196
Crewe and Nantwich	1175	163
Crickhowell	3323	203
Cricklade	3008	197
Cromer	1393	166
Crowborough	1598	171
Croydon M.C.	2732	71

	Ct No	Page
Cullompton	1478	168
Cumbernauld D.C.	9531	145
Cumnock D.C.	9460	146
Cupar	9717	129
Cupar D.C.	9485	129
Cwmbran	3202	201
Cynon Valley	3262	109

D

	Ct No	Page
Dacorum	1878	177
Darlington	1577	170
Dartford	1954	180
Dartford and Gravesham	1969	181
Darwen	2000	181
Daventry	2322	63
De Brycheiniog	3350	101
Deben	2861	194
De Ceredigion	3136	200
Defynock	3324	203
De Maldwyn	3352	204
Denbighshire	3061	106
Dengie and Maldon	1614	171
Derby	1419	167
Derby and South Derbyshire	1427	167
	1431	167
Derby County and Appletree	1420	167
Derwentside	1578	170
Devizes	3009	197
Dewsbury	2986	196
Dewsland	3115	199
Dewsland-Haverfordwest	3133	200
Deytheur	3325	203
Dickering	1927	179
Dickering and North Holderness	1904	178
Didcot and Wantage	2718	190
Dinefwr	3140	102
Dingwall	9721	121
Dingwall D.C.	9500	121
Diss	1387	166
Doncaster	2771	58
Dorchester	1504	169
Dore and Bredwardine	1848	176
Dorking	2836	193
Dornoch	9722	121
Dorset, East	1522	48
Dorset, West	1523	50
Dover and East Kent	1955	180
Down	9018	115
Downham Market	1386	166
Drayton	3275	198
Droitwich	1849	176
Droxford	1763	175
Dudley	2911	17
Dumbarton	9723	140
Dumbarton D.C.	9576	141
Dumfries	9724	146
Dumfries D.C.	9446	147
Dumfries and Galloway D.C. at Annan	9445	146

INDEX

	Ct No	Page
Dumfries and Galloway D.C. at Dumfries	9446	147
Dumfries and Galloway D.C. at Kirkcudbright	9447	148
Dumfries and Galloway D.C. at Sanquhar	9449	147
Dumfries and Galloway D.C. at Stranraer	9450	149
Dundee	9726	129
Dundee, City of, D.C.	9456	129
Dunfermline	9727	130
Dunfermline D.C.	9486	130
Dungannon	9019	115
Dunheved	1261	163
Dunhevid and Stratton	1284	164
Dunmow	1615	171
Dunmow and Saffron Walden	1632	172
Dunoon	9728	141
Dunoon D.C.	9427	142
Duns	9729	133
Dunstable	1053	160
Durham	1579	170
Durham (North)	1583	33
Durham (South)	1584	34
Dursley	1675	173
Dwyfor	3236	202
Dyffryn Clwyd	3053	199

E

	Ct No	Page
Ealing M.C.	2734	77
Easington	1580	170
Easingwold	2544	187
East Ayrshire D.C. at Cumnock	9460	146
East Ayrshire D.C. at Kilmarnock	9461	143
East Berkshire	1072	96
East Cambridgeshire	1166	22
East Coquetdale Ward	2339	185
East Cornwall	1289	45
East Derbyshire	1429	167
East Dereham	1388	166
East Dorset	1522	48
East Dunbartonshire D.C. at Kirkintilloch	9465	139
East Dunbartonshire D.C. at Milngavie	9466	141
East Elloe	2057	183
East Gwent	3208	201
East Hertfordshire	1888	9
East Kent	1957	61
East Kilbride D.C.	9565	139
East Lothian D.C. at Haddington	9470	134
East Middle	1262	163
East Oxfordshire	2717	190
East Penwith	1263	163
East Powder	1264	163
East Radnor	3343 / 3344	204 / 204
East Renfrewshire D.C. at Giffnock	9474	144
East Retford	2553	187
East South	1265	163

	Ct No	Page
East Tyrone	—	115
East Ward	1366	165
Eastbourne	1599	171
Eastbourne and Hailsham	1605	171
Eastleigh	1764	175
Eccles	1737	174
Eccleshall	2783	191
Eden	1324	38
Edinburgh	9741	133
Edinburgh (City of) D.C.	9478	134
Eifionydd	3225	202
Elfionydd and Pwllheli	3236	202
Elgin	9742	122
Ellesmere Port and Neston	1176	163
Elloes	2076	63
Ely	1138	162
Enfield M.C.	2757	78
Epping and Ongar	1616	171
Epsom	2837	193
Epworth and Goole	1928	179
Esher and Walton	2838	193
Essex, Mid-North	1612	10
Essex, Mid-South	1610	10
Essex, North-East	1613	10
Essex, North-West	1619	11
Essex, South-East	1629	12
Essex, South-West	1626	12
Estimaner	3226	202
Everley and Pewsey	3010	197
Evesham	1850	176
Exeter	1479	168
Exeter and Wonford	1497	169
Exmouth	1480	168

F

	Ct No	Page
Fairford	1676	173
Fakenham	1389	166
Falkirk	9751	130
Falkirk D.C.	9482	130
Falmouth	1266	163
Falmouth and Kerrier	1283	164
Falmouth-Penryn	1281	164
Fareham	1765	175
Faringdon	2674	188
Farnham	2839	193
Faversham	1956	180
Faversham and Sittingbourne	1967	181
Felixstowe	2818	192
Feltham M.C.	2769	82
Fenland	1167	23
Fenny Stratford	1116	161
Fermanagh	9020	116
Fishguard	3116	199
Fife D.C. at Cupar	9485	129
Fife D.C. at Dunfermline	9486	130
Fife D.C. at Kirkcaldy	9487	131
Flint	3054	199
Flintshire	3059	107
Folkestone and Hythe	1957	180
Forest	1066	160

INDEX

	Ct No	Page
Forest of Dean	1695	174
Forfar	9752	131
Fort William	9753	122
Fort William D.C.	9502	122
Freshwell and South Hinckford	1617	171
Frome	2704	189
Furness and District	1398	38
Fylde	2001	181
Flyde Coast	1992	39

G

	Ct No	Page
Gainsborough	2058	183
	2075	63
Gateshead	2850	31
Giffnock D.C.	9474	144
Gilling East	2528	186
Girvan D.C.	9561	146
Glasgow and Strathkelvin	9761	138
Glasgow (City of) D.C.	9495	138
Glendale Ward	2340	185
Glossop	1421	167
Gloucester	1692	174
Gloucester (City)	1677	173
Gloucester County	1690	173
Gloucester (County)	1678	173
Gloucestershire	1698	49
Godstone	2840	193
Gogledd Ceredigion	3135	200
Gogledd Preseli	3141	201
Goole and Howdenshire	1928	58
Gosport	1766	175
Grantham	2059	183
	2077	64
Gravesham	1958	180
Great Yarmouth	1391	166
	1443	23
Greenock	9762	142
Greenwich M.C.	2643	72
Greenwich Y.C.	6656	73
Grimsby and Cleethorpes	1940	58
Grimsby (Borough)	1929	179
Grimsby (County)	1930	179
Guildford	2841	193
Gwent	3211	110
Gwent (North West)	3209	201
Gwent (South East)	3210	201
Gwynedd	3244	107
Gwyrfai	3227	202

H

	Ct No	Page
Hackney Y.C.	6650	83
Haddington	9771	134
Hailsham	1600	171
Halesowen	2912	195
Halifax	2982	196
Hallikeld	2529	186
Halstead	1618	172
Halstead and Hedingham	1628	172
Halton	1177	27

	Ct No	Page
Hamilton	9772	147
Hamilton D.C.	9566	148
Hammersmith and Fulham Y.C.	6658	83
Hampstead M.C. (CLOSED)	2740	190
Hang, East	2530	186
Hang, West	2531	186
Haringey M.C.	2742	80
Harlow	1619	172
Harrogate	2527	89
Harrow M.C.	2760	80
Hartismere	2819	192
Hartlepool	1247	32
Harwich	1620	172
Hastings	1601	171
Hastings and Rother	1606	171
Hatfield	1879	177
Havant	1767	175
Haverfordwest	3117	199
Haverhill	2825	192
Haverhill and Sudbury	2864	194
Havering M.C.	1837	81
Hawarden	3055	199
Hawkshead	1367	165
Helensburgh D.C.	9428	140
Helston and Kerrier	1267	163
Hendon M.C.	2741	76
Henley	2675	188
Hereford (City of)	1851	176
Hereford (County)	1852	176
Herefordshire	1841	17
Hertford and Ware	1888	178
Hertfordshire (East)	1888	9
Hertfordshire (West)	1893	12
Hexham	2341	185
High Peak	1422	167
	1430	42
High Wycombe	1117	161
Highbury Corner M.C.	2663	77
Highland D.C. at Dingwall	9500	121
Highland D.C. at Dornoch	9501	121
Highland D.C. at Fort William	9502	122
Highland D.C. at Inverness	9503	123
Highland D.C. at Kingussie	9504	123
Highland D.C. at Nairn	9505	123
Highland D.C. at Portree	9506	125
Highland D.C. at Tain	9509	126
Highland D.C. at Wick	9508	127
Hitchin	1881	177
Holme Beacon	1931	179
Honiton	1481	168
Horncastle	2060	183
Horseferry Road M.C.	2660	188
Horsham	2930	196
Houghton-le-Spring	2854	32
Hounslow L.J.A.	—	82
Hove	1602	171
Howdenshire	1932	179
Huddersfield	2987	89
Hull and Holderness	1943	58

INDEX

	Ct No	Page
Hundred House	1853	176
Hungerford and Lambourn	1067	160
Hunstanton	1394	166
Huntingdon	1161	162
Huntingdon and Norman Cross	1157	162
Huntingdonshire	1168	23
Hurstingstone	1140	162
Hyndburn	2010	39
Hythe (Hants.)	1768	175

I

	Ct No	Page
Ilkeston	1423	167
Ilminster	2705	189
Inner London F.P.C.	6700	87
Inverclyde D.C. at Greenock	9514	142
Inverness	9781	123
Inverness D.C.	9503	123
Inverurie D.C.	9407	120
Ipswich	2820	192
	2830	193
Irvine D.C.	9526	143
Isle of Wight	1945	54
Isles of Scilly	1268	163
Islington Y.C.	6650	83

J

	Ct No	Page
Jedburgh	9791	135
Jedburgh D.C.	9551	135

K

	Ct No	Page
Keighley	2979	89
Kendal	1368	165
Kendal and Lonsdale	1382	166
Kennet	3025	198
Kensington and Chelsea Y.C.	6658	83
Keswick	1369	165
Kettering	2323	64
Kidderminster	1854	176
Kidderminster	1842	17
Kilmarnock	9801	142
Kilmarnock D.C.	9461	143
Kineton	2895	194
Kingsbridge	1482	168
King's Lynn	1392	166
Kingston upon Hull	1933	179
Kingston-upon-Thames M.C.	2812	83
Kington	1855	176
Kingussie D.C.	9504	123
Kirkcaldy	9803	131
Kircaldy D.C.	9487	131
Kirkcudbright	9804	148
Kirkcudbright D.C.	9447	148
Kirkintilloch D.C.	9465	139
Kirkwall	9805	124
Knighton	3326	203
Knowsley	2266	27

L

	Ct No	Page
Lackford (renamed Mildenhall)	2821	192

	Ct No	Page
Lambeth Y.C.	6649	83
Lampeter	3118	200
Lanark	9811	148
Lanark D.C.	9567	149
Lanbaurgh East	1248	32
Lancaster	2002	39
Larne	9024	116
Lawford's Gate	1014	159
Ledbury	1856	176
Leeds	2988	197
Leeds District	2992	90
Leek	2784	191
Leicester (City)	2039	182
Leicester (County)	2040	182
Leicester	2048	64
Leigh	1743	174
Leighton Buzzard	1054	160
Leominster and Wigmore	1857	176
Lerwick	9812	124
Lesnewth	1269	164
Lewes	1603	171
Lewes and Crowborough	1607	171
Lewisham Y.C.	6656	73
Lichfield	2785	191
Lichfield and Tamworth	2860	194
Limavady	9025	116
Lincoln (City)	2061	183
Lincoln (County)	2072	183
Lincoln District	2079	64
Lincoln (Kesteven)	2062	183
Lincolnshire (North)	1903	59
Lindsey (Lincoln and Wragby)	2063	183
Linlithgow	9813	135
Linslade	1118	161
Linton	1141	162
Lisburn	9026	116
Liskerrett	1270	164
Liverpool	2267	28
Livingston	9815	135
Llandeilo	3119	200
Llandovery	3120	200
Llandrindod Wells (renamed Radnorshire and North Brecknock)	3327	203
	3351	204
Llandyssul	3121	200
Llanelli	3122	102
Llanfyllin	3328	203
Llanidloes	3329	203
Lliw Valley	3358	204
Lochgilphead D.C.	9429	142
Lochmaddy	9814	124
London (City of) M.C.	2631	70
Londonderry	9028	117
Long Ashton	1015	159
Lonsdale Ward	1370	165
Loughborough	2041	182
	2049	65

INDEX

	Ct No	Page
Louth	2064	183
	2070	183
Lower Rhymney Valley	3263	202
Lowestoft	2822	192
Luton	1055	160
Luton and South Bedfordshire	1055	9
Lutterworth	2042	182
Lydney	1679	173
Lymington	1769	175

M

	Ct No	Page
Macclesfield	1178	28
Machynlleth	3330	203
Magherafelt	9029	117
Maidenhead	1068	160
Maidstone	1959	180
Makerfield	1744	174
Maldon and Witham	1630	172
Malmesbury	3011	197
Malton	2542	186
Malvern	1858	176
Malvern Hills	1870	177
Manchester City	1733	52
Mansfield	2566	42
Mansfield (Borough)	2554	187
Mansfield (County)	2555	187
Margate	1960	180
Market Bosworth	2043	182
	2050	65
Market Harborough	2044	182
Market Harborough and Lutterworth	2051	65
Market Rasen	2065	183
	2081	184
Marlborough	3012	197
Marlborough Street M.C. (CLOSED)	2644	188
Marlow	1119	161
Marylebone M.C.	2646	188
Maryport	1371	165
Mathrafal	3331	203
Matlock	1424	167
Medway	1961	180
Meirionnydd	3239	202
Melksham	3013	197
Melton and Belvoir	2045	182
Melton, Belvoir and Rutland	2045	65
Mendip	2715	5
Merthyr Tydfil	3264	110
Merton L.J.A.	—	84
Middle Holderness	1934	179
Middleton and Heywood	1735	174
Mid Hertfordshire	1890	178
Midhurst	2931	196
Mid Kent	1959	180
Mid Northants	2324	184
Mid-North Essex	1612	10
Mid-South Essex	1610	10
Mid Staffordshire	2795	192
Mid Staffordshire and Rugeley	2799	192
Mid Sussex	2932	196

	Ct No	Page
Mid Warwickshire	2903	195
Mid Worcestershire	1872	177
Midlothian D.C. at Loanhead	9518	134
Mildenhall	2821	192
Milford Haven	3123	200
Milngavie D.C.	9466	141
Milton Keynes	1124	97
Miskin	3265	110
Mold	3056	199
Monmouth	3204	201
Montgomery	3332	203
Montgomeryshire	3355	103
Moray D.C. at Elgin	9522	122
Moreton and Wallingford	2676	188
Morley	2989	197
Morpeth Ward	2342	185
Motherwell D.C.	9532	147
Moyle	9030	117

N

	Ct No	Page
Nairn D.C.	9505	123
Nant Conwy	3228	202
Narberth	3124	200
Neath	3359	204
Neath Port Talbot	3359	103
New Forest	1779	54
New Radnor	3333	203
New Spelthorne (renamed Feltham)	2769	82
New Windsor	1070	160
Newark	2556	187
Newark and Southwell	2567	42
Newbury	1069	160
Newcastle and Ogmore	3266	111
Newcastle Emlyn	3125	200
Newcastle-under-Lyme	2786	191
Newcastle-under-Lyme and Pirehill North	2797	192
Newcastle upon Tyne	2851	33
Newent	1680	173
Newham L.J.A.	—	84
Newmarket	1142	162
Newmarket (Cambs)	1164	162
Newmarket (Suffolk)	2823	192
Newnham	1681	173
Newport	3205	201
Newport Pagnell	1120	161
Newry and Mourne	9032	117
Newtown	3334	203
	3347	204
	3352	204
Newtownabbey	9033	117
Norman Cross	1143	162
North and East Surrey	2845	193
North Anglesey	3229	202
North Antrim	—	118
North Avon	1021	6
North Ayrshire D.C. at Irvine	9526	143
North Bedfordshire (renamed Bedford and Mid Bedfordshire)	1051	8

211

INDEX

	Ct No	Page
North Cotswold	1694	174
North Devon	1291	46
North Down	9034	118
North Durham	1583	33
North East Derbyshire and Dales ...	1432	43
North-East Essex	1613	10
North East Hampshire	1780	55
North East Suffolk	2863	23
North Gloucestershire	1696	174
North Herefordshire	1868	177
North Hertfordshire	1889	11
North Hinckford	1621	172
North Holderness	1935	179
North Kent (Dartford)	1966	61
North Kent (Medway)	1966	61
North Lanarkshire D.C. at Coatbridge	9530	145
North Lanarkshire D.C. at Cumbernauld	9531	145
North Lanarkshire D.C. at Motherwell	9532	147
North Lincolnshire	1903	59
North Lonsdale	1372	165
North Meirionnydd	3221	201
North Norfolk	1444	24
North Oxfordshire	2677	189
North Oxfordshire and Chipping Norton	2702	189
North Pembrokeshire	3139	201
North Sefton	2269	28
North Somerset	1023	6
North Staffordshire	{ 2791 / 2798	18 / 192
North Surrey	2849	92
North Tyneside	2852	34
North Walsham	1397	166
North West Essex	1619	11
North West Gwent	3209	201
North West Hampshire	1781	55
North West Suffolk	2862	194
North West Surrey	2846	193
North West Surrey	2857	93
North West Wiltshire	3026	49
North Wiltshire	3022	198
North Witchford	1144	162
Northallerton	2543	186
Northallerton and Richmond	2543	90
Northampton	2325	66
Northern Oxfordshire	2775	97
Northleach	1682	173
Norwich	{ 1385 / 1445	166 / 24
Nottingham	2568	43
Nottingham (City)	2557	187
Nottingham (County)	2558	187
Nuneaton	2896	194

O

	Ct No	Page
Oban	9841	143
Oban D.C.	9430	143
Odiham	1770	175
Odsey	1882	178
Okehampton	1483	168
Oldham	1734	52
Old Street M.C. (CLOSED)	2648	188
Omagh	9035	118
Ormskirk	2003	40
Orwell	2824	192
Oswestry	3277	198
Oundle and Thrapston	2326	184
Oxford	{ 2678 / 2777	189 / 98

P

	Ct No	Page
Painscastle	3335	203
Paisley	9851	143
Peebles	9852	136
Pembroke	3126	200
Pembrokeshire	3356	104
Pencader	3127	200
Pendle	2004	181
Penllyn	3230	202
Penrith	1373	165
Penrith and Alston	{ 1378 / 1384	166 / 166
Penryn	1271	164
Penwith	1272	164
Pershore	1859	176
Perth	9853	132
Perth and Kinross D.C. at Perth	9538	132
Peterborough	1162	24
Peterhead	9854	124
Peterhead D.C.	9408	125
Petersfield	1771	175
Petworth	2933	196
Pirehill North	2787	191
Plymouth	{ 1484 / 1290	168 / 46
Plympton	1485	168
Pontefract	2994	90
Pontypool	3206	201
Poole	1505	169
Port Talbot	3357	204
Portree	9855	125
Portree D.C.	9506	125
Portsmouth	1772	175
Powder Tywardreath	1273	164
Presteigne	3336	203
Preston	2005	40
Pudsey and Otley	2990	197
Pwllheli	3231	202
Pydar	1274	164

R

Radnor, East *see* East Radnor

	Ct No	Page
Radnorshire and North Brecknock	3351	104

INDEX

	Ct No	Page
Ramsey	1145	162
Ramsgate	1962	180
Reading	1071 / 1076	160 / 98
Reading and Sonning	1076	160
Redbridge M.C.	2815	85
Redditch	1860	176
Reigate	2842	193
Renfrewshire D.C. at Paisley	9542	144
Rhayader	3337	203
Rhuddlan	3057	199
Rhydlewis	3128	200
Ribble Valley	2008	181
Richmond	2545	187
Richmond and Gilling West	2533	186
Richmond upon Thames M.C.	2768	85
Ringwood	1773	175
Ripon Liberty	2534	186
Risbridge (renamed Haverhill)	2825	192
Rochdale	1736	174
Rochdale, Middleton and Heywood	1750	52
Rochford	1622	172
Rochford and Southend-on-Sea	1629	172
Romsey	1774	175
Ross	1861	177
Rossendale	2006	181
Rotherham	2772	59
Rothesay	9861	144
Rugby	2897	195
Rugeley	2788	191
Rutherglen D.C.	9568	139
Rutland	2046	182
Ryedale	2535 / 2546	186 / 187

S

	Ct No	Page
Saffron Walden	1623	172
St. Albans	1883	178
St. Clears	3129	200
St. Edmundsbury	2826 / 2832	192 / 193
St. Edmundsbury and Stowmarket	2865	194
St. Helens	2268	28
Salford	1738	174
Salford (City of)	1747	51
Salisbury	3014 / 3023	197 / 198
Sanquhar D.C.	9449	147
Saxmundham	2831	193
Scarborough	2536	90
Scottish Borders D.C. at Duns	9550	133
Scottish Borders D.C. at Jedburgh	9551	135
Scottish Borders D.C. at Peebles	9552	136
Scottish Borders D.C. at Selkirk	9553	137
Scunthorpe	1936	179
Scunthorpe, Brigg and Barton	1903	178

	Ct No	Page
Sedgefield	1581	170
Sedgemoor	2706	6
Seisdon	2789	191
Selby	2537	91
Selkirk	9871	137
Sevenoaks	1963	180
Severnminster (renamed Kidderminster)	1842	17
Shaftesbury	1506 / 1513	169 / 170
Sheffield	2773	59
Shepton Mallet	2707	189
Sherborne	1507	169
Shipston-on-Stour	2898	195
Shrewsbury	3279	198
Shrewsbury and North Shropshire	3278	18
Sittingbourne	1964	180
Skegness	2082	66
Skipton	2538	91
Skyrack and Wetherby	2991	197
Sleaford	2066 / 2080	183 / 66
Slough	1072	160
Sodbury	1016	159
Soke of Peterborough	1158	162
Solihull	2916	14
Somerton	2708	189
Southam	2899	195
Southampton	1775	56
South and Middle Holderness	1902	178
South Anglesey	3232	202
South Ayrshire D.C. at Ayr	9560	146
South Ayrshire D.C. at Girvan	9561	146
South Cambridgeshire	1163	162
South Cheshire	1187	29
South Derbyshire	1425	167
South Devon	1293	46
South Durham	1584	34
South East Cornwall	1280	164
South East Essex	1629	12
South East Gwent	3210	201
South East Hampshire	1782	55
South East Northumberland	2349	35
South East Staffordshire	2860	19
South East Suffolk	2866	25
South East Surrey	2847	193
South East Surrey	2856	93
South East Wiltshire	3027	50
Southend-on-Sea	1624	172
Southern Derbyshire	1428	43
Southern Oxfordshire	2774	98
South Gloucestershire	1693	174
South Hams	1496	169
South Hampshire	1783	56
South Herefordshire	1869	177
South Holderness	1937	179
South Hunsley and Beacon and Howdenshire	1901	178

213

INDEX

	Ct No	Page
South Hunsley Beacon	1901	178
	1938	179
South Lakeland	1323	40
South Lakes	1381	166
South Lanarkshire D.C. at East Kilbride	9565	139
South Lanarkshire D.C. at Hamilton	9566	148
South Lanarkshire D.C. at Lanark	9567	149
South Lanarkshire D.C. at Rutherglen	9568	139
South Meirionnydd	3235	202
South Mimms	1884	178
South Molton	1486	168
South Norfolk	1446	25
South Pembrokeshire	3142	201
South Powder	1275	164
South Ribble	2007	40
South Sefton	2270	29
South Somerset	2714	7
South Tameside	1741	174
South Tyneside	2853	35
Southwark Y.C.	6656	73
South Warwickshire	2902	195
Southwell	2559	187
South Western M.C.	2649	86
South West Essex	1626	12
South West Surrey	2848	93
South Worcestershire	1843	19
Spelthorne, New see New Spelthorne		
Spilsby	2067	183
Spilsby and Skegness (renamed Skegness)	2071	183
	2082	66
Stafford	2790	191
Staffordshire Moorlands	2796	192
Staincliffe (renamed Skipton)	2538	91
Staines and Sunbury	2843	193
Stamford	2068	183
Stevenage	1885	178
Steyning	2934	196
Stirling	9872	132
Stirling D.C.	9572	132
Stockport	1739	52
Stoke-on-Trent	2791	191
Stokesley	2539	186
Stone	2792	191
Stonehaven	9873	125
Stonehaven D.C.	9409	126
Stony Stratford	1121	161
Stornoway	9874	126
Stourbridge	2913	195
Stourbridge and Halesowen	2912	20
Stourport	1862	177
Stow	2827	193
Stow (renamed Stowmarket)	2833	193
Stowmarket	2833	193
Stow-on-the-Wold	1683	173
Strabane	9036	118
Stranraer	9875	149
Stranraer D.C.	9450	149

	Ct No	Page
Stratford M.C.	2721	84
Stratford-upon-Avon	2900	195
Stratton	1276	164
Stroud	1684	173
Sturminster	1508	169
Sudbury	2828	193
Sudbury and Cosford (renamed Sudbury)	2828	193
Sunderland	2855	36
Sussex (Central) L.J.A.	2950	94
Sussex (Eastern) L.J.A.	2948	94
Sussex (Northern) L.J.A.	2947	95
Sussex (Western) L.J.A.	2949	95
Sutton M.C.	2756	190
	2733	74
Sutton Coldfield	2909	14
Swaffham	1395	166
Swansea	3360	105
Swindon	3015	50

T

	Ct No	Page
Tain	9881	126
Tain D.C.	9509	126
Talgarth	3338	203
Talybont	3233	202
Tameside	1748	53
Tamworth	2793	191
Taunton Deane	2709	189
Taunton Deane and West Somerset L.J.A.	2709	7
Tavistock	1487	168
Teesdale and Wear Valley	1582	170
Teesside	1249	36
Teignbridge	1488	168
Telford & South Shropshire	3276	20
Telford & South Shropshire L.J.A.	3282	20
Tenbury	1863	177
Tenby	3130	200
Tendring	1625	172
Tetbury	1685	173
Tewksbury	1686	173
Thame and Henley	2719	190
	2778	191
Thames M.C.	2650	79
Thanet	1968	181
Thetford	1396	166
Thornbury	1017	159
Thurrock	1626	172
Tisbury and Mere	3016	198
Tiverton	1489	168
Todmorden	2983	196
Tonbridge and Malling	1965	181
Torbay	1490	168
Toseland	1147	162
Totnes	1491	168
Totton and New Forest	1776	175
Towcester	2327	66
Tower Bridge M.C.	2651	74
Tower Hamlets Y.C.	6650	83

INDEX

	Ct No	Page
Trafford	1742	53
Tregaron	3131	200
Trowbridge	3017	198
Truro and South Powder	1282	164
Truro and West Powder	1277	164
Tunbridge Wells and Cranbrook	1966	181
Tynedale	2346	36

U

	Ct No	Page
Upper Rhymney Valley	3267	203
Upton on Severn	1864	177
Usk	3207	201
Uttoxeter	2794	192
Uxbridge M.C.	2766	81

V

	Ct No	Page
Vale of Evesham	1873	177
Vale of Glamorgan	3349	111
Vale Royal	1179	29
Verge of the Palaces (The)	—	87

W

	Ct No	Page
Wadebridge	1278	164
Wakefield	2995	91
Wallington	2731	190
Walsall	2918	195
Walsall & Adridge L.J.A.	2917	21
Waltham Forest M.C.	2813	86
Walton Street M.C. (CLOSED)	2657	188
Wandsworth Y.C.	6649	83
Wansbeck	2343	185
Wansdyke	1018	159
Wantage	2679	189
Wantage and Faringdon	2682	189
Wareham	1509	169
Warley	2914	21
Warminster	3018	198
Warrington	1180	29
Warwick	2901	195
Warwickshire	2904	15
Watford	1886	178
Watlington	2680	189
Wellingborough	2328	67
Wells	2710	189
Wells Street M.C. (CLOSED)	2655	188
Welshpool	3339	203
	3341	204
	3346	204
Welwyn	1887	178
Wenlock	3281	198
West Allerdale	1379	166
West Allerdale and Keswick	1325	41
West Berkshire	1075	99
West Bromwich	2915	21
Westbury	3019	198
West Coquetdale Ward	2344	185
West Cornwall	1288	47
West Devon	1495	169

	Ct No	Page
West Dorset	1516	170
	1523	50
West Dunbartonshire D.C. at Clydebank	9575	141
West Dunbartonshire D.C. at Dumbarton	9576	141
West Elloe	2069	183
Western Isles D.C. at Stornoway	9584	126
West Ham M.C. (CLOSED)	2722	190
West Hertfordshire	1893	12
West Kent	1963	180
West London M.C.	2652	188
	2658	79
West Lothian D.C. at Livingston	9580	136
Westminster, Y.C.	6658	83
West Norfolk	1447	25
Weston-super-Mare	1019	159
West Somerset	2711	189
West Suffolk	2867	26
West Ward	1374	165
West Wiltshire	3024	198
Weymouth and Portland	1510	170
Whitby Strand	2540	186
Whitehaven	1375	41
Whitland	3132	200
Whitminster	1687	173
Whittlesey	1148	162
Whorwellsdown	3020	198
Wick	9891	127
Wick D.C.	9508	127
Wigan	1745	174
	1746	174
Wigan and Leigh L.J.A.	1749	53
Wigton	1376	165
Willesden M.C. (renamed Brent M.C.)	2762	76
Wilton Beacon	1939	179
Wimbledon M.C.	2763	84
Wimborne	1511	170
Wincanton	2712	189
Winchcombe	1688	173
Winchester	1777	175
Windsor	1074	160
Windsor County	1073	160
Winslow	1122	161
Wirral	2271	30
Wisbech	1160	162
Wisbech (Borough)	1149	162
Wisbech (Isle)	1150	162
Witham	1627	172
Witney	2703	189
	2779	191
Woking	2844	193
Wolds	2078	67
Wolverhampton	2919	21
Wonford	1492	168
Woodbridge	2829	193
Woodspring (renamed North Somerset)	1023	6

INDEX

	Ct No	Page		Ct No	Page
Woodstock	2701	189	Wrexham Maelor	3058	107
Woolwich M.C.	2643	72	Wycombe	1127	161
Worcester (City of)	1865	177	Wycombe and Beaconsfield	1130	99
	1874	177	Wycombe (County)	1123	161
Worcester (County)	1866	177	Wymondham	1390	166
Worcester (County)(Motorway)	1867	177	Wyre	2009	182
Workington	1377	165			
Worksop	2560	187	**Y**		
Worksop and Retford L.J.A.	2569	44	Yeovil	2713	189
Worthing	2935	196	Ynys Mon/Anglesey	3238	108
Worthing and District	2937	196	York	2541	91
Wrekin (The)	3280	198	Ysrtadgynlais	3340	203

PART IV

**LIST OF CORONERS
AND
ADDRESSES OF CORONERS' OFFICERS**

PART IV

LIST OF CORONERS AND ADDRESSES OF CORONERS' OFFICERS

NOTE: The names of Coroners' Districts are shown in bold type

District	Coroner	
ABERCONWY AND COLWYN – see **CENTRAL NORTH WALES**		
ANGLESEY – see **NORTH WEST WALES**		
AVON	*Coroner:* P. E. A. Forrest	
	Coroner's Court, The Courthouse, Old Weston Road, Flax Bourton, Bristol BS48 1UL	Tel: 01275 461920 Fax: 01275 462749
	E-mail: coroner's_office@bristol-city.gov.uk	
BATH AND NORTH EAST SOMERSET – see **AVON**		
BEDFORDSHIRE AND LUTON	*Coroner:* David S. Morris	
Bedford	Coroner's Office, 8 Goldington Road, Bedford MK40 3NF	Tel: 01234 273011/2 (Officers) 273013 (Secretary) Fax: 01234 273014
Luton	Coroner's Office, Jansel House, Hitchin Road, Luton LU2 7XH	Tel: 01234 270443/4 (Officers) 273013 (Secretary) Fax: 01582 481261
BERKSHIRE	Coroner Peter J. Bedford	
	Yeomanry House, 131 Castle Hill, Reading, Berkshire RG1 7TA	Tel: 0118 901 5193 Fax: 0118 901 5448
	E-mail: peter.bedford@reading.gov.uk	
	Coroner's Officers:	
	TVP Langley Police Station SL3 8NF	Tel: 01753 211826 Fax: 01753 211823
	TVP Bracknell Police Station	Tel: 01344 823432 Fax: 01344 823499
	Royal Berkshire Hospital, Craven Road, Reading RG1 5AN	Tel: 0118 986 3116 Fax: 0118 975 6594
	Police Station, Mill Lane, Newbury RG14 5QU	Tel: 01635 264745 Fax: 01635 264651
BLAENAU GWENT – see **GWENT**		
BOURNEMOUTH – see DORSET: **BOURNEMOUTH, POOLE AND EASTERN DORSET**, p. 6 *post*		
BRIDGEND AND GLAMORGAN VALLEYS [PEN-Y-BONT A CHYMOEDD MORGANWG]		
	Coroner: P. M. Walters	
	3 Victoria Square, Aberdare CF44 7LA	Tel: 01685 872593 872595 Fax: 01685 872573
	Coroner's Officers:	
	Police Station, Swan Street, Merthyr Tydfil	Tel: 01685 724228 Fax: 01685 724263
	Police Station, Mill Street, Tonyrefail	Tel: 01443 743698 Fax: 01443 743699
	Police Station, Pandy Road, Aberkenfig	Tel: 01656 762968 Fax: 01656 762969

LIST OF CORONERS AND ADDRESSES OF CORONERS' OFFICERS

District	Coroner	
BRIGHTON AND HOVE – see SUSSEX p. 18 *post*		
BRISTOL CITY – see **AVON**		
BUCKINGHAMSHIRE:	*Coroner:* R. A. Hulett 3 High Street, Marlow, Buckinghamshire SL7 1AU	Tel: 01844 214454 Fax: 01844 358186 DX 80580 THAME
	Coroner's Officers: Thames Valley Police, Police Station, High Wycombe, Bucks HP11 1BE Thames Valley Police, Police Station, Aylesbury, Bucks.	Tel: 01494 686180 Fax: 01494 686012 Tel: 01296 396116 Fax: 01296 396036
CAERNARFONSHIRE AND MERIONETHSHIRE – see **NORTH WEST WALES**		
CAERPHILLY – see **GWENT**		
CAMBRIDGESHIRE:		
SOUTH AND WEST CAMBS.	*Coroner:* David S. Morris Shire Hall, Castle Hill, Cambridge CB3 0AP	Tel: 01223 717486 (Coroner's Officer) 01223 718621 (Coroner's Officer) Fax: 01223 717586
	Coroner's Officer: Huntingdon Police Station, Ferrars Road, Huntingdon, Cambs. PE29 6DQ	Tel: 01480 375511/375527 Fax: 01480 375517
NORTH AND EAST CAMBS.	*Coroner:* W.R. Morris, LL.B. 1 & 2 York Row, Wisbech, Cambs. PE13 1EA	Tel: 01945 461456 Fax: 01945 461364
PETERBOROUGH	*Coroner:* G.S. Ryall 10 Briggate Quay, Whittlesey, Peterborough PE7 1DH	Tel: 01733 351010 Fax: 01733 351141 E-mail: ryallg@btconnect.com
	Coroner's Officer: Cambridgeshire Constabulary, Bridge Street Police Station, Peterborough PE1 1EQ	Tel: 01733 424459 424450
[CAERDYDD A BRO MORGANNWG]		
CARDIFF AND THE VALE OF GLAMORGAN	*Coroner:* Mary Elizabeth Hassell Coroner's Court and Offices, Central Police Station, Cathays Park, Cardiff CF10 3NN	Tel: 029 2022 2111 ext 30699 and 30698 Fax: 029 2033 3886
CARDIGANSHIRE [SIR ABERTEIFI]	*Coroner:* P. L. Brunton 6 Upper Portland Street, Aberystwyth, Ceredigion SY23 2DU	Tel: 01970 612567 617931 Fax: 01970 615572
	Coroner's Officer: Aberystwyth Police Station, Boulevard St. Brieuc, Aberystwyth SY23 1PH	Tel: 01970 612791 Fax: 01970 625174 E-mail: enquiries@bruntonsaber.co.uk

LIST OF CORONERS AND ADDRESSES OF CORONERS' OFFICERS

District	Coroner	
CARMARTHENSHIRE [SIR GAERFYRDDIN]	*Coroner:* W.J. Owen Corner House, Llandeilo, Carmarthenshire SA19 6AG	Tel: 01558 822215 Fax: 01558 822933
CENTRAL NORTH WALES [CANOL COGLEDD CWMRU]	*Coroner:* J. B. Hughes Marbel House, Overton Arcade, High Street, Wrexham LL13 8LL	Tel: 01978 357775 Fax: 01978 358000 DX 26675 WREXHAM
	Coroner's Officers: Mr. T. D. Griffiths North Wales Police, Central Division Headquarters, Ffordd William Morgan, St Asaph Business Park, St Asaph, Denbighshire LL17 0HQ	Tel: 01745 588607
CHESHIRE	*Coroner:* N. L. Rheinberg The West Annexe, Town Hall, Sankey Street, Warrington, Cheshire WA1 1UH	Tel: 01925 444216 Fax: 01925 444219 E-mail: nrheinberg@warrington.gov.uk

CORNWALL:

CORNWALL	*Coroner:* Dr. E. E. Carlyon 14 Barrack Lane, Truro, Cornwall TR1 2DW	Tel: 01872 261612 Fax: 01872 262738
	Coroner's Officers: Truro Police Station, Tregolls Road, Truro, Cornwall	Tel: 01872 326064 326077 326207 326208 326210 Fax: 01872 326209
ISLES OF SCILLY	*Coroner:* I. M. Arrow Cary Chambers, 1 Palk Street, Torquay TQ2 5EL	Tel: 01803 380705 Fax: 01803 380704

CUMBRIA:

NORTH EAST CUMBRIA	*Coroner:* D. I. Osborne, Bourne House, Milbourne Street, Carlisle CA2 5XF	Tel: 01228 549462 Fax: 01228 548405
SOUTH CUMBRIA & FURNESS	*Coroner:* I. Smith Central Police Station, Market Street, Barrow-in-Furness, Cumbria LA14 2LE	Tel: 01229 848966 Fax: 01229 848953
NORTH & WEST CUMBRIA	*Coroner:* J. C. Taylor 38/42 Lowther Street, Whitehaven, Cumbria CA28 7JU	Tel: 01946 692461/3 Fax: 01946 692015

DARLINGTON see DURHAM: **DARLINGTON AND SOUTH DURHAM** p 6 *post*

DENBIGHSHIRE – see **CENTRAL NORTH WALES**

DERBYSHIRE:

DERBY & SOUTH DERBYSHIRE	*Coroner:* P. G. Ashworth St. Katherine's House, St. Mary's Wharf, Mansfield Road, Derby DE1 3TQ	Tel: 01332 613014 Fax: 01332 294942 Email: derby.coroner@btopenworld.com
SCARSDALE & HIGH PEAK	*Coroner:* T. Kelly 69 Saltergate, Chesterfield, Derbyshire S40 1JS	Tel: 01246 201391

LIST OF CORONERS AND ADDRESSES OF CORONERS' OFFICERS

District	Coroner	
DEVON:		
EXETER & GREATER DEVON	Coroner: Dr. Elizabeth Ann Earland, MBCh.B., D.A., Dip. Law, L.P.C. Raleigh Hall, Fore Street, Topsham, Exeter EX3 0HU	Tel: 01392 876575 Fax: 01392 876574
PLYMOUTH & SOUTH WEST DEVON	Deputy Coroner: I. M. Arrow (Acting) 3 The Crescent, Plymouth PL1 3AB	Tel: 01752 204636 Fax: 01752 313297
TORBAY & SOUTH DEVON	Coroner: I. M. Arrow Cary Chambers, 1 Palk Street, Torquay TQ2 5EL	Tel: 01803 380705 Fax: 01803 380704
	Torbay Hospital, Lawes Bridge, Torquay TQ2 7AA	Tel: 01803 655205
DORSET:		
BOURNEMOUTH, POOLE AND EASTERN DORSET	Coroner: Sheriff S. Payne The Coroner's Court, Stafford Road, Bournemouth, Dorset BH1 1PA	Tel: 01202 310049 Fax: 01202 780423 DX 7615 BOURNEMOUTH
	Coroner's Officers:	Tel: 01202 789057 780879 789353 789154 Fax: 01202 780423
WESTERN DORSET	Coroner: M. C. Johnston The Coroner's Office, The Plocks, Blandford Forum, Dorset DT11 7QB DX: 90100 BLANDFORD FORUM	Tel: 01305 223033 01258 453733 01747 811226 (out of hours) Fax: 01258 455747
DURHAM:		
DARLINGTON AND SOUTH DURHAM	Coroner: A. Tweddle Post Office House, Elliott Street, Crook, Co. Durham DL15 8QH	Tel: 01388 767770 Fax: 01388 766617
	Coroner's Officers: Police Office, 6 St. Cuthberts Way, Darlington, Co. Durham DL1 5LB	Tel: 01325 742194 Fax: 01325 742194
	Police Office, Woodhouse Lane, Bishop Auckland, Co. Durham DL14 6LB	Tel: 0845 606 0365 Fax: 01325 742323
NORTH DURHAM	Coroner: Andrew Tweddle, LL.B. Post Office House, Elliott Street, Crook, Co. Durham DL15 8QH	Tel: 01388 767770 Fax: 01388 766617
	Coroner's Officers: The Police Station, New Elvet, Durham City	Tel: 0191 375 2818/2824 375 2821
EAST RIDING AND HULL	Coroner: G. M. Saul Coroner's Office & Court, Essex House, Manor Street, Kingston upon Hull HU1 1YU	Tel: 01482 613009 613011 Fax: 01482 613020

LIST OF CORONERS AND ADDRESSES OF CORONERS' OFFICERS

District	Coroner	
EAST SUSSEX, see p. 18		
ESSEX:		
ESSEX AND THURROCK	*Coroner:* Mrs. Caroline Beasley-Murray Essex County Council, County Hall, P.O. Box 11, Chelmsford, Essex CM1 1LX	Tel: 01245 438011
Chelmsford	Police Headquarters, V Block, 33 Kingston Crescent, Springfield, Chelmsford, Essex CM2 6DA	Tel: 01245 457177 Fax: 01245 457115
Basildon Grays	The Old Police Station, 6-8 Hall Crescent, Hadleigh, Essex SS7 2QW	Tel: 01245 452270 Fax: 01702 557654
SOUTHEND AND SOUTH EAST ESSEX DISTRICT	*Coroner:* Dr. Peter Dean Old Hadleigh Police Station, 6-8 Hall Crescent, Hadleigh, Essex SS7 2QW	Tel: 01245 452554 Fax: 01702 553995
FLINTSHIRE – see **NORTH EAST WALES**		
GATESHEAD AND SOUTH TYNESIDE – see TYNE AND WEAR page 18 *post*		
GLOUCESTERSHIRE	*Coroner:* Alan C. Crickmore County Offices, St George's Road, Cheltenham, Glos. GL50 3PF	Tel: 01242 221064 Fax: 01242 226575
	Coroner: A. C. Crickmore Maitland House, Spa Road, Gloucester GL1 1UY	Tel: 01452 305661 Fax: 01452 412618
SOUTH GLOUCESTERSHIRE – see **AVON**		
GREATER MANCHESTER – see page 13		
GWENT	*Coroner:* D. T. Bowen Victoria Chambers, 11 Clytha Park Road, Newport, S. Wales NP20 4PB	Tel: 01633 264194 Fax: 01633 841146

LIST OF CORONERS AND ADDRESSES OF CORONERS' OFFICERS

District	Coroner	
HAMPSHIRE:		
CENTRAL HAMPSHIRE	*Coroner:* G. A. Short Coroner's Office, 19 St. Peter Street, Winchester, Hants. SO23 8BU	Tel: 01962 830006 Fax: 01962 830005
NORTH EAST HAMPSHIRE	*Coroner:* A. M. Bradley 76 Bounty Road, Basingstoke RG21 3BZ	Tel: 01256 322911 Fax: 01256 327811
	Coroner's Officer: David Richards Police Station, London Road, Basingstoke	Tel: 01256 405015 Fax: 01256 405001
PORTSMOUTH & SOUTH EAST HAMPSHIRE	*Coroner:* D. C. Horsley Room T20, The Guildhall, Guildhall Square, Portsmouth PO1 2AJ	Tel: 023 9268 8326 Fax: 023 9268 8331
	E-mail: coroners.office@portsmouthcc.gov.uk	
SOUTHAMPTON AND NEW FOREST	*Coroner:* K. S. Wiseman Southampton City Council, Coroner's Court, Civic Centre, Southampton SO14 7LY	Tel: 023 8071 0452 Fax: 023 8071 5671
	Coroner's Officer: Coroner's Office, Police Station, Civic Centre, Southampton SO14 7LG	Tel: 0845 045 4545 ext 3149/3349 or Direct Dial 023 8067 4266/7 Fax: 023 8071 5671
HARTLEPOOL	*Coroner:* C. W. M. Donnelly, LL.B. c/o Donnelly Adamson, Solicitors, 155 York Road, Hartlepool TS26 9EQ	Tel: 01429 274732 Fax: 01429 260199
HEREFORD & WORCESTER:		
HEREFORDSHIRE	*Coroner:* D. M. Halpern 36/37 Bridge Street, Hereford HR4 9DJ	Tel: 01432 355301 Fax: 01432 356619 DX 17207 HEREFORD
WORCESTERSHIRE	*Coroner:* G. U. Williams: The Court House, Bewdley Road, Stourport on Severn, Worcestershire DY13 8XE	Tel: 01299 824029 Fax: 01299 879238
	E-mail: coroner@worcestershire.gov.uk	
	Coroner's Officers at: Police Station, Castle Street, Worcester WR1 3AD Police Station, Grove Street, Redditch	Tel: 01905 331026 Fax: 01905 331025 Tel: 01527 586186 Fax: 01527 586116
HERTFORDSHIRE	*Coroner:* E. G. Thomas The Old Courthouse, St. Albans Road East, Hatfield, Herts. AL10 0ES	Tel: 01707 897411 Fax: 01707 897399
	Coroner's Officer: The Old Courthouse, St. Albans Road East, Hatfield, Herts. AL10 0ES DX 100702 HATFIELD	Tel: 01707 897407 Fax: 01707 897399

LIST OF CORONERS AND ADDRESSES OF CORONERS' OFFICERS

District	Coroner	
ISLE OF WIGHT	Coroner: J. A. Matthews 3-9 Quay Street, Newport, Isle of Wight PO30 5BB	Tel: 01983 520697 Fax: 01983 527678 E-mail: coroners@iow.gov.uk
ISLES OF SCILLY – see CORNWALL		
KENT:		
CENTRAL AND SOUTH EAST KENT	Coroner: Mrs. Helen Rachel Redman Elphicks Farmhouse, Hunton, Maidstone, Kent ME15 0SB	Tel: 01622 820412 Fax: 01622 820800
Ashford	Ashford Police Station, Tufton Street, Ashford, Kent TN23 1BT	Tel: 01233 896242 Fax: 01233 896449
Folkestone and Dover	Folkestone Police Station, Shorncliffe Road, Folkestone, Kent CT20 2SG	Tel: 01303 289147 Fax: 01303 289439
MID KENT AND MEDWAY	Coroner: R. J. Sykes The Coach House, Biddenden Road, Sissinghurst, Kent TN17 2JP	Tel: 01580 714182 Fax: 01580 714189
	Police Station, Palace Avenue, Maidstone ME15 6NF	Tel: 01622 604115 Fax: 01622 604119
	Medway Maritime Hospital, Windmill Road, Gillingham ME7 5NY	Tel: 01634 848773 Fax: 01634 845092
NORTH EAST KENT	Coroner: Miss R. M. Cobb 5 Lloyd Road, Broadstairs, Kent CT10 1HX	Tel: 01843 863260 Fax: 01843 603927
	Coroner's Officers: Margate Police Station, Fort Hill, Margate, Kent	Tel: 01843 222170/1 Fax: 01843 222172
NORTH WEST KENT	Coroner: Roger L. Hatch 23-25 Copperfields, Dartford DA1 2DE	Tel: 01322 226281 Fax: 01322 286324
	Coroner's Officers: Tunbridge Wells Police Station, Crescent Road, Tunbridge Wells, Kent TN1 2LU Dartford Police Station, Instone Road, Dartford, Kent DA1 1AA	Tel: 01892 502171/137 Fax: 01892 502172 Tel: 01322 283016/7 Fax: 01322 283019
KINGSTON-UPON-HULL – see **EAST RIDING AND HULL**		

LIST OF CORONERS AND ADDRESSES OF CORONERS' OFFICERS

District	Coroner	
LANCASHIRE:		
BLACKBURN, HYNDBURN AND RIBBLE VALLEY	*Coroner:* M. J. H. Singleton 7 Richmond Terrace, Blackburn BB1 7BB	Tel: 01254 263091 Mob: 07968 326068 Fax: 01254 274001
	Coroner's Officer: P.C. 2052 Farnworth, Lancashire Constabulary, Greenbank, Blackburn	Tel: 01254 294116
	CO John Schofield, Lancashire Constabulary, Greenbank, Blackburn	Tel: 01254 294116
BLACKPOOL/ FYLDE	*Coroner:* Anne V. Hind 283 Church Street, Blackpool, Lancs. FY1 3PG	Tel: 01253 625731 Fax: 01253 291915
	Coroner's Officers: Lancashire Constabulary, Montague Street, Blackpool	Tel: 01253 604207 Fax: 01253 291915
EAST LANCS	*Coroner:* Richard G. Taylor 6a Hargreaves Street, Burnley, Lancs. BB11 1ES	Tel: 01282 438446/ 446519 Fax: 01282 446525/ 425041 DX 23860 BURNLEY
PRESTON & WEST LANCS.	*Coroner:* Dr James Adeley, BSc, M.B.B.S., LL.B. Coroner's Court, Lawson Street, Preston, Lancs.	Tel: 01772 821788 Fax: 01772 828755
	Coroner's Officers: Police Station, Watling Street Road, Fulwood, Preston, Lancs.	Tel: 01772 209519 Fax: 01772 209532
	Ormskirk Police Station, 1 Derby Street, Ormskirk, Lancs.	Tel: 01695 566429 Fax: 01695 566365
	Chorley Police Station, St. Thomas's Road, Chorley, Lancs.	Tel: 01257 246207 Fax: 01257 246348
	Lancaster Police Station, Thurnham Street, Lancaster, Lancs.	Tel: 01524 596675 Fax: 01524 596732
LEICESTERSHIRE:		
LEICESTER CITY & SOUTH LEICESTERSHIRE	*Coroner:* J. M. Symington The Town Hall, Leicester LE1 9BG	Tel: 0116 225 2534 2535 2538 Fax: 0116 225 2537 E-mail: symij900@leicester.gov.uk
RUTLAND AND NORTH LEICESTERSHIRE	*Coroner:* T. H. Kirkman 34 Woodgate, Loughborough, Leicestershire LE11 2TY	Tel: 01509 268748 Fax: 01509 210 744

LIST OF CORONERS AND ADDRESSES OF CORONERS' OFFICERS

District	Coroner	
LINCOLNSHIRE:		
BOSTON & SPALDING	*Coroner:* Miss M. Taylor	
	Coroner's Officer: J. Bradwell County Police Station, Lincoln Lane, Boston PE21 8QS	Tel: 01205 312217 Mob: 07768 503329 Fax: 01205 312353
	E-mail: James.Bradwell@lincs.pnn.police.uk	
LOUTH	*Coroner:* S. P. G. Fisher 19 South St Mary's Gate, Grimsby, N.E. Lincolnshire DN31 1JE	Tel: 01472 316645 Mob: 07831 171029 Fax: 01472 311500
	Coroner's Officer: N. J. Jones County Police Station, Lincoln Lane, Boston, Lincolnshire PE21 8QS	Tel: 01205 312330 Mob: 07887 578980 Fax: 01205 312353
SPILSBY	*Coroner:* S. P. G. Fisher 19 South St Mary's Gate, Grimsby, N.E. Lincolnshire DN31 1JE	Tel: 01472 316645 Mob: 07831 171029 Fax: 01472 311500
	Coroner's Officer: N. J. Jones County Police Station, Lincoln Lane, Boston PE21 8QS	Tel: 01205 312330 Mob: 07887 578980 Fax: 01205 312353
STAMFORD	*Coroner:* G. S. Ryall 10 Briggate Quay, Whittlesey, Peterborough PE7 1DH	Tel: 01733 351010 Fax: 01733 351141
	E-mail: ryallg@btconnect.com	
	Coroner's Officer: Lincolnshire Police Divisional HQ, St. Catherine's Road, Grantham, Lincs. NG31 9DD	Tel: 01476 403217 Fax: 01476 403217
WEST LINCOLNSHIRE	*Coroner:* R. D. Atkinson, M.A., LL.M. H.M. Coroner's Office, 4 Lindum Terrace, Lincoln LN2 1NN	Tel: 01522 530055 Fax: 01522 560055
	E-mail: Lincs@Coroner.FSBusiness.co.uk	
	Coroner's Officers: Area Police HQ, West Parade, Lincoln LN1 1YP	Tel: 01522 885217 Fax: 01522 885344
	Area Police HQ, Grantham NG31 9DD	Tel: 01476 403217 Fax: 01476 403217

NORTH LINCOLNSHIRE – see **NORTH LINCOLNSHIRE AND GRIMSBY** p. 14

NORTH EAST LINCOLNSHIRE – see **NORTH LINCOLNSHIRE AND GRIMSBY** p. 14

LIST OF CORONERS AND ADDRESSES OF CORONERS' OFFICERS

District	Coroner	
LONDON:		
CITY OF LONDON	*Coroner:* Paul Matthews, B.C.L., LL.D. City of London Coroner's Court, Walbrook Wharf, 78-83 Upper Thames Street, London EC4Y 3TD	Tel: 020 7332 1598 Fax: 020 7601 2714
EAST LONDON	*Coroner:* Dr. E. J. Stearns Coroners Court, Queens Road, Walthamstow E17 8QP	Tel: 020 8496 5000 Fax: 020 8496 3378
INNER NORTH LONDON	*Coroner:* Dr. A. S. Reid St. Pancras Coroner's Court, Camley Street, London NW1 0PP Poplar Coroner's Court, 127 Poplar High Street, London E14 0AE	Tel: 020 7387 4882 Fax: 020 7383 2485 Tel: 020 7987 3614 Fax: 020 7538 0565
INNER SOUTH LONDON	*Coroner:* John Sampson Southwark Coroner's Court, 1 Tennis Street, London SE1 1YD Greenwich Office	Tel: 020 7525 4200 Fax: 020 7525 6356 Tel: 020 7525 6340 Fax: 020 7525 6344
INNER WEST LONDON	*Coroner:* P. A. Knapman Westminster Coroner's Court, 65 Horseferry Road, London SW1P 2ED Battersea Office, 48 Falcon Road, London SW11 2LR	Tel: 020 7802 4750 Fax: 020 7828 2837 Tel: 020 7228 6044 Fax: 020 7738 0640
NORTH LONDON	*Coroner:* W. F. G. Dolman Hornsey Coroner's Court, Myddelton Road, Hornsey N8 7PY Edgware Police Station, Whitchurch Lane, Edgware, Middx. HA8 6LA	Tel: 020 8348 4411 Fax: 020 8347 5229 Tel: 020 8733 3567 Fax: 020 8733 3514
SOUTHERN DISTRICT OF LONDON	*Coroner:* Dr. Roy Palmer Croydon Coroner's Court, Barclay Road, Croydon CR9 3NE	Tel: 020 8681 5019 Coroner's P.A. (Mrs. Bellingham): 020 8688 4691 (Part-time) Fax: 020 8686 3491
Bromley and Bexley Office:	Kingfisher House, 21-23 Elmfield Road, Bromley BR1 1LT	Tel: 020 8315 7580 Fax: 020 8315 7588
Croydon and Sutton Office:	150 Thornton Road, Thornton Heath, Surrey CR7 6BB	Tel: 020 8684 2758 Fax: 020 8684 2796
WEST LONDON	*Coroner:* Alison Mary Thompson 25 Bagleys Lane, Fulham, London SW6 2QA	Tel: 020 8753 6800/02 Fax: 020 8753 6803

LUTON – see **BEDFORDSHIRE AND LUTON** p. 3 *ante*

LIST OF CORONERS AND ADDRESSES OF CORONERS' OFFICERS

District	Coroner	
GREATER MANCHESTER:		
MANCHESTER	Coroner: N. S. Meadows, H.M. Coroner's Office, Crown Square, Deansgate, Manchester M60 1PR	Tel: 0161 830 4222 Fax: 0161 830 4328
MANCHESTER NORTH	Coroner: Simon R. Nelson Coroner's Office, Fourth Floor, Telegraph House, Baillie Street, Rochdale OL16 1QY	Tel: 01706 924815 Fax: 01706 640720 E-mail: coroners@rochdale.gov.uk
MANCHESTER SOUTH	Coroner: J. S. Pollard 10 Greek Street, Stockport SK3 8AB	Tel: 0161 476 0971 Fax: 0161 476 0972 E-mail: john.pollard@stockport.gov.uk
Trafford	Trafford General Hospital Mortuary, Davy Hulme, Manchester	Tel: 0161 746 2503
Stockport	Stepping Hill Hospital Mortuary, Stockport	Tel: 0161 419 5632
Tameside	Tameside General Hospital Mortuary, Ashton under Lyne	Tel: 0161 331 6528
MANCHESTER WEST	Coroner: M. Jennifer Leeming Paderborn House, Civic Centre, Howell Croft North, Bolton BL1 1JW	Tel: 01204 338 799 Fax: 01204 338 798 E-mail: jennifer.leeming@bolton.gov.uk
MERSEYSIDE:		
SEFTON, KNOWSLEY & ST HELENS		
	Coroner: Christopher Kent Sumner Southport Town Hall, Lord Street, Southport PR8 1DA	Tel: 0151 934 2746/9 Fax: 01704 534321
Sefton North, Sefton South	Southport Police Station, Law Courts, Southport	Tel: 0151 777 3480 Fax: 01704 512784
Knowsley & St. Helens	Coroners Office, Whiston Hospital, Whiston, Merseyside	Tel: 0151 430 1238 Fax: 0151 426 6694
LIVERPOOL	Coroner: A. J. A. Rebello H.M. Coroner's Court, The Cotton Exchange, Old Hall Street, Liverpool L3 9UF	Tel: 0151 233 4709/4713 Fax: 0151 233 4710
WIRRAL	Coroner: C. W. Johnson Midland Bank Building, Grange Road, West Kirby, Wirral CH48 4EB	Tel: 0151 625 6538 Fax: 0151 625 7757 E-mail: westkirbycoroner@btconnect.com

MERTHYR TYDFIL – see **BRIDGEND AND GLAMORGAN VALLEY**

MIDDLESBROUGH – see **TEESSIDE**

LIST OF CORONERS AND ADDRESSES OF CORONERS' OFFICERS

District	Coroner	
MILTON KEYNES	*Coroner:* R. H. G. Corner 10 Market Square, Buckingham MK18 1NJ	Tel: 01280 822217 Fax: 01280 813269 E-mail: rcorner@btconnect.com
	Coroner's Officer: Milton Keynes Police Station, 302 North Row, Witan Gate East, Central Milton Keynes MK9 2DS	Tel: 01908 686031 Fax: 01908 686160

MONMOUTHSHIRE – see **GWENT**

NEATH AND PORT TALBOT
[CASTELL-NEDD A PHORT TALBOT]

	Coroner: Dr. D. J. Osborne Pontardawe Police Station, High Street, Pontardawe, County Borough of Neath Port Talbot SA8 4HU	Tel: 01792 562784 Fax: 01792 562750

NEWPORT – see **GWENT**

NORFOLK:

GREAT YARMOUTH	*Coroner:* K. M. Dowding 29 Poplar Drive, Filby, Great Yarmouth, Norfolk NR29 3HU	Tel: 01493 369364 Fax: 01493 369125
	Coroner's Officers: James Paget Hospital, Gorleston, Gt. Yarmouth, Norfolk NR31 6LA	Tel: 01493 452477 Fax: 01493 452177
GREATER NORFOLK	*Coroner:* William J. Armstrong	
	Coroner's Officers: 124 Barrack Street, Norwich NR3 1TL	Tel: 01603 663302 Fax: 01603 665511
	Queen Elizabeth Hospital, Gayton Road, Kings Lynn, Norfolk PE30 4ET	Tel: 01553 613478 Fax: 01553 613469
	Kings Lynn Police Station, St. James Street, Kings Lynn, Norfolk PE30 5DE	Tel: 01553 691211 Fax: 01553 769084

NORTH EAST LINCOLNSHIRE – see **NORTH LINCOLNSHIRE AND GRIMSBY** below

NORTH EAST SOMERSET – see **AVON**

NORTH EAST WALES
[GOGLEDD DWYRAIN CYMRU]

	Coroner: J. B. Hughes Marbel House, Overton Arcade, High Street, Wrexham LL13 8LL	Tel: 01978 357775 Fax: 01978 358000 DX 26675 WREXHAM
	Coroner's Officer: Mr. G. Williams Eastern Control Room, Police Station, Bodhyfryd, Wrexham LL12 7BW	Tel: 01978 294554 294555

NORTH LINCOLNSHIRE AND GRIMSBY

	Coroner: J. S. Atkinson H.M. Coroner's Office, The Town Hall, Knoll Street, Cleethorpes, North East Lincolnshire DN35 8LN	Tel: 01472 324005 Fax: 01472 324007

NORTH WEST SOMERSET – see **AVON**

NORTH WEST WALES
[GOGLEDD GORLLEWIN CYMRU]

	Coroner: D. Pritchard Jones 37 Castle Square, Caernarfon, Gwynedd LL55 2NN	Tel: 01286 672804 Fax: 01286 675217

LIST OF CORONERS AND ADDRESSES OF CORONERS' OFFICERS

District	Coroner	
NORTH YORKSHIRE – see p. 20		
NORTHAMPTONSHIRE		
Northampton	*Coroner:* Mrs. A. Pember	
	300 Wellingborough Road, Northampton NN1 4EP	Tel: 01604 624732 Fax: 01604 232282
	Campbell Square Police Station, Northampton NN1 3EB	Tel: 01604 703618/9 Fax: 01604 703716
Kettering	Kettering Police Station, London Road, Kettering, Northants. NN15 7PQ	Tel: 01536 534827 Fax: 01536 534717
NORTHUMBERLAND:		
NORTH NORTHUMBERLAND		
	Coroner: I. G. McCreath, M.B.E. *Deputy Coroner:* Tony Brown, LL.M.	
	4 Quay Walls, Berwick-upon-Tweed TD15 1HD	Tel: 01289 304318 Fax: 01289 330323 E-mail: igm@sm-e.co.uk
	Coroner's Officer: Northumbria Police, Lintonville Terrace, Ashington, Northumberland NE63 9JX	Tel: 01661 872555 ext 61654 Fax: 01661 861658
SOUTH NORTHUMBERLAND		
	Coroner: E. Armstrong	
	3 Stanley Street, Blyth, Northumberland NE24 2BS DX 62601 BLYTH	Tel: 01670 354777 Fax: 01670 797891
NOTTINGHAMSHIRE	*Coroner:* N. D. Chapman	
	50 Carrington Street, Nottingham NG1 7FG	Tel: 0115 941 2322 Fax: 0115 950 0141
OXFORDSHIRE	*Coroner:* N. G. Gardiner	
	Southern House, 1 Cambridge Terrace, Oxford OX1 1RR	Tel: 01865 721451 Fax: 01865 251804
	Coroners' Officers: Coroner's Office, The Old School House, High Street, Cumnor, Oxon OX2 9PE	Tel: 01865 681912 Fax: 01865 864207
	Coroner's Office, Level One, John Radcliffe Hospital, Oxford OX3 9DU	Tel: 01865 764681 Fax: 01865 742453
PEMBROKESHIRE [SIR BENFRO]	*Coroner:* M. S. Howells	
	The Town Hall, Hamilton Terrace, Milford Haven, Pembs. SA73 3JW	Tel: 01646 698129 Fax: 01646 690607
	Coroners Officer: Jeremy Davies The Police Station, Charles Street, Milford Haven SA73 2HP	Tel: 01646 697375 Fax: 01646 698873
POOLE – see DORSET: **BOURNEMOUTH, POOLE AND EASTERN DORSET**		
PORTSMOUTH – see HAMPSHIRE: **PORTSMOUTH AND SOUTH EAST HAMPSHIRE**		

LIST OF CORONERS AND ADDRESSES OF CORONERS' OFFICERS

District	Coroner	
POWYS [POWYS]	*Coroner:* G. U. Williams, LL.B. 4 Lion Street, Brecon, Powys LD3 7AU	Tel: 01874 622106 Fax: 01874 623702 DX 200350 BRECON
REDCAR AND CLEVELAND – see **TEESSIDE**		
RHONDDA, CYNON, TAFF – see **BRIDGEND AND GLAMORGAN VALLEY**		
THE ROYAL HOUSEHOLD	*Coroner:* M. J. C. Burgess H.M. Coroner's Court Station Approach, Woking, Surrey GU22 7AP	Tel: 01483 776138 (when court sitting)
RUTLAND AND NORTH LEICESTERSHIRE – see under LEICESTERSHIRE page 10 *ante*		
SHROPSHIRE:		
MID & NORTH SHROPSHIRE	*Coroner:* J. P. Ellery c/o West Mercia Constabulary, Police HQ, Clive Road, Monkmoor, Shrewsbury SY2 5RW	Tel: 01743 237445 Fax: 01743 264879
SOUTH SHROPSHIRE	*Coroner:* A. F. T. Sibcy, LL.B. 6 Mill Street, Ludlow, Shropshire SY8 1AZ	Tel: 01584 879709 Fax: 01584 878364 E-mail: anthony.sibcy@shropshire-cc.gov.uk
	Coroner's Officer: The Police Station, Lower Galdeford, Ludlow, Shropshire SY8 1SA Note: All telephone calls and enquiries to be made in the first instance to the Coroner's Officer.	Tel: 08457 444888 Ext. 4608 Fax: 01743 264736
TELFORD AND WREKIN	*Coroner:* M. T. Gwynne Edgbaston House, Walker Street, Wellington, Telford, Shropshire TF1 1HF	Tel: 01952 641651 Fax: 01952 247441/ 388466 E-mail: telford.coroners@telford.gov.uk
SOMERSET:		
EASTERN SOMERSET	*Coroner:* T. Williams Argyll House, Bath Street, Frome, Somerset BA11 1DP	Tel: 01761 411030 Fax: 01761 416272 E-mail: info@hmcoroner.co.uk
WESTERN SOMERSET	*Coroner:* Michael Rose Blackbrook Gate, Blackbrook Park Avenue, Taunton, Somerset TA1 2PG	Tel: 01823 445380 Fax: 01823 445825 DX 97175 TAUNTON E-mail: coroner@clarkewillmott.com
	Coroner's Officer: The Police Station, Shuttern, Taunton, Somerset TA1 3QA	Tel: 01823 363271 Fax: 01823 363103
NORTH EAST SOMERSET – see **AVON**		
NORTH WEST SOMERSET – see **AVON**		
SOUTH GLOUCESTERSHIRE – see **AVON**		
SOUTH YORKSHIRE – see p.21		
SOUTHAMPTON – see HAMPSHIRE: **SOUTHAMPTON AND NEW FOREST**		

LIST OF CORONERS AND ADDRESSES OF CORONERS' OFFICERS

District	Coroner	
STAFFORDSHIRE:		
STAFFORDSHIRE SOUTH	*Coroner:* A. A. Haigh, B.A. Coroner's Office, 79 Eastgate Street, Stafford ST16 2NG	Tel: 01785 276127 Fax: 01785 276128 DX 712320 STAFFORD 5
	Coroner's Officers:	
Stafford	Stafford Borough Police Station, Eastgate Street, Stafford	Tel: 01785 234083
Burton on Trent	Burton Police Station, Horninglow Street, Burton on Trent	Tel: 01785 234783
Cannock	Stafford Borough Police Station, Eastgate Street, Stafford	Tel: 01785 234019
STOKE-ON-TRENT AND NORTH STAFFORDSHIRE	*Coroner:* I.S. Smith, LL.B. Coroner's Court & Chambers, 547 Hartshill Road, Hartshill, Stoke on Trent, Staffordshire ST4 6HF	Tel: 01782 234777 Fax: 01782 234783
STOCKTON-ON-TEES – see **TEESSIDE**		
STOKE-ON-TRENT – see STAFFORDSHIRE above		
SUFFOLK	*Coroner:* Dr. Peter Dean Suffolk Constabulary, Criminal Justice Unit, Shire Hall, Bury St. Edmunds, Suffolk IP33 2AP *Coroner's Officers:* Criminal Justice Unit, Shire Hall, Bury St. Edmunds, Suffolk IP33 2AP Ipswich Police Station, Civic Drive, Ipswich IP1 2AW Suffolk Police, Old Nelson Street, Lowestoft, Suffolk	Tel: 01284 774167 Fax: 01284 774204 Tel: 01284 774167 Fax: 01284 774204 Tel: 01473 383167 Fax: 01473 383207 Tel: 01986 835167 Fax: 01986 835174
SURREY	*Coroner:* M. J. C. Burgess H.M. Coroner's Court, Station Approach, Woking, Surrey GU22 7AP Police Station, Garfield Road, Addlestone, Surrey KT15 2NW Police Station, High Street, Ripley, Surrey GU23 6AE	Tel: 01483 776138 (when court sitting) Tel: 01932 205346 Tel: 01483 222078

LIST OF CORONERS AND ADDRESSES OF CORONERS' OFFICERS

District	Coroner	
SUSSEX:		
CITY OF BRIGHTON AND HOVE	*Coroner:* Veronica Hamilton-Deeley, LL.B. The Coroner's Office, Woodvale, Lewes Road, Brighton BN2 3QB	Tel: 01273 292046 Fax: 01273 292047
	Coroner's Officers: Brighton Police Station, John Street, Brighton, East Sussex BN2 2LA	Tel: 01273 665525 Fax: 01273 665543
EAST SUSSEX	*Coroner:* A. R. Craze, LL.B. 28/29 Grand Parade, St. Leonard-on-Sea TN37 6DR	Tel: 01424 200144 Fax: 01424 200145
Hastings & Rother Districts	The Police Station, Bohemia Road, Hastings, East Sussex TN34 1BT	Tel: 01424 456009 Fax: 01424 456096
Eastbourne, Wealden and Lewes Districts	The Police Station, George Street, Hailsham, East Sussex BN27 1AB	Tel: 01323 414067 Fax: 01323 414083
WEST SUSSEX	*Coroner:* Roger J. Stone 50 Westgate, Chichester, West Sussex PO19 3HE	Tel: 01243 530388 Fax: 01243 530389
	Coroner's Officers Police Station, Kingsham Road, Chichester, West Sussex	Tel: 01243 520217 Fax: 01243 520354
	Centenary House, Durrington Lane, Worthing, West Sussex	Tel: 01243 843507 Fax: 01243 843566
	Police Station, Bolnore Road, Haywards Heath, West Sussex	Tel: 01444 445808 Fax: 01444 445955
	Police Station, Hurst Road, Horsham, West Sussex	Tel: 01243 520286 Fax: 01243 520315
CITY AND COUNTY OF SWANSEA [ABERTAWE]	*Coroner:* Philip Rogers The Coroner's Office, County Hall, Oystermouth Road, Swansea SA1 3SN	Tel: 01792 636237 Fax: 01792 636603
	Coroner's Officer: Central Police Station, Grove Place, Swansea	Tel: 01792 450698
TEESSIDE	*Coroner:* M. J. F. Sheffield Register Office, Corporation Road, Middlesbrough, Cleveland TS1 2DA	Tel: 01642 729350 Fax: 01642 729948 DX 60532 MIDDLESBROUGH-1
THAMESDOWN – see **WILTSHIRE AND SWINDON**		
TORFAEN – see **GWENT**		
TYNE AND WEAR:		
GATESHEAD AND SOUTH TYNESIDE	*Coroner:* T. Carney Law Court Chambers, 2 Coronation Street, South Shields, Tyne and Wear NE33 1AP	Tel: 0191 483 8771 Fax: 0191 428 6699
	Coroner's Officers: Northumbria Police HQ, Millbank, Station Road, South Shields	Tel: 0191 454 7555 Fax: 0191 563 5052
	Northumbria Police HQ, High Street West, Gateshead	Tel: 0191 454 7555 Fax: 0191 221 9188

LIST OF CORONERS AND ADDRESSES OF CORONERS' OFFICERS

District	Coroner	
NEWCASTLE UPON TYNE	*Coroner:* David Mitford Coroner's Department, Civic Centre, Barras Bridge, Newcastle upon Tyne NE1 8PS	Tel: 0191 277 7280 Fax: 0191 261 2952
NORTH TYNESIDE	*Coroner:* E. Armstrong 3 Stanley Street, Blyth, Northumberland NE24 2BS	Tel: 01670 354777 Fax: 01670 797891 DX 62601 BLYTH
CITY OF SUNDERLAND	*Coroner:* D. Winter, LL.B., Solicitor Advocate, Morton's Solicitors, 112 High Street West, Sunderland SR1 1TX	Tel: 0191 514 4323 Fax: 0191 514 8100

WALES – see **CENTRAL NORTH WALES** p. 5, **NORTH EAST WALES** p. 14 and **NORTH WEST WALES**, p. 15

VALE OF GLAMORGAN – see **CARDIFF AND THE VALE OF GLAMORGAN**

WARWICKSHIRE	*Coroner:* M. F. Coker 42 Warwick Street, Leamington Spa CV32 5JS	Tel: 01926 422101 Fax: 01926 450568 DX 11861 LEAMINGTON SPA 1
	Coroner's Officers:	
Leamington Spa	The Police Station, Priory Road, Warwick CV34 4NA	Tel: 01926 684348/9 Fax: 01926 415607
Nuneaton and Bedworth	The Police Station, High Street, Bedworth CV12 8NH	Tel: 02476 483368
Rugby	County Police Office, Newbold Road, Rugby CV21 2DH	Tel: 01788 853749 Fax: 01788 853869
Stratford Upon Avon	County Police Office, Rother Street, Stratford Upon Avon	Tel: 01789 444521 Fax: 01926 415728

WEST MIDLANDS:

BIRMINGHAM/ SOLIHULL	*Coroner:* Aidan Keith Cotter LL.B., M.B.A., CMD Coroner's Court, 50 Newton Street, Birmingham B4 6NE	Tel: 0121 303 4274 Fax: 0121 233 4841
COVENTRY	*Coroner:* D. R. Sarginson Police HQ, Little Park Street, Coventry CV1 2JZ	Tel: 024 7653 9018 Fax: 024 7653 9804
BLACK COUNTRY	*Coroner:* Robin J. Balmain Highfields, High Street, West Bromwich, West Midlands B70 8RJ	Tel: 0121 500 2713 Fax: 0121 500 2717 E-mail: barbara_powles@sandwell.gov.uk
	Coroner's Officers: Highfields, High Street, West Bromwich, West Midlands B70 8RJ	Tel: 0121 500 2714/5 Fax: 0121 500 2712
	Highfields, High Street, West Bromwich, West Midlands B70 8RJ	Tel: 0121 500 2710/1 Fax: 0121 500 2712
	Green Lane Police Station, Walsall, West Midlands WS2 8HL	Tel: 01922 439018 Fax: 01922 439223
WOLVERHAMPTON	*Coroner:* R. J. Allen Bilston Street Police Station, Wolverhampton WV1 3AA	Tel: 01902 649211 Fax: 01902 649202

LIST OF CORONERS AND ADDRESSES OF CORONERS' OFFICERS

District	Coroner	
WEST SUSSEX – see p. 18		
WEST YORKSHIRE – see p. 21		
WILTSHIRE AND SWINDON	*Coroner:* David C. Masters	
	Lloyds Bank Chambers, 6 Castle Street, Salisbury, Wiltshire SP1 1BB	Tel: 01722 326870 Fax: 01722 332223
	Coroner's Officers:	
	Divisional Police HQ, Wilton Road, Salisbury, Wiltshire SP2 7HR	Tel: 01722 435293 Fax: 01722 435240
	Divisional Police HQ, Hampton Park West, Melksham, Wiltshire SN12 6QQ	Tel: 01249 449633 Fax: 01249 449690
	Divisional Police HQ, Police Station, Gablecross, Shrivenham Road, South Marston, Swindon SN3 4RB	Tel: 01793 507841 Fax: 01793 507840
WORCESTERSHIRE – see HEREFORD AND WORCESTER p. 8.		
WREXHAM – see **NORTH EAST WALES**		
YORK	*Coroner:* W. D. F. Coverdale, LL.B.	
	Sentinel House, Peasholme Green, York YO1 7PP	Tel: 01904 716000 Fax: 01904 716100 DX 61510 YORK
	Coroner's Officer:	
	N. Yorkshire Police Divisional HQ, Fulford Road, York YO1 4BY	Tel: 01904 669332 Fax: 01904 479965
YORKSHIRE:		
EAST RIDING – see **EAST RIDING AND HULL** p. 6		
NORTH YORKSHIRE **EASTERN DISTRICT**	*Coroner:* M. D. Oakley	
	Forsyth House, Market Place, Malton, North Yorkshire YO17 7LR	Tel: 01653 600070 01439 788339 Mob: 07860 789957 Fax: 01653 600049 DX 63700 MALTON
	Coroner's Officers:	
	Police Station, Northway, Scarborough YO12 7AD	Tel: 01723 509332 Fax: 01723 509373
	Police Station, 72 High Street, Northallerton DL7 8BR	Tel: 01609 789458 Fax: 01609 789413
WESTERN DISTRICT	*Coroner:* G. L. Fell	
	21 Grammar School Lane, Northallerton, North Yorkshire DL6 1DF	Tel: 01609 533805 533843 (Secretary) Fax: 01609 780793
	Coroner's Officers:	
	North Yorkshire Police, North Park Road, Harrogate, North Yorkshire HG1 5PJ	Tel: 01423 539332 Fax: 01423 539313
	Police Station, 72 High Street, Northallerton DL7 8BR	Tel: 01609 789458 Fax: 01609 789413
	Police Station, Portholme Road, Selby YO8 4QQ	Tel: 01904 669654 Fax: 01904 669613

LIST OF CORONERS AND ADDRESSES OF CORONERS' OFFICERS

District	Coroner	
SOUTH YORKSHIRE		
EAST	*Coroner:* E. S. Hooper	
Doncaster	Coroner's Court & Office, 5 Union Street, Off St. Sepulchre Gate West, Doncaster DN1 3AE	Tel: 01302 320844 Fax: 01302 364833
Rotherham	The Police Station, Main Street, Rotherham S60 1QU	Tel: 01709 832031 Fax: 01709 832145
WEST	*Coroner:* C. P. Dorries	
	Medico-Legal Centre, Watery Street, Sheffield S3 7ET	Tel: 0114 273 8721 Fax: 0114 272 6247
	Barnsley Police Station, Churchfield, Barnsley, South Yorkshire	Tel: 0122 673 6031 Fax: 0122 673 6295
WEST YORKSHIRE		
EASTERN DISTRICT	*Coroner:* D. Hinchliff	
	Coroner's Office, 71 Northgate, Wakefield WF1 3BS	Tel: 01924 302180 Fax: 01924 302184
	Coroner's Officers:	
Leeds	Symons House, Belgrave Street, Leeds LS2 8DD	Tel: 0113 241 4037 0113 241 4103/4/5 Fax: 0113 245 4892
Wakefield	71 Northgate, Wakefield WF1 3BS	Tel: 01924 293270 293265 Fax: 01924 302184
WESTERN DISTRICT	*Coroner:* R. Ll. Whittaker	
	Coroner's Office, The City Courts, Bradford BD1 1LA	Tel: 01274 391362
	Coroner's Officers:	
Bradford	Trafalgar House Police Station, Nelson Street, Bradford BD5 0EW	Tel: 01274 376510 Fax: 01274 376477
Keighley	West Yorkshire Police, Keighley Division, Keighley	Tel: 01535 293481
Dewsbury	West Yorkshire Police, Dewsbury Division, Aldams Road, Dewsbury	Tel: 01924 431070
Huddersfield	West Yorkshire Police, Huddersfield Division, Civic Centre, Huddersfield	Tel: 01484 436700
Halifax	H.M. Coroner's Office, 8 Carlton Street, Halifax HX1 2AL	Tel: 01422 354606 Fax: 01422 380153

ALPHABETICAL INDEX TO CORONERS' DISTRICTS

	Page		Page		Page
Avon	3	Hull – see East Riding and Hull		Powys	16
Bedfordshire and Luton	3	Isle of Wight	9	Preston & West Lancashire	10
Berkshire	3	Isles of Scilly	5	Royal Household	16
Birmingham/Solihull	19	Kent, Central and South East	9	Rutland and North Leicesterhsire	10
Black Country	19	Kent, Mid and Medway	9		
Blackburn, Hyndburn and Ribble Valley	10	Kent, North East	9	St. Helens – see Sefton, Knowsley and St. Helens	
Blackpool/Fylde	10	Kent, North West	9		
Boston and Spalding	11	Knowsley – see Sefton, Knowsley and St. Helens		Scarsdale & High Peak	5
Bournemouth, Poole and Eastern Dorset	6	Lancashire, East	10	Sefton, Knowsley & St. Helens	13
Bridgend and Glamorgan Valleys	3	Leicester City & South Lecistershire	10	Shropshire, Mid and North	16
Brighton and Hove	18	Lincolnshire, West	11	Shropshire, South	16
Buckinghamshire	4	Liverpool	13	Sleaford	11
Cambridgeshire, North and East	4	London, City of	12	Somerset, Eastern	16
		London, East	12	Somerset, Western	16
Cambridgeshire South and West	4	London, Inner North	12	South Yorkshire, East	21
		London, Inner South	12	South Yorkshire, West	21
Cardiff and the Vale of Glamorgan	4	London, Inner West	12	Southampton and New Forest	8
		London, North	12		
Cardinganshire	4	London, Southern District of	12	Southend and South East Essex District	7
Carmarthenshire	5	London, West	12		
Central North Wales	5	Louth	11	Spilsby	11
Cheshire	5	Luton – see Bedfordshire and Luton		Staffordshire, South	17
City of London	12			Stamford	11
Cornwall	5	Manchester	13	Stoke-on-Trent and North Staffordshire	17
Coventry	19	Manchester, North	13		
Cumbria, North East	5	Manchester, South	13	Suffolk	17
Cumbria, North & West	5	Manchester, West	13	Sunderland, City of	19
Darlington and South Durham	6	Milton Keynes	14	Surrey	17
		Neath and Port Talbot	14	Sussex East	18
Derby and South Derbyshire	5	Newcastle upon Tyne	19	Sussex West	18
Dorset, Western	6	North Lincolnshire and Grimsby	14	Swansea, City and County of	18
Durham, North	6			Teesside	18
East Riding and Hull	6	North Yorkshire, Eastern District	20	Telford and Wrekin	16
East Sussex	18			Thamesdown – see Wiltshire and Thamesdown	
Essex and Thurrock	7	North Yorkshire, Western District	20		
Exeter and Greater Devon	6			Torbay & South Devon	6
Furness & South Cumbria	5	Northamptonshire	15	Tyneside, North	19
Gateshead and South Tyneside	18	Northumberland, North	15	Wales, Central North	5
		Northumberland, South	15	Wales, North East	14
Gloucestershire	7	Nottinghamshire	15	Wales, North West	14
Greater Norfolk	14	Oxfordshire	15	Warwickshire	19
Great Yarmouth	14	Pembrokeshire	15	Watford – see St. Albans/Watford	
Grimsby – see North Lincolnshire and Grimsby		Peterborough	4		
		Plymouth & South West Devon	6	West Sussex	18
Gwent	7			West Yorkshire, Eastern	21
Hampshire, Central	8	Poole – see Bournemouth, Poole and Eastern Dorset		West Yorkshire, Western	21
Hampshire, North East	8			Wiltshire and Swindon	20
Hartlepool	8	Port Talbot – see Neath and Port Talbot		Wirral	13
Herefordshire	8			Wolverhampton	19
Hertfordshire	8	Portsmouth & South East Hampshire	8	Worcestershire	8
				York	20

PART V

LIST OF PROBATE REGISTRARS
AND
ADDRESSES OF PROBATE COURTS

PROBATE COURTS

Town, Type of Probate Court and Registrar	Probate Manager and Court Offices	Opening Times

BANGOR
Sub-Registry
Registrar: Mr. P. Curran
(Cardiff DPR)
	Mr. R. Perry,
	City Council Offices,
	Ffordd Gwynedd,
	Bangor,
	Gwynedd,
	Wales LL57 1DT
	  Switchboard: 01248 362410
	  General Fax: 01248 364423
	DX 23186 Bangor 2
		Court building open: 9.30 a.m.
		Court building closed: 4.00 p.m.
		Court counter open: 9.30 a.m.
		Court counter closed: 4.00 p.m.

BIRMINGHAM
District Registry
Registrar: Miss P. Walbeoff
	Mrs. J. O'Dwyer,
	The Priory Courts,
	33 Bull Street,
	Birmingham,
	West Midlands B4 6DU
	  Switchboard: 0121 681 3400
	  General Fax: 0121 236 2465
	DX 701990 Birmingham 7
		Court building open: 9.30 a.m.
		Court building closed: 4.00 p.m.
		Court counter open: 9.30 a.m.
		Court counter closed: 4.00 p.m.

BODMIN
Sub-Registry
Registrar: Mr. R. Joyce
(Bristol DPR)
	Mrs. Emma Sherwin,
	Market Street,
	Bodmin,
	Cornwall PL31 2JW
	  Switchboard: 01208 72279
	  General Fax: 01208 269004
	DX 136847 Bodmin 2
		Court building open: 9.30 a.m.
		Court building closed: 4.00 p.m.
		Court counter open: 9.30 a.m.
		Court counter closed: 4.00 p.m.

BRIGHTON
District Registry
Registrar: Mr. P. R. Ellwood
	Mrs. S. Catt,
	William Street,
	Brighton,
	East Sussex BN2 2LG
	  Switchboard: 01273 573510
	  General Fax: 01273 625845
	DX 98073 Brighton 3
		Court building open: 9.30 a.m.
		Court building closed: 4.00 p.m.
		Court counter open: 9.30 a.m.
		Court counter closed: 4.00 p.m.

BRISTOL
District Registry
Registrar: Mr. R. H. P. Joyce
	Mrs. Teresa Peacock,
	Ground Floor,
	The Crescent Centre,
	Temple Back,
	Bristol BS1 6EP
	  Switchboard: 0117 927 3915
	  General Fax: 0117 925 3549
	  Switchboard: 0117 926 4619
	DX 94400 Bristol 5
		Court building open: 9.30 a.m.
		Court building closed: 4.00 p.m.
		Court counter open: 9.30 a.m.
		Court counter closed: 4.00 p.m.

CARDIFF
Probate Registry of Wales
Registrar: Mr. P. Curran
	Veronica Thomas,
	P.O. Box 474,
	2 Park Street,
	Cardiff,
	South Wales CF10 1TB
	  Switchboard: 029 2037 6479
	  General Fax: 029 2022 9855
	DX 122782 Cardiff 13
		Court building open: 9.30 a.m.
		Court building closed: 4.00 p.m.
		Court counter open: 9.30 a.m.
		Court counter closed: 4.00 p.m.

PROBATE COURTS

Town, Type of Probate Court and Registrar	Probate Manager and Court Offices	Opening Times
CARLISLE *Sub-Registry* Registrar: Mrs. M. C. Riley (Newcastle DPR)	Miss Judith Graham, Courts of Justice, Earl Street, Carlisle, Cumbria CA1 1DJ Direct Line: 01228 521751 DX 63034 Carlisle	Court building open: 9.30 a.m. Court building closed: 4.00 p.m. Court counter open: 9.30 a.m. Court counter closed: 4.00 p.m.

CARMARTHEN
 	
Sub-Registry
 	
Registrar: Mr. P. Curran
(Cardiff DPR)
	Mrs. Maureen Roberts,
	14 King Street,
	Carmarthen,
	Carmarthenshire SA31 1BL
	   Switchboard: 01267 242560
	   General Fax: 01267 229067
	DX 51420 Carmarthen
		Court building open: 9.30 a.m.
		Court building closed: 4.00 p.m.
		Court counter open: 9.30 a.m.
		Court counter closed: 4.00 p.m.

CHESTER
 	
Sub-Registry
 	
Registrar: Mrs. K. Clark-Rimmer
(Liverpool DPR)
	Mrs. W. M. Bevan,
	2nd Floor,
	Civil Justice Centre,
	Trident House,
	Little St John Street,
	Chester CH1 1RE
	   Switchboard: 01244 345082
	   General Fax: 01244 348709
		Court building open: 9.30 a.m.
		Court building closed: 4.00 p.m.
		Court counter open: 9.30 a.m.
		Court counter closed: 4.00 p.m.

EXETER
 	
Sub-Registry
 	
Registrar: Mr. R. H. P. Joyce
(Bristol DPR)
	Mr. G. R. Bower,
	1st Floor,
	Exeter Crown and County
	   Courts,
	Southernhay Gardens,
	Exeter,
	Devon EX1 1UH
	   Switchboard: 01392 415370
	   General Fax: 01392 415608
	DX 98442 Exeter 2
		Court building open: 9.30 a.m.
		Court building closed: 4.00 p.m.
		Court counter open: 9.30 a.m.
		Court counter closed: 4.00 p.m.

GLOUCESTER
 	
Sub-Registry
 	
Registrar: Mr. R. R. D. Costa
(Oxford DPR)
	Miss Claire Mahon,
	2nd Floor,
	Combined Court Building,
	Kimbrose Way,
	Gloucester,
	Gloucestershire GL1 2DG
	   Switchboard: 01452 834966
	   General Fax: 01452 834970
	DX 98663 Gloucester 5
		Court building open: 9.30 a.m.
		Court building closed: 4.00 p.m.
		Court counter open: 9.30 a.m.
		Court counter closed: 4.00 p.m.

IPSWICH
 	
District Registry
 	
Registrar: Miss H. Whitby
	Miss S. Hadley,
	Ground Floor,
	8 Arcade Street,
	Ipswich,
	Suffolk IP1 1EJ
	   Switchboard: 01473 284260
	   General Fax: 01473 231951
	DX 3279 Ipswich
		Court building open: 9.30 a.m.
		Court building closed: 4.00 p.m.
		Court counter open: 9.30 a.m.
		Court counter closed: 4.00 p.m.

PROBATE COURTS

Town, Type of Probate Court and Registrar	Probate Manager and Court Offices	Opening Times

LANCASTER
 	
Sub-Registry
 	
Registrar: Mrs. K. Clark-Rimmer (Liverpool DPR)
	Miss E. Limont-Brown,
	Room 111,
	Mitre House,
	Church Street,
	Lancaster LA1 1HE
	  Switchboard: 01524 36625
	  General Fax: 01542 35561
	DX 63509 Lancaster
		Court building open: 9.30 a.m.
		Court building closed: 4.00 p.m.
		Court counter open: 9.30 a.m.
		Court counter closed: 4.00 p.m.

LEEDS
 	
District Registry
 	
Registrar: Mrs. A. Parry
	Mrs. Sally Holding,
	Coronet House,
	3rd Floor,
	Queen Street,
	Leeds,
	West Yorkshire LS1 2BA
	  Switchboard: 0113 386 3540
	  General Fax: 0113 247 1893
	DX 26451 Leeds Park Square
		Court building open: 9.30 a.m.
		Court building closed: 4.00 p.m.
		Court counter open: 9.30 a.m.
		Court counter closed: 4.00 p.m.

LEICESTER *Probate Sub Registry* Registrar: Mr. R. R. D'Costa (Oxford DPR)	Mr. Tony Smith, Crown Court Building, 90 Wellington Street, Leicester, Leicestershire LE1 6HG Switchboard: 0116 285 3380 DX 17403 Leicester3	Court building open: 8.00 a.m. Court building closed: 5.00 p.m. Court counter open: 9.30 a.m. Court counter closed: 4.00 p.m.

LINCOLN
 	
Sub-Registry
 	
Registrar: Mrs. A. Parry (Leeds DPR)
	Mr. N. Kitching,
	360 High Street,
	Lincoln,
	Lincolnshire LN5 7PS
	  Switchboard: 01522 523648
	  General Fax: 01522 539903
	DX 703233 Lincoln 6
		Court building open: 9.30 a.m.
		Court building closed: 4.00 p.m.
		Court counter open: 9.30 a.m.
		Court counter closed: 4.00 p.m.

LIVERPOOL
 	
District Registry
 	
Registrar: Mrs. K. Clark-Rimmer
	Mrs. D. Shone,
	Queen Elizabeth II Law Courts,
	Derby Square,
	Liverpool,
	Merseyside L2 1XA
	  Switchboard: 0151 236 8264
	  General Fax: 0151 227 4634
	DX 14246 Liverpool 1
		Court building open: 9.30 a.m.
		Court building closed: 4.00 p.m.
		Court counter open: 9.30 a.m.
		Court counter closed: 4.00 p.m.

PROBATE COURTS

Town, Type of Probate Court and Registrar	Probate Manager and Court Offices	Opening Times
LONDON Probate Department Manager: Kevin Donnelly Customer Service Officer: Ade Ojo	Tina Constantinou, London Probate Department, PRFD, First Avenue House, 42-49 High Holborn, Ground Floor, Holborn, London WC1V 6NP Probate Helpline: 0845 3020 900 Safe custody/Caveat and Summons enquiries: 020 7947 7022/6948 Personal application enquiries: 020 7947 6939/6043 Solicitors' enquiries: 020 7947 7431/6953 General Fax: 020 7947 6946 DX 941 London Chancery Lane	Court building open: 10.00 a.m. Court building closed: 4.30 p.m. Court counter open: 10.00 a.m. Court counter closed: 4.30 p.m.
MAIDSTONE *Sub-Registry* Registrar: Mr. P. Ellwood (Brighton DPR)	Mr. A. Connor, The Law Courts, Barker Road, Maidstone, Kent ME16 8EQ Switchboard: 01622 202048 Switchboard: 01622 202000 DX 130066 Maidstone	Court building open: 9.30 a.m. Court building closed: 4.00 p.m. Court counter open: 9.30 a.m. Court counter closed: 4.00 p.m.
MANCHESTER *District Registry* Registrar: Mr. P. A. Burch	Mr. K. Murphy, 9th Floor, Astley House, 23 Quay Street, Manchester, Greater Manchester M3 4AT Switchboard: 0161 837 6070 General Fax: 0161 832 2690 DX 14387 Manchester 1	Court building open: 9.30 a.m. Court building closed: 4.00 p.m. Court counter open: 9.30 a.m. Court counter closed: 4.00 p.m.

NOTE: With effect from 24th October 2007 Manchester DPR will be located at 1 Bridge Street West, Manchester M60 9DJ. Tel: 0161 240 5000

MIDDLESBROUGH *Sub-Registry* Registrar: Mrs. M. C. Riley (at Newcastle DPR)	Mr. Mark Burden (at Newcastle DPR), 1 Waterloo Square, Newcastle-upon-Tyne, Tyne & Wear NE1 4AL Switchboard: 01962 430001	Court building open: 10.00 a.m. Court building closed: 3.00 p.m. Court counter open: 10.00 a.m. Court counter closed: 3.00 p.m.
NEWCASTLE *District Registry* Registrar: Mrs. M. C. Riley	Mr. M. Burden, 1 Waterloo Square, Newcastle-upon-Tyne, Tyne & Wear NE1 4AL Switchboard: 0191 211 2170 General Fax: 0191 211 2184 DX 61081 Newcastle-upon-Tyne 14	Court building open: 9.30 a.m. Court building closed: 4.00 p.m. Court counter open: 9.30 a.m. Court counter closed: 4.00 p.m.

PROBATE COURTS

Town, Type of Probate Court and Registrar	Probate Manager and Court Offices	Opening Times

NORWICH
Sub-Registry
Registrar: Miss H. Whitby (Ipswich DPR)
	Mr. T. Harvey,
	Combined Court Building,
	The Law Courts,
	Bishopgate,
	Norwich,
	Norfolk NR3 1UR
	  Switchboard: 01603 728267
	  General Fax: 01603 627469
	DX 5202 Norwich
		Court building open: 9.30 a.m.
		Court building closed: 4.00 p.m.
		Court counter open: 9.30 a.m.
		Court counter closed: 4.00 p.m.

NOTTINGHAM
Sub-Registry
Registrar: Mr. P. Burch (Manchester DPR)
	Mr. J. Hill,
	Butt Dyke House,
	33 Park Row,
	Nottingham,
	Nottinghamshire NG1 6GR
	  Switchboard: 0115 941 4288
	  General Fax: 0115 950 3383
	DX 10055 Nottingham
		Court building open: 9.30 a.m.
		Court building closed: 4.00 p.m.
		Court counter open: 9.30 a.m.
		Court counter closed: 4.00 p.m.

OXFORD
District Registry
Registrar: Mr. R. R. D'Costa
	Mrs. F. C. Herdman,
	Combined Court Building,
	St. Aldates,
	Oxford,
	Oxfordshire OX1 1LY
	  Switchboard: 01865 793050
	  Switchboard: 01865 793055
	  General Fax: 01865 793090
	DX 96454 Oxford 4
		Court building open: 9.30 a.m.
		Court building closed: 4.00 p.m.
		Court counter open: 9.30 a.m.
		Court counter closed: 4.00 p.m.

PETERBOROUGH
Sub-Registry
Registrar: Miss H. Whitby (Ipswich DPR)
	Miss Hina Pankhania,
	1st Floor,
	Crown Building,
	Rivergate,
	Peterborough,
	Cambridgeshire PE1 1EJ
	  Switchboard: 01733 562802
	  General Fax: 01733 313016
	DX 12327 Peterborough 1
		Court building open: 9.30 a.m.
		Court building closed: 4.00 p.m.
		Court counter open: 9.30 a.m.
		Court counter closed: 4.00 p.m.

SHEFFIELD
Sub-Registry
Registrar: Mrs. A. Parry (Leeds DPR)
	Ms. Lisa Joel,
	P.O. Box 832,
	The Law Courts,
	50 West Bar,
	Sheffield,
	South Yorkshire S3 8YR
	  Switchboard: 0114 281 2596
	  General Fax: 0114 273 0848
	DX 26054 Sheffield 2
		Court building open: 9.30 a.m.
		Court building closed: 4.00 p.m.
		Court counter open: 9.30 a.m.
		Court counter closed: 4.00 p.m.

PROBATE COURTS

Town, Type of Probate Court and Registrar	Probate Manager and Court Offices	Opening Times

STOKE-ON-TRENT
Sub-Registry
Registrar: Miss P. Walbeoff
(Birmingham DPR)
	Mrs. Linda Best (Acting),
	Combined Court Centre,
	Bethesda Street,
	Hanley,
	Stoke-on-Trent,
	Staffordshire ST1 3BP
	  Switchboard: 01782 854065
	  General Fax: 01782 274916
	DX 703363 Hanley 3
		Court building open: 9.30 a.m.
		Court building closed: 4.00 p.m.
		Court counter open: 9.30 a.m.
		Court counter closed: 4.00 p.m.

WINCHESTER
District Registry
Registrar: Mr. A. Butler
	Mrs. B. Phillips,
	4th Floor,
	Cromwell House,
	Andover Road,
	Winchester,
	Hampshire SO23 7EW
	  Solicitors' Enquiries:
	  01962 897024
	  Personal Applications:
	  01962 897029
	  General Fax: 01962 840796
	DX 96900 Winchester 2
		Court building open: 9.30 a.m.
		Court building closed: 4.00 p.m.
		Court counter open: 9.30 a.m.
		Court counter closed: 4.00 p.m.

YORK
Sub-Registry
Registrar: Mrs. M. C. Riley
(Newcastle DPR)
	1st Floor,
	Castle Chambers,
	5 Clifford Street,
	York,
	North Yorkshire YO1 9RG
	  Switchboard: 01904 666777
	  Switchboard: 01904 666770
	  Switchboard: 01904 666781
	  General Fax: 01904 666776
	DX 720629 York 21
		Court building open: 9.30 a.m.
		Court building closed: 4.00 p.m.
		Court counter open: 9.30 a.m.
		Court counter closed: 4.00 p.m.

APPENDIX I

THE CROWN PROSECUTION SERVICE (CPS)

	Page
Crown Prosecution Service Headquarters	3

Crown Prosecution Service Areas:

CPS Avon and Somerset	5
CPS Bedfordshire	6
CPS Cambridgeshire	7
CPS Cheshire	8
CPS Cleveland	9
CPS Cumbria	9
CPS Derbyshire	11
CPS Devon and Cornwall	12
CPS Dorset	13
CPS Durham	13
CPS Dyfed Powys	14
CPS Essex	15
CPS Gloucestershire	17
CPS Greater Manchester	18
CPS Gwent	20
CPS Hampshire and Isle of Wight	20
CPS Hertfordshire	22
CPS Humberside	23
CPS Kent	24
CPS Lancashire	26
CPS Leicestershire	27
CPS Lincolnshire	28
CPS London	29
CPS Merseyside	33
CPS Norfolk	35
CPS Northamptonshire	36
CPS Northumbria	36
CPS North Wales	38
CPS North Yorkshire	39
CPS Nottinghamshire	40
CPS South Wales	41
CPS South Yorkshire	43
CPS Staffordshire	43
CPS Suffolk	44
CPS Surrey	45
CPS Sussex	45
CPS Thames Valley	47
CPS Warwickshire	48
CPS West Mercia	48
CPS West Midlands	49
CPS West Yorkshire	51
CPS Wiltshire	53

APPENDIX I

THE CROWN PROSECUTION SERVICE (CPS)

The Crown Prosecution Service is responsible for prosecuting cases investigated by the police in England and Wales (with the exception of cases conducted by the Serious Fraud Office and certain minor offences).

The Director of Public Prosecutions is the Head of the Service and discharges his statutory functions under the superintendence of the Attorney General.

The Service comprises Headquarters Offices in London and York and 43 Areas covering England and Wales corresponding to each current police force in England and Wales outside London, and one for London. Each of the CPS Areas is headed by a Chief Crown Prosecutor supported by an Area Business Manager.

CROWN PROSECUTION SERVICE HEADQUARTERS

50 Ludgate Hill, London EC4M 7EX
Tel: 020 7796 8000
DX 300850 LUDGATE EC4

Director of Public Prosecutions (SCS): Ken Macdonald Q.C.
Chief Executive (SCS): Peter Lewis

CPS DIRECT

6th Floor, United House, Piccadilly, York YO1 9PQ
Tel: 01904 545594
Fax: 01904 545698
DX 65204 YORK 6

CCP: Barry Hughes
ABM: Sue Barrand

CPS AREAS

CPS AVON AND SOMERSET

Chief Crown Prosecutor: Mr David Archer

Area Business Manager: Ms Sarah Trevelyan

Area Address: 2nd Floor, Froomsgate House, Rupert Street, Bristol BS1 2QJ
Tel: 0117 930 2800   Fax: 0117 930 2810   DX 78120 BRISTOL

Branch Address	Courts Covered	
	Crown Courts	Magistrates' Courts
TAUNTON TRIALS UNIT Riverside Chambers, Castle Street, Taunton, Somerset TA1 4AP Tel: 01823 623100 Fax: 01823 623111 DX 115643 TAUNTON 3	Taunton	
SOUTHERN CRIMINAL JUSTICE UNIT Taunton Police Station, Shuttern, Taunton, Somerset TA1 4ET Tel: 01823 363066 Fax: 01823 363626 DX 115643 TAUNTON 3		Bridgwater (Sedgemoor) Yeovil (South Somerset) Taunton (Taunton Deane) Minehead (West Somerset)
NORTHERN CRIMINAL JUSTICE UNIT 4th Floor, Froomsgate House, Rupert Street, Bristol BS1 2QJ Tel: 0117 952 9814 Fax: 0117 952 9863		North Avon Bath Bristol Wells (Mendip) Frome (Mendip) Weston Super Mare (Woodspring) Flax Bourton (Woodspring)
BRISTOL CROWN COURT TRIALS UNIT 2nd & 3rd Floor, Froomsgate House, Rupert Street, Bristol BS1 2QJ Tel: 0117 930 2800 DX 78120 BRISTOL	Bristol	

CPS AREAS

WITNESS CARE UNIT
1st Floor,
Froomsgate House,
Rupert Street,
Bristol BS1 2QJ

Tel: 0117 930 2879

Fax: 0117 930 2842

DX 78120 BRISTOL

CPS BEDFORDSHIRE

Chief Crown Prosecutor: Mr. Richard Newcombe

Area Business Manager: Mr. Timothy Riley

Area Address: Sceptre House, 7-9 Castle Street, Luton, Beds. LU1 3AJ
Tel: 01582 816600   Fax: 01582 816678   DX 120503 LUTON 6

Branch Address	Courts Covered	
	Crown Courts	Magistrates' Courts
CRIMINAL JUSTICE UNIT Sceptre House, 7-9 Castle Street, Luton, Beds. LU1 3AJ Tel: 01582 394451 (Luton) 01234 275020 (Bedford) Fax: 01582 816679 DX 120503 LUTON 6		Bedford and Mid Bedfordshire (Bedford) Luton and South Bedfordshire (Luton)
CRIMINAL JUSTICE UNIT Sceptre House, 7-9 Castle Street, Luton, Beds. LU1 3AJ Tel: 01582 816609 Fax: 01582 816678 DX 120503 LUTON 6	Luton	

CPS AREAS

CPS CAMBRIDGESHIRE

Chief Crown Prosecutor: Mr Richard Crowley

Area Business Manager: Mr Adrian Mardell

Area Address: Justinian House, Spitfire Close, Ermine Business Park, Huntingdon, Cambridgeshire PE29 6XY   Tel: 01480 825200   Fax: 01480 825205
DX 123223 HUNTINGDON 5

	Courts Covered	
Branch Address	Crown Courts	Magistrates' Courts
NORTHERN CRIMINAL JUSTICE UNIT (PETERBOROUGH) Thorpe Wood Police Station, Peterborough, Cambridgeshire PE3 6SD Tel: 01733 424134 Fax: 01733 553934 DX 123371 PETERBOROUGH		Peterborough Wisbech
SOUTHERN CRIMINAL JUSTICE UNIT (CAMBRIDGE) Parkside Police Station, Cambridge CB1 1JG Tel: 01480 825213 Fax: 01223 823242 DX 133564 CAMBRIDGE 7		Cambridge Ely
TRIALS UNIT Justinian House, Spitfire Close, Ermine Business Park, Huntingdon, Cambridgeshire PE29 6XY Tel: 01480 825288 Fax: 01480 825206 DX 123223 HUNTINGDON 5	Peterborough Cambridge Northampton Norwich	
SOUTHERN CRIMINAL JUSTICE UNIT (HUNTINGDON) Justinian House, Spitfire Close, Ermine Business Park, Huntingdon, Cambridgeshire PE29 6XY Tel: 01480 825213 Fax: 01480 825208 DX 123223 HUNTINGDON 5		Huntingdon

CPS AREAS

CPS CHESHIRE

Chief Crown Prosdecutor: Mr Ian Rushton

Area Business Manager: Mrs Angela Garbett

Area Address: 2nd Floor, Windsor House, Pepper Street, Chester CH1 1TD
Tel: 01244 408600   Fax: 01244 408657   DX 20019 CHESTER

Branch Address	Courts Covered	
	Crown Courts	Magistrates' Courts
SOUTH CHESHIRE DIVISION 2nd Floor Windsor House, Pepper Street, Chester CH1 1TD Tel: 01244 408600 Fax: 01244 408657 DX 20019 CHESTER	Chester Knutsford Mold Warrington	Chester, Ellesmere Port and Neston (Chester) Vale Royal (Northwich, Winsford)
SUB-OFFICE CREWE 3rd Floor, Crewe Police Station, Civic Way, Crewe CW1 2DQ Tel: 01270 509841 Fax: 01270 509851	Chester Knutsford Mold Warrington	Chester
NORTH CHESHIRE DIVISION Bankside Chambers, 1-4 Bankside, Crossfield Street, Warrington WA1 1UP Tel: 01925 425300 Fax: 01925 425348 (Warrington Team) 425349 (Halton/Macclesfield Team) DX 17769 WARRINGTON	Chester Knutsford Mold Warrington	Halton (Runcorn)

CPS AREAS

CPS CLEVELAND

Chief Crown Prosecutor: Mr Martin Goldman

Area Business Manager: Mrs Margaret Phillips

Area Address: 5 Linthorpe Road, Middlesbrough, Cleveland TS1 1TX
Tel: 01642 204500   Fax: 01642 204503   DX 60551 MIDDLESBROUGH 12

Branch Address	Courts Covered	
	Crown Courts	Magistrates' Courts
TEESSIDE BRANCH 5 Linthorpe Road, Middlesbrough, Cleveland TS1 1TX Tel: 01642 204500 Fax: 01642 204503 DX 60551 MIDDLESBROUGH 12	Teesside	Lanbaurgh East (Guisborough) Teesside (Middlesbrough) Hartlepool
HARTLEPOOL BRANCH Hartlepool Police Station, Avenue Road, Hartlepool TS24 8AB Tel: 01642 302500 Fax: 01642 302513		Hartlepool

CPS CUMBRIA

Chief Crown Prosecutor: Claire Lindley

Area Business Manager: Mr John Pears

Area Address: 1st Floor, Stocklund House, Castle Street, Carlisle, Cumbria CA3 8SY
Tel: 01228 882900   Fax: 01228 882910   DX 63032 CARLISLE

Branch Address	Courts Covered	
	Crown Courts	Magistrates' Courts
NORTHERN COMBINED UNIT:		
CARLISLE TEAM 1st Floor, Stocklund House, Castle Street, Carlisle, Cumbria CA3 8SY Tel: 01228 882900 Fax: 01228 882910 DX 63032 CARLISLE	Carlisle	Carlisle

CPS AREAS

WORKINGTON TEAM
Prosper House,
Regents Court
Guard Street,
Workington,
Cumbria CA14 4EW

Tel: 01900 734100

Fax: 01900 734110

DX 62857 WORKINGTON

Carlisle

West Allerdale (Workington)
Whitehaven

SOUTHERN COMBINED UNIT:

BARROW-IN-FURNESS OFFICE
5th Floor,
Furness House,
The Mall,
Barrow-in-Furness,
Cumbria LA14 1HL

Tel: 01229 814400

Fax: 01229 814410

DX 63903 BARROW

Barrow
Lancaster
Preston

Furness and District
(Barrow-in-Furness)

KENDAL TRIALS UNIT
New Magistrates' Court Building,
Burneside Road,
Kendal,
Cumbria LA9 4RT

Tel: 01539 815540

Fax: 01539 815541

DX 63452 KENDAL 2

Barrow-in-Furness
Carlisle
Lancaster
Preston

KENDAL CRIMINAL JUSTICE UNIT
Kendal Police Station,
Busher Walk,
Kendal LA9 4RJ

Tel: 01539 815540

Fax: 01539 815541

(Magistrates' Courts)
Kendal
Penrith

CPS AREAS

CPS DERBYSHIRE

Chief Crown Prosecutor: Mr Brian Gunn

Area Business Manager: Mr Chris Mitchell

Area Address: 7th Floor, St. Peter's House, Gower Street, Derby DE1 1SB
Tel: 01332 614000   Fax: 01332 614009   DX 725818 DERBY 22

	Courts Covered	
Branch Address	Crown Courts	Magistrates' Courts
DERBYSHIRE BRANCH 5th Floor, St. Peter's House, Gower Street, Derby DE1 1SB Tel: 01332 614000 Fax: 01332 614050 DX 725818 DERBY 22		
DERBYSHIRE SOUTH CRIMINAL JUSTICE UNIT 5th Floor, St. Peter's House, Gower Street, Derby DE1 1SB Tel: 01332 614021 DX 725818 DERBY 22		Derby Ilkeston
DERBYSHIRE NORTH CRIMINAL JUSTICE UNIT Derbyshire Constabulary, 4th Floor, Chesterfield Divisional HQ, Beetwell Street, Chesterfield S40 1QP Tel: 01246 522568 Fax: 01246 275495		Chesterfield Buxton Glossop
TRIALS UNIT 5th Floor, St. Peter's House, Gower Street, Derby DE1 1SB Tel: 01332 614063 Fax: 01332 614085 DX 725818 DERBY 22	Derby Manchester Nottingham	

CPS AREAS

CPS DEVON AND CORNWALL

Chief Crown Prosecutor: Mr Roger Coe-Salazar

Area Business Manager: Julie Heron

Area Address: Hawkins House, Pynes Hill, Rydon Lane, Exeter, Devon EX2 5SS
Tel: 01392 288000   Fax: 01392 288008   DX 135606 EXETER 16

Branch Address	Courts Covered	
	Crown Courts	Magistrates' Courts
EXETER OFFICE Argal House, Peninsular Business Park, Rydon Lane, Exeter, Devon EX2 7NT Tel: 01392 356700 Fax: 01392 356703 DX 151400 EXETER 25	Barnstaple Exeter Plymouth	Barnstaple Exeter and Wonford (Exeter) Teignbridge (Newton Abbott) Torbay (Torquay) Totnes
Truro Office 2nd Floor, Lysnoweth, Infirmary Hill, Truro, Cornwall TR1 2XG Tel: 01872 243000 Fax: 01872 243032 DX 140883 TRURO 5	Truro	Bodmin Dunheved and Stratton (Launceston) East Penwith (Camborne) Isles of Scilly Penwith (Penzance) South East Cornwall (Liskeard) Truro and South Powder (Truro)
Plymouth Office 1st Floor, St. Andrews Court, 12 St. Andrews Street, Plymouth PL1 2AH Tel: 01752 602700 Fax: 01752 602740 DX 98473 PLYMOUTH 7	Plymouth	Plymouth

CPS AREAS

CPS DORSET

Chief Crown Prosecutor: Ms Kate Brown

Area Business Manager: Mr Jason Putman

Area Address: Ground Floor, Oxford House, Oxford Road, Bournemouth BH8 8HA
Tel: 01202 498700   Fax: 01202 498860   DX 7699 BOURNEMOUTH

	Courts Covered	
Branch Address	Crown Courts	Magistrates' Courts

DORSET AREA
Ground Floor,
Oxford House,
Oxford Road,
Bournemouth BH8 8HA
 	
Tel: 01202 498700
 	
Fax: 01202 498860
  (Area Secretariat)
  01202 498748
  (Crown Court Unit)
  01202 498701
  (Magistrates' Court Unit)
 	
DX 7699 BOURNEMOUTH
	Blandford
	Bournemouth
	Dorchester
	Poole
	Sherborne
	Winchester
		Bournemouth
		Bridport
		Gillingham
		Weymouth
		Wimborne

CPS DURHAM

Chief Crown Prosecutor: Ms Portia Ragnauth

Area Business Manager: Ms Lyn Burke

Area Address: Elvet House, Hallgarth Street, Durham DH1 3AT
Tel: 0191 383 5800   Fax: 0191 383 5801   DX 60227 DURHAM

	Courts Covered	
Branch Address	Crown Courts	Magistrates' Courts
NORTH DURHAM BRANCH Elvet House, Hallgarth Street, Durham DH1 3AT Tel: 0191 383 5800 Fax: 0191 383 5801 DX 60227 DURHAM	Durham Newcastle upon Tyne Teesside	Derwentside (Consett) Durham Easington (Peterlee)
SOUTH DURHAM SUB BRANCH Newton Aycliffe Police Station, Central Avenue, Newton Aycliffe, Co. Durham DL5 5RW Tel: 01325 742588	Durham Teesside	Darlington Sedgefield (Newton Aycliffe) Teesdale and Wear Valley (Bishop Auckland)

CPS AREAS

CPS DYFED-POWYS

Chief Crown Prosecutor: Mr Iwan Jenkins

Area Business Manager: Mr Jeff Thomas

Area Address: Heol Penlanffos, Tanerdy, Carmarthen, Dyfed SA31 2EZ
Tel: 01267 242100   Fax: 01267 242111   DX 51411 CARMARTHEN

| Branch Address | Courts Covered ||
	Crown Courts	Magistrates' Courts
DYFED POWYS BRANCH Heol Penlanffos, Tanerdy, Carmarthen, Dyfed SA31 2EZ Tel: 01267 242100 Fax: 01267 242111 DX 742440 CARMARTHEN 9	Carmarthen Haverfordwest Swansea	Carmarthen Ceredigion (Aberystwyth) Dinefwr (Ammanford, Llandovery) Llanelli Ystradgynlais
NEWTOWN SUB BRANCH Afon House, The Park, Newtown, Powys SY16 2PQ Tel: 01686 616700 Fax: 01686 616709 DX 29233 NEWTOWN (POWYS)	Chester Merthyr Tydfil Mold	De Brycheiniog (Brecon) Radnorshire and North Brecknock (Llandrindod Wells) Welshpool
HAVERFORDWEST SUB BRANCH PO Box 92, Police Station, Haverfordwest, Pembrokeshire SA61 9AG Tel: 01437 772700 Fax: 01437 765641 DX 98281 HAVERFORDWEST 1		North Pembrokeshire (Cardigan, Haverfordwest) South Pembrokeshire (Tenby)

CPS AREAS

CPS ESSEX

Chief Crown Prosecutor: Paula Abrahams

Area Business Manager: Ms Susan Stovell

Area Address: County House, 100 New London Road, Chelmsford, Essex CM2 0RG
Tel: 01245 455800   Fax: 01245 455964   DX 139160 CHELMSFORD 11

Branch Address	Courts Covered	
	Crown Courts	Magistrates' Courts
BASILDON CRIMINAL JUSTICE UNIT Police Station, Durham Road, Laindon, Basildon, Essex SS15 6PH Tel: 01268 410101 Fax: 01268 410118 DX 144040 BASILDON 11		Basildon Grays
SOUTH WEST ESSEX PROSECUTION TEAM County House, 100 New London Road, Chelmsford, Essex CM2 0RG Tel: 01245 455872 Fax: 01245 455964 DX 139160 CHELMSFORD 11	Basildon Chelmsford Southend	
SOUTH EAST ESSEX PROSECUTION TEAM County House, 100 New London Road, Chelmsford, Essex CM2 0RG Tel: 01245 455872 Fax: 01245 455964 DX 139160 CHELMSFORD 11	Basildon Chelmsford Southend	
NORTH EAST ESSEX PROSECUTION TEAM **Crown Court Team** County House, 100 New London Road, Chelmsford CM2 0RG Tel: 01245 455875 Fax: 01245 455929 DX 139160 CHELMSFORD 11	Chelmsford	

CPS AREAS

COLCHESTER CRIMINAL JUSTICE UNIT
Magistrates' Court Team
Police Station,
10 Southway,
Colchester,
Essex
CO3 3BU

Chelmsford
Colchester
Harwich
Witham

DX 722462 COLCHESTER 8

NORTH WEST ESSEX PROSECUTION TEAM
Crown Court Team
County House,
100 New London Road,
Chelmsford
CM2 0RG

Chelmsford

Tel: 01268 455901

Fax: 01268 455928

DX 139160 CHELMSFORD 11

HARLOW CRIMINAL JUSTICE UNIT
Magistrates' Court Team
Police Station,
The High,
Harlow,
Essex
CM20 1HG

Epping
Harlow

Tel: 01279 641212

Fax: 01279 418039

DX 142260 HARLOW 6

SOUTHEND CRIMINAL JUSTICE UNIT
Police Station,
Victoria Avenue,
Southend,
Essex SS2 6ES

Southend

Tel: 01702 431212

Fax: 01702 423162

DX 142000 SOUTHEND 6

CPS AREAS

CPS GLOUCESTERSHIRE

Chief Crown Prosecutor: Mr Adrian Foster

Area Business Manager: Mr Neil Spiller

Area Address: 2 Kimbrose Way, Gloucester, Gloucestershire GL1 2DB
Tel: 01452 872400   Fax: 01452 872406   DX 7544 GLOUCESTER

Branch Address	Courts Covered	
	Crown Courts	Magistrates' Courts
TRIALS UNIT 2 Kimbrose Way, Gloucester, Gloucestershire GL1 2DB Tel: 01452 872400 Fax: 01452 872430 DX 7544 GLOUCESTER	Bristol Gloucester	
CRIMINAL JUSTICE UNIT (B DIVISION) Gloucester Police Station, Bearland, Longsmith Street, Gloucester GL1 2JP Tel: 01452 335372 Fax: 01452 528981		Forest of Dean (Coleford) Gloucester
CRIMINAL JUSTICE UNIT (A & C DIVISIONS) 2 Kimbrose Way, Gloucester, Gloucestershire GL1 2DB Tel: 01452 872400 Fax: 01452 872453		Cirencester, Fairford and Tetbury (Cirencester) North Gloucestershire (Cheltenham) South Gloucestershire (Stroud)

CPS AREAS

CPS GREATER MANCHESTER

Chief Crown Prosecutor: Mr John Holt

Area Business Manager: Ms Jean Ashton

Area Address: P.O. Box 237, 8th Floor, Sunlight House, Quay Street, Manchester M60 3PS
Tel: 0161 827 4700   Fax: 0161 827 4932   DX 710288 MANCHESTER 3

	Courts Covered	
Branch Address	Crown Courts	Magistrates' Courts
CITY OF MANCHESTER BRANCH P.O. Box 29, 8th Floor, Sunlight House, Quay Street, Manchester M60 3PT Tel: 0161-827 4700 Fax: 0161-827 4935 DX 710309 MANCHESTER 3	Manchester	Manchester
BOLTON AND WIGAN BRANCH 1st Floor Bolton Division, Police Headquarters, Scholey Street, Bolton BL2 1HD Tel: 01204 543300 Fax: 01204 543340	Bolton Liverpool Manchester	Bolton
WIGAN SUB-BRANCH 1st Floor, Wigan Police Station, Robin Park Road, Wigan WN5 0UP Tel: 0161-856 6699 Fax: 01942 230549	Liverpool Bolton Manchester	Leigh Wigan
OLDHAM AND TAMESIDE (HYDE) BRANCH 1-2 Cromwell Court, Oldham OL1 1ET Tel: 0161-856 5800 Fax: 0161-343 8616	Manchester	Oldham
TAMESIDE (HYDE) SUB-BRANCH Wharfingers House, Manchester Road, Hyde SK14 2BX Tel: 0161-882 5200 Fax: 0161-882 5202	Manchester	Tameside (Ashton-under-Lyne)

CPS AREAS

ROCHDALE AND BURY BRANCH
4th Floor,
Newgate House,
Newgate,
Rochdale OL16 1XA

Tel: 01706 515600

Fax: 01706 515620

Bolton
Manchester

Rochdale, Middleton and Heywood
(Middleton, Rochdale)

BURY SUB-BRANCH
4th Floor,
Newgate House,
Newgate,
Rochdale OL16 1XA

Tel: 01706 515600

Fax: 01706 515620

Bolton
Manchester

Bury

STOCKPORT AND SALFORD BRANCH
P.O. Box 28,
4th Floor,
Sunlight House,
Quay Street,
Manchester
M60 3PP

Tel: 0161-827 4945

Fax: 0161-827 4938/9

DX 718173 MANCHESTER 3

Manchester

City of Salford
Stockport

SALE SUB-BRANCH
P.O. Box 28,
4th Floor,
Sunlight House,
Quay Street,
Manchester
M60 3PP

Tel: 0161-827 4944

Fax: 0161-827 4939

DX 718173 MANCHESTER 3

Manchester

Stockport
Trafford (Sale)

CPS AREAS

CPS GWENT

Chief Crown Prosecutor: Christopher Woolley (Acting)

Area Business Manager: Mr Clive Parish (Acting)

Area Address: 6th Floor, Chartist Tower, Upper Dock Street, Newport, Gwent NP20 1DW
Tel: 01633 261100   Fax: 01633 261106   DX 33232 NEWPORT (GWENT)

Branch Address	Courts Covered	
	Crown Courts	Magistrates' Courts
NORTH WEST GWENT CRIMINAL JUSTICE UNIT 6th Floor, Chartist Tower, Upper Dock Street, Newport, Gwent NP9 1DW Tel: 01633 261115 Fax: 01633 261105 DX 33232 NEWPORT (GWENT)		Abertillery Blackwood Caerphilly
SOUTH WEST GWENT CRIMINAL JUSTICE UNIT Tel: 01633 844741		Abergavenny and Chepstow Cwmbran Newport
GWENT CROWN COURT UNIT Tel: 01633 261137	Cardiff Newport	

CPS HAMPSHIRE AND ISLE OF WIGHT

Chief Crown Prosecutor: Mr Nick Hawkins

Area Business Manager: Mrs Denise Bailey

Area Address: 3rd Floor, Black Horse House, 8-10 Leigh Road, Eastleigh, Hampshire SO50 9FH
Tel: 02380 673800   Fax: 02380 673854   DX 148581 EASTLEIGH 4

Branch Address	Courts Covered	
	Crown Courts	Magistrates' Courts
SOUTHAMPTON AND NEW FOREST CRIMINAL JUSTICE UNIT Portswood Police Station, 15-17 St Deny's Road, Portswood, Southampton, Hampshire Tel: 02380 674 484 Fax: 02380 674 025 DX 144940 SOUTHAMPTON 36	Southampton Winchester	Eastleigh New Forest (Lyndhurst) Southampton

CPS AREAS

SOUTHAMPTON TRIALS UNIT
Western Range,
83 London Road,
Southampton,
Hampshire SO15 2AA

Tel: 023 8071 4000

Fax: 023 8071 4053

DX 34149 EASTLEIGH

BASINGSTOKE AND ALDERSHOT CRIMINAL JUSTICE UNIT
Basingstoke Police Station,
1st Floor,
London Road,
Basingstoke,
Hampshire RG21 4AD

Tel: 01256 405390 (B'stoke)
        406499 (A'shot)

Fax: 01256 405038 (B'stoke)
        405368 (A'shot)

DX 145160 BASINGSTOKE 18

Aldershot Police Station,
Wellington Avenue,
Aldershot,
Hampshire GU11 1NZ

DX 145111 ALDERSHOT 4

Winchester

North East Hampshire (Aldershot, Alton)
North West Hampshire (Andover, Basingstoke)

ISLE OF WIGHT CRIMINAL JUSTICE AND TRIALS UNIT
6 Langley Court,
Pyle Street,
Newport,
Isle of Wight PO30 1LA

Tel: 01983 538666

Fax: 01983 538603/4

DX 98463 NEWPORT 2

Isle of Wight (Newport)

Isle of Wight (Newport)

PORTSMOUTH CRIMINAL JUSTICE UNIT
Central Police Station,
Winston Churchill Avenue,
Portsmouth,
Hampshire PO1 2DG

Tel: 023 9289 1584

Fax: 01329 233145

DX 98493 PORTSMOUTH 5

South Hampshire (Fareham)
South East Hampshire (Portsmouth)

CPS AREAS

PORTSMOUTH TRIALS UNIT Portsmouth
Crown House,
Winston Churchill Avenue,
Portsmouth,
Hampshire PO1 2PJ

Tel: 023 9285 6210

Fax: 023 9285 6211/12

DX 98493 PORTSMOUTH 5

CPS HERTFORDSHIRE

Chief Crown Prosecutor: Mr Charles Ingham

Acting Area Business Manager: Ms Linda Fox

   Area Address: Queen's House, 58 Victoria Street, St. Albans, Hertfordshire AL1 3HZ
          Tel: 01727 798700   Fax: 01727 798795   DX 120650 ST. ALBANS 7

	Courts Covered	
Branch Address	Crown Courts	Magistrates' Courts
HERTFORDSHIRE CROWN COURT UNIT Queen's House, 58 Victoria Street, St. Albans, Hertfordshire AL1 3HZ Tel: 01727 799707 Fax: 01727 798794 DX 120650 ST. ALBANS 7	Luton St. Albans	
CRIMINAL JUSTICE UNIT CENTRAL Queen's House, 58 Victoria Street, St. Albans, Hertfordshire AL1 3HZ Tel: 01727 798788 Fax: 01727 798805 DX 120650 ST. ALBANS 7		St. Albans
CRIMINAL JUSTICE UNIT WEST County Police Station, Shady Lane, Watford WD1 1DD Tel: 01923 472414 Fax: 01923 472419 DX 51538 WATFORD 2		Watford Dacorum

CPS AREAS

CRIMINAL JUSTICE UNIT EAST
County Police Station,
192 Ware Road,
Hertford SG13 7HD

Tel: 01992 533489

Fax: 01992 533439

DX 57907 HERTFORD

Hertford
Stevenage
Cheshunt

CPS HUMBERSIDE

Chief Crown Prosecutor: Mr Nigel Cowgill

Area Business Manager: Miss Caron Skidmore

Area Address: Citadel House, 58 High Street, Hull HU1 1QD
Tel: 01482 621000   Fax: 01482 621002   DX 11922 HULL

Courts Covered

Branch Address	Crown Courts	Magistrates' Courts
HULL AND EAST RIDING CRIMINAL JUSTICE UNIT Citadel House, 58 High Street, Hull HU1 1QD Tel: 01482 621018 Fax: 01482 621002 DX 11922 HULL		Beverley and the Wolds (Beverley) Bridlington Hull and Holderness (Kingston Upon Hull) Goole
HULL AND EAST RIDING TRIALS UNIT Citadel House, 58 High Street, Hull HU1 1QD Tel: 01482 621023 Fax: 01482 621002 DX 11922 HULL	Hull	
GRIMSBY COMBINED CRIMINAL JUSTICE UNIT/TRIALS UNIT Heritage House, Fisherman's Wharf, Grimsby, South Humberside DN31 1SY Tel: 01472 243900 Fax: 01472 243901 DX 13515 GRIMSBY 1	Grimsby	Grimsby and Cleethorpes (Grimsby) North Lincolnshire (Scunthorpe)

CPS AREAS

SCUNTHORPE CRIMINAL JUSTICE BOARD
Scunthorpe Police Station,
Corporation Road,
Scunthorpe DN15 6QB

Tel: 01724 274227

CPS KENT

Chief Crown Prosecutor: Miss Elizabeth Howe

Assistant Chief Crown Prosecutor (West Kent): Vacant

Assistant Chief Crown Prosecutor (East Kent): Kate Rushbrook

Area Business Manager: Mr Ken Mitchell

Area Address: Priory Gate, 29 Union Street, Maidstone, Kent ME14 1PT
Tel: 01622 356300   Fax: 01622 356399   DX 4830 MAIDSTONE

Branch Address	Courts Covered	
	Crown Courts	Magistrates' Courts
EAST KENT TRIALS UNIT Riding Gate House, 37 Old Dover Road, Canterbury, Kent CT1 3JG Tel: 01227 866000 Fax: 01227 866001 DX 5349 CANTERBURY 1	Canterbury Maidstone	
WEST KENT TRIAL UNIT Priory Gate, 29 Union Street, Maidstone, Kent ME14 1PT Tel: 01622 356300 Fax: 01622 356359 DX 4830 MAIDSTONE	Maidstone	
CANTERBURY CRIMINAL JUSTICE UNIT Police Station, Old Dover Road, Canterbury, Kent CT1 3JQ Tel: 01227 866000 Fax: 01227 866030 DX 5350 CANTERBURY		Canterbury Thanet

CPS AREAS

FOLKESTONE CRIMINAL JUSTICE UNIT
Police Station,
Bouverie House,
Bouverie Road West,
Folkestone,
Kent CT20 2RW

Tel: 01227 866000

Fax: 01227 866079

DX 4935 FOLKESTONE

Dover
Ashford
Folkestone

DEDICATED ORGANISED CRIME UNIT
Riding Gate Centre,
37 Old Dover Road,
Canterbury,
Kent CT1 3JG

Tel: 01227 866000

DX 5349 CANTERBURY 1

SPECIAL CASEWORK UNIT
Priory Gate,
29 Union Street,
Maidstone,
Kent ME14 1PT

Tel: 01622 356300

DX 4830 MAIDSTONE

MEDWAY CRIMINAL JUSTICE UNIT
Police Station,
The Brook,
Chatham,
Kent ME4 4LD

Tel: 01622 356300

Fax: 01622 356350

DX 13199 ROCHESTER 2

Medway

MAIDSTONE CRIMINAL JUSTICE UNIT
Police Station,
Palace Avenue,
Maidstone,
Kent ME4 4LD

Tel: 01622 356300

Fax: 01622 356358

DX 51966 MAIDSTONE 2

Maidstone
Sittingbourne

GRAVESEND CRIMINAL JUSTICE UNIT
Police Station,
Windmill Street,
Gravesend,
Kent DA12 1DB

Tel: 01622 356300

Fax: 01622 356330

Dartford
Sevenoaks

CPS AREAS

CPS LANCASHIRE

Chief Crown Prosecutor: Robert Marshall

Area Business Manager: Angela Walsh

Area Address: 2nd Floor Podium, Unicentre, Lords Walk, Preston PR1 1DH
Tel: 01772 208100   Fax: 01772 278277   DX 723740 PRESTON 20

	Courts Covered	
Branch Address	Crown Courts	Magistrates' Courts
PRESTON BRANCH 3rd Floor, Unicentre, Lords Walk, Preston PR1 1DH Tel: 01772 208100 Fax: 01772 208144 DX 723741 PRESTON 20	Preston	Chorley Ormskirk Preston South Ribble (Leyland)
BURNLEY DISTRICT Burnley Wharf, Manchester Road, Burnley BB11 1JG Tel: 01282 478500 Fax: 01282 478505 DX 23866 BURNLEY	Burnley Preston	Blackburn, Darwen and Ribble Valley (Blackburn) Burnley and Pendle (Burnley, Reedley) Hyndburn (Accrington) Rossendale
FYDE DISTRICT – BLACKPOOL **COMBINED UNIT** 2nd Floor, Prudential House, Topping Street, Blackpool, Lancashire FY1 3AB Tel: 01253 743800 Fax: 01253 743843 DX 17040 BLACKPOOL 1	Lancaster Preston	Blackpool and Fylde Lancaster Wyre (Fleetwood)
LANCASTER SUB – DISTRICT **COMBINED UNIT** Rosemary House, North Road, Lancaster LA0 1LU Tel: 01524 386700 Fax: 01524 386707		

CPS AREAS

CPS LEICESTERSHIRE

Chief Crown Prosecutor: Ms Janet Meek

Area Business Manager: Ms Jane Robinson

Area Address: Beaumont Leys Police Station, 2 Beaumont Way, Beaumont Leys, Leicester LE4 1DS
Tel: 0116 222 2222   Fax: 0116 262 4713   DX 10899 LEICESTER 1

	Courts Covered	
Branch Address	Crown Courts	Magistrates' Courts
LEICESTER COUNTY CRIMINAL JUSTICE UNIT Princes Court, 34 York Road, Leicester LE1 5TU Tel: 0116 204 6700 Fax: 0116 204 6733 DX 10899 LEICESTER 1	Leicester	Ashby-de-la-Zouch (Coalville) Leicester Loughborough Market Bosworth (Hinckley) Market Harborough and Lutterworth (Market Harborough) Melton, Belvoir and Rutland (Oakham, Melton Mowbray)
TRIALS UNIT Princes Court, 34 York Road, Leicester LE1 5TU Tel: 0116 204 6700 Fax: 0116 204 6733		
LEICESTER/MARKET HARBOROUGH CRIMINAL JUSTICE UNIT 34 York Road, Leicester LE1 5TU Tel: 0116 204 6704 Fax: 0116 204 6711		

CPS AREAS

CPS LINCOLNSHIRE

Chief Crown Prosecutor: Mr Colin Chapman

Area Business Manager: Ms Sue Lloyd

Area Address: Crosstrend House, 10A Newport, Lincoln LN1 3DF
Tel: 01522 585900   Fax: 01522 585958   DX 15562 LINCOLN 4

Courts Covered

Branch Address	Crown Courts	Magistrates' Courts
LINCOLNSHIRE CRIMINAL JUSTICE UNIT Crosstrend House, 10A Newport, Lincoln LN1 3DF Tel: 01522 585900 Fax: 01522 585958 DX 15562 LINCOLN 4		Gainsborough Lincoln Louth Skegness
LINCOLNSHIRE TRIALS UNIT Crosstrend House, 10A Newport, Lincoln LN1 3DF Tel: 01522 585900 Fax: 01522 585959 DX 13362 LINCOLN 4	Lincoln	
GRANTHAM CRIMINAL JUSTICE UNIT The Old Barracks, Sandon Road, Grantham, Lincolnshire NG31 9AS Tel: 01476 512100 Fax: 01476 512101 DX 712150 GRANTHAM		Bourne Grantham Sleaford Spalding Stamford Boston

CPS AREAS

CPS LONDON

Chief Crown Prosecutor: Ms. Dru Sharpling

Directors: René Barclay (Director, Serious Casework), Simon Clements (Director, London South Sector), Wendy Williams (Director, London North and East Sector), Nazir Afzal (Director, London West Sector)

Operations Director: Ms Lesley Burton

CPS Fraud Prosecution Service Director: David Kirk

Legal Practice and Quality Assurance Director: Raj Joshi

Area Address: CPS London HQ, 50 Ludgate Hill, London EC4M 7EX
Tel: 020 7796 8000 Fax: 020 7796 8651 DX 300850 LUDGATE EC4

Branch Address	Courts Covered	
	Crown Courts	Magistrates' Courts
NORTH LONDON PROSECUTION SERVICE Edmonton Police Station, PO Box 44918, Edmonton N9 0XR Switchboard: 020 8884 6400 General Fax: 020 8884 6473/6477 DX 36266 EDMONTON 2	Wood Green	Enfield Haringey
EAST LONDON PROSECUTION SERVICE 3rd Floor, Solar House, 1–9 Romford Road, Stratford, London E15 4LJ Switchboard: 020 8221 3500 Fax: 020 8221 3501 DX 5449 STRATFORD (LONDON)	Snaresbrook	Barking Stratford Havering Redbridge Waltham Forest
CAMDEN AND ISLINGTON TEAM 8th Floor, Holborn Police Station, PO Box 36822, 10 Lamb's Conduit Street, London WC2 3NR Switchboard: 020 7061 3900 General Fax: 020 7061 3905 DX 475 LONDON CHANCERY LANE		Highbury Corner

CPS AREAS

EAST CENTRAL LONDON PROSECUTION SERVICE
3rd Floor,
50 Ludgate Hill,
London EC4M 7EX

Switchboard: 020 7796 8000

General Fax: 020 7796 8268

DX 300850 LUDGATE

Southwark

Thames

BEXLEY BOROUGH UNIT
Bexleyheath Police Station,
2 Arnsberg Way,
Bexleyheath,
Kent DA7 4QS

Tel: 020 8248 9259

Fax: 020 8248 9217

CITY OF LONDON TEAM
Bishopsgate Police Station,
182 Bishopsgate,
London EC4M 4WZ

Switchboard: 020 7696 4700

General Fax: 020 7696 4714

DX 561 LONDON CITY

City of London

SOUTH EAST LONDON PROSECUTION SERVICE
The Cooperage,
8 Gainsford Street,
London SE1 2NE

Switchboard: 020 7378 4100

General Fax: 020 7378 4248

DX 80712 BERMONDSEY

Blackfriars
Woolwich

Bexley
Greenwich
Woolwich

SOUTH LONDON PROSECUTION SERVICE
8th and 9th Floor,
Prospect West,
81 Station Road,
Croydon CR0 2RD

Switchboard: 020 8662 2800

General Fax: 020 8662 2828/2843

Croydon

Bromley
Croydon

SOUTH CENTRAL LONDON PROSECUTION SERVICE
The Cooperage,
8 Gainsford Street,
London SE1 2NE

Switchboard: 020 7378 4100

General Fax: 020 7378 4248

DX 80712 BERMONDSEY

Inner London

Camberwell Green
Tower Bridge

CPS AREAS

INNER LONDON YOUTH PROSECUTION SERVICE
The Cooperage,
8 Gainsford Street,
London SE1 2NE

Switchboard: 020 7378 4100

General Fax: 020 7378 4248

DX 80712 BERMONDSEY

Inner London

Thames (Youth Court)
West London (Youth Court)
Balham (Youth Court)
Camberwell (Youth Court)

CENTRAL LONDON PROSECUTION SERVICE
Hillgate House,
26 Old Bailey,
London EC4M 7HW

Switchboard: 020 7029 4600

General Fax: 020 7029 4602/3/4

DX 89 CHANCERY LANE

Middlesex
Guildhall

Bow Street
Horseferry Road
Marylebone

LONDON TRAFFIC PROSECUTION SERVICE
6th Foor,
Marlowe House,
109 Station Road,
Sidcup DA15 7ES

Switchboard: 020 8217 9919

General Fax: 020 8217 9924

DX 31706 SIDCUP

Greenwich (Regional Gateway Court)
Highbury (Regional Gateway Court)
Marylebone (Regional Gateway Court)
Redbridge (Regional Gateway Court)
Wimbledon (Regional Gateway Court)

WEST CENTRAL LONDON PROSECUTION SERVICE (WEST SECTOR)
4th Floor,
50 Ludgate Hill,
London EC4M 7EX

Switchboard: 020 7796 8000

General Fax: 020 7796 8268

DX 300850 LUDGATE

Blackfriars

West London

NORTH WEST LONDON PROSECUTION SERVICE
2nd Floor,
Kings House,
Kymberley Road,
Harrow HA1 1YH

Switchboard: 020 8901 5700

General Fax: 020 8901 5919

DX 4204 HARROW 1

Harrow

CPS AREAS

BARNET TEAM
Colindale Police Station,
Grahame Park Way,
London NW9 5TW

Switchboard: 020 8200 2650

General Fax: 020 8200 2670

Barnet
Hendon
Brent

WEST LONDON PROSECUTION SERVICE
2nd Floor,
Kings House,
Kymberley Road,
Harrow HA1 1YH

Switchboard: 020 8901 5700

General Fax: 020 8901 5919

DX 4204 HARROW 1

Isleworth

Uxbridge
Feltham
Ealing

SOUTH WEST LONDON PROSECUTION SERVICE
17th and 18th Floor,
Tolworth Tower,
Surbiton,
Surrey KT6 7DS

Switchboard: 020 8335 1500

General Fax: 020 8335 1600

DX 57549 TOLWORTH

Kingston

Kingston
Richmond
South Western
Sutton
Wimbledon

CENTRAL CRIMINAL COURT PROSECUTION SERVICE (SERIOUS CASEWORK SECTOR)
4th Floor,
50 Ludgate Hill,
London EC4M 7EX

Switchboard: 020 7796 8000

General Fax: 020 7796 8670

DX 300850 LUDGATE EC4

Central Criminal

LONDON SPECIAL CASEWORK PROSECUTION SERVICE
4th Floor,
50 Ludgate Hill,
London EC4M 7EX

Switchboard: 020 7796 8000

General Fax: 020 7796 8670

DX 300850 LUDGATE EC4

CROWN COURT CENTRAL CRIMINAL COURT
Tel: 020 7248 3277

CPS AREAS

FRAUD PROSECUTION UNIT
3rd Floor,
South Wing,
Rose Court,
2 Southwark Bridge Road,
London SE1 9HS

Tel: 020 7796 8000

Fax: 020 7796 8647

DX CPS ROSE COURT 300851 LUDGATE

POLICE COMPLAINTS SECTION
Tel: 020 7710 6023/3385

**SPECIAL CASEWORK UNIT
(SERIOUS CASEWORK SECTION)**
Tel: 020 7796 8267

CPS MERSEYSIDE

Chief Crown Prosecutor: Mr Paul Whittaker

Area Business Manager: Ms Anne Reilly (Acting)

Area Address: 7th Floor (South) Royal Liver Building, Pier Head, Liverpool L3 1HN
Tel: 0151 239 6400   Fax: 0151 239 6420   DX 700596 LIVERPOOL 4

Branch Address	Courts Covered	
	Crown Courts	Magistrates' Courts
MERSEYSIDE CROWN COURT BRANCH 7th Floor (South), Royal Liver Building, Pier Head, Liverpool L3 1HN Tel: 0151 239 6400 Fax: 0151 239 6420 DX 700596 LIVERPOOL 4	Liverpool	
NORTH LIVERPOOL COMMUNITY JUSTICE CENTRE Boundary Lane, Liverpool L5 2QD Tel: 0151 298 3600 Fax: 0151 298 3601		

CPS AREAS

MERSEY NORTH DISTRICT
Heron House,
Hougoumont Avenue,
Crosby,
Liverpool
L22 0LL

Tel: 0151 966 6900

Fax: 0151 966 6911

DX 13636 WATERLOO

Knowsley (Huyton)
North Sefton District (Southport)
St. Helens
South Sefton District (Bootle)

MERSEYSIDE WITNESS CARE UNIT
5th Floor,
Tithebann House,
Tithebann Street,
Liverpool L2 2NZ

Tel: 0151 777 1700

Fax: 0151 777 1742/1743

WIRRAL DISTRICT   Liverpool   Wirral (Birkenhead, Wallasey)
4th Floor,
St. Mark's House,
2 Conway Street,
Birkenhead CH41 6QD

Tel: 0151 650 8400

Fax: 0151 650 8448

DX 17860 BIRKENHEAD

LIVERPOOL DISTRICT   Liverpool   Liverpool
7th Floor,
Royal Liver Building,
Pier Head,
Liverpool L3 1HN

Tel: 0151 239 6400

Fax: 0151 239 6420

DX 13636 WATERLOO

CPS AREAS

CPS NORFOLK

Chief Crown Prosecutor: Mr Peter Tidey

Area Business Manager: Ms Catherine Scholefield

Area Address: Carmelite House, St James' Court, White Friars, Norwich, Norfolk NR3 1SL
Tel: 01603 693000   Fax: 01603 693001   DX 5299 NORWICH

Branch Address	Courts Covered	
	Crown Courts	Magistrates' Courts
EASTERN COMBINED UNIT Carmelite House, St James' Court, White Friars, Norwich, Norfolk NR3 1SL Tel: 01603 693000 Fax: 01603 693001 DX 5299 NORWICH	King's Lynn Norwich	Cromer Great Yarmouth
WESTERN COMBINED UNIT Carmelite House, St James' Court, White Friars, Norwich, Norfolk NR3 1SL Tel: 01603 693000 Fax: 01603 693001 DX 5299 NORWICH		King's Lynn Swaffham Thetford
CENTRAL COMBINED UNIT Carmelite House, St James' Court, White Friars, Norwich, Norfolk NR3 1SL Tel: 01603 693000 Fax: 01603 693001 DX 5299 NORWICH		Norwich

CPS AREAS

CPS NORTHAMPTONSHIRE

Chief Crown Prosecutor: Grace Ononiwu

Area Business Manager: Miss Fiona Campbell

Area Address: Beaumont House, Cliftonville, Northampton NN1 5BE
Tel: 01604 823600   Fax: 01604 823651   DX 18512 NORTHAMPTON

	Courts Covered	
Branch Address	Crown Courts	Magistrates' Courts
NORTHAMPTONSHIRE BRANCH Beaumont House, Cliftonville, Northampton NN1 5BE Tel: 01604 823600 Fax: 01604 823651 DX 18512 NORTHAMPTON **SOUTH COMBINED UNIT** Tel: 01604 823613 **NORTH COMBINED UNIT** Tel: 01604 773890 **WITNESS CARE UNIT** Tel: 01604 235811	Northampton	Corby Daventry Kettering Northampton Towcester Wellingborough

CPS NORTHUMBRIA

Chief Crown Prosecutor: Miss Nicola Reasbeck

Area Business Manager: Mrs Adele Clarke

Area Address: St Ann's Quay, 122 Quayside, Newcastle-upon-Tyne NE1 3BD
Tel: 0191 260 4200   Fax: 0191 260 4241   DX 61006 NEWCASTLE-UPON-TYNE

	Courts Covered	
Branch Address	Crown Courts	Magistrates' Courts
TRIAL UNIT St Ann's Quay, 122 Quayside, Newcastle-upon-Tyne NE1 3BD Tel: 0191 260 4200 Fax: 0191 260 4242/4243/4330 DX 61006 NEWCASTLE-UPON-TYNE	Newcastle-upon-Tyne	

CPS AREAS

CRIMINAL JUSTICE UNIT NORTH
TYNESIDE   North Shields
North Shields Police Station,
Upper Pearson Street,
North Shields,
Tyne and Wear NE30 1AB

Tel: 01661 863880

Fax: 0191 257 8461

CRIMINAL JUSTICE UNIT SOUTH
SOUTH TYNE TEAM   South Tyneside
Milbank Police Station,
South Shields,
Tyne & Wear
NE33 1RR

Tel: 0191 563 5909

Fax: 0191 497 5207

CRIMINAL JUSTICE UNIT NORTH   South East Northumberland
Bedlington Police Station,   (Bedlington)
Bedlington,
Northumberland
NE22 7LA

Tel: 01661 863749

Fax: 01670 823252

NEWCASTLE   Gosforth (Youth Court)
St Ann's Quay,   Newcastle-upon-Tyne (Gosforth,
122 Quayside,   Newcastle-upon-Tyne)
Newcastle-upon-Tyne   Tynedale (Hexham)
NE1 3BD   Alnwick
                                                  Berwick-upon-Tweed
Tel: 0191 260 4200

Fax: 0191 260 4329

DX 61006 NEWCASTLE-UPON-TYNE

CRIMINAL JUSTICE UNIT SOUTH
GATESHEAD TEAM   Gateshead
Gateshead Police Station,   Blaydon
High West Street,
Gateshead,
Tyne & Wear NE8 1DT

Tel: 0191 221 9608

Fax: 0191 477 8962

CRIMINAL JUSTICE UNIT SOUTH
SUNDERLAND TEAM   Sunderland
Sunderland Police Station,   Houghton-le-Spring
Gillbridge Avenue,
Sunderland
SR1 3AP

Tel: 0191 563 6871

Fax: 0191 563 8439

CPS AREAS

CPS NORTH WALES

Chief Crown Prosecutor: Mr Ed Beltrami

Area Business Manager: Wray Ferguson

Area Address: Bromfield House, Ellice Way, Wrexham LL13 7YW
Tel: 01978 346000   Fax: 01978 346001   DX 723100 WREXHAM 5

Branch Address	Courts Covered	
	Crown Courts	Magistrates' Courts
CENTRAL UNIT Llys Eirias, Heritage Gate, Abergele Road, Colwyn Bay, Conwy LL29 8BW Tel: 01492 806807 Fax: 01492 806859 DX 718060 COLWYN BAY 3	Caernarfon Chester Dolgellau Mold Knutsford	Llandudno Denbigh Prestatyn
EASTERN UNIT Bromfield House, Ellice Way, Wrexham LL13 7YW Tel: 01978 346000 Fax: 01978 346060 DX 723100 WREXHAM 5	Caernarfon Chester Dolgellau Mold	Flintshire (Flint, Mold) Wrexham Maelor
WESTERN UNIT Llys Erias, Heritage Gate, Abergele Road, Colwyn Bay, Conwy LL29 8BW Bromfield House, Ellice Way, Wrexham LL13 7YW Tel: 01492 806800 Fax: 01492 806801	Chester Knutsford Mold Caernarfon Dolgellau	Pwllheli Dolgellau Holyhead Llangefni

CPS AREAS

CPS NORTH YORKSHIRE

Chief Crown Prosecutor: Mr Robert Turnbull

Area Business Manager: Mr Andrew Illingworth

Area Address: Athena House, Kettlestring Lane, Clifton Moor, York YO30 4XF
Tel: 01904 731700 Fax: 01904 731764 DX 729960 YORK 29

Branch Address	Courts Covered	
	Crown Courts	Magistrates' Courts
HARROGATE COMBINED UNIT 3rd Floor, The Exchange, Station Parade, Harrogate HG1 1TS Tel: 01423 539950 Fax: 01423 539990 DX 722500 HARROGATE 8		Harrogate Northallerton Selby Skipton York
YORK COMBINED CRIMINAL JUSTICE UNIT/TRIALS UNIT Athena House, Kettlestring Lane, Clifton Moor, York YO30 4XF Tel: 01904 731700 Fax: 01904 731724 DX 729960 YORK 29	Teeside York Leeds	Harrogate Northallerton Richmond Selby Skipton York
SCARBOROUGH COMBINED CRIMINAL JUSTICE UNIT/TRIALS UNIT Scarborough Police Station, Northway, Scarborough, North Yorkshire YO12 7AD Tel: 01723 509870 Fax: 01723 368622 DX 68892 SCARBOROUGH 4	York	Scarborough (Pickering, Scarborough, Whitby)

CPS AREAS

CPS NOTTINGHAMSHIRE

Chief Crown Prosecutor: Ms Kate Carty

Area Business Manager: Mrs Gail Pessol

Area Address: 2 King Edward Court, King Edward Street, Nottingham NG1 1EL
Tel: 0115 852 3300   Fax: 0115 852 3380   DX 729100 NOTTINGHAM 48

Branch Address	*Courts Covered*	
	Crown Courts	Magistrates' Courts
CRIMINAL JUSTICE UNIT 2 King Edward Court, King Edward Street, Nottingham NG1 1EL Tel: 0115 852 3411 Fax: 0115 852 3567 DX 729101 NOTTINGHAM 48	Nottingham	Nottingham
COUNTY TEAM AND COUNTY CRIMINAL JUSTICE UNIT Holmes House, Ratcliffe Gate, Mansfield, Nottinghamshire NG18 2JW Tel: 01623 483970 Fax: 01623 483070	East Retford (Retford) Mansfield Newark and Southwell (Newark) Worksop	Nottingham City
TRIALS UNIT 2 King Edward Court, King Edward Street, Nottingham NG1 1EL Tel: 0115 852 3340 Fax: 0115 852 3453 DX 729102 NOTTINGHAM 48		

CPS AREAS

CPS SOUTH WALES

Chief Crown Prosecutor: Mr Christopher Woolley

Area Business Manager: Ms Helen Phillips (Temporary)

Area Address: 20th Floor, Capital House, Greyfriars Road, Cardiff CF10 3PL
Tel: 029 2080 3900   Fax: 029 2080 3930   DX 33056 CARDIFF 1

Branch Address	Courts Covered	
	Crown Courts	Magistrates' Courts
CENTRAL/RUMNEY UNIT 19th/21st Floor, Capital House, Greyfriars Road, Cardiff CF10 3PL Tel: 029 2080 3800 Fax: 029 2080 3840 DX 33056 CARDIFF 1	Cardiff	
MERTHYR OFFICE Cambria House, Merthyr Tydfil Industrial Park, Pentrebach, Merthyr Tydfil, Mid Glamorgan CF48 4XA Tel: 01443 694800 Fax: 01443 694804 DX 53411 MERTHYR		Cynon Valley (Aberdare) Merthyr Tydfil Pontypridd
SWANSEA PRINCESS HOUSE UNIT Princess House, Princess Way, Swansea SA1 3LY Tel: 01792 452900 Fax: 01792 452930 DX 92056 SWANSEA 3	Swansea	
CARDIFF/VALE DIVISION 21st Floor, Capital House, Greyfriars Road, Cardiff CF10 3PL Tel: 029 2080 3800 Fax: 029 2080 3840 DX 33050 CARDIFF 1	Cardiff	

CPS AREAS

COMPLEX CASEWORK UNIT
SWANSEA OFFICE
2nd Floor,
Central Police Station,
Grove Place,
Swansea SA1 5AE

Tel: 01792 555587

Fax: 01792 452910

DX 92056 SWANSEA 3

SWANSEA GROVE POLICE UNIT
Swansea Central Police Station,
Grove Place,
Swansea SA1 5DB

Tel: 01792 555600

Fax: 01792 476558

DX 39580 SWANSEA

BARRY/FAIRWATER UNIT
2nd Floor,
Barry Police Station,
Gladstone Road,
Barry CF63 1TD

Tel: 01446 731670

Fax: 01446 749599

DX 38555 BARRY

Vale of Glamorgan (Barry)

MERTHYR SOUTH UNIT
1st Floor,
Bridgend Police Station,
Brackla Street,
Bridgend CF31 1BZ

Tel: 01656 679590

Fax: 01656 667482

DX 38043 BRIDGEND

Newcastle
Ogmore (Bridgend)

MERTHYR NORTH UNIT
Merthyr Police Station,
2nd Floor,
Swan Street,
Merthyr Tydfil CF47 8ES

Tel: 01685 724310

Fax: 01685 389914

CPS AREAS

CPS SOUTH YORKSHIRE

Chief Crown Prosecutor: Mrs Judith Walker

Area Business Manager: Mr Christopher Day

Area Address: Greenfield House, 32 Scotland Street, Sheffield S3 7DQ
Tel: 0114 229 8600   Fax: 0114 229 8607   DX 711830 SHEFFIELD 18

Branch Address	Courts Covered	
	Crown Courts	Magistrates' Courts
SOUTH YORKSHIRE CRIMINAL JUSTICE UNIT Greenfield House, 32 Scotland Street, Sheffield S3 7DQ Tel: 0114 229 8600 Fax: 0114 229 8618 DX 711830 SHEFFIELD 18		Barnsley Doncaster Rotherham Sheffield
SOUTH YORKSHIRE TRIALS UNIT Greenfield House, 32 Scotland Street, Sheffield S3 7DQ Tel: 0114 229 8600 Fax: 0114 229 8729 DX 711830 SHEFFIELD 18	Doncaster Sheffield	

CPS STAFFORDSHIRE

Chief Crown Prosecutor: Mr Harry Ireland

Area Business Manager: Mr Brian Laybourne

Area Address: Building 3, Etruria Valley Office Village, Etruria, Stoke-on-Trent ST1 5RU
Tel: 01782 664560   Fax: 01782 664555   DX 701706 HANLEY 2

Branch Address	Courts Covered	
	Crown Courts	Magistrates' Courts
NORTH STAFFORDSHIRE BRANCH Building 3, Etruria Valley Office Village, Etruria, Stoke-on-Trent ST1 5RU Tel: 01782 664500 Fax: 01782 664501 DX 701706 HANLEY 2	Stoke-on-Trent	Newcastle-under-Lyme Fenton Stoke-on-Trent (Fenton)

CPS AREAS

SOUTH STAFFORDSHIRE BRANCH
2 Parker Court,
Staffordshire Technology Park,
Stafford ST18 0EZ

Tel: 01785 272200

Fax: 01785 272290

DX 709193 STFFORD 4

Stafford

Burton-upon-Trent
Cannock
Stafford
Tamworth

CPS SUFFOLK

Chief Crown Prosecutor: Mr Ken Caley

Area Business Manager: Ms Caroline Gilbert

Area Address: St. Vincent House, 9th Floor, 1 Cutler Street, Ipswich, Suffolk IP1 1UL
Tel: 01473 282100   Fax: 01473 282101   DX 3266 IPSWICH

Branch Address	Courts Covered	
	Crown Courts	Magistrates' Courts
TRIALS UNIT St Vincent House, 9th Floor, 1 Cutler Street, Ipswich, Suffolk IP1 1UL Tel: 01473 282100 Fax: 01473 282103 DX 3266 IPSWICH	Bury St. Edmunds Ipswich	
IPSWICH CRIMINAL JUSTICE UNIT Ipswich Police Station, Civic Drive, Ipswich, Suffolk IP1 2AW Tel: 01473 383152 Fax: 01473 288413 DX 3265 IPSWICH		Ipswich
LOWESTOFT CRIMINAL JUSTICE UNIT Police Station, Old Nelson Street, Lowestoft, Suffolk NR32 1PE Tel: 01986 835193 Fax: 01502 530814 DX 41223 LOWESTOFT		Lowestoft

CPS AREAS

BURY ST EDMUNDS CRIMINAL JUSTICE UNIT
Shire Hall,
Bury St Edmunds,
Suffolk IP33 2AP

Tel: 01284 774164

Fax: 01284 764252

DX 57235 BURY ST. EDMUNDS

Bury St. Edmunds
Mildenhall
Sudbury

CPS SURREY

Chief Crown Prosecutor: Ms Tracy Easton

Area Business Manager: Mr Ben Widdicombe

Area Address: Saxon House, 3 Onslow Street, Guildford, Surrey GU1 4YA
Tel: 01483 468200   Fax: 01483 468202   DX 122041 GUILDFORD 10

Branch Address	Courts Covered	
	Crown Courts	Magistrates' Courts
SURREY COMBINED UNIT 3 Onslow Street, Guildford, Surrey GU1 4YA Tel: 01483 468200 Fax: 01483 468203 DX 122041 GUILDFORD 10	Central Criminal Court Guildford	South East Surrey (Dorking, Reigate) North East Surrey (Staines) North West Surrey (Woking) South West Surrey (Guildford)

CPS SUSSEX

Chief Crown Prosecutor: Sarah Jane Gallagher

Area Business Manager: Mr Iain Everett

Area Address: City Gates, 185 Dyke Road, Brighton, East Sussex BN3 1TL
Tel: 01273 765600   Fax: 01273 765605   DX 149840 HOVE 6

Branch Address	Courts Covered	
	Crown Courts	Magistrates' Courts
BRIGHTON CRIMINAL JUSTICE UNIT Brighton Police Station, John Street, Brighton, East Sussex BN2 2LA Tel: 01273 665987 Fax: 01273 818743 DX 94303 BRIGHTON	Lewes and Hove	Brighton/Lewes

CPS AREAS

CRAWLEY CRIMINAL JUSTICE UNIT
Police Station,
Northgate Avenue,
Crawley,
West Sussex
RH10 8BF

Tel: 01293 583957

Fax: 01293 583920

DX 146680 CRAWLEY 14

Chichester
Lewes

Crawley
Horsham
Mid Sussex (Haywards Heath)

EAST SUSSEX BRANCH – BRIGHTON TRIAL UNIT
City Gates,
185 Dyke Road,
Brighton,
East Sussex
BN3 1TL

Tel: 01273 765600

Fax: 01273 765641

DX 149840 HOVE 6

Lewes and Hove
Brighton

EASTBOURNE CRIMINAL JUSTICE UNIT
1st Floor,
27 St. Leonards Road,
Eastbourne,
East Sussex BN21 3NN

Tel: 01323 636500

Fax: 01323 636501
       636502

DX 141690 EASTBOURNE 5

Lewes

Eastbourne
Hastings
Lewes

WEST SUSSEX BRANCH
Sussex Suite,
2-4 City Gates,
Southgate,
Chichester,
West Sussex PO19 2DJ

Tel: 01243 523900

Fax: 01243 523950

DX 97464 CHICHESTER 2

Chichester

Chichester
Worthing

CPS AREAS

CPS THAMES VALLEY

Chief Crown Prosecutor: Baljit Ubhey

Area Business Manager: Mrs Karen Sawitzki

Area Address: Eaton Court, 112 Oxford Road, Reading RG1 7LL
Tel: 01235 551975   Fax: 01235 551971   DX 40104 READING

	Courts Covered	
Branch Address	Crown Courts	Magistrates' Courts
BERKSHIRE BRANCH Eaton Court, 112 Oxford Road, Reading, Berkshire RG1 7LL Tel: 01189 513600 Fax: 01189 513666 DX 40104 READING	Reading	East Berkshire (Slough, Bracknell, Maidenhead) Reading West Berkshire (Newbury)
BUCKINGHAMSHIRE BRANCH 4-7 Prebendal Court, Oxford Road, Aylesbury, Buckinghamshire HP19 3EY Tel: 01296 414800 Fax: 01296 414801 DX 4117 AYLESBURY	Aylesbury Luton Northampton Reading	Central Buckinghamshire (Aylesbury) Milton Keynes Wycombe and Beaconsfield (High Wycombe)
OXFORDSHIRE BRANCH Gemini One, Oxford Business Park South, Garsington Road, Oxford OX4 2LL Tel: 01865 233400 Fax: 01865 233401 DX 45417 COWLEY	Oxford	Didcot Banbury Bicester Witney

WITNESS CARE UNIT

Berkshire
Eaton Court,
112 Oxford Road,
Berkshire RG1 7LL

Tel: 01189 513660

Fax: 01189 513666

Buckinghamshire
Aylesbury Police Station,
Wendover Road,
Aylesbury,
Buckinghamshire HP21 7LA

Tel: 01296 396310

Fax: 01865 835531

CPS AREAS

CPS WARWICKSHIRE

Chief Crown Prosecutor: Mr Mark Lynn

Area Business Manager: Mr Ian Edmondson

Area Address: Rossmore House, 10 Newbold Terrace, Leamington Spa, Warwickshire CV32 4EA
Tel: 01926 455000   Fax: 01926 455002/3   DX 11881 LEAMINGTON SPA

Branch Address	Courts Covered	
	Crown Courts	Magistrates' Courts
WARWICKSHIRE BRANCH Rossmore House, 10 Newbold Terrace, Leamington Spa, Warwickshire CV32 4EA Tel: 01926 455027 (Magistrates' Court Unit) 01926 455020 (Crown Court Unit) Fax: 01926 455002 (Magistrates' Court Unit) 01926 455003 (Crown Court Unit) DX 11881 LEAMINGTON SPA	Warwick	Atherstone Mid-Warwickshire Nuneaton Rugby South Warwickshire

CPS WEST MERCIA

Chief Crown Prosecutor: Mr Chris Enzor

Area Business Manager: Mr Laurence Sutton

Area Address: Artillery House, Heritage Way, Droitwich, Worcester WR9 8YB
Tel: 01905 825000   Fax: 01905 825100   DX 179491 DROITWICH 4

Branch Address	Courts Covered	
	Crown Courts	Magistrates' Courts
SHROPSHIRE COMBINED UNIT Lakeside House, Holsworth Park, Bicton Heath, Shrewsbury SY3 5HJ Tel: 01743 263700 Fax: 01743 263749 DX 703280 SHREWSBURY 4	Shrewsbury	Bridgnorth Drayton (Market Drayton) Ludlow Oswestry Shrewsbury Telford Whitchurch

CPS AREAS

HEREFORD AND WORCESTER COMBINED UNIT
Artillery House,
Heritage Way,
Droitwich,
Worcester WR9 8YB

Tel: 01905 825010

Fax: 01905 825102

DX 179490 DROITWICH 4

Hereford
Worcester

Hereford
Kidderminster
Redditch
Worcester

REDDITCH & KIDDERMINSTER COMBINED UNIT
Artillery House,
Heritage Way,
Droitwich
WR9 8YB

Tel: 01905 825010

Fax: 01905 825102

DX 179490 DROITWICH 4

CPS WEST MIDLANDS

Chief Crown Prosecutor: Mr David Blundell

Area Business Manager: Mr Mike Grist

Area Address: Colmore Gate, 2 Colmore Row, Birmingham B3 2QA
Tel: 0121 262 1300   Fax: 0121 262 1307   DX 719540 BIRMINGHAM 45

Branch Address	Courts Covered	
	Crown Courts	Magistrates' Courts
BIRMINGHAM CENTRAL
Colmore Gate,
2 Colmore Row,
Birmingham
B3 2QA
Tel: 0121 262 1300
Fax: 0121 262 1500
DX 719540 BIRMINGHAM 45	Birmingham	
BIRMINGHAM OUTER
Colmore Gate,
2 Colmore Row,
Birmingham B3 2QA
Tel: 0121 262 1300
Fax: 0121 262 1500
DX 719540 BIRMINGHAM 45		Birmingham
Sutton Coldfield

CPS AREAS

WALSALL CRIMINAL JUSTICE UNIT
Police Station,
Green Lane,
Walsall WS2 8HL

Tel: 01922 423750

Fax: 01902 638139

DX 12108 WALSALL

BLACK COUNTRY CRIMINAL JUSTICE UNITS
St. George's House,
Lever Street,
Wolverhampton WV2 1EZ

Tel: 01902 872800

Fax: 01902 872870

DX 702349 WOLVERHAMPTON 5

Aldridge and Brownhills
Dudley
Stourbridge and Halesowen
Walsall
Warley (Oldbury)
West Bromwich
Wolverhampton

COVENTRY AND SOLIHULL CRIMINAL JUSTICE UNITS
Friars House,
Manor House Drive,
Coventry CV1 2TE

Tel: 024 7650 8400

Fax: 024 7650 8440/4

DX 11247 COVENTRY 1

Coventry

EASTERN TRIAL UNIT & CRIMINAL JUSTICE UNITS GROUP TRIAL UNIT
Friars House,
Manor House Drive,
Coventry CV1 2TE

Tel: 024 7650 8400

Fax: 024 7650 8440/4

DX 11247 COVENTRY 1

Coventry
Warwick

WEST BROMWICH CRIMINAL JUSTICE UNIT
West Bromwich Police Station,
New Street,
West Bromwich B70 7PS

Tel: 01902 872800

DX 14618 WEST BROMWICH

BRIERLEY HILL CRIMINAL JUSTICE UNIT
Police Station,
Bank Street,
Brierley Hill DY5 3DH

Tel: 01902 872910

Fax: 01902 872925

DX 22755 BRIERLEY HILL

CPS AREAS

HALESOWEN CRIMINAL JUSTICE UNIT
Police Station,
Bank Street,
Laurel Lane,
Halesowen B63 3JA

Tel: 01902 872905

Fax: 01902 872914

DX 14524

SOLIHULL   Solihull
Solihull Police Station,
Homer Road,
Solihull B91 3QL

Tel: 024 7650 8400

Fax: 024 7650 8440
               8444

DX 713381 SOLIHULL

WOLVERHAMPTON TRIALS UNIT AND   Wolverhampton
BLACK COUNTRY CRIMINAL JUSTICE
GROUP
St. George's House,
Lever Street,
Wolverhampton
WV2 1EZ

Tel: 01902 872800

Fax: 01902 872810

DX 702439 WOLVERHAMPTON 5

CPS WEST YORKSHIRE

Chief Crown Prosecutor: Mr Neil Franklin

Area Business Manager: Ms Karen Wright

Area Address: Oxford House, Oxford Row, Leeds LS1 3BE
Tel: 0113 290 2700   Fax: 0113 290 2707   DX 26435 LEEDS PARK SQUARE

	Courts Covered	
Branch Address	Crown Courts	Magistrates' Courts
WESTERN AREA Windsor House, 10 Manchester Road, Bradford, W. Yorks. BD5 0QH Tel: 01274 301100 Fax: 01274 301101/2/3 DX 11766 BRADFORD 1	Bradford	

CPS AREAS

EASTERN AREA
Oxford House,
Oxford Row,
Leeds LS1 3BE

Tel: 01132 902700

Fax: 01132 902707

DX 26435 LEEDS PARK SQUARE

CITY AND HOLBECK DIVISION
3rd Floor,
Oxford House,
Oxford Row,
Leeds LS1 3BE

Tel: 0113 290 2966

WAKEFIELD DIVISION
Wakefield Police Station,
Wood Street,
Wakefield WF1 2HJ

Tel: 01924 932254

Leeds

Castleford
Leeds
Pontefract
Wakefield
Wetherby

CHAPELTOWN DIVISION
Oxford House,
Oxford Row,
Leeds LS1 3BE

Tel: 0113 290 0966

DX 26435 LEEDS PARK SQUARE

BRADFORD NORTH AND KEIGHLEY DIVISION
Lawcroft House Police Station,
Lilycroft Road,
Manningham,
Bradford BD9 5AF

Tel: 01274 301182

BRADFORD SOUTH DIVISION
Bradford Central Police Station,
The Tyrls,
Bradford BD1 1TR

Tel: 01274 301182

Fax: 01274 376740

CALDERDALE DIVISION
Richmond Close Police Station,
Halifax,
W. Yorks. HX1 5TW

Tel: 01422 350210

Fax: 01422 363664

CPS AREAS

HUDDERSFIELD DIVISION
1st Floor,
Castlegate Police Station,
Huddersfield,
W. Yorks. HD1 2NJ

Tel: 01484 558000

Fax: 01484 558001

Bradford
Bingley
Halifax
Dewsbury
Huddersfield

PONTERFRACT DIVISION
Pontefract Police Station,
Sessions House Yard,
Pontefract
WF8 1BN

Tel: 01977 601005

WESTWOOD AND PUDSEY DIVISION
Oxford House,
Oxford Row,
Leeds LS1 3BE

Tel: 0113 290 2966

DEWSBURY DIVISION
Police Station,
Aldams Road,
Dewsbury
WF12 8AR

Tel: 01924 431184

KILLINGBECK DIVISION
Oxford House,
Oxford Row,
Leeds LS1 3BE

Tel: 0113 290 2740

CPS WILTSHIRE

Chief Crown Prosecutor: Mrs Karen Harrold

Area Business Manager: Mrs Kim O'Neill

Area Address: Fox Talbot House, Bellinger Close, Malmesbury Road, Chippenham, Wiltshire SN15 1BN Tel: 01249 766100 Fax: 01249 766101 DX 98644 CHIPPENHAM 2

Branch Address	Courts Covered	
	Crown Courts	Magistrates' Courts
WILTSHIRE BRANCH Fox Talbot House, Bellinger Close, Malmesbury Road, Chippenham, Wiltshire SN15 1BN Tel: 01249 766100 Fax: 01249 766101 DX 98644 CHIPPENHAM 2	Bristol Salisbury Swindon Winchester	Kennett (Devizes) North Wiltshire (Chippenham) Salisbury Swindon West Wiltshire (Trowbridge)

APPENDIX II

CROWN OFFICE AND PROCURATOR FISCAL SERVICE (SCOTLAND)

	Page
Crown Office	3
Procurator Fiscal Service Areas	
Area: Grampian	5
Area: Highland and Islands	6
Area: Tayside	8
Area: Central	9
Area: Fife	10
Area: Argyll and Bute	11
Area: Ayrshire	12
Area: Glasgow	13
Area: Lothian and Borders	14
Area: Lanarkshire	15
Area: Dumfries and Galloway	16

APPENDIX II

CROWN OFFICE and PROCURATOR FISCAL SERVICE (SCOTLAND)

The aim of the Procurator Fiscal Service is to serve the public interest by providing a system of independent public prosecution and to allay public anxiety by investigating all sudden, unexplained and suspicious deaths.

Crown Office is the departmental headquarters of the Procurator Fiscal Service. The Scottish Law Officers – the Lord Advocate and the Solicitor General – are based in Crown Office as is the Crown Agent, who is the Head of the Service.

Scotland is now divided into 11 Sheriffdoms. With the exception of Glasgow, each is made up of a number of Sheriff Court Districts. The senior member of the Procurator Fiscal Service in each Sheriffdom is the Area Procurator Fiscal, who is also the Procurator Fiscal for the district in which his own office is situated. Each other Sheriff Court District has its own (District) Procurator Fiscal.

CROWN OFFICE

25 Chambers Street, Edinburgh EH1 1LA
  Tel: 0131-226 2626
  Fax: 0131-226 6564 and 0131-226 6910

Crown Agent/Chief Executive: N. McFadyen
Deputy Crown Agent: J. Brisbane
Deputy Chief Executive: W. McQueen

AREA:- GRAMPIAN

Area Procurator Fiscal: Miss. M. A. McLaughlin

AREA OFFICE: Atholl House, 84-88 Guild Street, Aberdeen AB11 6QA
Tel: 01224 585111   Fax: 01224 585550

District Office	*Sheriff Court*	*District Court(s)*
ABERDEEN Atholl House, 84-88 Guild Street AB11 6QA Tel: 01224 585111 Fax: 01224 585550	Aberdeen	City of Aberdeen D.C. D.C. of Aberdeenshire at Inverarie
BANFF Sheriff Court AB4 1AU Tel: 01261 812131/815318 Fax: 01261 818282	Banff	D.C. of Aberdeenshire at Banff
ELGIN Sheriff Court IV30 1BU Tel: 01343 547133/543594 Fax: 01343 544146	Elgin	Moray D.C. at Elgin
PETERHEAD 70 St. Peter Street AB4 6QD Tel: 01779 476628 Fax: 01779 490284	Peterhead	D.C. of Aberdeenshire at Peterhead
STONEHAVEN Sheriff Court AB3 2JD Tel: 01569 762048 Fax: 01569 765614	Stonehaven	D.C. of Aberdeenshire at Stonehaven

AREA:- HIGHLAND AND ISLANDS

Area Procurator Fiscal: A. S. D. Laing

AREA OFFICE: 2 Baron Taylor's Street, Inverness IV1 1QL
Tel: 01463 224858   Fax: 01463 711187

District Office	Sheriff Court	District Court(s)
DINGWALL County Buildings, Ferry Road IV15 9QK Tel: 01349 862122/864058 Fax: 01349 862715	Dingwall	Highland D.C. at Dingwall
DORNOCH Sheriff Court IV25 3FD Tel: 01862 810248/810930 Fax: 01862 811196	Dornoch	Highland D.C. at Dornoch
FORT WILLIAM Sheriff Court PH33 6BR Tel: 01397 703874 Fax: 01397 701476	Fort William	Highland D.C. at Fort William
INVERNESS 2 Baron Taylor's St. IV1 1QL Tel: 01463 224858 Fax: 01463 711187	Inverness	Highland D.C. at Inverness Highland D.C. at Kingussie Highland D.C. at Nairn
KIRKWALL Sheriff Court KW15 1PD Tel: 01856 873273 Fax: 01856 870505	Kirkwall	
LERWICK Sheriff Court ZE1 0HD Tel: 01595 692808 Fax: 01595 695152	Lerwick	
LOCHMADDY Sheriff Court PA82 5AE Tel: 01876 500243 Fax: 01876 500432	Lochmaddy	Western Isles D.C. at Stornoway

HIGHLAND AND ISLANDS

District Office	*Sheriff Court*	*District Court(s)*
PORTREE Sheriff Court IV51 9EH Tel: 01478 612510 Fax: 01478 613499	Portree	Highland D.C. at Portree
STORNOWAY County Buildings PA87 2JF Tel: 01851 703439 Fax: 01851 704618	Stornoway	Western Isles D.C. at Stornoway
TAIN 1 Tower Street IV19 1DY Tel: 01862 892472 Fax: 01862 892883	Tain	Highland D.C. at Tain
WICK Sheriff Court KW1 4AJ Tel: 01955 602197 Fax: 01955 606507	Wick	Highland D.C. at Wick

AREA:– TAYSIDE

Area Procurator Fiscal: D. J. Howdle

AREA OFFICE: Caledonian House, Greenmarket, Dundee DD1 1QX
Tel: 01382 227535   Fax: 01382 202719

District Office	Sheriff Court	District Court(s)
ARBROATH Aitken House, 15 Hill Street DD1 1BR Tel: 01241 876555 Fax: 01241 430052	Arbroath	Angus D.C. at Arbroath
DUNDEE Caledonian House, Greenmarket DD1 1QX Tel: 01382 227535 Fax: 01382 202719	Dundee	City of Dundee D.C.
FORFAR Sheriff Court DD8 3LA Tel: 01307 463296 Fax: 01307 463589	Forfar	Angus D.C. at Brechin Angus D.C. at Forfar
PERTH 52 Tay Street PH1 5TR Tel: 01738 637272 Fax: 01738 622673	Perth	Perth & Kinross D.C. at Perth

AREA:– CENTRAL

Area Procurator Fiscal: Mrs G. M. Watt

AREA OFFICE: Sheriff Court, Stirling FK8 1NH
Tel: 01786 462021   Fax: 01786 446823

District Office	*Sheriff Court*	*District Court(s)*
ALLOA Sheriff Court FK10 1HR Tel: 01259 214561/721736 Fax: 01259 219577	Alloa	Clackmannanshire D.C. at Alloa
FALKIRK Mansionhouse Road, Camelon FK1 4LW Tel: 01324 638396 Fax: 01324 628841	Falkirk	Falkirk D.C.
STIRLING Sheriff Court FK8 1NH Tel: 01786 462021 Fax: 01786 446823	Stirling	Stirling D.C.

AREA:- FIFE

Area Procurator Fiscal: C. Ritchie

AREA OFFICE: Wing D, Carlyle House, Carlyle Road, Kirkcaldy KY1 1DB
Tel: 01592 268661   Fax: 01592 261120

District Office	Sheriff Court	District Court(s)
CUPAR Sheriff Court KY15 4LS Tel: 01334 654991 Fax: 01334 656041	Cupar	Fife D.C. at Cupar
DUMFERMLINE Sheriff Court, Carnegie Drive KY12 7HW Tel: 01383 723688 Fax: 01383 624828	Dunfermline	Fife D.C. at Dunfermline
KIRKCALDY 3 East Fergus Place KY1 1XG Tel: 01592 268661 Fax: 01592 261120	Kirkcaldy	Fife D.C. at Kirkcaldy

AREA:- ARGYLL AND BUTE

Area Procurator Fiscal: J. Watt

AREA OFFICE: 106 Renfrew Road, Paisley PA3 4DX
Tel: 0141 887 5225   Fax: 0141 887 6172

District Office	*Sheriff Court*	*District Court(s)*
CAMPBELTOWN Sheriff Court PA28 6AN Tel: 01586 553383 Fax: 01586 554967	Campbeltown	Argyll & Bute D.C. at Bowmore Argyll & Bute D.C. at Campbeltown
DUMBARTON St. Marys Way G82 1NL Tel: 01389 730972 Fax: 01389 731182	Dumbarton	West Dumbartonshire D.C. at Dumbarton West Dumbartonshire D.C. at Clydebank Argyll & Bute D.C. at Helensburgh East Dumbartonshire D.C. at Milngavie
DUNOON Sheriff Court PS23 8BQ Tel: 01369 702292 Fax: 01369 702191	Dunoon	Argyll & Bute D.C. at Dunoon Argyll & Bute D.C. at Lochgilphead
GREENOCK Sheriff Court, Nelson Street PA15 1TR Tel: 01475 728316 Fax: 01475 724488	Greenock	Inverclyde D.C. at Greenock
OBAN Sheriff Court PA34 4AL Tel: 01631 564088 Fax: 01631 570352	Oban	Argyll & Bute D.C. at Oban
PAISLEY 1 Love Street PA3 2DA Tel: 0141-887 5225 Fax: 0141-887 6172	Paisley	Renfrewshire D.C. at Paisley East Renfrewshire D.C. at Giffnock
ROTHESAY Sheriff Court PA20 9AB Tel: 01700 502105 Fax: 01700 504112	Rothesay	Argyll & Bute D.C. at Rothesay

AREA:– AYRSHIRE

Area Procurator Fiscal: J. Dunn

AREA OFFICE: St. Marnock Street, Kilmarnock KA1 1DZ
Tel: 01563 536211   Fax: 01563 571786

District Office	Sheriff Court	District Court(s)
AYR 29 Miller Road KA7 2AX Tel: 01292 267481/260748 Fax: 01292 611415	Ayr	South Ayrshire D.C. at Ayr South Ayrshire D.C. at Girvan East Ayrshire D.C. at Cumnock
KILMARNOCK St. Marnock Street KA1 1DZ Tel: 01563 536211 Fax: 01563 571786	Kilmarnock	East Ayrshire D.C. at Kilmarnock North Ayrshire D.C. at Irvine

AREA:– GLASGOW

Area Procurator Fiscal: Mrs. C. P. Dyer

AREA OFFICE: 10 Ballater Street, Glasgow G5 9PS
Tel: 0141 429 5566   Fax: 0141 418 5177

District Office	*Sheriff Court*	*District Court(s)*
GLASGOW 10 Ballater Street G5 9PS Tel: 0141-429 5566 Fax: 0141-418 5177	Glasgow & Strathkelvin	City of Glasgow D.C. East Dumbartonshire D.C. at Kirkintilloch South Lanarkshire D.C. at East Kilbride South Lanarkshire D.C. at Rutherglen

AREA:- LOTHIAN AND BORDERS

Area Procurator Fiscal: F. Mulholland

AREA OFFICE: 29 Chambers Street, Edinburgh EH1 1LG
Tel: 0131 226 4962   Fax: 0131 247 2636

District Office	Sheriff Court	District Court(s)
EDINBURGH 29 Chambers Street, Edinburgh EH1 1LG Tel: 0131-226 4962 Fax: 0131-247 2636	Edinburgh	City of Edinburgh D.C. Midlothian D.C. at Penicuik
LINLITHGOW Stuart House, 181/201 High Street EH49 7EN Tel: 01506 844556 Fax: 01506 670102	Linlithgow	West Lothian D.C. at Livingston
SELKIRK Sheriff Court TD7 4LE Tel: 01750 20345 Fax: 01750 21113	Selkirk	Scottish Borders D.C. at Selkirk
PEEBLES Sheriff Court EH45 8SW Tel: 01721 720345 Fax: 01721 729583	Peebles	Scottish Borders D.C. at Peebles
JEDBURGH Sheriff Court TD8 6AR Tel: 01835 862345 Fax: 01835 864514	Jedburgh	Scottish Borders D.C. at Jedburgh
DUNS Sheriff Court TD11 3DU Tel: 01361 882345 Fax: 01361 882060	Duns	Scottish Borders D.C. at Duns

AREA:- LANKARKSHIRE

Area Procurator Fiscal: Mrs. J. E. Cameron

AREA OFFICE: Cameronian House, 3/5 Almada Street, Hamilton ML3 0LG
Tel: 01698 284000   Fax: 01698 422929

District Office	*Sheriff Court*	*District Court(s)*
AIRDRIE Sheriff Court, Graham Street ML6 6EE Tel: 01236 747027 Fax: 01236 747677	Airdrie	North Lanarkshire D.C. at Coatbridge North Lanarkshire D.C. at Cumbernauld
HAMILTON Cameronian House, 3/5 Almada Street ML3 0HG Tel: 01698 284000 Fax: 01698 422929	Hamilton	South Lanarkshire D.C. at Hamilton North Lanarkshire D.C. at Motherwell
LANARK Sheriff Court ML11 7NE Tel: 01555 661669 Fax: 01555 663716	Lanark	South Lanarkshire D.C. at Lanark

AREA:- DUMFRIES AND GALLOWAY

Area Procurator Fiscal: T. S. Dysart

AREA OFFICE: Sheriff Court, Buccleuch Street, Dumfries DG1 2AN
Tel: 01387 263034   Fax: 01387 259356

District Office	Sheriff Court	District Court(s)
DUMFRIES Sheriff Court, Buccleuch Street DG1 2AN Tel: 01387 263034 Fax: 01387 259356	Dumfries	Dumfries and Galloway D.C. at Annan Dumfries and Galloway D.C. at Dumfries Dumfries and Galloway D.C. at Lockerbie Dumfries and Galloway D.C. at Sanguhar
STRANRAER Sheriff Court DG9 7AA Tel: 01776 704321 Fax: 01776 889465	Stranraer	Dumfries and Galloway D.C. at Stranraer
KIRKCUDBRIGHT Sheriff Court DG6 4JW Tel: 01557 331403 Fax: 01557 331764	Kirkcudbright	Dumfreis and Galloway D.C. at Kirkcudbright

APPENDIX III

PENAL ESTABLISHMENTS

ENGLAND AND WALES

	Page
Headquarters Establishments	3
High Security Estate	6
Local Prisons and Remand Centres	6
Training Prisons	8
Adult Male Open Prisons	11
Foreign National Prison	11
Therapeutic Community	12
Male Semi-Open with Resettlement Regime	12
Female Open with Resettlement Regime	12
Female Semi-Open with Resettlement Regime	12
Young Offender Institutions	12
Short Sentence Institutions	14
Juvenile Institutions	14
Immigration Removal Centres	15
Special Hospitals	15

NORTHERN IRELAND

Headquarters Establishments	16
Prisons	16
Young Offenders Centre	16

SCOTLAND

Headquarters	17
Prison Service College	17
Prisons	17
Young Offender Institutions	18
State Hospital	18

APPENDIX III

Postal Addresses and Telephone Numbers of

PENAL ESTABLISHMENTS

ENGLAND AND WALES

HEADQUARTERS

HM Prison Service Headquarters, Cleland House, Page Street, London SW1P 4LN   Tel: 020 7217 6000   Fax: 020 7217 6403
Website: www.hmprisonservice.gov.uk

Director General: Phil Wheatley. Tel: 020 7217 6777
Deputy Director General: Michael Spurr. Tel: 020 7217 6393
Director of Finance: Ann Beasley. Tel: 020 7217 6822
Director of High Security Prisons: Steve Wagstaffe. Tel: 020 7217 6397
Director of Personnel: Robin Wilkinson (Acting). Tel: 020 7217 6584
Director of Operations: Michael Spurr. Tel: 020 7217 6393
Director of Prison Health: Richard Bradshaw. Tel: 020 7972 4767

AREA OFFICES

EASTERN

Area Manager: Drayton Old Lodge, 146 Drayton High Road, Drayton, Norwich NR8 6AN Tel: 01603 264100 Fax: 01603 264111

- HM Prison Bedford
- HM Prison Blundeston
- HM Prison Bullwood Hall
- HM Prison/YOI Chelmsford
- HM Prison Edmunds Hill
- HM Prison Highpoint
- HM Prison/YOI Hollesley Bay Colony
- HM Prison Littlehey
- HM Prison The Mount
- HM Prison/YOI Norwich
- HM Prison/YOI Warren Hill
- HM Prison Wayland

EAST MIDLANDS

Area Manager: Empriss House, Unit C, Harcourt Way, Meridian Business Park, Leicester LE19 1WP Tel: 0116 281 4000 Fax: 0116 281 4060

- HM Prison Ashwell
- HM Prison/RC Foston Hall
- HM Prison Gartree
- HMYOI Glen Parva
- HM Prison Leicester
- HM Prison Lincoln
- HM Prison Morton Hall
- HM Prison North Sea Camp
- HM Prison Nottingham
- HM Prison Onley
- HM Prison Ranby
- HM Prison Stocken
- HM Prison Sudbury
- HM Prison Wellingborough
- HM Prison Whatton

LONDON

Area Manager: Room 726, Cleland House, Page Street, London SW1P 4LN Tel: 020 7217 6180 Fax: 020 7217 2893

- HM Prison Brixton
- HMYOI/RC Feltham
- HM Prison Holloway
- HM Prison Latchmere House
- HM Prison Pentonville
- HM Prison Wandsworth
- HM Prison Wormwood Scrubs

AREA OFFICES

NORTH EAST

Area Manager: 2 Artemis Court, St Johns Road, Meadowfield, Durham DH7 8XQ
Tel: 0191 378 6000 Fax: 0191 378 6001

HM Prison Acklington
HMYOI Castington
HMYOI Deerbolt
HM Prison Durham

HM Prison Holme House
HM Prison Kirklevington
HM Prison Low Newton

NORTH WEST

Area Manager: Stirling House, Ackhurst Business Park, Foxhole Road, Chorley PR7 1NY Tel: 01257 248600 Fax: 01257 248604

HM Prison Buckley Hall
HM Prison Garth
HM Prison Haverigg
HM Prison/YOI Hindley
HM Prison Kennet
HM Prison Kirkham
HM Prison Lancaster Castle

HMYOI Lancaster Farms
HM Prison Liverpool
HM Prison Preston
HM Prison Risley
HM Prison/YOI Styal
HMYOI Thorn Cross
HM Prison Wymott

SOUTH CENTRAL

Area Manager: 2nd Floor, White Rose Court, Oriental Road, Woking, Surrey GU22 7PJ
Tel: 01483 716607

HM Prison Albany
HM Prison/YOI Aylesbury
HM Prison Bullingdon
HM Prison Camp Hill
HM Prison Coldingley
HM Prison Downview
HM Prison Grendon/Springhill
HMIRC Haslar

HM Prison High Down
HM Prison Huntercombe
HM Prison Kingston
HM Prison Parkhurst
HM Prison/YOI Reading
HM Prison Send
HM Prison Winchester

KENT AND SUSSEX

Area Manager: 80 Sir Evelyn Road, Rochester, Kent ME1 3NF Tel: 01634 673000
Fax: 01634 673048

HM Prison Blantyre House
HM Prison Canterbury
HM Prison/YOI Cookham Wood
HMIRC Dover
HM Prison/YOI East Sutton Park
HM Prison/YOI Elmley

HM Prison Ford
HM Prison/YOI Lewes
HM Prison Maidstone
HMYOI Rochester
HM Prison Standford Hill
HM Prison Swaleside

SOUTH WEST

Area Manager: 1 Tortworth Road, Leyhill, Wotton under Edge, Gloucestershire GL12 8BQ Tel: 01454 264053 Fax: 01454 264065

HM Prison Bristol
HM Prison Channings Wood
HM Prison Dartmoor
HM Prison Dorchester
HM Prison Erlestoke
HM Prison Exeter

HM Prison Gloucester
HM Prison/YOI Guys Marsh
HM Prison Leyhill
HMYOI Portland
HM Prison Shepton Mallett
HM Prison The Verne

AREA OFFICES

WALES

Area Manager: 102 Maryport Street, Usk, Gwent NP15 1AH Tel: 01291 674850 Fax: 01291 674865

HM Prison Cardiff
HM Prison/YOI Parc
HM Prison Swansea

HM Prison Usk
HM Prison Prescoed

WEST MIDLANDS

Area Manager: P.O. Box 458, HM Prison Shrewsbury, The Dana, Shrewsbury, Shropshire SY1 2WB Tel: 01743 284543 Fax: 01743 280051

HM Prison Birmingham
HM Prison Blakenhurst
HMYOI Brinsford
HM Prison Brockhill
HM Prison/YOI Drake Hall
HM Prison Featherstone

HM Prison Hewell Grange
HM Prison Shrewsbury
HM Prison Stafford
HMYOI Stoke Heath
HMYOI Swinfen Hall
HMYOI Werrington

YORKSHIRE AND HUMBERSIDE

Area Manager: 2 Marston House, Audby Lane, Wetherby, West Yorkshire LS22 7FD Tel: 01937 544500 Fax: 01937 544501

HM Prison Askham Grange
HM Prison Everthorpe
HM Prison Hull
HM Prison Leeds
HM Prison Lindholme
HM Prison Moorland Closed

HM Prison Moorland Open
HM Prison New Hall
HMRC Northallerton
HM Prison Wealstun
HMYOI Wetherby

DIRECTORATE OF HIGH SECURITY

Director: Room 512/513, Cleland House, Page Street, London SW1P 4LN Tel: 020 7217 2888 Fax: 020 7217 6664

HM Prison Belmarsh
HM Prison Frankland
HM Prison Full Sutton
HM Prison Long Lartin

HM Prison Manchester
HM Prison Wakefield
HM Prison Whitemoor
HM Prison Woodhill

COMMISSIONER'S SUPPORT BUREAU

Area Manager: Elizabeth House, Unit 2, Forder Way, Cygnet Park, Hampton, Peterborough PE7 8GX Tel: 01733 440400 Fax: 01733 425230

HM Prison Altcourse
HM Prison Ashfield
HM Prison Bronzefield
HMYOI Doncaster
HM Prison Dovegate
HMYOI Forest Bank

HM Prison Lowdham Grange
HMYOI Parc
HM Prison Peterborough
HM Prison Rye Hill
HM Prison The Wolds

HIGH SECURITY ESTATE

FRANKLAND The Governor, H.M. Prison Frankland, Brasside, Durham DH1 5YD
Tel: 0191 332 3000   Fax: 0191 332 3001

FULL SUTTON The Governor, H.M. Prison Full Sutton, York YO41 1PS
Tel: 01759 475100   Fax: 01759 371206

LONG LARTIN The Governor, H.M. Prison Long Lartin, South Littleton, Evesham, Worcestershire WR11 8TZ
Tel: 01386 835100   Fax: 01386 835101

MANCHESTER The Governor, H.M. Prison, Southall Street, Manchester M60 9AH
Tel: 0161 817 5600 Fax: 0161 871 5601

SWALESIDE The Governor, H.M. Prison, Swaleside, Brabazon Road, Eastchurch, Isle of Sheppey, Kent ME12 4AX
Tel: 01795 804100 Fax: 01795 804200

WAKEFIELD The Governor, H.M. Prison, Love Lane, Wakefield, West Yorkshire WF2 9AG
Tel: 01924 246000 Fax: 01924 246001

WHITEMOOR The Governor, H.M. Prison Whitemoor, Longhill Road, March, Cambridgeshire PE15 0PR
Tel: 01354 602350 Fax: 01354 602351

WOODHILL The Governor, H.M. Prison Woodhill, Tattenhoe Street, Milton Keynes, Buckinghamshire MK4 4DA
Tel: 01908 722000 Fax: 01908 867063

LOCAL PRISONS AND REMAND CENTRES

(i) FOR MALES

ALTCOURSE The Director, H.M. Prison Altcourse, Higher Lane, Fazakerley, Liverpool L9 7LH
Tel: 0151 522 2000 Fax: 0151 522 2121

BEDFORD The Governor, H.M. Prison, St. Loyes, Bedford MK40 1HG
Tel: 01234 373000 Fax: 01234 273568

BELMARSH The Governor, H.M. Prison Belmarsh, Western Way, Thamesmead, London SE28 0EB
Tel: 020 8331 4400 Fax: 020 8331 4401

BIRMINGHAM The Governor, H.M. Prison, Winson Green Road, Birmingham B18 4AS
Tel: 0121 345 2500 Fax: 0121 345 2501

BLAKENHURST The Governor, H.M. Prison Blakenhurst, Hewell Lane, Redditch, Worcestershire B97 6QS
Tel: 01527 400500 Fax: 01527 400501

BRISTOL The Governor, H.M. Prison, Cambridge Road, Bristol BS7 8PS
Tel: 0117 372 3100 Fax: 0117 372 3013

BRIXTON The Governor, H.M. Prison, P.O. Box 369, Jebb Avenue, London SW2 5XF
Tel: 020 8588 6000 Fax: 020 8588 6296

BULLINGDON The Governor, H.M. Prison, PO Box 50, Bicester, Oxon OX25 1WD
Tel: 01869 353100 Fax: 01869 353101

CARDIFF The Governor, H.M. Prison and Remand Centre, Knox Road, Cardiff CF24 0UG
Tel: 029 2092 3100 Fax: 029 2092 3318

CHELMSFORD The Governor, H.M. Prison, 200 Springfield Road, Chelmsford, Essex CM2 6LQ
Tel: 01245 272000 Fax: 01245 272001

DONCASTER (Serco Ltd) The Director, H.M. Prison Doncaster, Marshgate, Doncaster, S. Yorks DN5 8UX
Tel: 01302 760870 Fax: 01302 760851

DORCHESTER The Governor, H.M. Prison, North Square, Dorchester, Dorset DT1 1JD
Tel: 01305 214500 Fax: 01305 214501

DURHAM	The Governor, H.M. Prison, Old Elvet, Durham DH1 3HU Tel: 0191 332 3400 Fax: 0191 332 3401
ELMLEY	The Governor, H.M. Prison, Church Road, Eastchurch, Sheerness, Kent ME12 4DZ Tel: 01795 882000 Fax: 01795 882001
EXETER	The Governor, H.M. Prison, 30 New North Road, Exeter, Devon EX4 4EX Tel: 01392 415650 Fax: 01392 415691
FOREST BANK	The Governor, H.M. Prison Forest Bank, Agecroft Road, Pendlebury, Manchester M27 8FB Tel: 0161 925 7000 Fax: 0161 925 7001
GLOUCESTER	The Governor, H.M. Prison, Barrack Square, Gloucester GL1 2JN Tel: 01452 453000 Fax: 01452 453001
HIGHDOWN	The Governor, H.M. Prison, High Down Lane, Sutton, Surrey SM2 5PJ Tel: 020 7147 6300 Fax: 020 7147 6301
HOLME HOUSE	The Governor, H.M. Prison Holme House, Holme House Road, Stockton-on-Tees, Cleveland TS18 2QU Tel: 01642 744000 Fax: 01642 744001
HULL	The Governor, H.M. Prison, Hedon Road, Hull HU9 5LS Tel: 01482 282200 Fax: 01482 282400
LEEDS	The Governor, H.M. Prison, 2 Gloucester Terrace, Armley Road, Leeds, West Yorkshire LS12 2TJ Tel: 0113 203 2600 Fax: 0113 231 9005
LEICESTER	The Governor, H.M. Prison, Welford Road, Leicester LE2 7AJ Tel: 0116 228 3000 Fax: 0116 228 3001
LEWES	The Governor, H.M. Prison, Brighton Road, Lewes, East Sussex BN7 1EA Tel: 01273 785100 Fax: 01273 785101
LINCOLN	The Governor, H.M. Prison, Greetwell Road, Lincoln LN2 4BD Tel: 01522 663000 Fax: 01522 663001
LIVERPOOL	The Governor, H.M. Prison, 68 Hornby Road, Liverpool L9 3DF Tel: 0151 530 4000 Fax: 0151 530 4001
NORWICH	The Governor, H.M. Prison and Remand Centre, Knox Road, Norwich, Norfolk NR1 4LU Tel: 01603 708600 Fax: 01603 708601
NOTTINGHAM	The Governor, H.M. Prison, Perry Road, Sherwood, Nottingham NG5 3AG Tel: 0115 872 3000 Fax: 0115 872 3001
PARKHURST	The Governor, H.M. Prison Parkhurst, Newport, Isle of Wight PO30 5NX Tel: 01983 554000 Fax: 01983 554001
PENTONVILLE	The Governor, H.M. Prison Pentonville, Caledonian Road, London N7 8TT Tel: 020 7023 7000 Fax: 020 7023 7001
PETERBOROUGH (KALYX)	The Director, H.M. Prison Peterborough, Saville Road, Westfield, Peterborough PE3 7PD Tel: 01733 217500 Fax: 01733 217501
PRESTON	The Governor, H.M. Prison, 2 Ribbleton Lane, Preston, Lancs. PR1 5AB Tel: 01772 257734 Fax: 01772 886810
READING	The Governor, H.M. Prison, Forbury Road, Reading, Berkshire RG1 3HY Tel: 0118 908 5000 Fax: 0118 908 5001
SHREWSBURY	The Governor, H.M. Prison, The Dana, Shrewsbury, Shropshire SY1 2HR Tel: 01743 273000 Fax: 01743 273001
SWANSEA	The Governor, H.M. Prison, Oystermouth Road, Swansea SA1 3SR Tel: 01792 485300 Fax: 01792 485430
WANDSWORTH	The Governor, H.M. Prison Wandsworth, P.O. Box 757, Heathfield Road, Wandsworth, London SW18 3HS Tel: 020 8588 4000 Fax: 020 8588 4001
WINCHESTER	The Governor, H.M. Prison, Romsey Road, Winchester, Hants. SO22 5DF Tel: 01962 723000 Fax: 01962 723001

WORMWOOD SCRUBS	The Governor, H.M. Prison, Wormwood Scrubs, P.O. Box 757, Du Cane Road, London W12 0AE Tel: 020 8588 3200 Fax: 020 8588 3201

(ii) FOR FEMALES

BRONZEFIELD (KALYX)	The Director, H.M. Prison Bronzefield, Woodthorpe Road, Ashford, Middlesex TW15 3JZ Tel: 01784 425690 Fax: 01784 425691
EASTWOOD PARK	The Governor, H.M. Prison Eastwood Park, Falfield, Wooton under Edge, Gloucestershire GL12 8DB Tel: 01454 382100 Fax: 01454 382101
FOSTON HALL	The Governor, H.M. Prison Foston Hall, Foston, Derby DE65 5DN Tel: 01283 584300 Fax: 01283 584301
HOLLOWAY	The Governor, H.M. Prison and Young Offender Institution, Parkhurst Road, Holloway, London N7 0NU Tel: 020 7979 4400 Fax: 020 7979 4401
LOW NEWTON	The Governor, H.M. Prison and Young Offender Institution Low Newton, Brasside, Durham DH1 5YA Tel: 0191 376 4000 Fax: 0191 376 4001
NEW HALL	The Governor, H.M. Prison and Young Offender Institution New Hall, Dial Wood, Flockton, Wakefield, West Yorkshire WF4 4XX Tel: 01924 803000 Fax: 01924 803001
PETERBOROUGH (KALYX)	The Director, H.M. Prison Peterborough, Saville Road, Westfield, Peterborough PE3 7PD Tel: 01733 217500 Fax: 01733 217501

TRAINING PRISONS

(i) PRISONS FOR MALE OFFENDERS

CLOSED

ACKLINGTON	The Governor, H.M. Prison Acklington, Nr. Morpeth, Northumberland NE65 9XF Tel: 01670 762300 Fax: 01670 762301
ALBANY	The Governor, H.M. Prison Albany, 55 Parkhurst Road, Newport, Isle of Wight PO30 5RS Tel: 01983 556300 Fax: 01983 556332
ASHWELL	The Governor, H.M. Prison Ashwell, Oakham, Leicestershire LE15 7LF Tel: 01572 884100 Fax: 01572 884101
BLUNDESTON	The Governor, H.M. Prison Blundeston, Lowestoft, Suffolk NR32 5BG Tel: 01502 734500 Fax: 01502 734501
BROCKHILL	The Governor, H.M. Prison Brockhill, Hewell Lane, Redditch, Worcs. B97 6RD Tel: 01527 552650 Fax: 01527 552651
BUCKLEY HALL	The Governor, H.M. Prison, Buckley Hall Road, Rochdale, Lancashire OL12 9DP Tel: 01706 514300 Fax: 01706 514399
BULLWOOD HALL	The Governor, H.M Prison Bullwood Hall, High Road, Hockley, Essex SS5 4TE Tel: 01702 562800 Fax: 01702 562801
CAMP HILL	The Governor, H.M. Prison Camp Hill, Newport, Isle of Wight PO30 5PB Tel: 01983 554600 Fax: 01983 554647
CHANNINGS WOOD	The Governor, H.M. Prison, Channings Wood, Denbury, Newton Abbot, Devon TQ12 6DW Tel: 01803 814600 Fax: 01803 814601
COLDINGLEY	The Governor, Shaftesbury Road, Bisley, Woking, Surrey GU24 9EX Tel: 01483 804300 Fax: 01483 804427

DARTMOOR	The Governor, H.M. Prison Dartmoor, Princetown, Yelverton, Devon PL20 6RR Tel: 01822 892000 Fax: 01822 892001
DOVEGATE (Serco Home Affairs)	The Director, H.M. Prison Dovegate, Uttoxeter, Staffordshire ST14 8XR Tel: 01283 829400 Fax: 01283 820066 (General)
EDMUNDS HILL	The Governor, H.M. Prison Edmunds Hill, Stradishall, Newmarket, Suffolk CB8 9YN Tel: 01440 743100 Fax: 01440 743560
ERLESTOKE	The Governor, H.M. Prison Erlestoke, Devizes, Wiltshire SN10 5TU Tel: 01380 814250 Fax: 01380 814273
EVERTHORPE	The Governor, H.M. Prison, Beck Road, Brough, East Yorkshire HU15 1RB Tel: 01430 426500 Fax: 01430 426501
FEATHERSTONE	The Governor, H.M. Prison, New Road, Featherstone, Wolverhampton WV10 7PU Tel: 01902 703000 Fax: 01902 703001
GARTH	The Governor, H.M. Prison Garth, Ulnes Walton Lane, Leyland, Preston, Lancashire PR26 8NE Tel: 01772 443300 Fax: 01772 443301
GARTREE	The Governor, H.M. Prison Gartree, Gallow Field Road, Market Harborough, Leicestershire LE16 7RP Tel: 01858 436600 Fax: 01858 436601
GUYS MARSH	The Governor, H.M. Prison Guys Marsh, Shaftesbury, Dorset SP7 0AH Tel: 01747 856400 Fax: 01747 856401
HAVERIGG	The Governor, H.M. Prison Haverigg, Millom, Cumbria LA18 4NA Tel: 01229 713000 Fax: 01229 713001
HIGHPOINT	The Governor, H.M. Prison Highpoint, Stradishall, Newmarket, Suffolk CB8 9YG Tel: 01440 743100 Fax: 01440 743092
KINGSTON (Portsmouth)	The Governor, H.M. Prison, 122 Milton Road, Portsmouth, Hampshire PO3 6AS Tel: 023 9295 3100 Fax: 023 9295 3181
LANCASTER CASTLE	The Governor, H.M. Prison, The Castle, Lancaster LA1 1YL Tel: 01524 565100 Fax: 01524 565101
LINDHOLME	The Governor, H.M. Prison Lindholme, Bawtry Road, Hatfield Woodhouse, Doncaster, S. Yorkshire DN7 6EE Tel: 01302 524700 Fax: 01302 524750
LITTLEHEY	The Governor, H.M. Prison Littlehey, Perry, Huntingdon, Cambridgeshire PE28 0SR Tel: 01480 333000 Fax: 01480 333070
LONG LARTIN	The Governor, H.M. Prison Long Lartin, South Littleton, Evesham, Worcestershire WR11 8TZ Tel: 01386 835100 Fax: 01386 835101
LOWDHAM GRANGE (Serco Ltd)	The Governor, H.M. Prison Lowdham Grange, Lowdham, Nottingham NG14 7DA Tel: 0115 966 9200 Fax: 0115 966 9220
MAIDSTONE	The Governor, H.M. Prison, County Road, Maidstone, Kent ME14 1UZ Tel: 01622 755300 Fax: 01622 755301
MOORLAND	The Governor, H.M. Prison, Bawtry Road, Hatfield Woodhouse, Doncaster DN7 6BW Tel: 01302 523000 Fax: 01302 523001
THE MOUNT	The Governor, H.M. Prison The Mount, Molyneaux Avenue, Bovingdon, Hemel Hempstead, Hertfordshire HP3 0NZ Tel: 01442 836300 Fax: 01442 836301
ONLEY	The Governor, H.M. Prison and Young Offender Institution Onley, Wiloughby, Rugby, Warwickshire CV23 8AP Tel: 01788 523400 Fax: 01788 523401
RANBY	The Governor, H.M. Prison Ranby, Retford, Nottinghamshire DN22 8EU Tel: 01777 862000 Fax: 01777 862001

RISLEY	The Governor, H.M. Prison, Warrington Road, Risley, Warrington, Cheshire WA3 6BP Tel: 01925 733000 Fax: 01925 733001
RYE HILL (GSL Ltd)	The Director, H.M. Prison Rye Hill, Onley, Willoughby, Nr. Rugby, Warwickshire CV32 8SZ Tel: 01788 523300 Fax: 01788 523111
SHEPTON MALLET	The Governor, H.M. Prison, Cornhill, Shepton Mallet, Somerset BA4 5LU Tel: 01749 823300 Fax: 01749 823301
STAFFORD	The Governor, H.M. Prison, 54 Gaol Road, Stafford ST16 3AW Tel: 01785 773000 Fax: 01785 773001
STOCKEN	The Governor, H.M. Prison, Stocken Hall Road, Stretton, Nr. Oakham, Rutland, Leicestershire LE15 7RD Tel: 01780 795100 Fax: 01780 410767
USK	The Governor, H.M. Prison Usk, 47 Maryport Street, Usk, Monmouthshire NP15 1XP Tel: 01291 671600 Fax: 01291 671752 (Linked with Prescoed)
THE VERNE	The Governor, H.M Prison The Verne, Portland, Dorset DT5 1EQ Tel: 01305 825000 Fax: 01305 825001
WAYLAND	The Governor, H.M. Prison Wayland, Griston, Thetford, Norfolk IP25 6RL Tel: 01953 804100 Fax: 01953 804220
WEALSTUN	The Governor, H.M. Prison Wealstun, Wetherby, West Yorkshire LS23 7AZ Tel: 01937 440000 Fax: 01937 440001
WELLINGBOROUGH	The Governor, H.M. Prison, Millers Park, Doddington Park, Wellingborough, Northamptonshire NN8 2NH Tel: 01933 232700 Fax: 01933 232701
WHATTON	The Governor, H.M. Prison, New Lane, Whatton, Nottinghamshire NG13 9FQ Tel: 01949 803200 Fax: 01949 803201
WOLDS (GSL Ltd)	The Director, H.M. Prison Wolds, Sands Lane, Everthorpe, Brough, East Yorkshire HU15 2JZ Tel: 01430 428000 Fax: 01430 428001
WYMOTT	The Governor, H.M. Prison Wymott, Ulnes Walton Lane, Leyland, Preston, Lancashire PR26 8LW Tel: 01772 442000 Fax: 01772 442001

OPEN

FORD	The Governor, H.M. Prison Ford, Arundel, West Sussex BN18 0BX Tel: 01903 663000 Fax: 01903 663001
KIRKLEVINGTON GRANGE	The Governor, H.M. Prison Kirklevington Grange, Yarm, Cleveland TS15 9PA Tel: 01642 792600 Fax: 01642 792601
STANDFORD HILL	The Governor, H.M. Prison Standford Hill, Church Road, Eastchurch, Sheerness, Kent ME12 4AA Tel: 01795 884500 Fax: 01795 884638
WEALSTUN	The Governor, H.M. Prison Wealstun, Wetherby, West Yorkshire LS23 7AZ Tel: 01937 440000 Fax: 01937 440001

SEMI-OPEN

BLANTYRE HOUSE	The Governor, H.M. Prison Blantyre House, Round Green Lane, Goudhurst, Kent TN17 2NH Tel: 01580 213223/4 Fax: 01580 213201

(ii) PRISONS FOR FEMALE OFFENDERS

CLOSED

COOKHAM WOOD	The Governor, H.M. Prison and Youth Offending Institution Cookham Wood, Sir Evelyn Road, Rochester, Kent ME1 3LU Tel: 01634 202500 Fax: 01634 202501
DOWNVIEW	The Governor, H.M. Prison, Sutton Lane, Sutton, Surrey SM2 5PD Tel: 020 8929 3300 Fax: 020 8929 3301
FOSTON HALL	The Governor, H.M. Prison Foston Hall, Foston, Derby DE65 5DN Tel: 01283 584300 Fax: 01283 584301
SEND	The Governor, H.M. Prison, Ripley Road, Send, Woking, Surrey GU23 7LJ Tel: 01483 471000 Fax: 01483 471001
STYAL	The Governor, H.M. Prison and Young Offender Institution Styal, Wilmslow, Cheshire SK9 4HR Tel: 01625 553000 Fax: 01625 553001

SEMI-OPEN

MORTON HALL	The Governor, H.M. Prison Morton Hall, Swinderby, Lincoln LN6 9PT Tel: 01522 666700 Fax: 01522 666750

ADULT MALE

OPEN

HEWELL GRANGE	The Governor, H.M. Prison Hewell Grange, Redditch, Worcestershire B97 6QQ Tel: 01527 552000 Fax: 01527 552001
HOLLESLEY BAY	The Governor, H.M. Prison and Young Offender Institution Hollesley Bay, Hollesley, Woodbridge, Suffolk IP12 3JW Tel: 01394 412400 Fax: 01394 412758
KIRKHAM	The Governor, H.M. Prison, Freckleton Road, Kirkham, Preston, Lancashire PR4 2RN Tel: 01772 675400 Fax: 01772 675401
LEYHILL	The Governor, H.M. Prison Leyhill, Wotton-under-Edge, Gloucestershire GL12 8BT Tel: 01454 264000 Fax: 01454 264001
NORTH SEA CAMP	The Governor, H.M. Prison North Sea Camp, Freiston, Boston, Lincolnshire PE22 0QX Tel: 01205 769300 Fax: 01205 769301
PRESCOED	The Governor, H.M. Prison Prescoed, Coed y Paen, Nr. Pontypool, Torfaen NP14 0TB Tel: 01291 675000 Fax: 01291 675158 (Linked with Usk. Please send all correspondence to Usk address)
SPRING HILL	The Governor, H.M. Prison Spring Hill, Grendon Underwood, Aylesbury, Buckinghamshire HP18 0TL Tel: 01296 443000 Fax: 01296 443002
SUDBURY	The Governor, H.M. Prison, Sudbury, Derby DE6 5HW Tel: 01283 584000 Fax: 01283 584001

FOREIGN NATIONAL PRISON FOR MALE OFFENDERS

CLOSED

Canterbury	The Governor, H.M. Prison, Longport, Canterbury, Kent CT1 1PJ Tel: 01227 862800 Fax: 01227 862801

THERAPEUTIC COMMUNITY

DOVEGATE
(Serco Home Affairs)
The Director, H.M. Prison Dovegate, Uttoxeter, Staffordshire ST14 8XR
Tel: 01283 829400 Fax: 01283 820066 (General)

GRENDON
The Governor, H.M. Prison Grendon, Grendon Underwood, Aylesbury, Buckinghamshire HP18 0TL
Tel: 01296 443000 Fax: 01296 443001

MALE SEMI-OPEN WITH RESETTLEMENT REGIME

LATCHMERE HOUSE
The Governor, H.M. Prison Latchmere House, Church Road, Ham Comman, Richmond, Surrey TW10 5HH
Tel: 020 8588 6650   Fax: 020 8588 6698

FEMALE OPEN WITH RESETTLEMENT REGIME

ASKHAM GRANGE
The Governor, H.M. Prison and Young Offender Institution Askham Grange, Askham Richard, York YO23 3FT
Tel: 01904 772000 Fax: 01904 772001

EAST SUTTON PARK
The Governor, H.M. Prison and Young Offender Institution East Sutton Park, Sutton Valance, Maidstone, Kent ME17 3DF
Tel: 01622 845000 Fax: 01622 845001

FEMALE SEMI-OPEN WITH RESETTLEMENT REGIME

DRAKE HALL
The Governor, H.M. Prison and Young Offender Institution Drake Hall, Eccleshall, Staffordshire ST21 6LQ
Tel: 01785 774100   Fax: 01785 774010

YOUNG OFFENDERS

(i) YOUNG OFFENDERS INSTITUTIONS FOR MALE OFFENDERS

CLOSED

ASHFIELD
The Director, H.M. Young Offender Institution, Shortwood Road, Pucklechurch, Bristol BS16 9QJ
Tel: 0117 303 8000 Fax: 0117 303 8001

AYLESBURY
The Governor, H.M. Young Offender Institution, Bierton Road, Aylesbury, Buckinghamshire HP20 1EH
Tel: 01296 444000 Fax: 01296 444001

BRINSFORD
The Governor, H.M. Young Offender Institution and Remand Centre, Brinsford, New Road, Featherstone, Wolverhampton WV10 7PY
Tel: 01902 532450 Fax: 01902 532451

CASTINGTON
The Governor, H.M. Young Offender Institution, Castington, Morpeth, Northumberland NE65 9XG
Tel: 01670 382100 Fax: 01670 382101

CHELMSFORD
The Governor, H.M. Prison, 200 Springfield Road, Chelmsford, Essex CM2 6LQ
Tel: 01245 272000   Fax: 01245 272001

DEERBOLT
The Governor, H.M. Young Offender Institution, Deerbolt, Bowes Road, Barnard Castle, Co. Durham DL12 9BG
Tel: 01833 633200 Fax: 01833 633201

FELTHAM
The Governor, H.M. Young Offender Institution and Remand Centre, Bedfont Road, Feltham, Middlesex TW13 4ND
Tel: 020 8844 5000 Fax: 020 8844 5001

GLEN PARVA
The Governor, H.M. Young Offender Institution, 10 Tigers Road, Wigston, Leicester LE18 4TN
Tel: 0116 228 4100 Fax: 0116 228 4000

GUYS MARSH
The Governor, H.M. Prison Guys Marsh, Shaftesbury, Dorset SP7 0AH
Tel: 01747 856400 Fax: 01747 856401

HINDLEY	The Governor, H.M. Prison and Young Offenders Institution Hindley, Gibson Street, Bickershaw, Hindley, Wigan, Lancashire WN2 5TH Tel: 01942 663000 Fax: 01942 663101
LANCASTER FARMS	The Governor, H.M. Youth Offender Institution and Remand Centre Lancaster Farms, Far Moore Lane, Stone Row Head off Quernmore Road, Lancaster LA1 3QZ Tel: 01524 563450 Fax: 01524 563451
MOORLAND	The Governor, H.M. Prison, Bawtry Road, Hatfield Woodhouse, Doncaster DN7 6BW Tel: 01302 523000 Fax: 01302 523001
NORTHALLERTON	The Governor, H.M. Young Offender Institution, 15a East Road, Northallerton, North Yorkshire DL6 1NW Tel: 01609 785100 Fax: 01609 785101
ONLEY	The Governor, H.M. Prison and Young Offender Institution Onley, Wiloughby, Rugby, Warwickshire CV23 8AP Tel: 01788 523400 Fax: 01788 523401
PORTLAND	The Governor, H.M. Young Offender Institution, Easton, Portland, Dorset DT5 1DL Tel: 01305 825600 Fax: 01305 825601
ROCHESTER	The Governor, H.M. Young Offender Institution Rochester, 1 Fort Road, Rochester, Kent ME1 3QS Tel: 01634 803100 Fax: 01634 803101
STOKE HEATH	The Governor, H.M. Prison Stoke Heath, Market Drayton, Shropshire TF9 2JL Tel: 01630 636000 Fax: 01630 636001
SWINFEN HALL	The Governor, H.M. Prison and Young Offender Institution Swinfen Hall, Lichfield, Staffordshire WS14 9QS Tel: 01543 484000 Fax: 01543 484001

OPEN

MOORLAND OPEN	The Governor, H.M. Young Offender Institution Moorland Open, Thorne Road, Hatfield, Doncaster, South Yorkshire DN7 6EL Tel: 01405 746500 Fax: 01405 746501
THORN CROSS	The Governor, H.M. Young Offender Institution, Arley Road, Appleton Thorn, Warrington, Cheshire WA4 4RL Tel: 01925 805100 Fax: 01925 805101

(ii) YOUNG OFFENDER INSTITUTION FOR FEMALE OFFENDERS

CLOSED

EASTWOOD PARK	The Governor, H.M. Prison Eastwood Park, Falfield, Wooton under Edge, Gloucestershire GL12 8DB Tel: 01454 382100 Fax: 01454 382101
HOLLOWAY	The Governor, H.M. Prison and Young Offender Institution, Parkhurst Road, Holloway, London N7 0NU Tel: 029 7979 4400 Fax: 020 7979 4401
PETERBOROUGH (KALYX)	The Director, H.M. Prison Peterborough, Saville Road, Westfield, Peterborough PE3 7PD Tel: 01733 217500 Fax: 01733 217501
NEW HALL	The Governor, H.M. Prison and Young Offender Institution New Hall, Dial Wood, Flockton, Wakefield, West Yorkshire WF4 4XX Tel: 01924 803000 Fax: 01924 803001
STYAL	The Governor, H.M. Prison and Young Offender Institution Styal, Wilmslow, Cheshire SK9 4HR Tel: 01625 553000 Fax: 01625 553001

OPEN

ASKHAM GRANGE The Governor, H.M. Prison and Young Offender Institution Askham Grange, Askham Richard, York YO23 3FT
Tel: 01904 772000 Fax: 01904 772001

SEMI-OPEN

DRAKE HALL The Governor, H.M. Prison and Young Offender Institution Drake Hall, Eccleshall, Staffordshire ST21 6LQ
Tel: 01785 774100 Fax: 01785 774010

(iii) SHORT SENTENCE INSTITUTIONS

EASTWOOD PARK The Governor, H.M. Prison Eastwood Park, Falfield, Wooton under Edge, Gloucestershire GL12 8DB
Tel: 01454 382100 Fax: 01454 382101

(iv) JUVENILE INSTITUTIONS

CASTINGTON The Governor, H.M. Young Offender Institution, Castington, Morpeth, Northumberland NE65 9XG
Tel: 01670 382100 Fax: 01670 382101

COOKHAM WOOD The Governor, Juvenile Unit, H.M. Prison and Youth Offending Institution Cookham Wood, Sir Evelyn Road, Rochester, Kent ME1 3LU
Tel: 01634 202500 Fax: 01634 202501

DOWNVIEW The Governor, H.M. Prison, Sutton Lane, Sutton, Surrey SM2 5PD
Tel: 020 8929 3300 Fax: 020 8929 3301

EASTWOOD PARK The Governor, H.M. Prison Eastwood Park, Falfield, Wooton under Edge, Gloucestershire GL12 8DB
Tel: 01454 382100 Fax: 01454 382101

FELTHAM The Governor, H.M. Young Offender Institution and Remand Centre, Bedfont Road, Feltham, Middlesex TW13 4ND
Tel: 020 8844 5000 Fax: 020 8844 5001

FOSTON HALL The Governor, H.M. Prison Foston Hall, Foston, Derby DE65 5DN
Tel: 01283 584300 Fax: 01283 584301

HINDLEY The Governor, H.M. Prison and Young Offender Institution Hindley, Gibson Street, Bickershaw, Hindley, Wigan, Lancashire WN2 5TH
Tel: 01942 663000   Fax: 01942 663101

HUNTERCOMBE The Governor, H.M. Young Offender Institution, Huntercombe Place, Nuffield, Henley-on-Thames, Oxon RG9 5SB
Tel: 01491 643100 Fax: 01491 643101

STOKE HEATH The Governor, H.M. Prison Stoke Heath, Market Drayton, Shropshire TF9 2JL
Tel: 01630 636000 Fax: 01630 636001

WARREN HILL The Governor, H.M. Young Offender Institution, Warren Hill, Hollesley, Woodbridge, Suffolk IP12 3JW
Tel: 01394 412400 Fax: 01394 412767

WERRINGTON The Governor, H.M. Young Offender Institution, Werrington House, Werrington, Stoke-on-Trent, Staffordshire ST9 0DX
Tel: 01782 463300 Fax: 01782 463301

WETHERBY The Governor, H.M. Young Offender Institution, York Road, Wetherby, West Yorkshire LS22 5ED
Tel: 01937 544200   Fax: 01937 544201

(v) IMMIGRATION REMOVAL CENTRES

DOVER — The Centre Manager, Dover Immigration Removal Centre, The Citadel, Western Heights, Dover, Kent CT17 9DR
Tel: 01304 246400 Fax: 01304 246401

HASLAR — The Manager, Haslar Immigration Removal Centre, 2 Dolphin Way, Gosport, Hampshire PO12 2AW
Tel: 02392 604000 Fax: 02392 604001

LINDHOLME — The Governor, H.M. Prison Lindholme, Bawtry Road, Hatfield Woodhouse, Doncaster, S. Yorkshire DN7 6EE
Tel: 01302 524700 Fax: 01302 524750

E – SPECIAL HOSPITALS (DOH)

Broadmoor Hospital, Crowthorne, Berks. RG11 7EG
Tel: 01344 773111   Fax: 01344 754848

Rampton Hospital, Retford, Notts. DN22 0PD
Tel: 01777 248321   Fax: 01771 248442

Ashworth Hospital, Parkbourn, Maghull, Liverpool L31 1HW
Tel: 0151 473 0303   Fax: 0151 526 6603

PENAL ESTABLISHMENTS

NORTHERN IRELAND

A – HEADQUARTERS ESTABLISHMENTS

HEADQUARTERS......... Prison Service Headquarters, Dundonald House, Upper Newtownards Road, Belfast BT4 3SU
Tel: 028 9052 2922
Fax: 028 9052 4330

PRISON SERVICE COLLEGE......... Head of Training and Development, Prison Service College, Woburn House, Millisle, Co. Down BT22 2HS
Tel: 028 9186 3000
Fax: 028 9186 3022

B – PRISONS

MAGHABERRY............. The Governor, Maghaberry Prison, Old Road, Ballinderry Upper, Lisburn, Co. Antrim BT28 2PT
Tel: 028 9261 1888
Fax: 028 9261 9516

MAGILLIGAN................ The Governor, Magilligan Prison, Point Road, Limavady, Co. Londonderry BT49 0LR
Tel: 028 7776 3311
Fax: 028 7775 0819

C – YOUNG OFFENDERS CENTRE AND PRISON

HYDEBANK WOOD...... The Governor, Hydebank Wood Young Offenders Centre and Prison, Hospital Road, Belfast BT8 8NA
Tel: 028 9025 3666
Fax: 028 9025 3668

PRISONS

PERTH .... The Governor, H.M. Prison, 3 Edinburgh Road, Perth PH2 8AT
Tel: 01738 622293   Fax: 01738 630545

PETERHEAD .... The Governor, H.M. Prison, Peterhead, Aberdeenshire AB42 2YY
Tel: 01779 479101   Fax: 01779 470529

SHOTTS .... The Governor, H.M. Prison, Scott Drive, Shotts, Lanarkshire ML7 4LE
Tel: 01501 824000   Fax: 01501 824001

D – YOUNG OFFENDER INSTITUTIONS

CORNTON VALE .... The Governor, H.M. Y.O.I., Cornton Vale, Cornton Road, Stirling FK9 5NU
Tel: 01786 832591   Fax: 01786 833597

POLMONT .... The Governor, H.M. Y.O.I., Brightons, near Falkirk, Stirlingshire FK2 0AB
Tel: 01324 711558   Fax: 01324 714919

E – STATE HOSPITAL

State Hospital, Carstairs Junction, Lanark ML11 8RP

Tel: Carnwath (0155 584) 0293
Fax: 01555 840 100

PENAL ESTABLISHMENTS

SCOTLAND

A – HEADQUARTERS

HEADQUARTERS......... Calton House, 5 Redheughs Rigg, Edinburgh EH12 9HW
Tel: 0131-244 8745   Fax: 0131-244 8774

B – PRISON SERVICE COLLEGE

SCOTTISH PRISON...... Head of College, Scottish Prison Service College, Newlands Road,
SERVICE COLLEGE   Brightons, Falkirk, Stirlingshire FK2 0DE
Tel: Polmont (01324) 710405   Fax: 01324 710401

C – PRISONS

ABERDEEN.................. The Governor, H.M. Prison, Craiginches, 4 Grampian Place,
Aberdeen AB11 8FN
Tel: 01224 238300   Fax: 01224 896209

BARLINNIE.................. The Governor, H.M. Prison, Barlinnie, Glasgow G33 2QX
Tel: 0141-770 2000   Fax: 0141-770 2060

CASTLE HUNTLY .... The Governor, HMP Open Estate, Castle Huntly, Longforgan, Near
Dundee DD2 5HL
Tel: 01382 319333   Fax: 01382 319350

CORNTON VALE .... The Governor, H.M. Prison, Cornton Vale, Cornton Road, Stirling FK9 5NY
Tel: 01786 832591   Fax: 01786 833597

DUMFRIES.................... The Governor, H.M. Prison, Terregles Street, Dumfries DG2 9AX
Tel: 01387 261218   Fax: 01387 264144

EDINBURGH .... The Governor, H.M. Prison, Edinburgh, 33 Stenhouse Road,
Edinburgh EH11 3LN
Tel: 0131-444 3000   Fax: 0131-444 3045

GLENOCHIL.................. The Governor, H.M. Prison, King O'Muir Road, Tullibody,
Clackmannanshire FK10 3AD
Tel: 01259 760471   Fax: 01259 762003

GREENOCK .... The Governor, H.M. Prison, Gateside, Greenock PA16 9AH
Tel: 01475 787801   Fax: 01475 783154

INVERNESS .... The Governor, H.M. Prison, Porterfield, Duffy Drive, Inverness
IV2 3HH
Tel: 01463 229000   Fax: 01463 229010

KILMARNOCK .... The Director, H.M. Prison, Bowhouse, Mauchline Road, Kilmarnock
(Serco Home Affairs)   KA1 5AA
Tel: 01563 548800   Fax: 01563 548845

NORANSIDE .... The Governor, H.M.P. Open Estate, Noranside, Fern, by Forfar, Angus
DD8 3QY
Tel: 01382 319333   Fax: 01356 650245